BANDITS AND LIBERALS, REBELS AND SAINTS

BANDITS AND LIBERALS, REBELS AND SAINTS

LATIN AMERICA SINCE INDEPENDENCE

Alan Knight

UNIVERSITY OF NEBRASKA PRESS   LINCOLN

The University of Nebraska Press is part of a land-
grant institution with campuses and programs on the
past, present, and future homelands of the Pawnee,
Ponca, Otoe-Missouria, Omaha, Dakota, Lakota, Kaw,
Cheyenne, and Arapaho Peoples, as well as those of the
relocated Ho-Chunk, Sac and Fox, and Iowa Peoples.

Library of Congress Cataloging-in-Publication Data
Names: Knight, Alan, 1946– author.
Title: Bandits and liberals, rebels and saints: Latin
America since independence / Alan Knight.
Other titles: Latin America since independence
Description: Lincoln: University of Nebraska Press,
[2022] | Includes bibliographical references and index.
Identifiers: LCCN 2021034616
ISBN 9781496229427 (hardback)
ISBN 9781496229786 (paperback)
ISBN 9781496230898 (epub)
ISBN 9781496230904 (pdf)
Subjects: LCSH: Latin America—History—1830– | Latin
America—Politics and government—1830–1948. |
BISAC: HISTORY / Latin America / Mexico |
HISTORY / Latin America / South America
Classification: LCC F1413 .K65 2022 |
DDC 980.03—dc23/eng/20211007
LC record available at https://lccn.loc.gov/2021034616

Set in Adobe Caslon by Mikala R. Kolander.
Designed by N. Putens.

For April and Aria

(Bandits or Liberals? Rebels or Saints? Time Will Tell)

Contents

List of Illustrations
ix

List of Tables
xi

Acknowledgments
xiii

Introduction
1

1. Back to Banditry
25

2. Toward an Explanation of Liberalism in
Nineteenth-Century Latin America
49

3. Religion and Conflict in Latin America, 1820–1930
87

4. The Little Divergence: Peru and Mexico
Compared, 1780–1940
113

5. Informal Empire and Internal Colonialism in
Latin America, 1820–1930
135

6. Hovering Dwarf: Britain and Latin American
Revolutions in the Twentieth Century
169

7. Workers and Peasants, Liberals and Jacobins:
The Mexican Revolution in Comparative Global Perspective
193

Notes
219

Selected Bibliography
379

Index
405

Illustrations

1. The evolution of liberalism in Latin America

65

Tables

1. Peru and Mexico: Exports/GDP per capita in U.S. dollars

305

Acknowledgments

I SHOULD FIRST LIKE TO THANK THE UNIVERSITY OF NEBRASKA Press for renewing our old partnership and publishing this book of essays.[1] In particular, I would like to thank Bridget Barry, Emily Casillas, and Sara Springsteen for shepherding the book through to publication, as well as Mary Hill for her scrupulous editing and the two anonymous readers who gave helpful and constructive comments on the manuscript.

Second, I should recognize the provenance of the chapters in this book, all of which derive from conference papers or lectures that, for various reasons, were never published; so all of what follows is substantially new. I wrote chapter 1 for a London conference ("History after Hobsbawm") held in homage to Eric Hobsbawm in April 2014, where I organized a "Latin American" panel, along with Prof. Joan Martínez-Alier and Prof. Paulo Drinot. Interestingly, none of the Latin American papers made it to the final edited volume—which does, however, include essays on Cambridgeshire village folklore and industrialization "viewed through some key Welsh woolen objects."[2] The volume skimps on Hobsbawm's important Latin American work and omits banditry entirely. Peru gets one passing reference, Argentina gets none, and Mexico appears, fleetingly, as a source of migrant workers to the United States. There are also several references to a fictional country called San Domingo.[3] In other words, Hobsbawm's breadth of historical vision is hardly well served by the volume compiled in his name.

Chapter 2 was written at the invitation of Prof. Paula Alonso, whom I would like to thank, for a panel on Latin American liberalism held at the Latin American Studies Association Congress in Chicago in May 2014. It proved too long to fit into an academic journal and so had to find another home. I wrote chapter 3 in response to a request from Dr. Evelyn Brouwers, who was editing a symposium on violence and the Catholic Church. Unfortunately, my contribution did not quite fit the desired template, so we happily parted company. Rather less happily, I wrote chapter 4 at the invitation of Prof. Ben Fallaw, who was coediting a symposium on the comparative history of Peru and Mexico and who approached me, requesting a concluding chapter for the proposed volume, which, after I had plowed my way through the book manuscript, I duly produced. However, for reasons never clearly or adequately explained, the solicited conclusion was then axed from the published volume. So it has now found another, rather more intellectually suitable home.

Chapter 5 was originally given as the Costa Lecture at Ohio University in September 2008: I would like to thank Prof. Patrick Barr-Melej for the invitation and for hosting an enjoyable trip to Athens. So it not only is the oldest of the chapters but also has even older origins—going back about fifty years, in fact—and by way of further acknowledgment, I would like briefly to mention those origins. I first ventured into Latin American history—then, for me, terra incognita—at the suggestion of Prof. Jack Gallagher, who tutored me in British foreign policy and imperial history when I was an undergraduate at Balliol College, Oxford, in the late 1960s.[4] When I expressed an inchoate desire to undertake research in that broad area, he suggested that Latin America was an interesting but—in the United Kingdom, at least—a sadly neglected field. (He was right then and would be even more right today, especially in my own university, Oxford, where the chair of Latin American history, which I held for twenty years, has been frozen—like a mammoth deep in the Siberian tundra—since I retired seven years ago. There is therefore no full-time Latin Americanist in a faculty of 120.)[5] Providentially, however, back in the 1960s the British government had experienced a rare moment of lucidity and, alarmed by the Cuban Revolution, had modestly sponsored a few graduate research grants in Latin American studies, one of which I got. So I should probably thank Fidel as well. At any rate, I started work on Latin America as an arena of foreign economic penetration and Great Power rivalry; and while that "imperial" focus soon faded as I became immersed in the domestic history of the region (Mexico and the Mexican Revolution, in particular), I never entirely relinquished that initial interest in the "imperial" connection. So when the opportunity arose, I decided to try to sum up some ideas about "informal empire" in Latin America. As readers will see, my approach is, in the best Gallagher-and-Robinson tradition, decidedly "excentric" (i.e., focused on "peripheral" rather than "metropolitan" chains of causality). Hence, I seek to link "informal empire" to "internal colonialism."

Chapter 6 is loosely related in that it concerns Britain's relations with and perceptions of Latin America, specifically, those Latin American countries that, in the twentieth century, experienced major revolutions. It was written for a panel at the International Congress of Americanists held in Vienna in 2012, for which I thank my old University of Texas colleague Jonathan Brown. Finally, chapter 7 was written for a conference on revolutions held at University College Dublin in October 2016, for which I thank Dr. Mark Jones, who organized and hosted the event, and Prof. Erik Zürcher, another participant, who gave me the benefit of his expert knowledge of Turkish history. My old Essex comrade, now Oxford colleague, Prof. S. A. Smith—that rare bird, a genuine (Russo-Chinese) comparative historian—helpfully commented on an early draft of the chapter; and an abbreviated Spanish version was given at a conference on revolutions held at the Universidad Andina Simón Bolívar, Quito, Ecuador, in 2019, organized by another friend and colleague, Dr. Enrique Ayala Mora.

The fact that these essays all derive from invitations and conference presentations may suggest a certain intellectual inertia on my part: I write things when given a prod and sometimes the added incentives of a trip to Dublin or Quito and participation in an interesting academic forum. However, there is so much potentially absorbing history "out there" (not least in Latin America), thus so many possible topics for fruitful research, that some process of selection has to be followed, and I take the serendipitous view that relying on the (somewhat) random roll of the academic dice (thus, responding to invitations that happen to drop on the doormat) is not a bad way to proceed. But I am, therefore, indebted to these several academic hosts and to the different publics who attended, endured, questioned, and commented.

Two final acknowledgments. I took a passing potshot at Oxford University for its serial neglect of Latin American history. However, the university's Latin American Centre, built on the ancient and solid foundations laid down by colleagues like Alan Angell, Malcolm Deas, and Rosemary Thorp (all now also retired), has not only survived but even, in respect to history, quietly prospered, a triumph over adversity and indifference that has crucially depended on the dedicated work of Prof. Eduardo Posada-Carbó. Eduardo has not only kept the local flame of Latin American history flickeringly alive but also found time to make his own major contributions to the field, from which, as my endnotes indicate, I have learned a good deal. He thus confounds the stereotype, today all too common, whereby those professors who climb the greasy pole of university politics and administration relinquish, if they ever had it in the first place, their intellectual vitality.

I previously mentioned Prof. Paula Alonso, who, I hope, will not mind me commending her, an Argentine, for successfully marrying an Englishman. My own wife, Lidia Lozano, also a *porteña* born and bred, made the same brave decision, which, at least from my own selfish point of view, has afforded me a great deal of (unpaid) help when it comes to writing, traveling, translating, and negotiating modern technology. So the old Anglo-Argentinian liaison, touched on in chapter 5, still has some life in it, despite the long-term decline and recurrent reverses—on the football field or elsewhere—that it has suffered since the good old days of Rosas and Roca.

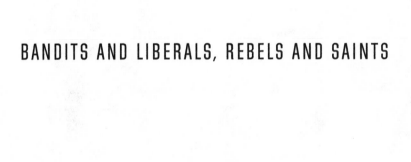

BANDITS AND LIBERALS, REBELS AND SAINTS

Introduction

AS I MENTION IN THE ACKNOWLEDGMENTS, ALL THESE ESSAYS—
previously unpublished—were written in response to successive invitations
that happened to land on the doormat. To that extent, the selection of
topics has a somewhat stochastic character in a way that the late George
Cockcroft (alias Luke Rhinehart) would have approved.[1] They do, however,
reflect some eclectic interests and approaches that I have pursued over the
years, so to that extent, there is some coherence. They may be unplanned
children, but they display a certain family likeness. And in this short
introduction, I shall try to pull together some recurrent themes, provide
signposts for the reader, and, I hope, make the claimed coherence more
explicit. I shall do so first by setting out the themes, then by draping them
on a rough chronological framework. Along the way, I will loose a few shafts
in the direction of recent historiography, its fads, fashions, and failures.

Several of the chapters deal with Latin American political economy in
the period from independence to, roughly, the mid-twentieth century.[2]
"Political economy" neatly encapsulates two interlocking themes: economic
relations and the role of the state. The latter is crucial since, for all the
casual talk of nineteenth-century Latin America being a region where
laissez-faire economic liberalism increasingly held sway, that is a something
of a myth. (I shall mention several myths as I proceed.) Throughout the
period, and even in their alleged "liberal" guise, Latin American states

regularly and often robustly intervened in society: they taxed, imposed heavy tariffs, regulated property relations, confiscated assets, experimented with currencies, pioneered public works, exercised tough social control, forcibly recruited conscripts, and dragooned labor. The "liberal" Latin American state, as I stress in chapter 2, was often highly illiberal, which should come as no surprise, since state (and party) nomenclature—remember Europe's many postwar "democratic" and "socialist" republics—is often misleading. One might also query how "Bolivarian" the current Venezuelan regime is, but then it is not at all clear what "Bolivarian" means. To put it differently, Latin American states, while they often served as the "agents" of dominant social classes (in the nineteenth century, typically the landed "oligarchy"), also enjoyed a genuine measure of "relative autonomy."[3] Either they pursued what they conceived as the national interest, over and above sectional interests, or they dispensed perks and patronage to their followers, as governments habitually do, or they simply feathered their own personal nests, as governments also habitually do.[4]

If the political economy approach addresses material and collective (often class) interests and thus has at least a *marxisant* flavor, I don't believe that ideas and ideologies are invariably just superstructural reflections of the socioeconomic infrastructure. Often—and I give several examples—the old base/superstructure model *does* make good historical sense: liberalism, positivism, socialism, and anarchism appealed to distinct social groups for good material reasons that had to do with their resources (or lack of resources) and their place within the political economy of the time. Sometimes, the "social groups" in question were discernible and antagonistic classes, for example, the planters and campesinos of Morelos, Mexico, on the eve of the Mexican Revolution.[5] Sometimes, of course, sectoral interest cut across class lines: depreciating currencies favored exporters, debtors, and domestic industrialists, as we see in Mexico, Chile, and Brazil in the 1890s, but importers—and governments concerned to service the foreign debt and to maintain national creditworthiness—preferred strong currencies, ideally pegged to the gold standard.[6] Or, to take a specific and nasty example, the Díaz regime, an "oligarchic" regime that usually respected the interests of the landed elite, sought to quash the Yaqui rebellion in northwestern Mexico by harsh repression and wholesale deportations, but the hacendados of Sonora were uneasy not because they sympathized with the Yaquis or were untainted by racism but because they objected to the forced removal of their best laborers.[7] Elites, or "oligarchies," may have shared a common concern for social order and a collective fear of popular dissidence, but they could still disagree on important issues relating to economic policy, the church, or the politics of regionalism.[8]

Simplistic class reductionism, whereby oligarchs and bourgeois, peasant and workers, perform their choreographed roles in accord with a priori theory, rarely work very well in practice.[9] The so-called liberal bourgeoisie, to take one recurrent example, is another Latin American myth, since the "bourgeoisies" of the region have often supported highly illiberal—authoritarian, clerical/conservative, and even fascistic—causes.[10] On the other hand, as I discuss in chapter 2, "popular" liberalism, espoused by workers and peasants, is now an accepted feature of Latin American sociopolitical history. And it would be rash and rather presumptuous to attribute this to plebeian "false consciousness." Often, there was a clear rationale to such political alignments, whether they concerned workers and peasants or, indeed, oligarchs and bourgeois. These people of the past may not have conformed precisely to the rigid model of "rational actors" beloved by today's political scientists (though some probably did or at least came close), but their sociopolitical alignments can still be rationally investigated and explained.

In pursuing such investigation and presenting explanations, the historian, whether of Latin America or, I would argue, anywhere else in the world, needs to steer a middle course between the Scylla of sheer contingency and the Charybdis of grand determinist "metanarratives." The latter are now widely and often rightly discredited. Divine Providence and the Hegelian dialectic are no more than quaint period pieces. The grand Marxist meta-narrative, whereby modes of production unfold across centuries according to their own inexorable internal logic, culminating in socialism, is also something of a spent force, though, unlike its two (Christian and Hegelian) predecessors, it has at least left a useful theoretical legacy, in terms of class analysis, as well as some classic historical "case studies," such as E.

P. Thompson's *Making of the English Working Class.*[11] Indeed, Marxist and marxisant history has also been an important and often positive current in Latin American historiography, where it has informed perceptive case studies that can be appreciated without requiring unqualified acceptance of the old Marxist metanarrative.[12] In other words, we can accept that the Zapatista revolution was substantially a class conflict provoked by peasant resistance to engrossing landlords without believing that those peasants were passengers riding a mechanical escalator from feudalism to capitalism and ultimately socialism.[13]

On the other hand, having eagerly junked metanarratives, a good many of today's historians, including those who locate themselves on the left, capitulate to notions of extreme contingency. Historical events, far from following a grand pattern, follow no pattern at all. The escalator is replaced by a mass of pollen grains jiggling about in random "Brownian motion." This collapse into contingency, whereby historians tell "just-so" stories that yield no substantial conclusions, comparisons, or regularities, is sometimes justified by ritual invocations of historical "complexity," along with rote obsequies, implicit if not explicit, of the old defunct metanarratives. The linguistic turn, with its routine emphasis on free-floating texts and rebuttal of alleged "positivism," has no doubt encouraged this embrace of contingency, even though its adherents seem quite happy to echo Foucauldian mantras that straddle vast areas of time and space ("archaeology," "discursive formations," "signs," "signifiers and signified").[14] Metanarratives may be defunct, but metaconcepts—portmanteau terms that can blithely travel the world—are just fine, especially if they depart from Paris Charles de Gaulle.

We can all agree that history is complex: even minute local studies can be very complex, just as some grand world histories can be banally simplistic. But history need not be willfully myopic, a blur of random events lacking pattern or connection. Regarding "random," we can also agree that some important events are "contingent," if that means that they involved either (1) individual decisions that could have turned out differently (e.g., decisions to make war, launch rebellions, assassinate political leaders, etc.) or (2) "accidents" that largely defy human control—unplanned and unforeseen events such as earthquakes and epidemics that dramatically disrupt "the best-laid plans of mice and men."[15] But even allowing for such contingency, which is real enough, there remains a great swath of historical processes that are not, in either of these two senses, contingent and that display patterned regularities and rationales—especially, perhaps, in the realm of social and economic history, where big numbers and large social groups are involved. And it is the task of the historian, where possible, to discern, clarify, and depict those patterns, not to shroud their just-so stories in a fog of scholastic minutiae and gratuitous neologisms.

The most obvious case of the "relative autonomy" of ideas and ideology concerns religion, the topic of chapter 4. Latin America has a rich, diverse, and contentious religious history in which different traditions blend and collide. Like all majoritarian Catholic regions of the world, Latin America experienced severe church/state conflict, incipient in the late colonial period, reaching a crescendo in the mid-nineteenth century, and in Mexico, at least, continuing into the early twentieth century. (That timing and the salient role of Mexico are both interesting questions, which I address in chapter 3.) Despite some desperate efforts to do so, it is futile to reduce church/state, Catholic/anticlerical conflict simply to prior socioeconomic interests, for example, depicting the Cristero rebels of the 1920s essentially as sturdy smallholders (rancheros) threatened by land reform or, worse, as peons pressed into service by reactionary landlords, all of them mobilized in order to resist the revolutionary *reparto de tierras*.[16] Certainly, church/state conflict reflected broad, often secular issues, but "secular" does not necessarily mean "material" or class-derived. These issues included the conflicting claims made upon Mexicans' loyalty by the two powerful institutional rivals; growing friction between local, regional, and central authorities in the context of revolutionary political flux; and cultural tensions relating to education, gender, family ties, and public rituals. But strictly religious ideas and beliefs also mattered, and when it comes to religion (and thus, some would add, immortal souls) it is clearly impossible to reduce such allegiances and antipathies to some prior (rational and/or material) interest. Again, historians have to exercise *their* powers of rational inquiry and analysis, even if the *actors* they study are not, in the conventional secular sense, "rational." Although, if you pause for open-minded thought, you might well conclude that, even allowing for infinite "temporal discounting," immortality represents the biggest chunk of "utility" any rational individual could ever envisage. In which case, striving for immortality makes a lot of sense. And that, after all, was the gist of Pascal's wager, and Pascal was a very smart and, by his own lights, very rational gambler.[17]

It is a commonplace that Latin America is a highly diverse region—ethnically, topographically, climatically—and that the twenty countries that, according to the conventional twentieth-century count, comprise it are also highly diverse. Costa Rica is very different from Brazil. And several of the countries are, like Brazil, extremely large and, again, diverse. Indeed, even a small country like Costa Rica is richly diverse.[18] Much of the best recent historiography of Latin America has adopted a regional or local perspective, and although I can claim no credit for this trend (I have no adoptive historiographical *patria chica*), I have learned a great deal from local and regional studies. Arguably, the countries of Latin America were even more diverse in the nineteenth century, and regionalism was even more important. Some superficial analysts (e.g., of twentieth-century Mexico) like to claim that with development and "modernity" (whatever that is), countries have emerged from some kind of bland "traditional" uniformity and become more complex, variegated, and pluralist, and this process, it is also sometimes said, has favored recent democratization. This seems to me to be another myth. Over decades—and the late nineteenth century is a key period in this long process—state power has tended to grow, education and literacy have expanded, and economies have become more tightly integrated by means of improved communications, modern mass media, and enhanced flows of goods, capital, and labor. Countries have consequently become more, not less, homogeneous and integrated (and I see no clear or necessary correlation between these trends and democratization). In the nineteenth century, Alberto Flores Galindo observed, "the Peruvian coast was closer to Asia than to its Andean hinterland," but that was no longer the case in the twentieth.[19] Much of the spadework of integration, which turned introverted regional economies and semiautonomous political fiefs into more coherent national units, was performed in the period that this book covers.

Of course, the diversity of Latin America endured both within and between countries. Costa Rica is very different from Brazil, but Rondônia is also very different from São Paulo. Some stern critics, flaunting their elementary expertise, tell us that the label "Latin America" is too broad and encompasses too much. (They also tell us it was invented by Napoleon III, which may be true, but of course, the meaning and utility of such labels depend on their current usage, not their distant origins.) However, querying "Latin America" as a common label is too pernickety for my taste: the region possesses a loose common history that derived from three centuries of Iberian colonial rule and that imparted shared features—political, cultural, and economic. The Latin American states roughly replicate the old colonial administrative units. Spanish and Portuguese are the region's two lingua francas, and in the realm of religion, the Catholic Church is dominant. (Indeed, it was more dominant between 1800 and 1950 than it is today.) And some enduring—"structural"—features of Latin American society have colonial roots: ethnic makeup, patterns of settlement, the spatial geography of the major cities. The so-called colonial legacy does not rigidly determine later development (or underdevelopment), and during the two centuries since independence, there have been many examples of national divergence (as I examine, regarding the specific cases of Peru and Mexico, in chapter 4). But the shared colonial past is not a mere figment, and the "Latin American" label therefore remains both useful and appropriate.

There are, of course, ways of usefully disaggregating the catch-all "Latin America," apart from simply resorting to the convenient "givens" of national or, indeed, subnational political units: countries, states/provinces, districts, and municipalities. Particularly useful is the rough tripartite division proposed in chapter 2, which distinguishes (1) temperate highlands, historically populated by dense, ancient, sedentary, tribute-paying, indigenous communities, characterized by peasant farming, often coupled with mining (the norm in central and southern Mexico, Guatemala, and the huge Andean zone, from Colombia through Ecuador, Peru, and Bolivia); (2) the pastoral plains, suitable for extensive stock-raising, site of a footloose "cowboy" (gaucho) culture, as well as mobile indigenous populations who maintained a stubborn resistance to white/mestizo control (in northern Mexico, southern Chile, the sprawling Argentine pampas); and (3) the tropical, coastal lowlands, dedicated to cash crops such as sugar and cacao, often destined for export and worked by imported African slaves (e.g., Cuba, Brazil, the Colombian littoral).[20] This typology is neither static nor exhaustive, but it has quite broad explanatory power.[21] It derives, obviously, from climate, topography, location, economic activity, and labor supply, a set of interlocking determinants that are basically materialist but that have broader consequences touching upon, among other things, religion and politics.

The colonial church, for example, put down deeper roots in the highlands, where dense populations yielded labor and revenue and, in general, produced more devout concentrated Catholic communities. For similar reasons, the colonial state usually established its headquarters in the highlands: Mexico, Quito, Bogotá (Lima was the exception, typifying Peru's sharp polarization between Spanish/mestizo coast and Indian sierras). As a result, nineteenth-century Conservative parties, committed to centralism, wedded to the Catholic Church, and sometimes sympathetic to protectionist lobbies, tended to flourish in the cities of the highlands, while liberalism took root on the coasts, where the church was weak, where port populations tended to support free trade and federalism, and where the presence of both free Black communities and foreign immigrants favored religious heterodoxy and incipient anticlericalism. The contrast is evident if we compare Mexico City and Veracruz, Quito and Guayaquil, Bogotá and Barranquilla, even, to some degree, Santiago and Valparaíso. (Lima, perched on the coast yet more clerical/Catholic than Peru's Indian highlands, is again a partial exception, as well as a good example of the "path dependency" created by early colonial arrangements.)

The tripartite perspective also helps when it comes to tracing major episodes in the long Latin America saga: the Spanish conquest involved seizing a strategic center (Mexico City, Lima) and slowly asserting control over recalcitrant hinterlands, but the cause of independence began on the coastal lowlands (of Venezuela and Argentina) before finally overcoming the last bastions of colonial power in the heartlands of Peru and Mexico.

And during the later nineteenth century, economic and demographic growth tended to favor the old hinterlands at the expense of the historic centers. Buenos Aires and Montevideo boomed, Guayaquil overtook Quito, south-central Brazil (especially São Paulo) outstripped Bahía and the northeast, and northern Mexico began its long trajectory of growth, which was both illustrated and accelerated by the triumph of the northern revolutionaries, the Sonorans in particular, as a result of the 1910 Revolution.

Two final themes deserve mention. First, revolutions and, more broadly, political and/or criminal violence. Another prevalent myth is that Latin America is a notably revolutionary region.[22] A UK cigarette advert from the 1980s, urging brand loyalty, suggested: "If you want a revolution, go to Latin America." Recently, the news from Latin America, especially Mexico and Colombia, that tenuously filters through to a largely indifferent and ignorant European public focuses obsessively on criminal violence.[23] It is true, of course, that, following independence, Latin America, like other recent postcolonial regions (e.g., much of Africa after the Second World War), experienced recurrent political instability, as the old—partial and dwindling—legitimacy of the Crown was finally lost and new states struggled to acquire new postcolonial legitimacies.[24]

But there is instability and instability. Some early Latin American states did achieve a measure of stability (Portalian Chile, Argentina under Rosas, the mature Brazilian Empire), while others experienced recurrent coups and cuartelazos. Often, however, the latter were of very limited scope and severity. Anatole France's description of the French Third Republic ("a tranquil people governed by harassed legislators") has some relevance for nineteenth-century Latin America. Society ticked over, as yet unrevolutionized (since independence did not bring a transformative social revolution), but political life was in flux, and new collective actors, notably the armed forces (regular and irregular), now played a more prominent role and, arguably, a politically destabilizing role. But compared to the previous generation—the generation of the Great Andean rebellion of the 1780s or the Mexican insurgency of the 1810s—that of the postindependence decades lived quieter lives. Of course, there were exceptions: "external" wars (i.e., wars involving non–Latin American belligerents and, usually, aggressors) severely affected Mexico in the 1840s and 1860s, Central America in the 1850s, and Cuba in the 1860s and 1890s. In this respect, the history of the circum-Caribbean, a cockpit of imperialist conflict, was notably more violent than that of South America. Regarding the latter, although the countries of Latin America have fought fewer and much less costly wars among themselves than the Europeans, Chile twice defeated Peru (1836–39, 1879–84), and Paraguay was devastated by Brazil, Argentina, and Uruguay in the War of the Triple Alliance (1864–70).

Nevertheless, the incidence and impact of war, whether civil or international, have been quite limited in postindependence Latin America, arguably less than in Europe or, indeed, Asia and Africa in the same period.[25] As for major social revolutions, they have been few and far between. In the nineteenth century, perhaps only the Mexican Reform and the two Cuban insurgencies have claims to "social revolutionary" status, but they are claims, and they are certainly disputable.[26] In the twentieth century, as more radical forms of mass politics emerged, so the tally of "social revolutions" arguably increased, as I discuss in chapters 6 and 7: Mexico 1910, Bolivia 1952, and Cuba 1959.[27] However, three or four such revolutions among twenty countries over, let's say, the hundred years of the twentieth century, making two thousand "country-years," does not indicate a particular penchant for (social) revolution. Eastern Europe evinces a much more revolutionary twentieth-century history (consider the climacterics of, roughly, 1918, 1945, and 1990). So—and this should come as no surprise—we should not base our history on advertising catchphrases.

Furthermore, we should recall that some analysts of Latin America, past and present, have stressed not its volatile instability but its somnolence, torpor, and quiescence. The region is less a violent volcano than a stagnant pond, not Popocatépetl but the Paraguayan Pantanal.[28] Again, popular images such as taco advertisements capture this stereotype: the image of the "lazy Mexican," for example, involves a sleeping Mexican, slumped under a broad sombrero, propped up against a saguaro cactus (an image rarely to be seen in real life for the good reason that leaning against a cactus is hardly conducive to a good siesta). More important, scholars subscribe to the stereotype. In the 1960s—thus, in the wake of the Cuban

Revolution, no less—expert Latin Americanists commonly emphasized the "politics of conformity" and the "obstacles to change" that affected and retarded the region.[29] In doing so, they echoed—I suspect unwittingly-those censorious foreign travelers who, a century earlier, had lamented the Latin Americans' indifference to work, progress, and innovation and who, like many of their well-to-do Latin American contemporaries, concluded that it was necessary to crack the whip in order to galvanize otherwise "lazy natives" into productive work (as I discuss in chapter 5).

So should we see Latin America as an unstable volcano or a stagnant pond? It is, of course, "une question mal posée." The region is not uniform, nor is its history. Whether the story is one of continuity or change, stability or upheaval, depends on where and when you look. (The same would, of course, be true of Europe: compare 1914–45 and post-1945.) The hugely destructive wars of independence presaged a century of reduced violence and upheaval; the massive upheaval of the Mexican Revolution (1910–20) ushered in decades of relative political stability. So, too, did the much less violent Cuban Revolution of 1959 and the brief Costa Rican civil war of 1948. Political upheaval and political stability, far from being chronic, congenital conditions from which Latin America cannot escape, tend to come in cycles, in part because they are causally connected. Long periods of stability, especially of an authoritarian kind, may incubate growing pent-up discontent, leading eventually to a social explosion, but bouts of upheaval may provide release and an opportunity for political reform and renovation. The grim memory of upheaval, it has been shown, can inhibit radical or violent protest, but with time, the memory fades, and protest may acquire fresh appeal.[30]

Violence also comes in many forms. In fact, if we were able to calibrate the incidence of violence across the two centuries since independence, I suspect that the two biggest contributors would be not political insurgency or social revolution but, on the one hand, low-level, local violence associated with crime, banditry, xenophobia, feuds, and family disputes, examples of which are given in chapters 1 and 3, and, on the other, "top-down" repression by states—what R. J. Rummel has called "death by government"—involving professional police and armies and directed against (supposed) rebels, dissidents, and subversives.[31] In chapters 3 and 5 I mention how top-down violence of this kind increased in the late nineteenth century as well-armed forces repressed troublesome peasants, frontier Indians, religious dissidents, and incipient labor organizations. And, of course, the twentieth century has witnessed yet more extreme forms of state repression, carried out by both the "bureaucratic-authoritarian" states of the Southern Cone and the ethnocidal regimes of Central America (themes that lie beyond the scope of this book). Yet more recently, drug- and crime-related violence has burgeoned, notably in Mexico, Central America, and Colombia. So to the extent that Latin America is violent, we need to disaggregate the forms, incidence, and rationale of violence, and one clear-cut conclusion would be that "revolutionary" violence—violence perpetrated in pursuit of radical political goals—is not and has rarely been the most common variety. If you really want a violent revolution, don't go to Latin America.

The final theme I wish to broach concerns Latin America's external relations, although the argument I develop in chapter 5 is that "external" relations are inextricable from "internal" economic and sociopolitical arrangements and that, to anticipate the conclusion of that chapter, a form of "internal colonialism" obviated any need for "informal empire" to be converted into "formal empire," as was happening in much of Asia and most of Africa in the later nineteenth century. During and after the 1960s, the influential "dependency" school of thought argued that, following independence, Latin America escaped Iberian tutelage only to fall under the sway of the new global hegemon, Britain, which thus established an informal empire in the region.[32] Later, the 1890s being seen as a watershed, the United States embarked on its own imperialist penetration of Latin America, which, again, involved largely "informal" control and influence, especially in South America. (In the circum-Caribbean it was a different story, involving U.S. armed interventions and protectorates.) In making its claim, the dependency school echoed, in rather different and discordant tones, arguments previously made by Marxist analysts such as Lenin, Rosa Luxemburg, and Rudolf Hilferding to the effect that European— and incipient American—imperialism, driven by the voracious demands of "finance" or "monopoly" capital, needed to expand overseas, whether by means of direct conquest during the Scramble for Africa or by more indirect and devious methods, as in Latin America.[33] The dependistas also echoed historians of (British) imperialism who, though they sharply and rightly dissented from the Marxist diagnosis of finance/monopoly capital, agreed that Latin America was a crucial area of British economic expansion and penetration, involving a degree of force and arm-twisting that might justifiably be called "informal imperialism" or "paramountcy" or something on those lines. The classic exposition of this view, summed up in just fifteen eloquent pages, was penned by John Gallagher and Ronald Robinson, who, stressing the continuity of British economic expansion through the nineteenth century, tacitly agreed with the Marxist emphasis on basic economic drivers but dismissed the alleged connection between finance capital and the Scramble for Africa.[34] They argued—convincingly, I think—that the British economy did not experience some sudden quantum shift (to finance/monopoly capital) in the late nineteenth century and that imperial expansion, both formal (with conquest) and informal (without), was a story of continuity throughout the century.[35]

The final piece of the jigsaw concerned what we could call "peripheral causality" (associated with Gallagher and Robinson's "local crisis" thesis). If we ask, why did Britain, the preeminent imperial power, sometimes opt for formal empire (e.g., in India and sub-Saharan Africa), sometimes for informal relations (in Latin America, especially Argentina), the answer lies in events and processes in the periphery; it has little or nothing to do with the dynamics of finance/monopoly capitalism. And, we should stress, this is a key question-and-answer: under formal empire, your country is painted red on the map, and the British run your affairs, taxing, administering, and conscripting; under informal empire, your country, though constrained by a close and influential British liaison, remains independent, governed by its own "collaborating elites." Argentina thus resembled Australia in important respects, but no Argentines died at Gallipoli. These formal/informal alternatives, therefore, although they exist on a broad spectrum, are significantly different, and the difference can be a matter of life or death. The same alternatives also apply in respect to later U.S. imperialism, although the United States, as I argue, placed much greater weight on geopolitical considerations in Latin America, especially the circum-Caribbean, than the British ever did. While decisions either to intervene or to abstain have to be taken by the "metropolitan" power, the causality is largely "peripheral" (or, as Robinson put it, "excentric"), since it is events in the periphery that determine whether the informal liaison remains viable (i.e., safe, secure, and profitable) or whether, typically as a result of a "local crisis," the liaison ruptures and the imperial/metropolitan power decides, perhaps reluctantly, to intervene. ("Intervention" can cover a range of actions, but I am assuming that a measure of force, leading to a measure of outright control, is essential.)

Of course, this did not happen in Latin America. In the first half of the nineteenth century, the British had intervened, forcibly but sporadically; thus, they combined coercion and cajolery in the hope of promoting their interests, which meant encouraging political stability, favoring congenial, commerce-friendly elites, and promoting conditions conducive to profitable trade and investment. (Again, in later decades, the United States would adopt similar priorities, overlaid with more pressing geopolitical concerns.) These early British interventions were not noticeably successful; Gallagher and Robinson, who were not, I repeat, Latin American experts, tended to exaggerate the success, though not the scale, of British efforts. But by the later nineteenth century—and the timing varies from country to country—the need for intervention receded, because Latin American elites were now putting their troubled houses in order. Internally, this meant the imposition of order, social control, and a more business-friendly environment, a package of policies that I describe in chapter 5 under the loose description of "internal colonialism," the justification for the term being that these policies often replicated those undertaken by colonial regimes for much the same reasons elsewhere in the world. And in highly schematic terms, we can say that internal colonialism obviated the need for formal imperialism. Why would the imperial power waste blood and treasure when local elites were doing a pretty good job on their own?[36] The later nineteenth century thus witnessed fewer imperialist interventions, and when the United States began its interventionist spree after 1898, it was largely confined to the circum-Caribbean. South America remained off-limits. If my argument holds, we thus identify an intimate connection between, on the one hand, the evolution of the Latin American domestic political economy, the rise of the state, and the positivistic mutation of liberalism and, on the other, the changing modalities of "imperialist" power and "informal empire." The internal and external stories are two halves of the same walnut.

Finally, I will revert to the historian's default mode: chronology and periodization. The aim is to show how the stories already mentioned wove their sinuous way through some five generations of Latin American life. Those generations can be roughly identified with the following very approximate periods, which are defined in politico-economic terms: independence (ca. 1780–1820), early state-building (ca. 1820–50), midcentury liberalism (ca. 1850–80), the positivist project (ca. 1880–1920), and a rather open-ended catch-all that will receive cursory treatment, the onset of mass politics (ca. 1920–50).[37]

Traditional nationalist historians hailed independence as a heroic break with an oppressive colonial past, lionizing the *próceres de la patria*—the pleiad of great men (and a few women) who defeated Spain and thus ended the long dark night of colonial obscurantism and oppression. From the beginning, this highly partisan account was challenged by conservative and Catholic opponents who deplored the violence and destruction, the anticlericalism and xenophobia associated with the Wars of Independence while lamenting that Spanish rule, which had brought order, hierarchy, and Catholicism to the Americas, had come to a gratuitously violent end.[38] Both views, of course, were caricatures or, if you prefer, myths. But they were potent myths that influenced postindependence political thinking and provided some of the ideological inspiration for the embryonic liberal and conservative parties of the nineteenth century.

More to the point, serious historians have continued to debate the causes and consequences of independence. Regarding causes, recent revisionist historiography, which I mention at several points in the book, has tended to play down the internal structural factors that provoked protest and eventually brought about the fall of the empire: class and ethnic conflict (including the rivalry of criollos and peninsulares); the enhanced taxation, centralization, and social control associated with the Bourbon Reforms; and the fraying of the bonds that had historically tied throne and altar together in mutually advantageous alliance. Instead, the revisionists stress external and contingent causes, particularly the Napoleonic invasion of Spain and the decapitation of the Spanish monarchy, which generated a legitimation crisis in the Americas. The crisis came from outside, disrupting a colonial pact that was still solid, legitimate, and viable; indeed, it has been counterfactually suggested that the Spanish Empire could have reformed itself into an enlightened transatlantic Iberian commonwealth, acceding to moderate colonial demands while maintaining the monarchy and the empire intact.[39]

As I suggest at several points, this revisionist debunking of the old orthodoxy (of mass patriotic insurrection against oppressive colonial regimes) has, like many revisionist exercises of this kind, advanced from sensible critique to overblown orthodoxy; it has overshot the mark and, in doing so, has created an unconvincing myth of its own. It mistakes a trigger—the Napoleonic invasion—for a basic cause. It forgets that Spain had gone through a previous monarchical crisis (the War of the Spanish Succession, 1701–14), which had triggered no major anticolonial insurrections. It chooses to overlook or downplay the series of major protests and rebellions that preceded 1808: the resistance provoked, notably in Paraguay and Mexico, by the expulsion of the Jesuits in the 1750s and 1760s; the Comunero rebellion, which shook New Granada in 1781; and the Great Andean revolt, which was, in effect, three "massive rebellions" that convulsed Peru and Upper Peru in the 1780s.[40] It confuses the ostensible prosperity of the late Bourbon period (basically, the Crown's successful extraction of bullion) with general well-being, when, in fact, fiscal rapacity coincided with and arguably contributed to declining living standards.[41] And it exaggerates the reformist potential of the Spanish Crown. After all, the restoration of Fernando VII in 1814 signaled a return to hard-line absolutism, and even the Spanish liberals, who briefly triumphed in 1821, showed little sign of deferring to colonial demands for home rule and representation.

It is certainly true that the independence movements themselves were confused and fractured and did not exhibit a common, consensual, proactive program for state- and nation-building. But that is par for the course with most major revolutions.[42] As chapter 7 illustrates, revolutions rarely achieve ideological or programmatic unity, but that does not stop them from being real revolutions underpinned by profound ("structural") socio-political grievances and leading to rapid substantial change (a diagnostic requirement of successful revolutions). And if gung-ho revisionists deny or downplay those basic grievances, a gaping explanatory hole remains: What were people fighting and dying for, in large numbers, on both sides of the barricades? As the parallel with the War of the Spanish Succession suggests, contingent external events do not of themselves cause major con-flagrations, even if they supply the spark, as in 1808. In order to burn the house down, a conflagration requires plenty of dry, flammable, domestic fuel.

So much for the causes; what of the consequences? It helps to draw a distinction, albeit somewhat artificial, between the economic and the political. In the 1960s and after, the so-called dependency school, men-tioned a few pages back, reacted against positive and patriotic accounts of independence, arguing that Latin America swapped decrepit Iberian *formal* imperial control for a more robust and aggressive *informal* impe-rialism, deployed by Britain and, later, the United States. "Dependency," the condition of being a reflex economy in thrall to a metropolitan master, thus continued in a different form, and it stymied hopes of independent Latin American development (except, some proponents argued, logically but fancifully, in countries such as Dr. Francia's Paraguay, which kept the imperialists at bay and pioneered autonomous national development). Nowadays, the dependency paradigm is dead or at least moribund.[43] As I mention in chapter 5, Britain did entertain high hopes of commercial bonanzas in Latin America, but in the decades after independence, these were often disappointed. Latin America did not rapidly succumb to a new dependency, which in turn stymied development. The dependistas were therefore wrong, but as already mentioned, Gallagher and Robinson (who were not, of course, Latin American experts) also exaggerated both the scale of British commercial penetration and the impact of "informal empire."

However, after the mid-nineteenth century (and the timing varied from place to place, depending crucially on "peripheral" factors), the Anglo–Latin

American economic liaison deepened, especially in regard to investment. And in general, Latin America now rapidly integrated into global circuits of trade, capital flow, and international migration. This approximate periodization reinforces the notion, now quite widely accepted, of a "middle period" in Latin American economic history, spanning the late colonial period and the early postindependence decades (roughly 1750–1850). Independence, by formally terminating Spain's already shaky mercantilist control, accelerated the region's opening to global trade. But it is hard to see it as a profound economic watershed in itself.

In political terms, however, independence *was* a genuine revolution, which is why, inter alia, we should not hesitate to refer to the Wars of Independence as revolutions rather than mere "civil wars." The old regime of throne and altar collapsed, and the new republics had to grapple with formidable problems of state- and nation-building in a chaotic postcolonial context. The postindependence generation was therefore one of political opening, experiment, and—with qualifications—instability. As the early liberal hopes of representative republican government faded, a conservative and clerical backlash gathered strength, and (again, at different times in different places) political opening gave way to closure. Faith in politico-constitutional solutions faded; the franchise was restricted; and while the clerical conservatives looked back to the colony for inspiration, the more radical liberals concluded that far-reaching institutional reform was necessary if their countries were to stabilize and prosper. What I termed "institutional" liberalism thus targeted the corporate property of the church and of peasant—often indigenous—communities. Anticlericalism, hitherto a secondary issue, emerged as a key political litmus. The embryonic liberal/conservative dichotomy became more salient, divisive, and institutionally entrenched (notably in Mexico and Colombia). It also penetrated society more deeply as elite skirmishing gave way to broader and often more violent mass mobilization. As a result, specific regions, communities, and families acquired distinct political loyalties, typically liberal or conservative, often in opposition to local or regional rivals. National politics rode on the back of these subnational conflicts. The outcome varied according to the balance of forces in different countries, so we could identify a slew of "divergences" both great and small. Brazil, again, was an outlier, since the monarchy had quite successfully contained and managed liberal/conservative conflict within constitutional bounds. However, the fall of the empire, coming on the heels of the abolition of slavery, provoked social protest—often couched in religious or messianic terms—and harsh state repression.

Again, the conflicts of one generation provoked reactions in its successor. During approximately the last quarter of the nineteenth century, the classic liberal/conservative conflict tended to diminish as a measure of elite consensus emerged that spanned party lines and that was committed to a positivistic project of economic development. Contentious politics had to be shelved in the interests of peace, order, and economic progress. The positivistic project was, in some cases (e.g., Argentina and Uruguay), roughly compatible with liberal representative government, but often, particularly in "Indo-America," it involved authoritarian and exclusionary policies, enacted by stronger, more muscular states. Hence, as I argue in chapter 5, the neat fit between, on the one hand, "informal empire" (in the sense of much tighter insertion into the global economy, including close alignment with its economic imperatives) and, on the other, a form of racially inflected "internal colonialism."

Finally, we come to the twentieth century, to the notional fifth generation and what I glibly label the age of mass politics. This book in no sense offers a broad coverage of twentieth-century Latin America: it focuses—in chapters 6 and 7—on the specific question of revolution, which is but one big theme among many. But to conclude this prospectus, I shall offer a very brief overview, if only to locate "revolution" within a broader context. Since independence Latin American politics had always embodied a measure of rumbustious popular participation (a feature it shared with the United States, however much Americans might dislike or ignore the parallel). Perhaps, as a Mexicanist, I am prone to exaggerate this feature, since Mexico is the arguably classic case of recurrent popular political mobilization.[44] But there are plenty of instances elsewhere, symptoms of Latin America's precocious politicization, its early adoption of representative republican regimes, and thus its long tradition of mass involvement in politics, whether violent or electoral, local, regional, or national.[45] But the twentieth century witnessed the growth of more formal and enduring mass institutions (parties, sindicatos, peasant leagues); the spread of new ideologies of both Left and Right (anarchism, communism, social Catholicism, liberation theology, fascism, the latter assuming both secular and clerical-Catholic guises); and the evolution of stronger states, heirs of the late nineteenth-century positivist regimes, which now had to respond to renewed mass politicization at home and a fast-changing global environment abroad. The responses varied, involving harsh repression, more subtle co-optation, or, sometimes, populist promotion—irresponsible "rabble-rousing," in the eyes of alarmed conservatives.

Regarding economic policy, there was no sudden paradigm shift from laissez-faire to state intervention, since, as I have stressed, the nineteenth-century Latin American state had never been a minimalist "nightwatchman" to begin with. But twentieth-century political elites now began to grapple with the "social question" (roughly, urban growth, disease, and deprivation linked to incipient working-class mobilization). They became belatedly aware of ethnic exclusion and oppression (hence the rise of *indigenismo*), and they came to see the utility of acquiring mass support, particularly in the cities, among the burgeoning working class. (The rural poor, especially when they were brown and indigenous, remained, in many cases, marginal to "official" politics: indigenismo, therefore, was often more rhetorical than real.)

The most spectacular example of these trends was Mexico, where the revolution—discussed in chapter 7—brought to power a new elite, committed, whether out of idealism or self-interest, to land and labor reform, to a robust cultural nationalism, and to the emancipation, sometimes real, often rhetorical, of Mexico's indigenous population. For all its corruption and opportunism, the Mexican Revolution embodied a genuine reform of the state and its relation to a newly mobilized population. Elsewhere, as the paired comparison with Peru reveals, reform tended to be more skin-deep: the *indigenista* rhetoric of President Augusto Leguía was hardly translated into practical policy, land reform remained off the agenda, and even the "allure of labor" had a cosmetic quality.[46] But even where Leguía's state dragged its feet, important critics such as the Alianza Popular Revolucionaria Americana (APRA) and José Carlos Mariátegui's small but vocal Socialist Party shifted the terms of political debate.[47] Elsewhere in Indo-America (e.g., in Central America), reform lagged; at best, Guatemala had to settle for the personalist populism of Jorge Ubico, while in Nicaragua Augusto César Sandino was eliminated and, with American connivance, the Somoza dynasty took power. "He may be a sonofabitch, but at least he's our sonofabitch," as FDR—perhaps— said of Anastasio Somoza García, a succinct summary of the ethics and mechanics of "informal empire."[48]

But in the Southern Cone, liberal representative politics had now taken root, further bolstered by Argentina's Sáenz Peña Law of 1912, which introduced compulsory universal male suffrage and the secret ballot. If the countryside remained politically marginal (the most troublesome "peasants" were the insurgent Swiss settlers of Santa Fé), the "social question," fueled by mass immigration, agitated the cities, where anarchism briefly flourished.[49] After 1916, Hipólito Irigoyen's Radical government combined repression with modest overtures to organized labor. Meanwhile, across the Río de la Plata, José Batlle y Ordóñez pioneered a novel form of social democracy, grafting welfarism onto liberalism, as Asquith and Lloyd George were doing in the United Kingdom. Although the Mexican revolutionary example appealed to nationalist reformist sectors elsewhere in the region (such as Peru's APRA and, later, the more progressive wing of Colombia's Liberal Party), governments and elites remained leery, especially in Indo-America.[50] Southern Cone reformers also disdained the distant, rabble-rousing example of Mexico: for them, progressive (white) Europe was a more suitable and decorous model. The Mexican Revolution, though it served as an example—good or bad—to some Latin Americans, remained a political outlier, and renewed revolutionary experiments had to await the 1950s. Revolution, as I have said, was not a standing dish in Latin America.

Finally, the region's external relations also underwent significant changes in the twentieth century. By 1914 integration into global markets had proceeded apace; British "hegemony" was fading, and especially in the circum-Caribbean and northern South America, the economic role of the United States grew, substantially accelerated by the two world wars. By the 1950s the British had become largely passive observers of revolution in Bolivia and Cuba; the Americans were now the major foreign players, although—in arguably "paranoid style"—they readily detected and exaggerated foreign challenges (German, Japanese, Russian) to their Monrovian hegemony in the Americas.[51] The British and their "collaborating elites," we could say, had done the spadework of integration and infrastructural investment back in the nineteenth century; now, as the Second Industrial Revolution, based on mass production, chemicals, cars, steel, oil, and electricity, supplanted the First (the revolution of steam, coal, and textiles), the United States became the chief beneficiary and by 1945 the new global hegemon, committed to waging a bipolar Cold War. However, this process was no seamless narrative. Latin America was jolted by two world wars and the Great Depression, external shocks that were all the more severe, given the previous phase of global integration, which now made the region acutely vulnerable to capricious vicissitudes in foreign demand, commodity prices, and capital flows.[52]

Two concluding observations about the book. First, these essays are fairly wide-ranging and—sometimes implicitly, often explicitly—comparative in approach. Broad-brush history of this kind has no intrinsic merit, nor, indeed, do minutely detailed historical monographs.[53] Both genres can be good or bad. However, nowadays we hear a good deal about "global" and "transnational" history—a reflection, perhaps, of trends in the "real world" beyond academia. However, like a good many fashionable neologisms, "transnational" is vague and often serves as a fancy nom-de-plume for old and familiar themes. And when it comes to global history, though there are some genuine and original examples of the genre, quite often the claim to "global" involves little more than linking yet another narrow case study to broader supranational trends or influences, often assuming a crudely diffusionist view of how the world works.[54]

I do not therefore claim that the essays in this book are "global" or "transnational" (although chapter 7 has claims), simply that they deal with big themes, often in comparative terms. Comparison, of course, can be supranational (Brazil and Costa Rica) or subnational (Rondônia and São Paulo). Furthermore, most historians—if they retain a glimmer of intellectual curiosity—engage in regular comparisons, even if they are not explicit about them. (By the same token, they also engage in tacit counterfactuals.) Usually, when it comes to writing history, historians remain attached like limpets to particular rocks (places and periods), and their comparisons serve to shed light on the rocks they have chosen to inhabit, which is fine. "Vaulting ambition which o'erleaps itself" is probably best avoided by both historians and medieval Scottish lords.[55] Occasionally, historians venture beyond their rocks and hazard more ambitious comparisons, which, though they can be difficult, are also commendable, if they are done in a sensible, scholarly fashion, that is, by relying on a wide range of good sources, reading with critical discrimination, and skeptically steering clear of both vapid neologisms and prepackaged metanarratives. One good reason for occasionally attempting broad-brush, comparative, even global history is that, if historians don't do it, the field is surrendered to others: glib commentators like Francis Fukuyama or those historical sociologists who, devising ingenious neologisms, like to "play pick-and-mix in the sweetshop of history."[56] The sweets—or, if you prefer, candies—have already been mixed, baked, wrapped, shipped, and retailed by workaday historians. The historical sociologists then swallow the ones they like. It seems reasonable, therefore, that—changing the metaphor—those who make the bricks in the first place should sometimes have a say in the subsequent design and construction of the big building.

This brings me to my last point. One important comparative advantage enjoyed by historians (compared to sociologists and the like) is a due regard for the provenance and utility of historical data. Historians are, as we have seen, well aware of "complexity," but they also know, or should know, that evidence needs to be assembled carefully and critically. "Facts" can't be wrenched out of context and pressed into the service of some grand, possibly a priori, and often anachronistic scheme (like Fukuyama's "end of history"). The bricks and the clay that goes into them have to be fit for purpose. Synthetic historiography, of which these several essays are examples, depends crucially on using the right (secondary, published) sources both carefully and correctly. The endnotes that accompany the essays are, I sheepishly admit, quite numerous and bulky. This may partly reflect a personal idiosyncrasy: I consider (substantive) endnotes to be interesting, rewarding, and deserving of scholarly support.[57] But there is also a practical point. I set out to present the main arguments in the text, using fairly bold strokes and illustrative examples, without wearying the reader with too many details, caveats, or qualifications. Where, it seemed to me, additional evidence, clarifications, and occasional and relevant digressions were advisable, I have squirreled them away in the notes. (By "relevant digressions" I mean those that link the central discussion to interesting connections and comparisons.) Equally, some of my more intemperate remarks are also buried in the notes. In short, I am sympathetic to Leopold von Ranke's approach—as described by Anthony Grafton—that notes crucially serve to bolster and reinforce the basic arguments advanced in the text: "A serious work of history must travel on an impregnably armoured bottom, rather like a tank."[58] "Lay readers" may prefer to skip the notes and concentrate on the text; picky experts, critics, and reviewers, on the other hand, may wish to inspect my armor-plated bottom.

CHAPTER I

Back to Banditry

ERIC HOBSBAWM WAS, ALONG WITH VICTOR KIERNAN, THE MOST cosmopolitan of the British Marxist historians.[1] Though his earliest published work dealt with British labor history, his initial interest in French North Africa having been stymied by the outbreak of the Second World War, he soon diversified, chiefly to Europe but also to Asia, Africa, and the Americas, including Latin America.[2] Apart from some firsthand research, chiefly on contemporary (1960s) Peru, his Latin American forays were based almost entirely on secondary sources.[3] However, Hobsbawm had a proven knack for choosing good secondary sources on which to build his ambitious surveys, so his work, while bullish and broad-brush in approach, is not strewn with the errors and simplifications that often mar such works of synthesis.

At least three major concepts of Hobsbawmian provenance have entered the Latin American historiographical mainstream: the general crisis of the seventeenth century; the invention of tradition; and, as a subset of primitive/"prepolitical" rebellion, social banditry, which has been the subject of some lively debate.[4] His book *Bandits*—the more popular follow-up to *Primitive Rebels*—focused heavily on Europe, but it contains several references to Latin American cases, and in some recent editions, Pancho Villa, the celebrated Mexican bandit turned revolutionary, graces the cover.[5] (More surprisingly, a recent Spanish version of *Rebeldes primitivos* carries on its cover what looks suspiciously like a Mexican-revolutionary scene, which is very odd, since the Mexican revolutionaries—being "revolutionaries" rather than "prepolitical" rebels—were quite rightly absent from the pages of *Primitive Rebels*.)[6]

Whatever one might think about Hobsbawm's discussion of banditry and its contribution to Latin American history, we should recognize at the outset that it served to bring bandits in from the cold, rescuing them from the clutches of romantics and folklorists. That sort of rescue of "subaltern" actors from the "enormous condescension of posterity," once it's done, can begin to appear natural, a statement of the historiographically obvious; thus, we may underestimate the original novelty of the approach and the credit that is due for introducing a (historiographical) novelty and successfully naturalizing it.[7]

The key novelty was the concept of social banditry, that is, of banditry that had a strongly social dimension, involving popular support, and that made banditry a form of popular resistance (or, indeed, "primitive rebellion").[8] On the basis of wide, if sometimes rather superficial, reading (which, in *Bandits*, now encompassed the world, including Brazil, Mexico, and Peru), Hobsbawm argued that this was a global phenomenon, displaying common features regarding bandit organization, motivation, recruitment, and modus operandi. Some generalizations display a characteristic Hobsbawmian chutzpah, for example, the breezy generalization that "the bulk of bandits speak no kind of argot but simply a version of the local peasant dialect" or—perhaps my favorite—when Hobsbawm tosses off a reference to "the well-known [*sic*] Bulgarian ballad . . . 'Stoian and Nedelia.'"[9]

It was a tribute to the appeal and originality of the work—both *Primitive Rebels* and, even more, *Bandits*—that it provoked plenty of comment, a good deal of it critical. Several critics pointed out, correctly, that Hobsbawm had relied almost entirely on secondary sources; that these were often literary (in the broad sense: novels, poems, ballads); and that available primary sources, notably, police and similar government documents, were largely neglected, even when they were accessible.[10] Thus, when Hobsbawm boldly states that "the documents are unanimous," one may reasonably ask *which* documents and how comprehensive Hobsbawm's search for "documents" had been.[11] Sources mattered because, it was further alleged, Hobsbawm's reliance on literary texts seriously distorted reality. And in his case, reality mattered: given his robust defense of empirical history, he could hardly plead a fashionable postmodern indifference to positivistic facts.[12] Indeed, Hobsbawm recognized that myths about the "noble bandit" could mislead, and "in all cases we need independent evidence of his actions."[13]

In particular, Anton Blok penned a cogent but not entirely negative critique based on his deep knowledge of the Sicilian mafia, arguing that "his" bandits were mostly mercenary criminals who preyed on the peasantry and often did so in the service of local elites.[14] The classic case of Salvatore Giuliano would seem to clinch the argument.[15] However, Blok argued on the basis of what he knew, and on that basis he could not—and did not—dismiss the notion of social banditry altogether.[16] Showing that Sicilian bandits were unsocial or antisocial did not tell us anything about bandits in, for example, the sierras of northern Mexico, the hill country of central Cuba, or the *sertão* of northeastern Brazil.

Latin American specialists soon weighed in, often adopting a similarly critical stance. Billy Jaynes Chandler, in one of the best (biographical) studies of Latin American banditry, questioned both Hobsbawm's methodology and the application of the "social bandit" label to his own subject, the Brazilian bandit Lampião: Hobsbawm's "discussions . . . are neither closely reasoned nor adequately supported by reliable evidence," and his interpretation of banditry, "although [it] . . . may make a considerable contribution to the analysis of myths about bandits, contributes little to . . . the study of bandits themselves."[17] Linda Lewin, recounting the career of Lampião's predecessor Antonio Silvino, roughly concurred: though Silvino seemed to fit the "noble robber" / Robin Hood category, this legend obscured "his actual historical role as an instrument for maintaining the established order on behalf of local agrarian elites."[18] For Mexico, Paul Vanderwood analyzed banditry and rural policing in the later nineteenth century, arguing that bandits were mercenary criminals who were out for monetary gain and who rationally chose a life of crime and had no qualms about fleecing the peasantry. In his contribution to a 1987 symposium (which also took a critical line toward social banditry), Vanderwood concluded that bandits were, in the main, "mercenaries," "profit-seeking" individualists, and "outsiders who wanted in."[19] Vanderwood's student Rosalie Schwartz replicated the argument for nineteenth-century Cuba, in direct contrast to Louis Perez's distinctly Hobsbawmian interpretation of the island's bandit gangs.[20] By way of summing up the Latin American experience (a notoriously risky thing to do, given the scale and heterogeneity of the region), Richard Slatta, editor of the previously cited symposium on Latin American outlaws, boldly concluded that the social bandit thesis did not work in Latin America; nor, he added for good measure, did it work in the world at large, there being "few historical figures to match Hobsbawm's model" (though Slatta at least gave Hobsbawm a parting pat on the back for his "inspired and original hypothesis").[21] In contrast, Gilbert Joseph, in what is probably the most comprehensive review of the literature on Latin American banditry, was more positive, at least to the extent that he chose to assimilate social banditry to broader forms of peasant resistance and protest, thus indirectly justifying the social bandit approach.[22]

My own take on the subject is somewhat closer to Joseph's (than to Slatta's or Vanderwood's), but I don't intend following precisely the same "dead-end trail" into a "swamp of conceptual relativity" (I hope).[23] Of course, each case has to be judged on its merits, but I can see sufficient evidence to grant *some* Mexican bandits "social" status (and not just in the realm of myth), and that being the case, I am disposed to believe that other Latin American bandits may have displayed social characteristics (e.g., in Cuba, where, on the basis of admittedly limited knowledge, I would locate myself somewhere between the contrasting views of Schwartz and Perez).[24] However, we can go beyond a simple yes/no debate by considering the modalities of (social) banditry, including how bandits were recruited, how they operated, and—a crucial question—how perceptions of them depended on both time and place. Finally, we can hazard some thoughts about the political status of bandits, particularly in revolutionary contexts. Here, somewhat in contrast to Joseph, I would place greater stress on the role of the state and the dialectical relationship between banditry and state power (rather than focusing overmuch on the place of banditry within the panorama of peasant resistance, a theme that certainly merits attention and that has received plenty of it in recent years).

Before launching into the analysis, a few words of initial clarification may help, if only to clear away some conceptual clutter. First, we can roughly define bandits as those who illegally and violently acquire goods (including money) that are not theirs. Hence in the eyes of the law they are criminals. (What "society" thinks of them is another matter and is, of course, a key item in the "social banditry" debate.) Bandits may acquire those goods by robbery or by extortion (i.e., by forcing victims to pay up), but in contrast to, say, forgers, embezzlers, pickpockets, con men, burglars, and, perhaps, hedge-fund traders, bandits acquire their ill-gotten gains not by deceit and subterfuge but by direct confrontation involving the threat or use of violence. Hence, while certainly criminal, they can be seen as bold, brave, and macho in a way that forgers, embezzlers, pickpockets, and the rest are not. (History throws up no "noble embezzlers" or "social burglars," as far as I know.) There is some discrepancy in the literature between those who see banditry as necessarily collective (a question of gangs) and those who would admit solo outlaws (such as Dick Turpin, who, incidentally, seems to have been a thoroughly antisocial bandit).[25] Euclides da Cunha—not a wholly reliable guide, it is true—referred to "the solitary bandit who arrived with his blunderbuss on his shoulder" at the messianic community of Canudos in the Brazilian backlands.[26] We certainly hear of bandits such as Pancho Villa who occasionally pulled jobs on their own.[27] I do not see this as crucial to the argument (in other words, it is how the bandit operates, not the size of the group, that matters); however, as a matter of fact the great majority of the bandits I have looked at or heard of in Mexico and elsewhere operated in groups. (I shall later suggest some ballpark figures.) Furthermore, even solo outlaws such as Dick Turpin needed their network of supporters and sympathizers, as I shall also discuss.

A more important discrepancy concerns whether bandits are necessarily rural or also urban. Hobsbawm, linking banditry to "primitive rebellion," took the former view, which Gilbert Joseph, by locating banditry within the broader spectrum of "peasant resistance," tended to follow. This is important, because a rural or peasant emphasis strongly suggests that banditry is a product of the past, a phenomenon of "traditional" rural or peasant societies that is destined to disappear with the advance of "modernity" (whatever that is) or, more concretely, with the growth of cities, industry, literacy, markets, globalization (take your pick). And Latin America, we should note, is now heavily urban, industrial, literate, market-oriented, and globalized. It is true that many of the famous bandits whom we know about were (primarily) rural, but some also operated in or on the edges of urban settings, such as Isaac Mendicoa, "The Tiger of the Pedregal," and, perhaps, the notorious Grey Automobile Gang, which preyed on a crime-ridden Mexico City in the late 1910s.[28] In Cuba (by Latin American standards, a precociously urban country) bandits clustered not in remote rural regions but rather, Schwartz shows, "on the fringes of a throbbing capital city [Havana] in the most heavily populated and urban part of the island."[29] Smaller provincial towns, like the tobacco and cigar town of Bejucal, also witnessed banditry and harbored, particularly among the tobacco workers, "admirers and supporters" of the local outlaws.[30] More recently, Mexico's narco gangs have—necessarily—operated in town and country alike; they are also involved in extensive and complex transnational networks. So if they are bandits, social or unsocial, they seem to have negotiated Mexico's transformation to an urban, industrial, and, if you like, "modern" society with some success.[31] Maybe banditry isn't as typically "traditional" (i.e., rural, "primitive," and peasant-based) as Hobsbawm and others supposed, which also means that it is not destined to wither in the bright light of "modernity" (whatever "modernity" may be).

I now suggest a more positive point: if we review the phenomenon broadly and comparatively, banditry seems to cluster in certain times and places, which suggests some degree of underlying—if you like, "structural"—causation; it is not just a question of random individual criminality or psychopathology.[32] Major wars generated bouts of banditry, a phenomenon evident in Europe at the time of the Thirty Years War and the French-revolutionary and Napoleonic wars and again apparent in Latin America following the War of the Pacific (in Peru), the Ten Years War in Cuba, and, as I shall later note, the Mexican Revolution of 1910–20.[33] In Brazil, too, an "epidemic" of banditry broke out in the later nineteenth and early twentieth centuries, stimulated, it would seem, both by socioeconomic "push" factors (recurrent drought, overpopulation, and volatile migration, associated with the end of slavery and the Amazon rubber boom-and-bust) and political "permissive" factors (the shift in 1889 from the centralized monarchy to the highly decentralized Old Republic, which allowed local clans—*parentelas*—to engage in ferocious familial and political feuds).[34]

There are also clear spatial patterns. In Mexico at the time of the revolution, banditry appears to have clustered in the Bajío (and the center/west of the country more broadly), along the southern Gulf Coast (southern Veracruz and Tabasco), and in the Sierra Madre Occidental in the center/ north.[35] Though climatically very different, they had in common relatively commercial economies, cash-crop (and/or mining) production, and a mix of villages, small towns, and sizeable farms or ranches. In the dense, sedentary peasant zones of central Mexico (such as Morelos, Zapata's state), banditry was weaker, certainly during the revolutionary period.[36] In Brazil, too, there was a clear geographical pattern: the classic bandit zone was to be found in the northeastern sertão, where conditions were particularly harsh and "state failure" exacerbated the traditional propensity toward clan vendettas and blood feuds.[37] (This was also the primary region of messianic movements, which have been seen, in part, as responses to severe social upheaval and anomie.)[38] In contrast, the economically buoyant southeast of Brazil, dominated by coffee and the burgeoning metropolis of São Paulo, remained relatively unscathed. Two principal factors would seem to be at work: in the southeast the economy was more prosperous and the state was stronger (it enjoyed greater resources and was arguably more legitimate).[39] Young men—the typical recruits to bandit gangs—had career alternatives, and the authority of the state was respected to a greater extent than it was, for example, in the backwoods of the northeast. In Cuba, too, late nineteenth-century banditry clustered in the center of the island, in the sugar zone south and east of Havana, where commercial vicissitudes were combined with agrarian dispossession and land concentration; the east—notably, the province of Oriente, where a more traditional peasantry subsisted and where banditry would later flourish alongside revolutionary insurrection in the twentieth century—was comparatively quiet and orderly.[40]

These patterns suggest that banditry is not just a random individual phenomenon; some sort of structural causation relating to both broad historical trends (wars, migrations, droughts, economic cycles) and socio-political geography (settlement, population, the frontier, the reach of the state) is at work. But whether the structural preconditions produce Hobsbawmian social grievances, class solidarity, and social banditry, on the one hand, or anti-Hobsbawmian mercenary criminality, on the other, remains an open question. To anticipate my rough conclusion, I think that the story in Mexico and, to some extent, Cuba is compatible with a Hobsbawmian explanation (banditry acquired a social and political dimension), but in Brazil and Peru (perhaps Peru especially) the link is less apparent. That does not mean that Brazilian and Peruvian banditry was simply random happenstance. It was just as structurally determined, but in these cases the combination of causality and context generated mercenary, factionalized banditry linked to elite interests and often very destructive of peasant lives and livelihood.[41]

Here, the key factor concerns the bandit's place within society; it is a "relational question" analogous to related questions concerning, say, "legitimacy" and "charisma."[42] Are bandits genuinely popular figures who are seen by "the people" as "noble robbers" or righteous "avengers"?[43] Have they typically been driven to banditry by oppressive authorities and their elite allies? Do bandits merit popular sympathy because, in their bandit activities, they rob the rich while sparing or even succoring the poor? Or, as Vanderwood and others argue, are bandits common criminals who are out for loot and lucre and who have chosen a life of crime? While they may rob the rich (since it's the rich who have the money and goods worth robbing: remember the wise words of Willie Sutton), are they also happy to fleece the poor, relying on fear and intimidation and, on occasion, even serving as the hired mercenaries of exploitative elites?[44] Merely posing these causal alternatives, of course, raises a series of further imponderables ("known unknowns," as Donald Rumsfeld would have said), such as, Who are "the people"? How important, when it comes to bandit careers, is the initial causality (i.e., is it "moral outrage" or mercenary rationality that provides the initial fuel)?[45] Is some kind of redistribution, à la Robin Hood, a sine qua non of "social" banditry, or is it sufficient that the poor should be exempt from bandit exactions?

One important methodological point should be made at the outset: in many cases, these are questions of degree. Rather than dividing bandits into "social" sheep and "antisocial" goats, as if these were two discrete species, we should instead think in terms of a spectrum of social/unsocial banditry (from the noblest Robin Hood at one end to the most mercenary criminal terrorist at the other). It is not simply a question of whether X or Y was a social bandit but rather the degree of "social" (or unsocial) "banditness" evident in his (or occasionally her) career.[46] And, as I shall argue, the answer to this question is often heavily influenced by time and space: individual bandits (and their gangs) shift along the spectrum, depending on where and when they operate. In fact, the several subquestions just mentioned are also questions of degree: How wide must "popular" support be? How much redistribution is required? And, indeed, the utility of the "social bandit" concept is itself a matter of degree, since while it could be argued that the confirmation of *at least one* bona fide social bandit would, in some logical sense, validate Hobsbawm's thesis (against his more robust critics, at least), it would be a lot better for the thesis's usefulness if we could come up with several, as I think we can.[47]

It is obvious to all students of the subject that bandits need some degree of wider support. This is true even of the solo highwaymen; it is even truer of larger gangs, which need food, ammunition, mounts, intelligence, and protection, as well as the networks that enable them to dispose of their ill-gotten gains. But how broad is this support, and on what is it based? Like the states that they confront and defy, bandits have several means of garnering support. (In broaching this tendentious comparison we should recall St. Augustine's famous equation of bandit gangs and secular states, and we could repeat that "relational" concepts such as "legitimacy" and "charisma" are relevant in both contexts.)[48] I will divide these means into three: (1) security (the protection of life and property); (2) material benefits (goods and/or money; clearly, there is some overlap between points

1 and 2); and (3) psychological rewards (e.g., seeing your heroes and allies triumphant, your enemies defeated and humbled). Thus, the state may offer (1) security (the basic task of the "night-watchman state"); (2) food, public works, or modern-day transfer payments; and (3) uplifting ritual, often of a nationalistic kind. (The last two categories—material rewards and ritual—are well exemplified by Rome's policy of panem et circenses.) So too the bandit, in competition with the state, can (1) protect against abusive authorities or, indeed, rival bandits; (2) provide material benefits (if he is a "noble bandit," particularly to the poor and needy); and (3) elicit popular sympathy for his bold, brave, generous, and successful bandit exploits.[49] States and bandits thus compete for hearts and minds. The successful, sometimes "social," bandit is one who wins the competition, and banditry certainly tends to flourish in times and places where, as I have suggested, the state—and what we might call "state-related elites"—are inept and/or abusive.[50] Failed states greatly favor banditry.

Of course, as Hobsbawm's critics have correctly pointed out, some bandit handouts may be entirely rational, even cynical; they are a way of buying some useful support, without which crime cannot flourish. Successful bandits, such as Lampião, are often skillful practitioners of public relations.[51] The narco bosses of contemporary Mexico have also been adept at burnishing their reputations, even in the face of adverse publicity.[52] But that alone does not make them "social" bandits, any more than successful PR men (or women) are ipso facto "social" activists (recall Prime Minister David Cameron's brief prepolitical career). Handouts in themselves are not sufficient proof of "social" status. The provision or denial of protection is similarly ambivalent: it could be purely calculating and prudential (good bandit policy), or it could reflect some stirrings of social conscience. We are again in the murky realm of motivation.[53] In both cases, we have to consider the scale of the activity, the beneficiaries, and (though this is often difficult, if not impossible, to establish) the bandits' own motives: Are these the calculated strategies of a mercenary "rational actor" or the normative manifestations of some kind of social conscience and commitment?

Both handouts and protection are, in a sense, "instrumental" (as against "expressive"): they relate to the practical consequences of bandit activity in terms of material welfare and personal security.[54] When it comes to psychological rewards, we tread upon rather looser "expressive" terrain. Here, the key question is how people appraise bandit as against state activity: Do they consider the bandit(s) to be sympathetic victims and popular heroes or, rather, nasty predators and elite hatchet men? Hobsbawm, as I have said, was widely criticized for relying overmuch on legends and literature that fostered positive images of bandits but often from a vantage point very far removed in time and/or space from the original scene of bandit action. This was a telling criticism. Legends and literature are relatively easy to research (you can often do it from the comfort of your study or university library), while getting into the hearts and minds of people at the scene of the action can be very difficult, requiring either arduous anthropological fieldwork or serious primary research in, very possibly, distant dusty archives. And even if contemporary primary documents are available, they often reflect the opinion of the authorities and have to be read, subaltern studies style, "against the grain."[55] A legitimate criticism of some revisionist (anti-Hobsbawmian) scholarship is that by delving into the archives (and, for good reason, discounting published myth and legend), historians may risk contagion from the "official mind"; that is, they begin to think like the officials who created the archival documents, which can lead to an overly cynical view of "bandits" as amoral utility maximizers or, indeed, mindless thugs.[56] So the archives are invaluable, but I repeat, they have to be read "against the grain"—without, of course, using this as an excuse for flights of authorial fancy. If read ("deconstructed"?) sensibly, they are an essential counterweight to Hobsbawm's clearly excessive reliance on poems, ballads, and novels.[57]

By way of trying to make sense of these complexities, I now offer a fairly straightforward tripartite model of banditry based heavily on my Mexican knowledge but also informed by some other Latin American cases, including Brazil, Peru, and Cuba. In terms of its social context, a successful bandit organization may be said to consist of three concentric rings of relationships.[58] The inner core consists of the gang and, perhaps, a few very closely connected allies (the regular and reliable contacts who provide shelter, resources, and intelligence). The size of the gang may well fluctuate.[59] There are often desertions and, of course, betrayals (sometimes leading to the classic bandit demise: death by betrayal). The inner core typically contains family members, as well as close "clan" allies, and it often derives from a particular locality, as I note below. This is as true of mercenary as of social banditry; it seems to apply to old-time traditional bandits, as well as to some modern criminal groups (such as Mexican narco gangs, at least in their infancy, e.g., the pioneering Sinaloan "cartel"). It is a key organizational feature but not a very useful criterion for distinguishing social from social banditry, since it clearly straddles the social/unsocial boundary.

Second, turning to the middle ring of three, bandit groups often enjoy broader support within a given region. How far such support is purely instrumental or further bolstered by "expressive" sympathies will vary and may be difficult to measure; however, the broader and stronger the support, the more likely it embodies expressive sympathy, premised, for example, on class—or ethnic, regional, or patriotic—solidarity, which makes it more committed and durable, less transactional and time-serving.[60] After all, it is likely to be difficult for any bandit operation to sustain the material resources of a large population in the way that a functioning welfare state might. A few ancien régime states, of course, have managed the grain supply (ancient Rome being the classic case, but Rome had a huge empire to squeeze). Bandits lack resources, since they often operate in relatively poor rural environments, and they have no effective bureaucracy at their disposal.[61] On the contrary, bandit redistribution, though it occurs, tends to be highly personal and ad hoc; in other words, it is the antithesis of rational bureaucratic procedures. The key feature of such support is that it is based on direct experience, on "local knowledge," to use the good old Geertzian term. Or, as Elizabeth Bott puts it, making a similar distinction, it is "direct" rather than "constructed."[62] In many cases, it may even depend on a face-to-face contact with the bandits, especially the leader. Within this second concentric circle, people know the bandits and, in some senses, approve of them (which is to say that they also *dis*approve of the bandits' enemies: the authorities, the police, and associated local elites).[63] This sympathetic public may on occasion be the beneficiary of the bandits' material and practical help (so their support is instrumental), but they may sympathize also on the basis of an expressive, normative solidarity. But they are not part of the inner circle of fighters and close allies. The bigger and more durable this second circle, the better the bandits' claim to "social" status (and the better their chances of surviving).

All detailed studies of banditry stress the importance of the "bandit support network" (*coheiteros*, to use the Brazilian Portuguese term): they are the "relatives, friends, protectors, supporters, spies [and] auxiliaries" who make the operations of the gang—the inner circle—possible.[64] Pancho Villa, prior to the 1910 Revolution, "had a network of contacts which extended throughout the state of Chihuahua and Durango, [consisting] of compadres, friends, accomplices, lovers, and scattered protégés [*favorecidos dispersos*] who had received, at Villa's hands, some money, a cow, a pig, a piece of clothing, or some other object of some value" and on whom Villa could therefore count for support.[65] Manuel García, the most famous Cuban bandit of the late nineteenth century, "could not travel more than a few miles" across his Havana bailiwick—from which most of his gang hailed—"before bumping into a relative or friend who would give them food and shelter."[66] Such supportive networks could span society; they might include not only peasants and workers but also sympathetic landlords, hacienda foremen, and corrupt officials.[67] In Peru, too, bandits such as Aurelio Vargas could establish safe havens in rough country where, "given their intimate knowledge of the terrain, their secure base, and efficient network of informers," they could elude government pursuit.[68]

Thanks to Schwartz's meticulous study of bandits in the province of Havana, it is possible to make a very rough assessment of the ratio of the inner to the middle circle in this scheme and of both circles to the total population. As I mentioned, Cuban gangs appear to have been quite small (e.g., compared to Lampião's). Schwartz reckons that active bandits—"full-time members of gangs engaged in organized criminality"— numbered fewer than 200 in the province of Havana in the 1880s (in a rural population of 200,000 or a total provincial population of 450,000). Manuel García, the preeminent bandit leader, had a gang of twenty (the inner circle), divided into three subgroups, but they in turn counted on "three or four hundred other residents [who] participated in the gang's exploits occasionally, as intermediaries in kidnappings, collectors of protection money, horse thieves, or lookouts."[69] Thus, while both the model and the data are necessarily imprecise, this example would suggest a ratio of perhaps 1:150 or 1:200 between the inner circle of permanent, "professional" bandits and the middle circle of direct helpers, sympathizers, and beneficiaries.

Finally, the third and outer ring consists of the more diffuse and *in*direct sympathy enjoyed by the bandit(s). This is not based on "local knowledge," on face-to-face relationships, or on instrumental payoffs; it is entirely "expressive" or, in Bott's term, "constructed" (and, in some cases, the timing of the "construction" can be quite precisely dated).[70] It comprises, too, the realm of legend and literature to which, his critics say, Hobsbawm was excessively attached. Thus, it depends on print literature, art, film, radio, and television. (Today in Mexico it includes narco corridos and narco blogs, as I mention below.) While we might reasonably assume that as the mass media grew throughout the twentieth century, so the speed of transmission—from local to regional and finally to national celebrity/notoriety—increased, we should not underestimate how fast news, rumor, and reputation could travel in earlier times. Thus, as early as February 1914, when Pancho Villa's rapid rise to power in northern Mexico was under way but far from complete, rebels at the other end of Mexico, 1,750 miles away in Abalá, Yucatán, rose in revolt to the cry of "¡Viva Villa!"[71]

Clearly, the insurgents of Abalá had no direct experience of Villa as either bandit or caudillo. He was a distant symbol and example. Here, in the outer third circle, attitudes were formed quite differently compared to the two inner circles, where direct knowledge and experience counted. Just as Hobsbawm was criticized for romanticizing bandits, so the inhabitants of this outer circle may entertain positive notions that are at odds with those of the middle circle, whose occupants are familiar, at firsthand, with bandit behavior, including bandit abuses (a case in point being the people of Chihuahua who had to live with Pancho Villa during his descent into gangsterism after 1915).[72] In Brazil, too, Chandler notes, "bandits achieved greater acceptance among intellectuals who surveyed the happenings from afar than among the inhabitants of the zones in which the bandits spread their destruction."[73]

But the contrast may go the other way: the public at large—being fed, inter alia, a diet of official propaganda—may fear and denigrate the bandit (even the bona fide revolutionary officially miscalled a "bandit"), while local people who know what the bandit/revolutionary really stands for are sympathetic and supportive.[74] "Bandit" often served as a convenient smear, rather like "terrorist" today.[75] This was the case with the "early" Pancho Villa, as well as other northern Mexican bandits.[76] It applied even more clearly to Emiliano Zapata, who, branded as a ruthless bandit, became a fearsome bogeyman for the *chilangos*—the inhabitants of Mexico City— who expected to be slaughtered in their beds when the Zapatistas entered the city in 1914. Yet when the Zapatistas came, nothing much happened: "Calm was restored and businesses reopened their premises."[77] The fears and prejudices of the outer ring were proven to be wildly exaggerated. As I later note, there are similar discrepancies in Mexican public opinion today.

The concentric circle model thus helps explain marked fluctuations in bandit reputations; it also suggests grounds for assessing whether bandits merit the term "social" or not. As I just mentioned, Pancho Villa went from fearsome bandit (1910–11) to respectable revolutionary caudillo (1913–15) and back to fearsome bandit (1916–20).[78] After 1920 (and particularly after 1923, when Villa died a classic bandit death, gunned down while driving through the streets of Parral), his reputation as a champion of the poor and symbol of Mexican nationalism flourished again.[79] These shifts partly derived from objective changes in Villa's behavior (i.e., the degree of rapacity and indiscriminate violence he displayed), but they also reflected subjective evaluations made by different groups of people on the basis of different "evidence": direct firsthand evidence in the middle circle, indirect secondhand evidence in the outer circle.

The model also works for some late twentieth-century Mexican narco organizations that have enjoyed genuine local support based on the protection they provided (e.g., for illegal marijuana producers), the material benefits they distributed (jobs, perks, charity, and public works), and the sense that they were "one of us," "us" being, in the classic case, a resident of Sinaloa or, more specifically, the highland municipality of Badiraguato, which spawned the notorious Sinaloa "cartel."[80] These sources of sympathy were all the greater when the state appeared as repressive, corrupt, alien, and generally good-for-nothing. Again, bandit reputation generally stands in inverse proportion to that of the state. However, Mexican public opinion as a whole was not so sympathetic. During the drug boom of the 1980s and 1990s, when the Mexican economy was performing poorly and the established hegemony of the ruling party—the PRI—was in sharp decline, attitudes somewhat shifted. A wide swath of opinion was seduced by narco culture: music, dress, films, gunplay, trucks, planes, and so-called narco bling.[81]

A distinct, if related, phenomenon was the popular "canonization" of bandits, usually those who had died at the hands of the authorities. The phenomenon is not confined to recent times or to Mexico.[82] But the violence and upheaval associated with narco activities and their heavy-handed repression by the state seem to have boosted bandit cults, the most obvious case being that of San Jesús Malverde, whose shrine in Culiacán, Sinaloa, attracts devotees (and tourists), not all of them Sinaloan or even Mexican.[83] The cult clearly speaks to a broad desire for help and reassurance in dangerous times (as does the burgeoning cult of Santa Muerte, "Holy Death").[84] Jesús Malverde himself was, at best, a minor bandit whose posthumous cult far outstrips his intrinsic historical significance.[85] Like Robin Hood, he is much more myth than reality.

Regarding contemporary reality, the marked increase in narco violence since 2006 has attenuated the "social" content of narco "banditry": public opinion in general has become more critical, and even some local communities have turned to vigilantism in order to combat narco gangs, who seem to have lost much of their erstwhile "social" gloss.[86] As the established cartels fragmented and feuded among themselves while, at the same time, combatting a militarized state, so egregious—even psychopathological—violence mounted, and with it the annual body count. There was also a generational shift as the rags-to-riches bosses of the past—self-made men who, like the mafioso of old, were reputedly "men of respect," businesslike, and even honorable in their dealings—gave way to the so-called narco juniors of the present: affluent spoiled brats who flaunted their wealth and (like the Arellano Félix brothers of Tijuana) appeared to revel in violence.[87] Yet some of the old local—"middle circle"—sympathy and support remain, hence the protest demonstrations mounted in Sinaloa that greeted the arrest in 2014 of the preeminent narco capo, "Chapo" Guzmán.[88]

These are changes over time that we can trace by means of "diachronic" analysis, in other words, by telling stories. But we can also adopt a static ("synchronic") view of banditry, stressing spatial rather than temporal differences. Bandits tend to be strongly territorial creatures who rely heavily on local networks and their intimate familiarity with the territory—what Mexicans call the patria chica—where they operate and where their origins usually lie. Thus, Luis Orozco, for a time a bandit comrade of Pancho Villa, quit Parral (Chihuahua), where the gang was operating, in order to return to Durango "because he could not exist so far from his country [*su tierra*] and his family."[89] In Mexico and probably elsewhere (in Latin America at least), bandits capitalize not only on local roots and popularity but also on traditional enmities that pit village against village, town against town, and region against region.[90] Frequently, the inhabitants of community X consider those of community Y (which may lie close by, across the river or over the hill) as criminals and troublemakers, and vice versa.[91] While dyadic antagonisms of this kind are too common and, we might say, too stereotypical to reflect reality, it is true that some communities acquired justifiably criminal reputations as havens for hoodlums, smugglers, and troublemakers who lived for crime and from crime.[92]

Here, the two inner circles encompassed the community (broadly defined), ensuring the bandit help, protection, shelter, intelligence, and recruits. However, roaming beyond the patria chica took the bandit into potentially foreign, even hostile territory, where his firsthand intelligence was inferior and popular support could not be counted on; where he might clash with rival bandits; and where, his network and legitimacy being lacking, he tended to rely more on sheer coercion.[93] Hence the marked territoriality of many bandits, perhaps especially of the minor ones, about whom we know less. The kingpins, becoming more mobile and ambitious, began to hit the headlines, like Lampião, or even converted themselves into national revolutionary caudillos, like Pancho Villa.[94] On the other hand, bandits could hardly stay put, stuck like limpets to their local rocks. As parasites, they had to extract resources from their hosts (the territory and communities that they exploited), and if the extraction was excessive, the host would be killed off or, more likely, would slough off the greedy parasite. In other words, the bandits, forfeiting popular support, would be resisted and finally repressed.

Parasitism therefore had to be finely calibrated, such that for the social bandit or even the mercenary bandit who preferred a "capital-intensive" to "coercion-intensive" approach, it screwed the rich and spared the poor. One successful strategy was to exploit rich concentrations of resources, such as the mines and bullion trails of northern Mexico or, indeed, the border towns where vice and contraband flourished.[95] Not surprisingly, the northern Mexican borderlands and neighboring sierras were noted for their banditry. More recently, of course, drugs—production and cross-border shipment—have supplied an unusually valuable concentration of exploitable resources. In central Mexico, the old camino real from Veracruz up to Mexico City was notoriously prone to banditry, while in the deep south, tropical plantations were vulnerable, and bandits could take advantage of the major rivers to intercept goods and, sometimes, to make speedy fluvial escapes.[96]

Bandits could also roam farther afield, seeking fresh resources and sparing their host communities.[97] But when they did so, their "social" character was likely to atrophy; they appeared not as local heroes but as passing predators who confirmed the stereotype of criminal outsiders and who had to be resisted and/or denounced to the authorities. A basic conclusion emerges: it is often wrong to call a particular bandit "social" tout court; "sociality" may depend on the time, the locality, and the community whose sentiments confer—or deny—"social" status. A bandit may be "social" back in the patria chica and a troublesome interloper elsewhere. Or, contrariwise, he may be a local predator who nevertheless acquires a heroic (pseudosocial?) reputation among the broader public, who do not know him firsthand but who depend on the unreliable print or other mass media. Bandits in the latter category are grist to the anti-Hobsbawmian mill (and, by definition, they often include the most celebrated individuals, who received the most publicity). But we should not forget the lesser local bandits who occupy the former category, for example, the outlaws, smugglers, and "bad Indians" who inhabited the coastal lagoons of Chiapas in the 1900s, whom the local people protected, and, indeed, whom they "employ[ed] to avenge their grievances against the authorities and outsiders for matters concerning the common land of the village."[98] These tend to be minor, even anonymous figures; hence, they may be more easily underestimated, which is to say that there may have been more (minor, mute, inglorious) social bandits than Hobsbawm's critics perhaps allow.

Thus, bandits faced a dilemma: if the "carrying capacity" of their patria chica dwindled, they had to turn the screw on local people or range farther afield; but ranging farther afield detached them from their base and eroded their "social" claims. Such was the case with Lampião, who, over time, covered a vast swath of the northeastern sertão of Brazil but in the process became increasingly violent and rapacious.[99] Some bandits, however, could be saved from this dilemma by providential national events, notably wars and revolutions. Latin America offers two good examples: Cuba's wars of national liberation (1868–78 and 1895–98) and Mexico's great revolution (1910–20). Thus, while most bandits (certainly those of Brazil and Peru) met early deaths or, if they were lucky, retired into discreet obscurity, a few made the transition to revolutionary warlords (some, in China, even laid claim to the mandate of heaven and became emperors, though these will not concern us here).[100] The classic bandit turned revolutionary was Pancho Villa, who has already been mentioned several times. While he is in some respects exceptional (at one point he was Mexico's mightiest caudillo, and he seemed destined to rule the country), he embodies several features of the bandit turned revolutionary that deserve brief attention.

Revolutions—or wars of national liberation—attract bandits for two obvious reasons: bandits have an aptitude for violence, and they are and are known to be hostile to the authorities. They have the necessary skills to confront the authorities, since that is what they do for a living. They are familiar with firearms, often possess horses, know the terrain, and have networks of support (the middle circle) that they can rely upon. They can be elusively mobile: Villa was known as *nalgas de fierro* (iron buttocks), since he could withstand long days in the saddle; Chávez García could, allegedly, sleep on horseback.[101] They are also "men who deserve respect": they have stood up to police, political officials, and landlords and have got away with it. This was certainly the case with Villa, who came from a long lineage of bandits in the Durango/Chihuahua region. Whether Villa had been a "social" bandit in the years prior to the outbreak of revolution in 1910 is a matter of debate; so, too, is the cause of his initial turn to banditry in 1894, when he was just sixteen. The two imponderables are connected: if Villa was driven to banditry by the oppression of local elites, then he fits the role of the reluctant victim, who might in turn sympathize with fellow victims while garnering their support. If, instead, he deliberately chose crime, then his bandit career appears more "rational" and mercenary. There is no doubt that he came from a poor family, and it seems *probable* that a confrontation with the authorities (and/or local elites), *perhaps* connected to the dishonoring of his sister (or mother), impelled him into a life of crime.[102] So, pace Paul Vanderwood, it looks very much as if harsh circumstances rather than rational choice determined the outcome.[103] The subsequent evidence for "social" banditry is thin; it could be that Villa robbed the rich for much the same reason that Willie Sutton robbed the banks.

Either way, it is worth noting that Villa was not alone: a prominent ally was the ex-bandit Tomás Urbina (graphically described by John Reed, who encountered him in his Durango headquarters in 1913), while elsewhere the incipient revolution of 1910–11 counted on the valuable support of erstwhile bandits, for whom the switch from outlawry to guerrilla war (the inevitable first stage of the Mexican Revolution) was an easy transition.[104] After all, it meant doing much the same as before—scouring the local countryside; evading pursuit; collecting guns, ammunition, horses, and recruits; skirmishing with the police; and drawing on the support of sympathetic communities. In a context of social revolution, banditry easily merged into the popular mobilization.[105] The same was true of Cuban bandits—whom Schwartz calls "patriot-brigands"—during the two wars of national liberation.[106] War and revolution afforded bandits status and a political banner. No doubt some were cynical; the banner legitimized and facilitated more mercenary banditry. But some, particularly the more "social" bandits, nurtured not only a hatred of the authorities (in the Cuban case, Spanish colonial authorities) but also a sense of solidarity with the common people from whom they had sprung. This, I think, was the case with Villa, who enjoyed widespread popular support while giving ample evidence of a kind of plebeian social reformism.

Bandits, it has often been said, are not revolutionaries; they do not seek to overturn the social order.[107] Nor, of course, do most people, however disgruntled and put-upon they may be. But when revolution heaves into sight, often rather unexpectedly, the scene changes. What once might have seemed like utopian fantasy becomes attainable; the world is turned upside down. In this new context, bandits are quite capable of espousing social reform, as Villa clearly did during his brief heyday in northern Mexico in 1913–15. He did not sponsor a major land distribution, but he gave generous handouts to the poor, provided for widows and orphans, and was genuinely keen to promote popular education.[108] He also delighted in deposing and humiliating the powerful ruling clique in Chihuahua, the Creel/Terrazas faction, who were widely disliked and whose deposition and humiliation were therefore applauded. And he expelled Spanish priests from his fief, more because they were Spaniards than because they were priests.[109]

This package of policies did not constitute a fully fledged social revolution (though some of Villa's supporters went further in their desire to codify social reform), and we should note, when Villa settled down to his short-lived but comfortable retirement on the hacienda of Canutillo (1920–23), he presided over an efficient commercial hacienda, not a utopian commune.[110] But he did surround himself with old comrades and retainers. This was in part good politics (and personal insurance), but it also suggested that Villa, while he was no doctrinaire revolutionary, did espouse notions of social reform and popular betterment. For this reason, I once referred to Villismo, as a political movement, as "social banditry writ large," that is, the logical culmination of plebeian sentiments of popular solidarity allied to a hatred of powerful elites and a vague commitment to social improvement, for example, through education.[111]

Two other features of Villa are worth mentioning in this context. First, he was governed by a somewhat bandit-like "territorial imperative": his chief priority was his north-central heartland (chiefly Chihuahua and Durango, including the rich cotton country of La Laguna), and though he ranged farther afield (he fought his final major battles on the plains of Bajío, to the south), he does not seem to have been overly concerned to seize hold of Mexico City, still less the remote south of the country. Unlike his Carrancista enemies, who finally triumphed in 1915, Villa did not dispatch expeditionary forces to the south, nor did he strike an alliance with organized labor, as the Carrancistas did. His vision of Mexico remained somewhat limited, even parochial. Social banditry, even when it was "writ large," was not a great traveler. Thus, after 1915, as he faced defeat, Villa fell back on his northern heartland, but he was now obliged to squeeze its resources—of both men and matériel—to the detriment of his local reputation.

However, at the same time (1915–20), Villa enhanced his reputation as a macho Mexican patriot. Understandably aggrieved by U.S. support for his archenemy, Venustiano Carranza, Villa made reprisals against American companies in his zone (which were many) and raided across the border, shooting up the garrison town of Columbus, New Mexico, in March 1916. In response, President Woodrow Wilson sent the so-called Punitive Expedition into Mexico in order to kill or apprehend this troublesome bandit. The Punitive Expedition failed, and Villa, drawing on his old bandit experience, cleverly eluded pursuit while also embroiling the United States and Mexico in a risky armed confrontation. In Chihuahua, his old heartland, Villa's popularity now slumped, but in Mexico as a whole he came to be seen as a daring fighter who had challenged the *coloso del norte* and got away with it.[112] Somewhat similar nationalist, anti-American sentiments underpin the popularity, dwindling though it may be, of today's narco gangs in Mexico, whose exploits involve systematically fooling the U.S. authorities, especially the hated *migra*.[113] Needless to say, Cuba's "patriot-brigands" also acquired nationalist credentials in their service against the Spanish colonial authorities. We may contrast this outcome with the fate of bandits in Brazil or Peru, where no social revolution and no war of national liberation offered the opportunity for bandits to turn their skills to a grand, popular, political cause.[114] Instead, they faced death and defeat or, in a few lucky cases, a quiet but obscure retirement. Pancho Villa became a national hero (for some, even something of a popular saint), the reward for being in the right place at the right time.[115]

Lastly, in this recurrent sequence, as armed revolution recedes and, eventually, as new regimes start to achieve a measure of order and stability, bandits become superfluous and potentially troublesome. This was an old problem in Mexico; back in the 1860s Benito Juárez had partly addressed the problem by recruiting bandits into the rural police.[116] The Mexican revolutionary regime certainly incorporated plenty of pistoleros and fighters into its official ranks, while, as we have seen, Villa, like other caudillos, was amnestied and rewarded. In addition, by the 1920s the caudillos of the revolution were ageing and, following years of arduous campaigning, were showing signs of early physical decline. (Villa himself suffered from a gammy leg and rheumatic joints.) But not everyone could be so accommodated, and the late 1910s were full of stories of bandit gangs that could not or would not submit to the new authorities and that eked out a dangerous living in the hills, robbing and raiding.[117] Though their resistance to the authorities was applauded by some (e.g., by Catholics who resented revolutionary anticlericalism), most of these bandits were distinctly "unsocial," the most extreme case being José Inés Chávez García, a savage leader who led a large irregular force in the Bajío capable at times of resisting government forces in open battle.[118]

Over time, as they both repressed and recruited bandit/revolutionaries, the authorities prevailed. Banditry never disappeared, but through the 1920s and 1930s it noticeably diminished.[119] The new revolutionary state never achieved a "monopoly of legitimate violence" in the land, but it increasingly held the whip hand, especially as it could now rely on better logistics, communications, and weaponry (telephones, radio, trucks, jeeps, planes, and, later, helicopter gunships). No less important, the new state enjoyed a surer basis of popular support. It incorporated mass political parties, labor unions, and peasant communities (notably, the ejidos, the new agrarian reform communities). All of these deployed their pistoleros and paramilitaries, but the latter were increasingly subject to central and civilian control; furthermore, as a regime that was both more popular and more populist than its (Porfirian) old regime predecessor, the revolutionary state enjoyed greater legitimacy. It also presided over a burgeoning economy. And a legitimate effective state, coupled with economic opportunity, is probably the surest guarantee against the contagion of banditry, both social and unsocial. It was not until the 1980s and 1990s, when the state eroded and the economy nose-dived, that extensive banditry again reared its head, now in the nasty guise of the narco cartels.

To conclude: while many Latin American bandits may not have been "social" (in that, the revisionists are probably correct), some certainly were (and if they were the more anonymous ones, perhaps they have been underestimated). Hobsbawm exaggerated the scale and incidence of "social banditry," just as he went way too far in asserting the sameness of banditry across time and space. Such generalizations were, perhaps, heroic, but they were also hyperbolic. His exaggeration was clearly related to his overreliance on published, often literary texts and his neglect of both anthropological and archival sources. But the critical response—the revisionist school— went too far, especially when, as revisionist schools often do, it overshot the mark, arguing that the social bandit was a figment of Hobsbawm's fertile imagination and that real bandits were profit-maximizing rational actors straight out of the pages of American economic textbooks.

Latin America, perhaps particularly Mexico, does yield cases of genuine social bandits or, as I have suggested, cases of banditry that oscillate on a continuum from social to unsocial or antisocial, depending on time and place. So, used discriminatingly, on the basis of good evidence (including primary sources read "against the grain"), the concept retains some validity, and we would be conceptually poorer if we ditched it. Like Voltaire's God, if it did not exist (which, thanks largely to Hobsbawm, it does), then we would have to invent it. Not surprisingly, I therefore agree with Gilbert Joseph (when he agrees with me) to the effect that even if the concept is "problematic," it is premature to show the social bandit the door and wave goodbye.[120]

CHAPTER 2

Toward an Explanation of Liberalism in Nineteenth-Century Latin America

ONE OF THE FIRST ACADEMIC PAPERS I GAVE AND LATER PUB-
lished dealt with Mexican liberalism in the later nineteenth century.[1] It
was written for a (UK) History Workshop conference on liberalism, and if
it embodied any novelty, it was its stress on the role of popular, especially
peasant, liberalism as a force to be taken seriously. This concept was novel
to the extent that the prevailing view (ca. 1980) tended to see liberalism as
an imported, cosmopolitan, elite philosophy or project repudiated by the
majority of the Mexican—or, indeed, Latin American—people, particularly
the peasantry.[2] Though my claim was based on fairly skimpy evidence
derived from secondary sources (so it was more a historical hunch than a
considered conclusion based on years of archival toil), it was not wholly
wrong, and to use one of today's favorite clichés, it gained traction over
time as more serious scholars of Mexican liberalism stressed the scale and
examined the nature of Mexican popular patriotic liberalism.[3]

That was nearly forty years ago. The Bourbons, having returned to the
French throne after an absence of a mere twenty years, had, allegedly,
"learned nothing and forgotten nothing." Since writing "El liberalismo
mexicano" I think I have learned a certain amount, but I have certainly
forgotten a good deal too. (Indeed, the rate of forgetting is probably now
overtaking the rate of learning.) Meanwhile, Mexican liberalism has been

studied from a local, regional, and "bottom-up" perspective (hence the stress on popular patriotic liberalism); it has thus benefited from both the "decentering" of Mexican history (away from Mexico City and from national elites and leaders) and the renewed interest in the political and electoral history of the early nineteenth century (which, in turn, reflected the "new political history" of recent years, as well as the immediate stimulus given by the bicentenary of independence and of the Constitution of Cádiz).[4] In addition, the "neoliberal" turn of the last generation—the repudiation of statist and "populist" models of development in favor of privatization, market-friendly reform, and *desarrollo hacia afuera* (outward-looking development)—has prompted a reevaluation, often positive, of "liberal" economic policy and its accomplishments, especially as they unfolded in the later nineteenth century. Thus, the so-called liberal era of Mexican and Latin American development (roughly post-1870) has attracted greater and more sympathetic attention.[5]

Since these trends have not been confined to Mexico but can be seen in Latin America more broadly, it makes sense to reconsider Mexican liberalism in both its political and its economic incarnations within a wider context. Of course, the task is huge, so the treatment will be superficial and no doubt vulnerable to various objections. These are likely to be (1) empirical: this or that particular interpretation is factually wrong; (2) conceptual: the "organizing concepts" are unclear or unhelpful; or (3) historiographical: there is nothing new here; we've heard it all before. (Objection 3 would, to my mind, be the most disappointing.) In what follows, therefore, I take another look at Mexican liberalism, rethinking some of the arguments of thirty or forty years ago while introducing comparisons with other Latin American cases.

I should stress at the outset that I am chiefly interested in liberalism as a set of ideas, policies, and, perhaps, "national projects," that is, nineteenth-century Latin American liberalism in action. Interesting and occasionally important though they may be, I will say little about the great *pensadores* of liberalism (whether Latin American or, more remotely, European or North American), and I will not be chasing up intellectual debts and genealogies (a pursuit that can lead to sterile and hypothetical imputations of "influence," typically among a handful of male intellectuals whose works are easily accessed by a later generation of desk-bound fellow intellectuals).

That said, it is probably necessary to offer a very brief definitional guide.[6] It seems to me that liberalism as a philosophy centers on the rights, freedom, and autonomy of individuals, from which premise (I will not say "essence") several further postulates and practices can be derived: the rule of law, freedom of expression, and government by consent (thus, involving some sort of representation, perhaps even popular sovereignty). All this stands in opposition to varieties of absolutism, autocracy, theocracy, arbitrary or despotic rule, and ascriptive hierarchies.[7] Clearly, there can be degrees of liberalism, some being more radical than others, and we may wish to subdivide the phenomenon in other ways, as I will in the analysis that follows. One obvious subdivision involves political and economic liberalism and their contentious relationship (which I touch on), and some scholars stress a basic difference between, say, French/Continental and British/"Anglo-Saxon" liberalism.[8] My analysis does not dwell on the latter distinction, but neither does it reject it out of hand. Also, in any political system, practical reality may well diverge sharply from theoretical or constitutional principle (James Scott's "public transcript"), and this divergence must be taken into account.[9] Finally, while in practice liberalism *can* consort with democracy (hence the familiar tandem, "liberal democracy") and the two may indeed be said to enjoy an "elective affinity" (i.e., given its individualist premise, liberalism may well tend toward democracy), nevertheless, in practice many historic liberals have, like Tocqueville, resisted that tendency, so the tandem is by no means automatic or typical, especially not for the nineteenth century.[10]

Liberalism: Typology and Timing

My analysis of nineteenth-century Mexican liberalism involved three roughly generational stages.[11] In the first stage, associated with independence and its aftermath, great faith was placed in constitutional architecture, which was hardly surprising, since the basic political question concerned the form that the emergent postcolonial state would take.[12] Having shaken off colonial rule, Mexico could establish a new polity that was liberal in the sense of espousing representative government, free elections (with a wide male suffrage), division of powers, protection of civil rights, popular sovereignty, universal citizenship (therefore, the abolition of caste distinctions), and federalism. All these elements are evident in the foundational Constitution of 1824, which in turn built upon Cádiz. A similar pattern was evident in, for example, New Granada, Central America, and several other succession states of Spain's American empire.[13] Even if we qualify this early stage of Latin American liberalism as "moderate," it still represented a dramatic political change following three centuries of monarchical and colonial rule.[14]

Economic liberalism and liberal anticlericalism were already apparent, but they were not, it seems to me, the dominant concerns of these early Latin American liberals (a good many of whom were priests anyway) or of their (conservative) enemies.[15] Economic liberalism, as I shall shortly suggest, spanned a wide range of political opinion, including a good many "conservatives," while anticlericalism did not become a dominant issue until rather later in the century.[16] This is another way of making the point that the definition of liberalism vis-à-vis conservatism took some time to emerge (David Bushnell, for Colombia, dates it to the War of the Supremes in 1839–43) and that, in respect to economic policy, the definition never attained the clarity that some analyses suggest (with liberals supposedly being gung-ho for free trade and conservatives clinging to protectionism).[17] Indeed, at this early stage, Simon Collier argues (for Chile) that "both Conservative and Liberal outlooks fell within the boundaries of nineteenth-century liberalism," while for Mexico, José Antonio Aguilar Rivera suggests that the ideological founding fathers of liberalism and conservatism—José María Luis Mora and Lucas Alamán—"shared many ideas" and "were in good measure inspired by the same writers."[18]

Of course, when it came to the crucial task of constructing new postindependence constitutions, the choice between federalist or centralist options remained open, with liberals, according to taste and circumstances, inclining both ways. Thus, while federalism and liberalism perhaps enjoyed a certain kinship (another "elective affinity," if you like), the relationship was not inevitable; some liberals, like Bernardino Rivadavia in the Río de la Plata, espoused centralization as a means to better establish—even impose-a liberal order.[19] This Jacobin/Napoleonic option—top-down centralizing liberalism—would, of course, become a recurrent theme throughout the nineteenth century, a theme to which I will return.[20] Finally, we should note that from these early days, liberals in power tended to be more centralizing and even authoritarian than those who were out of power (for whom federalism might exert a stronger appeal).[21] In some cases, centralization of power was, for embattled incumbent liberals, a matter of political survival as much as ideological preference.[22] Political necessity trumped ideological preference.

However, this early emphasis on constitutionalism soon faded. By the 1830s Mexican liberalism was in retreat, and a resurgent conservatism had taken power, imposing in 1836 a substantially different—centralist—constitution.[23] Ideological differences now grew sharper, as did official repression; the role of the Catholic Church became salient; and political disillusionment—the loss of faith in constitutional solutions—was paralleled by mounting economic and fiscal problems, which also blighted the optimistic hopes of the early liberals. Conservatives concluded that Mexico had to retain or revert to old colonial beliefs and practices: strong centralized government, the alliance of "throne" (i.e., state) and altar, even colonial systems of taxation such as the *capitación* (head tax).[24]

The conservative revival was apparent in other parts of Latin America too where, during the 1830s and 1840s, a political mood of "pessimism and conservatism" prevailed, the product of "economic crisis, earlier bouts of political instability and . . . social reactions against reforms."[25] Long before, amid the upheaval of the Wars of Independence, Simón Bolívar had concluded that centralized, quasi-monarchical rule best suited Latin America. (He also concluded that constitutions were so much paper and that dictatorial rule might be a necessary antidote to chaos and bankruptcy.)[26] Diego Portales in Chile, followed by Juan Manuel de Rosas in Argentina, established strong regimes that were, to varying degrees, authoritarian and, in some measure, "neocolonial."[27] Rafael Carrera, carried to power by a "powerful conservative reaction," headed a regime of conservative clerical makeup in Guatemala.[28] Colombia, like Mexico, shifted from a federal to a centralist regime in 1843; in the same year Ecuador acquired a conservative constitution (the "charter of slavery," as outraged liberals called it).[29] In Paraguay, a conservative "reaction" was hardly required, since the regime of José Gaspar Rodríguez de Francia continued colonial forms without a significant liberal interlude.[30] Even in Brazil, which, in various obvious respects, diverges from the Spanish American norm, federalism and decentralization had, by the 1840s, given way to a reassertion of central government power, which was facilitated by the coming of age of Pedro II.[31] In all these cases, the church and the military (usually the regular army, sometimes, as in Chile, the National Guard) were important components of the conservative reaction: their rights (*fueros*) and privileges were respected, and in many cases, they supplied the key personnel of conservative rule. The Vatican, now veering toward a reactionary ultramontanism, applauded, and a new generation of Latin American clerics took their cue from Rome, preaching (sometimes literally, from the pulpit) "authoritarianism and ultramontane orthodoxy."[32]

If *political* change, involving centralist rule and tightly restricted suffrage, was widely apparent, in *economic* and fiscal terms, the liberal retreat was less significant, since the liberals had never established thoroughgoing free-trade regimes, and their conservative opponents, if sometimes more comfortable with protectionist measures, were also keen to boost exports and to build infrastructure. Decisions on the tariff often involved complex trade-offs between regions and sectors (evident, e.g., in Mexico's cotton and textile sectors and Colombia's cattle and coffee), so party or ideological consistency was hard to achieve. The debate between protectionists and free-traders "cut across party lines" in Colombia; Tomás Cipriano Mosquera, a "Ministerial" or "proto-Conservative" of Bolivarian beliefs, proved, as president, an eager economic reformer who promoted foreign trade, lower tariffs, and a "liberal economic program designed to free private initiative from obsolete restrictions and thereby lay the basis for an aggressively outward-oriented development strategy."[33] In Central America, some liberals rejected free trade, while "leaders in both factions . . . recognized the need for more modern, rational approaches to the economy."[34] The classic example of this economic bipartisanship was Ecuador's Gabriel

García Moreno, a cultural conservative, a fervent Catholic, and a believer in exemplary repression who, on the basis of "liberal economic theory that recognized the importance of free markets, progress and development," sought to promote public works, communications, education (of a sort), and exports.[35] In Brazil, too, Liberals and Conservatives adopted bipartisan economic policies.[36]

The first generation of postindependence Latin Americans thus experienced a pendulum swing from liberal to conservative. But around midcentury, liberalism was renewed necessarily by a second generation that had not lived through the hopes and disappointments of independence but that had, in some cases, been inspired by the example of the European revolutions of 1848.[37] They pioneered what I previously called an "institutional" liberalism, designed to change the basic institutions and "customs" of society (several, it was said, backward vestiges of colonialism) in order to make liberalism more feasible and successful.[38] At the same time, they sought to undermine the basis of their enemies' political, material, and even cultural power. In Mexico, this Liberal counterattack took shape with the Reform, which abolished the military and ecclesiastical fueros (the Ley Juárez, 1855) while promoting the disentailment (*desamortización*) of civil corporations (the Ley Lerdo, 1856), which included both church and corporate (including village) property. Both measures were famously embodied in the Constitution of 1857, the Magna Carta of Mexican liberalism. Facing strenuous opposition, as well as indifference, the liberals had to impose their reforms by force majeure, hence, the War of the Reform and its convoluted sequel, the French Intervention, in the course of which church and state were separated, corporate property was nationalized and sold off, and Mexican conservatism suffered an ignominious defeat in alliance with foreign invaders.[39]

Again there are, mutatis mutandis, Continental parallels: the rise to power of a second generation of ("institutional") liberals who realized that, if they were to hold power and achieve their liberal objectives, they would have to adopt more radical policies and ram them through in the face of strenuous opposition, opposition that was not confined to a narrow conservative or clerical elite but that included substantial sectors of society.[40]

Mexico's *puros* (radical liberals) had their counterparts in Chile's Equality Society (Sociedad de la Igualdad) or Colombia's Gólgotas. (The Colombian equivalent of Mexico's *moderados* were, rather oddly, called Draconianos because they favored retention of the death penalty.)[41] More broadly, Frank Safford discerns a "second wave of federalism," stretching from Mexico to Peru, between 1845 and 1870, but he stresses that the key feature of this "wave" was less constitutional design (since "positions on the centralist-federalist issue tended to be more rhetorical and tactical") than intense conflict over the status of the church (which now generated "strong emotions and deep commitments").[42] The scale of the ensuing conflict of course varied, depending on the strength of the church, the immoveable object and the impact of liberal anticlericalism, the unstoppable force. In Mexico and Colombia, where a powerful church confronted a vigorous liberalism, the issue was salient. In Argentina, where, again, a new liberal generation (Bartolomé Mitre, Domingo Faustino Sarmiento, Nicolás Avellaneda) came to power following the fall of Rosas in 1852, anticlericalism played second fiddle to questions of constitutional arrangement (Buenos Aires versus the provinces).[43] And, of course, the impact of desamortización varied too, being most decisive in countries where a dense, often Indian peasantry risked losing access to land as privatization forged ahead (as I discuss below).

As this second generation of Latin American liberals struggled to gain power and enact their "institutional" reforms, the old logic of Jacobinism (roughly, statist liberalism) became even more obvious and compelling. To achieve victory, liberals had to show a robust and combative spirit, they had to acquire and deploy military force (by definition, a somewhat illiberal thing to do), and they had to defeat their enemies and impose "liberal" measures in the face of strenuous opposition.[44] In the process, they needed to forge alliances and win popular support. One consequence was the rise of a more radical, popular, or "social" liberalism (discussed below). Unlike in Mexico, however, where the liberals finally secured an overwhelming if costly triumph, the liberal victory elsewhere in Latin America was usually partial and temporary.[45] Liberals and conservatives continued to compete for office (both peacefully and violently). The degree of genuine liberalization depended above all, I will argue, on basic questions of political economy, which determined that, for example, Argentina and Uruguay would take a more liberal path than Peru or Bolivia. The Mexican outcome—a clear-cut liberal hegemony—was unusual, the product of contingent circumstances: foreign invasion and liberal/patriotic resistance. For that reason, I will later attempt a brief discussion of nationalism and its relation to liberalism.

The third and final episode of the nineteenth-century story was what I, rather inelegantly, called "developmental" liberalism. This corresponds in Mexico to the Porfirian mutation, a genetic blending of liberalism and positivism that, true to its positivist inheritance, stressed economic causality and maintained that Mexico had to avoid destabilizing ideological partisanship in order to concentrate on strong solid government (so, *mucha administración y poca política*) while promoting economic development by means of foreign trade and infrastructural investment.[46] Of course, previous governments had espoused these goals: they were, one could say, the Latin American equivalents of motherhood and apple pie. And as I have suggested, there was a degree of bipartisanship when it came to economic policy. The great majority of conservatives, too, had favored boosting trade and building infrastructure.

"Developmental" liberals, while they eagerly looked forward to a future economy based on free markets and laissez-faire, believed that in the here-and-now (a here-and-now of political instability and economic backwardness) the state would have to adopt robust measures by way of keeping social order, protecting property rights (including those of foreigners), stimulating the market, promoting infrastructure (e.g., with generous subsidies for railway companies), and facilitating the supply of labor (whether by means of emigration from abroad or forms of recruitment, often coercive, from within). As I discuss in chapter 5, such projects were made possible, as well as attractive, by the dramatic growth of world trade in the later nineteenth century and the massive export of capital from Europe, especially Britain.[47] However, contra the more extreme versions of dependency theory, foreign inputs did not determine, even though they made possible, this new phase of *desarrollo hacia afuera*, often under authoritarian yet "liberal" and occasionally "Liberal" auspices.[48]

Again, the parallels between Mexico and the rest of Latin America are very apparent, though I will later make a basic distinction between those countries (such as Argentina and Uruguay) where economic development followed more liberal (or less illiberal) lines and, in so doing, permitted a real measure of political liberalization, eventually democratization, and those (Porfirian Mexico, most of Central America, Peru, and Bolivia) where "developmental" liberalism, even if economically "successful," was clearly associated with political closure and even outright authoritarianism. Chile and Colombia, I would suggest, occupy an approximate middle ground: for example, Colombia under Rafael Núñez, a devotee of Herbert Spencer, adopted a "rigidly centralist" constitution in 1886, and the Regeneración regime of that time embodied a "positivist-Conservative Reaction" that was loosely analogous to Mexico's Porfiriato. (Colombia, like Mexico, had just emerged from a costly bout of civil war.)[49]

During this period, "liberal" regimes and leaders were common, and the entire period, roughly 1870–1914 (or 1930) is often denominated "liberal."[50] But "developmental" liberalism was in many respects profoundly *il*liberal: it favored strong centralized governments, deployed force against its own citizens, and intervened systematically in the workings of the market. All this could be justified in terms of the ends justifying the means: in the short or medium term, the state had to take such steps in order to bring about growth, development, and "progress" (note: not "modernity" or "modernization").[51] Portales in Chile had foreseen and advocated such a trajectory, which the Científicos of Porfirian Mexico would eagerly espouse.[52] Once achieved—once the necessary "stage" of development had been reached—illiberal measures could, like a chrysalis, be sloughed off, and the beautiful butterfly of liberalism (a liberalism both political and economic) could finally take flight.

Developmental liberalism was, in a sense, a kind of neo-Jacobinism, now infused with a strong economistic and, I repeat, positivistic rationale. The state became a social engineer. Mexicans and others had to be forced not just to be free and, perhaps, patriotic but also to be productive, hardworking, sober, and conscientious. Thus, developmental liberalism was committed—again, very illiberally—to a social engineering project that would, by means of education, exhortation, and, when necessary, coercion, create not just patriotic citizens (which was an old liberal/Jacobin dream) but also productive workers (and peasants). "Liberty," as a Peruvian congressional report declared in 1866, "requires great effort and sharp sufferings to bear its fruit."[53] And Peru was a clear-cut case of such illiberal liberalism. In the southern highlands, "liberal notions turned from a moralising, hopeful call for emancipation of all groups from the strictures of Spanish 'medieval' tyranny into the justification of exclusionary pretensions to social excellence and political power."[54] Indians in general therefore suffered exclusion and coercion; estate workers (*colonos*) had to be "correct[ed] with toughness so that they mend their ways and cease being rascals."[55] One consequence was that the popular peasant (and Indian) constituency that had backed liberal leaders and movements in the decades after independence (notably in Huanta) now atrophied, marginalized by "liberal" racism and exclusion. As a result, Cecilia Méndez observes, "Peruvian liberalism thereby lost the popular appearance in the second half of the [nineteenth] century which it had been able to display during the first."[56] Similar trends are apparent elsewhere in Andean America with García Moreno's combination of "modernizing project" and "coercive colonial practices" in Ecuador and Manuel Melgarejo's aggressive ("liberal") assault on Indian corporate landholdings in Bolivia.[57]

Such ends/means trade-offs are not, of course, confined to liberalism, though perhaps liberalism, with its central stress on individual choice and autonomy, is particularly vulnerable to the inconsistency and hypocrisy that such trade-offs encourage.[58] Building socialism has also involved some not very socialistic measures (as liberal critics are fond of pointing out). But liberal inconsistency, hypocrisy, even apostasy were, in this instance, egregious: in the name of a philosophy of individual freedom, regimes denied representation and expression, repressed their people (peasants, workers, and artisans), and forced them to work, often in very harsh environments, from the lumber camps of Chiapas and the tobacco fields of the Valle Nacional in Mexico to the rubber forests of the Amazon basin, the tin mines of Bolivia, and the nitrate fields of the Atacama desert.[59] And the hypocrisy was all the more apparent when, as often happens in such situations, supposedly short-term means became enduring ends in themselves, which came about because they proved profitable and attractive to the elite beneficiaries of "developmental liberalism," who, in turn, had the power to turn means into ends.[60]

My 1985 analysis confined itself to this tripartite typology: constitutional, institutional, and developmental liberalism, these being successive waves impelled by both regional (Latin American) and global circumstances. They followed a chronological, perhaps dialectical, sequence, in that institutional (or "radical") liberalism represented a critique of its constitutional predecessor, just as "developmental liberalism" (or, if you prefer, "illiberal liberalism" or "pseudoliberalism") was a further mutation that was critical of its predecessor and induced by both the philosophical appeal of positivism and the practical incentives (profit, revenue, graft) of *desarrollo hacia afuera*. While these shifting beliefs and practices attached to generations—to men (by and large) who were products of their time—this did not mean that each wave entirely displaced its predecessor. Die-hard adherents of the old lived on—or were reborn in later generations. Radical undercurrents coursed through the Latin American body politic long before leftist movements ever attained power, while the alleged perversion of liberalism by the Porfirian regime caused a younger generation of liberals to hark back to their fathers and grandfathers, invoking the spirit of Juárez or Mora in opposition to the "order and progress" dictatorship of Porfirio Díaz, Francisco Madero being the classic example.[61] Similarly, the Argentine liberals of the 1850s looked back to the "reformist mood of the 1820s" for inspiration.[62]

The third stage—developmental (Porfirian) liberalism—represented an illiberal and statist option designed to obviate the alleged failings of earlier liberalism, in particular, its promotion of weak governments, political polarization, and thus severe instability, which prejudiced economic progress. But this was not the only exit from the liberal labyrinth. In Mexico, as in Latin America and, indeed, Europe, other alternatives to (or, to resume an earlier metaphor, mutations of) mid-nineteenth-century liberalism existed. Two deserve mention: anarcho-liberalism and social liberalism. (By thus further complicating the typology, I run the risk of making an already "overwrought" analysis even more intricate.[63] But then, historical reality is complicated, and simplistic schemes can wreak havoc with that reality.)

The kinship between liberalism and anarchism is clear both philosophically and, in some cases, practically.[64] Liberals value individual freedom and autonomy and are suspicious of the powers of the state, which they typically seek to limit and to divide up. Anarchism carries this further, to the point of annulling the state and relying on individuals to achieve voluntary cooperation among themselves.[65] Historically, Spanish Liberalism, as represented by Francisco Pi y Margall in the Second Spanish Republic, easily elided into anarchism, which, of course, became a major current in Spanish politics.[66] Latin America also produced vigorous anarchist movements during the same period, roughly 1870–1920. Radical liberalism and anarchism tended to appeal to the same social sectors (above all, literate urban artisans); they valued voluntary political sociability, open debate, and print culture.[67] In Latin America, as in Spain, their opposition to the authority of the state was combined with a robust critique of the often powerful Catholic Church. And since the state, not least in its "liberal" developmentalist guise, was currently flexing its muscles and imposing "order and progress," the infant anarchist movements did not lack for obvious authoritarian targets. Thus, developmental liberalism and anarcho-liberalism were, in a sense, two sides of the same coin: on the one hand an ambitious affirmation, on the other a radical repudiation of *desarrollo hacia afuera* and enhanced state power.

The mutation of liberalism into anarchism is very clear in Mexico, where the radical Partido Liberal Mexicano of the 1900s was born as a conventionally liberal protest party, attracting mainstream and often middle-class liberals in opposition to the Porfirian regime (and to the church), but it rapidly shifted to the left, adopting more radical anarchist policies and eschewing electoral politics (which proved a dead end) in favor of armed insurrection.[68] Yet the "Liberal" label was retained: Out of inertia? To fool the public? Or because (radical) liberalism remained a suitable label for a party and program that now veered toward anarchism?[69] At any rate, during the lead-up to the Mexican Revolution in 1910, there was a clear overlap in terms of ideas, motifs, and personnel between Maderista liberalism and Magonista radicalism. Perhaps the Mexican case was unusual, but there is some evidence of similar overlap elsewhere in Latin America, notably Argentina, while Nicaragua's Augusto Sandino, a Liberal, also cobbled together an eclectic ideology combining liberalism, nationalism, Freemasonry, and religious heterodoxy.[70]

If anarcho-liberalism offered one way out of the labyrinth, another was provided by what we could call "social" liberalism. Now this term has suffered, at least in the Mexican context, because of its opportunistic adoption by the administration of Carlos Salinas de Gortari (1988–94), which, in order to sweeten the pill of neoliberal reform, invoked the notion of "social liberalism," which traced back to the seminal thinking of Ponciano Arriaga and other mid-nineteenth-century left-wing liberals (alias puros).[71] Arriaga was a radical or, if you prefer, "social" liberal who stood on the left of the Juarista Liberal Party, and indeed, he had been thus identified by the influential Priísta historian/theorist/ideologue Jesús Reyes Heroles, who sought to link the revolution, which indirectly gave birth to the PRI, to its influential liberal/Juarista origins.[72]

"Social liberalism" exemplified a liberal concern for social problems and policies, which Reyes Heroles associated with the PRI (at least, the PRI of his enlightened aspirations) and which, twenty years later, Salinas and his "organic intellectuals" were keen to reappropriate for the new, neoliberal PRI of the late 1980s. The Salinista discursive ploy may have enjoyed some short-term success (not least because it was linked to creative clientelism in the guise of the Programa Nacional de Solidaridad), but we should not let that passing political episode acquire a monopoly of the "social liberal" brand. Reyes Heroles's more historically grounded analysis remains valid: social liberalism arose on the left of the mid-nineteenth-century Liberal Party (Arriaga indeed being a key exponent), and it proposed more radical solutions to the perceived "social question" of the day, including the protection of labor and a measure of land reform. Roberto Gargarella discerns similar concerns and solutions among several Latin American countries and radical liberal movements in the nineteenth century.[73] "Social" liberalism was therefore a logical response to the so-called social question, a "question" that, prompted by the rapid advance of capitalism, urbanization, and proletarianization, preoccupied both Europe and Latin America in the late nineteenth century and after.[74]

In terms of their concerns, as well as their constituencies (which included artisans, workers, peasants, and dissident members of the petty bourgeoisie), "social" liberals rubbed shoulders with anarcho-liberals. But they differed—and differed increasingly—regarding the solution. Where the anarchists advocated the dissolution of the oppressive, authoritarian state, the "social liberals" believed that the state had a key role to play in making genuine liberalism work. That is, in order to enable individuals to achieve their full autonomy and potential (the philosophical bedrock of liberalism), the state had to reorder and regulate society, providing not just law and order but also education, protection of workers (including women and children), social security, and perhaps land reform.[75] Such policies involved greater state intervention in society and the economy and hence were a clear departure from the strict principles of laissez-faire, so for some, this was an unforgivable derogation of "true" (economic) liberalism. But social liberals could reasonably retort that without socially responsible state intervention, liberal values remained, at best, hollow aspirations: How could uneducated workers and peons, toiling in field and factory, achieve freedom, autonomy, and personal development? Only the state could create the conditions in which such worthy goals became practically feasible.[76]

Furthermore, this was not just a moral issue: the "social question" involved serious fears on the part of states, elites, and the well-to-do concerning the growth of cities, the erosion of old paternalist ties, the formation of a rootless proletariat, and the sociopolitical tensions and conflicts that resulted. These years witnessed serious, sometimes bloody labor disputes: Cananea and Río Blanco in Mexico (1906–7), Iquique in Chile (1907), general strikes in Argentina (1902, 1919) and Peru (1919), and a burst of prewar labor militancy in Brazil.[77] Social liberalism therefore obeyed both a prudential and an altruistic rationale. It offered a way—alongside the usual resort to repression—of assuaging social tensions and channeling popular dissidence into more acceptable, less challenging courses. A classic case was Francisco Madero's creation of Mexico's Department of Labor in 1912, an institution designed to monitor and resolve industrial disputes, thus averting conflict and showing the workers that the state could play a positive (nonrepressive) role. It was also designed to undercut the appeal of radical working-class movements, such as the anarchistic Casa del Obrero Mundial.[78]

Social liberalism was a staple feature of fin-de-siècle Europe, especially northern and western Europe. In Britain, where T. H. Green and L. T. Hobhouse had supplied the philosophical justification for a socially conscious, state-interventionist liberalism, it was the Liberal Party and its massive working-class constituency that pioneered social welfare reform in the 1900s.[79] When it came to state-sponsored social welfare, southern Europe lagged behind: in Spain and Italy the state lacked comparable resources, was more corrupt, and faced a more militant—in part anarchist—organized working class. Latin America, as you would expect, more closely resembled southern Europe. (The resemblance, of course, went further, since Latin America was also overwhelmingly Catholic, and the combination of a corrupt, *caciquista* state and a powerful Catholic Church provided fertile ground for the growth of anarchism.) But there were exceptions, notably Uruguay, which developed a precocious welfare state under the leadership of José Batlle y Ordóñez and his ("social liberal") Colorado Party, which, given its "populist reformism" and qualified respect for the rule of law, appealed to some radical groups, such as the tailors' union, which, it has been plausibly argued, evolved from "anarchism" to "anarcho-Batllismo."[80]

The typology I have just outlined can be roughly depicted as seen in figure 1. Of course, all this is highly schematic: it offers a rough way to conceptualize the sprawling, shape-shifting thing we call "liberalism." In the remainder of this chapter I want to introduce three additional perspectives that complicate the scheme but, I hope, make it more congruent with Latin America's complex and dynamic reality: political economy and class relations, culture (religious and, at greater length, popular culture), and, finally, nationalism.

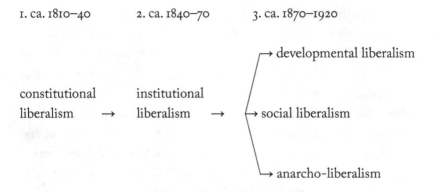

1. ca. 1810–40   2. ca. 1840–70   3. ca. 1870–1920

developmental liberalism

constitutional   institutional
liberalism   →   liberalism   →   social liberalism

anarcho-liberalism

1. THE EVOLUTION OF LIBERALISM IN LATIN AMERICA.

Political Economy and Class Relations

First, my goal is to clarify "really existing liberalism," that is, liberalism as a program of government or a movement of social and political activism.[81] The writings of the great liberals—Mora, Sarmiento, Arriaga—should, of course, be taken seriously (and have been taken seriously by some notable scholars, especially Charles Hale). But the liberal canon no more explains the whole history of liberalism than the writings of Marx and Engels explain world Communism. I have already suggested how Latin American liberalism mutated in response to changing circumstances: the great Victorian boom at midcentury; the growth of world trade and capital flows; and processes of urbanization, proletarianization, and commercialization, which in turn provoked the so-called social question at the end of the century. While these tides of global change washed over the whole of Latin America, from Tijuana to Tierra del Fuego, their local or national impact varied a good deal. The key difference—and here I will advance a frankly materialist explanation that some may consider economically reductionist—concerns how trade, investment, and production generated divergent but far from random outcomes throughout nineteenth-century Latin America.[82]

In respect to class relations and political economy, there are two principal and contrasting patterns: the Indo-American and the neo-European.[83]

However, a third, more slippery category is also required, one that I will call "neopatrimonial" (apologies for yet more "overwrought" typologies). In what might be called Indo-America (Central America, Peru, Bolivia, Ecuador, and, to a lesser degree, Mexico and Colombia), a dense peasantry of Indian ethnic origin coexisted with commercial haciendas and mining. After a "long hiatus"—roughly, the generation following independence— both haciendas and mines began to respond to quickening global and national demand, a response made possible by infrastructural investment (ports, telegraphs, and, above all, railways).[84] There is little evidence to suggest that conservatives were any less keen on this kind of "progress" than their liberal enemies (to put it differently, their ideological differences did not hinge primarily on questions of political economy). True, the liberals tended to favor free trade in principle, but they were not at all averse to government intervention in the economy, as already mentioned. Elites of both conservative and liberal persuasion also favored the protection and expansion of private property rights, even when this meant (via desamortización) the dispossession of corporate peasant, often Indian land. Again, the liberals may have been rather keener (the conservatives being leery of a policy that attacked both the church and the villages), but once the process was under way and the profits became apparent, conservative elites were happy to take advantage and did not try to put the clock back.[85] A similar liberal/conservative elite consensus was apparent when it came to carving up public land (*terrenos baldíos*) from Mexico to Argentina.[86] In blunt terms, the class—perhaps also ethnic—interests of Latin American elites tended to trump their ideological (conservative/liberal) differences.

However, the context in which they acted varied greatly. In Indo-America the process of land commercialization, peasant dispossession, and integration into world markets was violent and conflictual.[87] It involved what Marx called "primary accumulation," which he further defined as "those moments when great masses of human beings were suddenly and forcibly torn away from the means of subsistence and hurled into the labour market as masterless proletarians."[88] "Primary accumulation," in the Indo-American case, came at the expense of Indian and mestizo peasants who had the ability to resist; that is, they had resources, material, human, and cultural, to draw upon. They could resist peacefully by means of litigation and lobbying, and they could resort to evasion, but they could also take up arms in sporadic revolts or, in the case of Mexico, in a major popular revolution.[89] In such circumstances, liberalism faced an uphill struggle. Committed to respect for individual rights, the division of powers, the rule of law, and representative government, liberals—and others—found themselves resorting to coercion and repression.[90] The result was a highly illiberal form of "liberalism," or, if you prefer, "pseudoliberalism."

The Mexican dénouement—the Revolution of 1910—was unusually dramatic and decisive: it halted, then reversed, the process of peasant dispossession. No other major "peasant war" interrupted the course of primary accumulation in Indo-America during the so-called liberal period. But peasant resistance in the form of sporadic rebellion, as well as litigation, footdragging, and obstruction (the famous "weapons of the weak"), substantially slowed it down in both Central and Andean America. Political and economic elites realized that they had to reckon with serious popular opposition in which class and ethnic tensions were combined; meanwhile, they complained bitterly about lazy Indians who, from time to time, turned into vicious savages. Only state coercion could counter the "near impenetrable stupidity" of (Guatemalan) Indians or discipline the "lazy" and "shameless" Indians of southern Peru, who, being "refractory to learning," languished "in the lair of their ancestral vices," stigmatized by "slovenliness and innate apathy."[91]

Not surprisingly, it proved difficult to establish genuinely liberal regimes in Indo-America: Madero failed in Mexico, while within Central America, Costa Rica was at best a small and incipient exception. Conversely, hardline developmental liberalism reached its apogee in Indo-American countries, for example, in the Mexico of Porfirio Díaz, the Guatemala of Manuel Estrada Cabrera, or Peru's Aristocratic Republic. The result was a series of authoritarian regimes, some highly corrupt and personalistic, and in consequence, popular discontent could rarely take a peaceful electoral path. Instead, Indo-America witnessed a series of major revolts (and repressions): Zapatismo, the prolonged Yaqui insurgency in northwestern Mexico, the rebellion of Pablo Zárate ("el temible Willka") on the Bolivian altiplano (1898), the major Chayanta revolt in southern Bolivia (1927), and the Rumi Maqui revolt of 1915–16 in Peru's southern highlands, itself part of an entire "cycle of protest and rebellion" in that region between 1915 and 1924.[92]

In contrast, the "neo-Europes"—to use Alfred Crosbie's phrase—were more hospitable to liberal practices.[93] Argentina, as Tulio Halperín famously commented, was a country "born liberal," although it took some time for its liberal birthright to achieve practical expression.[94] However, as the Argentine economy grew (and the old problem of Buenos Aires's relationship to the provinces was resolved), so later nineteenth-century Argentina did acquire a liberal and representative though not yet democratic regime, which crystallized under the rule of Julio Roca and the PAN.[95] And after 1916, "oligarchic" liberalism evolved into a genuine form of democratic liberalism: Argentina thus followed a loosely western European pattern, a fact of which Europhile Argentines were well aware and vocally proud. It did so in part because Argentina's landed elite, being rich and influential, believed that they could weather a democratic transition; indeed, some even welcomed it as a means to curtail the power of corrupt political bosses (caudillos).[96] Uruguay traced a somewhat similar path from caudillismo to civilian and eventually democratic—indeed, *social* democratic—government.[97] In these two cases, economic growth involved mass European migration, the significance of this being not that European migrants carried democracy in their bones (after all, most came from Italy and Spain, which were far from being model democracies at the time) but that they migrated to expanding, free-market, capitalist economies that possessed abundant land and relied on cash incentives rather than coercion to recruit labor to work the land (and service the cities).[98] A free market of this kind may also have been particularly conducive to the creation of "a vigorous civil society" involving a lively press, a plural "public sphere," and "an unprecedented expansion of associative practices," in short, a "solid foundation for a free and republican society."[99] In the absence of coercion, which in Indo-America was needed first to dispossess the peasantry and then to set them to work as peons or proletarians, Argentina and Uruguay could attract mass migration and rely on the market to ensure a supply of labor and increase production. Since the migrants boosted the domestic market, that production included a significant measure of import-substitution industrialization. Of course, as time went by, as the social question loomed, and as workers, including immigrants, began to organize and protest, so repression ensued (notably in 1919). But this occurred within a really-existing liberal polity, and again, it was not radically different from what happened in Europe in the same period.

My third, rather looser category is "neopatrimonial."[100] By this I mean a society in which a strong landed class enjoys political influence and social status, based on a combination of clientelism and coercion, in the (relative) absence of densely settled peasant communities that might resist the landlords' largely informal and hence neopatrimonial authority. Rather less prosperous than their *porteño* counterparts, landlords in the central valley of Chile and northeastern Brazil controlled relatively poor rural societies, represented by Chile's *inquilinos* and Brazil's *caboclos*, who in turn lacked the lively traditions and related organizational power of Mexican and Andean peasant villages.[101] (In Brazil they were also ethnically diverse, which added to their social disaggregation.) In the Brazilian sertão, violent political factionalism prevailed; in Chile's Central Valley, landlords maintained a more peaceful and robust form of (neo)patrimonial hegemony, successfully resisting the inroads of urban radicalism until the period after the Second World War.[102] Neither environment was propitious for promoting liberal rights, still less democratic representation.[103] When democracy finally penetrated these places, to the accompaniment of demands for land reform, it proved highly destabilizing; hence, in Brazil in the 1960s and Chile in the 1970s, popular mobilization and agrarian reform were the prelude to military interventions.[104]

Culture

Religion

So far I have stressed broadly socioeconomic trends bound up with global transformations but mediated through the policies of Latin American states and elites, especially the landlord class. Alongside these trends we can discern sociocultural shifts too: the rise of education (which, certainly in Mexico, could help create loyal liberal constituencies, brought up to revere Juárez and the *próceres* of the Reform and French Intervention) and the crucial role of the Catholic Church, which had to react to the same trends while confronting—and often opposing—what was seen as a serious liberal threat to its own material and institutional interests. As I mention in chapter 3 of this book, at the time of independence, liberalism and Catholicism sometimes dovetailed: at least, plenty of early liberals were priests, and the great majority of liberals were also Catholics.[105] But with the rise of anticlerical "institutional" liberalism in the mid-nineteenth century, the church proved intransigent, as befitted a body led by the reactionary Pius IX.[106] A generation later, as the "social question" reared its head and liberals, in the ways just suggested, groped to find their own solutions, so the church also began to experiment with more creative and reformist responses, even, with Rerum Novarum (1891), opting to work with the liberal state, if only for fear of meeting something worse. Catholics and liberals thus danced their own complicated quadrille, and both the nature and the impact of liberalism must be assessed in light of Catholic opposition (or, occasionally, collaboration).

Of course, the Catholic/clerical question was most pressing in those countries where the church was unusually strong, rooted, and popular: in Mexico, for example, where anticlericalism was a key item of policy (and source of conflict) in the mid-nineteenth century and again, even more virulently, after the revolution broke out in 1910. The church was also strong in Ecuador, where the liberals failed to mount a decisive challenge until the 1890s, while in contrast, the Venezuelan church was "too weak to put up a good fight against the anticlericals."[107] In the Southern Cone (including, for these purposes, Brazil), the church was also weaker than in Mexico, Colombia, or Ecuador; in Argentina, neither Roca's PAN nor Hipólito Irigoyen's Radical Party targeted the church. Church/state squabbles in Argentina tended to be minor and provincial.[108] Argentine radicalism, in particular, while ticking most of the boxes of liberal policy and resembling its French (radical) namesake in several respects, never adopted a vigorous anticlerical stance, because it did not see the church as either a major problem or a serious rival (indeed, it sometimes saw the church as a useful bulwark against social subversion), so the anticlerical mantle therefore fell to the Socialists (who, as observers noted, more closely resembled European, i.e., French or Italian, radicals).[109]

The religious makeup of the "neopatrimonialist" lands varied. In Chile a powerful church underpinned landlord hegemony and, as in Colombia, proved a loyal ally of the Conservative Party well into the nineteenth century. But in northern Brazil the church was weaker; thus, landlord "hegemony" (if that is the right word) depended more on brute force and naked clientelism (i.e., the provision of jobs and protection), and the partial religious vacuum was filled, inter alia, by millenarian and messianic movements.[110] Thus, depending on the balance of forces, liberalism might, as in Mexico, espouse a robust anticlericalism, which would deeply color national politics, or it might consider the church either too weak (Venezuela) or too inoffensive (Argentina) to warrant making anticlericalism a central plank in the liberal platform. I shall return to the anticlerical question very briefly when I address the character of popular liberalism.

The Raw and the Cooked

If "really existing" liberalism is to be understood as an active political force as well as a theoretical canon, it must be related to class relations and cultural (including religious) context, as just mentioned. Religion and anticlericalism—which, I assume, can be uncontentiously considered "cultural" questions—do not, however, exhaust the cultural dimension of nineteenth-century Latin American liberalism. There is an additional, perhaps less obvious dimension that can perhaps be described in terms lifted from Claude Lévi-Strauss (via Eric Van Young): "the raw and the cooked."[111] An alternative formulation of this distinction, following Robert Redfield, would be "Great Tradition" and "Little Tradition" liberalism.[112] By this I mean, roughly, popular ("raw," "Little Tradition") liberalism versus elite ("cooked," "Great Tradition") liberalism, a distinction that is now all the more pertinent following the historiographical "discovery" and investigation of a significant strand of popular liberalism in Latin America.[113]

Any powerful and broad-based "ism" necessarily embraces a variety of classes or social sectors.[114] In Latin America, Catholicism would be the classic example, "folk" versus "elite" Catholicism being the basic but not the sole division. To the extent that liberalism also acquired a broad following, it acquired both popular and elite forms: the "raw" and the "cooked." An older view of Latin American liberalism—still influential, even dominant, when I wrote my 1985 article—was that liberalism was essentially an elite philosophy/project imported from abroad and imposed on an indifferent or even hostile population. That view, espoused by Claudio Veliz and others, has since been substantially revised: popular liberalism has now become a standard explanatory concept, from Mexico to Argentina, and liberalism is no longer seen as an alien import, lacking Latin American roots.[115] Of course, the relative strength of popular liberalism varied both *within* countries (as I shall later mention) and *between* countries. (It was more salient in Mexico than in Guatemala, while within Central America, El Salvador and Nicaragua displayed a stronger popular-liberal tradition than Guatemala. Colombian liberalism also developed a popular wing that, by way of comparison, was much weaker in Peru.) Some of the socioeconomic and cultural-religious reasons for these divergences have been touched on.

But popular and elite liberalism also adopted rather different forms.[116] Almost by definition, elite liberalism was more cerebral and sophisticated: it was epitomized by political intellectuals like Mora and Sarmiento, and it appealed to a small literate (usually urban) public who, perhaps, had some direct familiarity with John Stuart Mill or Spencer and who followed the news from Europe (notably in 1848). Conservative critics in Colombia "deplored [the] Liberals' fondness for heterodox European writers as against traditional Catholic thinkers."[117] Given its makeup, elite liberal "mobilization" tended to take the form of parties of notables, which, if they prospered, mutated into mass parties with a popular base: Argentina's Unión Cívica Radical, the Colombian Liberal Party, Madero's Partido Antirreeleccionista. In order to get their message across, such parties, again largely urban, relied on newspapers, broadsheets, speeches in the plaza, and electoral campaigns. (Hence, I repeat, their success depended a good deal on whether they operated in a more open pluralist polity, such as Buenos Aires or Montevideo, rather than one in which repression and neopatrimonial clientelism prevailed, such as the provincial towns of Peru, northern Brazil, or even central Chile.) While we should not underestimate the important role of ideas, symbols, and international news in the formation of popular liberalism (Hobsbawm's notion of "prepolitical" peasants is now seen, I think, as somewhat simplistic and even wrong), it remains true that popular ("raw") liberalism assumed rather different forms compared to its elite ("cooked") counterpart.[118]

For one thing, popular liberalism was a rural as much as an urban phenomenon, and even when it was urban, it affected small towns and the working-class barrios of larger cities, where it recruited, above all, aspiring artisans.[119] In Mexico, as Rodney Anderson shows, liberalism was the principal ideology of the late-Porfirian working class.[120] And while Mexico may have been a special case (see below), working-class liberalism sprang up elsewhere in Latin America, for example, in Arequipa, Peru, and Bogotá, where artisans supported the moderate (Draconiano) wing of the Liberal Party.[121] But popular liberalism also had rural roots. Zapatismo, though it soon became a popular revolutionary movement, adhered to liberal notions and traditions, and these can be traced back at least to the mid-nineteenth century, when Juan Alvarez, the caudillo of the South, and his rough peasant retainers (many of them of Afro-mestizo origin) played a key role in the War of the Reform.[122] In Colombia, too, General José María Obando led popular liberal levies, which included recently emancipated slaves. (Since the liberals claimed the credit for Colombia's belated emancipation in 1851, they were able to "capture and retain the overwhelming allegiance of the nation's blacks.")[123]

Popular liberalism was "raw" in the sense of attracting people of lower status and less literacy. They often looked, dressed, and sounded different from their more suave, educated, urban middle- and upper-class counterparts. Latin American political "culture" is not short of terms that capture this division between plebs and patricians. In postindependence Oaxaca (Mexico), for example, the well-to-do "oil" faction battled with its plebeian "vinegar" rival.[124] In contemporary Guatemala, liberals were called *cacos* (thieves) and conservatives *bacos* (drunks), but these labels were soon swapped for *fievres* (firebrands) and *serviles* (lackeys).[125] Such (emic) vocabulary captures something of contemporary social and political polarization and adds a cultural flavor to the more desiccated (etic) terms that we as historians (or social scientists) tend to use: elite, mass, worker, peasant, subaltern. And they counted at the time: in the 1840s the Arequipa liberal Manuel Ignacio de Vivanco resisted the Peruvian caudillo Agustín Gamarra, promising to restore government—enlightened, progressive, liberal government—to "the capable and the cultured."[126]

Such class and status—sometimes also ethnic—divisions did not strictly correspond to (liberal/conservative) ideological affiliations; they also ran through both liberal and conservative constituencies. It seems likely that, compared to its elite counterpart, popular liberalism owed more to local ("little") traditions maintained within relatively parochial oral minicultures. People became liberals not because they read Mill or admired the French Third Republic but because their family/clan/barrio/community had come to adopt a liberal label, revered liberal heroes, and commemorated liberal anniversaries.[127] Quite often, certainly in Mexico, this local liberal identity was reinforced by dyadic rivalries with neighboring conservative (and clerical) communities, the classic case being San José de Gracia, in Michoacán, which, as a conservative, Catholic, mestizo community, looked askance at neighboring Mazamitla, which was liberal, Indian, and later revolutionary.[128] Traditions were also sustained by local organizations, not so much the learned *tertulias* (soirées) of the educated bourgeois (though we should not discount the earnest gatherings of literate, aspiring artisans, such as Colombia's "Democratic Societies") but, rather, the ubiquitous military bands of central Mexico, which, we could say, spread liberalism to the beat of the drum and the sound of the sometimes ill-tuned trumpet.[129]

The fact that popular liberalism of this kind relied on family or local tradition allied to oral or even musical forms of inspiration (rather than a more purely cerebral/textual/literate appeal) does not disqualify it from membership in the great global liberal family. After all, plenty—perhaps the majority—of elite liberals also adhered to the cause on the grounds of family allegiance or local/regional inclination. Recent research also suggests that political attitudes and preferences in general may be more "irrational" (I would prefer "affective") than dominant rational-actor models assume.[130]

At any rate, whatever the motivation or mode of conversion, popular liberalism was a vigorous force in the politics of many Latin American countries. It also diverged from its elite counterpart in some significant ways. I will briefly mention just three relevant areas of divergence (there may be more): anticlericalism, agrarianism, and local autonomy. Finally, I will touch on the related question of popular liberal mobilization and nationalism.

Anticlericalism, Agrarianism, and Autonomy

I noted the importance of church/state relations in defining liberal/conservative party lines. However, liberalism, as a broad and diverse movement, was not uniformly anticlerical. Rather, it seems that popular anticlericalism, where it existed, tended to be less virulent than the anticlericalism of the educated middle class or well-to-do. Or, to be more precise, *rural* popular liberalism was rarely as strongly anticlerical as its *urban* counterpart (i.e., the difference was in part spatial-cultural [urban vs. rural] and in part socioeconomic [elite vs. popular]). This was certainly the case in Mexico, where peasant rebels like the Zapatistas, while strongly committed to the liberal cause, were relaxed as regards the church and, following a long tradition that dated back to independence, even included a few liberal *curas* in their camp. In contrast, radical liberal (alias "Jacobin") anticlericalism was most evident among the urban petty bourgeoisie (Plutarco Elías Calles being a classic case) or in radical artisan circles, where the presence of a priest would have been unthinkable.[131] It was also stronger in the hot coastal lowlands than in the temperate highlands. Popular liberal anticlericalism, though sometimes associated with outright rationalism, also drew sustenance from religious heterodoxy, including Spiritualism and variants of Protestantism, especially Methodism.[132] The case of Sandino suggests that this connection was not confined to Mexico.[133]

Attitudes toward the church were also gendered: liberal anticlericals generally believed that the church depended—for its "ideological hegemony," we might say—on women, especially devout older women (*beatas*), who played a key role in everyday religious observances (services, pilgrimages, fiestas). And this was not merely a macho misperception. Women often sprang to the defense of clerical rights and privileges (in opposition to liberal reforms), while conversely, radical anticlericalism tended to be a male preoccupation.[134] This gendered divergence—a tendency, I should stress, not an absolute—may relate to a broader feature of nineteenth-century liberalism: while notions of citizenship and representation, the kernel of liberalism, benefited men, including, often enough, men of the lower classes, they systematically excluded women, who did not enjoy the vote and remained politically excluded.[135] Indeed, it is arguable that, during the nineteenth century, women lost political ground relative to men: the liberal *apertura* (opening) tended to be a male preserve.[136] This radical macho tradition was carried well into the twentieth century by some (not all) radical and anarchist movements.[137]

Second, popular peasant liberalism also helped create a tension at the heart of the movement, which had to do with land tenure and (potential) agrarian reform. Mid-nineteenth-century ("institutional") liberals had favored breaking up corporate property and turning it into freehold, thus promoting, it was hoped, the growth of a sturdy and prosperous farmer class on Jeffersonian lines. In some (Mexican) cases, this hope was realized: in Oaxaca, for example, in the Estado de Mexico, or in the Huasteca, where the farmer/ranchero sector was bolstered by the Reforma and, in consequence, its liberal affiliation was fortified.[138] Elsewhere (e.g., in much of Jalisco or Michoacán), rancheros were too close to the Catholic Church to convert to liberalism: religious allegiance trumped socioeconomic reward. However, some peasant communities, including many that had supported Juárez, resented the process of desamortización, since it made possible the concentration of land in private hands, including both rising rancheros and rich hacendados. As a result, the Revolution of 1910 contained a strong agrarian element. Yet *agraristas* such as the Zapatistas also proclaimed their allegiance to Juárez, even though he had (indirectly at least) helped to bring about the "planters' progress" in Morelos.[139] Other communities managed to combine a liberal—and soon to be revolutionary—reputation with a commitment to agrarian reform, reform that necessarily attacked property rights and, implicitly at least, represented a critique of Juarista liberalism. In contrast, elite liberals such as Francisco Madero set great store by private property rights, and while sometimes recognizing the need for a more equitable division of land, they believed that reform had to be consensual, legal, and respectful of those rights. In the context of 1910–20, that probably meant little or no reform at all.[140]

So we face something of a paradox: Mexican popular rebels proclaimed their liberalism but set out to reverse a major item of (nineteenth-century) liberal policy. (There is an analogous paradox that might be profitably explored, though it will not be addressed here: why urban artisans, potential victims of free trade, supported supposedly free-trading liberals. One brief answer, already touched on, is that, regarding the question of free trade versus protection, party lines were more blurred than often supposed.) Of course, paradox is common enough in history, and "no ideology is wholly consistent."[141] So an easy explanation—not to say a cop-out—might be that people are inconsistent and hence capable of entertaining opposed principles without too much mental anguish. While no doubt true, this only gets us so far, since if people (in this case, nineteenth-century Latin Americans) can happily adhere to any number of contradictory ideas and allegiances, then the explanatory power of the latter evaporates. Ideas count for nothing.[142]

There are, however, some important factors that help explain and thus reduce the inconsistency. I shall mention two in particular. First, there is the obvious question of timing. Liberal desamortización was placed firmly on the Mexican political agenda in the 1850s.[143] But it took time for legislation to take effect; and as Juárez battled the Conservatives and then the French, the pace of land privatization and, more important, land concentration was slow, being retarded, in a good many cases, by peasant resistance.[144] It accelerated after Díaz's seizure of power in 1876, as the Pax Porfiriana brought political stability, as the new railway network was built, as population grew, and as national and overseas markets exerted a strong demand. Landlords sought to expand their holdings under the auspices of a benign state, and indeed, the Porfirian state further accelerated the process with its colonization laws, which threw open public lands for "denunciation" and privatization.[145] Now the dispossession of the peasantry gathered pace, and quite logically the dispossessed peasants—including Zapata and his family—blamed the Díaz regime and the local landlords, such as the egregious Pablo Escandón, who were both the economic beneficiaries and, increasingly, the political representatives of that regime.[146] Juárez's culpability was a distant memory, outshone by his heroic and patriotic aura; the abuses that agrarian rebels sought to correct were more recent, immediate, and recognizably "Porfirian." So it was not so illogical for an agrarian rebel to be Juarista but anti-Porfirian.

Second, we should bear in mind both the *purpose* and the *outcome* of liberal desamortización. Many liberals genuinely believed (as far as we know) that breaking up corporate property would indeed benefit small farmers, and in some cases, as I have mentioned, they were right.[147] The Jeffersonian ideal of a prosperous yeomanry was not historically preposterous: witness the American Midwest or large swaths of rural France following the revolution.[148] The problem was not the *goal* of liberal policy, which certainly appealed to agrarian rebels such as the Zapatistas, but rather its *consequences*, which, given several other intervening factors (the Pax Porfiriana, caciquismo, the railways, market demand), jeopardized the very existence of peasant communities such as Zapata's hometown, Anenecuilco.[149] In very general terms, we could say, liberalism was perfectly compatible with a dense peasantry pursuing independent small-scale production. But when liberalism promoted untrammeled property rights within a market economy (another good liberal tradition), the tendency was for land concentration to grow, to the detriment of peasant smallholding. Liberals had to decide which had priority: property rights or peasant welfare. Some liberal regimes clearly opted for the second: in postrevolutionary France, in late nineteenth-century Ireland, even in colonial West Africa, where we see policies designed to protect peasant farming and curtail the power of big landowners. Infringing property rights in order to protect or promote small farmers was just another of the several compromises that "social liberalism" adopted in order to save the spirit of liberalism, even if it meant departing from letter. After 1917 the Mexican revolutionaries performed similar contortions when they created the ejido, the agrarian reform community. The ejido was designed to protect and promote peasant holdings while curtailing latifundismo, but many of its proponents, such as Cabrera and Calles, saw it as a means to promote not communal miniutopias but a prosperous farmer class. The Jeffersonian vision remained, but it required some novel measures to bring it about.[150]

Drawing direct parallels between Mexico's agrarian trajectory and that of the rest of Latin America would be ambitious and, in some respects, unhelpful.[151] It seems clear that, as already mentioned, the timing is roughly similar in Peru and, to a lesser extent, Bolivia: agrarian commercialization, backed by the power of the state, accelerated in the later nineteenth century, provoking peasant dispossession and protest. In Peru, as Méndez argues, this trend had the predictable effect of undermining peasant support for liberalism.[152] In Bolivia, liberal forces could still count on that support, notably in 1899, but following the revolt of that year, those "Aymara Liberals" were vilified and punished, while Liberals and Conservative elites "reconciled their differences by generating negative images of the Aymara population."[153] Land reform—and, with it, some genuine empowerment of the Bolivian peasantry—had to await the 1940s and 1950s, at which time the peasantry's key allies were the military and the semifascistic MNR. In experiencing a revolution that obeyed liberal inspiration but that resulted in extensive agrarian reform, Mexico was unusual, certainly for the so-called liberal period of Latin American history (ca. 1870–1930).

A third feature of "raw" popular liberalism that gave it strength and stamina was its emphasis on local or maybe regional autonomy. Of course, this was an old tradition: throughout the nineteenth century, liberals, both elite and popular, had championed local and regional rights of self-government in the face of often conservative centralism. The War of the Reform in Mexico pitted a "liberal circle" of states and regions—"a vast arc of territory that slices from Veracruz up through San Luis Potosí, Zacatecas, Guanajuato, Jalisco, then down through Michoacán, and ends in Guerrero and Oaxaca"—against the power of the "center" in Mexico City and its surrounding valley.[154] The Revolution of 1910–14 roughly reprised this geopolitical pattern. The provinces resented central control—taxation, forced recruitment, political impositions—and liberalism was a suitable (but not the sole) banner under which to express that resentment. But the same pattern was replicated at the regional level, where small towns chafed under the weight of metropolises such as Puebla, Guadalajara, and Monterrey, and even locally, where *sujetos* (dependent towns/villages) sought to free themselves from the authorities of *cabeceras* (head towns). Such politico-spatial conflicts could assume a variety of ideological forms, but one, and one that had a certain logic, involved liberal assertions of state or municipal autonomy in the face of centralizing pressures from above.

Similar patterns are evident throughout Latin America. Conservatism tended to be strong in Bogotá, while liberalism flourished on the Colombian periphery: in Panama and along the Caribbean coast.[155] Just as the liberals of northern Chile spurned the hidebound conservatism of the Central Valley, so southern Peruvian liberals resisted Limeño centralization, drawing on effective popular support.[156] In Central America, El Salvador's historic liberalism derived from resentment at the predominance, both political and commercial, of Guatemala City, while in Nicaragua, León became a "hotbed of liberal thought and action" in opposition to conservative Granada.[157] More generally, local politics in Central American often reflected, in Ralph Lee Woodward's words, "an adolescent desire to be free of their respective immediate superiors."[158]

Furthermore, the late nineteenth-century triumph of "developmental liberalism," with its commitment to centralized state power, ratcheted up the tension within the loose liberal movement. Now the rural and provincial proponents of autonomy could claim a greater fidelity to liberal principles (of freedom, self-government, perhaps federalism, and "subsidiarity") than their centralizing, "developmental," and even authoritarian "liberal" opponents. Thus, some autonomist movements (which I have elsewhere referred to generically as *serrano*) readily adopted a liberal label.[159] They responded to Madero in 1910 in part because he proclaimed a liberal affiliation but also because he was mounting a challenge to the overweening Porfirian state and its creatures—creatures who, in the main, happened to call themselves "liberals" too.

Mobilization and Nationalism

Finally, irrespective of goals and motives, the fact of popular ("raw") liberalism was important in practical terms, since it provided the liberals with a stout rural constituency that outnumbered and, at critical moments, outgunned urban opponents. Since nineteenth-century Latin America was, with few exceptions, overwhelmingly rural, the opinions and actions of the rural population counted for a good deal. And, as I have suggested, the idea of "prepolitical" peasants sunk in "rural idiocy" and indifferent to national events and processes is no longer tenable. Supracommunal organization might have been difficult (hence, popular revolts were often highly localized), but this did not mean that the rural population lacked knowledge of or interest in what happened beyond the purview of the church tower.[160] Rural people also made better combatants, especially when guerrilla warfare was on the agenda.[161] They knew the terrain and had access to guns and horses (or, failing those, machetes and mules). Juan Alvarez, the liberal caudillo of the South, was instrumental in the triumph of the Revolution of Ayutla.[162] José María Obando, who was "cordially detested and feared by many conservatives" while enjoying "the admiration of the liberal rank-and-file," raised his popular forces in Pasto, where they included recently liberated slaves; in Cauca, just to the north, the Conservatives sneered at their enemy rank-and-file for being "multitudes of blacks and mulattos."[163] As already mentioned, the peasants of Huanta and the artisans of Arequipa provided Peruvian liberals with valuable manpower, as did the insurgent Aymara of 1899 in highland Bolivia.[164]

In 1910–11, when Mexico's major cities remained firmly under the thumb of the Porfirian authorities, rural guerrillas carried the fight to the regime, many proclaiming a liberal allegiance.[165] Neither the War of the Reform, nor the War of the French Intervention, nor the Revolution of 1910–14 would have been won by liberal/progressive forces without the decisive agency of rural insurgents carrying liberal banners. Sandino, of course, affords another example of a twentieth-century liberal rebel who waged a dogged guerrilla war against both Nicaragua's conservatives and their American allies. His struggle in the Segovias "began in the name of the Constitution and liberal principles, and continued in the name of national sovereignty and dignity," the mixture fortified by a dose of religious heterodoxy and Arielismo.[166]

Of course, liberalism had no monopoly of rural insurgency. There were, in Mexico and elsewhere, plenty of Catholic (including Catholic/conservative) rebellions, as well as rebellions premised on ethnic identity, factional advantage, or, later, more explicitly socialist principles. Some, like Lozada's revolt in northwestern Mexico, were enduring; some, like Carrera's in Guatemala, achieved lasting power. But it is important to recognize that a large swath of rural (including class/ethnic) protest carried a liberal label (which should not be dismissed as an indicator of "false consciousness" or "rural idiocy") and that, given the nature of nineteenth-century Latin America, armed protest was often more effective in the countryside than in the city.[167]

A final ingredient needs to be tossed into the mix: nationalism (or patriotism: for the purposes of this analysis, they are interchangeable). Again, there is an interesting debate to be had concerning the relationship between liberalism and nationalism. On the one hand, classic nineteenth-century liberalism was leery of nationalism, since liberals typically believed in free trade, peaceful commercial intercourse, and the Cobdenite vision of a world of *doux commerce*. Nationalism, whether it took the form of armed warfare or aggressive protectionism, offended liberal sensibilities (and anarchist sensibilities too, of course). On the other hand, in a world of empires (and, notwithstanding certain clichés to the contrary, the nineteenth century *was* a world of empires), nationalism affirmed the rights of free peoples to govern themselves under regimes of their own choosing.[168] So nationalism and liberalism went hand in hand in Risorgimento Italy and elsewhere.[169] In late colonial Iberian America, nationalism (or "protonationalism," if we want to hedge our bets) also displayed an "elective affinity" with liberalism. That is not to say that all patriots (or protopatriots) were liberals nor that all liberals were (proto)patriots. But there was a degree of kinship, just as there was a clear correlation between (Bourbon) imperial rule and absolutist (i.e., illiberal) government. The Bourbons, it is true, had flirted with some liberal *economic* measures, as well as an Erastian anticlericalism, but for obvious reasons that went beyond the reactionary personal opinions of Fernando VII, Spain found it difficult to concede liberal political rights throughout the empire, since such a concession would have jeopardized the empire as it was currently constituted. Indeed, even Spanish liberals were reluctant to make that concession.[170]

Thus, in colonial contexts, nationalism and liberalism were natural allies; once independent nation-states were established, however, the alliance lost much of its logic.[171] After all, nations could be—and often were—legitimized on conservative and religious grounds. Such legitimation was evident during the Mexican independence struggle, in nineteenth-century Ecuador, or at the birth of the Brazilian monarchy.[172] So there is no reason to assume that liberalism enjoyed any across-the-board advantage when it came to claiming patriotic credentials. However, when anticolonial or anti-imperialist struggles were on the agenda it was a different matter. A standard interpretation says that Communist movements that came to power by means of wars of national liberation proved inherently stronger and more durable than those lacking a clear nationalist mandate: in China, Yugoslavia, and, perhaps, Cuba.[173] The same can be said of liberal movements. The classic case happens to be Mexico, and the sheer strength of Mexican liberalism—as a vital movement claiming popular support—was clearly a product of the war against the French and their Mexican allies. As a result of this successful struggle, liberalism and nationalism fused, and the conservatives were seriously discredited. In a sense, conservatism did not recover as an articulate national force until the late twentieth century, when the revived PAN took advantage of the discredited PRI.[174] As I mentioned earlier, some of Juárez's failings—his abuse of power, his espousal of desamortización—were eclipsed by his heroic leadership in a war of national liberation. Conversely, Maximilian, for all his genuinely liberal impulses, was impaled on the horns of an insoluble dilemma: how to impose a liberal regime by coercive methods in alliance with a foreign army.

The Mexican case may be the clearest and most consequential, but there have been a few others. Liberals played a role in the Cuban struggle against Spanish rule (and later against U.S. intervention). And in the 1920s the United States emulated Napoleon III by invading a weak Latin America country (Nicaragua), seeking to impose a preferred (Conservative) government in the face of strenuous Liberal resistance, in which Sandino was prominent. In contrast, some seventy years earlier, a rather different—freelance—American invasion by William Walker had compromised and discredited Central American, especially Nicaraguan, liberals while boosting the fortunes of the Conservatives, who had resisted.[175] These contrasting Latin American examples seem to bear out the general proposition: liberalism has no inherently stronger claim to patriotic status than conservatism, except in those situations where foreign powers seek to impose regimes, and the liberal commitment to self-government and autonomy can, as a result, forge a natural alliance with nationalism.[176] Such situations have occurred often enough in Latin America—chiefly in Mexico and the circum-Caribbean—for a syndrome of nationalist liberalism to become established; however, in South America, where, following independence, foreign interventions have been fewer and less consequential, that syndrome is relatively absent. International wars in South America, while certainly productive of nationalism, have not encouraged a distinctly *liberal* nationalism; indeed, such wars, fought between Latin American neighbors, have often been fought under military and/or authoritarian auspices (e.g., Paraguay and the War of the Triple Alliance [1864–70], the War of the Pacific [1879–83], and the Chaco War [1932–35]).

Conclusion

Latin American liberalism is diverse and complicated, but it is worth trying to discern some patterns amid the complexity. I have suggested that the Mexican generational pattern of three successive waves of liberalism (constitutional, institutional, and developmental) has some relevance for the rest of Latin America. Indeed, unless one views history as a random series of disconnected events and/or "Latin America" as an entirely meaningless concept, it would be surprising if the Mexican story did not "resonate" with that of other countries in the region. Of course, there was plenty of contingent foam riding on the crest of these waves: liberals out of power, for example, tended to be more genuinely liberal and often federalist; once in power they succumbed to the lure of centralism and Jacobinism. The generational pattern also followed a certain logic, beginning with early constitutional experiments, proceeding to more radical institutional reforms in the mid-nineteenth century (when anticlericalism became more pronounced and divisive), then lapsing into a more authoritarian "developmental" mode in the later nineteenth century.

Global economic trends played a part, and a comparison of Latin American political economies ("Indo-American," "neo-European," and, perhaps, "neopatrimonial") helps explain why, in terms of practical politics, liberalism put down deeper roots in some countries than others. Political regimes (liberal, democratic, authoritarian) depended a good deal on political economies, which in turn involved questions of labor recruitment, land tenure, migration, and exports. At the same time, cultural factors—in particular, the strength and role of the Catholic Church—were also important. Liberalism waxed or waned in a dialectical struggle with the church, the outcome reflecting national and regional differences. In almost all cases, a form of genuine popular liberalism evolved (proving that liberalism was not just a shallow, elitist, imported product), and popular liberalism displayed distinct (again, if you like, "cultural") characteristics. Especially in its rural form, it tended to be less anticlerical; it embodied some "raw" populist characteristics, which offended high-toned liberals weaned on Mill or Spencer; and it supplied much of the manpower for both electoral and, crucially, armed struggles.[177] Finally, a key exogenous factor was provided by nationalism. Conservatives often had just as good a claim to patriotism as their liberal rivals, but when it came to combatting foreign imperialism (chiefly in Mexico and the circum-Caribbean) liberalism and nationalism formed a logical and powerful partnership, with decisive historical consequences.

CHAPTER 3

Religion and Conflict in Latin America, 1820–1930

THIS CHAPTER EXAMINES THE RELATIONSHIP BETWEEN RELI-gion and conflict, including violent conflict, in Latin America during roughly the long nineteenth century. A personal motivation was to place Mexico, the country I know best, in a broader comparative context (partly on the grounds that comparison can help refine arguments about a particular case). I hoped to clarify why church/state conflict, sometimes involving serious and sustained violence, though evident throughout Latin America's modern history, was especially acute in Mexico and why, in particular, the Cristero War of 1926–29, which I come to in conclusion, was the most extreme and bloody example of such conflict.

The essay focuses on the role of religion as a *cause* of conflict, episodes when religion, typically in conjunction with secular factors, provoked contention and violence. "In conjunction" signals an important initial point: "purely" religious violence was very rare for the obvious reason that the church lacked the autonomous capacity to deploy violence. (As Stalin cynically asked: "How many divisions has the pope?") With few exceptions, the Latin American church lacked the sword-wielding bishops or armed religious orders of medieval Europe: when force was deployed, the church either relied on secular allies (armies, warlords, paramilitaries) or recruited support, on a smaller, local scale, among the so-called fanatical laity.[1] It was often a church militant, but it could never be a military church.

Apart from *causing* violence, religion also *facilitated* it, supplying not necessarily the basic motivation but rather collective solidarity and organization.[2] We should also note, however, that religion occasionally *deterred* violence, when, for example, priests counselled peace and conciliation, motivated, perhaps, by biblical injunctions ("blessed are the peacemakers") or, more likely, by sociopolitical concerns, including connivance with ruling elites keen to preserve the status quo.[3] So religion could serve as both a stimulant and a sedative (or "opium," in Marx's famous formulation). However, space being limited, I focus on the stimulation rather than the sedation.

Concepts and Collective Actors

Some further clarifications are required. Two, concerning time and space, are straightforward; two, regarding the basic concepts of "violence" and "religion," demand longer treatment. First, "Latin America" refers to the successor states of the Iberian (Spanish and Portuguese) Empires in the Americas: the eighteen Spanish-speaking republics, plus Brazil and Haiti.[4] Regarding periodization, I address the "long" century from the 1820s, when, with the exception of Cuba, those countries achieved independence, to 1930, that year being a more meaningful (and conventional) watershed than either 1900 or 1914.[5] However, we cannot understand the nineteenth century without considering the influential "colonial legacy" created over the three previous centuries. Covering the history of twenty countries over 110 years (so some 2,200 "country/years") is difficult. True, the shared Iberian background—including a powerful Catholic Church—affords some commonalities, but "Latin America" is also highly diverse, so the story involves multiple plotlines.

But there is a greater analytical problem. Nineteenth-century Latin America was both very religious and, on the face of it, very violent, so there seems to be a prima facie case for addressing these twin phenomena and their relationship. The region boasted a rich religious tradition (primarily but not solely Catholic), and it experienced recurrent bouts of conflict and violence. Historians have amply addressed the institutional conflict between church and state in these decades, but there is rather more to the story than this theme, important though it is.

Regarding international warfare, postindependence Latin America—rather like Europe in the century after Waterloo—largely avoided massive wars.[6] Five major international wars were fought, three involving non–Latin American belligerents: the Mexican-American War (1846–48), the French Intervention in Mexico (1861–67), and the prolonged Cuban insurgency against Spain (1868–78 and 1895–98). Of these, only the first had a clear religious dimension, since it pitted overwhelmingly Catholic Mexico against the predominantly Protestant United States. Catholic exhortation and an occasional priest on horseback bolstered Mexican resistance.[7] The Cuban insurgency involved issues of race, class, and nationalism, but religion was marginal.[8] The two major "intra–Latin American" armed conflicts—the War of the Triple Alliance (Argentina, Brazil, and Uruguay against Paraguay [1864–70]) and the War of the Pacific (Chile against Peru [1879–83])—involved Catholic countries and were in no sense "religious wars." Of course, religious exhortations and legitimations played their part. The commander in chief of the Chilean army that invaded Peru in 1879, Erasmo Escala, was a paid-up Conservative, seen by his Liberal opponents as a "religious fanatic," inept, irascible, and said to be in thrall to his confessor; at the Battle of San Francisco he "unfurled a banner of Our Lady of Carmen, proclaiming that 'it has given us victory.'" José Francisco Vergara, Escala's personal secretary, soon to be promoted to war minister, demurred: "We owe more to our valour and bayonets than what this good image can do for us."[9]

Latin America also experienced a constant cycle of internal violence, sometimes involving religion: coups, rebellions, and civil wars, many of them minor and inconsequential (in terms of casualties, political polarization, and social upheaval), some—such as the Mexican War of the Reform (1858–61), the Colombian War of the Thousand Days (1899–1902), and the Mexican Cristiada (1926–29)—both costly and serious. Catholicism fueled the first, was indirectly involved in the second, and provided the basic motivation of the third. In addition, Latin America lived with a constant undercurrent of quotidian, decentralized, disorganized violence, the product of popular protest, land disputes, frontier expansion, banditry (both "social" and "unsocial"), smuggling, urban riots, ethnic and xenophobic conflict, and common ("mercenary") crime. Religious factors played a part in some of this endemic but unquantifiable violence, as I mention later.

The character of the Latin American state was crucial to the unfolding of this story. In the earlier decades (roughly 1820–70), the state was, with few exceptions (such as Chile and Brazil), weak, unstable, and unable to maintain anything remotely resembling Max Weber's "monopoly of the exercise of legitimate violence" throughout the region's vast, rugged, underpopulated territory. After ca. 1870 Latin American states, like the Latin American church, grew stronger, recruiting personnel, acquiring new "technologies of power," and achieving greater control over their populations. This trend did not eliminate violence, but it meant that "bottom-up," decentralized violence yielded to "top-down," state-orchestrated violence. Again, religious factors were relevant.

So I will first address cases of religion, usually Catholicism, provoking or sanctioning violence, typically in tandem with political goals and secular actors. Then I will briefly consider "bottom-up" examples of popular religious violence and the usually repressive reactions of the state. The range of violent phenomena is extensive, but there are deliberate omissions. I omit "mercenary" or "criminal" violence that lacked any politico-religious rationale.[10] Violence of this kind, though common, sought material reward, not political office, policy changes, or regime transformation. In the terminology of a recent debate, it was motivated by "greed" rather than "grievances."[11] Thus, "unsocial" bandits—mercenary bandits who lack the popular support enjoyed by "social bandits" like Robin Hood—do not pursue political goals, nor do they espouse religious causes, even if, like the majority of the population, they adhere to the beliefs and practices of popular religion.[12] Indeed, yesterday's bandits—like today's narco pistoleros—may be conspicuously "religious" or "superstitious," because they follow a very dangerous occupation.[13] However, that occupation is geared to material reward and obeys no political or religious rationale.

One final clarification. Both political and mercenary violence were basically "instrumental." Violence served particular goals, whether material or political; it was planned and premeditated; it was motivated by either "greed" or "grievances." However, students of violence—psychologists, particularly—also identify "affective" violence, violence that obeys no ulterior purpose, that is not (rationally, instrumentally) premeditated, and that obeys psychological, even psychopathological urges.[14] Familial and interpersonal violence, including wife-beating, street fights, and barroom brawls, were commonplace in Latin America. Often, they involved a matter of perceived personal "honor" and what in Spanish is delicately referred to as "una cuestión de faldas" (literally, "a question of skirts," i.e., a dispute over a woman).[15] Often, they were also fueled by alcohol.

It is plausible that religion figured in these events, for example, in popular fiestas (notoriously rowdy and drunken) or in those private households, very common throughout Latin America, where irreligious men cohabited with devout women (*beatas*, as they were sometimes contemptuously called).[16] But for lack of both space and (historical) data, I have to overlook these important social phenomena.

Regarding the catchall concept of "religion" (or, more specifically, "Catholicism"), matters are a bit simpler. Violence is typically "epiphenomenal" (which does not mean unimportant): it arises for a bewildering array of reasons (instrumental and affective, political and mercenary). Any analysis of "violence" leads the analyst into labyrinthine explanations. While religion may sometimes be "epiphenomenal" (the classic "opium of the people" thesis says as much), often it is not, and as recent research has shown, reductionist arguments that reduce religion to underlying political or economic imperatives, denying it autonomous agency, are often unconvincing.[17] Religion may sometimes serve ulterior purposes (I will give examples), but it also has an autonomous existence that cannot simply be reduced to an underlying secular rationale.

But "religion" embodies several dimensions (rituals, ethics, cosmologies, sacred spaces, aesthetics, institutions). Some disaggregation is essential. One central fact helps anchor the analysis: Latin America was and is overwhelmingly Catholic. Under colonial rule, Catholicism in its diverse dimensions was the only tolerated religion; rivals to Catholicism (Protestantism, Islam, "animist" beliefs brought in by African slaves, and the rich heritage of pre-Conquest indigenous religion) were systematically repressed. The colonial regime rested on a close alliance of throne and altar, whereby the church preached submission to the state, and the state supported the church.[18] Over three centuries, the church acquired ample spiritual power and vast material resources (land, buildings, capital, and religious artifacts). It was the colony's major banker and the chief provider of both education and charity. Although senior officials in church and state sometimes quarreled over specific issues, the alliance of throne and altar remained the bedrock of colonial rule.[19]

However, in the late eighteenth century, tensions mounted, foreshadowing the serious conflicts of the nineteenth century. The Bourbon Reforms (the Pombaline Reforms in Portugal and Brazil) sought to strengthen state power and metropolitan control of the colonies. Designed to emulate—and resist—rival colonial powers (Britain and France), the reformist project involved administrative reorganization, heavier taxation, and the creation of standing armies in the Americas. The church—the Jesuit Order in particular—was targeted: it was an overmighty subject whose power needed to be curbed and a source of wealth that the cash-strapped state coveted. The Crown expelled the Jesuits, sought to promote a more austere brand of Catholicism, and, under the fiscal pressure of war, confiscated church assets. The historic alliance of throne and altar was severely strained; and the Crown came to rely increasingly on the secular and coercive power of army and officialdom rather than the ideological "hegemony" of church and Catholicism. As David Brading put it, "Where the Habsburgs used priests, the Bourbons employed soldiers."[20]

However, the monopolistic Catholic Church was a diverse and sometimes divided institution. Like the state, it was divided between Spanish-born (*peninsular*) appointees who were loyal to the Crown and creoles (born in the Americas) who felt an attachment to their American homeland.[21] Thus, the Mexican Jesuit Francisco Clavijero, exiled to Italy, penned a paean to his homeland, demonstrating an incipient Mexican "protopatriotism" in opposition to Spanish colonial oppression.[22] Even before independence, then, Catholicism and nationalism could happily coexist.

The institutional church also involved a stretched hierarchy, with rich, powerful, often Spanish prelates at the top and a host of parish priests (*curas*), mostly creoles and mestizos (people of mixed Spanish/Indian ancestry), who served poor rural parishes, often in straitened circumstances, at the bottom. Thus, in the early nineteenth century, clerical coverage was patchy: stronger in the cities than the countryside, stronger in some colonies/countries (such as Mexico and Peru) than others (such as Bolivia, Argentina, and Brazil). The quality of the lower clergy was also patchy. Many priests cohabited and fathered children.[23] While this shocked censorious Protestant observers, it did not necessarily offend parishioners, who often preferred a cura who was "one of them," respectful of local cults and customs and, indeed, of local women: cohabiting curas were perhaps less sexually predatory. But some curas were considered rapacious and arrogant: they charged excessive fees for clerical services (baptisms, marriages, and funerals), obliged their parishioners to feed and serve them, and sometimes disparaged local religious practices (fiestas, pilgrimages, the cult of the saints). As a result, colonial society produced a current of popular anticlericalism reminiscent of medieval movements like Lollardy, whereby the common people, while cleaving firmly to Catholicism, protested against overweening or corrupt priests.[24] Occasionally, such protests involved violence.[25]

While the Catholic Church—a massive, sprawling, internally diverse institution—dominated religious life, it did not enjoy a perfect monopoly of religious belief and practice. Four rivals, each in their different way illicit and subversive, challenged Catholic domination. Two were feeble rivals. Protestantism made few inroads, and only gradually, as Protestant immigrants trickled in through the nineteenth century, did they contribute a modest extra ingredient to Latin America's religious mix.[26] Freethinking—the repudiation of Catholicism or religion in general—was also rare, probably confined to a small, educated, urban minority. Furthermore, freethinking, apart from running the risk of official sanction, lacked both institutional organization and effective means of public communication, whether written or verbal. The Catholic Church, of course, enjoyed both.[27]

Much more important were the two main forms of popular religious heterodoxy: imported African religions and the still-strong vestiges of pre-Conquest Indian religions. In the hot coastal lowlands, where dense

Indian populations were lacking and profitable cash crops such as sugar and cacao required a large, regimented labor force, the Europeans introduced vast numbers of African slaves. Northeastern Brazil, lowland Colombia, and the Caribbean islands of Cuba and Hispaniola became bastions of plantation agriculture worked by African slaves, who brought with them both Islam and African animist beliefs. Though extensive Catholic conversion occurred, it was always partial, in part because some planters favored a policy of "divide and rule" regarding both religion and ethnicity. Islam and animism therefore survived and sometimes blended with Catholicism in hybrid forms. The resulting popular beliefs underpinned slave identity and, at key moments, helped legitimize slave rebellions.

In Haiti, the site of the greatest and most successful slave insurrection in history, African beliefs (often loosely labeled "Voodoo") sustained the 1790s rebellion, serving as "an instrument of solidarity and communication."[28] Furthermore, while independence brought about the swift abolition of slavery in some countries (Mexico, Venezuela, Argentina), Brazil continued to import slaves en masse until ca. 1850 (and slavery survived until 1888), while Cuba, still a Spanish colony, followed a similar trajectory. In 1835 Bahía, in northeastern Brazil, witnessed a massive insurrection by black slaves and free black allies who professed Islam: the rebels were motivated by specific grievances (harsh treatment and arbitrary masters), as well as a collective class rejection of servitude, but Islam gave the movement cohesion and an additionally threatening aspect.[29] Cuba also experienced slave rebellions, notably in 1843; again, religious attachments—African animist beliefs hybridized with Catholicism—provided vital inspiration and organizational capacity.[30] That said, all bar the Haitian revolution were brutally put down.

But the biggest challenge to the religious supremacy of (orthodox) Catholicism came from the survival of pre-Conquest Indian religions. Logically, this phenomenon was most evident in those regions where a large sedentary Indian population survived, clustered in ancient communities, where they provided the basis of the colonial political economy, especially in Mexico, Central America, and the huge Andean region (Colombia, Ecuador, Peru, and Bolivia).[31] Here, the Spaniards hijacked existing indigenous states and societies (Aztec, Maya, Inca, and others). Fearful of Indian religions, which they equated with diabolism, the Spaniards sought to extirpate them, often violently. However, a process of genuine conversion also took place as Indians perceived the attractions of Catholicism, one attraction being that many Catholic icons (like the Virgin Mary and the saints) and Catholic practices (sacrifice, mortification, fiestas) followed pre-Conquest precedents, thus softening the sharp edge of the so-called spiritual conquest.[32] The classic example was the creation of the major Mexican cult of the Virgin of Guadalupe (the "brown Virgin"), whose apparition in 1531 occurred at a spot sacred to the Aztec goddess Tonantzin.[33]

At first viscerally hostile to Indian beliefs, the church came to see the advantage of selectively incorporating some elements into a so-called syncretic (hybrid) religion, the distinctive and exuberant Baroque Catholicism of colonial—and independent—Latin America. This process was most successful in Mexico, where, despite exceptions on the northern and southern frontiers, the Indian population was thoroughly Christianized, even if their Christianity—often loosely termed a "folk religion"—embodied discreetly disguised pre-Conquest features and involved rowdy fiestas that offended elite sensibilities.[34] Such popular religiosity was effectively sustained by local lay organizations: the cofradias (sodalities), which were dedicated to the cult of the saints and which often functioned fairly autonomously of the institutional church. By ca. 1800, the Mexican authorities, both clerical and secular, were more concerned to moderate such Baroque excesses in the interests of an enlightened religion than to extirpate a threatening religious deviance.[35] Popular religious heterodoxy—the resort to magic and shamans, for example—was now seen as foolish superstition, an example of Indian infantilism rather than a subversive threat to the social order. Culprits needed to be reprimanded and reeducated, not brutally punished.

Similar trends can be observed in Andean America (notably in Ecuador, where the church put down deep roots), but in highland Peru and Bolivia the Catholic Church was stretched, its proselytization was very partial, and pre-Conquest beliefs and practices survived more lustily. While Lima was a clerical city where orthodox Catholicism prevailed, sustained by a dense network of churches, parishes, convents, and seminaries, by contrast, in the villages, estates, and mining centers of the high Andes, the old cults, legacies of Inca culture (such as the Pachamama, the Andean Earth Mother), endured vigorously.[36] Indeed, in marked contrast to Mexico (where no one seriously advocated an Aztec restoration), highland Peru and Bolivia retained a lingering attachment to Inca rule mediated through an influential indigenous aristocracy, as the massive Tupac Amaru revolt of 1780 revealed.[37]

Thus, in regions of dense Indian population, a syncretic religion evolved, in some regions, such as central Mexico, closer to orthodox (but popular or "folk") Catholicism, in others, such as Bolivia, more heterodox, even downright deviant. These colonial patterns survived long after independence and were crucial in determining the scale and character of religious conflict in the nineteenth century.

Church/State Conflict in the Nineteenth Century

Religion played an important role in the independence struggles of 1808–25, which, except for Cuba, resulted in the downfall of the old Iberian empires and the creation of new would-be nation-states. However, that role was complicated and, indeed, bilateral. Both royalists and patriots invoked religious symbols; the clergy was seriously split, with a significant minority—especially the lower clergy, those, typically creoles and mestizos, more closely integrated into local communities—supporting independence (or, at least, a variety of "home rule," national autonomy in loose association with the metropolis). In Mexico, where clerical authority was strongest, the two great popular leaders of the independence struggle, Miguel Hidalgo José María Morelos, were both parish priests, though of a distinctly heterodox kind. (Hidalgo had been investigated by the Inquisition, while Morelos had a common-law wife and children.) But the higher clergy, notably the Spanish (*peninsular*) prelates, concentrated in the major cities, typically supported the Crown. As the struggle unfolded, these clerical rivals brandished their respective religious symbols, the "brown" Virgen de Guadalupe being espoused by the Mexican insurgents, while the royalists invoked the Virgen de los Remedios.[38]

In Argentina, too, where independence came rapidly (economic interests and grievances being the drivers), the clergy often lent their support to the cause, proof that it was quite possible to combine Catholicism and moderate liberal patriotism.[39] In Brazil, where independence took an unusual course (less violent, more negotiated, and leading to a constitutional monarchy), priests again showed that Catholicism was compatible with national independence, liberalism, and (limited) representative government.[40] The union of throne and altar did not have to be absolutist or despotic.

The struggle for independence, finally resolved in the 1820s, transformed Latin America: two ancient empires gave way to a congeries of independent states; the extensive fighting and the rupture with Iberia dislocated the economy; and the already dwindling legitimacy of the Crown gave way to unstable states, typically republics (monarchical Brazil being the exception), in which the military emerged as a key player. Those states now had to forge a new legitimacy, whether monarchical, republican, constitutional, authoritarian, or religious.

The situation of the church was paradoxical. Its economic resources were reduced by social upheaval, material destruction, and wartime taxation (even outright confiscation). But it now confronted a state that was even poorer, in some cases chronically bankrupt, and whose legitimacy was questionable. Politically, the old alliance between throne and altar, seriously strained by the Bourbon Reforms, now had to be renegotiated in the new context of fragile nation-states. The latter still claimed the old right of royal patronage (the right of the state to nominate bishops), and in most cases, states were disposed to maintain Catholicism as the sole official religion.[41] Rome, leery of both liberalism and popular rebellion, delayed recognizing the newly independent states, and Rome's disengagement, coupled with domestic instability, meant that bishoprics and parishes often remained vacant for years, even decades.[42] The institutional weakness of the church, especially across the vast expanses of the South American countryside, was thus compounded.

However, the church now enjoyed greater autonomy: the pope was a distant, distracted master, and the new states lacked the muscle of their royal predecessors. Crucially, there is scant evidence that Catholicism—in all its kaleidoscopic variety—seriously declined with independence. The institutional reach of the church shrank, but popular beliefs and practices still flourished, often sustained by those local lay organizations already mentioned. Indeed, beliefs and practices may have been invigorated by the absence of censorious clerical control; by the reassertion, with independence, of peasant autonomy; and, perhaps, by the stimulus that war and upheaval sometimes give to religious observation.[43] Only among a small minority of literate, urban Latin Americans did freethinking ideas begin to take root, for example, in the ranks of the Masonic lodges or among the readers of the newspapers that sprang up after independence.[44]

Given this novel and uncertain balance between church and state, outright conflict was rare. Though organized warfare subsided after independence, Latin America remained both politically unstable and violent, affected, as already mentioned, by international and civil wars, as well as "quotidian" violence, both criminal and interpersonal. But religion was not usually a salient issue. Northeastern Brazil experienced the dramatic Moslem slave rebellion of 1835, but the majority of the many rebellions that affected Brazil in the 1820s through 1840s concerned secular issues: regionalism, federalism, liberalism, and nationalism (Brazilians vs. Portuguese). And liberalism, here and elsewhere, did not necessarily carry an anticlerical, still less an anti-Catholic, charge. Priests served in the higher echelons of the new Brazilian empire; in Mexico, too, priests were to be found on both sides of the emergent liberal/conservative, federalist/centralist divide, just as they had been found on both sides during the independence struggles. Indeed, it has been convincingly argued that in Mexico, as in France, liberalism was compatible with Catholicism and, in fact, derived some of its appeal from religious conviction.[45]

But this wary coexistence did not last. It prevailed during the first generation after independence, when political conflict hinged upon questions concerning constitutions, the forms of government (federalist vs. centralist), and the new borders, both internal and external, that the infant states of Latin America would adopt. The position of the church was not usually central to these questions. In the mid-nineteenth century, however, things changed, and conflict, including violent conflict, spiked. The change came about, first, because the papacy, in the hands of Pius IX (1846–78), adopted a more aggressive and "reactionary" policy, seeking to impose "ultramontane" control on the Catholic Church in Latin America as elsewhere.[46] Second, and more important, a new political generation came to power in Latin America alarmed by the instability that had plagued the region and retarded "progress" since the 1820s. Its members sought root-and-branch reform that would go beyond constitutional design and eliminate the heavy institutional baggage that, they believed, burdened Latin American societies. An influential model, sometimes openly acknowledged, was the liberal, progressive United States. Logically, these reformers now gathered under the formal label of "Liberal" parties.

These second-generation reformers targeted what they saw as the dead weight of the colonial legacy, especially the Catholic Church. They enacted economic reforms that were designed to break up the church's massive landholdings by converting them into private property and thus supposedly invigorating the market and fostering the growth of prosperous yeoman farmers. But they also sought to weaken the institutional church, eliminating the church's separate jurisdiction (its so-called *fueros*, the privileges that exempted priests from secular justice) and separating church and state, thus relinquishing state control of tithes and ecclesiastical patronage while enabling citizens to go through rites of passage (births, marriages, and deaths) without recourse to the church. Finally, the radical liberals banned the regular orders (monks, friars, and nuns) and, following Bourbon precedent, expelled the Jesuits. Mexico offers the clearest case of this new anticlerical liberalism, but similar measures were adopted throughout Latin America between the 1840s and 1870s.[47]

This onslaught on the church required and in turn provoked widespread violence. In Mexico, the Liberal/Conservative conflict was exacerbated by the disaster of the Mexican-American War, which in turn further polarized politics. The Liberals advocated root-and-branch reform (including the anticlerical measures just mentioned), which would fortify the republic and galvanize the economy; in short, they argued that Mexico had to emulate the United States in order to resist the United States. Their Conservatives enemies were even more hostile to the United States, but they believed that the solution lay in a return to old colonial values: a centralist and even authoritarian regime buttressed by a strong and privileged church.[48]

The resulting War of the Reform (1858–61) greatly exceeded, in scale, ferocity, and casualties, the many coups and rebellions of previous decades. Although many—probably most—Liberals were Catholics, the church as an institution threw its weight behind the Conservatives (as did Rome). Priests pronounced anathemas from the pulpit and thus "helped to inflame devout opinion and undoubtedly drove many men into rebellion against the radical government."[49] The capital and the more clerical cities of central Mexico favored the Conservatives, while the Liberals drew support from the historically federalist and less clerical periphery (Oaxaca, Michoacán, Zacatecas). The far north and the coastal lowlands (e.g., Veracruz, hugging the long Gulf Coast) also tended toward liberalism, in part because in these regions the church was historically weak, in part because "federalist" antipathy to Mexico City ran deep.[50] This was no mere elite quarrel: the common people—the urban plebeians and the mass of the peasantry—were deeply involved in the growing political polarization and the ensuing violence.

Elsewhere in Latin America, the same conflict generated violence, but on a lesser scale. Explaining national variations is not easy. One could posit a kind of game-theory explanation. In Mexico, the balance of rival forces—Liberal/anticlerical versus Conservative/clerical—was pretty even. Mexican Catholicism was strong; hence, attacks on the church provoked an angry response from both elites and plebeians. But as the War of the Reform and the French Intervention showed, Mexican Liberalism was also an increasingly formidable force endowed with solid regional and popular bases. Neither side overawed the other, but neither could deliver a knock-out blow. Hence, attritional conflict spanned the best part of two decades (1851–67). Furthermore, like other protracted wars, this conflict tended to entrench divisions as each side acquired its heroes, martyrs, and collective memories.

The closest South American equivalent was Colombia, where, again, the institutional church was strong (especially in the highlands and the far south) and where, similarly, the two parties, emerging in their Conservative/

Liberal form in the 1840s, contested for decades, the pendulum swinging to and fro. One index of this pendular process was the status of the Jesuits, who, having been expelled by the Crown in 1773, were recalled by the Conservatives in 1842, expelled in 1850, and welcomed back again in 1858. Over time, Colombian politics acquired a deeply rooted Liberal/Conservative, "Red/Blue" cleavage, and recurrent wars engendered enduring "hereditary hatreds" between the two parties.[51] Religion was not the sole cause or marker of this political partisanship, but starting with the War of the Supremes (1839–41), "the one consistent difference between the parties had to do . . . with the status of the Church," and "priests often acted as political organizers," typically in the Conservative interest.[52] Religious partisanship triggered the "war of the schools" in 1876 and still partially defined the rival Liberal and Conservative forces in the bloody "War of 1,000 Days" of 1899–1902.[53]

Elsewhere, this approximate parity was absent. In Argentina and Brazil, the church was relatively weak, more easily dominated by the state, whether the authoritarian rule of caudillo Juan Manuel Rosas in Argentina (1827–54) or the more enlightened constitutional rule of Emperor Pedro II of Brazil (1831–89). Rosas ran Argentina as a kind of private fief in which the church served as a docile partner.[54] Pedro II, whose personal views were educated and enlightened, happily employed clerics in his administration but did not shrink from confronting the church when he chose.[55] In Chile, the church was stronger, especially in the dominant Central Valley around Santiago, but the Chilean state, constructed by the wily conservative Diego Portales in the 1830s, was unusually strong, centralized, and powerful, endowed with an effective administration and—by Latin American standards—a formidable army. The Chilean Liberals, who entered government in the 1850s, enacted a mild version of Mexico's reform laws, but they had no intention of destabilizing the state that they inherited, and for its part, the church had no desire to risk an open conflict.

An interesting example is Ecuador. According to an old adage (still, perhaps, tenuously relevant today), Venezuela was historically ruled by soldiers, Colombia by lawyers, and Ecuador by priests. (We could add: *highland* Ecuador in particular, since, here as elsewhere in Latin America, the coast—notably the commercial port of Guayaquil—tended to favor Liberalism in opposition to the clerical Conservatism of the more populous Indian highlands.)[56] Given the strength of the church, Liberal anticlericalism made little headway through much of the nineteenth century. Indeed, during the midcentury decades when liberalism was advancing elsewhere, the preeminent Ecuadorian president was Gabriel García Moreno (1861–65, 1869–75), a devoted Catholic who supported the church, invited the Jesuits back from exile, favored Catholic education, and dedicated his country to the new (ultramontane) cult of the Sacred Heart of Jesus.[57] García Moreno showed that red-blooded clerical conservatism could win mass support and provide effective government. In Guatemala, too, a similarly poor, largely Indian country, clerical power underpinned the Conservative regime of Rafael Carrera (1844–48, 1851–65).[58]

International factors also counted. Mexico's turbulent external relations heightened political polarization: the American threat, soon to be followed by the French intervention, made Mexicans acutely aware of national weakness and encouraged a search for radical solutions. Far from promoting national unity and consensus, this sense of crisis fostered sharp polarization. (We could compare France in the 1930s and 1940s.) No other Latin American country faced such severe external threats. (Unless we include Cuba, still a Spanish colony, where nationalist insurgents fought two bitter civil wars in order to achieve independence.)

Thus, while the balance of forces and the outcomes varied, it is clear that church/state conflict became more systematic and acute during the mid-nineteenth century. Violence was common, though not inevitable. Liberal/Conservative conflict was not solely about religion: other political cleavages (federalism vs. centralism, broader vs. narrower political representation, free trade vs. protection) were also crucial. But religion—more strictly, the status of the Catholic Church—was now a salient political issue that served both to provoke and to sustain hostile confrontations.

However, the long-term outcome was not an ascending spiral of unstoppable violence. Mexico, where the midcentury crisis was particularly acute, was again an outlier, and again international factors played a major role. Having lost the War of the Reform to the Liberals, a cabal of defeated and disgruntled Conservatives took the drastic step of opting for monarchy, inveigling the naive emperor Napoleon III into deploying a French army to bring this about. The result was a yet more costly and bitter war—a combined civil war and foreign invasion—which, again, the Liberals, led by the indomitable Benito Juárez, decisively won.[59] The Conservative Party was defeated and disgraced; the Liberals, now trailing clouds of patriotic glory, achieved a near monopoly of political power.

However, the chief beneficiary of this Liberal triumph was a young general, Porfirio Díaz, who, taking advantage of Mexico's war-weary condition, constructed a durable authoritarian regime that lasted thirty-five years (1876–1911). Though originally a radical Liberal, Díaz sought to allay church/state conflict in the interests of peace and stability. He allowed the crestfallen Conservatives to reenter politics (selectively, on his terms, and stripped of partisan labels). His regime focused on maintaining order and fostering economic growth. The sharp political divisions of the past were deliberately blurred; the official positivistic ideology of the regime—derived from Comte, advocated by Díaz's Científico advisors, and summed up in the slogan "order and progress"—involved a stress on material progress and the abandonment of the misguided "metaphysical" concerns of the past (liberal rights, representative electoral government, and anticlerical priest-bashing). While some die-hard Liberals clung to their old principles, many went along with Díaz's positivistic project.[60]

Díaz relaxed but did not formally abolish the anticlerical provisions of the Reform and tolerated a marked resurgence of the church.[61] For alongside Díaz's successful state-building project, the church, too, was recovering from the years of damaging conflict and rebuilding its institutions. This partly responded to papal initiative: the abandonment of the reactionary ultramontanism of Pius IX and the commitment to Catholic social and political engagement evident in Leo XIII's encyclical Rerum Novarum (1891). But the church's resurgence also depended on Mexican circumstances: the stability and outward prosperity of the Díaz regime; the growth of towns and cities; and the new technology that the church, like the state, could use to enhance its power and appeal. Railways, telegraphs, and mass circulation newspapers helped knit the country together, and the church—which was no obscurantist ostrich, hiding its head in dank medieval sand—was willing and able to use these innovations to spread its message. By 1910, when the Mexican Revolution began, the Catholic press was an important political voice, and within months an effective Catholic political party was formed. Some Catholic activists (a minority, I believe) espoused the new brand of "social Catholicism," which advocated active social and political engagement, not least to address Mexico's so-called social question (rapid urbanization, squalor, and poverty).[62]

But more important was the organizational and spiritual advance of the church as a whole (a church that still harbored sizeable conservative, even reactionary, elements): the creation of new parishes, the training of more and better priests, and the formation of lay associations of workers and peasants, of men, women, and children. In some communities, such as San José de Gracia, in Michoacán, the church acquired unprecedented local power and influence. Here in the 1890s the new young cura, Othón Méndez, became the key figure in the community, not only overseeing services, cults, and charities but also promoting education, construction, artisanry, and theater (all of suitably Catholic character), thus fulfilling his mission of "modelling a nascent small-town society."[63] San José was not typical of small-town Mexico (no one community was), but it represented, perhaps in accentuated form, a common pattern, especially in central and west-central regions of the country where resurgent clerical influence reigned. Thus, on the eve of the 1910 Revolution (of which more in conclusion), the Mexican church was on the march, benefiting from the Pax Porfiriana (the "peace of Porfirio") and the church/state detente that accompanied it.

Again, we see similar trends throughout Latin America. That is, the later nineteenth century witnessed rapid economic growth involving increased foreign trade and investment; the formation of more stable, effective governments endowed with greater territorial control and fiscal strength; the dilution of the old political enmities of the past (Conservatives vs. Liberals, church vs. state); and, by way of ideological glue, the adoption, formally or informally, of positivist doctrines of "order and progress," the slogan that, following the fall of the Brazilian monarchy and the creation of the republic in 1889, now adorned the new national flag. The doctrinaire positivists disdained religion, but they sought to avoid distracting "metaphysical" disputes and valued "order and progress," to which end they repressed popular dissidence and could, at least tacitly, make common cause with the church. Even if Catholicism was a farrago of superstitions, the Catholic Church underpinned social stability. Thus, in Argentina under Julio Roca (president 1880–86, 1898–1904), in Chile following the so-called Fusion of Liberals and Conservatives (1858–73), and in Colombia under the Regeneración regime of Rafael Núñez (president 1880–82, 1884–86), the later nineteenth century saw a measure of Liberal/Conservative détente at a time when economic development took priority and church/state conflict waned.[64] A striking, if belated example was Peruvian president/dictator Augusto Leguía (1919–30), who, breaking the traditional Liberal/Conservative mold, combined authoritarian rule with aggressive economic development and a cozy alliance with the church ("no public appearance of Leguía was complete without a cluster of bishops on the platform or in the cavalcade").[65] Though the attempt to dedicate Peru to the Sacred Heart of Jesus was foiled by political protest (in which the nascent Alianza Popular Revolucionaria Americana [APRA] played a prominent role), Leguía did at least receive the papal honor of Knight of the Supreme Military Order of Christ.[66]

Popular Religious Violence

The growth in the later nineteenth century of more powerful states in cahoots with (or at least pragmatically tolerant of) the church did not mean that "religious violence"—violence prompted and sustained by religious convictions—disappeared from the landscape. Rather, it assumed new forms. Thus far, I have focused on formal church/state conflict and the ways in which that conflict, often intertwining with secular issues, stimulated violence. This violence tended to be organized, political, and often "top-down": it was violence deployed by rival elites in pursuit of power on the basis of political goals and "grievances." Though "top-down," it often involved extensive popular involvement, especially as church/state, Conservative/Liberal confrontations peaked in the middle decades of the century, notably in countries such as Mexico and Colombia.

But as previously mentioned, Latin America also experienced sub-currents of endemic popular violence, which, though hard to measure, cannot be ignored. Some involved both religious motives and a measure of popular autonomy (they were not controlled from above, nor were they closely linked to "macropolitical" conflicts). So a brief "bottom-up" look at popular religiosity and violence is needed. Latin American "folk religion," though demonstrably Catholic, was variable, heterodox, and often resistant to intrusive clerical control. Especially in rural and Indian regions such as southern Mexico and the high Andes, peasants ran their own religious lives with scant clerical oversight. Indeed, priests who tried to reform what they saw as wayward practices, such as "superstitious" rituals and drunken fiestas, sometimes provoked angry anticlerical reactions. In and around Mexico City, late colonial prelates imbued with enlightened Bourbon ideas sought to crack down on the buying and selling, drinking and eating that accompanied—and, in their view, sullied—major religious festivals such as Holy Week and Corpus Christi. Such practices, these priests complained, turned "solemn religious acts into causes of diversion, excess and impudence"; in one case, members of Indian guilds (cofradias) marched through the streets of Mexico City "almost naked."[67] However, attempts to wrest control of the cofradias from their traditional (Indian) leaders so that right-thinking Spaniards might replace them were strenuously resisted, even in the heartland of Spain's richest colony.[68] Out in the sticks, matters were—from the clerical point of view—even worse: in about one-fifth of the eighteenth-century village uprisings in central Mexico studied by William Taylor, priests were the targets (local officials fared only slightly worse); however, though priests were often humiliated, menaced, and occasionally injured by "flying rocks," they were almost never killed.[69] The cloth provided some residual protection.

Resistance to clerical authority was not confined to ancient Indian communities. The footloose gauchos (cowboys) of the sprawling Argentine pampas likewise adhered to a heterodox religion that was regarded by outsiders as crudely superstitious and was largely untouched by priestly oversight. Churches were few and far between, and clerical fees (e.g., for burials) could be prohibitively expensive; hence, even the basic rites of passage were rarely observed: "A peon seldom graced the inside of a church even in death."[70] Not that crossing the threshold was essential: as an American observed in 1832, the gauchos of the pampas, "untaught either in letters, manners, religion or morals," were so attached to their mounts that they even "hear mass . . . on horseback."[71]

One feature of this, we could say, autonomous or "unsupervised" popular religiosity was violence directed against alleged Protestants, Jews, and heretics. This syndrome also formed part of the colonial legacy; it was the product of centuries of preaching against heresy, of persecuting Protestants (few though they were), and of encouraging anti-Semitic attitudes (after all, the Jews had been coresponsible for killing the Son of God).[72] When the Napoleonic invasion of Spain triggered a political crisis in the Americas, the confused popular response included denunciations of culpable Jews, Protestants, and atheistic French revolutionaries.[73]

After independence, these entrenched attitudes survived. As mercantilist barriers fell and the new nations of Latin America allowed foreign trade and foreign merchants to penetrate their hitherto protected markets, a xenophobic backlash ensued. In part, this reflected economic self-interest: local merchants resented foreign competition, and urban artisans resisted the influx of cheap European, usually British, goods.[74] But there was a distinct religious dimension too. Taught that Protestants were diabolical heretics, people believed that the British concealed tails in their trousers (the telltale sign was the way they rode on horseback).[75] Foreigners, whether travelers or immigrants, who showed insufficient respect for Catholic rituals (e.g., not doffing their hats when the Host was processed through the streets) risked being beaten up, even killed.[76] Rites of passage were also a source of conflict: acrimonious disputes arose concerning the status of cemeteries (who could be buried where according to which rites), while marriage between Protestants and Catholics was frowned on. A go-ahead English sheep farmer who set up in Argentina in the mid-nineteenth century married "a lady of Spanish blood, of a good family, city born and bred," a marriage that took place "in spite of opposition from her people and of the tremendous difficulties in the way of a union between one of the Faith and a heretic."[77]

The attitude of the authorities to such displays of popular religious prejudice was ambivalent. Some, including liberal policy-makers like Bernardino Rivadavia who were advocates of free trade and immigration, condemned religious prejudice and sought to facilitate the foreign/Protestant presence.[78] But more conservative leaders condoned, encouraged, and, perhaps, shared these sentiments. The Argentine gauchos' contempt for Europeans and dislike of Protestants fitted snugly within the discursive framework of the populist dictator Rosas, and lesser local warlords such as Angel Peñaloza of La Rioja incited popular hatred of foreigners, heretics, and Protestants.[79]

Like popular religious prejudices elsewhere, these were not easily or quickly quelled. (Hostility to Jews and Protestants spiked in the big bustling metropolis of Mexico City as late as the 1940s.) A key example was the famous Tandil massacre of 1872, when, on the pampas of Argentina, a bunch of fifty armed men—loosely, gauchos nurtured in a violent and footloose world—killed thirty-six European migrants (Spaniards, Italians, French, and British).[80] The killers alleged that they had been incited by a popular priest, folk healer, and miracle worker named Gerónimo de Solané, who urged them to "exterminate the enemies of God and religion"; their war cries were "long live religion," "death to the Masons," and "kill [the] gringos and Basques."[81] The Tandil case was extreme and has been well-researched, but as John Lynch reminds us, it "was not a solitary atrocity."[82]

Through the mid-nineteenth century in Argentina and elsewhere, the authorities were often unable or unwilling to curb such prejudice, which some of the "authorities" may well have shared. The state was often weak and had other preoccupations. But as state power waxed in the later nineteenth century, benefiting from railways, telegraphs, and improved armies and police forces, so it began to crack down on such manifestations of popular xenophobia and religiosity. Not only did they besmirch the state's "Weberian" image, they also deterred foreign trade and immigration while raising the threat of foreign punitive measures. They were readily seen as sad manifestations of superstition, backwardness, and indiscipline, which the "positivistic" governments of Latin America, bent on "progress" and eager to promote "civilization" over "barbarism," were keen to extirpate.[83]

So even as they "conquered the desert," that is, eliminated the Indians of the Argentine pampas and repressed the insurgent Yaqui and Maya Indians in Mexico, the Latin American authorities combatted what they saw as dangerous religious dissent, all in the name of "order and progress."[84] In Mexico in 1892, the Díaz government ruthlessly crushed the northern village of Tomóchic, where local grievances over land and politics combined with a revivalist cult.[85] On a grander scale, the new Brazilian Republic—officially positivist and led, initially, by army officers—repressed two major millenarian movements at different ends of the country: the Canudos community, led by "Antonio the Counsellor" in the desperately poor, drought-afflicted northeast (1896–97), and the Contestado insurrection in the southern state of Santa Catarina (1912–16).[86]

These were clear cases of top-down, official, exemplary repression designed to eliminate both millenarian and monarchical allegiances. In a third case, that of Juazeiro, also in the northeast, the heterodox Catholic priest Father Cícero presided over the growth of a flourishing town that, despite quarrels with both church and state, survived for decades under his politico-religious rule.[87] In all these cases, the Catholic Church tended to side with the Brazilian state: the church also felt threatened by religious dissidence and was generally happy to see the state stamp it out—or, in the case of Juazeiro, reach a pragmatic modus vivendi. Compromise was sometimes possible because these movements, combining messianism, millenarianism, and, occasionally, a residual monarchism, did not preach class conflict or social revolution; rather, springing up as they did in regions of endemic poverty, violence, banditry, and political factionalism, they offered desperate local people a measure of order and stability.[88] At Juazeiro, church and state grudgingly tolerated Padre Cícero's regime; at Canudos and the Contestado they drowned dissent in blood.

The Cristero War

By way of conclusion, I have saved the best—or worst—till last, that is, the biggest case of religious violence during the entire period: Mexico's Cristero War of 1926–29, in which over one hundred thousand people died.[89] The war flared up in west-central Mexico in the wake of the

Mexican Revolution, when revolutionary anticlericals, led by President Plutarco Elías Calles (1924–28), ramped up the old church/state conflict in the context of extensive political mobilization and social reform. Where the nineteenth-century Liberal anticlericals had separated church and state and confiscated church property, Calles and his fellow revolutionaries went further, seeking to subject the church to state regulation, to eliminate Catholic primary education, and to inculcate a secular, scientific worldview among Mexico's benighted population (women and peasants in particular). A minority of revolutionary *enragés* sought the elimination of religion altogether. In response, lay Catholics in those western states where the institutional church was strongest mounted protests, boycotts, and, in 1926, a full-scale armed rebellion. The rebellion was led by radical lay Catholics, sworn enemies of the new revolutionary state; although some priests were involved, it was not a clerical-led movement; and Rome was distinctly leery, bending its efforts to restrain the rebels and, ultimately, to reach an agreement with the state (which finally occurred in 1929).

Some historians, including old-style Marxists, attribute the Cristero War to the machinations of local landlords who, hostile to the revolutionary state and its incipient agrarian reform, manipulated the religious question to whip up gullible, God-fearing peasants, victims of "false consciousness." While some vested interests certainly sought to take advantage of the revolt, its motivation—as Jean Meyer has convincingly shown—was clearly religious.[90] However, recent research has added an important rider: here, as in earlier times, religion intertwined with secular concerns; thus, revolutionary anticlericalism, when it attacked Catholic priests and practices (fiestas, shrines, pilgrimages), was seen to subvert local ways of life, imposing an alien authority on proud, historically autonomous communities.[91] So the Cristero War was certainly a religious war, but "religion" embraced a range of political, cultural, and collective sensibilities. Or, we could say, while this was the clearest case of extreme macropolitical religious violence, it derived its force partly from local, micropolitical loyalties.

The war "ended" with a grudging compromise in 1929, though church/state conflict simmered for another decade. In terms of its scope and impact, it was the most serious Latin American religious war of the period, and it was, without doubt, a *religious* war. Even if religion served as a rallying cry for local dissidents who sought, more broadly, to resist the intrusive revolutionary state, it was significant that religion—rather than any suitable secular ideology such as liberalism or federalism—played this mobilizing and agglutinative role. And as Meyer and others stress, sincere religious sentiments, offended by aggressive official anticlericalism, were crucial in motivating Cristero resistance. This hardly seems an implausible argument, given that autonomous religiosity has fueled plenty of popular uprisings in the past in Mexico, Latin America, and beyond. Furthermore, the Cristeros' anticlerical enemies were also fired by their own autonomous ideological inspiration: although anticlericalism may have obeyed ulterior motives (the expansion of centralized state power or, less plausibly, the desire to distract Mexicans from mundane socioeconomic problems), Calles and his allies were often genuine in their belief that Catholicism was an obscurantist throwback that served as a brake on the country's progress and as blinkers inhibiting the vision of its benighted followers (women in particular).[92]

On both sides, therefore, the war involved intransigent leaders and extreme brutality; the military camaraderie, even chivalry, that sometimes characterized the armed conflicts of the Mexican Revolution of the 1910s, fought between rival political factions, was largely absent. After all, this was a battle between rival worldviews in which middle-of-the-road compromise was impossible. Immortal souls were at stake. In the end, the Cristeros, prodded by Rome and the moderate bishops, realized that victory (the overthrow of the revolutionary state) was unattainable. In fact, the church's decision to abandon insurrectionary struggle in favor of peaceful mobilization by means of charitable good works, new lay organizations, and discreet lobbying proved to be sensible and, in the long term, successful.

The Cristero War was unique to Mexico because the Revolution of 1910 was also unique. No other Latin American country experienced such a massive sociopolitical upheaval. (And none would until the 1950s; furthermore, as I suggest in chapter 7, the Bolivian and Cuban revolutions of that decade failed to generate the religious conflict that had afflicted

Mexico.) The revolution raised fundamental questions concerning property rights, education, state power, and political organization in a context of unprecedented mass mobilization. It made strong and exclusive claims on the allegiance of patriotic Mexicans. Given the historic strength of the Catholic Church and its own, similarly exclusive claims, a bitter conflict was bound to ensue. The 1910 Revolution was not born virulently anticlerical, but as it advanced, radicalized, and consolidated state power, a confrontation with the church became inevitable. This hypothesis is confirmed not only *negatively* (by the absence of any comparable conflict in the rest of nonrevolutionary Latin America) but also *positively* by the outbreak of a similar and even more violent religious war in Spain in the 1930s, again in a context of unprecedented social upheaval and mass mobilization. In Spain anticlerical violence and violent Catholic responses were even more severe and sustained than in Mexico.[93] And, of course, the outcome was very different: the church won, the revolution lost. Nevertheless, Mexico in the 1920s and Spain in the 1930s could be seen as symptoms of a new, more extreme form of church/state conflict that, reflecting the mounting tensions of mass society and the aggressive claims of these two historic antagonists, went far beyond nineteenth-century precedents.

CHAPTER 4

The Little Divergence

Peru and Mexico Compared, 1780–1940

WHY ATTEMPT AN EXPLICIT COMPARISON OF MEXICO AND PERU? Of course, both countries regularly get bundled into overviews of Latin American history, but such overviews are rarely explicitly comparative (though they may involve implicit, unspoken comparisons). Political scientists, especially those who inhabit teeming departments of "comparative politics," are compelled to attempt broad and ambitious cross-national comparisons. Spatially broad, such comparisons are often temporally limited: they tend to offer ("synchronic") global snapshots, not ("diachronic") traversals of time. Typically, they cover a large number of cases ("$N = 183$"), and they highlight particular variables ("trust," parochialism, attitudes to democracy, etc.) in the hope, as I understand the comparative-political approach, of revealing generalities, be they "laws," tendencies, or "elective affinities" that hold across a wide range of disparate cases.

By contrast, historians, also by definition, take a diachronic approach while stressing peculiarities and contingencies.[1] Furthermore, while political scientists seek generalities, historians are more likely to use comparisons in order to deepen their understanding of particular cases. Thus, regarding the Mexico-Peru comparison presented here, we might ask (as Florencia Mallon did) why Mexican resistance to foreign (French) invasion in 1862–67 proved more tenacious and successful than Peruvian resistance to foreign (Chilean) invasion in 1879–83.[2] Or why Mexico experienced a major social revolution in the early twentieth century when Peru didn't, even though many of the factors regularly cited as causes of the Mexican Revolution were, as I shall suggest, also present in Peru. Or, finally, why President Calles launched an assault on the Mexican Catholic Church in the 1920s when his Peruvian counterpart, Augusto Leguía, sought to dedicate his country to the Sacred Heart of Jesus.[3] Exploring these contrasts—and as I mentioned, there are also similarities that could be usefully addressed— will not lead us to general laws regarding Latin American sociopolitical development, but they might shed light on the cases that, as historians of Peru, or Mexico, or, more superficially, Latin America as a whole, we are interested in.

Limiting the number of cases under consideration to just a couple pretty much rules out any contribution to grand theory.[4] But it may have countervailing merits. First, it is possible to do justice to the complexity of particular cases, taking into account multiple, interlocking factors rather than abstracting a handful of factors—or, worse, "proxies"—often chosen because they lend themselves to quantitative analysis, however contrived. Second, a limited comparison can draw upon the historian's detailed grasp of those cases—a grasp that is frequently not amenable to straightforward quantification but involves nonquantifiable judgements concerning what is more or less significant.[5] And third, as already mentioned, such a comparison offers a dynamic "diachronic" narrative as opposed to a static snapshot.

That said, even "small *n*" historical comparisons are not at all easy, especially when they involve large and complicated countries whose regional disparities often make national generalizations tricky. Perhaps that is why, regarding Mexico and Peru, explicit comparisons—as opposed to occasional nods of mutual recognition—are fairly rare.[6] Given the risks involved, I shall adopt a fairly straightforward narrative (or, again, "diachronic") approach, tracing the course of Peruvian and Mexican history from the late eighteenth century through the nineteenth into the mid-twentieth century. However, to avoid a tedious and inconsequential "one-damn-thing-after-another" story, I shall use the notions of *convergence* and *divergence* to try to tease out some conclusions from the story. Two initial clarifications may help.

First, what does "divergence/convergence" mean? Perhaps the historical example that attracted most attention was the presumed *con*vergence of the United States and the Soviet Union during the period of the Cold War, a proposition that, once in vogue but now rarely addressed, drew upon modernization theory, Weberian notions of bureaucratization, and grand sociological models of industrial society (à la Talcott Parsons).[7] More specifically, more recently, and, I would say, more convincingly, Kenneth Pomerantz has analyzed the *di*vergence between China and "the West" over several centuries.[8] And in similar style, economic historians of Latin America have tried, also with some success, to explain "why Latin American fell behind," that is, why Latin America diverged from the United States in terms of growth and output in the postindependence period.[9] These studies are chiefly concerned with economic development, and there are good reasons for thinking that *economic* di/convergence—being both potentially quantifiable and amenable to sophisticated economic analysis—is a particularly fruitful line of inquiry. (It may also be seen, rightly or wrongly, as practically relevant and therefore more important.)[10] In the analysis that follows, therefore, I give priority to economic—or, more accurately, "politico-economic"—trends and periodization.

When it comes to more narrowly political and, perhaps, sociocultural trends, the picture is cloudier.[11] Political trajectories can be seriously affected by "accidental" factors such as wars, rebellions, invasions, individual deaths, and idiosyncratic decisions—the kinds of events that are often "underdetermined" and that prompt legitimate counterfactual speculation.[12] Santa Anna, by obstinately refusing to relinquish Texas, ensured that Mexico would lose California, Arizona, and New Mexico. Calles's onslaught on the Catholic Church, it has been suggested, was motivated by his illegitimate origins.[13] In other words, political trajectories—more so, I would suggest, than economic ones—are subject to causal factors that, though important (they can have decisive effects), are random and nongeneralizable. What if Santa Anna had died—as he nearly did—when his leg was riddled with shrapnel in 1838? What if Calles's well-to-do father had dutifully married Calles's socially inferior mother, thus removing the taint of illegitimacy? Finally, when it comes to "culture," something of a capacious catchall category, the causal chains are often obscure and mystifying; for that reason, I will—with one notable exception (the Catholic Church)—tend to steer clear of "culture" and stick to a broadly politico-economic approach.

Even though my concern is the "long" nineteenth century, it is logical to start with the colonial period, during which many of the basic institutions and practices were established. And, as we all know, the resulting "colonial legacy" cast a long shadow across postindependence Peru and Mexico. At first glance, the similarities between Mexico and Peru are striking; thus, they strongly suggest a common starting point for the story that follows. Both were conquered by Spain in the sixteenth century, their respective indigenous empires being violently decapitated, their dwindling populations squeezed into new exploitative institutions (encomiendas, haciendas, *congregaciones, reducciones*). Both countries also underwent a "spiritual conquest" as Catholicism was imposed and pre-Conquest beliefs and practices were repressed. Just as they had been the seats of the two great indigenous empires in the Americas, Mexico and Peru became—thanks to the random coincidence of dense populations and rich mineral deposits—the twin poles of Spanish mercantilist imperialism, the two brightest jewels in the colonial crown.[14] First to be conquered and subjugated in the early sixteenth century, they were also the last to be "liberated" three hundred years later at the time of independence.[15]

So far, so similar. These undoubted common features suggest that the Mexico/Peru comparison makes good sense, since we are not comparing countries/cultures that are so radically different (e.g., Denmark and China) that the whole exercise becomes rather futile.[16] But the colonial legacies were also significantly different, and it is crucial to consider whether those initial differences determined later divergent trajectories. In other words, to the extent that Mexico and Peru reveal contrasting paths of development after independence, was that divergence the product of prior *colonial* differences (as James Mahoney suggests), or did it arise because of events and processes that took place *after* independence (as Hillel Soifer proposes)?[17]

Perhaps the salient colonial contrast relates to integration (political, economic, cultural). Both Mexico and Peru were huge, sprawling, poorly integrated countries/kingdoms/colonies traversed by mountain ranges and carved up into regional and local units. (Again, those units could be defined in political, economic, perhaps even cultural terms.) But arguably, Mexico was the more integrated of the two in political, economic, and perhaps also cultural terms.[18] Mexico City, standing on the ruins of Aztec Tenochtitlan, commanded the densely populated central highlands; its authority over the high plains of the North and distant tropical Southeast was tenuous, but it had stronger claims to be an effective capital city than Lima, a Spanish creation that was perched on the coast and was far removed, both geographically and culturally, from the indigenous communities of the Sierra (North and South).[19] As Alberto Flores Galindo polemically put it regarding both the colonial and national periods, "The Peruvian coast was closer to Asia than to its Andean hinterland"—a proximity evident in terms of trade, migration, and, we could say, elite mentality.[20]

Economically, too, colonial Mexico possessed more integrated markets, evident in the flow of goods, livestock, and credit; with this, it seems, went greater regional specialization and interdependence, as well as higher per capita income.[21] In Peru the money economy was more restricted, regions and localities tended to be more autarkic (which is not to say that they were "closed economies"), and per capita income was lower. Furthermore, the gap appears to have widened in the final decades of the colonial period.[22] One indicator of both economic and political integration was that the per capita tax yield of Mexico (New Spain) was substantially greater than that of Peru.[23]

In both countries the legacy of conquest was an ethnically stratified society, but in Mexico ethnic stratification was less marked, while hybridization (mestizaje) had proceeded farther and faster. One eye-catching indication of this trend was the famous Mexican *casta* paintings of the later eighteenth century.[24] On the eve of independence, the supposed Indian population of Peru, relative to total population, was perhaps roughly similar to that of Mexico.[25] But even if this is correct (and there may be doubts), the Indian presence in Peru was more marked, the ethnic dividing line more entrenched.[26] Quechua constituted a genuine lingua franca for much of the population; in Mexico the major Indian languages, such as Nahuatl and Maya, were more regionally circumscribed.[27] Numbers aside, the *mancha india* (Indian stain) was a bigger blot on the Peruvian landscape; that is to say, the Indian population remained distinct, subordinate, exploited, and resentful. For centuries, Indian labor was forcibly recruited by means of the *mita*, a system of indirect control whereby the colonial state obliged community authorities to recruit labor, especially for the mines. (Similarly, those authorities were responsible for tribute payments.) And traditional coercive systems continued to function well into the nineteenth century (and even beyond).[28]

In Mexico forced labor—both slavery and the early encomienda drafts—largely died out, such that by the eighteenth century the booming mining industry relied on "free" labor, whose recruitment did not require extensive state coercion.[29] Mexican haciendas, too, recruited and retained labor by their own "entrepreneurial" efforts; debt peonage, traditionally seen as a form of coercive semiservitude, often relied on voluntaristic (and/or customary) relations between landlord and peon.[30]

Caste divisions appear to have been more strictly maintained in Peru than in Mexico, where the process of mestizaje was more advanced: mestizos constituted perhaps 40 percent of the Mexican population at the end of the colonial period, compared to 23 percent in Peru.[31] By the time Mexico gained independence, "Indian" had become, in many cases, a fiscal rather than an ethnic/cultural category.[32] One cause of this initial (colonial) divergence was the scope and influence of the Mexican Catholic Church, which meant that Mexico experienced greater religious as well as politico-economic integration. We need not accept the excessively lyrical version of Mexico's "spiritual conquest" to reach the reasonable conclusion that by the later colonial period, the Catholic Church had put down deep roots in Mexican society in all regions among all ethnic groups.[33] One suggestive straw in the wind was nomenclature: in Mexico, William Taylor has noted, the names "María" and "Guadalupe" grew substantially in popularity in the eighteenth century as the cult of the Virgin of Guadalupe spread—evidence, we might say, of an extensive religious cult with "protopatriotic" implications.[34] In Peru, the church was stretched and superficial: its strong presence in Lima contrasted with its sketchy influence in the highlands, where Indian beliefs and practices still flourished.[35] In Mexico, by contrast, idolatry was seen more as a lingering childish superstition than as a worrying subversive threat.[36]

Popular rebellion offers a telling illustration of this contrast. In the 1780s highland Peru witnessed a massive popular—in large part indigenous—rebellion that not only challenged the authority of the colonial government in Lima but also threatened to subvert Spanish rule entirely. The rebels harked back to the Incas, and as the violence spiraled upward, the conflict assumed the form of a "caste" or ethnic war. In Mexico, prior to 1810, violent popular protest tended to be highly local, limited, and tactical—what has (elsewhere) been called "bargaining by riot."[37] Of course, the Mexican (independence) insurgency of 1810, while embodying a great deal of such local protests, went much further in forging supralocal links and, in some cases, advancing a bold and radical agenda that embodied class and caste/ethnic antagonism, as well as popular religious, protopatriotic, and democratic notions.[38]

Thus, while the Andean rebels of the 1780s shared with their Mexican counterparts of 1810 both class and ethnic grievances, their respective ideologies were noticeably different. The Mexican version was, if you like, more forward-looking, innovative, and "proactive," while in Peru, revolt adopted a more "reactive," nostalgic, and prescriptive character.[39] There was a corresponding difference in terms of class, too: the Hispanophobic hosts of Father Hidalgo were recruited among the floating population of the Bajío (an embryonic proletariat, one might say), not among the indigenous communities of the central highlands, including the Valley of Mexico, Puebla, and Oaxaca, where communities were leery of Hidalgo's cause.[40] And to my knowledge, no Mexican rebels advocated a return to Aztec rule, nor was there an extant Aztec—or, for that matter, Tarascan or Tlaxcalan lineage—that could be called upon to supplant the ruling Spaniards. Traditionally, as already mentioned, Mexican rebels and protestors had worked within the existing (colonial) system; thus, when litigation and petitioning failed, they sought redress by riot, and in many cases they got results. Major insurrectionary outbursts were unusual and confined to the outer peripheries of New Spain (e.g., Chiapas and New Mexico), yet even there, rebels often deployed Catholic notions and images.[41] Among the elites of New Spain, too, notions of a distinct national identity—a kind of inchoate "protopatriotism"—seem to have been stronger than in Peru, where caste and ethnic divisions tended to trump any sense of common Peruanidad.

As a result, although both Mexico and Peru were the last colonies (or kingdoms) to achieve independence, their respective trajectories were somewhat different and indicative of a prior colonial divergence. Peru generated powerful insurgent movements (e.g., those centered on Cuzco in the southern highlands), but the struggle for independence was weaker than in Mexico, in part because the Tupac Amaru revolt and repression of a generation earlier had frightened Peru's elites, intimidated Peru's Indians, and created a tougher carapace of social control.[42] In Mexico, both Hidalgo and Morelos were defeated and executed; however, the movements they led could not be snuffed out, and eventually, independence was achieved more or less autonomously, that is, as a result of events unfolding in Mexico (and Spain).[43] In Peru, of course, "liberation" came from without, as Bolívar and San Martín invaded from north and south, respectively.

Thus, despite some obvious similarities in respect to the colonial experience—which, putting it simply, mean that Mexico resembled Peru much more closely than, say, it resembled Argentina or Cuba—there were also important differences.[44] Again, to put it simply, Mexico was a more effectively integrated society, politically, economically, and culturally (e.g., in terms of religion). Ethnic tensions, though strong, were less dominant and divisive; thus, the bases of subsequent nationhood were somewhat more solid in Mexico than in Peru.

Both Peru and Mexico became independent in the 1820s (although Spain did not at once acquiesce, and indeed, it attempted quixotic reconquests of both republics in later decades). If we take, as a point of comparison, the period immediately following independence, roughly the 1820s through the 1840s, the similarities are striking—which is to say, we see a process of *con*vergence rather than *di*vergence.[45] Both national states were weak and unstable, lacking both solid legitimacy and sound finances.[46]

Political independence could not change basic geographical facts: both countries lacked viable communications (railways came late to both and had to overcome formidable natural obstacles); regional divisions remained strong and regularly generated political contention and even outright rebellion. In the absence of strong legitimate central government, regional caudillismo flourished, the product of a centrifugal process of "political feudalization."[47] National boundaries were as yet indeterminate: Peru and Bolivia were briefly united (then torn apart by Chilean aggression); Mexico relinquished Central America, retained Chiapas, and in 1848 lost its vast northern territories to the expansionist United States.

Since the mining economy had suffered from both wartime destruction and the flight of Spanish capital, government revenue slumped. Facing what Barbara Tenenbaum calls—in the Mexican context—the "politics of penury," both states were tempted to revive the colonial head tax (capitación), thus perpetuating creaky colonial fiscal structures long after independence.[48] Similarly, while the collapse of colonial mercantilism had promoted a surge in foreign imports and a spate of foreign loans, neither could be sustained; the loans soon defaulted, and sluggish exports could not generate the foreign exchange required to continue importing (high tariffs also deterred importers). In short, the first postindependence decades were a period of economic stagnation—a "long wait" until new circumstances jolted these stick-in-the-mud economies out of their respective ruts.[49]

If this politico-economic scenario is well-known, the sociopolitical consequences are, perhaps, less obvious. Since both states were relatively weak, lacking both resources and legitimacy, landed elites could not confidently depend on the strong arm of the state to defend their class interests; at best, they had to rely on the shifting and uncertain power of local and regional caudillos. As a result, the balance of class power shifted somewhat in favor of the popular classes, chiefly the peasantry, including the Indian peasantry.[50] The reintroduction of the head tax implied a material cost, but at least in Peru, it signified the continuation of the historic "tributary pact," whereby Indian communities retained a measure of recognized autonomy in return for obeying—and financing—a distant government.[51] More broadly, peasant, including Indian, communities in both countries emerged from the upheaval of independence with their power and autonomy somewhat enhanced. They now confronted weaker states and elites; also, especially in Mexico, popular insurgency left a legacy of organization and even weaponry.[52] Popular caudillos such as Juan Alvarez of Guerrero, in southwestern Mexico, built their durable careers on the basis of peasant support and mobilization.[53] In Chalco and elsewhere in Mexico, as John Tutino has shown, peasant communities, including a rising ranchero class, were able to litigate, resist, at times fight, and thus maintain or even expand their landholdings.[54] Compared to the late colonial period, landlords lacked both the power and the incentive to battle assertive peasant communities. Thus, Mexico and Peru underwent what has been called a process of agrarian "decompression" as both commercial and coercive pressures attenuated.[55] Adrian Pearce has further shown that, as in the past, politico-economic trends had broader cultural consequences, since, enjoying de facto greater autonomy, (Peruvian) indigenous communities could reassert their identity, spurning Spanish in favor of Quechua.[56] Postindependence Peru was, in this sense, "reindigenized."

In short, in these early decades of independence, Mexico and Peru tended to follow similar—perhaps "neocolonial"—paths; their initial "colonial divergence" grew no wider; and both countries offer a contrast with, for example, the centralized state-building achieved under the Portalian system in Chile or the Brazilian Empire of Pedro II or with the economic quickening evident both in the authoritarian Argentina of Rosas and on the *siempre fiel* (always faithful) island of colonial Cuba as the sugar boom and precocious railway investment forged ahead.

Around midcentury, however, more or less as the second postindependence generation came to power, the fortunes of Mexico and Peru sharply diverged. Hence this conjuncture could be called the "first divergence" in the period under consideration; to be more specific, it could be called the "great guano divergence." This first—alias guano—divergence was the product of changing economic trends coupled with the more stochastic roll of the international geopolitical dice.

After ca. 1840 European demand for fertilizer prompted the exploitation and export of Peru's offshore guano deposits, which by the following decade had generated an unprecedented boom.[57] Apart from making individual fortunes, guano hugely boosted state revenue, making possible a bigger payroll and ambitious public works.[58] Revenue facilitated political stability (since factions could be more easily bought off); it enhanced the repressive power of the state (the Peruvian army became "the richest military clan on the planet") while strengthening Lima vis-à-vis the provinces; and it fostered a new collaborative relationship between the Peruvian state, which owned the guano deposits, and overseas business interests, making possible heavy foreign borrowing.[59] However, it left the indigenous population of the sierra relatively unaffected, and it benefited coastal elites, including the slave-owning planters, who were richly recompensed when slavery was abolished in 1854.[60] By the 1850s, the planters of the northern coast in particular were expanding production of sugar, cotton, and staple foodstuffs.[61] Though stronger and more stable, the guano state nevertheless remained disconnected from society as a whole (in other words, it lacked "social penetration"), since it declined to invest in social provision or education and left the indigenous communities of the sierra in a condition of at best benign neglect.[62] Furthermore, the guano boom was a—perhaps *the*—classic example of a freakish commodity boom that depended on foreign demand and finite resources while—relatively speaking—lacking linkages to the broader Peruvian economy.[63]

Peru's guano boom occurred during a period of relative calm in the country's foreign relations. It was sandwiched between two defeats at the hands of Chile: the latter's defeat of the short-lived Peru-Bolivia Confederation (1836–39) and the more serious and consequential War of the Pacific (1879–83). (In contrast, the 1864–66 conflict with Spain was purely naval and, unlike the two land wars, resulted in a Peruvian victory.) For Mexico, in contrast, these midcentury decades were defined by bloody and costly international conflicts. Indeed, Mexico's experience could be seen as part of a global spike in violence that upset the long post-Napoleonic peace: the Revolutions of 1848 and the protracted Italian Risorgimento (1858–66), the Crimean War (1853–56), the American Civil War (1861–65), and China's Taiping Rebellion (1850–56). The United States invaded Mexico in 1846, making off with half of the national territory, and French forces occupied much of Mexico in 1861–66 in a vain attempt to prop up the empire of Maximilian. Furthermore, the French invasion occurred following a major Mexican civil war—the War of the Reform (1858–61), which the Liberals won, only to have the fruits of victory (temporarily) wrested from their grasp by Maximilian, Napoleon III, and their Conservative Mexican allies. Needless to say, three successive wars, costing tens of thousands of Mexican lives, devastated the economy, delaying for a generation any hope of sustained economic growth.[64]

So while Peru boomed, Mexico stagnated. This contrast was hardly written in the stars, nor could it have been confidently predicted by intelligent and informed observers of the two countries. The guano boom, as I have said, was a freakish commodity boom, while Mexico's grim fate at the hands of foreign (non–Latin American) powers stemmed from the vagaries of international geopolitics. True, the country's geographical location, linked to its reputation as a vast unexploited treasure house, made it unusually vulnerable, at least compared to other Latin American nations, but the Mexican-American War was in part a war of choice (chosen by the Mexicans—or, at least, by Santa Anna and others in power at the time), while the French adventure was a characteristic product of Napoleon III's meddlesome, militaristic inclinations, which Mexican Conservatives cleverly exploited.[65]

So the first/guano divergence obeyed no deep structural determinism. It occurred because Peru's Pacific coast was rich in fish, which fed seabirds whose mountainous droppings, accumulating over the centuries, met a growing demand from European agriculture and because—in contrast to the South American experience-Mexico fell victim to predatory (non–Latin American) powers, which the country's leaders failed to assuage and at times perversely encouraged. But if the causes of the divergence were, in a sense, stochastic, their consequences were profound: Peru experienced a precocious, if superficial and ephemeral, prosperity, while Mexico suffered a generation of war, territorial loss, economic stagnation, and political polarization.[66]

In the last quarter of the nineteenth century, however, the roles were reversed. During this—the second or, we could say, "Porfirian" divergence—Mexico achieved unprecedented political stability under authoritarian personalist rule, while Peru now faced foreign invasion, defeat, and territorial loss. The rule of Porfirio Díaz stretched over a long generation (1876–1911); though distinctive political and socioeconomic subperiods can be usefully demarcated, it is reasonable, for the purpose of broad comparison, to consider the period/regime as a whole.[67] Seizing power in 1876, Díaz represented both a generational shift and a transition from Liberal civilian to Liberal caudillo rule. He inherited a war-weary country that was disposed to acquiesce in Porfirio's effective blend of tough top-down sociopolitical control and constructive economic "progress"—a combination legitimized, at least in the eyes of his elite collaborators, the Científicos, in terms of enlightened Comtean positivism. Foreign investment poured into the country, making possible the infrastructure (railways, telegraphs, ports) that bolstered centralized political authority while fostering market integration, both national and international.[68] As Tom Passananti has argued, the Porfirian/Científico project was no supine surrender to foreign imperialism; it obeyed a coherent initial rationale, it served the national interest (at least as Díaz and the Científicos conceived it), and the project was, by its own criteria, strikingly successful.[69] However, as I shall shortly mention, the regime contained the seeds of its own downfall, since it became increasingly remote, racist, and unpopular (without necessarily realizing it); in addition, at least from the 1890s, its ostensibly successful economic policy proved to be socially regressive and politically provocative.[70]

But for the time being, the Porfirian regime looked to be a successful and enviable model. Peru, meanwhile, regressed. Just as, at midcentury, Peru had boomed while Mexico was devastated by war, so, in the 1870s and 1880s, Mexico's economic revival contrasted with war, defeat, and instability in Peru. True, the War of the Pacific concerned intra–Latin American warfare, Chile being, in some respects, a less threatening adversary than either the United States or the France of Napoleon III.[71] And Peru's territorial losses were minor in comparison. However, the War of the Pacific had serious political and economic effects, the more so because it coincided with the end of the guano boom.[72] Furthermore, Juárez's final defeat of the French and their Belgian, Austrian, and Mexican allies in 1867 helped cauterize the wound of 1848: it showed that Mexico could mount a successful patriotic resistance to foreign invasion, and it created the political platform for the creation of the subsequent Porfirian regime.[73] Mallon's comparative study suggests that Mexican popular mobilization, in support of the liberal-patriotic cause, contrasted with Peru's inability to mount a coherent, cross-class, multiethnic resistance.[74] Whatever the causes of this contrast, the consequences were profound.[75] Mexico acquired both a powerful myth of integrative patriotism and, more importantly perhaps, a solid political base (i.e., the decisive victory of the Liberals and their "modernizing" project) upon which Porfirio could construct a durable "modernizing" regime, blending liberal and conservative elements and capitalizing on the war-weariness of the Mexican people.[76]

In contrast, Peru's political counterparts, the Civilistas, were strikingly less successful. True, the economy revived following the disaster of the war; infrastructure, exports, and foreign investment increased; and Civilista ideology—like that of Mexico's Científicos—legitimized export-led growth and firm, authoritarian government. But there were important differences, albeit of degree. Mexican growth was more sustained and extensive.[77] The proximity of the United States facilitated both exports and foreign investment; the new railway system was transformative, generating major savings and—I would hypothesize—greater economic output in Mexico than in Peru.[78] Politically, the Mexican Liberal Party—even as it mutated into a Liberal-Positivist amalgam, stressing economic growth over political rights—enjoyed a near monopoly of national power. Foreigners fawned on Díaz, the architect of "order and progress," comparing him to Moses, Alexander the Great, Julius Caesar, Cromwell, Washington, Napoleon, and Bismarck.[79] The Peruvian state was weaker, more factionalized, less capable of controlling its sprawling territory and rival centers of power.[80] We could thus see the Civilista regime as a poor man's Porfiriato: seeking similar goals by similar means but lacking the political muscle and thus failing to achieve either the political stability or the sustained growth of the Porfiriato. The result was ideological *con*vergence (the two regimes espoused similar goals) but practical *di*vergence (the Mexican regime was much more successful at achieving those goals).[81]

But the Peruvian project at least had the virtues of its defects. That is, given the nature of these evolving "order and progress" regimes, too much ostensible success (à la mexicana) could prove a potential risk, while relative failure (à la peruana) could diminish that risk. In other words, the rapid and severe sociopolitical "compression" created by the Porfiriato led to a sociopolitical explosion: the Mexican Revolution of 1910 and its consequences, the final dramatic—"revolutionary"—divergence between the two countries. In Peru and, for that matter, the rest of Latin America, the compression was less, the risk was reduced, and no comparable explosion occurred.[82] There were, it is true, many minor outbursts: protests, riots, and rebellions, some of which coalesced into serious regional insurrections, such as "the wave of violent peasant revolts that swept through the southern highlands" of Peru in the 1910s, including the radical antilandlord, neo-Incaista Rumi Maqui insurgency of 1915.[83] In addition, the Peruvian state could not extirpate chronic banditry (as the Porfirian state had done).[84] And by the early twentieth century, major strikes had begun to affect the big commercial sugar plantations of the North.[85] But these were repressed, or accommodated, or both, and they never gelled into a social revolution comparable to the Mexican experience of the 1910s.[86] So here we see a clear example of how comparison can help us understand major historical conjunctures. The example suggests, to my mind, that popular grievances were more acute and extensive in Mexico; that the capacity for broad popular insurgency (evident throughout nineteenth-century Mexican history) was an important facilitating condition; and that the Porfirian state, though ostensibly much stronger than the Peruvian, failed to provide escape valves for popular discontent and, on the contrary, came to believe, hubristically and even suicidally, in its own indisputable—and racist—right to rule.[87]

Of course, the causes of the Mexican Revolution—thus, of the last major "divergence" to be considered—are many and contentious. Here, I will simply present my own interpretation, which others might well query. The revolution, as I have said, was a genuinely popular social revolution (not just "a great rebellion"), and it was provoked precisely by those Porfirian policies that the boosters of Don Porfirio had regularly lauded and applauded: a strong, authoritarian, centralized government that denied broad political representation, not least to the burgeoning middle class; tough top-down social control enacted by the arbitrary officials of the central government; rapid repression of political, social, and ethnic dissent, the victims including mestizo peasants, the incipient labor movement, and insurgent Indians (Yaqui and Maya in particular); an agrarian project that boosted commercial production, exports, and land values, thus favoring big landowners to the disadvantage of peasant communities while encouraging repressive exploitation of rural workers; and a policy toward urban labor that, though slightly more nuanced, did little to mitigate growing fluctuations in the business cycle or, from the 1890s, at least, declining real wages, declining living standards, and even declining physical stature.[88]

These mounting tensions and grievances came dramatically to light after 1910. Previously, during the prior belle époque of the late Porfiriato, they had remained in the shadows, only occasionally illuminated by sudden outbreaks of protest that were followed by rapid exercises in repression (such as the Cananea and Río Blanco labor disputes).[89] As a result, "informed" observers penned their paeans to Don Porfirio and confidently asserted that rebellion was out of the question.[90] Here, the comparison with Peru is fruitful. Pretty much all the factors evident in Porfirian Mexico can be discerned, if less clearly, in contemporary Peru. Here, too, as the market quickened and exports grew, landlords grew richer and more aggressively expansionist; state policy and infrastructural investment usually served their interests. Hence, as I mentioned, we see recurrent peasant protest. Indeed, prior to 1910, peasant protest was more common and—in the short term—more consequential in Peru than in Mexico.[91] We might reasonably hypothesize that protest in turn inhibited landlord expansion.[92] In Mexico the demands of the market and power of the state were both appreciably stronger, making landlords both overweening and overconfident.

There was also a structural contrast that harks back to the "initial divergence" mentioned earlier. In Mexico, dense, often ancient peasant settlements clustered in central and southern regions, as well as in pockets of the North. These settlements now confronted aggressively expansion- ist landlords. Generations of uneasy coexistence between haciendas or ranchos, on the one hand, and peasant communities, on the other, now gave way to agrarian polarization, a zero-sum struggle for resources (land, water, and labor) in the context of market expansion and state coercion.[93] The ensuing armed conflict was therefore most severe in regions where this polarization was particularly acute: in Morelos, parts of Puebla and Tlaxcala, La Laguna, the Yaqui Valley, and the valleys of the Sierra Madre in western Chihuahua.

As is well known, agrarian rebellion was much less pronounced in southern Mexico—and not because the campesinos of the South were better off and contented. Here, state and landlord repression was more severe (Yucatán being a classic case), and in states such as Oaxaca and Chiapas, lowland landlords were often more concerned to acquire peasant *labor* than peasant *land*. This they did either by imposing forms of extreme labor coercion (debt peonage in its classic, semiservile form) or by luring labor from highland communities by offering advances and short-term contracts. Hence, we see the system of *enganche* typical of Chiapas— and of neighboring Guatemala and Peru.[94] Historically, such enganche systems, embodying, in Marxist terms, an "articulation of modes of production," linked highland (subsistence) peasants to lowland (commercial) landlords, with venal local officials as the key intermediaries.[95] Though by any reasonable criteria they were exploitative and abusive, enganche systems generated less popular resistance and protest than the direct dispossession of peasants by landlords (as occurred in central and parts of northern Mexico, as well as in certain pockets of the Peruvian sierra). Such direct dispossession marked the crossing of a decisive threshold, from peasant to proletarian, campesino to peon; it represented a cultural as well as socioeconomic derogation; and it effectively mobilized large swaths of the community in aggrieved opposition.

Zapatismo was the classic case, and we can discern mini-Zapatismos in Peru at the same time. But Zapatismo, as I have argued elsewhere, was simply the most vigorous and sustained agrarista movement among many, and taken together, Mexican agrarismo achieved a critical mass that determined both the course of the armed revolution (1910–20) and the ensuing project of the "revolución hecha gobierno" (revolution made government) through the 1920s and 1930s. In Peru, peasant movements, though common enough, did not gel into a broad national movement; in some cases they were snuffed out, but in others they put up a dogged resistance to landlord claims, in the process inhibiting landlord expansion.[96] Furthermore, although in some Peruvian provinces (e.g., Azángaro), peasant rebels targeted expansionist landlords, elsewhere (e.g., neighboring Puno), insurgents chiefly resisted the fiscal demands of the state—such as the salt tax—and the rapacious officials (*gamonales*) who were locally responsible. The Puno protest thus harked back to late colonial and early nineteenth-century precedents and testified to the weakness of the market and the archaic predatoriness of the state. In a context of more vigorous market activity, Azángaro had witnessed the "wholesale transfer of land from smallholders to hacendados," which in turn provoked popular agrarian insurrection.[97] The latter could be seen as a more "Mexican"—and arguably a more "modern"—sociopolitical syndrome. For in Mexico, the sustained and aggressive process of landlord expansion (or "agrarian compression," if you prefer) facilitated by the stronger Porfirian state brought about the state's own sociopolitical downfall.

Of course, the Mexican Revolution involved more than purely *agrarista* mobilization. The radical organized working class also played a secondary role during the armed insurrection and, after 1920, a more salient role as a key ally of the new state, in return for which it received significant benefits.[98] The progressive middle class—rather larger, in both absolute and relative terms, in Mexico than in Peru—also contributed to the labyrinthine course of the revolution (both violent and institutional), championing classic democratic liberalism under Madero and a more radical but somewhat authoritarian Jacobinism under Obregón and Calles, leaders who rode a mounting wave of radical anticlericalism.[99] And although the causal importance of nationalist, anti-imperialist, and anti-American sentiment has often been exaggerated, the pervasive patriotism that revolutionary Mexico inherited from its liberal-Juarista past was now revived and radicalized in the context of both armed insurrection and sporadic American intervention south of the border. The new nationalism of the revolution now also embodied a significant indigenista dimension: an effort, often rhetorical but sometimes also practical, to emancipate and uplift the oppressed indigenous populations, especially in the "nonrevolutionary" southeast of the country.[100] This mélange of policies, projects, and collective actors, unique in Latin America at the time, made possible the distinctive revolutionary state of the 1920s and 1930s: agrarista, *obrerista*, nationalist, centralizing, indigenista, and inclusionary but also, depending on time and place, authoritarian, anticlerical, and Jacobin.[101]

Peru, like the rest of Latin America, experienced no comparable national upheaval. The social ingredients of the Mexican Revolution were all evident in Peru: an aggrieved peasantry, a nascent working class, a small progressive urban middle class. The harsh peonage of Chiapas had its even harsher counterpart in the Putumayo rubber boom. But the critical mass was lacking; so, too, was the agglutinative cement of nationalism. Perhaps, too, the distant memory of Tupac Amaru, sustained by recurrent Indian protests through the nineteenth century, made Peruvian elites more cautious about making mass appeals for armed insurrection.[102] "Micropolitical" violence—sporadic and localized, unable to subvert either the state or the social status quo—was common enough, but Peru did not experience the macropolitical effects of social revolution. (Then or since, we might add: the military regime of 1968–80 undertook top-down nationalist reform, while Sendero Luminoso failed in its attempt to impose its brutal brand of Maoism.) Of course, within Latin America as a whole, Mexico was the outlier, not Peru.

We come, therefore, to the final chapter in this comparison. If the Civilista regime was, as I have suggested, a "poor man's Porfiriato," so Augusto Leguía was, we could say, a mini-Calles.[103] Leguía dominated Peruvian politics during the *oncenio* (1919–30), much as his contemporary Calles dominated Mexico from the mid-1920s to the mid-1930s. Their respective regimes display several superficial similarities: a commitment to economic modernization (road-building being a particular concern of both presidents); a belief in strong, if necessary authoritarian, government, requiring somewhat greater state revenue and spending; and a measure of indigenismo designed to integrate disparate indigenous populations into national society.[104]

But as the product of a genuine social revolution, Calles proved much more radical, above all because he had to take note of popular pressures, including militant unions and armed agraristas. Thus, he sponsored a genuine land reform (which Leguía never did), and as a patron of organized labor, he went much further than Leguía, empowering unions and the Confederación Regional Obrera Mexicana (Mexican Regional Workers Confederation, CROM), thus alarming employers, both foreign and Mexican.[105] Calles's indigenismo was rather more red-blooded (which is to say that Leguía's was more superficial and rhetorical).[106] Calles's nationalism, too, was all the more robust, given the looming proximity of the United States. (Leguía, in contrast, was and is criticized for being obsequiously deferential to the United States.)[107] The Mexican state also promoted mass rural education and actively espoused a brand of assertive cultural nationalism for which there was (to my knowledge) no close Peruvian counterpart.[108] Finally, perhaps the most clear-cut contrast, while Calles battled the Catholic Church, Leguía sought to dedicate Peru to the Sacred Heart of Jesus. As a result, Calles was widely regarded as a dangerous "Bolshevik"—an accusation Leguía never faced (again, to my knowledge). In the subsequent decade of the 1930s, Mexican president Lázaro Cárdenas enacted a reform project that was even more radical—indeed, avowedly "socialist" in respect to education—at a time when Peru swung to the right, falling under the semidictatorial and conservative rule of President Oscar Benavides (1933–39).[109]

I am not trying to play Mark Antony to Calles's Caesar.[110] The contrast is not meant to demean Leguía as a feeble lackey of the church (or of imperialism) nor to laud Calles as a noble tribune of the people. To do so would be to impose extraneous value judgments upon historical processes and people.[111] The task of the historian is not to judge but to explain—in this case, to explain the final big divergence, which involved Mexico acquiring a stable, reformist, inclusionary, and increasingly civilian regime endowed with a real measure of "social penetration," while Peru remained in thrall to a more narrowly oligarchic and exclusionary regime, the oncenio being, according to some perceptive historians, a refurbished, updated, and authoritarian version of Civilismo.[112] Indeed, the closest contemporary Peruvian counterparts of Calles and the infant PNR were Víctor Raúl Haya de la Torre and the Alianza Popular Revolucionaria Americana (APRA), as Haya himself stressed; yet, of course, Haya and Leguía were political enemies, and APRA remained not a radical nationalist party of government but a strenuous oppositional force that faced repression at the hands of both Leguía and Benavides.

This comparison suggests one final tentative conclusion. If we wish to evaluate the impact of the Mexican Revolution, we need, implicitly or (better) explicitly, to consider how Mexico would have evolved in the absence of the revolution—if, for example, Díaz had parlayed his succession with more skill and foresight (which was entirely possible). Given certain basic similarities between Peru and Mexico and given, too, that Civilismo and Porfirismo shared certain broad ideological goals, the trajectory that Peru followed may offer some useful clues when it comes to Mexican counterfactuals. If, for example, Díaz had tapped Bernardo Reyes to be his successor (Reyes being an experienced político who was no less authoritarian than Díaz but who was committed to a measure of top-down reform and enjoyed genuine middle-class support), then perhaps revolution might have been avoided.[113] Mexico under a notional Reyes regime would have looked rather like Peru under Leguía, that is, socially stable, politically oligarchical and exclusionary, and superficially progressive. (As governor of Nuevo León, for example, Reyes, had—in paternalist Bismarckian fashion—shown some awareness of working-class demands and interests.)[114] It would be risky to regard a hypothetical Reyes regime—or the actual oncenio—as purposive "revolutions from above," since those regimes (hypothetical or actual) hardly merit the "revolutionary" label, however qualified. But they have some kinship with Barrington Moore's seminal concept.[115] In reality, of course, Díaz missed the bus, botched the succession, and opened the door to "revolution from below." The result, if we compare Mexico and Peru during the first half of the twentieth century, was the biggest and most consequential divergence of them all, one that would determine the contrasting trajectories of the two countries through the twentieth century.[116]

CHAPTER 5

Informal Empire and Internal Colonialism in Latin America, 1820–1930

IN THE TWENTY-FIRST CENTURY, EMPIRE HAS COME BACK INTO fashion. By the same token, if we define imperialism as the means whereby empire is established and justified, imperialism is also back in fashion. I refer not just to real-world facts and trends (although a case could be made there too) but rather to academic production and debate, which are somewhat easier to measure. In recent years, major books on empire that address both the British and American variants, as I will in this chapter, include robust critiques such as Chalmers Johnson's *Blowback*; revisionist defenses such as Niall Ferguson's *Empire* and *Colossus*, Deepak Lal's *In Praise of Empire* (the title tells it all), and, with qualifications, Max Boot's *The Savage Wars of Peace*; and, finally, more neutral—one might also say Olympian—surveys such as John Darwin's *After Tamerlane* and Charles Maier's *Among Empires*.[1]

On the British side, Sir John Wheeler-Bennett, writing back in the 1960s, referred to "that splendidly unregenerate period before 'empire' became a 'dirty' word."[2] Now, it seems, the dirt has been at least partially washed from Britannia's grubby paws, and apologists of empire, such as Ferguson and Lal, applaud the British Empire for espousing free trade, integrating the global economy, and fostering commerce and investment while providing (as an international "hegemon" supposedly should) the valuable "public goods" of peace and security to the benefit of all.[3] British hegemony, of course, embraced both formal and informal empires. (I shall define them shortly. For the moment, we can say that the formal empire was painted red on the map; the rest, including much of Latin America, was painted other colors.) American hegemony has been largely informal; hence, as Donald Rumsfeld stated (in one of his more pithy and straightforward observations), "We don't do empire," an old and familiar American claim that is broadly valid, but only if "empire" is defined in formal terms, that is, with respect to dependencies painted red on the map.[4]

If the United States has an empire (as Ferguson says it does and indeed should have), then it is primarily an informal empire. The biggest bit of Britain's "informal empire" was Latin America; indeed, it is plausible to see Latin America's external relations—some would say the continent's "dependency"—shifting from Britain to the United States in the period I am discussing (and I will come to that). Therefore, an analysis of Latin America should in some measure help us understand what, if anything, "informal empire" is and, perhaps, whether it is, as Ferguson assures us, what Sellar and Yeatman would call "A Good Thing."[5]

First, how should we define "informal empire"? Many students of empire recognize that there are forms of hegemony (or "paramountcy," "imperium," "overlordship," "ascendancy"—the concepts keep coming) that in turn sustain corresponding conditions of "dependency" or "neocolonialism" yet that do not involve formal control, as in fully fledged colonies or protectorates. Indeed, there is a loose consensus, embracing both Marxist analysts and their non-Marxist ("bourgeois"?) counterparts, that such a category exists (even if they give it different labels) and that "empire" cannot simply be reduced to colonies and protectorates. However, if "empire does not mean just the accumulation of lands abroad by conquest," there is no consensus regarding precise positive definition of "informal empire."[6] My first best shot at a definition would be that informal empire involves a marked, unequal, and enduring relationship between countries that may combine political, military, economic, and, perhaps, cultural elements but that falls short of direct formal colonial control. The "metropolitan" country exercises nonreciprocal power and influence over its "peripheral" counterpart while avoiding direct control or conquest.

However, in historical reality, things are, as usual, rather more complicated. The "formality" of formal empire embraces two distinct notions: first, the direct exercise of metropolitan—say, British or American—power, and second, a general recognition of the legitimacy of that power, resulting in the decision to paint certain bits of the map red and have people take it seriously. Both of these notions involve a continuum (you can have more or less of each): some metropolitan power is direct, hands-on, meddlesome, and intense; some is indirect, partial, and mediated through "host" authorities, such as Indian princes and West African emirs (or, if you take imperial Rome as an example, through "friendly kings," i.e., puppet rulers like Herod the Great and Ptolemy of Mauretania).[7] Thus, within *formal* colonies such as British India and Nigeria there were degrees of *indirect* rule. In some British colonies (the so-called White Dominions), metropolitan power receded, and by the late nineteenth century, a large measure of self-government prevailed (so this was "indirect rule" of a very different kind). At the same time, British colonial rule was sometimes long-lasting and legitimate (at least in the eyes of many, including the "international community"), but sometimes it was short-lived and contentious (e.g., the Palestine Mandate). Thus, if we unpack the bits that are painted red on the map, we find quite different degrees of formality and informality; for this reason, some of Britain's supposed "informal empire" (e.g., Argentina) may, in terms of the imperial liaison, resemble "formal" possessions such as Canada and Australia more often than is supposed.[8]

So, too, with the putative American Empire. It combines, first, footholds that are formal in the sense of being both directly and "legitimately" ruled (e.g., Puerto Rico, as well as a string of U.S. military bases around the world, from Okinawa to Guantánamo).[9] These do not show up as big slabs of red on the map but rather as a global scattering of colored dots. However, they embody the twin elements of formality: direct rule and, usually, legitimacy.[10] Second, there are places that, for the time being, may be subject to direct rule but without any pretension to enduring legitimacy (e.g., Nicaragua, Haiti and the Dominican Republic in the 1910s and 1920s, or Baghdad or Kabul in the 2000s).[11] Finally, there are countries (e.g., in Latin America) where U.S. power and influence are neither direct nor legitimate but depend on many-stranded informal ties, political, economic, and cultural. Of course, since ties of this kind are ubiquitous and growing (that's what "globalization" is all about), the presence of such ties alone does not constitute "empire," since empire—as commonly and correctly understood—must involve an enduring and clear-cut imbalance, or nonreciprocity, of power and influence between unequal countries. Globalization may involve informal imperialism, but it is not the same thing.

Now why should a Great Power (Britain in the nineteenth century, America in the twentieth) opt for formal as against informal power, or vice versa? Why, to put it succinctly, was there a "scramble for Africa" in the late nineteenth century that involved a wholesale land grab, an extensive painting of the map (chiefly red), yet no equivalent "scramble for Latin America"? (It is true that some historians do refer to a nineteenth-century "scramble for Latin America," but they mean a much more pacific run-of-the-mill competition for trade and investment, a qualitatively different "scramble" that should not be confused with the huge and violent upheaval experienced in Africa. Latin American–style "scrambles" are the default mode of international capitalism; the scramble for Africa—an example of Great Power "grand larceny"—was a one-off colonialist carve-up.)[12] So why no Latin American "scramble" (in the strong and strict sense)? After all, given events around the world, including the Americas, during the later eighteenth and early nineteenth centuries, "there was no good reason to suppose that Great Britain would refrain from annexing territory in Latin America."[13] So why did that not happen?

The formal/informal variation derives from the interplay of metropolitan goals and motives, on the one hand (thus, the perceived interests of the Great Powers), and the character and reaction of the "peripheral" society, on the other. So we can speak of metropolitan and peripheral explanations, respectively. I shall say something about metropolitan goals and motives first, even though I will go on to argue that "peripheral" factors are arguably more crucial—and, in my view, more interesting. Hence, in the terminology of the relevant debate, I will be presenting what Ronald Robinson called a largely "excentric"—or, we could say, "peripheral"—interpretation of Latin America in the period.[14]

When the Spanish conquistadors embarked on their bloody exploits in the Americas, they responded—by their own account—to three main motivations, which can be alliteratively summed up as glory, God, and gold. Nurtured in the martial and chivalric traditions of the Reconquista (the traditions that Cervantes lampooned in *Don Quixote*), they sought glory for themselves and the Spanish Crown; at the same time, they espoused a genuine Christian mission (and, of course, the Catholic Church became a powerful and successful engine of Spanish imperialism in the New World); finally, more than some might accept, they had a thirst for material gain, especially bullion.[15] (In using "gold" as shorthand for material gain in general, I believe I am using that most fashionable of current figures of speech, a "synecdoche.")

In order to extend this simple threefold set of motivations to more recent times, we can roughly equate glory with national prestige and security, God with cultural and ideological proselytization, and gold, very obviously, with material acquisition.[16] Empire-builders sought to augment the power, the cultural influence, and the wealth of their people, not least themselves.[17] The British are the simplest case. For them, informal empire in Latin America—but not necessarily elsewhere—was a matter of gold, that is, of material gain accrued initially by means of trade: the export of British manufactures (particularly textiles) and the import of Latin American primary products (hides, silver, guano, wool, wheat, cotton, meat, nitrates, copper) and, increasingly through the later nineteenth century, by means of extensive investment, both direct (mines, railways, public utilities) and indirect (government debt). The British did not come to convert (the British missionary effort went elsewhere), and they did not garner much by way of glory. Britain's wars in Latin America were small sideshows, and some (like the brief occupations of Buenos Aires and Montevideo in 1806–7) were distinctly inglorious.[18] If the archetypal Spanish imperialist was a conquistador or friar, his archetypal British counterpart was a banker, a railway engineer, or a weathered naval captain responsible for shipping bullion and occasionally showing the flag in sultry tropical ports.[19] Of course, as the globe shrank and, to put it crudely, sixteenth-century feudal/militaristic values gave way to nineteenth-century bourgeois commercial calculation, so "glory" became, for the purposes of my analysis, a preoccupation with the national interest and with the projection and maintenance of national power. Thus, as Macaulay famously remarked, colonies became pawns and battlegrounds in the great imperialist wars of the eighteenth and early nineteenth centuries.[20] But for Britain, enjoying a measure of naval mastery after Trafalgar, Latin America was not a crucial strategic region; no major rivals threatened British access to Latin American markets; and Britain was, for the time being, the "workshop of the world." Hence, as I said, the threefold motivation of the Spaniards now came down to a single overriding British concern: gold, that is to say, commercial profit. Furthermore, that profit, derived from trade with Latin America (especially the export of textiles), was a key item in Britain's global balance sheet.[21]

The United States, as I shall later discuss, became a major player in the circum-Caribbean toward the end of the nineteenth century and extended its power and influence to the south during and after the First World War (taking advantage of and, indeed, actively promoting Britain's relative decline). Like the British, the Americans came to Latin America looking for profit, so gold remained preeminent. But unlike the British, the United States regarded parts of Latin America as strategically key, notably Mexico, where American expansionism triumphed in 1848 and—to the relief of the United States—French expansionism dramatically failed twenty years later; Central America, the scene of American filibustering in the 1850s and armed interventions in the 1910s and 1920s; and the Caribbean, where Puerto Rico was annexed and Cuba, Haiti, and the Dominican Republic were intermittently occupied between 1898 and 1934. The completion of the Panama Canal in 1914 (following Roosevelt's connivance at Panamanian secession from Colombia in 1903) reinforced this strategic imperative.[22] Panama was to the United States what Suez was to Britain: a vital interest and therefore a recurrent stimulus to armed interventions and the creation of protectorates—the British in Africa, the Americans in the circum-Caribbean.[23]

Furthermore, given the more democratic and demotic character of American politics, "glory"—that is, the pursuit of national security and, in the 1840s and again in the 1890s, of national expansion—had a direct impact on domestic politics to a greater degree than in Victorian Britain.[24] Hence William Randolph Hearst's espousal of a forward policy in Cuba ("give me the pictures and I'll give you the war," as he supposedly told Frederic Remington) and Theodore Roosevelt's rapid rise from Rough Rider to Progressive president.[25] Finally, the United States also conceived of Latin America in missionary terms in a way that Britain never had. In part, this involved conventional (Protestant) missionary work, an admittedly slow and at times risky business in the Catholic South. But the American "mission" also embraced more secular ideological proselytization: initially, of common liberal-republican values in the face of threatening European monarchism and colonialism and later, of American "corporate culture," "a bold vision of a world remade in the image . . . of the United States."[26] Much more than Britain, therefore, the United States adopted a multipronged approach to Latin America: it certainly looked to make money, as Britain had, but it also perceived vital national security interests, and it entertained ambitious cultural goals, not only religious but also, more importantly, political and corporate.[27]

Given this repertoire of goals, how did the "imperial" powers set about achieving them in Latin America? Again, in very schematic, scene-setting terms, I would argue that these powers, like all imperial powers (Roman, Spanish, French, Russian), had to do two things if their "empires" were to grow and prosper: they had to keep out threatening rivals, and they had to mold the host or peripheral society to their needs. The first activity leads us into the realm of Great Power conflict; the second, on which I will focus more fully, involves the liaison between the Great Powers and their (formal or informal) dependencies. Since there has never been a single monopolistic world empire, all imperialist states have had to reckon with rivals.[28] However, different empires have dealt with different rivals in different ways. Spain sought to encase Spanish America in a mercantilist straitjacket so that the gains of trade, especially the bullion trade, would redound to Spain alone. Foreign imports were severely restricted, and in cultural terms, Spain maintained an intolerant Catholic monopoly. (Portugal adopted a rather more relaxed stance, in part out of weakness; hence, the story in Brazil was significantly different, and the transition to independence and commercial openness was rather smoother.)

Successful for generations, Spanish imperial control faltered in the late eighteenth century. Paradoxically but not unusually, it faltered precisely as the regime sought to impose tighter fiscal and administrative controls—the famous Bourbon Reforms. Domestic dissent combined with international war to weaken Spain's colonial grip. After 1800 foreign imports, chiefly British, surged into the colonies, initially in the form of contraband. By around 1820 Valparaiso was so chock-full of English goods and traders that it seemed like "a coast town in Britain." A few short years later, the religious images in the churches of Buenos Aires were clad in "coarse English cotton," while Lima and other Peruvian towns boasted English tables, chairs, crockery, earthenware, knives, forks, glassware, women's linen and cotton dresses, and men's coats and cloaks.[29] Foreign ideas, in particular, those of the Enlightenment, also penetrated Iberian America. And foreign (again, chiefly British) armed interventions chipped away the fine facade of the Spanish Empire: Havana fell, briefly, in 1767, Buenos Aires and Montevideo, also briefly, in 1805–6, and Sir Arthur Wellesley was nearly sent to "liberate" Mexico in 1807 (the Napoleonic invasion of Spain induced a providential change of plan).[30]

By the 1820s, the entire Spanish Empire in the Americas, bar Cuba and Puerto Rico, was independent, mercantilist control had collapsed, and a new, more open relationship with the world economy, particularly the British economy, began to take shape. I will discuss the crucial Latin American side of this relationship shortly. For the British, the old dream of cracking open Latin American markets was now realized. As is common with such dreams, they are easier to entertain than to realize. (Consider the great twentieth-century mirage of the China market, which has belatedly become the China industrial juggernaut, exporting rather than importing and using its huge surplus to accumulate assets around the world.)

In nineteenth-century Latin America, the benefits from trade, though substantial, were variable by time and place, and early British investments—direct investment, chiefly in mining, and portfolio investment in government bonds—proved disappointing.[31] In addition, as discussed below, Latin American societies threw up serious obstacles to successful commercial relations: chronic political instability, hostile interest groups such as domestic manufacturers and artisans, and popular xenophobia reinforced by religious prejudice. Even as these obstacles were reduced in the course of the nineteenth century, so Britain lost its global economic preeminence and began to face stiffer European and American competition in Latin America (Argentina and Uruguay being partial exceptions). But even as British trade declined relative to competitors, so British direct and indirect investment surged ahead. By 1914 Argentina figured alongside Canada, Australia, and South Africa as a recipient of British capital, and even little Uruguay had more British investment than all British West Africa put together.[32]

While Spain had sought to maintain its imperial position by means of mercantilist controls, Britain had no such pretensions; increasingly, Britain favored free trade both at home (hence the repeal of the Corn Laws in 1846) and abroad. In its relations with the infant Latin American states, Britain sought openings to trade, which were often codified in trade treaties, but no special advantage: in the jargon of the time, "a fair field and no favour."[33] Hence both Ferguson and Lal applaud the British Empire for being an engine of free trade and global integration. With respect to *late* nineteenth-century Latin America, they are partly right, but they are less right regarding the region pre-1850, as I shall note, and they are also less right about other parts of the world—the political economy of the "Company Raj" in India was no paragon of free trade.[34] Free trade was fine so long as Britain was the dominant industrial power, thanks to its decisive head start in the first industrial revolution, the revolution of steam, coal, textiles, and railways. Since Britain could beat its competitors on price, quality, and security of delivery, there was no need for special favors.[35] The British state played a key role in protecting commerce and, from time to time, enforcing respect for British lives and property. The Royal Navy was, therefore, a crucial, if very costly, asset.[36] But, increasingly, British trade with and investment in Latin America were driven by the market, and as the dominant player for much of the century, Britain was keen for free trade and open markets, just as the United States, the successor "hegemon," would be similarly keen during the post-1945 economic boom.[37]

Market dominance of a country, a company, a commodity is never permanent, of course, and by 1900 Britain was being fast overtaken in terms of industrial production and exports—though not, as yet, overseas investment—by both the United States and European competitors, chiefly Germany. Hence, as I mentioned, the so-called (and misnamed) scramble for Latin America heightened competition for Latin American markets, leading to a relative decline in Britain's position. There was not a lot Britain could do about this. In the formal empire, where Britain not only traded and invested but also ruled (above all, in India), a form of neomercantilism could be attempted under the guise of "imperial preference."[38] The 1933 Roca-Runciman agreement between Britain and Argentina was a diluted form of such neomercantilism that was typical of the depression years (we could compare the U.S.-Cuban Reciprocity Treaty of 1934) and illustrative of the Anglo-Argentine special relationship.[39] But elsewhere in Latin America the result was a rapid relative decline of British trade, investment, and influence, usually to the advantage of the United States. During the two world wars the U.S. government clearly set out to accelerate this process, displacing Britain's commercial position: first, after 1914, in Mexico and northern South America, and finally, post-1939, in the last redoubt of British power in the Southern Cone.[40]

However, the chief driver was not government policy but rather U.S. economic power, now premised on the second industrial revolution (that of steel, chemicals, electricity, machine tools, oil, and mass-produced consumer goods, in all of which the United States had a huge comparative advantage over Britain). British governments, being aware of the problem, took a few feeble steps to counter British decline: the Roca-Runciman pact (following glitzy visits of the Prince of Wales to Buenos Aires in 1925 and 1931) was one such step.[41] Britain could also try to parlay its creditor power into commercial benefits in both Argentina and Brazil. But to little avail. Two costly world wars massively drained British resources, and as a highly informal "empire" (if, indeed, it was an "empire" at all), Latin America could not be constrained by dwindling British power. The lure of American goods, technology, markets, and money proved irresistible.[42]

Furthermore, as already mentioned, Latin America was not strategically crucial for Britain. The British Empire—the formal geopolitical empire—hinged on India, the route to India, and the way stations that maintained that route: Gibraltar, Suez, the Cape of Good Hope, and beyond to Singapore.[43] The Falklands may have been the scene of a significant First World War naval battle, and twenty-five years later the German pocket battleship *Graf Spee* may have been cornered and scuttled in the estuary of the River Plate.[44] But by and large, Latin America was not geopolitically crucial, so Britain—now, in Joseph Chamberlain's phrase, an overburdened and "weary Titan"—had no desire to take on fresh political or military responsibilities across the Atlantic. Increasingly, therefore, Britain deferred to American hegemony in the Americas: with respect to the Venezuelan border question (1895), the (potential) Panama Canal (1900), and the Mexican Revolution (1910).[45]

Since the geopolitical imperative was weak and the economic challenge was insurmountable, Britain had to resign itself to a progressive loss of markets and influence in Latin America. The chief beneficiary was the United States. (Germany, also a major rival, was even more seriously knocked back than Britain by the two world wars.) The twentieth century was, in Henry Luce's famous phrase, the "American century," and perhaps nowhere more than in Latin America.[46] Following my suggestion that imperial powers look to shut out rivals while molding their dependencies, how did the American experience in Latin America compare with the British with regard to the first? (I shall turn to processes on the ground in Latin America in conclusion.) Just as American goals in the Americas were more diverse than British goals, so, too, American fears of rivals were more acute. But the rivalry—and the fears—were geopolitical more than economic. Thanks to the two world wars, coupled with its own economic size and dynamism, the United States came to dominate the external economic relations of the Americas.[47] Though competition continued and sharp elbows could be used, this was generally a fairly low-key game in which the Americans had conspicuous advantages.

A greater threat was posed by geopolitical rivals, especially when they seemed to find ready allies within the Latin American countries. American sensitivity to such threats had been made clear as early as 1821 with the

Monroe Doctrine, which sought to fend off European monarchism and (formal) empire-building in the Americas. But for decades the Monroe Doctrine was enforceable (or, we could say, was enforced chiefly by the Royal Navy); hence, the United States did nothing to prevent the British acquisition of the Falklands, the creeping expansion of British Honduras in the 1830s, or the French invasions of Mexico in 1838 and 1861–67. (True, in the 1860s the United States was embroiled in its own domestic difficulties.)[48] Similarly, American territorial designs on Nicaragua or Cuba remained no more than designs espoused by a jingo minority. The United States was not yet seen as a formally imperialist power. Like Russia, its territorial expansion was continental, not maritime; it built a land empire (at the expense of Mexico, it is true) and, throughout the nineteenth century, eschewed overseas acquisitions. Here, ideology, sectional interests, and military constraints all played a part.

By the 1890s, however, the United States had acquired greater muscle, including naval muscle, and its efforts to extend and enforce the Monroe Doctrine had become more ambitious and even strident.[49] Historically, the British had been seen as serious rivals in the Americas. But, as I mentioned, the British had perforce become more deferential toward the United States: in Central America, in Venezuela, and in Mexico at the time of the revolution when the desire of maverick British minister Sir Lionel Carden to stand up to the Americans was frustrated by Whitehall's insistence that good Anglo-American relations were paramount. By now, the United States perceived a greater threat in an expansionist imperial Germany, while in the Pacific, there were premonitory symptoms of the U.S.-Japanese rivalry that would culminate in Pearl Harbor, Midway, and Hiroshima.[50] Especially once the Panama Canal was under construction, the United States became acutely sensitive to perceived threats in the circum-Caribbean (in "its own backyard").

The critical invasion of Cuba in 1898 obeyed several motives, but it was not fundamentally an economic undertaking: it sought to accelerate the withdrawal of Spain from its last imperial redoubt in the Americas, to prevent any renewed European intervention in the island, and, as I shall note in conclusion, to ensure that the new Cuban regime was broadly favorable to U.S. interests.[51] Domestic political concerns, inflamed by the yellow press, also played a part. Similar geopolitical motives propelled the United States into Nicaragua in 1912, Haiti in 1915, and the Dominican Republic in 1916.[52] Compared to Cuba, U.S. trade with and investment in these small, underdeveloped countries was relatively insignificant. By intervening, the United States sought to promote its national security and geopolitical power, and U.S. decision-makers, operating in a demotic political system, sought to enhance their popularity and further their careers.[53]

And, while the Cold War—in its quintessential, post-1945 form—lies beyond the scope of this essay, it is clear that similar reflexes governed U.S. perceptions of the Soviet threat. Indeed, as early as the 1920s the United States saw Bolshevism stalking its southern border, infecting Mexico and spilling over into Nicaragua (where the marines unsuccessfully combated Augusto Sandino) and Cuba (where Sumner Welles played his proconsular role in 1933, ensuring that the revolution against Gerardo Machado would result in a congenial regime run by Fulgencio Batista rather than a worryingly radical one under Ramón Grau San Martín).[54] Thus, while the rise of the Soviet Union to superpower status upped the stakes, the classic confrontations of the Cold War in the Americas—the CIA's intervention in Guatemala in 1954, the Cuban missile crisis, the invasion of the Dominican Republic in 1965—all reflected a traditionally hypersensitive U.S. concern for national security in the circum-Caribbean (a region, of course, of small, vulnerable countries), a concern that dated back decades but that was further exacerbated by the bipolar ideological confrontation of post-1945.[55]

Thus, just as Britain was drawn into imperial intervention for fear of losing Suez (in 1882, 1896, and, the last, worst example, in 1956), so the United States felt obliged to counter external threats by adopting an aggressive policy in the circum-Caribbean. In Latin America more broadly, of course, similar concerns, heightened by the Cold War, were evident. But the geopolitical stakes were rather lower: a Soviet presence in, for example, landlocked Bolivia was not the same as one in Cuba or Guatemala, so the United States adopted a more subtle, conciliatory, and successful policy toward the Bolivian Revolution of 1952.[56] Furthermore,

Argentina or Brazil (or, indeed, Mexico) could hardly be invaded like the Dominican Republic. In those bigger, often more remote countries, the United States had to rely on informal, less coercive methods to promote its national interests. Invading Brazil was out of the question, but cozying up to the Brazilian military was entirely feasible and desirable.[57]

Having reviewed Great Power—"imperialist"—motivations, I now turn to a yet more crucial set of considerations: the reality on the ground in Latin America. Imperialist expansion, though often haphazard and piecemeal, typically followed a kind of cost-benefit logic, perhaps especially in the case of the British. The latter did not desire expansion for its own sake. They had definite priorities, and where possible, they usually favored informal empire (which was relatively cheap) over formal empire (which was costly in terms of both blood and treasure).[58] In simple terms, how many resources should be devoted to a particular "imperialist" interest? Calibration involved both cost and benefit. The defense of the Raj was paramount and elicited huge efforts, but some assets were expendable. Later U.S. policy displayed similar priorities: the Bolivian Revolution was less crucial than the Mexican or the Cuban; it was one thing to invade the Dominican Republic (or Grenada or Panama), but an invasion of Brazil (or even Venezuela today) was quite another matter.

Regarding the costs of intervention, a key consideration is the disposition of the "intervened" people. Can intervention work, militarily and politically, thus securing the benefits—in terms of security, profit, or conversion—that are expected by the intervening imperialist power? Of course, calculations often go wrong. Woodrow Wilson thought the Mexicans would welcome the U.S. Marines as liberators when they took Veracruz in April 1914, but they didn't.[59] (More egregious recent examples spring to mind, such as Iraq.) The British entertained similar delusions when they seized Buenos Aires in 1806. Thereafter, Lord Castlereagh resolved, Britain should avoid such risky interventions. However, in 1843–45, Lord Aberdeen, sending the navy to protect Montevideo, to blockade Buenos Aires, and to force open a passage upriver to Paraguay, overlooked that resolution and came to regret it.[60]

More often than not, European and American armed interventions in Latin America have proven costly failures. The biggest exception was the Mexican-American War of 1846–48, a very successful landgrab by an aggressive territorial (not yet maritime) empire that was followed by swift withdrawal and the absorption of the spoils into the American body politic. But the British failed in the River Plate (twice), and the French intervention in Mexico in the 1860s, designed not to grab contiguous territory but to set up a congenial client regime, was a massive and expensive failure. Lesser armed interventions—blockades, bombardments, brief seizures of ports—had mixed fortunes, but often they were ill-conceived decisions that proved counterproductive. FDR's Good Neighbor Policy, which President Hoover had tentatively anticipated, was a recognition that thirty years of sustained interventions in Central America and the Caribbean had proved more trouble than they were worth.[61] So the American forces withdrew, and the U.S. government made a formal commitment to (military) nonintervention. That commitment lasted for some twenty years, that is, until the post-1945 Cold War prompted renewed interventions in Guatemala, Cuba, the Dominican Republic, and Nicaragua. However, the Americans kept an insurance policy in their back pocket: they worked with (in some cases, proactively installed) collaborative regimes, typically of authoritarian makeup: Batista in Cuba, Rafael Trujillo in the Dominican Republic, the Somozas in Nicaragua. A key item in this new liaison (at least in Nicaragua and the Dominican Republic) was the National Guard, which was initially set up under American auspices and which provided the basis for enduring (pro-American) authoritarian regimes. As Lars Schoultz sums up the process, it was a question of "removing the Marines and installing the puppets."[62]

Discreet and pacific informal imperialism based on a measure of consent and collaboration—what Geir Lundestad has called, in the very different European context, "empire by invitation"—has usually been more durable and successful.[63] This has been the case because the Latin American nation-states, for all their alleged imperfections—their instability, internal factionalism, ethnic and class diversity—are relatively old nations, older than most in the world; they have strong nationalist traditions; and they have proven the strength of these traditions by resisting not only imperialist invasions but also those of their Latin American neighbors (e.g., the War of the Triple Alliance [1864–70] and the War of the Pacific [1879–84]). Twice victims of an incipient nationalism in Buenos Aires, the British thereafter avoided land invasions, while after 1898 the United States limited its armed interventions to Mexico and—more consequentially—the small nations of the circum-Caribbean. (And even there the costs outweighed the supposed geostrategic benefits, hence, as I have said, the birth of the Good Neighbor Policy in 1933.) Furthermore, during this period the Latin American states strengthened their military resources (I shall give examples shortly): they became tougher nuts to crack. We can compare this fairly successful nation-building process with the progressive dissolution of traditional regimes in China or the Ottoman Empire, which made them vulnerable to imperialist aggression, or with the inability of stateless peoples in sub-Saharan Africa to resist European penetration—politically, militarily, and technologically.[64]

Thus, having thrown off one set of imperial masters—the Spaniards and Portuguese—Latin Americans were not ready to submit to renewed imperial control. (Indeed, with the possible exception of eastern Europe, modern history offers few or no examples of genuinely postcolonial states that have succumbed to a new formal colonialism: one bout of empire, perhaps followed by a successful "national liberation struggle," seems to inoculate the body politic against a second bout.) Of course, Cuba exchanged Spanish formal empire for American protectorate status in 1898, but the latter did not last, in part because Cuban nationalism—in recent decades one of the principal props of the Castro regime—would not allow it.[65] And throughout Latin America, nationalist and sometimes xenophobic sentiments have checked what was seen as unwarranted foreign interference, first by the British and later, more systematically, by the Americans. The recent crop of nationalist and sometimes anti-American leaders in Latin America—Castro, Chávez, Morales, the Kirchners—stand in an old tradition, which traces back to Martí, Sandino, Carranza, Calles, and Perón. These all stand on the left of the political spectrum, but Latin America also boasts a long history of Catholic conservative hostility to Protestant outsiders.

By raising a substantial barrier to imperialist intervention, Latin

American nationalism imposed a potentially heavy cost on such intervention. This cost had to be offset against the potential benefits. I now turn, in slightly greater detail, to the question of Latin American political economy and "elite collaboration." As Adam Smith argued (even if many of his more dogmatic latter-day disciples appear to have forgotten), markets do not operate in a vacuum; the "propensity to truck, barter and exchange" can only be fully realized in the right circumstances, where there is a measure of order, suitable legal codes, protection of property, a currency, adequate communications, demand for goods and services, and, finally, sources of capital, raw materials, energy, and labor that can meet that demand.[66] Firms and individuals can supply some of these desiderata through market mechanisms, but as the "new institutional economics" persuasively argues, there is no case of a well-developed market economy flourishing in a state of anarchy, that is to say, in the absence of a state that can provide the necessary "public goods."[67] Of course, a bloated, rapacious, rent-seeking state can also choke off the market; the ideal, for a functioning market society, is a balance between Anarchy and Leviathan.

Achieving the balance can be a long and arduous process.[68] Even in England, the cradle of market capitalism, it took centuries.[69] In Latin America, three centuries of Iberian rule had laid down vital foundations (which were not to be found in some other parts of the world, e.g., in sub-Saharan Africa). Spain and, mutatis mutandis, Portugal conquered and created colonies out of a congeries of Native American societies that ranged from the hierarchical, densely populated, partially urban empires of the Aztecs and Incas, through intermediate city-states and chiefdoms, to stateless peoples who lived as egalitarian farmers or hunter-gatherers. Over three hundred years, Spain created a durable colonial state and church; introduced a (largely silver) currency; imposed head and trade taxes; established property rights (at least for the large private sector of haciendas, ranchos, and estancias, while village property often remained corporate, i.e., communally owned); introduced law courts, which were regularly used by both Indians and Spaniards; demarcated administrative units, which would eventually become, more or less, the nations and provinces of the nineteenth century; made Spanish the language of church and state; and experimented with different forms of labor recruitment, some, but not all, coercive (slavery, encomienda, repartimiento, peonage). Thus, the Spanish colonial state advanced a long way from Anarchy toward Leviathan, even if it remained a somewhat creaking, corrupt, and ponderous Leviathan. The Bourbon Reforms of the late eighteenth century were in part an effort to rejuvenate the beast, following the example of Spain's more efficient and powerful European rivals, France and England. But, as already mentioned, the reforms were riddled with contradictions and provoked widespread opposition, which contributed to the independence movements of the 1810s.

Thus, when the Spanish Empire finally collapsed and the infant nation-states were opened up to foreign trade and investment, the latter encountered fairly favorable circumstances. In particular, there existed functioning, if somewhat unstable, states that were keen for foreign loans and foreign trade. (We could contrast the reclusive Chinese Empire, whose emperor famously told Sir George Macartney that "we possess all things . . . and have no use for your country's manufactures.")[70] Latin American consumers, especially urban consumers, were familiar with a cash economy and eager for European goods.[71] Hence the British clothes, fashions, and household items that, by the 1820s, could be seen in Valparaiso and dozens of other Latin American cities. Hence, too, the high hopes of the bountiful Latin American market entertained by British merchants, investors, and boosters, such as Benjamin Disraeli, who honed his fictional talents writing prospectuses for Latin American mining ventures.[72]

However, a range of obstacles remained. Some were inherent in what were still relatively backward economies: despite notable exceptions, Latin America lacked buoyant exports; the old staple of silver had suffered from the destructive wars of independence; and, without exports, there was no foreign exchange with which to purchase foreign imports or to service the early foreign loans (which rapidly defaulted).[73] Communications remained primitive; overland travel was prohibitively expensive; and, compared to the United States, Latin America lacked river and canal transportation. The 130 miles between Mexico City and Veracruz, Mexico's main port, took seven days by mule train or five by jolting stagecoach; the 580 miles between Buenos Aires and Mendoza took fifty days by oxcart; thus, given the relative costs of land versus sea transport, it was thirteen times more expensive to shift a ton of freight from Salta to Buenos Aires than from Buenos Aires to Liverpool.[74] Railways were still some way off: the key decades for railway "takeoff" were the 1860s for Argentina, the 1880s for Mexico (well behind western Europe and the United States but ahead of China and Africa). Ecuador, something of a socioeconomic laggard, did not acquire a rail link between the two principal cities of the republic, Quito and Guayaquil, until 1908. To begin with, therefore, the British were trying to make money in highly imperfect, sluggish, often shallow markets. Well into the nineteenth century, foreign travelers were struck by the lack of imported goods and the poverty of material life in provincial Latin America (i.e., away from the major cities and ports, where the middle class clustered). In Colombia in the 1850s, for example, the well-to-do of Bogotá had glass sash-windows, but glass was "unknown . . . in all other places" in the country; clocks, too, were "rather uncommon." Imported soap was expensive, and furniture was usually simple artisanal stuff, "as elegant as might be expected from the hand of a carpenter in a land where the lathe is unknown."[75]

In addition to these infrastructural blockages to foreign trade and investment, Latin America also displayed sociopolitical obstacles. Key sectors of the population, such as domestic merchants and artisans, resented cheap foreign imports and advocated protection, which some political leaders were disposed to provide. Dr. Francia ran Paraguay as a closed economy for some thirty years after independence, a mini-China in the heart of South America.[76] Political instability and interstate warfare—perhaps the inevitable consequences of violent decolonization in Latin America as elsewhere—prejudiced trade and investment while prompting arbitrary taxation, sequestration, and destruction of property.[77] Governments, such as the Mexican, faced chronic bankruptcy, which embroiled them with aggressive foreign governments, aggrieved bondholders, and victims seeking redress.[78] In addition, foreigners incurred cultural hostility. The Catholic Church was leery of foreign, especially Protestant, inroads into its hitherto monopolistic domain.[79] Popular prejudice ran deep, occasionally breaking out into violence: after all, Protestants were subversive heretics who, as their style in the saddle made clear, concealed tails inside their trousers.[80] Hence, the Protestant missionary effort made scant headway until the later twentieth century. Again, therefore, the British found themselves swimming upstream.

Taken together, these material, political, and cultural obstacles inhibited British commercial penetration. There were pockets of success, such as the relatively stable Brazilian Empire, which counted on sugar and coffee exports, or Portalian Chile, which produced grain, copper, and, later, nitrates. But during the first generation after independence (roughly 1820–60), the scale of British trade and investment did not match early expectations.[81] Latin America was partially capitalist, thanks largely to the prior spadework of the Spanish Empire, but there was more spadework to be done by way of converting either "natural economies" or, more commonly, economies that were poorly integrated and monetized into functioning markets profitable to British merchants and investors.

Frustrated, some British policy-makers flirted with force: in 1843 a fleet was dispatched to the River Plate to coerce the recalcitrant dictator of Argentina, Rosas.[82] In Peru, Central America, and even Brazil (where the slave trade was a bone of contention), British diplomats lobbied, arm-twisted, and threatened reprisals.[83] Off the coast of western Mexico, naval vessels protected British merchants (even when they were shipping contraband silver), and in the 1860s Britain joined France and Spain in the coercion of a bankrupt Mexico.[84] Back in Whitehall, Latin American experts toyed with the idea of striking alliances with unstable states or seizing key points such as the Falkland Islands (which were, of course, seized) or San Francisco, California, then a remote outpost of a shaky Mexican nation-state that soon fell into American rather than British hands.[85]

Thus, the early (pre-1850) British liaison with Latin America was far from peaceful or purely mediated through the market. Britain behaved like an ancien régime state. Indeed, as C. A. Bayly reminds us, victory over Napoleon served to "give the old regime a new lease of life."[86] Governed by the likes of Wellington (architect of that victory), Britain remained stoutly monarchical, ruled by an unreformed parliament and steeped in

Anglican deference. Meanwhile, abroad, Britain readily resorted to force in order to open up markets and protect far-flung commercial interests.[87] Of course, the Latin American interventions were not on the scale of the contemporary Opium Wars: China had to be forcibly broken open, while, thanks to three centuries of Iberian imperialism, Latin America was already half-open, and the task of the British was to prize the door farther ajar and ensure that, once inside, the British were adequately protected. As Palmerston put it in his bullish way, Latin American governments, being a feckless lot, needed a "dressing down ever eight or ten years to keep them in order."[88] We should note: a "dressing down," a short, sharp lesson, not outright invasion or annexation. Even limited armed intervention such as the blockade of the River Plate in 1843 proved costly and counterproductive, while aggressive diplomacy and lobbying (e.g., in Peru) had scant success.[89]

This combination of commercial penetration backed by recurrent threats and coercion seems to me sufficient to justify the use of the "informal imperialist" label, as Gallagher and Robinson proposed; though, as their chief critic, D. C. M. Platt, pointed out, the success of this policy, both commercially and politically, was much less than they imagined.[90] British commerce did not swamp the infant Latin American republics; it seeped in gradually and partially, slowly transforming more stable and receptive political economies but facing frustration in others. Brazil and the Southern Cone proved more welcoming than Mexico, Central America, and Andean America, and with the key exception of imported textiles, which penetrated the length and breadth of the continent, the cities—still, by modern standards, very small—took the bulk of foreign imports, leaving the vast rural hinterland to work, travel, and eat (but not to dress) as they had for generations.[91]

However, during the later nineteenth century—at different times and speeds in different countries—Latin America underwent a socioeconomic transformation, the so-called Second Conquest.[92] The vicious circle of unstable governments, defaults, wars, arbitrary exactions, coercive interventions, poor communications, scant exports, and low demand gave way to a virtuous circle: governments became solvent and more stable; property rights were extended and better protected; foreign investment, stimulated by state incentives, built the major railway systems, along with ports and telegraph networks; exports increased in response both to external demand (rising population and consumption in an industrializing Europe) and to internal supply-side factors (improved transport and the better protection of property rights, already mentioned); the enforcement of social order; and enhanced systems of labor recruitment and control. In other words, Latin American societies—chiefly, their ruling elites—put their house in order in accordance with the criteria of global and especially British capitalism.

The elites did so because it was in their own perceived interests. They may have constituted what Gallagher and Robinson called "collaborating elites," but that did not make them callow traitors or evil Quislings.[93] Many probably believed they were benefiting their countries (we should never underestimate politicians' ability to conflate personal, party, and national interest), and they certainly benefited from their liaison with British capital, whether individually—often corruptly—or collectively—and legally. Thanks to foreign trade, investment, and credit, elites could forge more stable states endowed with greater power. Another rule of thumb: never underestimate incumbent politicians' desire to centralize and accumulate power, irrespective of the ideology they may have espoused before they took office. As I argue in chapter 2, Latin American liberals *in power* proved much more authoritarian and centralizing than liberals *out of power*. From the British point of view, therefore, the need to coerce—or to try to coerce—Latin American governments to behave correctly was much reduced. Governments and elites had internalized the norms of market, though not necessarily "gentlemanly," capitalism, norms that served as a kind of political superego, mandating protection of property, respect for contracts, the repayment of debts. Conscience, we could say, had replaced coercion. As a result, the British could, by and large, call off the gunboats. Palmerstonian "dressings down" had become superfluous.

Thus, by the late nineteenth century, Argentina was a congenial and profitable collaborator with British interests, and the days of the British invasions and blockades were long gone. A mutually beneficial economic relationship—beneficial, at least, to powerful vested interests on both sides of the Atlantic—obviated the use or even the threat of force.[94] When in 1890 the Argentine bubble burst and Barings Bank, being heavily exposed, faced collapse, Prime Minister Salisbury could take a lofty, noninterventionist stance, since he was confident that his Argentine counterpart, President Carlos Pelligrini, would strive manfully to ride out the crisis without jeopardizing the key Anglo-Argentine relationship. As, indeed, he did.[95]

Some might reasonably ask whether the relative absence of force in this intimate Anglo-Argentine relationship meant that it was in no sense "imperialist."[96] Of course, it depends on one's definition of "imperialism" and whether the use of force is a diagnostic requirement. But two points are relevant: first, the balance of power between the two parties (irrespective of the actual use of force), and second, perhaps more important, the displacement of coercion from the international to the domestic context. The Anglo-Argentine relationship remained highly unequal: the Baring crisis shook Buenos Aires much more than it shook London (which is why Lord Salisbury could feel relatively relaxed), and Argentina needed British trade and (above all) investment more than Britain needed Argentine goods, markets, and investment opportunities.[97]

Argentina is an exemplary case. However, other Latin American countries, including other large countries, also wrestled with a comparable nonreciprocal economic "dependency" that could have a deep impact on their societies. Thus, as the guano boom petered out, Peru defaulted on its foreign debt (1876), lost the costly War of the Pacific to Chile (1879–83), and agreed to the controversial Grace Contract (1890), which gave the foreign-controlled Peruvian Corporation management of the country's railways and guano income.[98] However, like the Baring crisis, the Peruvian settlement was negotiated (with the Peruvians playing a weak hand); it was not imposed by foreign warships steaming into Callao harbor.[99] Some would go further and see the tentacles of dependency snaking deep into Latin American society. Thus, it has been argued that the serious urban riots that affected belle époque Rio de Janeiro in 1893, 1904, and 1916 were caused not just by specific grievances, such as tax increases and compulsory vaccination, but also by a more general socioeconomic malaise: "Different from the crowds of Europe or the United States . . . [the Rio rioters] came up against companies owned by foreign monopolists, taxes imposed to pay for loans from British banks, and urban renewal projects designed to make Rio look more like London and Paris. Thus, Brazil's dependence . . . had a profound effect on the particular function of the capital city and on the nature of social protest."[100]

Furthermore, the absence of outright coercion did not mean that the ultima ratio of force had entirely disappeared from the scene. Force majeure might have receded, but historical memories and lessons could not be entirely erased.[101] After all, Argentina had never sent a fleet up the Thames estuary to blockade London. And elsewhere in Latin America, a few "rogue states"—like the Venezuela of Cipriano Castro—that failed to follow the Argentine path to congenial collaboration suffered coercive retribution well into the twentieth century (hence the Anglo-German naval blockade of Venezuela in 1902–3).[102] If many Latin America states had now acquired a respectable ruling superego, the old irresponsible id still lurked in some parts of the continent, and when it raised its ugly head, it risked reprisals.

The integration of Latin America—Argentina in particular—into a global economy dominated by Britain was, of course, a question of action more than attitude. Collaborating elites, be they civilian parliamentarians, landed oligarchs, or gold-braided generals, had to ensure that their societies were attractive sites for foreign trade and investment. To put it more schematically, they had to turn closed, backward, sometimes "natural" economies into more open, expanding, market economies; they had to convert suspicious peasants, Indians, and city artisans into factory, mine, plantation, and port workers; and they had to provide foreigners with basic protection and facilities, including, for example, their own chapels and cemeteries, even when these appeared to contravene the legal monopoly of the Catholic Church.[103] Thereby, these elites benefited themselves and some of their citizens, and they removed a primary cause of foreign intervention and possible foreign takeover. Crudely put, functioning *informal* empire made *formal* empire unnecessary and mutually undesirable. The transition—essentially a peripheral or "excentric" story—required action by Latin American elites (and some Latin American "subalterns" too), and it involved a good deal of violence. But the violence was the work of Latin Americans on fellow Latin Americans; the "imperialist" foreigners looked on, often applauding, occasionally censuring, but ultimately benefiting.[104]

The relevant policies were many, complicated, and variable from country to country. Argentina was not like Guatemala. But some common elements were apparent; furthermore, they were apparent not only in Latin America but also in many European colonies where comparable state-building and developmental policies were being attempted. The difference, of course, was that in the formal European colonies these policies were the work of colonial rulers, whereas in Latin America the initiative came from "indigenous" elites. Such policies could, at a pinch, be called instruments of "internal colonialism." That is to say, wittingly or not, they reproduced, in the context of independent states, goals, policies, and rationalizations evident in the European colonial orbit.[105] By way of conclusion, I shall briefly identify six such policies.

First, governments had to establish financial stability, honor debts, and establish credit. One standard instrument to bring this about was the adoption of the gold standard, the lynchpin of Britain's global commercial system. Historically, Latin American economies had relied on silver and paper currency, and throughout the nineteenth century they experienced recurrent monetary vicissitudes.[106] Toward the end of the century, as silver fast depreciated, as servicing foreign debts became more onerous, and as the need to attract and retain foreign investment became more compelling, Latin America shifted, piecemeal, to the gold standard (or, in some cases, to hybrid bimetallic or "gold exchange" standards). The solutions were various, but the problem was a common one: how to better manage Latin America's increasingly close integration into global markets, at least in the eyes of official policy-makers. In adopting the gold standard, Latin America followed in the footsteps not only of Britain, much of Europe, and the United States but also of British dependencies, notably India, Egypt, and the Straits Settlements (where the underlying rationale was similar). Key American policy-makers, while keen to outcompete the British, agreed on the benefits—indeed, the almost mystical virtues—of the gold standard and duly set about exporting it to the United States' newly acquired dependencies: Puerto Rico, the Philippines, and, with less success, Cuba.[107] American experts such as Jeremiah Jenks built careers by advising foreign governments on how to switch to the gold (or "gold exchange") standard. Jenks duly played a role in both Nicaragua and Mexico.

Indeed, Mexico, under the authoritarian rule of Porfirio Díaz (1876–1911), was an apt pupil. During the last quarter of the nineteenth century, the country emerged from chronic bankruptcy and became a model debtor. In 1906 Mexico, though a major silver producer, followed several Latin American countries in converting to the gold standard, a move designed to bolster financial stability, facilitate servicing of the foreign debt, and reassure foreign creditors (which it did).[108] At the same time, the decision represented a clear victory for the Científicos, a clique of cosmopolitan businessmen, bankers, and policy-makers unofficially led by finance minister José Yves Limantour, and it riled both their political enemies (such as presidential aspirant General Bernardo Reyes) and the beneficiaries of peso depreciation, including Mexico's silver miners. Apart from thus aggravating divisions within the Porfirian elite, the currency reform also constrained export earnings and led to credit restrictions. Coupled with other conjunctural factors (bad harvests and the 1907 recession), the currency reform arguably contributed to the growing discontent that presaged the Mexican Revolution of 1910.[109]

Second, monetary reform in Latin America rode on the back of material advance. Advance—growing investment and production, especially for export—made monetary reform both possible and, given the key role of foreign direct investment, desirable. While the Latin American regimes of the day often lauded free trade and even called themselves "liberal" (a label historians have readily, if misleadingly, adopted), they were happy to use state resources to build infrastructure, especially railways. Although foreign capital—and, of course, foreign technology—were essential for the creation of Latin America's railway systems, the state (as well as domestic private capital) played a key role, especially in the initial phase (ca. 1850–75). The early railways were often state-owned, or they depended on crucial state incentives: direct subsidies, guaranteed returns, and easy access to land and labor. Once this initial spadework was done and as the Latin American economies rapidly expanded, foreign capital, both European and American, poured in, especially during the 1880s.[110] The state also pumped money into ports (such as Veracruz, Buenos Aires, and Callao) and telegraph systems, the latter essential both to stimulate international trade and to enhance internal state power.[111] The logic, both political and economic, was much the same in these countries as it was in British India.[112]

Third, governments improved their armies and police forces. This was partly a question of importing new technology: crucially, the breech-loading rifle, which fired faster and more accurately than the old smoothbore muskets of the Napoleonic era; mobile field artillery, suitable for long-range punitive expeditions; and, by the 1900s, the Maxim and Gatling guns, which had recently speeded the advance of European imperialism in Africa.[113] Now the same military technology could serve Latin American states as they embarked on campaigns of frontier conquest against the Yaquis and Maya in Mexico, Chile's Mapuche people, and the Indians of the Argentine pampas.[114] Superior technology, including field artillery, troop trains, and, by the 1900s, machine guns, also enabled states to snuff out popular rebellions: at Tomóchic in northern Mexico; Canudos in north-eastern Brazil and the Contestado in the south; Chayanta in southern Bolivia.[115] Gunboats and pontoons were used by the Porfirian military to cut off and subdue the Maya rebels of the Yucatán peninsula, thus ending over fifty years of dogged resistance.[116] Dissident elites, too, now thought twice about confronting states that possessed better communications and greater firepower.

As armies grew more professional, often under the guidance of French or German military advisors, so the old, informal, caudillo-led militias of the past declined, and a career officer corps came to dominate the military establishment.[117] Early photographs depict officers and men in distinctly colonial guise, the officers generally paler, with moustaches and European-style helmets (including the Prussian pickelhaube), and the rank-and-file darker, often smaller, resembling some colonial native levy (and there is "hard" evidence to confirm this visual impression).[118] Where the French military influence was pronounced (e.g., in Peru), the key figures were often "colonials" such as Joseph Gallieni and Hubert Lyautey, vocal advocates as well as hardened practitioners of French imperialism.[119] Coercive power was thereby centralized—it gravitated from the provinces to the central government—and it could serve the "developmental" project of that government: positively, by engaging in public works (such as surveying, roadbuilding, and stringing telegraph cables); negatively, and more importantly, by crushing dissent.[120] This buildup of centralized military power, of course, gave the army both greater political leverage and a greater sense of its own importance, to the potential detriment of civilian rule.[121] Police forces such as the famous Mexican rurales also underwent centralization as the tentacles of social control snaked out from the cities into what had previously been a vast undergoverned and underpoliced rural hinterland.[122] The victims of this enhancement of central state power were not only bandits, insurgents, and frontier Indians; the footloose cowboys of the plains, in particular, the gauchos of the Argentine pampas, now also faced greater control, discipline, and exclusion.[123] By the later nineteenth century, the classic gaucho had become more a national stereotype and literary trope than a pillar of the basic pastoral economy.

Enhanced social control was necessary since, fourth, states were keen to enforce stricter private property rights. A series of "liberal" reforms—liberal in theory if not always in practice—swept Latin America as the corporate property of church and peasantry was privatized, supposedly by way of fostering a prosperous "propertied yeomanry" but frequently bolstering the assets of big landowners.[124] In addition, supposedly virgin public lands (*baldíos*) were carved up among private landowners, and in the vast frontier zones of northern Mexico and the Southern Cone (the Argentine Pampas, Chile south of the Bío-Bío), what had once been "desert" was "conquered" and parceled out as freehold, usually as big chunks, among favored elites.[125] The old Latin American hacienda was thus amplified and strengthened, making it better equipped to meet overseas demand for agricultural and pastoral products: Mexican henequen; Argentine beef and grain; Brazilian and Central American coffee; Peruvian sugar, cotton, and wool.[126] While it would be a misleading exaggeration to call nineteenth-century Latin American countries "white-settler societies," as Richard Gott has done (since "white" elites had lived in these lands for generations), there are evident parallels with the huge contemporary land grab undertaken by Europeans in sub-Saharan Africa.[127]

By way of contrast, we may note that some colonial regimes— "Dominion" governments in Canada and Australia and even, to a degree, British authorities in Ireland and West Africa—took steps to protect smallholders and to restrict the accumulation of land in large estates.[128] The motivation, of course, was less disinterested social justice than concern for social stability and stable governance. In Latin America, however, there was no formal colonial government to hold the ring in this fashion; instead, landed elites, who were usually political elites as well, could advance their interests in relative freedom. No "relatively autonomous" state blocked their path. Of course, land privatization and accumulation provoked resistance and protest, especially in regions such as Mexico and the Andean countries where a dense, often Indian peasantry sought to protect its patrimony. (Agrarian protest was much less evident in regions of recent migration, such as Argentina and southern Brazil, where peasants were few and European immigrants—real "white settlers," in this case—could enjoy a measure of social mobility without prejudicing the interests of the "native" population.)

Fifth, the story of land was inseparable from the story of labor in Latin America as in the colonies. Economic development demanded a larger, more disciplined, and reliable labor force, one that was inured to what E. P. Thompson called the "time and work discipline of industrial (and agrarian) capitalism" and did not disappear at harvest time or regularly observe San Lunes ("St. Monday," the traditional day off following a boozy weekend).[129] No one has emulated Thompson's masterpiece and written *The Making of the Latin American Working Class*, but such a process surely occurred, and even more than in England it occurred as a result of deliberate policy and often involved violence. The most obvious historical example was slavery, which still underpinned Cuban and Brazilian plantation production in the third quarter of the nineteenth century. Thereafter, slavery rapidly declined, a victim of the abolition of the slave trade and the harsh demographic logic of Latin American slave societies. The end of slavery did not, however, mark the end of coercive labor. While some labor could be secured by the mechanism of the free market—as in western Europe and the postbellum United States—and while land concentration by dispossessing peasants usefully swelled the surplus labor pool, this was not sufficient, and Latin American landlords regularly complained that production was crimped by labor shortages and inefficiencies (such as San Lunes, again).[130]

Thus, in order to supplement the growing pool of proletarian labor, the state intervened actively and often coercively in the labor market: it subsidized migrants from Europe and coolies from China; it built roads and railways with corvée labor in Ecuador, Peru, and Guatemala; it allowed or promoted forms of *enganche* (debt peonage) and *mandamiento* (compulsory labor drafts) in Peru, Ecuador, southern Mexico, and Guatemala; and it put deported prisoners to work in Yucatán and Cuba.[131] Draconian labor systems were most apparent where "liberal" states (in this context, a grotesque misnomer) sought to extract labor from recalcitrant Indian populations—populations who retained land, who were reluctant to undertake harsh and unhealthy work far from home, and who could be easily depicted as "lazy Indians" (another colonial stereotype) who would work only if compelled. "The Indian," as they said in Yucatán, "hears only through his butt" (*el indio no oye sino por las nalgas*).[132]

The most extreme form of labor coercion occurred in the Putumayo region of the upper Amazon basin, where Brazil borders Peru and Colombia and where, around the turn of the century, rubber companies established a horrific form of predatory exploitation that had all the hallmarks of the contemporary Congo of King Leopold. The rubber boom, which, like all booms, was followed by a bust, responded to burgeoning international demand linked to the automobile industry; it involved a rapacious exploitation of forest resources in a region where the state (Peruvian, Brazilian, or Colombian) conceded ample autonomy to freelance entrepreneurs; and it demanded the labor of indigenous people who, hitherto, had largely avoided contact with the cash economy and who, being "lazy natives," had to be coerced into hard labor.[133] A similar syndrome—a "mode of extraction" rather than a "mode of production"—was evident in southern Mexico, notably in the notorious *monterías* (logging camps) of Chiapas.[134]

These examples suggest a final parallel between the Latin American and the European-colonial experience. As Latin American elites set out to emulate the Europeans in the ways I have suggested, they naturally borrowed European ideas and attitudes. This was an old practice, of course (it explains why Latin America is Catholic, after all). In the early nineteenth century, liberalism—a genuine representative political liberalism—exercised broad appeal, as I discuss in chapter 2. By the later nineteenth century, however, though the name was often retained, liberalism had mutated into a kind of developmental positivism that, following Auguste Comte, placed less emphasis on so-called metaphysical political rights and much more on technology and material development.[135] The result was the "order and progress dictatorships" that populated Latin America in the period, especially in the Andean and Mesoamerican regions. They still called themselves "liberal," but they were happy to strong-arm their populations, especially their brown peasant populations, in the several ways mentioned. Positivism became a crucial legitimizing ideology, rather as "socialism" did in some postcolonial African states; it inspired the Mexican Científicos, and its slogan was emblazoned on the Brazilian flag. Positivism coexisted happily with Spencerian notions of social Darwinism, as well as with outright racism. It was, we might reasonably conclude, easier to browbeat "lazy Indians" if "science" demonstrated that they were inferior beings who benefited from browbeating. Indeed, labor coercion was an enlightened means to inculcate civilization.[136]

Similarly, fashionable norms of "progress" justified eliminating the footloose cowboys of the pampas. The "organic intellectuals" of developmental regimes—Domingo Sarmiento in Argentina, Justo Sierra in Mexico—thus recycled the ideas and slogans of both the United States and imperialist Europe.[137] Sarmiento's insistence on the need for "civilization" to overcome "barbarism" is well-known, but it is worth looking at the examples of "barbarism" that, writing in the 1840s, he recurrently invokes. Arabs, whom he had seen firsthand in North Africa, strongly resemble Argentines; pastoral societies, like that of the pampas, recall "the Asiatic plains," dotted with "Kalmuck, Cossack or Arab tents" whose inhabitants are "living a life essentially barbarous and unprogressive."[138] The violent atrocities of the Rosas regime were similar to those committed by "other barbarous and Tartaric chiefs"; Facundo, the exemplary Argentinian caudillo, resembles Attila and Tamerlane.[139] The pampas Indians are "American Bedouins"; "in Africa, at the present day, there exists the same struggle between civilization and barbarism" as in Argentina.[140] These several associations are summed up in Sarmiento's association of the color red—"the symbol of violence, blood, and barbarism"—with Facundo and Rosas and also, with respect to flags, with "Algiers, Tunis, Japan, Turkey, Siam, the Africans, [and] the savages."[141]

Sarmiento, of course, was no lone intellectual voice crying in a political wilderness: he served for six not very successful years as president of Argentina (1868–74), and his advocacy of "civilization"—but "civilization" attained by means of coercive and even "colonialist methods"—offered intellectual rationalization for the violence that was already endemic along the frontier. As Charles Darwin, an eyewitness, noted in 1833, Indian men, women, and children were indiscriminately massacred in Argentina, since "everyone here is fully convinced that this is the most just war, because it is against barbarians."[142] Furthermore, Sarmiento's advocacy only grew stronger with time. His last "major book," *Conflictos y armonías de las razas en América* (1883), reprises his admiration for the United States as a dynamic expansionist society, but blending racism and positivism, it also praises the advance of European imperialism in Africa, where "everyone feels that its [Africa's] hour of justice, dignity and redress has come."[143] Thirty years later (1915), as those same European imperialists were busy slaughtering each other, the prominent Argentine socialist José Ingenieros could still pen a florid eulogy of Sarmiento's worldview.[144]

Sarmiento's discourse was not the mindless parroting of irrelevant imported slogans: the slogans made sense because the regimes of the day were often enacting policies similar to those of colonial regimes—or, indeed, of the U.S. and tsarist Russian regimes, as they built their vast land empires westward and eastward, respectively. Yet this kind of "project," this transformation of the political economy, involving a rapid, often harsh incorporation of people and places into a dynamic expanding capitalist system, was not happening in this way everywhere, of course. It was not happening, for example, in Britain, Belgium, France, Germany, or Scandinavia, in all of which countries the process of capitalist accumulation and related state-building was much older; hence, the task was largely complete. There were few subsistence peasants, no Indians, no slaves, no peons, and not much of a frontier. The same was true of New England and, increasingly, much of the American Midwest. (The South, populated by slaves and, later, peons, is a different matter.) When Latin American elites looked for political models, it was France, the France of the Third Republic, that often topped the list, as Georges Clemenceau was glad to report.[145] Anglophilia was a common feature of prominent Brazilian politicians, intellectuals, and businessmen, while the United States—the dynamic, civilized, urban United States of Boston, New York, Philadelphia, and Cleveland—also exerted a strong appeal.[146] The attachment to the "liberal" label reflected this commitment to progressive sociopolitical values (as I discuss in chapter 2 of this book).

But when it came to the crucial question of socioeconomic development, which, the Positivists plausibly argued, was the top priority and the necessary prerequisite of liberal politics, the Latin American elites found their models and methods elsewhere. In Argentina and Uruguay there was, at least by the 1900s, a tolerable fit between socioeconomic project and political practice: an incipient liberal politics rode on the back of a genuinely liberal, free-market economy (though, of course, it had taken a good deal of time and conflict to get there, as it had in liberal-democratic Europe). But more usually in Latin America, the fit proved elusive. Hence the paradox at the heart of much late nineteenth-century Latin American liberalism: in order to espouse progress and development, thus to catch up with Europe and, at the same time, to obviate the risk of an imperialist scramble in the continent, governments had to adopt profoundly *illiberal* measures. As Sierra, the organic intellectual of Mexico's Porfirian regime, put it, in the late 1870s, as the Americans looked to extend their new transcontinental railways into Mexico, "their object was to dominate our markets to the profit of their industry." This could be done by "declaring [Mexico] to be in a state of anarchy and intervening," or "it could be satisfied in a normal, pacific manner if they could be convinced that there was a stable and viable government in Mexico whose word in treaties and contracts could be trusted."[147] Irrespective of whether Latin American elites—not just Mexican elites—actively feared foreign "imperialist" chastisement, the logic of the situation demanded that those elites should undertake the spadework of state-building, peace-making, and export-led "development." Such spadework in turn demanded a good deal of illiberal coercion and social engineering. Internal colonialism, one might say, was the price to be paid for avoiding external imperialism, for ensuring that there would be no "scramble for Latin America," as there was a "scramble for Africa," and for thus guaranteeing that the continent would, like Jacob's coat of many colors, remain prettily polychromatic on maps of the world.

CHAPTER 6

Hovering Dwarf

*Britain and Latin American Revolutions
in the Twentieth Century*

THIS CHAPTER CONSIDERS HOW THE BRITISH—CHIEFLY HIS/HER Majesty's government but also British economic actors and, in some measure, British travelers and intellectuals—reacted to revolutions in Latin America, in particular the Mexican (1910), the Bolivian (1952), and the Cuban (1959).[1] The chief aim is to use British reactions and reportage as a lens through which to view these three revolutionary experiences. Those experiences had rather little to do with British policy: only in Mexico did British policy count, and even there British influence was secondary and fast declining. In each of the three cases, the United States was the significant diplomatic "other" whose reactions mattered and whose policies counted.[2] If the United States was, in respect to Latin American revolutions, a "hovering giant," Britain was, at least by the 1950s, a hovering dwarf: small and getting smaller.[3] The British role, therefore, is interesting chiefly as that of observer—an observer of both internal "revolutionary" events and external, especially American, policy and its impact.

So with some qualifications in respect to Mexico (especially Mexico prior to 1914), this is a story in which the British are not principal actors but part of the chorus, whose chief claim on our, the audience's, attention is their recounting of events. And this British narrative contains, I think, a couple of elements of interest. First, there is the basic reportage: the British telling us what happened, even if they could not much influence the outcome. Of course, we must allow for bias and prejudice, of which there was a great deal, but read with caution, occasionally "against the grain," the British sources, by virtue of being foreign but not American (therefore, in no sense "hegemonic"), can be useful; they tell us things that domestic (Mexican, Bolivian, and Cuban) sources do not tell us; and, of course, while they often and, indeed, increasingly echo American voices, they are still distinct and, therefore, sometimes disposed to dissent from and even criticize American opinions and policies. Thus, they offer a modest counterweight to the latter. Clearly, the loss of British influence during the twentieth century, of which British actors in Latin America were well aware, means that what the British *did* was of scant significance (often they did very little), so what they *thought* is, by the same token, fairly irrelevant in practical terms. The British were, I repeat, members of the chorus, not principal actors, and while what the chorus says may be interesting and enlightening (by way of telling us what is happening in the play) it is not the same thing as strutting the stage in the guise of Hamlet or Henry V.

The second feature of British involvement in the three revolutions has to do with the bias and prejudices just mentioned. One consequence of the "cultural turn" in historiography, perhaps particularly in the United States, has been a focus on foreign perceptions of the "other," in this case, the Latin American revolutionary "other." Historians, often genuflecting in the general direction of Edward Said, have tried to reveal the "Orientalist"—or, in the case of Latin America, "Occidentalist"—presumptions that underwrite "Western" beliefs, attitudes, and policies regarding the rest of the world.[4] Revealing "Orientalism/Occidentalism" is, perhaps, a valid but often quite easy task; it can usually be done sitting in a comfortable armchair reading books (so no hours of toil in the archives, least of all distant archives in refractory foreign countries). Furthermore, some historians rest content with the act of revelation, showing that "Western" travelers, writers, statesmen, and diplomats (very rarely actual businessmen, as far as I can see) entertained prejudiced—usually elitist, racist, right-wing, and patriarchal—views about the Latin American "other." These historians fail to show how or when these views had a practical impact on, say, policy or patterns of trade and investment. The result is a rather rarefied *Ideengeschichte*, or "intellectual history," often of people who are not intellectual heavyweights and whose views—surprise, surprise!—tend to reflect those of the elites to which they belong. That is to say, they tend to be elitist, racist, right-wing, and patriarchal.

In this essay I do dabble in British attitudes and prejudices (as I've said, they are quite easy to recover, so I plead guilty to coasting downhill on a few occasions), but I don't believe that these attitudes and prejudices were necessarily consequential. First, the British lacked *palanca* (i.e., leverage), so what they may have thought *in foro interno* hardly mattered *in foro externo* (i.e., in practice).[5] Second, it is not at all clear that when the British or anybody else (including the Americans) exercised their palanca, they did so on the basis of prior attitudes and prejudices. Of course, general worldviews, "cognitive maps," and "mindsets" count, even for bankers and businessmen, as well as for statesmen and diplomats, but to return to my extended thespian metaphor, these form part of the backdrop and may not determine the plot in any given situation.[6]

One reason is that worldviews are usually pretty vague and fungible and thus can be invoked to justify quite different policy responses. For example, racism, providentialism, and notions of American exceptional-ism can legitimize both aggressive imperial expansion and America-First isolationism and hostility to overseas empire-building.[7] A more specific and relevant example would be the contrasting American responses to the almost contemporaneous Bolivian, Guatemalan, and Cuban revolutions. Here, the American "official mind" of the time (supposedly internationalist, anti-Communist, Monroeist, etc.) proved strangely schizoid, capable of devising quite different policies in these two cases: more subtle diplomatic and financial engagement in Bolivia, outright confrontation and boycott in the cases of Guatemala and Cuba.[8] The differences had less to do with a uniform "official mind."[9] Instead, they were derived from contrasting situations (and bilateral relations) that were framed by geopolitics and political economy and filtered through individual perceptions and reac-tions.[10] Borrowing the language of imperialist studies, we could say that the chief determinants were "excentric" rather than metropolitan; and, for that reason, they had much more to do with material interests and geopolitics than with a determining metropolitan mindset.[11]

The British "official mind," which was probably more institutionally coherent than its American counterpart, certainly existed and can, to some extent, be dissected.[12] Dissection reveals a couple of interesting but hardly momentous conclusions: first, variations among British observers, which may relate to individual idiosyncrasies, and second, much more important, variations of a more systemic character, which suggest an evolution in the official mind during the twentieth century. As we will see, as the century advanced and Britain fought two costly world wars, so British power plummeted; the empire, having briefly achieved its post–First World War apogee, entered a terminal decline; and British attitudes necessarily changed. Again, interests and "events" counted for more than elite attitudes, which usually limped some way behind: this disjunction lay at the heart of Dean Acheson's famous comment that, post-1945, Britain had "lost an empire but not found a role." (The Tony Blair premiership showed that this existential dilemma had still not been finally resolved, at least not in the minds of giddy policy-makers. More recently, the successful Brexit campaign depended on a toxic mixture of mendacity and nostalgic delusion.) Perhaps, though I have been unable to come up with conclusive evidence, the body politic that housed the official mind also changed, such that British representatives in, for example, Bolivia and Cuba in the 1950s were of a rather different mentality and makeup compared to their predecessors in Mexico in the 1910s. Indeed, there is some evidence of attitudinal change among the British in Mexico through the 1920s and 1930s, though whether this change reflected, endogenously, the maturation of the Mexican Revolution or, rather, exogenous shifts in the social and mental formation of British representatives in Mexico is hard to say; I suspect the first was more important.

There is one last (small) pay-off from this analysis of British reactions to revolution in Latin America. Irrespective of the reportage that the British produced or of the ideas and prejudices that may have conditioned that reportage, the documents also remind us of something that, as historians, we are well aware of but that we occasionally underestimate. Since we work with hindsight (hence, we know the historical outcomes), we tend to assume inevitability and underestimate the uncertainty and ignorance of historical actors (or, I should say, reporters). In other words, we can retrospectively peer through the "fog of war" that enveloped and confused contemporaries. Reviewing British coverage of these three revolutions (and revolutions are, of course, fast-moving processes with radical outcomes, so they are particularly stringent tests of contemporary insight and prediction), we see just how fallible observers—even intelligent, perceptive, informed observers—actually were. As the great medievalist F. W. Maitland put it, "It is hard to think away out of our heads a history which has long lain in a remote past but which once lay in the future."[13] And the same is sometimes also true of history that lies in the recent past, for example, in our own lifetimes. It is, perhaps, a truism that *we* know how things turned out and tend to see the outcome as set in stone, while contemporaries had no such privileged insight; nevertheless, we should bear it in mind as we review the fallible efforts of British diplomats (and others) as they strove to understand the dynamic and deceptive processes of Latin American revolutions.

Let me first sketch the context, chiefly to illustrate Britain's loss of palanca. Since the Bolivian and Cuban revolutions roughly coincided, they can be taken together and contrasted with the earlier experience of Anglo-Mexican relations at the beginning of the twentieth century. Regarding Mexico, Britain had by 1910 already ceded economic and financial preeminence to the United States, but Britain remained an important player.[14] Díaz had unusually close relations with Weetman Pearson (Lord Cowdray), whose construction company was "almost considered a minor department of state" and whose oil company, El Aguila, was locked in fierce competition with American rivals.[15] The Díaz government was keen to cultivate British and European economic ties precisely to offset the growing and ineluctable influence of the United States.[16]

This balancing act, which later Mexican administrations would seek to replicate, gave rise to convoluted conspiracy theories: that the 1910 revolution was the work of disgruntled American economic interests (above all, the oil companies) who resented Díaz's alleged partiality toward the British and who, in throwing their weight behind Madero, not only deployed their financial power but also induced the U.S. government to support the revolution and end the long honeymoon with Porfirio Díaz.[17] Like any conspiracy theory, this cannot be definitively disproved (after all, the best of all conspiracies is one that leaves no trace). But it is highly suspect, lacking both supportive evidence and corroboration on the basis of cui bono? That is to say, it is very hard to see why the U.S. government—the conservative, cautious, and legalistic Taft administration—would dabble in revolution and discard an old partner who had brought peace south of the border along with ample opportunities for U.S. business.[18] The British may have lamented the fall of Díaz, but so did many American business interests and Mexico watchers.[19] Furthermore, within a year the U.S. ambassador, Henry Lane Wilson, began filing vitriolic reports, berating not only the incompetence but also the authoritarianism and corruption of the new Madero administration.[20] Notoriously, he collaborated with the anti-Madero *golpistas* (coup leaders) in early 1913, thus helping bring about Madero's assassination and the establishment of Victoriano Huerta's authoritarian regime.

The British played no such consequential role in the events of 1910–13, but like many of their American business and diplomatic counterparts, they lamented the fall of Díaz, expressed mounting doubts about Madero's risky liberal experiment, and applauded Huerta's seizure of power.[21] Lionel Carden, who became British minister shortly after the coup, was an avowed Huertista (and anti-American) who, apart from penning positive reports to London, lobbied for financial support and even gave the dictator his personal advice regarding counterinsurgency operations (such as building blockhouses to protect the vulnerable railways, as the British had done in the South African [Boer] War).

Thus, when U.S. policy turned against Huerta and President Woodrow Wilson eventually resolved to drive the dictator from office in order to promote democracy (and a measure of social reform), the British and the Europeans were aghast, though somewhat divided between those who blamed Wilson's self-righteous naivete and those who saw American support for the revolution as a Machiavellian plot to promote disorder and then subjugate Mexico to the United States.[22] Either way, British official opinion strongly favored Huerta and frowned on the revolution. The notion that the latter stood—as Wilson came to believe—for self-determination and progressive social reform was, as the British minister to Mexico, Thomas Hohler, put it, so much "bosh."[23] The revolutionaries were bandits and demagogues, and Mexico was a country that needed strong authoritarian rule along the lines of Díaz—or Huerta.[24] The "constitutionalist" label was humbug; Mexicans, not least Mexican peons like the "arch-scoundrel" Pancho Villa, were plainly incapable of self-government.[25] President Wilson's policy of blackballing Huerta and endorsing the revolution was, in the words of a British oilman, "sheer madness."[26]

We see here something of an anticipation of the Versailles Peace Conference five years later: Old World Realpolitik confronting New World liberal idealism. But in both cases, particularly in Mexico, the New World was ascendant; hence, the British had to defer to American sensibilities, however much they disliked doing so. As Peter Calvert's meticulous account of the "diplomacy of Anglo-American conflict" shows, the British had to put up with Wilsonian policy ("bleeding-heart liberalism," avant la lettre, we might call it), and so Carden was hung out to dry, and British support for Huerta (never that committed or efficacious) evaporated.[27] That did not stop Wilson's ill-informed emissary, John Lind, from detecting British imperialist machinations behind Huerta's dogged resistance to the revolution.[28] (We may see this as an example of a recurrent phenomenon: the tendency of Great Powers to attribute "agency" to other Great Powers, usually their antagonists, rather than to uppity "Third World" actors, who are too easily depicted as compliant puppets.)[29] Lind's intemperate reports in early 1914 were instrumental in prompting Wilson and Bryan to launch their senseless invasion of Veracruz in April of that year.[30]

The contrast between British and American, Old and New World, diplomacy had deep roots; hence, we see its fruits in quite different contexts, such as revolutionary Mexico and postwar Europe. The basic difference was the British commitment to imperialist values and rationales. The United States still subscribed, at least rhetorically, to liberal-international notions, harking back to the days and the doctrine of American independence;

those notions included "an unqualified commitment to the right of revolutionary self-determination."[31] This tension, which would resurface with the Atlantic Charter of 1941, reflected not just American political values but also American economic self-interest, namely, the need for an open global economy where burgeoning America business would face neither imperialist barriers to trade and investment nor, as Mexico would soon exemplify, the "Chinese wall" of Third World economic nationalism.[32] While the Wilsonian view of Mexico was of a people struggling for freedom and democracy, that of the British, conditioned by generations of empire-building, was of a turbulent native population who needed a firm hand (like Díaz's or Huerta's) if they were to be kept in order and put to productive work.

Again, we see both a political and an economic rationale. Mexico, a country of illiterate peasants and Indians, was palpably unfit for democratic self-government; Madero's liberal promises had merely unleashed mayhem and, some said, xenophobia. Strong government meant either the "iron hand" (Porfirian or Huertista) or, as a last resort, American intervention—but intervention of a red-blooded coercive kind, not Wilson's meddlesome do-gooding.[33] And if Mexico was to prosper, as it had under Díaz, it needed both strong government and a large dose of foreign investment linked to export earnings—in so many words, *desarrollo hacia afuera* (outward-looking development). Prosperity—and therefore profits for British banks and bondholders, railways and mines—required not only political stability but also a regime capable of developing, if necessary coercively, Mexico's latent factors of production: land, minerals, oil, primary exports, and, most important, labor, labor that, without discipline and direction from above, would vegetate in subsistence peasant communities, fecklessly indifferent to market signals. Both the vision and the conclusion were colonial: Mexico's authorities, like those of colonial Africa, had to keep order, control "lazy" native labor, protect investments, and promote exports. Dallying with democracy was a recipe for anarchy, as Wilson's naive policy showed.[34]

As I have argued in the previous chapter, the parallels with colonial Africa (and elsewhere) were sometimes explicit in at least two distinct senses. First, Mexican campesinos were feckless natives, like Egypt's fel-laheen: good enough workers when inured to discipline but prone to relapse (hence, the phenomenon of San Lunes and the "backward-sloping supply curve of labor") and entirely unsuited to political democracy.[35] (We should recall that universal male suffrage did not come to Britain itself until 1918.) Second, Mexican reformers and radicals—usually seen as demagogic mestizos—were subversive troublemakers, peddlers of half-baked anarchist/nationalist/Bolshevik theories whose progressive rhetoric masked ruthless self-interest. In other words, they resembled the emergent nationalist elites of the empire (and beyond): like India's babus they were half-educated rabble-rousers who preyed on the gullibility of the peasant (the "ignorant and barbarian peon"), gratuitously prompting protest and unrest, not least by the promise of "some chance of looting."[36] (By the 1920s, some were labeled Communist or Bolshevist, but this was more an offensive add-on, not the gravamen of the charge against Mexican radicals.)

These colonialist attitudes were, again, the product of interests and experience; they did not spring out of thin air. British representatives in Mexico came with CVs colored by imperial (which could be formal or informal imperial) service: Hohler, for example, had served in St. Petersburg, Cairo, Tokyo, Addis Ababa, and Constantinople. Businessmen, though generally more pragmatic and focused in their concerns, might also bring their imperial experience to bear. Interestingly, the Americans, once they had acquired a new empire—part formal, part informal—after 1898, also began to circulate quasi-imperial elites, both diplomatic and financial (including the famous "money doctors").[37]

But British attitudes and Mexican realities were increasingly contradic-tory. Carden might want to stand up to the Americans in opposition to the revolution, but he failed. His Majesty's government denied him support (indeed, it told Carden to appease the Americans), Huerta was ousted, and Carden soon received his passports from the new revolutionary regime. The long retreat of British influence in the circum-Caribbean, flagged by the Hay-Pauncefote Treaty of 1901, was accelerated, above all by the First World War. Politically, militarily, and financially beholden to the Ameri-cans, Britain could no longer pursue an independent policy in America's backyard.[38] British armed intervention was explicitly ruled out, and in order to protect British interests in northern Mexico, the government had to call on America's good offices.[39] However, this de facto retreat did not stop British representatives in Mexico from continuing to carry the quasi-colonial torch: attitudes lagged behind reality. When two British oilmen were killed down on the isthmus in 1917, the response of the British consul was one of imperial outrage, but the outrage was compounded by a sense of impotence.[40] And so it went on as the revolutionary regime consolidated, drawing up the radical Constitution of 1917 and embarking on policies of land and labor reform, anticlericalism, and (modest) economic nationalism. Members of the consular old guard like P. G. Holms and H. Cunard Cummins continued to rail against Mexican demagogy and duplicity; Cunard Cummins was expelled for his strenuous defense of Rosalie Evans, whose death at the hands of agraristas prompted a characteristic tirade by Holms: "This wicked and abominable act against a lonely woman should rouse the world against the monsters who are at the head of this government."[41]

Of course, the Americans, too, bridled at Mexican radicalism and nationalism, and the British came to rely on American pressure to mitigate radical reform, especially in respect to oil. But as the Mexicans themselves were well aware, Britain was no longer a major threat to be reckoned with: naval coercion was out of the question, and British commercial and financial leverage had dwindled.[42] When British oil assets—which exceeded American in output and value—were expropriated in 1938, the government threw a tantrum, and diplomatic relations were broken. The United States, in contrast, had been pursuing a policy of détente for over a decade, starting with Dwight Morrow in the late 1920s, and the Cárdenas administration, for all its genuine radicalism, knew that relations with the United States were paramount. At a time when the Mexican Communist Party—a frail plant—enjoyed a brief efflorescence, it did so as a junior ally of the regime, and the regime was at pains to depict itself as a Mexican version of the New Deal, not an offshoot of the Third International.[43] Despite loose talk of "Bolshevism," informed observers of Mexico, both American and British, rarely saw Mexico as a pawn of the Kremlin (after all, Calles had ruthlessly repressed the Mexican Communist Party after 1929).

Indeed, there is suggestive evidence that by the 1930s British representatives in Mexico had—belatedly—come to terms with the revolution and ditched their old imperialist hauteur. Vice-Consul Stanley Dutton-Pegram, reporting from La Laguna, was surprisingly positive about the sweeping Cardenista land reform of 1936 (even though it affected British interests such as the Tlahualilo Company).[44] At the same time, the Aguila Company's representative in Mexico City, J. A. Assheton, was a good deal more pragmatic and realistic than the boss of Royal Dutch Shell, who, cleaving to old colonialist values, regarded Assheton as "half a Bolshevik."[45] A particularly telling example of the British bending with the wind concerned the Cuernavaca hotelier Rosa King. In her 1936 memoirs, recalling the revolution in Morelos and her flight from the advancing Zapatistas in 1914, she treats Zapata as an honest, idealistic local hero leading doughty Indians who were fighting to reverse four centuries of bondage and oppression.[46] At the time, however, her (1914) eyewitness account was quite different: the "savage Zapatistas," "cruel beyond belief," led by "the wicked and cruel Emiliano Zapata," "respect nothing and no person, man or woman"; they conduct a "cowardly" form of warfare (they "never come out to fight but are always hidden"); so, she concludes, "no punishment can be too good for Zapata and his followers."[47] The British minister, Hohler, considered this account "wholly reliable," while a Foreign Office official, reviewing the story five thousand miles away, was taken aback. "The Zapatistas evidently stop at nothing," he reflected, and since their atrocities could not be considered "terrorist, like the Germans," he was forced to conclude that "presumably they act out of pure devilry."[48]

In part, this "discursive" change may have represented a generational shift as younger men (and, occasionally, women), products of the postwar era, replaced the old prewar "imperialists." But, very clearly in the case of Rosa King, the change was not generational so much as individual and based on personal experience: it reflected a realistic appreciation that the revolution was here to stay and could not be rolled back either by domestic counterrevolution (which had failed in 1913–14, 1923–24, and 1926–29) or by foreign (i.e., U.S.) intervention. Foreign residents and observers therefore had to come to terms with—even pay lip service to—the new revolutionary Mexico and, we could add, its official discourse, in which Zapata was a noble hero with a white horse, no longer the vengeful "Attila of the South."[49] Whatever the motive, it seems clear that British reportage on Mexico evolved between, roughly, 1910 and 1940, becoming more restrained and realistic, less racist and colonialist.

However, it is worth noting that, among the British intelligentsia, the old attitudes died hard. Celebrated British writers who visited Mexico in the 1920s and 1930s were often viscerally hostile to the revolutionary regime, which they saw as corrupt, mercenary, and authoritarian. Graham Greene came to record and denounce the persecution of the Catholic Church, even though that persecution was in fact fast abating. While it is not surprising that he denounced the godless state and all its works, he went much further, swiping at Mexican art, archaeology, culture, and kitsch.[50] Evelyn Waugh, another Catholic and avowed conservative whose trip was funded by British oil money, lavished unabashed praise on the old Porfiriato and excoriated its revolutionary successor.[51] Such attitudes were, in part, products of Britain's interwar (highbrow) culture, which disdained mass politics and mass consumerism.[52] As such, they had little to do with Mexican reality. (Greene admitted that he had "very poor Spanish," while Waugh, who rarely left Mexico City, spent most of his time—and gathered much of his "data"—in the Ritz Hotel.)[53] Mexico was just a convenient canvas on which to daub their splenetic opinions. But the reactionary stance of the likes of Greene and Waugh—a stance that they brought with them from Britain and that was not much contaminated by daily and open-minded contact with Mexican society—strongly suggests that it was that contact that induced realism on the part of the diplomats, consuls, and businessmen of the 1930s, while transient intellectual tourists, who came and went in a matter of weeks (and who did not speak Spanish), could keep their "Occidentalist" prejudices intact. Also, the former had to transact business (in the broad sense) with real-life Mexicans, while the latter were peddling their copy largely to a domestic (British) audience. Then as now, sensationalism was a feature of "literary" reportage back home, but it was a luxury that British interests on the ground in Mexico, where they had to make a living, could not afford.

Now let us fast forward twenty years to the 1950s. First, Britain's eco-nomic power had sharply declined, while that of the United States was at its apogee (in relative terms). Compared to the British stake in Mexico (ca. 1910), British assets in Bolivia and Cuba in the 1950s were very small.[54] There were two British railways in Bolivia, while the Williams, Harvey smelter at Liverpool was a major destination of Bolivia's tin ore. Both therefore became issues as the Bolivian Revolution unfolded.[55] British assets in Cuba, which in the nineteenth century had been substantial, were, by the 1950s, greatly reduced; the railways were gone, and Britain's investment consisted of one (Shell) oil refinery, recently (1957) constructed and soon (1961) to be expropriated, as well as "a number of insurance companies."[56] The British presence was therefore dwarfed by that of the United States.[57] True, American interests in Bolivia were much less than those in Cuba (which was significant for U.S. policy), but the United States was the principal supplier of Bolivian imports (not least food imports), and it would soon become a major source of aid. (To put it the other way round, after the revolution, Bolivia became the biggest recipient of U.S. aid in Latin America.)[58] In both cases, therefore, the United States was the key player, and Britain's role was marginal. Indeed, in the Bolivian case, Germany—which participated in the Triangular Plan (1961), designed to stabilize the Bolivian economy—played a greater role, while in Cuba, of course, it was the Soviet Union that soon became the chief external guarantor of the revolution.[59]

As a result, British deference toward the Americans, already appar-ent—to Carden's chagrin—at the time of the Mexican Revolution, now became a basic tenet of policy. No maverick British representative could—like Carden—contemplate pursuing an anti-American line. (Indeed, since 1910, the power and autonomy of diplomatic representatives in general had declined as metropolitan governments achieved greater central control, thanks to enhanced bureaucratization and swifter, easier communications.) The British role was reduced to reporting on what the Americans were up to and sometimes seeking American support for particular British interests. Meanwhile, the global context and the role of the United States within it had substantially changed since 1910. Not only had the United

States emerged as the global superpower at the end of the Second World War, it now confronted the Soviet Union in a bipolar world in which regional and local conflicts were readily defined in Cold War terms. At the time of the Mexican Revolution, no such Manichaean framework of explanation existed. Great Power politics was a poker game with several players (though the players might vary from game to game): the United States and Britain combatted the Germans (hence the febrile diplomacy and espionage of 1914–18, not least in Mexico, and the renewed hostility of the late 1930s and after), but by 1945 the German threat had evaporated, and by the 1960s, the truncated Federal Republic of Germany was collaborating with the United States in the revival of Bolivia's finances.[60] In the old days, too, the United States and Britain had their differences (witness Lind versus Carden in Mexico), and at least since the 1890s, the United States had bent its efforts toward usurping Britain's economic role—in some countries, a preponderant role—in Latin America.[61] Two world wars ensured an American victory; thus, Anglo-American economic rivalry, like Anglo-American-German geopolitical conflict, became largely a thing of the past. Instead, the United States focused primarily on a single enemy, once again exaggerating Soviet "agency" and viewing events in Latin America through the distorting lens of anti-Communism.[62]

In Mexico, the "Bolshevist" threat had surfaced in the later 1910s and become a familiar specter in the 1920s, but it was always something of a stage ghost designed to frighten the easily frightened. As I mentioned, when the Mexican regime lurched to the left under Cárdenas, it maintained good relations with the United States (whose chief fear at the time was the Axis powers, not the Soviet Union). By the 1950s the United States was committed to a Cold War perspective, which other powers had to take into account. Governments and elites in Latin American became adept at playing on American fears of Communism: Bolivia's Movimiento Nacionalista Revolucionario (MNR), which enjoyed the dubious distinction of "semifascist" origins, was thus able to parlay its anti-Communism into substantial U.S. aid, while Batista, when facing domestic dissent, easily succumbed to the "temptation . . . to seek popular and United States support by ascribing opposition tactics to the Communists."[63] The Cold

War thus gave "Third World" governments a useful extra string to their bow, one that they soon learned to exploit to their own—personal, party, or national—advantage. By the 1960s, when the Cuban Revolution hove into sight, the MNR's bargaining position had strengthened: informed observers came to see President Paz Estenssoro and the MNR as the only (acceptable) game in town. "The only other choice would be chaos or Communism," a nice alliteration but a faulty judgment, since it overlooked a third alternative: military intervention.[64] In Cuba itself, of course, the revolution produced a startling transformation in the island's geopolitical role: under Batista, the British ambassador reported in August 1957, Cuba "tends to follow the lead of the United States and is perfectly sound on the question of Soviet Russia and Communism in general," so "in any war between East and West, Washington would ensure that Cuba was on the side of the angels."[65] Five short years later, Cuba had made a deal with the devil and become a threatening Soviet bridgehead in the Americas.

Throughout these years the British shared the Americans' Cold War mentality; thus, reports from both Bolivia and Cuba regularly revolve the question of Communist involvement, its scale, character, and impact.[66] Two (interrelated) forms of such involvement were detected: first, the direct intervention of the Soviet Union (or occasionally one of its eastern European proxies) by way of aid, trade, counsel, or military backing; and second, the activities of "domestic" (i.e., Bolivian or Cuban) "Communists," be they parties, unions, or individuals, the "Communist" label being, of course, quite loosely and liberally applied (recall Ambassador Patterson's famous "duck test").[67] In Bolivia, both before and after the 1952 revolution, fears of Communism focused chiefly on the unions, especially the miners, who were "led by a Communist-indoctrinated militant few" bent on the "sovietization of Bolivia."[68] Oddly, British reports do not (to my knowledge) recognize the Trotskyist tradition among the Federación Sindical de Trabajadores Mineros de Bolivia (FSTMB) and tend instead to lump all Marxists/Communists together under the same "Soviet" rubric. In Cuba, the prerevolutionary Communist presence was evident; but the Partido Socialista Popular's dalliance with Batista (and distinctly ambivalent attitude toward the 26th of July Movement) made them less threatening and hence less suitable for conventional conspiracy theories. However, Cuba's militant students (of whom more anon) could be tarred with the Communist brush, and Fidel Castro was included partly on the basis of his supposed participation in "Communist-inspired riots in Bogotá" in 1949.[69]

As this case makes clear, varieties of the domino theory—premised on the notion that subversion entered the body politic from outside, like an alien contagion—were attractive, perhaps because they offered easy answers and, again, attributed agency to foreign agitators, thus providing a convenient alibi for domestic governments. In 1950 an alleged "South American Communist Party" was meant to be spreading subversion in Bolivia—as well as Brazil, Argentina, Ecuador, Chile, Paraguay, and Peru; its supposed leader, the Brazilian Luis Carlos Prestes, was designated "the President of the Soviet Union of South America."[70] Of course, the Cuban Revolution gave a great boost to the regional domino theory (which some Latin American governments again chose to cultivate and exploit). The "principal question" hanging over Bolivia at the start of 1962, the British ambassador reported, was "whether Bolivia could preserve her national revolution intact or whether she was destined to go the way of Cuba."[71] A more encouraging kind of domino was offered by Mexico: perhaps the MNR would emulate the PRI, creating a strong, stable, nationalist, and "revolutionary" but generally congenial state.[72] As we know, Bolivia finally followed neither the Cuban nor the Mexican path.

The bipolar perspective of the Cold War was imposed on Latin America societies, which, of course, were diverse and dynamic. Bolivia and Cuba were very different in terms of wealth, literacy, and "development," and both of them, Cuba especially, were different from the Mexico of 1910, which had spawned the revolution. Thus, Mexico's literacy rate in 1910 was 20 percent, Bolivia's in 1950 was 31 percent, and Cuba's in 1953 was 76 percent.[73] Per capita GDP in 1920 prices stood at $223 in Mexico in 1913, $189 in Bolivia in 1950, and $534 in Cuba in 1960.[74] In terms of urbanization, Cuba far outstripped 1910 Mexico and 1952 Bolivia, as it also did in respect to cars and telephones per head of the population.[75] Such crude socioeconomic comparisons suggest that Bolivia (1952) resembled Mexico (1910) rather more than either resembled Cuba (1959).

However, in political terms—and political forms do not neatly reflect socioeconomic structures—Bolivia and Cuba stood closer together, with Mexico an outlier. Mexico in 1910 lacked mass political institutions; the latter (parties, sindicatos, peasant leagues) sprang up quite rapidly in the wake of the revolution, which was their progenitor. And we should not forget that this process of political massification had its Catholic and conservative manifestations too.[76] In Bolivia and Cuba, especially the latter, "massification" preceded the revolutions of the 1950s and, in large measure, was their root cause. Both countries had mass parties, significant trade unions, and, in Cuba at least, vocal farmer/peasant organizations.[77] By the mid-1950s Bolivia even boasted a "union of prison inmates."[78] Trade union delegations regularly visited Bolivia, and having a labor attaché was now seen as vital to the workings of embassies in La Paz.[79] Another group that was largely absent from the Mexican Revolution played a key role in Bolivia and Cuba: students, notably radical leftist students, products of the "massification" of higher education, even in a relatively poor and underdeveloped country like Bolivia.[80] British diplomats, for whom student radicalism was a rather new and unwelcome phenomenon, were sometimes dismissive of "childish student antics," but they could not ignore the impact of student mobilization, especially in Cuba.[81] This "massification" of 1950s politics is evident in the proliferating acronyms that we now encounter in diplomatic reports from that decade. Of course, 1950s Mexico was similar. But back in the days of the armed revolution in 1910–20, scarcely an acronym was to be seen—the first of any significance was the infant labor confederation, the Confederación Regional Obrera Mexicana (CROM, 1918). The relevant actors were presidents, generals, caudillos, and caciques; their followers were recruited (assuming they had not been carried off by the *leva*, the press gang) on the basis of local, regional, and personal ties. The later acronym soup was a recipe cooked up by the revolution, although, as the Bolivian and Cuban cases confirm, it also reflected broader global trends.

The international context had also undergone parallel organizational changes. Alongside the bipolarity of the Cold War there had sprung up a series of multilateral agencies, many of them creatures of the UN or the

Bretton Woods system. Some, of course, became proxies in the conflicts of the Cold War (such as the Organización Regional Interamericana de Trabajadores [ORIT]); others enjoyed a genuine independence of the rival superpowers.[82] Entirely absent at the time of the Mexican Revolution, they played an important role in the 1950s, especially in Bolivia, where UN representatives had become regular players in policy-making (to the extent that they went native, deferring to vested interests and thus failing to achieve necessary reform, or so the British believed).[83] By the 1960s, and chiefly because of the Cuban Revolution, the United States, through the Alliance for Progress, began to espouse policies of aid and development, in respect to which Bolivia would become a principal beneficiary (and Cuba an outcast pariah). In a sense this was an updating of the old policies of dollar diplomacy—that is, using the power of the dollar to achieve outcomes favorable to U.S. interests—but now cast in a more progressive, reformist, and statist form, since the dollars came directly from the U.S. government and its agencies, not private banks. U.S. aid missions now formed part of the new political landscape; the United States also sought to deploy "soft power" by means of cultural and educational programs such as Fulbright or the seductive celluloid images of Hollywood.[84] Where the old informal imperialists of the nineteenth century relied on the stick or, when it came to carrots, distributed them discreetly among chosen "collaborative elites," American "informal empire," though quite disposed to use force in the circum-Caribbean (Cuba, the Dominican Republic, Nicaragua, Panama), tended elsewhere in Latin America to rely on proxy agents of coercion (such as the Guatemalan or Brazilian armed forces) or on more "democratic" programs of cultural influence that were more consonant with the "mass" politics of the era.[85] The carrots, we could say, were now diced and distributed much more widely among Latin American mass publics.

Again, therefore, British representatives, especially those in Bolivia, found themselves operating in a new environment with a new vocabulary. The old issues of political and economic power remained, of course, but the format and the discourse had changed. And the British changed accordingly. (Did they change because of their own education and careers or because the circumstances in which they worked had changed? Again, the answer is probably both.) Back in the 1910s, British reportage from Mexico had been racist and elitist; democratic demands and social reform were seen, as I said, as so much "bosh." Thomas Hohler (who used the "bosh" word) also took aim at the Convention of Aguascalientes, the important revolutionary assembly that in 1914 sought to achieve revolutionary unity and a common sociopolitical program. The convention, Hohler said, "appears closely to resemble the Parliament of Monkeys described by Mr. Kipling in the Jungle Book."[86] Dismissive in its content, the comment is surely also significant in terms of its literary reference to Rudyard Kipling, the unofficial poet laureate of British imperialism. But Hohler (like Kipling) was an intelligent man who knew parts of the "Third World" pretty well; his comment reflected not crass stupidity but the prevailing wisdom of the time, when democracy and social reform were relatively new even in Britain and certainly not considered suitable exports to the brown Third Word, be it British India or Porfirian Mexico. By the 1950s, British representatives had moved, albeit reluctantly, with the times. Though racist allusions remained, Cuban or Bolivian politics were interpreted differently and were seen as less radically distinct from the politics of western Europe, a politics, therefore, in which parties, elections, trade unions, and programs of social reform were facts of life, even legitimate facts of life. (Vice-Consul Dutton-Pegram, with his positive evaluation of the Cardenista land reform in La Laguna, pointed the way.)

One example was the focus on organized labor and the detailed reportage on labor activism in all three countries. The "incorporation" of labor into Latin American politics was now a crucial fact of life that the British, who had some domestic experience of this story, had to take seriously.[87] The CVs of British representatives also looked rather different. Hohler, as I mentioned earlier, could draw on his experiences in Ottoman Turkey, Ethiopia, and Egypt, "Third World" states that, to varying degrees, were subject to "First World" browbeating. When Ambassador Gilbert Holliday sought to make sense of Bolivia in the 1960s, his points of reference were very different: he recalled Chile in 1934 and Poland in 1945; he compared the Aymara of the Bolivian Altiplano to the Lapps; and Cochabamba reminded him—rather implausibly—of Provence ("at any moment, as we drove along the herb-scented maquis, I expected a screen of poplar trees to part and reveal the Mont St. Victoire").[88] Colonial/imperial motifs thus gave way to a bizarre mélange of Latin American, Communist eastern European, and French touristic comparisons. The resulting discourse is a lot less red-bloodedly imperial and a good deal more eclectic, open-minded, and even whimsical.

Finally, by way of reviewing the changed landscape of the 1950s, we should note how British international priorities had shifted—and shrunk. At the time of the Mexican Revolution (a crucial decade in British and world history, of course, which witnessed the First World War and the revolutionary transformation of eastern Europe), Great Britain, as a major global and imperial power, was playing for high stakes. Latin America in general was fairly marginal to British concerns, although Mexico was a cockpit of Great Power rivalry, and of course the Zimmerman Telegram—imperial Germany's inept attempt to inveigle Mexico into a war with the United States—briefly catapulted the country into the global/military limelight.[89] Geopolitically, Mexico was important to Britain chiefly in terms of its relations with the United States; hence, Britain successfully finessed the Zimmerman Telegram incident in such a way as to induce U.S. entry into the war without divulging the source of its secret information.[90] Again during the Second World War, when Britain's profile in Mexico had been much reduced, combatting German influence absorbed a great deal of diplomatic time and effort.[91] By the 1950s, however, with the war won but Britain's global power further diminished as a result, the stakes were much smaller: now, far from enlisting Latin American support in pursuit of a life-or-death war effort, Britain was concerned about Cuban or Bolivian support at the UN with regard to Cyprus or Suez.[92] In other words, in pursuit of dwindling imperial assets and pretensions elsewhere, Britain sought Latin American backing in the new multilateral context of the postwar period.

I conclude with a couple of slightly anecdotal observations. First, the systemic trends already mentioned—the loss of British power, the "massification" of Latin American politics, and the transformation of the international environment—were, of course, subject to the vagaries of individual careers and personalities. Even back in the 1910s, some British observers of Mexico were more far-sighted and perceptive than others, and as late as the 1940s and 1950s, there were diplomatic dinosaurs whose reports, however stylishly readable, seem like throwbacks to an earlier time. Bolivia seems to have attracted rather more of these, or perhaps it would truer to say that Bolivia, being a more backward country, full of Indians, elicited comments that had gone out of fashion regarding contemporary Mexico and Cuba. As elections approached in 1960, the infantilized Bolivian voters "looked expectantly at their favoured candidates for the presidency as children regard a conjuror, believing that he will produce some happy surprise, but unable to say what it will be." (Quite unlike the sophisticated British electorate, of course.)[93] Generic cultural—perhaps racist?—stereotypes persist. The Cruceños (the people of the booming province of Santa Cruz) may have avoided the taint of the Indian masses, but being "mainly of Spanish stock," they are "arrogant, intelligent and lazy."[94] Indeed, Bolivian politics in general was blighted by the fact that "here, as elsewhere in Spanish America," one had to contend with "the incurable fickleness of the upper and middle classes."[95] Such "explanations" have a musty and outdated air to them; they are more rarely heard in Mexican or Cuban reports for the 1950s and 1960s.[96] Perhaps the Foreign Office put its dinosaurs out to pasture in Bolivia, perhaps Bolivia evoked such atavistic opinions, or perhaps the altitude addled diplomatic brains. Certainly, diplomats posted to La Paz felt slighted and therefore disdainful. As one British ambassador put it, swiping simultaneously at Bolivia and Latin America: "I . . . hardly think it worthwhile to engage time and attention in London to [sic] the futile politics and sorrows of this minor unit of a not too serious subcontinent."[97] Which we might—imaginatively—construe as: Why am I wasting my time and talent in La Paz rather than Paris or Washington?

My final point is an obvious but important one. All the representatives/reporters reviewed here were fallible, finding it difficult to penetrate the "fog of war" or, we could say, the murky mists of revolution. This is hardly surprising, but it is worth bearing in mind when we survey "expert" opinion both then and now. Given the nature of revolutionary circumstances, which were fast-moving and often chaotic, prediction was risky. In addition, British representatives, operating in opaque polities, often relied on a narrow range of contacts and informants, and in some cases, wishful thinking led them to report what they wanted to happen.[98] There was, in consequence, a bias in favor of favorable outcomes, a mode of thinking that psychologists regard as "universal" and that makes lotteries profitable.[99] Thus, Lionel Carden, a keen supporter of President Huerta, systematically exaggerated Huerta's strengths and the weaknesses of the revolution. In January 1914—when we know, with hindsight, that the tide was turning against him—Huerta still had plenty of assets, Carden stressed; a hostile U.S. administration might, under public pressure, change its stance; and, anyway, U.S. recognition was "not of such vital importance to him as generally thought."[100] A month later, when President Wilson lifted the arms embargo on the northern rebels, Carden contrived to see this as a benefit: it will "enormously strengthen Huerta's hands" by making the "peaceable people" of Mexico rally to his cause. (Which, of course, never happened; rather, the raising of the embargo enabled the rebels, notably Pancho Villa, to equip large conventional armies capable of beating the Federales at the battles of Torreón and Zacatecas.)[101] At the same time, Carden saw a ray of light in rebel dissensions. True, Carranza and Villa were uneasy allies, but Carden prematurely turned their incipient difficulties into a "final and complete break," which, in turn, might make possible a "rapprochement" between Huerta and Carranza (a wild fantasy).[102]

Carden's long trail of self-denial and wishful thinking was an extreme example—and the work, we should note, of a minister who reported from Mexico City, had scant contact with the insurgent provinces, and was chummy with the government. In Bolivia, where, perhaps, expectations and stakes were both quite low, wishful thinking was less apparent. However, in August 1964, three months before a military coup ousted the MNR, the British ambassador optimistically opined that Bolivia was "on the move" and that, given help and good luck, the Bolivian Revolution could "attain the same sort of stability and prosperity as has at last been achieved by the first—Mexican—Revolution."[103] In Cuba, we can detect a milder version of Carden's persistent optimism. The assault on the Moncada barracks, as we have seen, was dismissed as a hotheaded escapade. Three years later, the expedition of the *Granma* to Oriente was similarly scorned (and misreported). The revolt in Oriente had "petered out in the course of a couple of weeks . . . as it was bound to [do]," on which (ambassadorial) report Whitehall officials minuted: "Mr. Fordham's analysis seems eminently reasonable," and "Fidel Castro has now faded out of the picture."[104] Several months later, as it became clear that Castro had not faded from the picture and the Sierra Maestra insurgency was continuing, Fordham marginally revised his opinion. Castro might be alive, but he had lost the initiative; he could "do little more than inconvenience the regime"; he would have to break out from the Sierra or remain "a mere irritant."[105]

In other words, there seems to have been a systematic bias in favor of the outcomes favored by the British (which usually meant the status quo). The British wanted stability and continuity; they tended to take their cues from elites in the capital city; and revolution was troublesome and threatening, thus easily attributed either to bandits (as in Mexico), to "indoctrinated" Communists (in Cuba and Bolivia), or to "hotheads" and "fickle" Latins in general.[106] Over time, as I have argued, British power diminished, and British assessments became more balanced, less prejudiced. In part this may have reflected the changing "sociocultural" makeup of the Foreign Service, but more important, I suspect, was Britain's declining power and changing place in the world, which encouraged a less "imperial" view of events and processes in Latin America.[107] Britain, as Acheson said, may have lost an empire and failed to find a role, but in the process, the British perhaps acquired greater detachment and insight. For as the Americans demonstrated in Latin America and elsewhere, viewing the world through "imperial" spectacles could lead to serious distortions.

CHAPTER 7

Workers and Peasants, Liberals and Jacobins

The Mexican Revolution in Comparative Global Perspective

THIS CHAPTER ANALYZES THE MEXICAN REVOLUTION, THE historical case I know best, in a comparative global context.[1] Comparison is useful, even necessary, for at least two reasons: first, to try to arrive at some conclusions, positive or negative, about revolutions in general across time and space; and second (less ambitiously but more practically), to shed an oblique light on a particular case such as Mexico (since, as a Mexicanist, I am aware that a passing knowledge of other revolutions may prompt fresh questions and, perhaps, suggest new approaches to old questions). And although my main focus is on actual (i.e., successful, consequential) revolutions, I think it is important to consider both revolutionary and *non*revolutionary stories, if only to guard against the familiar fallacy of "post hoc, ergo propter hoc" (i.e., the fallacy of misattributed causality, which may involve stressing a "revolutionary" cause that, when detected in another time and place, proves to lack "revolutionary" significance).[2]

I shall begin by clearing the ground: this is a largely negative exercise that involves explaining what we can and—often—can't achieve when it comes to the comparative analysis of revolutions across time and space.[3] Clearing the ground involves a somewhat negative, skeptical, and "splitting" perspective (the perspective many historians prefer); when I get into the meat of this chapter, I will adopt a more positive and "lumping" point of view.[4] At that point, grounded skepticism gives way to a few leaps of faith.

Regarding what we can and can't do when comparatively analyzing revolutions, historians and social scientists (I am not sure that these are mutually exclusive categories, by the way) seem to agree that there is a useful concept of "revolution," meaning an uprising that is of greater substance and consequence than a (lesser) "revolt" or "rebellion" (a distinction that the duc de La Rochefoucauld-Liancourt presciently grasped back in 1789).[5] So "revolutions" are the big beasts in the extensive jungle of "revolts," "rebellions," and similar uprisings. A passing but important clarification: whether we are dealing with revolts or revolutions, we can often distinguish between successes and failures, between, on the one hand, those that (to some significant extent) achieved their goals or—a common outcome—brought about major change by way of *unintended* consequences and, on the other hand, those many revolts or revolutions that were repressed, defeated, or reversed (e.g., by counterrevolution, foreign intervention, or a combination of the two).[6]

Either way, the revolt/revolution distinction remains: Latin American history is littered with lesser revolts—including *golpes*, *cuartelazos*, and *pronunciamientos*—both successful and unsuccessful.[7] There have been a few unsuccessful (i.e., snuffed out) revolutions, such as that of Guatemala in 1954.[8] Beyond Latin America, examples of failed revolutions would include 1848 (in Austria, at least) or China's Taiping rebellion (1850–64), a "projected social and political revolution" that was bloodily repressed.[9]

Some analysts would go further and propose an elite class of very big revolutions, usually referred to as "great" or, perhaps, "social" revolutions, the usual candidates being the English, French, Russian, Chinese, and Cuban (and, I would add in passing, the Mexican).[10] As a rough rule of thumb, these "great" revolutions are usually seen as changing not just the political regime but also society as a whole, whereas (not-so-great, run-of-the-mill) revolutions may change *regimes* but not *societies* (successful anticolonial revolutions might be a case in point).

Thus, in terms of size, we have a roughly tripartite system: (mere) revolts, revolutions, and "great" or "social" revolutions. How we determine which is which is, of course, a tricky question, one that is hardly amenable to precise calibration and more a matter of informed judgment. But that is a common state of affairs when dealing with any number of big historical concepts ("state," "nation," "crisis," "hegemony"), and the fact that precision may be impossible is no good reason to abandon such concepts altogether. (Ultimately, the value of a concept is heuristic: Does it help us understand what happened? And for this, precision is an important but not overriding concern.)

These considerations acquire practical force if we look at the relevant historiography (whether of Mexico or elsewhere). Some analysts who are committed to a dogmatic, arguably ahistorical Marxist perspective would reserve the "revolutionary" label for politico-social upheavals that transform—or, we could say, slightly lowering the bar, substantially change—the "mode of production" of a given "social formation" (usually a country). Thus, some dogmatists assert, the French, Russian, and Chinese Revolutions, since they (allegedly) changed the "mode of production" (from feudal to capitalist or from capitalist to socialist), were real revolutions, while most, if not all, of the others, including the Mexican, weren't. But this is a somewhat stultifying perspective that excessively narrows the field and, arguably, misconstrues history (e.g., the history of France, whose revolution cannot convincingly be seen as bringing about a sudden transition from a "feudal" to "capitalist" mode of production, thus from seigneurial to bourgeois domination).[11]

One serious consequence of such a dogmatic view is that it eliminates "nationalist" or "anticolonialist" revolutions (which are by definition political but may also be "social"), including the American (1776) and Latin American independence revolutions (1808–25), the Italian Risorgimento (1848–71), the two Cuban Wars of Independence (the first, 1868–78, unsuccessful, the second, 1895–98, successful, albeit with qualifications), and the anticolonial struggles in Algeria and Vietnam in the 1950s through the 1970s.[12] It also distorts understanding of the Chinese Revolution, which is incomprehensible if its key nationalist dimension is lost sight of.[13] Other qualitative categories have been proposed, such as "modernizing" revolutions, a category that suffers from the original sin of invoking a woolly concept, "modernity," which habitually confuses more than it clarifies.[14] Of course, while the dogmatists may err by defining "real" revolutions in terms that are too narrow and demanding (i.e., by requiring structural transformation of the preexisting "mode of production"), it is important to maintain some analytical rigor, some rules regarding which candidates get admitted to the "revolutionary" club and which are blocked at the door. And, changing the metaphor, we should robustly resist the wholesale dilution—dilution of homeopathic proportions—of the term "revolution" when it is casually applied to consumer tastes or transient technological innovations.

So far, the discussion has been largely descriptive: it concerns roughly what revolutions look like and how they might be defined and typologized. Such discussion is necessary but neither path-breaking nor very informative. Some analysts would go much further, suggesting that we can discern either the "laws of motion" of revolution, as Trotsky believed, or particular stages through which revolutions typically—or necessarily?—pass, as Crane Brinton (and others) have suggested.[15] Here, I am frankly skeptical. Brinton's analysis is well worth reading, and to give him credit, his generalizations are hedged about with judicious qualifications. But as a fine historian of France, he tended to regard the French Revolution (and its supposed "stages": moderate, radical, Thermidorian reaction) as an explanatory template for other revolutions. But such Francocentric baggage does not travel well. There are no grounds for thinking that the French sequence, even assuming it is valid for France, applies to Mexico or Cuba (the two Latin American cases I know best and, more important, the two biggest Latin American revolutions of the twentieth century). And in some cases (not, in fact, Brinton's), Francocentrism involves a cavalier slighting of the earlier English and American Revolutions.[16]

"Stage" theories, which may work tolerably well when it comes to the broad sweep of economic history (consider analysts as diverse as Karl Marx, Walt Rostow, Alexander Gerschenkron, and Albert Hirschman), are unable to accommodate the multiple twists and turns of "conjunctural" revolutionary history.[17] This is particularly the case when we are dealing with large and variegated countries such as France, Mexico, and China that display marked regional variations, such that regional "stages," even if they can be discerned in the first place, may not correspond closely to national "stages."[18]

In this sense, revolutions are like wars (and, by analogy, "great" revolutions are like "total" wars): we can offer a useful definition, and by and large, we think we know one when we see one, but that does not mean that all wars—or "total" wars—follow a recognizable pattern. The pattern—the plot—is different in each case; as a result, revolutions, regarding both outbreak and trajectory, have been notoriously difficult to predict.[19] Two obvious reasons for this bewildering variety, which, I repeat, would be less striking in the case of economic trajectories (e.g., processes of industrialization), are, first, the role of individual decision-making, which can have decisive consequences for the course of wars or revolutions alike, and second, the part played by external actors, typically foreign powers that choose, usually unwisely and counterproductively, to intervene in revolutionary situations.[20] The First World War precipitated the Russian Revolution and was immediately followed by the abortive Allied intervention; while, in comparable fashion, the Allied campaigns against the Ottoman Empire culminated in the Greek invasion of 1919 and the Turkish "war of national liberation," which brought Atatürk to power.[21] The Japanese invasion, too, was crucial in determining the course and outcome of the Chinese Revolution.[22]

In contrast, the Mexican Revolution was largely self-contained: American intervention was limited to two major incursions (the Veracruz occupation of 1914 and the Punitive Expedition of 1916–17); neither involved extensive military campaigns, and neither, in my view, had decisive consequences for the revolution.[23] The Cuban Revolution also unfolded in fairly autonomous fashion during 1956–59; it was not until after the revolutionaries' triumphant entry into Havana in January 1959 that American hostility, culminating in the Bay of Pigs invasion (1961), became a determining factor in Cuba's revolutionary story.[24] Thus, while foreign intervention follows contrasting patterns—sometimes crucial (China, Turkey), sometimes marginal (Mexico), sometimes effective (Guatemala), sometimes abortive, even counterproductive (Russia, Cuba)—it is sufficiently common to constitute a key variable, and when that variable is combined with individual decision-making (again, analogous to decision-making in wartime), it contributes to the bewildering variety of revolutionary trajectories, which makes "stage theories" (and similarly mechanistic models) largely untenable.

However, while the plots of revolutions are, it seems to me, highly variable and "unpatterned" ("just so" stories, if you like), the actors involved may display common features that are worthy of comparison. By "actors" I mean collective groups (who, of course, may have their leaders, and those leaders may also provide useful labels—in the Mexican case, Madero for the Maderistas, Zapata for the Zapatistas, etc.). And as I shift into my more positive (faith-based) argument and start "lumping" instead of "splitting," I will focus on these collective groups. As will become apparent, these groups, while they are not reducible (even "in the last analysis") to social classes, do embody a strong class dimension, but this dimension needs to be supplemented by, we might say, a "politico-cultural" dimension. So if we wed class to politics and culture, we get the clumsy but serviceable qualifier "sociopolitico-cultural."

Thus, in a recent study of the Mexican Revolution and its collective actors, I noted the almost endless permutation of categories that could potentially be deployed (involving class, ethnicity, gender, locality/region, faction, generation, and ideology, both secular and religious).[25] But in seeking to escape from this labyrinth, I noted that some particular sociopolitico-cultural constellations—syndromes? persuasions? coalitions?—played a prominent role in the revolution and, furthermore, "made sense": for example, the poorly educated insurgent peasants who loyally followed Zapata in his home state of Morelos and who were agrarista in terms of their program, "popular liberal" by political tradition, and "folk Catholic" in respect to religion.[26] In contrast, other "constellations" were purely hypothetical and therefore irrelevant; for example, there were no female anarchist Indians to be found in the northeastern industrial city of Monterrey. In other words, these "constellations" embodied recognizable patterns (or, we could say, "elective affinities"). I also suggested that several of the main Mexican constellations had approximate counterparts in other revolutions, and it is this parallel that I will now pursue, eventually stressing one constellation in particular.

The analysis identifies five principal constellations—or six, if we include, as we should, the ancien régime against which the revolution fought and whose character inevitably affected the nature of the revolution itself. So, beginning with (1) the old regime, I go on to discuss (2) liberal constitutionalism; (3) working-class mobilization; (4) peasant protest; (5) Jacobin statism (the latter receiving somewhat privileged attention, since it is a more original and, probably, contentious category); and, very briefly, (6) statist socialism. Again, I stress that these categories combine both social (or class) makeup and politico-cultural attributes.[27]

The Old Regime

"Old regimes" are not, of course, monolithic, but for the sake of simplicity they can be categorized as the collective actors who stood behind the status quo, resisted rebellion, and were in turn targeted by rebels. In every case of successful revolution, the old regime was authoritarian. However, the basis of the authoritarianism varied, being in several cases dynastic (France, China, Russia, the Ottoman Empire) but in others republican/authoritarian (Mexico and Cuba).[28] (Thus, as Samuel Huntington concludes, no major revolution has overthrown a functioning democratic regime.)[29]

In Mexico, the social actors supportive of the old regime were landlords, the army, foreign business, and, with qualifications, the Catholic Church. Clearly, old regime coalitions varied from country to country: "foreign business" would be an anomalous category in eighteenth-century France, and the Ottoman army was a source of both revolutionary opposition and counterrevolutionary support for the old regime.[30] One feature of old regime resistance is worth highlighting, since it is apparent in several, if not all, cases: as old regime interests confronted revolution and were forced to react to early revolutionary victories, so they became more intransigent, nakedly coercive, and, arguably, illegitimate. When dynastic regimes collapsed, "men on horseback" briefly replaced kings and emperors: Yuan Shihkai seized power in China, driving Sun Yat-sen into exile and subverting the infant republic; while in Russia, Lavr Kornilov, having plotted against Alexander Kerensky's provisional government and failed to crush the Petrograd Soviet, led the White Russian counterrevolution, promising root-and-branch repression.[31] Both failed.

In Mexico, too, though there was no king to topple, the fall of the old president-dictator Porfirio Díaz in 1911 presaged the brief ultramilitarist regime of Victoriano Huerta in 1913–14.[32] Here, too, Huerta's militarized old regime, lacking dynastic legitimacy and facing mounting revolutionary opposition, soon collapsed, its chief historical legacy being to radicalize and extend the revolution that it sought to crush ("cost what it may," as Huerta liked to say). Of course, militarized old regimes sometimes succeed: witness Austria in 1848 or the military coup in Guatemala in 1954 (and its harshly repressive consequences).[33] France is an interesting example: Napoleon steered a middle course, endorsing (and exporting) much of the initial revolutionary program while subverting republican democracy and creating a new form of shaky but durable dynastic legitimacy.

Liberal Constitutionalism

Turning to the more important *revolutionary* collective actors, the first to identify would be liberal constitutionalism, typically espoused by enlightened educated leaders (usually of "bourgeois" origins) who enjoyed support among the urban middle and sometimes working classes, as well as certain sectors of the rural population. In Mexico, Francisco Madero, a well-to-do northern landlord and businessman, attracted widespread support in 1909-10, especially among the urban middle and working classes and to some extent from peasants (and rancheros) nurtured in the strong tradition of Mexican "popular liberalism."[34] Madero's program involved a bold commitment to liberal democracy ("bold," given Mexico's shaky democratic record and the authoritarian practices of the Porfirian old regime), but it lacked any clear-cut nationalist or anticlerical content, and when it came to social (i.e., land and labor) reform, Madero believed, optimistically, that progress could be made gradually and consensually through the ballot box. Meanwhile, property rights would be respected (at best, land reform might be given a nudge by judicious fiscal policy).[35]

The liberal-constitutionalist state would therefore be limited, democratic, and compatible with market capitalism of the kind that Madero, as a go-ahead northern businessman, had successfully practiced prior to the revolution.[36] Madero/Maderismo had clear analogies—mutatis mutandis—elsewhere: Antoine Barnave and the French Feuillants in 1789–92; the Society of Ottoman Liberals in Turkey and their contemporaries, the Chinese Constitutionalists; the Russian Kadets (Constitutional Democrats) in 1917; Manuel Azana and Juan Negrín in the Spanish Republic of the 1930s; and, finally, the liberal wing of the Cuban revolutionary coalition of the late 1950s.[37] All favored constitutional liberalism, a degree of democracy, and, at best, moderate socioeconomic reform. Education, too, was stressed as a means to uplift and improve the not necessarily very liberal masses.[38] Of course, there were important differences: in China and the Ottoman Empire, constitutional liberalism had a sharper nationalist edge that reflected widespread resentment against foreign tutelage.[39]

Again, we can note a common outcome. Constitutional liberalism typically failed, yielding to one of three alternative outcomes: military counterrevolution (Mexico and China in the short term, Spain in the long term), radical social revolution (Russia and Cuba from the start, China eventually), and what I will define as "Jacobin" revolution (France in the short term, Mexico and the Ottoman Empire in the long term).[40] Constitutional liberalism failed for numerous reasons: in the Mexican case, not because of its social radicalism but because the underlying sociopolitical consensus necessary for a functioning liberal democracy to take root was absent. And that consensus was absent because the revolution had unleashed latent social (and other) tensions that could not be peacefully accommodated within decorous electoral politics. In other words, revolutions—which by definition involve sharp sociopolitical polarization—are probably the worst environments in which to nurture an infant democracy.[41]

The same was true, in part, of Cuba (and Bolivia in 1952). In Cuba the revolutionary leadership showed scant regard for "bourgeois democracy" and, by virtue of their military triumph, had the power to take full control of a smallish, well-integrated, thus controllable island, ousting their erstwhile liberal-constitutionalist allies. Elsewhere, international warfare made the climate even more uncongenial to liberal democracy, which, in many cases, had shallower roots in society than it did in Mexico or Cuba. In Russia, Ottoman Turkey, and China, both structural and conjunctural factors conspired against the liberal-constitutionalist program. Typically, therefore, while revolutions often began with liberal-constitutionalist overtures, this motif tended to fade with time—sometimes quite quickly—and rival ideologies/coalitions determined the final outcome.

Working-Class Mobilization

A second collective actor would be the urban working class, a category that combines both spatial-cultural ("urban") and class-structural ("working-class") features.[42] The first feature connotes location in a densely populated environment that may present opportunities for both collective action (e.g., Red Petrograd) and old regime repression (e.g., Mexico in 1907 and again in 1910).[43] In many cases, repression seems to succeed (consider Germany in 1919 or Shanghai in 1927), which means either that the revolution fails or that it adopts an alternative (rural) path to victory, a strategy giving priority to "los de la sierra" (as Che Guevara put it) and producing what Huntington rather confusingly calls the "Eastern" path of popular revolution, whereby the forces of provincial insurgency converge on a conservative, if not counterrevolutionary, capital.[44] Provincial insurgency, of course, means mass peasant participation, as I shall mention in a moment.

The two big exceptions to this familiar—Mexican, Chinese, Cuban—pattern are France (i.e., Paris) in 1789 and Russia (St. Petersburg and Moscow) in 1917, these being cases in which urban working-class insurrection triumphed. But even this ostensible similarity conceals an obvious contrast: the French urban (Parisian) working class consisted of artisans and the city poor (roughly the *sans-culottes*), whereas the Russian workers were industrial proletarians, many of them congregated in large factories.[45] In this respect, Russia was the outlier, since factory production, including heavy industry, had grown rapidly under the stimulus of Sergei Witte's policy in the 1890s, followed by the pressing demands of the war after 1914.[46] The Russian industrial proletariat was thus a large and burgeoning class located in large and burgeoning cities.[47] Even if these proletarians were of fairly recent peasant extraction, the structure of production, coupled with tsarist intransigence and wartime privations, created a powerful, concentrated, urban revolutionary movement whose leadership the Bolsheviks adroitly assumed.[48]

With the exception of Germany, where somewhat similar conditions prevailed in 1919, the Russian story was unusual; elsewhere, industry was less developed, the industrial proletariat was too small to constitute a powerful revolutionary force, and the bulk of the urban working class consisted of artisans—some better off, some desperately poor—who resembled Parisian sans-culottes more than the metal workers of Red Petrograd. Mexico City in 1910 housed only ten thousand factory workers (barely 2 percent of the city's population); one-third of these were women; and the biggest proletarian concentrations were in textiles and cigarettes (where women constituted 20 percent and over 50 percent of the respective labor forces). Indeed, seamstresses and dressmakers were about as numerous as industrial factory workers, while both were greatly outnumbered by the sixty-five thousand female domestic servants, who constituted 30 percent of the city's total labor force, both male and female.[49] (Given the analysis that follows, we may note that late Ottoman industry resembled the Mexican pattern much more than the Russian, since "the Turkish working class was fragile and largely dispersed in small-scale enterprises.")[50]

The same argument can be put in different but familiar terms if we recall that major revolutions have typically occurred in "developing" countries/ economies where industry, especially heavy industry, is marginal, where artisan production is dominant, and where the peasantry remains a major component of society.[51] Or, a closely related argument, that revolutions are often the work not of confident "rising" classes (like Tawney's English gentry or Marx's bourgeoisie) but, rather, of embattled classes facing decline (such as peasants, artisans, or Trevor-Roper's downwardly mobile English gentry).[52]

Thus, we need to pay close attention to the artisan population and to the alliances that, in revolutionary times, artisans struck with other political groups. In the Mexican case, artisans not only outnumbered industrial proletarians but also displayed a distinct urban political culture based on tradition (going back, in some cases, to the colonial *gremios* [guilds]), as well as long-standing urban residence.[53] In short, Mexican artisans were not usually recent peasant migrants (as many Russian factory workers were); they formed part of a common urban culture that, at times, involved looking down on boorish country bumpkins; they were disproportionately literate (Mexico City had a literacy rate of 51 percent in 1910, when the national figure was 21 percent); and they were often proud of both their bookish culture and their capacity for earnest self-improvement.[54] This—the aspiring and often austere culture of working-class betterment—had many global parallels: among French artisans (such as the silk workers of Lyon) and the "labor sects" of nineteenth-century Britain, notably the primitive Methodists; and in the towns and cities of Spain, especially on the eastern seaboard and across the south, where anarchism flourished, proclaiming the emancipatory benefits of abstinence and education.[55] Russia, too, had its working-class advocates of austerity and self-improvement who looked down their noses at peasant vice and illiteracy, but they were a small and unrepresentative minority.[56]

Thus, in Mexico, urban artisans played a key role in both the initial electoral mobilization of 1909-10 and the formation of revolutionary armed forces in 1910–14. In the state of Veracruz, for example, where a large factory proletariat did exist and had, at great cost, pioneered unionization in the 1900s, the popular revolution was led by artisans and small tradesmen such as Gabriel Gavira (carpenter), Rafael Tapia (saddle-maker), and Camerino Z. Mendoza (shopkeeper).[57] And when the revolution triumphed, the lively radical politics of the port of Veracruz revolved around the *sindicato* (union) of prostitutes, the association of *inquilinos* (tenants, who were aggrieved at high rents and slum conditions), and the strategically placed stevedores' union, all under the loose leadership of the one-eyed Bohemian tailor Herón Proal.[58]

In Mexico City, too, working-class radicalism tended to be the work of artisans, who filled the ranks of the nascent Casa del Obrero Mundial after 1912.[59] These were men (and they were mostly men) who were steeped in the old Mexican liberal-patriotic tradition and for whom liberalism provided a bridge to more radical notions, some of distinctly anarchist character: a stress on austerity, education, and self-improvement and a suspicion of—if not an outright hostility to—the Catholic Church, its obscurantism, and its connivance with bosses and landlords.[60] And when it came to patriotism, traditional sentiments were accentuated by the role of Spanish (*gachupín*) businessmen, both industrial managers and retailers, in the urban economies of Mexico City, Puebla, and Veracruz.[61] As in China and Turkey, nationalism thus sharpened the edge of class conflict.[62] To the extent that more genuinely proletarian workers, grouped in larger units, played prominent roles in the revolution, they were to be found not in big factories but in the transport sector—typically, railwaymen and stevedores, both being groups involved in the export sector, where, again, they contested the authority of foreign management.[63]

Granted a common urban culture, a shared place of residence, and a historic commitment to often radical liberalism, these working-class spokesmen could forge alliances with middle-class (or, if you prefer, "bourgeois") activists; thus, a tentative détente under Madero (1911–13) eventually became a formal alliance in 1915, when the Casa struck a deal with Álvaro Obregón and the Constitutionalists and enrolled in the so-called Red Battalions.[64] While the notion that this alliance involved workers perversely taking up arms against their peasant comrades is rather too simple, it is clear that Casa leaders, true to their urban origins, often jibbed at peasant ignorance and superstition (while resenting the Zapatistas' interruption of the city's water supply or their forcing the closure of textile mills on the capital's southern flank).[65] Again, this was not a peculiarly Mexican phenomenon. In France, urban working-class recruits under the flag of the republic helped—not very expertly—in the ruthless repression of the rebels of La Vendée.[66]

The urban working class, not least the factory proletariat, thus played a major role in the Russian Revolution (a role that reflected Russia's greater level of industrial development and concentration, chiefly in Moscow and St. Petersburg). However, in Mexico, as in France, Spain, China, and Turkey, the role of the working class, though important, was ancillary and, given the greater importance of small-scale production, involved artisanal rather than industrial workers. Especially where they confronted an "obscurantist" Catholic Church, artisans mobilized in opposition to the old regime, typically in alliance with middle-class and petty-bourgeois liberals and radicals (as I discuss below). In the process—and here the Mexican case is exemplary—working-class anarchism, which had often evolved out of radical liberalism, faced an existential dilemma: whether to resist or to ally with (and perhaps succumb to) rivals on the left who embraced the state and, far from smashing it, sought to capture and use it.

In Russia, Bolshevik ultrastatism prevailed, and residual working-class anarchism was annihilated; a similar outcome later ensued in China. In Mexico, a different form of statism that was exemplified by Plutarco Elías Calles and, I will argue, can be usefully termed "Jacobinism" finally triumphed. The Casa was supplanted by the Confederación Regional Obrera Mexicana (Mexican Regional Labor Confederation, or CROM— the R for "Regional" suggests its anarchist origins), which became a close ally of the Sonoran ("Jacobin") state in the 1920s; and the Confederación General de Trabajo (General Confederation of Labor, CGT), which still carried aloft the old independent/anarchist banner, was marginalized by both the CROM and its 1930s successor, the Confederación de Trabajadores de México (Confederation of Mexican Workers, CTM), both of which contributed mightily to the consolidation of a strong state and an enduring political machine.[67] As Charles Maier has recently argued, from about the 1870s on, states embarked upon a century of robust growth in scope and strength, which political movements of all stripes had to reckon with, and Mexico was no exception.[68]

Peasant Protest

A third recurrent component involved peasant—or, if you prefer, popular rural—movements committed to a program of autonomy, land reform, and self-government. Such programs displayed both nostalgic, backward-looking features (e.g., the desire to restore the defunct or dying peasant community, perhaps suitably gilded) and radical, forward-looking goals (e.g., land reform and local democracy). (This retrospective/prospective distinction, often invoked, may at times be more trouble than it's worth.)[69] Some peasant rebels chiefly sought autonomy and self-government (in the Mexican context I have termed these *serranos*, roughly "highlanders").[70] Others (in Mexican terminology, agraristas) went further in demanding extensive land reform, which implied a transformation of property rights and even class relations. In the first instance, usually involving peripheral uplands, it was the state and its abuses (taxation, corrupt officialdom, military conscription) that principally provoked rebellion; in the second, where lowland commercial agriculture and peasant dispossession were the drivers, it was the landed elite, closely allied with the state, that was the chief target.[71]

Globally, peasant movements have assumed quite different "formal" ideologies (liberal, anarchist, socialist, communist, royalist, fascist, and religious/millenarian).[72] But common to many, perhaps most, was the desire for autonomy and self-government, often linked to notions of economic (i.e., landed) patrimony, these notions, as James Scott has stressed, frequently embodying the logic of the "moral economy."[73] And peasant mobilization has been key to several major revolutions, from the French, through the Mexican and Russian, to the Chinese. Thus, we might say, Bakunin (rather than Marx) was proved right in discerning the revolutionary potential of the rural poor in "backward" societies as against the supposed vanguard role of the industrial proletariat in "advanced" societies. The common causality, as Eric Wolf argued in his seminal work, *Peasant Wars of the Twentieth Century*, was the corrosive spread of market capitalism, in part made possible by the growth of stronger states endowed with greater political and technological power.[74]

This much is well-known—and, perhaps, not too contentious. When it comes to the ideological alignments of peasant movements, outcomes are, as I have suggested, widely diverse, a reflection, I would suggest, of peasant pragmatism. Given a basic interest in political and economic autonomy, peasants tended to favor programs and ideologies promising decentralization, self-government, and, where necessary, land reform, in particular, federalism, liberalism, and anarchism. Peasants might strike pragmatic alliances with centralizing movements such as Bonapartism and, more starkly, Chinese Communism, but the Bonapartist appeal involved the maintenance of the landed status quo achieved by the revolution, while the alliance with the Chinese Communist Party was forged in the furnace of the Japanese invasion, when the Communists alone seemed to promise honest, capable, and effective rule.[75]

More frequently and perhaps more logically, peasants aligned with federalist, liberal, decentralizing, and anarchist movements: Nestor Makhno in Ukraine; Zapata in south-central Mexico; the federalists and, later, the anarchists of Spain, especially southern and eastern Spain.[76] Ultimately, these alliances largely failed: both the Makhnovschina and the Andalusian anarchists were militarily defeated, and while the Zapatistas achieved a substantial measure of self-government and radical land reform during the 1920s, they did so by deferring to the authority of the new revolutionary state. To cite Maier again: the growth of the state ("Leviathan 2.0," to give it its trendy title) has been a constant since the later nineteenth century; hence, political movements premised on the demise or debilitation of the state have faced an uphill struggle that usually ends in either outright defeat or grudging compromise. As Maier puts it (using what now sounds like an unfortunate choice of words), from about the 1870s, "the organized national or imperial state was trump."[77]

Jacobin Statism

But defeat or grudging compromise with whom or what? If both constitutional liberalism and peasant anarchism lost out, who were the winners—the state builders who contributed to "Leviathan 2.0" and who successfully rode the tide of revolution to power? Apart from outright state repression, whether monarchical, fascist, or praetorian, there are, I think, two alternatives associated with successful revolutions.[78] The most obvious, already mentioned, would be Communist regimes involving powerful—critics would say totalitarian—states and parties and command economies. Communist success meant both the death of liberal constitutionalism ("bourgeois democracy") and the subjugation of the peasantry to the command economy, ultimately involving forced collectivization.[79] This grim outcome is well-known, and since it is an outcome that Mexico avoided (whatever conservative critics might say, its collective ejidos [community land grants] were nothing like Soviet *kolkhozy*), I shall give it a miss.

But there is a second, perhaps less obvious variant. This variant I would call the "Jacobin" option or "constellation." (As mentioned above, there are several terminological alternatives: I rather arbitrarily plumped for "constellation" over "syndrome" or "persuasion.") The Jacobin constellation sought the creation of a strong centralized state based on notions of republican citizenship and national sentiment while maintaining a broadly market-capitalist economy ("the Jacobins were great respecters of property"), albeit with an enhanced role for a regulatory but not asset-owning state.[80] Jacobinism made much of its popular legitimacy, but it was prepared, when the national interest and *raison d'état* demanded it, to ride roughshod over popular groups—not just fanatics and counterrevolutionaries but even its own popular (e.g., sans-culottes) allies.[81] A final key feature of the Jacobin constellation was its visceral hostility to the Catholic Church, even to religious belief in general, which it saw as antithetical to republican rule, national integration, and even economic progress (since the church promoted backward superstition and irrationalism while conniving with well-to-do conservatives in order to resist the revolution).[82]

"Jacobinism," of course, was originally a French invention, though the term—and, I would stress, the associated ideas and practices—cropped up elsewhere, from eighteenth-century England to nineteenth-century Argentina and twentieth-century Mexico.[83] It flourished particularly in the hothouse of revolution. Changing the metaphor, Jacobin currents swirled in the maelstrom of revolution in Russia and China, but Communist parties prevailed, cannibalizing Jacobinism and appropriating its centralizing, nationalist, republican, and anticlerical components while adopting radically different economic programs of *dirigisme*, forced industrialization, and rural collectivization.[84] In other cases, Jacobinism held its own and even triumphed. Obviously, France was one such case: Bonapartism compromised with the church, but on terms that permitted the establishment of a strong, centralizing, nationalist state.[85] Furthermore, the compromise between church and state did not last, and during the later nineteenth century, the struggle was resumed when, we might say, the neo-Jacobins of the Third Republic reasserted the power of the central state and set out to curtail the political and educational role of the Catholic Church. Then in France, as (later) in Mexico, schoolteacher and curé/cura confronted each other in a strenuous battle for hearts and minds.[86]

Mexico is a second case in point. As I have argued elsewhere, a Jacobin element played a major role in the armed revolution and, a fortiori, in the creation of the revolutionary state in the 1920s and 1930s.[87] In the process, the old regime was decisively defeated, constitutional liberalism wilted, and popular agrarianism had to come to terms with a centralizing (but reformist) state. Even when, under Lázaro Cárdenas (1934–40), the regime briefly flirted with socialism, Jacobinism survived and, arguably, outlived its (vaguely) socialist rival; thus, the regime of the PRI after 1946 was nationalist, republican, and centralizing while retaining vestiges of anticlericalism and coexisting happily with a capitalist (but a regulated capitalist) market. It would be a stretch to call the Priato—the post-1946 regime of the PRI—"Jacobin," tout court, but like the French Third Republic, it carried the genetic imprint of its origins.[88]

The emblematic leader of Mexican Jacobinism was Plutarco Elías Calles, a revolutionary caudillo (warlord) of the second rank but also the chief architect of the state of the 1920s, creator of the official party (the PNR, 1929), a dogged centralizer, robust nationalist, protagonist of popular education, science, and secularism, and visceral enemy of the Catholic Church.[89] As governor of the key northwestern state of Sonora (1915–19) and subsequently minister in the first "Sonoran" administration (1920–24), he served as president (1924–28) and *jefe máximo* (big boss) of the regime— sometimes referred to also as the "revolutionary family"—between 1928 and 1935.[90] In pursuit of his nationalist and centralizing goals, he battled the United States and foreign oil companies before finally reaching a modus vivendi with both. He curbed the power of regional caudillos and forged an alliance with organized labor. Though the term "socialism" was much bandied about, Calles had no intention of creating a command economy (indeed, he and his cronies acquired sizeable business interests); his goal was to achieve an "equilibrium" between labor and business, with the central state acting as arbiter.

Above all, Calles sought to combat the Catholic Church, which he saw as politically reactionary, hostile to the revolutionary state, and responsible for Mexico's economic and cultural backwardness.[91] He therefore set out to break the politico-cultural power of the church (its once-famed economic power was a thing of the past), resorting to both negative sanctions (restricting the numbers and the public role of priests, curtailing Catholic schooling, banning Catholic political activism) and positive incentives (the promotion of public education, secular fiestas and rituals, sport, science, and technology).[92]

It has been suggested that much of this was window-dressing, designed to distract the Mexican masses from serious social problems. But not only was Calles, as far as I can see, deadly serious; his anticlerical measures were also politically risky, even counterproductive, and he was too smart a politician to believe that those measures would win him easy popularity. He enacted them because he believed in them. Nor was he alone: the root-and-branch Jacobins were certainly a minority, perhaps even within the ruling elite, but they—Calles, Alvarado, Diéguez, Múgica, Garrido Canabál—were sufficiently powerful and committed to set their stamp on the regime.[93] And as a result of their policies, the state faced a major Catholic (Cristero) insurrection in west-central Mexico—Mexico's Vendée, it has been justly called—which raged for three years (1926–29).[94] After 1929, outright military confrontation was avoided, not least because Rome and the Mexican hierarchy reined in the Catholic radicals, but a "war of positions" continued for another decade, involving sporadic violence and, more important, Manichaean "culture wars" in streets, plazas, classrooms, and colleges.

Calles's maximalist goal—eliminating the Catholic Church as a major institution in Mexican life—was never realized; like other radical anticlericals in both France and Russia, he found the church—and religion—too tough a nut to crack.[95] The Mexican Schismatic Church of the 1920s and the secular fiestas and socialist baptisms of the 1930s did not put down deep roots.[96] Today, they remain quaint historical memories preserved in jerky black-and-white newsreels. They failed, I would argue, not because "secular religion" proved to be an inferior religion to its (Catholic) rival but because it was not really a religion at all, except in some loosely metaphorical sense. It could not connect to the supernatural (or, if you prefer, the transcendental), and it did not offer solace, however spurious, in times of suffering.[97] The majority of the Mexican people remained Catholic, and when that attachment did begin to fray in the later twentieth century, it was due not to "secular religion" but to evangelical Protestantism, which offered spiritual rapture, revivalism, faith healing, and hellfire sermons.[98]

The Jacobin state found it hard to change hearts and minds, but it could create—and veto—institutions: for decades it remained formally committed to lay public education, it maintained the ban on formally religious parties (so, unlike Chile, Mexico never acquired a self-styled Christian Democratic party), and, at least until the 1990s, it kept Rome and the hierarchy at arm's length.

The story of Mexican anticlericalism suggests two parallels, one obvious, one more recondite (but still, I suggest, valid). Catholic countries, including medieval and early modern England, often spawned anticlerical movements that, eventually, veered toward Jacobinism. If France was the pioneer, then Italy and Spain soon followed suit. Indeed, the parallels between Spain and Mexico are, not surprisingly, striking: both generated vigorous liberal parties and programs in the nineteenth century, as a result of which church corporate property came under attack (desamortización). Mexican liberalism achieved greater success, not least because it forged an indissoluble link with Mexican patriotism as a result of the French Intervention of the 1860s, while in Spain the Right benefited from its intimate association with the church, the patria (grande), and the empire. Spanish anticlericalism thus became even more strident and violent than its Mexican counterpart: in the Barcelona *semana trágica* of 1909 and across much of the country after 1936. Catholics (such as Graham Greene) complained of Mexico's vicious persecution of the church, yet Mexican anticlericalism, for all its radicalism and violence, was much less brutal and sanguinary than its Spanish counterpart.[99]

Nevertheless, in both countries, radical revolutionaries—Jacobins, socialists, and anarchists—saw the church as a formidable enemy that had to be combatted. Of course, the church fought back, much more successfully in Spain, where it lauded, legitimated, and marched alongside Franco's Nationalists. And in doing so, it set its indelible stamp on the post-1939 regime.

It should not be forgotten that the Communist revolutions of the twentieth century, for all their commitment to economic dirigisme and the building of socialism, also combatted religion. The Bolsheviks (in Paul Froese's hyperbolic phrase) hatched a "plot to kill God," at least until the Second World War obliged them to reach a (temporary) truce with Russian Orthodoxy.[100] In particular, literate aspiring workers in revolutionary Russia as in Spain and Mexico advocated personal austerity, a Puritan ethic, and "the rejection of religion."[101] In each case, however, revolutionary regimes found it impossible to extirpate religion (and the institutional church); though, perhaps more than Froese recognizes, they did contest and check its authority.

However, it is less the long-term outcome than the preceding process of conflict that concerns us. Given the political claims that they make on their populations, revolutionary regimes are very likely to target churches and religions, just as the latter are likely to resist. And resistance is all the greater in cases where the church itself is powerful and possessed of its own strong sense of mission. In largely Protestant societies that are characterized by religious diversity, the clash is muted; hence, as a general rule, Jacobin anticlericalism is much less evident in Britain, the United States, and Scandinavia.[102] Even in some Catholic countries where the church was weaker, revolutionary regimes felt less need to take up the anticlerical cudgels. The obvious example is Cuba, where the—historically weak—Catholic Church was outmatched by the revolutionary state, and eventually the two reached a modus vivendi.[103] There was no Cuban Vendée, no Cuban Cristiada.

However, a final case widens the analysis and suggests that revolutionary Jacobinism is not purely a feature of Christian Catholic societies. Mexico and Turkey are rarely compared, yet they offer some intriguing parallels: approximately similar levels of development; a fairly small industrial proletariat (already mentioned); a large rural/peasant sector; a vulnerable geopolitical location; and a period of mid-nineteenth-century liberal/constitutional reform (Turkey's Tanzimat period, the Mexican Reforma), each followed by a reversion to more authoritarian "order and progress" politics (the Hamidian regime, the Porfiriato).[104] Furthermore, although valid comparison does not demand ("emic") recognition on the part of historical actors, some Mexicans were aware of this parallel, and in the case of regional warlord Saturnino Cedillo, they admired Kemal Atatürk from afar.[105]

Cedillo's admiration was understandable. Like his Mexican revolutionary contemporaries, Atatürk came to power by military force, bent on deploying state power in order to radically reform what he saw as a backward society, the victim of predatory foreign powers.[106] Like Calles, Atatürk also sought to emulate his French Jacobin predecessors, striving, we might say, to "rationalize and nationalize" the disparate Turkish people; indeed, the French parallel is all the more valid, given Atatürk's taste for French social theory (Comte, Durkheim, Le Bon), which he shared with other Young Turks.[107] He did not espouse socialism: Kemalism is therefore seen as—yet another—"middle way" that rejects "individualism, liberalism, and socialism" in favor of a "solidaristic and corporatist" model couched in strongly nationalist discourse.[108]

This has been termed a "Turkish version of totalitarianism," and, certainly, it has an obvious kinship with fascism.[109] However, "fascism"—as manifested in "Third World" contexts such as Turkey and Latin America—had a different character and impact compared to the classic European cases of Italy and Germany, where Mussolini and Hitler were dedicated to destroying democracy and the Left. In contrast, the corporatism of Calles and Cárdenas—like Peronism or the radical nationalism of the Bolivian MNR—involved popular mobilization and genuine social reform. The Kemalist state—eventually a one-party state—was also committed to an ambitious kind of cultural revolution ("one of the greatest societal transformations of modern times"), which involved radical changes in Turkish life, involving Western script, judicial and sartorial reform (e.g., hats), (limited) rights for women, and a firm belief in the transformative power of education, most of which have clear contemporary Mexican parallels.[110]

In particular, Atatürk combatted Islam, which meant that an enlightened but authoritarian elite set about trying to subvert traditional popular beliefs and practices. As in the case of Calles, Atatürk's program involved developing and deepening anticlerical policies initiated by mid-nineteenth-century reformers, which had already "opened a chasm between the secular elite and the pious masses."[111] Under both leaders, that chasm greatly widened. And, like Calles, Atatürk was a devotee of secularism and science, something of an autodidact intellectual-in-politics.[112]

We could push the comparison further, if a little fancifully. Both leaders grew up in fatherless households (Atatürk also had a devout mother, a common pattern in Mexico, where anticlericalism tended to be a male, patriarchal preserve); both liked a drink or two; and, perhaps more significantly, both came from the outer (yet more "developed") periphery of their respective countries—the cosmopolitan city of Salonika (now Thessaloniki), in Atatürk's case, the big, bustling, arid, northwestern state of Sonora, in the case of Calles. They had lived on the borders of neighboring—but somewhat threatening—"modernity" (Europe and the United States); and their subsequent politico-cultural crusade involved the imposition of "modernity" on the backward heartland of their respective countries—Anatolia, "the new Fatherland" in the case of Atatürk, and "Indian" central and southeastern Mexico, in the case of Calles and the northern "proconsuls" who imposed their control on these "benighted" regions after 1915.[113] At the same time, both regimes invoked historical symbols drawn from that heartland: Hittite Sun symbols in Turkey and the iconic indigenismo displayed, for example, in Mexico's famous revolutionary murals.[114] In both cases, an aggressively "modernizing" (i.e., "rationalizing and nationalizing") project selectively incorporated both ancient history and the ethnic patrimony of peasant cultures (to which the "modernizers" did not belong and which, indeed, they set out to transform).

There may be a yet broader political pattern lurking here: the ruthless builders of revolutionary states/regimes often seem to hail from outlying provinces, whence they descend on a deliquescent "center" in order to seize control and, displaying the brusque contempt of outsiders, begin beating it into better shape. Such was the case with Calles and his fellow *fronterizos*; with Atatürk and a disproportionate number of the Young Turks, who came from Rumelia; with the Corsican Napoleon, the Ligurian Garibaldi, and the Georgian Stalin.[115] These were the "great men" of their respective revolutions, but a comparable phenomenon—whereby militant outsiders sought to "revolutionize" recalcitrant localities—was also evident lower in the political hierarchy, for example, in revolutionary France, where, Lynn Hunt notes, Jacobin militants were often "peripatetic politicians"—carpetbaggers, it could be said—who brashly inserted themselves into local politics.[116]

Atatürk's career and Turkey's national trajectory thus bear comparison with Calles and Mexico. And both cases can be subsumed under a loose "Jacobin" rubric. Of course, there were also major divergences: as targets of aggressive secularism, Islam and Catholicism were different in important respects (though both were formidable opponents); Mexico, while it had been a victim of predatory great powers in the nineteenth century, was more fortunate in the twentieth, even when it plunged into revolution; thus, its revolution was much less the product and plaything of Great Power ambition than was Turkey's. Furthermore, Turkey's substantial ethnic minorities, though they might be hypothetically compared to Mexico's substantial Indian population, presented far more formidable challenges to centralizing nationalist state builders.[117]

Atatürk presided over a polity from which his hometown of Salonika had been violently stripped away; in Calles's case, while there was some loose talk of Sonoran secession in 1913, it was never a real threat, since Sonora was too tightly linked to the Mexican nation-state, while the United States, a predatory land grabber in the 1840s, was, by the time of the revolution, well on the way to becoming Mexico's "Good Neighbor" (or, we could say more accurately, it had decided to relinquish coercive territorial expansion in favor of subtler forms of informal "imperialist" control and influence). Perhaps most important, the Young Turk revolution was a military "revolution from above," which, while it did not lack popular support, faced no counterbalancing "revolution from below" of the kind that the Mexican revolutionary leadership had to reckon with and that gave the Mexican Revolution its crucial popular, peasant, and agrarian dimension. Calles may have closely resembled Atatürk (and vice versa), but there was no Turkish Zapata, no sweeping Kemalist land reform. We should remember, however, that after the great *reparto* of the 1930s (the work of Cárdenas, carried through in the teeth of Callista opposition), the popular, populist, and agrarian thrust of the revolution was soon blunted. What emerged in Mexico post-1940, in the form of the Priísta regime, was arguably much more Callista than Cardenista, namely, a hegemonic party-state, nationalist and secular, tolerant of private enterprise but committed to state regulation, discursively reliant on the ageing myth of the revolution. Post-1940 Kemalism displayed many of the same characteristics, proof, I would suggest, of the tenacity of the Jacobin project that had been implemented in the 1920s and 1930s. And, to conclude, both Mexico and Turkey have, in recent years, witnessed the rollback of the old Jacobin project, involving a relaxation of religious restrictions and détente with clerical authorities. The Jacobin persuasion had a good run for its money, but like other politico-cultural revolutionary projects, it eventually faded, becoming more a matter of myth and memory than a practical political program.[118]

Notes

ACKNOWLEDGMENTS

1. When, in the late 1980s, Cambridge University Press declined to produce a paperback edition of my two-volume history of the Mexican Revolution, the University of Nebraska Press—a press known for its strong Mexican / Latin American list—stepped up to the plate: Alan Knight, *The Mexican Revolution*, 2 vols. (Lincoln: University of Nebraska Press, 1990).

2. John H. Arnold, Matthew Hilton, and Jan Rüger, eds., *History after Hobsbawm: Writing the Past for the Twenty-First Century* (Oxford: Oxford University Press, 2018). I don't doubt that the two chapters I refer to are excellent studies of Fenland folklore and Welsh woolen objects.

3. C. L. R. James, *The Black Jacobins: Toussaint L'Ouverture and the San Domingo Revolution* (London: Secker and Warburg, 1938) is probably the source of this odd usage. Just to be clear: the French colony of Saint-Domingue (later Haiti) is called Santo Domingo in Spanish.

4. See John Darwin, "John Andrew Gallagher, 1919–80," *Proceedings of the British Academy* 150 (2007): 57–75.

5. To be precise: there is one part-time historian of Latin America and one full-time historian of the pre-1800 Iberian world in a faculty of some 120.

INTRODUCTION

1. Luke Rhinehart, *The Dice Man* (New York: William Morrow, 1971).

2. As I later mention, the twentieth-century coverage is patchy, focusing chiefly on major revolutions, so the time period covered by the book as a whole is, roughly, the "long" nineteenth century, from independence to ca. 1930.

3. Some experts are leery of using the term "oligarchy," which carries a good deal of (negative) normative baggage and which—leaving Aristotle aside—is not a very well "theorized" concept. However, it is possible to use it with some objectivity and precision, and as an "organizing concept," it may be experiencing something of a revival: see, for example, Jeffrey A. Winters and Benjamin I. Page, "Oligarchy in the United States?" *Perspectives on Politics* 7, no. 4 (2009): 731–51, which, though focused on the United States, includes Singapore, Colombia, Russia, and Indonesia as putative "oligarchies." I use the term—in conjunction with "landed"—to describe the *hacendados/ estancieros/fazendeiros* of nineteenth-century Latin America, who arguably were the dominant socioeconomic class, even where they did not personally control the somewhat shaky and sometimes bloodstained levers of political power. Some, of course, did, but others delegated that power—whether out of choice or necessity—to "professional" politicians, such as caciques, *coroneis*, or regular and irregular military officers. Some landed "oligarchs" were go-ahead businessmen who diversified into trade and industry (so they could reasonably be called an "agrarian bourgeoisie"), but some were benighted rural backwoodsmen and/or exploiters of servile (slave) and semiservile (peon) labor for whom the "bourgeois" label would be inappropriate.

4. The Científicos of Porfirian Mexico (1876–1911), headed by Finance Minister Limantour, though closely aligned with the "landed oligarchy," devised and sought to implement a positivistic national "project" that went rather beyond the narrow interests of that class—interests that, of course, were diverse, not uniform. (Concerning tariffs, taxes, and currency reform, the henequen exporters of Yucatán did not necessarily agree with the grain producers of the Bajío.) Furthermore, the revolution that ousted the Científicos gave rise to a new state that enjoyed yet greater "relative autonomy" and, during the 1920s and 1930s, enacted policies—including land and labor reform—that incrementally undercut the oligarchy. That was unusual for Latin America at the time; however, other Latin American states—such as the Brazilian Empire, when it belatedly abolished slavery—occasionally adopted policies prejudicial to the landed interests (or to a significant section thereof).

5. John Womack Jr., *Zapata and the Mexican Revolution* (New York: Knopf, 1969), chap. 2, offers a graphic account.

6. Enrique Cárdenas Sánchez, *El largo curso de la economía mexicana: De 1780 a nuestro días* (Mexico City: FCE, 2015), 215–20; Simon Collier and William F. Sater, *A History of Chile* (Cambridge: Cambridge University Press, 1996), 166–67; Eugene Ridings, *Business Interest Groups in Nineteenth-Century Brazil*

(Cambridge: Cambridge University Press, 1996), 224–28. I discuss the role of the gold standard in chapter 5.

7. In the eyes of the *yori* (white/mestizo) population, the Yaquis were divided into *broncos*, "wild" Yaquis, who were prone to rebellion, and *mansos*, "tame" Yaquis, who were an important source of labor for the haciendas, mines, and urban economy of Sonora. In fact, the dividing line was porous, and the Porfirian policy of repression and deportation affected the state's labor supply as a whole. See Héctor Aguilar Camín, "The Relevant Tradition: Sonoran Leaders in the Revolution," in *Caudillo and Peasant in the Mexican Revolution*, ed. D. A. Brading (Cambridge: Cambridge University Press, 1980), 94–98.

8. If regionalism—the articulation of politics along regional (state or provincial) lines—was common to almost all Latin American countries, then Brazil was a particularly clear-cut case: under the Old Republic, which succeeded the empire in 1889, power was disproportionately shared between the coffee metropolis of São Paulo and the stock-raising state of Minas Gerais—the so-called *café com leite* (coffee with milk) alliance, which prevailed until 1930, when, under the leadership of Getulio Vargas, Rio Grande do Sul mounted a successful revolt. See the useful review article by Barbara Weinstein, "Brazilian Regionalism," *Latin American Research Review* 17, no. 2 (1982): 262–76.

9. John Mason Hart, *Revolutionary Mexico: The Coming and Process of the Mexican Revolution* (Berkeley: University of California Press, 1987) is a case in point.

10. What makes a bourgeoisie liberal—or fascistic, or clerical/conservative— obviously depends on a variety of historical factors, some of them politico-cultural (e.g., the role of the Catholic Church). But the socioeconomic context is crucial and can be very schematically summarized in terms of evolving class relationships. A bourgeoisie (a commercial, propertied class typically associated with urban interests) is, by definition, located between superordinate rivals above (the [feudal?] aristocracy, possibly allied with the [absolutist?] state) and subordinate plebeians (workers and peasants) below—plebeians who can potentially serve either as useful allies or as threatening enemies. The bourgeoise, we could say, can either "kick up," perhaps in alliance with the plebeians (e.g., England in the 1640s, France in 1789), or it can "kick down," combatting the plebeian threat, perhaps with the support of the residual aristocracy (e.g., Italy in the 1920s, Germany in the 1930s). The "kick-up" bourgeoisie will tend to espouse progressive, liberal, inclusive values; the "kick-down" bourgeoise will favor authoritarian and exclusionary solutions. The same crude syndrome is apparent, mutatis mutandis, in Latin America through the nineteenth and twentieth centuries.

11. E. P. Thompson, *The Making of the English Working Class* (Harmondsworth: Penguin, 1968).

12. Womack, *Zapata*, is a convincing account, flexibly Marxist in approach, that has stood the test of time. Or, looking beyond Mexico, Charles W. Bergquist, *Labor in Latin America: Comparative Essays on Chile, Argentina, Venezuela and Colombia* (Stanford: Stanford University Press, 1986), which, though it may not be convincing in every particular, also offers a perceptive comparative analysis in broadly Marxist terms. Plenty more citations could be given.

13. Which, taking into account the history of Mexico over the last century, is clearly not the case: "socialist" tendencies briefly peaked in the 1930s and subsequently declined as capitalism throve, first under the loosely nationalist/developmentalist aegis of the ruling PRI (1946–82), then, in even more red-blooded "neoliberal" guise, since the 1980s. Even the recent—rhetorical—abandonment of "neoliberalism" by President Andrés Manuel López Obrador has failed to reverse the process. In short, Mexico was, is, and, for the foreseeable future, remains thoroughly capitalist. If, as the Marxist metanarrative predicts, socialism is to emerge, it is taking its time, and its emergence will require some dramatic and unlikely change of direction. So, less an escalator than a roller-coaster.

14. I pluck these examples from Michel Foucault, *Archaeology of Knowledge* (London: Routledge, 2002), 12, 26, 36, where they float in a turgid soup of similar rarefied abstractions ("architectonic unities," "enunciative modalities," "points of diffraction/incompatibility/systematization," etc. [5, 55, 73]). It is probably a cheap shot, but this rambling, repetitive, and, in places, unreadable book carries a bit of blurb, contributed by Edward Said, that hails Foucault as a "brilliant writer" endowed with a "highly disciplined and coherent angle of vision." Yet even Foucault himself recognized that *Archaeology*—a "cautious, stumbling . . . text"—did not claim to offer a "coherent angle of vision": "At every turn, it stands back, measures up to what is before it, gropes towards its limits, stumbles against what it does not mean, and digs pits to mark out its own path" (pits into which some incautious followers have stumbled [18–19]). To be fair, Foucault's more focused historical work—such as *Discipline and Punish: The Birth of the Prison* (London: Penguin, 1991)—is rather more concrete and comprehensible, though not necessarily convincing.

15. In February 1913, when military rebels rose up against the Madero government in Mexico City, their leader, the old regime icon Bernardo Reyes, boldly led them across the Zócalo toward the presidential palace, expecting a tame

surrender; instead, shots rang out, Reyes was killed, the coup was hijacked by the reactionary Victoriano Huerta, and arguably the course of the Mexican Revolution underwent a decisive shift. (The young Alfonso Reyes, later one of Mexico's preeminent intellectuals, was also left fatherless.) Reyes's death was "contingent"—the bullet could have missed, he could have adopted a more prudent strategy—but it had important consequences. E. H. Carr, *What Is History?* (Harmondsworth: Pelican, 1964), 98, 101–2, similarly cites the sudden death of King Alexander of Greece in 1920, caused by a (contingent) monkey bite, which—according to Winston Churchill—triggered a political crisis, leading to thousands of deaths. Never one to shrink from hyperbole, Churchill declared that "a quarter of a million persons died of that monkey's bite." Carr, however, is more considered: recognizing that accidents will happen, he rightly queries Trotsky's odd argument (a desperate attempt to salvage society's inexorable "laws of motion") that "accidents" compensate and cancel each other out, leaving no net effect, but he also complains—again, correctly—that "the role of accident in history is nowadays seriously exaggerated by those who are interested to stress its importance" and that "when somebody tells me that history is a chapter of accidents, I tend to suspect him of intellectual laziness." A caveat that is worth remembering nowadays.

16. Nicolás Larín, *La rebelión de los cristeros (1926–1929)* (Mexico City: Ediciones Era, 1968), depicting the Cristero rebellion as a "clerical-feudal-imperialist conspiracy," is boilerplate Marxist history of the old school. A more subtle and scholarly study, but one that also leans toward a class/materialist interpretation, is John Tutino, *From Insurrection to Revolution in Mexico: Social Bases of Agrarian Violence, 1750–1940* (Princeton NJ: Princeton University Press, 1988), 342–47. Though much of the book (specifically, chapters 1 through 6) is convincing, it then veers somewhat off course, and the terse conclusion that "the Cristeros' demands were bluntly agrarian" is unconvincing. For a good résumé of the debate (as it then stood), see Ramón Jrade, "Inquiries into the Cristero Insurrection against the Mexican Revolution," *Latin American Research Review* 20, no. 2 (1985): 53–69; the summary of Larín's interpretation, as quoted above, appears on page 54.

17. Of course, Pascal's argument falls down if we accept Keynes's comment, apropos of long-run forecasts and planning, that "in the long run we are all dead." And, Keynes being an agnostic, "dead" for him meant dead, buried, defunct, not dead and providentially resurrected. Of course, the Cristeros agreed with Pascal, so they were, arguably, "rational," even if theirs was a

"bounded rationality"—that is, a rationality determined by their particular worldview, which not everyone shared.

18. In Latin America, ecological diversity and all that flows from it in terms of settlement, crops, and communications are particularly determined by altitude. Thus, the traveler who, in the 1900s, rode the "monster" train, hauled by a double locomotive, from the chilly highlands surrounding Mexico City down to the port of Veracruz descended three miles in the last one hundred miles of travel, passing from forested mountains across precipitous ravines and through warm valleys down to the "sweltering tropical swamps on the coast," witnessing, in this short trip, "all the climates of the world": Hans Gadow, *Through Southern Mexico* (London: Witherby and Co., 1908), 28–30. A similar pattern was evident in the Andes, where, since the time of the Incas, if not before, rural communities had organized production by exploiting such "vertical archipelagos": see the classic study of John V. Murra, *The Economic Organization of the Inka State* (Greenwich CT: JAI Press, 1980).

19. Alberto Flores Galindo, *Buscando un Inca: Identidad y utopía en los Andes* (Mexico City: Grijalbo, 1993), 274. By the twenty-first century, it should be noted, Peru's ties with Asia—both Japan and China—had significantly revived. It is also worth stressing that "integration" is not necessarily an unalloyed benefit for the "integrated" population; of itself, it does not guarantee welfare, income, rights, or representation; and it may, in fact, bring tighter social control, heavier taxation, and falling living standards. It all depends on the nature of the "integration."

20. Some analysts have flirted with the notion of "crop determinism" (my term): the notion that the nature of a region's crop has powerful social, economic, and even political consequences. The classic example was Fernando Ortiz's 1940 study of Cuban agriculture, which posited that tobacco was a smallholder product associated with a robust, patriotic Cuban yeomanry, while sugar was a colonial crop produced by slaves on large oppressive estates: *Cuban Counterpoint: Tobacco and Sugar* (Durham NC: Duke University Press, 1995). (Ortiz did not, of course, consider the consumption end of the story.) Some experts have also seen coffee as a distinctively smallholder crop, as opposed to sugar. And there is no doubt that extensive ranching has generated a footloose cowboy/gaucho culture while usually avoiding coercive labor systems such as slavery and peonage. Clearly, different crops require different ecological conditions, involve distinct processing systems, and tend to impose different labor regimes; to that extent, "crop determinism" does set some broad parameters. But, the parameters being broad, there is

ample scope for divergence. Coffee was a classic smallholder crop in Costa Rica but underpinned slave plantations in Brazil, notably São Paulo. Sugar promoted radical social protest in Mexico (1910s) and Cuba (1950s) but had no similarly radicalizing effect in Tucumán, Argentina; while in Peru, the traditional sugar-producing zones in the central departments of Lima and Ancash seem to have resembled Tucumán, but the boom-and-bust industry of the northern coast (Lambayeque and La Libertad) generated both a feisty labor movement (evident in the strikes of 1912, 1921, and 1931) and, by the 1930s, the radical nationalist movement APRA: see Peter F. Klaren, "The Sugar Industry in Peru," *Revista de Indias* 65, no. 233 (2005): 33–48. In other words, a great many additional variables intervene, diluting the effect of possible "crop determinism."

21. These seem to me to be the three principal and enduring economic-cum-ecological syndromes in Latin America, but there are others, albeit of less importance. Three that share a common feature also deserve mention. First, there were internal frontiers, which were often colonized by small farmers and ranchers (not big landowners) and which we see, for example, in Mexico and Colombia (coffee often being the key crop). The second syndrome involves what we could call "postplantation" rural societies, where, as in the Brazilian Northeast, commercial slave production ended, the market contracted, and a "new," usually very poor peasantry emerged from the ashes of the plantation: what Shepherd Forman, *The Brazilian Peasantry* (New York: Columbia University Press, 1975) calls a "precipitate peasantry." "Precipitate peasantries" also emerged in postemancipation Haiti, Jamaica, and the American South. Finally, the third syndrome concerns peasant communities reconstituted as a result of twentieth-century land reform programs that broke up big estates and distributed land to peasant farmers: the classic case was the Mexican *reparto* of the 1920s and 1930s, which created a massive new population of ejidatarios cultivating their ejidos (corporate land grants whose ownership was vested in the ejidal community, with individuals enjoying the usufruct). The common feature of all three is that they involve new—reconstituted or "precipitate"—peasantries, proof that peasant farming is not necessarily just a lingering vestige of an ancient traditional rural society.

22. Historians like to explode "myths" or, more prosaically, to question received opinions (as in: "it is commonly supposed that . . . but in fact . . ."). This is fair enough, since it promotes debate and, perhaps, historiographical progress. But it helps to know *whose* myths are being exploded and whether the "myths" are seriously considered opinions or just stereotypical straw men.

Some historians make a song-and-dance about debunking myths that few or no serious historians entertain (whatever the ill-informed opinion of the "Great British/American/Mexican public" might be). The notion that Latin America is distinctly revolutionary is, I think, a widespread popular misconception shared by much of the mass media: consider, for example, the iconographic salience of Pancho Villa, Frida Kahlo, and Che Guevara. Historians—or social scientists—probably know better. However, some of the other questionable myths that I mention (e.g., concerning Latin America's historic attachment to laissez-faire liberalism) are shared by respectable academics as well.

23. I feel reasonably confident in generalizing about the United Kingdom and, maybe, Europe, where Latin America is often ignored or, when not ignored, misunderstood. The United States is a more complicated case. Public awareness and knowledge of Latin America—indeed, the whole world beyond the borders of the United States—are known to be highly fallible. But where Latin America is concerned, there are important exceptions to this general rule, for example, communities along the southern border, colleges running Latin American programs (and sometimes university presses), and, finally, the huge Latin American diaspora, which now spreads far beyond Florida and the border states. That diaspora may nurture many misconceptions about Latin America (notably Cuba, Mexico, and Central America), but at least it is not carelessly indifferent.

24. "Postcolonial" is another much overdone adjective now promiscuously applied to entire branches of study (some of which have undergone a cosmetic change of name). Also, "postcolonialism," simply defined, is a very common condition in the history of the world—so common, in fact, that it lacks much specificity or explanatory power. Currently, the term tends to be applied to what used to be called the "Third World" (thus, Asia, Africa, and Latin America, and even there the diversity of "postcolonial" reality is enormous). But the United States, though it often seems to slip through the net, is very obviously "postcolonial"; so, arguably, are Greece, most of the Balkans, Italy, Spain and—if you go back far enough—Frankish Gaul and Anglo-Saxon England. Not much "postcolonial" commonality there.

25. A point well made in Miguel Angel Centeno, *Blood and Debt: War and the Nation-State in Latin America* (University Park: Penn State University Press, 2002). The relative absence of interstate warfare in Latin America may help explain the historically low and regressive tax systems of the region. To put it in positive terms, in Europe and the United States, major foreign wars have

served to push up government spending (which tends to be "downwardly sticky" even when the war is over), and more important, major—perhaps "total"—wars have often fostered a kind of social pact whereby the state demands sacrifice from its citizens in return for postwar social benefits (hence Britain's Beveridge Report or, in the United States, the GI Bill). Such wars being rare in Latin America, social pacts were largely absent, and social welfare lagged.

26. The vexed question of what qualifies as a "social" revolution depends, of course, on how we define these concepts and how high we set the bar—too high, and there are vanishingly few such revolutions in history; too low, and the category becomes hopelessly overpopulated. And the only criterion for preferring one definition over another is, in my view, analytical utility (as I mention in chapter 7). The Mexican Reform and the two Cuban insurgencies were political revolutions, regarding both process and eventual outcome, but I doubt that they changed society sufficiently to warrant "social revolutionary" status.

27. Regarding the twentieth century, I am confident about including Mexico, Bolivia, and Cuba. Nicaragua should perhaps be added, but here I plead lack of expertise and, perhaps, hindsight, so I play it safe by leaving it out. Hobsbawm considered the Colombian Violencia to be a "revolution manqué," but, stressing the adjective over the noun, I think it should be omitted.

28. The Pantanal is the world's biggest tropical wetland, straddling the borders of Paraguay, Brazil, and Bolivia.

29. Claudio Veliz, ed., *The Politics of Conformity in Latin America* (New York: Oxford University Press, 1967) and *Obstacles to Change in Latin America* (New York: Oxford University Press, 1965). A telling example of how the notion of Latin America as a region of socioeconomic inertia went mainstream is David S. Landes, *The Wealth and Poverty of Nations* (New York: W. W. Norton, 1999), chap. 20.

30. Linda S. Stevenson and Mitchell A. Seligson, "Fading Memories of Revolution: Is Stability Eroding in Mexico?" in *Polling for Democracy: Public Opinion and Political Liberalization in Mexico*, ed. Roderic Ai Camp (Wilmington DE: SR Books, 1996), 59–80.

31. R. J. Rummel, *Death by Government: Genocide and Mass Murder Since 1900* (New Brunswick NJ: Transaction Publishers, 1994). These categories are not, of course, watertight, and there may be debate about how particular forms of violence should be classified. However, historians and other social scientists often have to work with categories of this kind: it is more important that the categories should be useful than watertight.

32. For a good review of "dependency theory" by an outstanding historian, see Tulio Halperín Donghi, "'Dependency Theory' and Latin American Historiography," *Latin American Research Review* 17, no. 1 (1982): 115–30.

33. D. K. Fieldhouse, ed., *The Theory of Capitalist Imperialism* (London: Longman, 1974), 74–109, provides a selection from this extensive literature.

34. Gallagher and Robinson stressed that the defining feature of nineteenth-century Britain was its buoyant economic growth, which provided the (metropolitan) backdrop for dynamic global expansion, so the "first mover" of their theory, we could say, was metropolitan. But how that expansion played out in the "periphery" depended on "peripheral" factors; thus, they concluded, "imperialism . . . may be defined as a sufficient political function of this process of integrating new regions into the expanding economy" of Britain (John Gallagher and Ronald Robinson, "The Imperialism of Free Trade," *Economic History Review* 6, no. 1 [1953]: 5).

35. P. J. Cain and A. G. Hopkins, *British Imperialism: Innovation and Expansion, 1688–1914* (London: Longman, 1993) presents a different—and more convincing argument—to the effect that British capitalism, increasingly dominated by City financial interests, evolved a distinct form of "gentlemanly capitalism" to the detriment of industry and manufactured exports. We can see the effects in Latin America, since, during the late nineteenth century, Britain's share of the region's imports declined (relatively), while investment, both direct and indirect, increased. But at the same time, British politico-military interventionism faded as a result of changes taking place in (peripheral) Latin America, not the British metropolis. And as I stress in chapter 5, Latin American capitalism was not at all "gentlemanly."

36. The exceptions help support the argument: while most of Latin America was becoming more stable, respectable, and congenial (in British eyes), Venezuela bucked the trend and thus faced an Anglo-German naval blockade in 1902–3: Miriam Hood, *Gunboat Diplomacy 1895–1905: Great Power Pressure on Venezuela* (London: Allen and Unwin, 1983), chap. 10. And at the same time, U.S. interventions in the circum-Caribbean responded to similar perceptions of Latin American delinquency, coupled with fears of consequent European involvement.

37. "Generations" offer a useful way of periodizing and explaining long historical trajectories: see, for example, Luis González y González, *La ronda de las generaciones* (Mexico City: Clío, 1997). Of course, generations are not mathematical givens, and their definition is a matter of historical interpretation, in light of the pivotal events and experiences that constitute them. Furthermore, we

should beware of the "Harry Lime Theory of History": the notion, expressed by Harry in the movie *The Third Man*, that specific periods of history, such as the Renaissance, display a kind of seamless political, economic, social, and cultural unity. (The full text forms the epigraph to Centeno, *Blood and Debt*.) Of course, political, economic, social, and cultural histories interact, but they also display considerable mutual autonomy, and their respective trajectories move at different rhythms. My generational chronology is essentially politico-economic. There is no reason to assume that it would work for, say, art, architecture, science, philosophy, music, or literature.

38. The classic exponent of this emerging conservative political philosophy was the Mexican intellectual/businessman/statesman Lucas Alamán, who had witnessed the violence of the 1810 insurgency at first hand in Guanajuato: see Eric Van Young, *A Life Together: Lucas Alamán and Mexico, 1792–1853* (New Haven CT: Yale University Press, 2021). Brazil, of course, experienced a different, rather more peaceful and incremental path to independence under monarchical auspices; the Brazilian economy also depended heavily on slavery, which induced caution among elites, especially after the triumph of the Haitian Revolution. Cuba, the other major slave economy in Latin America, also avoided—or, rather, postponed—the upheaval of independence, remaining loyal to Spain. As the Cuban elite put it, "Cuba will be Spanish or it will be African."

39. Jaime Rodríguez O., *The Independence of Spanish America* (Cambridge: Cambridge University Press, 2009) is among the more persuasive purveyors of this thesis; however, I am not entirely persuaded.

40. Kenneth J. Andrien, *Andean Worlds: Indigenous History, Culture and Consciousness under Spanish Rule, 1532–1825* (Albuquerque: University of New Mexico Press, 2001), 207.

41. Again, there are variations within the huge and diverse Spanish Empire. The densely populated heartlands of "Indo-America" (especially Mexico and Peru) were arguably the chief victims of Bourbon policy; in Mexico, population growth coincided with bad harvests, producing severe dearths (e.g., in 1785–86 and again in 1809–10): Tutino, *From Insurrection to Revolution*, 74–82. The less populated and more commercially dynamic peripheries of South America—such as the Río de la Plata—benefited from enhanced trade (including contraband). For that reason, however, Spanish colonial restrictions chafed all the more.

42. As I discuss in chapter 7, most revolutions embody different currents—more moderate, more radical—and they often change over time under the pressure

of circumstances, so it is naive to expect—or to require—that a revolution must display internal coherence and consistency over time. In this context, it is also now quite common to see the wars of independence pointedly referred to as "civil wars" (which they certainly were). If the point of this usage is to stress that important sections of colonial population supported the Crown, that is also correct (but hardly a revelation). Sometimes, however, "civil war" is used, explicitly or implicitly, to deny the "revolutionary" claims of these struggles; they were, it is suggested, "just" civil wars, not "real" revolutions. Of course, some civil wars—like the English Wars of the Roses—have no revolutionary significance. But many civil wars (England in the 1640s, Russia after 1917, China in the 1930s and 1940s) are also revolutions, and any real revolution is also by definition a civil war (as Bolivia experienced, briefly, in 1952 and Cuba, more protractedly, in 1956–59; the only obvious exceptions might be the "velvet revolutions" of eastern Europe in the early 1990s). So we can all agree that the wars of independence were civil wars, but that tells us nothing about whether they were also revolutions—which I have no doubt they were in terms of both process and outcome.

43. Oddly, the "dependency" school flourished in the 1960s and 1970s when Latin America—especially the larger economies such as Mexico, Brazil, Argentina, and Chile—were relatively closed and dedicated to "import-substitution industrialization." Dependency thinking then withered as those economies began to adopt "neoliberal" policies of trade opening, export promotion, state shrinking, and increased reliance on foreign investment. By ca. 2000 Latin America was, arguably, much more "dependent"—on the United States, Japan, Europe, and, increasingly, China—than it had been forty years earlier, when "dependency theory" was in its heyday. Does this paradox—if it is a paradox—reveal the lamentable "false consciousness" that affects social scientists? In part, yes: "dependency" became such a dirty word that contemporary social scientists—economists, at least—would have nothing to do with it. More important, however, the neoliberal turn of the last forty years, apart from substantially changing economic policy (to the great advantage of some social sectors and the disadvantage of others), also wrought a more subtle paradigm shift in the social sciences (especially economics), whereby neoliberal, neoclassical, and rational-choice models came to prevail. Whatever might be happening in the real world (of Latin America), jobs, research grants, and promotions meant accepting the prevailing paradigm, especially in the United States and, increasingly, in the United Kingdom and much of Latin America too. Perhaps not surprisingly, the economists followed the money.

44. At least through the nineteenth century and into the twentieth: see Friedrich Katz, ed., *Riot, Rebellion and Revolution: Rural Social Conflict in Mexico* (Princeton NJ: Princeton University Press, 1988). After ca. 1940 Mexico's trajectory shifted, and the pacemakers of popular mobilization were to be found elsewhere: in Bolivia, Cuba, Argentina, and Central America.

45. Hilda Sabato, *Republics of the New World: The Revolutionary Political Experiment in Nineteenth-Century Latin America* (Princeton NJ: Princeton University Press, 2018) offers a broad overview; for a more detailed analysis, taking in the twentieth century, see Paul W. Drake, *Between Tyranny and Anarchy: A History of Democracy in Latin America, 1800–2006* (Stanford CA: Stanford University Press, 2009).

46. Paul Drinot, *The Allure of Labor: Workers, Race and the Making of the Peruvian State* (Durham NC: Duke University Press, 2011).

47. In 1928 Mariátegui founded the Peruvian Socialist Party, which, two years later, became the Communist Party. APRA (Alianza Popular Revolucionaria Americana) was founded by Víctor Raúl Haya de la Torre in 1924 and by the 1930s had become a major force in Peruvian politics—which it would continue to be well into the twenty-first century.

48. Possibly the "sonofabitch" in question was not Anastasio Somoza of Nicaragua but Rafael Trujillo of the Dominican Republic, and possibly FDR never used the phrase at all. Andrew Crawley, *Somoza and Roosevelt: Good Neighbour Diplomacy in Nicaragua, 1933–1945* (Oxford: Oxford University Press, 2007), 152–53, rather sniffily considers it to be "a wearyingly reiterated (and almost certainly apocryphal) vulgarity" possibly coined by Somoza himself, although Crawley also notes that the phrase was in common currency among American politicians at the time. At any rate, "vulgarity" or not, it captures the reality of U.S.-Nicaraguan relations and, in Giordano Bruno's words, "se non è vero è ben trovato" (even if it's not true, it's a good story). For example, a cabal of the American great and the good, meeting under the auspices of the Council on Foreign Relations in New York in 1949, agreed that "Somoza had three virtues: he propped Nicaragua open to private capital, allowed minimal state controls, and kept minimal order" (Walter LaFeber, *Inevitable Revolutions: The United States in Central America* [New York: W. W. Norton, 1984], 104). The quote is LaFeber's summation of the meeting, and as the author adds, the rationale was recycled thirty years later by Jeane Kirkpatrick, President Reagan's foreign policy advisor, by way of justifying support for authoritarian regimes in Latin America in general.

49. On these Swiss settlers, see Ezequiel Gallo, *La pampa gringa* (Buenos Aires: Editorial Sudamericana, 1983).

50. On reactions to the Mexican Revolution in Latin America, see Alan Knight, "La Revolución Mexicana en perspectiva global," in *La Revolución Bolchevique en América Latina*, ed. Santiago Aranguiz (Santiago: RIL, 2020), 147–70.

51. Richard Hofstadter, *The Paranoid Style in American Politics and Other Essays* (New York: Vintage Books, 1964), a book that has recently acquired renewed relevance and appeal.

52. Alan Knight and Paulo Drinot, eds., *The Great Depression in Latin America* (Durham NC: Duke University Press, 2014).

53. As Jan de Vries has cogently argued, "microhistorical" studies have of late become fashionable, but in the process, the genre has become perversely schizoid. Some examples, following an old tradition, consist of proper case studies that, addressing big themes within the context of a precise time and place on the basis of detailed archival evidence, are genuinely illuminating: a classic Mexican example would be Luis González y González's classic *Pueblo en vilo: Microhistoria de San José de Gracia* (Mexico City: El Colegio de Mexico, 1972). (Note that, since the first edition of this classic came out in 1968, over fifty years ago, we are not talking about some latter-day wonder.) As the author's other work showed, he was also a master of Mexican national history and hence could expertly weave national, regional, and local themes together. However, de Vries rightly complains, the "dominant form of microhistory" today, strongly influenced by "the cultural or linguistic turn," rather than seeking to test "large-scale paradigms," chooses to discard them altogether, burying itself in "petite narrative" and "essentializing the uniqueness of place and persons" (Jan de Vries, "Playing with Scales: The Global and the Micro, the Macro and the Nano," in *Global History and Microhistory*, ed. John-Paul Ghobrial, *Past and Present* 14 [2019]: 24–26).

54. Examples of genuinely original global history would include Eric R. Wolf, *Europe and the People without History* (Berkeley: University of California Press, 1982); Jared Diamond, *Guns, Germs and Steel: The Fates of Human Societies* (New York: W. W. Norton, 1997); Kenneth Pomerantz, *The Great Divergence: China, Europe and the Making of the Modern World Economy* (Princeton NJ: Princeton University Press, 2000); and James C. Scott, *Against the Grain: A Deep History of the Earliest States* (New Haven CT: Yale University Press, 2017). Chapter 5 of this book also cites several compendious—and genuinely global—histories of empire by, among others, Charles Maier, John Darwin, Jürgen Osterhammel, and Niall Ferguson.

55. William Shakespeare, *Macbeth*, act 1, scene 7, line 27.

56. Francis Fukuyama, *The End of History and the New Man* (London: Penguin, 1992), a work that, despite—or because of—its simplistic assumptions and dyed-in-the-wool Eurocentrism, caught the wave of post–Cold War hubris and has not aged well. But Fukuyama, who is nothing if not nimble, has managed to surf subsequent waves (e.g., the rise of nationalist populism) in similarly adroit fashion. For one of many critiques, see Louis Menand, "Francis Fukuyama Postpones the End of History," *New Yorker*, September 3, 2018. I should add that some historians, having forsaken the true path of their profession in order to engage in rent-a-quote punditry, yield to none in their capacity for glib comment. Regarding sociology, see the pungent critique of "grand historical sociology" by John H. Goldthorpe, "The Uses of History in Sociology: Reflections on Some Recent Tendencies," *British Journal of Sociology* 42, no. 2 (1990): 211–30 ("sweetshop" quote from 225).

57. So I agree with Chuck Zerby on the need to protect the "endangered footnote" from possible extinction: *The Devil's Details: A History of Footnotes* (New York: Touchstone, 2003), chap. 1.

58. Anthony Grafton, *The Footnote: A Curious History* (Cambridge MA: Harvard University Press, 1997), 56.

1. BACK TO BANDITRY

1. We may compare Hobsbawm's—and Kiernan's—pronounced cosmopolitanism with the Little Englandism that, some alleged, characterized E. P. Thompson's work and approach: see Thompson's rebuttal in *The Poverty of Theory and Other Essays* (Manchester: Merlin Press, 1978), iii (although his rebuttal concerns political causes rather than historiographical themes).

2. E. J. Hobsbawm, *Interesting Times: A Twentieth-Century Life* (London: Abacus, 2003), 153.

3. E. J. Hobsbawm, "A Case of Neo-feudalism: La Convención, Peru," *Journal of Latin American Studies* 1 (1969): 31–50.

4. In this essay I will focus on banditry, especially social banditry; I will not deal with the broader but also vaguer and more contentious notion of "primitive" and "prepolitical" protest, which has not stood the test of historiographical time very well (certainly not in Latin America), the thrust of much recent "bottom-up" research being that peasants and other "primitive" protesters, such as urban artisans, were clearly political and not at all "primitive." The essay builds upon and occasionally reprises an earlier piece written for a similar homage-to-Hobsbawm conference held at the Escuela Nacional de

Antropología e Historia in Mexico City in 2005: see Alan Knight, "Eric Hobsbawm, la historia mexicana y el bandolerismo social," in *Los historiadores y la historia para el siglo XXI: Homenaje a Eric J. Hobsbawm*, ed. Gumersindo Vera Hernández (Mexico City: CONACULTA/INAH, 2007), 429–61. Whereas that piece focused squarely on Mexico, this essay adopts a broader Latin American approach and is informed by a wider bibliography.

5. Editions published by Abacus, London, in 2000 and Paz e Terra, Rio de Janeiro, in 2010.

6. E. J. Hobsbawm, *Rebeldes primitivos* (Barcelona: Biblioteca del Bolsillo, 2010). Hobsbawm's "primitive rebels" were, in his formulation, "primitive" because they espoused archaic, "prepolitical" objectives and, therefore, could not be real "revolutionaries": see *Primitive Rebels: Studies in Archaic Forms of Social Movement in the 19th and 20th Centuries* (Manchester: Manchester University Press, 1974). And Hobsbawm certainly considered the Mexican Revolution to have been a real "revolution" waged by committed "revolutionaries," not "prepolitical" or "archaic" "primitive rebels."

7. "Enormous condescension of posterity" is from E. P. Thompson, *The Making of the English Working Class* (Harmondsworth: Penguin, 1968), 13. Perry Anderson, *Spectrum: From Right to Left in the World of Ideas* (London: Verso, 2005), 183, chides us that "by dint of repetition," this quote "risks becoming a PC tag," so, pace Perry, I plead guilty to parroting PC clichés.

8. Like many historiographical innovations, this one was not brand new; previous writers had addressed the social role of banditry and its connection to popular protest. For example, Mario Gill, "Heraclio Bernal: Caudillo frustrado," *Historia Mexicana* 4, no. 1 (1954): 138–58, depicts his subject as a classic "generous bandit." However, Hobsbawm formulated the hypothesis more systematically across a wide range of cases and contexts and thus greatly raised its scholarly profile.

9. E. J. Hobsbawm, *Bandits* (Harmondsworth: Penguin, 1972), 38, 63–64. The first statement is doubly risky: it presupposes a profound knowledge of innumerable cases that the author cannot have known in intimate detail, and it asserts a (qualified) negative, which historians should usually avoid doing.

10. Regarding Hobsbawm's reliance on secondary sources, see Ralph A. Austen, "Social Bandits and Other Heroic Criminals: Western Models of Resistance and Their Relevance for Africa," in *Banditry, Rebellion and Social Protest in Africa*, ed. Donald Crummey (London: James Currey, 1986), 89; Billy Jaynes Chandler, *The Bandit King: Lampião of Brazil* (College Station: Texas A&M

University Press, 1978), 240n10. On the range of accessible and useful sources (for Mexico), see Reidezel Mendoza Soriano, *Bandoleros y rebeldes*, 2 vols. (Mexico City: Ediciones del Azar, 2013), 1:11–12.

11. Hobsbawm, *Bandits*, 47.

12. On the "absolutely central distinction between established fact and fiction" and the "supremacy of evidence," see E. J. Hobsbawm, *On History* (New York: New Press, 1997), viii, 195, 271–72.

13. Hobsbawm, from the revised 1981 edition of *Bandits*, 142, quoted in Richard W. Slatta, "Eric J. Hobsbawm's Social Bandit: A Critique and Revision," *A Contracorriente* 1, no. 2 (2004): 24. A number of interesting recent studies have focused specifically on (Mexican) bandit myths, stories, and legends, making clear that they do not purport to tell us what real-life bandits actually did. Thus, Chris Frazer, *Bandit Nation: A History of Outlaws and Cultural Struggle in Mexico, 1810–1920* (Lincoln: University of Nebraska Press, 2006), 2, declares that "this book is a cultural history of banditry in Mexico from independence to the end of the revolution, based on narratives produced by Mexicans and English-speaking foreign visitors during the period"; it is not concerned with "whether or not certain outlaws were social bandits" but rather "how and why people told stories about them." So, notwithstanding its title, it is a "cultural history" not of banditry but of bandit myths and legends. A similar approach, also valuable within its own terms of reference, is Amy Robinson, "Bandits and Outlaws in Mexican Literature, 1885–1919" (PhD diss., University of Minnesota, 2003), from which derives "Mexican Banditry and Discourses of Class: The Case of Chucho el Roto," *Latin American Research Review* 44, no. 1 (2009): 5–31. Juan Pablo Dabove, *Nightmares of the Lettered City: Banditry and Literature in Latin America* (Pittsburgh: University of Pittsburgh Press, 2007) offers a broader analysis in the same genre, as does Pascale Baker, *Revolutionaries, Rebels and Robbers: The Golden Age of Banditry in Mexico, Latin America and the Chicano American Southwest* (Cardiff: University of Wales Press, 2015). However illuminating these studies may be in respect to literary/cultural images, they do not shed much light on the sociohistorical roots and role of banditry.

14. Anton Blok, "The Peasant and the Brigand: Social Banditry Reconsidered," *Comparative Studies in Society and History* 14 (1972): 495–504. We perhaps need a consensual adjective to describe the large universe of bandits who are not "social": "antisocial" or "unsocial" might be logical but sounds clumsy; a Colombian historian (see n. 114 below) refers to "lumpen" bandits; my own preference, pro tempore, is "mercenary."

15. Norman Lewis, *The Honoured Society: The Sicilian Mafia Observed* (London: Eland, 2013). Hobsbawm seems to grant Giuliano "social" status while making rather light of his repressive Mafia connections (*Primitive Rebels*, 14, 40); see also Hobsbawm, "The Bandit Giuliano," in *Uncommon People: Resistance, Rebellion and Jazz* (London: Weidenfeld and Nicolson, 1998), 191–99.

16. Blok, "The Peasant and the Brigand," 497.

17. Chandler, *Bandit King*, 241, 242–43. Regarding Lampião himself, Chandler is slightly ambivalent, conceding that perhaps he resembled Hobsbawm's "avengers" (241); however, Angelo Roque ("Labareda"), claimed by Hobsbawm to possess "the classic instincts of a Robin Hood" (*Bandits*, 61–62), was nothing of the sort (see Chandler, *Bandit King*, 242). More generally, Chandler accepts only a couple of those on Hobsbawm's bandit roster as genuine "social bandits" (Juro Janosik and Diego Corrientes), both of them "shadowy figures from the eighteenth century" (242). Oddly, Chandler then concludes his excellent book with the lame concession that, since "all banditry, broadly construed, may be called social banditry, involving as it does relations between people," then perhaps Lampião "was a social bandit, even if he was not a noble robber" (246–47).

18. Linda Lewin, "The Oligarchic Limitations of Social Banditry in Brazil: The Case of the 'Good Thief' Antonio Silvino," *Past and Present* 82, no. 1 (February 1979): 118. Correspondence in the *Past and Present* archive, in Oxford's Bodleian library, suggests that Hobsbawm oddly seems to have believed that Lewin's critique of his "social bandit" thesis actually confirmed it. Todd Diacon, *Millenarian Vision, Capitalist Reality: Brazil's Contestado Rebellion, 1912–1916* (Durham NC: Duke University Press, 1991), 139–40, suggests that Lewin may have underestimated the social implications of Silvino's activities. The debate hinges on Silvino's attacks on railways and telegraph lines: Were these simply tactical measures to impede pursuit, or did they embody some sort of rejection of unpopular processes of "modernization"? Like several arguments about banditry, this one concerns bandit motives, which, for obvious reasons, are notoriously difficult to ascertain.

19. Paul Vanderwood, *Disorder and Progress: Bandits, Police and Mexican Development* (Lincoln: University of Nebraska Press, 1981); Richard W. Slatta, "Introduction to Banditry in Latin America," in *Bandidos: The Varieties of Latin American Banditry*, ed. Richard W. Slatta (Westport CT: Praeger, 1987), 3–4.

20. Rosalie Schwartz, *Lawless Liberators: Political Banditry and Cuban Independence* (Durham NC: Duke University Press, 1989); compare Louis A.

Perez Jr., *Lords of the Mountain: Social Banditry and Peasant Protest in Cuba, 1878–1918* (Pittsburgh: University of Pittsburgh Press, 1989).

21. Slatta, "Eric J. Hobsbawm's Social Bandit," 30.

22. Gilbert M. Joseph, "On the Trail of Latin American Bandits: A Re-examination of Peasant Resistance," *Latin American Research Review* 25, no. 3 (1990): 7–53. See also Slatta's brief reply in *Latin American Research Review* 26, no. 1 (1991): 149–50; and several comments in the same volume, including Peter Singlemann, "Establishing a Trail in the Labyrinth," 152–55, and Christopher Birkbeck, "Latin American Banditry as Peasant Resistance: A Dead-End Trail?," 156–60.

23. Both phrases are taken from Birkbeck, "Latin American Banditry," 156, 158.

24. As I later argue, trying to segregate all bandits into social sheep and antisocial goats is too simple and even self-defeating; it is more helpful to think in terms of degrees of "sociality" versus mercenary criminality. That said, there are reasons for thinking that, given the historical circumstances, Mexico and Cuba may have been more productive of social bandits than, say, Brazil or Peru, as I tentatively conclude.

25. James Sharpe, *Dick Turpin: The Myth of the English Highwayman* (London: Profile Books, 2004). I am grateful to Prof. Kevin Middlebrook for drawing this book to my attention—indeed, for lending me a copy (which I think I still have).

26. Euclides da Cunha, *Rebellion in the Backlands* (Chicago: Phoenix Books, 1964), 149. Chandler, *Bandit King*, 7n6, warns against taking da Cunha too literally.

27. Mendoza, *Bandoleros y rebeldes*, 2:62.

28. Baltazar Gómez Pérez, *Isaac Medicoa: "El Tigre del Pedregal"* (Mexico City: Gobierno del DF, 2005). The *pedregal* is the volcanic zone to the south of Mexico City, now the home of the National University and the Aztec Stadium (therefore, an integral part of the great metropolis and a good place to be when there are earthquakes). At the time of Isaac Mendicoa's exploits in the early 1920s, it was a liminal zone between the city outskirts and the countryside beyond. But, even then, it was in no sense remote or inaccessible, and El Tigre operated in the city as much as the countryside. On the Gray Automobile Gang, a bunch of professional robbers (urban bandits?) who took advantage of revolutionary upheaval in Mexico City and of the new opportunities afforded by the motor car, see Pablo Piccato, *City of Suspects: Crime in Mexico City, 1900–1931* (Durham NC: Duke University Press, 2001), 178–79.

29. Schwartz, *Lawless Liberators*, 61.

30. Schwartz, *Lawless Liberators*, 74. Schwartz's descriptions are evocative and in many respects persuasive, but I am less convinced by her explanation of the tobacco workers' sympathy for the bandits, which she explains in terms of an (imputed) "penchant for personal autonomy" that made the workers admire the free-living, free-spending outlaws. Other "imputations"—more attuned to a collective, "social-bandit" interpretation—could just as well be advanced. We are back in the murky realm of motivation.

31. Frazer, *Bandit Nation*, 1, takes an even broader view, including among his "real and alleged outlaws in contemporary Mexico" groups as diverse as "narco-traffickers in [*sic*] the Gulf of Mexico, taxicab hijackers in Mexico City, or latter-day Zapatistas in Chiapas." The status of the first two could be legitimately debated (though the debate would, I think, rapidly discount their "social" claims); the third group, being popular political insurgents, should not be included at all.

32. What Chandler, *Bandit King*, 245, refers to as "human perversity."

33. Lewis Taylor, *Bandits and Politics in Peru: Landlord and Peasant Violence in Hualgayoc, 1900–30* (Cambridge: Centre for Latin American Studies, 1986), 15–21; Perez, *Lords of the Mountain*, 24–25; Schwartz, *Lawless Liberators*, 38–39.

34. Chandler, *Bandit King*, 6–7, 13–15; Amaury de Souza, "The Cangaço and the Politics of Violence in Northeast Brazil," in *Protest and Resistance in Angola and Brazil*, ed. Ronald L. Chilcote (Berkeley: University of California Press, 1972), 111–12. Lewin, "Oligarchic Limitations," 120–21, also relates earlier outbreaks of banditry to both drought and regime change, but she adds to the mix both the Paraíba cotton boom, which inflated land prices and market opportunities, and the closing of the frontier, which exacerbated land disputes. Clearly, this is a question of causal pick-and-mix; my tentative conclusion would be that a key common factor is social anomie, brought on by social and economic change (which may involve boom, or bust, or both), aggravated by both adverse climatic conditions and political incapacity (what is sometimes called "state failure").

35. Alan Knight, *The Mexican Revolution*, 2 vols. (Cambridge: Cambridge University Press, 1986), 1:351–67.

36. Some bandits sprang up amid the Zapatista rebellion, but they were relatively few and were either incorporated or snuffed out by the rebels: see Samuel Brunk, "'The Sad Situation of Civilians and Soldiers': The Banditry of Zapatismo in the Mexican Revolution," *American Historical Review* 101, no. 2 (April 1996): 331–53.

37. A similar syndrome—a chronically weak state and endemic factional vendettas—generated an epidemic of banditry in northern Peru: Taylor, *Bandits and Politics*, 65, refers to "a Hobbesian social climate, which . . . lacked the restraining presence of Leviathan."

38. Maria Isaura Pereira de Queiroz, "Messianism in Brazil," *Past and Present* 31 (1965): 62–86; Ralph della Cava, "Brazilian Messianism and National Institutions: A Reappraisal of Canudos and Joaseiro," *Hispanic American Historical Review* 48, no. 3 (1970): 402–20. I touch on this theme again in chapter 3.

39. I am conflating two aspects of the state: its strength in the sense of its social control and cognitive grasp and its legitimacy, that is, its capacity to elicit voluntary compliance and obedience. Ideally (from the state's point of view), these two attributes coincide and mutually reinforce each other. States can, however, be strong, even if illegitimate, or legitimate yet weak (each of these attributes being, I should add, points on a shifting continuum). In northeastern Brazil, as in northern Peru, the state was both weak and, at best, tenuously legitimate, hence the endemic elite feuds and associated banditry. The prerevolutionary (Porfirian) state was arguably lacking in legitimacy but enjoyed a real measure of social control, as did the Spanish colonial state in late nineteenth-century Cuba.

40. Schwartz, *Lawless Liberators*, and Perez, *Lords of the Mountain*, roughly agree on the geography of banditry and disorder, even if they disagree regarding their causes.

41. For, as Taylor shows, rival bandit gangs were controlled by elite factional leaders (such as Eleodoro Benel) who, in combatting their sworn political enemies, dragooned peasants into their ranks and devastated peasant communities. Even when the state sought to intervene and assert its flouted authority, peasants were again often the chief victims of military repression and extortion: see Taylor, *Bandits and Politics*, 73, 75, 80–4, 91, 99, 107.

42. Indeed, both charisma and legitimacy, while usually attributions of the state in its relation to its citizens, are also relevant when considering bandits and their social ties. On the "relational" quality of charisma, properly defined, see Douglas Madsen and Peter H. Snow, *The Charismatic Bond: Political Behavior in Time of Crisis* (Cambridge MA: Harvard University Press, 1991), 5–6.

43. While stressing the "amazing uniformity" of banditry across time and space, Hobsbawm also developed a more complex typology, including the Robin Hood bandit (the quintessential "noble robber"), the "avenger," and the bandit / guerrilla leader: see *Bandits*, 21, 23 and passim. Chandler, *Bandit*

King, 5, proposes a distinction between "brigandage" and "banditry," while Austen, "Social Bandits," adds the "self-helping frontiersman," the "populist redistributor," the "professional underworld," the "pícaro" ("rogue"), and the "urban guerrilla." Joseph, "On the Trail of Latin American Bandits," also goes in for further typologization. My own view is that this proliferation of bandit subtypes, many of which overlap, is confusing and misconceived; it derives from an essentialist intellectual impulse that makes us want to pigeonhole actors (and their actions) according to discrete categories. In fact, the categories bleed into each other, and individual bandits may shift between pigeonholes. Essentialization is therefore a bit like the old Ptolemaic cosmology: starting from partly false premises, it constantly has to invent new concepts and categories in order to meet the awkward demands of the evidence. My approach is to start with a simple descriptive model of what banditry is (thereby avoiding multiple functional subcategories) while retaining the crucial notion that the character and/or function of banditry in any particular context is strongly determined by class relations and state formation, the result of this dialectic being notably dynamic and shifting, as I go on to suggest.

44. Willie Sutton was the American bank robber who, when asked by the judge at his trial why he kept robbing banks, replied, "Because that's where the money is."

45. The notion of "moral outrage" is usefully discussed by Barrington Moore Jr., *Injustice: The Social Bases of Obedience and Revolt* (London: Macmillan, 1978).

46. Compare Henry Landsberger's discussion of "peasantness," which similarly— and correctly—seeks to avoid a simple essentialization of "peasant" status: Henry A. Landsberger, "The Role of Peasant Movements in Development," in *Latin American Peasant Movements*, ed. Henry A. Landsberger (Ithaca NY: Cornell University Press, 1969), 4–5. Having raised the question of gender, I should mention that in what follows, I assume that bandits and their followers/supporters of course include both women and men. There have been a few notable lady bandits (e.g., Lampião's partner, María Bonita; Phoolan Devi, the Indian dacoit; and, most recently, Mexico's "Queen of the Pacific," Sandra Avila Beltrán). Indeed, my impression is that recent banditry, such as Mexican narcocrime, has allowed women to play more prominent roles. A pioneer was Ignacia "La Nacha" Jasso, a key figure in the Ciudad Juárez drug business in the 1930s who survived for decades and whose example was followed by other women in the border zone as

the recent drug boom got under way: Nicole Mottier, "Drug Gangs and Politics in Ciudad Juárez, 1928–1936," *Mexican Studies / Estudios Mexicanos* 25, no. 1 (2009): 19–46; Elaine Carey and José Carlos Cisneros Guzmán, "The Daughters of La Nacha: Profiles of Women Drug Traffickers," NACLA *Report on the Americas: Mexico* (2011): 23–24. Historically, however, most major bandits have been men (as have been most politicians, prelates, generals, big businessmen, etc.). The bandits' social network, of course, includes women (and children) just as much as men; my "social" analysis is therefore gender—and generation—inclusive.

47. As already mentioned (see n. 17), Chandler detects only two genuine "social bandits," and these are pretty "shadowy" (i.e., inconclusive) cases. I do not find this convincing: given the sheer ubiquity of banditry (conventionally described) throughout history and throughout the world, it seems unlikely that there should be only two examples of a given category ("social bandit"). Either the category makes sense, in which case we would expect more, or it is mythical, and there are none.

48. Alexander Passerin d'Entreves, *The Notion of the State* (Oxford: Clarendon Press, 1967), 22.

49. The bandit can protect against abusive authorities and/or abstain from aggression against either favored social groups (à la Robin Hood) or favored families and individuals (thus, a protection racket). By way of historical examples, note that Lampião was famed for being trustworthy and generous toward his friends (of whatever social class) and ruthless and violent toward his enemies (Chandler, *The Bandit King*, 4, 40). Pancho Villa was similarly discriminating, protecting landlords—such as Francisco Rodríguez Villegas of the Hacienda El Pichagüe—who had helped him in the past. Despite the wealth of the estate, recalls Rodríguez's son, Villa and his partners "just laughed and took only some cartridges for their rifles. They all respected my father and never gave him trouble [nunca le hicieron caso]" (Mendoza, *Bandoleros y rebeldes*, 2:60).

50. By "state-related" I mean elites who are beneficiaries and even protagonists of state power and policy. Of course, particularly where rival elites were locked into internecine feuds (e.g., in northern Peru and northeastern Brazil), some—the "outs"—supported, recruited, and even joined the bandits. A similar elite/bandit alliance could, more rarely, occur in situations of revolution (e.g., northern Mexico in 1910–11) or, most clearly, in wars of national liberation, such as Cuba's in 1895–98. More typically, most elites aligned with the state, and the character of the state—its efficacy (strength) and legitimacy—was crucial in determining the scale and nature of banditry.

51. Chandler, *The Bandit King*, 244.

52. Elijah Wald, *Narcocorrido* (New York: HarperCollins, 2001) provides an excellent study of narcoculture in its various forms and functions.

53. Compare the debate over Silvino's destruction of railways and telegraphs, mentioned above (n. 18): Was it just a question of pragmatic tactics, or did it embody a sense of social protest?

54. The instrumental/expressive dichotomy crops up in psychology, criminology, and political science; for example, do voters decide preferences on the basis of the rational calculation of "utility," or do they rely on gut instincts, irrespective of such calculation? See Geoffrey Brennan and Loren Lomasky, *Democracy and Decision: The Pure Theory of Electoral Preference* (Cambridge: Cambridge University Press, 1993), 25, which contrasts "instrumental" or "outcome-causal" action with "expressive or symbolic action," which is "undertaken for its own sake rather than to bring about particular consequences." The distinction could be traced back—or, certainly, related—to Weber's discussion of *Zweckrationalität* versus *Wertrationalität*, but it would be unwise of me to try to unravel that connection here.

55. Allen Wells and Gilbert M. Joseph, *Summer of Discontent, Seasons of Upheaval: Elite Politics and Rural Insurgency in Yucatán, 1876–1915* (Stanford CA: Stanford University Press, 1996), 13, 213, which, in dealing with the Hunucma revolt of 1911, provides an example of officially designated "bandits"—responsible for "rustling, arson, robberies, hit-and-run attacks on henequen estates and bombings of municipal and prefectural offices"—who can just as well (or better) be seen as insurgent village rebels.

56. I am here influenced, I suspect, by my own work on the Mexican Revolution, for which official sources, both Mexican and foreign, painted an untenable picture of gullible plebs being duped by self-interested agitators and, indeed, "bandits." The course of events clearly disproved such a dumb explanation.

57. Ballads such as Mexican corridos and Brazilian *literatura de cordel* are tricky sources that may be, in some sense, "primary" (i.e., rapid, spontaneous responses to events that reflect an otherwise tacit public opinion), or "secondary" (i.e., composed long after the event and/or far away by people who may have a political or purely commercial agenda). Again, we confront an expressive versus instrumental dilemma, and only intimate knowledge of the case will enable us to say whether or to what degree a given source reflects either genuine popular sentiment or more contrived "instrumental" calculation. We know, for example, that many of today's narcocorridos, however popular they may be, have been written to order at the behest of

wealthy drug barons; they are, as Wald, *Narcocorrido*, 115, calls them, "paeans to high-powered narcos."

58. I sketched this model in a previous essay: Knight, "Eric Hobsbawm," 442. The current analysis is more broadly based and, I hope, more cogent for that. Schwartz, *Lawless Liberators*, 64, offers a rough empirical model of Cuban banditry that is not dissimilar, even though her premises and conclusions rather differ from mine. Richard White, "Bandas de forajidos en la Frontera Media: Los bandidos sociales norteamericanos," *Historia y Sociedad* 21 (July 2011): 33–59, also offers an analysis of midwestern American banditry that, I think, could be accommodated within the model I propose. (The original of White's article can be found in the *Western Historical Quarterly* 12 [October 1981]: 387–408.)

59. Lampião's band seems to have been quite large: at various junctures in the 1920s it comprised forty, fifty, and seventy members (Chandler, *The Bandit King*, 39, 41, 52, 55). Pancho Villa's prerevolutionary outfit was rather smaller, at most about a dozen, and Cuban gangs seem to have been no bigger.

60. Short-term ("instrumental") calculation involves asking the question: What have you done for me lately? We may contrast this to longer-term support and sympathy, which may well be "expressive" as well as "instrumental"— that is, based on affective sentiment, not just utilitarian calculus.

61. Mexico's modern drug cartels may be exceptions: alongside their thugs and smugglers, they employ lawyers and accountants, and if the "payroll" is more broadly defined, it includes a swath of functionally specific "employees," who may include singers, musicians, filmmakers, beauty queens, priests, policemen, and, of course, politicians. There is a hierarchy and, within it, elements of meritocracy. Thus, like other major organized crime networks, the big drug cartels—such as Sinaloa—display somewhat bureaucratic features.

62. Elizabeth Bott, cited in Blok, "The Peasant and the Brigand," 500.

63. Again, not necessarily all elites; some may throw in their lot with the bandits or even become bandits themselves (see n. 50 above).

64. Schwartz, *Lawless Liberators*, 88 ff.; compare Chandler, *The Bandit King*, 37, on the bandit Sebastião Pereira's "network of relatives, friends and protectors, some of whom were to perform valuable services for him [Lampião] in the coming years."

65. Mendoza, *Bandoleros y rebeldes*, 2:30.

66. Schwartz, *Lawless Liberators*, 58.

67. Nicolás Fernández, an hacienda foreman, was a close ally of Pancho Villa pre-1910. He later joined Villa's elite cavalry during the revolution, and by

the 1930s, long after his erstwhile leader's death, he became the leader of Mexico's fascistic Gold Shirts (Camisas Doradas): Mendoza, *Bandoleros y rebeldes*, 2:55, see also 49–50 for Villa's dealings with corrupt (i.e., conniving) judges. This was nothing new. Fanny Calderón de la Barca, writing in the mid-nineteenth century, observed a bandit "completely hand in glove" with a local judge; the two could be seen happily smoking cigars together in the judge's office: *Life in Mexico* (London: J. M. Dent, n.d. [1843]), 156.

68. Taylor, *Bandits and Politics*, 99.

69. Schwartz, *Lawless Liberators*, 64.

70. Chandler, *The Bandit King*, 21, notes that "until 1922 [Lampião] was known only locally"; he was "just another ordinary backlands bandit." After that date, his fame spread (as did his range of operations). The regional press began to write of the "renowned Lampião," and for the next sixteen years, until his death in 1938, he was rarely "out of the regional and national news."

71. Knight, *Mexican Revolution*, 2:127. Villa's star had begun to rise in late 1913, so by 1914 he was arguably more a revolutionary caudillo than a simple bandit (as I explore later). Nevertheless, the speed at which Villa's fame spread—essentially by means of the press and word of mouth—is striking.

72. Friedrich Katz, *The Life and Times of Pancho Villa* (Stanford CA: Stanford University Press, 1996), chap. 16.

73. Chandler, *The Bandit King*, 5. As already mentioned, da Cunha was an intellectual whose influential portrait of the backlands (banditry included) was based on very limited firsthand experience: Chandler, *The Bandit King*, 7n.6.

74. One example of official demonization was Carlos Agüero, a genuine veteran of the Ten Years War in Cuba, whom "for public consumption, [the authorities] . . . hunted and killed as a bandit" (Schwartz, *Lawless Liberators*, 105).

75. Wells and Joseph, *Summer of Discontent*, 238, 241.

76. Public opinion was scandalized by the alleged crimes of Sabás Baca, a Chihuahuan bandit who in 1900 had reportedly tortured a merchant, stabbed him to death, and then raped his wife; in fact, the merchant was not killed, nor was his wife violated: Mendoza, *Bandoleros y rebeldes*, 2:9.

77. Eugène Cuzin, *Diario de un francés durante la Revolución* (Mexico City: Conaculta, 2008), 158. The Zapatistas' docile occupation of the capital is described in Womack, *Zapata*, 219–21.

78. This trajectory is very evident in foreign (British and American) reports, but such reports usually mirrored Mexican elite opinion anyway. I should clarify that in his third incarnation, Villa did not just revert to square one (i.e., to

life as a fairly modest provincial bandit with his inner circles of cronies and collaborators); he now commanded large, better-armed forces whose ranks were sometimes filled by the press gang. Villa himself had become more violent and vengeful (some would say, with good reason), and—again—the context had changed, since the new (revolutionary) regime had a broader popular base than the old regime of Porfirio Díaz and, following years of warfare, the popular mood now favored peace and retrenchment.

79. Villa is a better example in this context than Zapata because Villa had been a genuine bandit pre-1910, and after 1915 he reverted to bandit-like behavior. Zapata was never a bandit, and his "bandit" reputation was entirely a product of government and elite disinformation.

80. There is a huge and growing literature on Mexico's recent narco boom (some of it is excessively superficial and sensationalist). For a short historical overview, see Alan Knight, "Narco Violence and the State in Modern Mexico," in *Violence, Coercion and State-Making in Twentieth-Century Mexico*, ed. Wil G. Pansters (Stanford CA: Stanford University Press, 2012), 115–34.

81. Wald, *Narcocorrido*; Knight, "Narco Violence."

82. For earlier "sanctified bandits," see Hugo Chumbita, "Bandoleros santificados," *Todo Es Historia* 340 (November 1995): 1–14.

83. James H. Creechan and Jorge de la Herrán García, "Without God or Law: Narcoculture and Belief in Jesús Malverde," *Religious Studies and Theology* 24, no. 2 (2005): 5–57, is a scholarly and well-illustrated discussion of the cult. Colombia also has its crop of popular "narco saints," such as the Virgen de los Sicarios (Medellín).

84. See Wil G. Pansters, ed., *La Santa Muerte in Mexico: History, Devotion, and Society* (Albuquerque: University of New Mexico Press, 2019).

85. Another case of, we might say, posthumous inflation is that of Juan Soldado: see Paul J. Vanderwood, *Juan Soldado: Rapist, Murderer, Martyr, Saint* (Durham NC: Duke University Press, 2004).

86. Notably in Michoacán, where the Mexican government recently (2014) decided to legitimize local vigilantism: Enrique Guerra Manzo, "Las auto-defensas de Michoacán: Movimiento social, paramilitarismo y neocaciquismo," *Política y Cultura* 44 (September 2015): 7–31. See also the perceptive analysis of Salvador Maldonado Aranda, "'We Are Men of War': Self-Defense Forces, Para-militarism and Organised Crime on the Mexican Periphery," *Global South* 12, no. 2 (2018): 148–65.

87. The younger narco generation not only produced and exported drugs, they also consumed them.

88. "Arman protestas en rechazo a detención del narcotraficante," *El Universal* (Mexico City), February 27, 2014.

89. Mendoza, *Bandoleros y rebeldes*, 2:40–41.

90. For a classic—and bloody—example, see Michael Kearney, *Los vientos de Ixtepeji* (Mexico City: Instituto Indigenista Interamericano, 1971), 28, 35–36, 47, 51, 57–58, 101.

91. Alan Knight, "Caciquismo in Twentieth-Century Mexico," in *Caciquismo in Twentieth-Century Mexico*, ed. Alan Knight and Wil Pansters (London: Institute for the Study of the Americas, 2005), 33–34, gives examples of such local "dyadic rivalries." Robert Redfield, researching in Morelos (Mexico) in the 1920s, noted how "a man sung as a bandit in one community may be sung as a redeemer in another": *Tepoztlán: A Mexican Village* (Chicago: University of Chicago Press, 1930), 9. Redfield, incidentally, is using "sing" literally, to refer to *corridos* (popular ballads).

92. For example, San Miguel Canoa, Puebla: Knight, *Mexican Revolution*, 1:123. Again, this was nothing new: see Calderón de la Barca, *Life in Mexico*, 152.

93. On clashes with rival bandits, see Mendoza, *Bandoleros y rebeldes*, 2:60. Charles Tilly, seeking to "model" the growth of state authority over centuries, makes a useful distinction between capital-intensive and coercion-intensive state formation: *Coercion, Capital and European States, AD 990–1992* (Oxford: Blackwell, 1992), 16–20. A similar distinction could be made regarding the growth of bandit power, which, closer to home, depends on capital (both literal and metaphorical, i.e., both material and reputational resources) yet which, as it roams farther afield, may come to rely more on outright coercion.

94. On the range of bandit operations, see, for Lampião, Chandler, *The Bandit King*, 57; also Schwartz, *Lawless Liberators*, 64. I discuss Pancho Villa's spatial domain later.

95. It was not easy for bandits to make off with heavy silver ingots, but the company payroll was another matter: see, for example, Mendoza, *Bandoleros y rebeldes*, 2:46. For a somewhat polemical version of this thesis, which links contemporary criminal violence in Latin America (especially Mexico) to "resource extraction" (mining, gas and oil), see Dawn Paley, *Drug War Capitalism* (Oakland CA: AK Press, 2014).

96. Sarah Wilson, "'In Pursuit of El Tigre de Acayucán': The Life and Death of a Social Bandit in Pre-revolutionary Veracruz (Mexico)" (undergraduate history thesis, Oxford University, 2011); Knight, *Mexican Revolution*, 1:363–64.

97. This kind of aggressive expansion should be distinguished from defensive dispersal, undertaken by bandits who, when hard-pressed, wanted to lie

low and escape from the authorities: see, for example, Taylor, *Bandits and Politics*, 75, on the dispersal of Raimundo Ramos's gang in 1918.

98. Knight, *Mexican Revolution*, 1:124. The report comes from a disgruntled rural policeman who also pleads that he is sadly ignorant of the local terrain and that he "face[s] the opposition of all the people of the villages and ranches that I pass." No need to read this report "against the grain."

99. The death of his brothers also seems to have made him more violent and vengeful. In other cases, bandits appear to have been affected by life-changing personal crises (usually for the worse): the antisocial Mexican bandit José Inés Chávez García, mentioned below, was said to have become meaner after a nasty bout of smallpox.

100. Angelo Roque, a member of Lampião's bandit gang, managed to retire from the fray and became—no less—a doorkeeper at the Bahía law courts: Hobsbawm, *Bandits*, 61–62. On China and bandits who aspired to dynastic rule, see Eric R. Wolf, *Peasant Wars of the Twentieth Century* (New York: Harper and Row, 1973), 107–8.

101. Mendoza, *Bandoleros y rebeldes*, 2:31; Knight, *Mexican Revolution*, 2:399.

102. Katz, *Life and Times*, 3–4.

103. Vanderwood, *Disorder and Progress*, tends to exaggerate the go-getting, even rational individualism of bandits who, he suggests, typically turn to crime as a matter of personal choice rather than harsh necessity.

104. John Reed, *Insurgent Mexico* (New York: D. Appleton, 1914), chaps. 1, 2; Knight, *Mexican Revolution*, 1:124–26.

105. As Brunk, "The Sad Situation," 333, points out, "The intentions and modes of social bandits are . . . rather indistinguishable from those of peasant revolutionaries engaged in a guerrilla war." The "modes" are certainly very similar; intentions are, again, hard to get at, but most historians would credit revolutionaries, especially peasant revolutionaries such as Zapata, with more clear-cut social goals than those entertained (as far as we know) by bandits, even "social bandits." Zapata's reform program, for example, was much more coherent and consistent than Villa's: see Knight, *Mexican Revolution*, 1:309–15, 2:115–29.

106. Schwartz, *Lawless Liberators*, 105–6. An earlier example would be José Artigas, the paladin of Uruguayan independence, who progressed from banditry and smuggling to guerrilla war and patriotic leadership: Hugo Chumbita, *Jinetes rebeldes: Historia del bandolerismo social en la Argentina* (Buenos Aires: Colihue, 2009), 39–43.

107. Chandler, *Bandit King*, 245; Hobsbawm, *Primitive Rebels*, 26–27, and *Bandits*, 65. Schwartz, *Lawless Liberators*, 88, goes even further, denying bandits even social-reformist goals.

108. Katz, *Life and Times*, chap. 11; Knight, *Mexican Revolution*, 2:119–20.

109. Katz, *Life and Times*, 242–44. Latin American bandits seem to have been broadly tolerant of priests; at least, I have not come across a stridently anticlerical brigand. Perhaps this was because anticlericalism tended to correlate with an urban background and a modicum of education, while bandits were typically rural and uneducated. Lampião was deferential toward priests (though he does not seem to have imbibed much by way of Christian charity). Fanny Calderón de Barca, *Life in Mexico*, 97, tells us that "the robbers are shy of attacking either soldiers or priests, the first from fear, the second from awe." On Peru, see Taylor, *Bandits and Politics*, 64.

110. Katz, *Life and Times*, chap. 19.

111. Knight, *Mexican Revolution*, 2:125.

112. Cf. Frazer, *Bandit Nation*, 3.

113. Wald, *Narcocorrido*.

114. An interesting case is Colombia, where the brutal civil war known as the Violencia, erupting in 1948 (its end date is disputed), claimed some two hundred thousand lives. In this context, a prominent Liberal warlord, Guadalupe Salcedo, who played a major role in the military campaigns in the Llanos Orientales (Eastern Plains), began life as a "lumpen bandit" (i.e., a mercenary brigand), then "transformed himself into a social bandit and ended up as a political *guerrillero* (guerrilla leader) and peace activist" (Orlando Villanueva Martín, *Guadalupe Salcedo y la insurrección llanera, 1949–1957* [Bogotá: Universidad Nacional de Colombia, 2012], 462–63). In terms of both his life and death, Salcedo was roughly typical of many such leaders: amnestied in 1953, he was gunned down by police in Bogotá four years later (521–39). Hobsbawm considered the Violencia to be a "classic social revolution" manqué (i.e., one that, unlike the Mexican or Cuban Revolution, failed to live up to its revolutionary potential): "The Revolutionary Situation in Colombia," *World Today* 19, no. 6 (June 1963): 248. There are grounds to question this judgment.

115. We could contrast this lucky outcome with the fate of Heraclio Bernal, who had the ill fortune to pursue his bandit career as the Pax Porfiriana was being ruthlessly enforced: Gill, "Heraclio Bernal"; Nicole Girón, *Heraclio Bernal: Bandolero, cacique o precursor de la Revolución?* (Mexico City: INAH, 1976).

116. Vanderwood, *Disorder and Progress*, chap. 5.

117. Knight, *Mexican Revolution*, 2:392–406.

118. Knight, *Mexican Revolution*, 2:397–403; Javier Garciadiego Dantán, "José Inés Chávez García: Rebelde, bandido social, simple bandolero o precursor de los Cristeros?" *Historia Mexicana* 60, no. 2 (2010): 833–95.

119. For the interesting case of Enrique Rodríguez, "El Tallarín" (the Noodle), whom the *New York Times* referred to as "one of Mexico's most noted bandits" and who, as bandit and/or rebel, roamed Zapata's home state of Morelos in the 1930s, see Salvador Salinas, *Land, Liberty and Water: Morelos after Zapata, 1920–1940* (Tucson: University of Arizona Press, 2018), chap. 5 (quote from 144).

120. Joseph, "On the Trail of Latin American Bandits."

2. LIBERALISM IN LATIN AMERICA

1. Alan Knight, "El liberalismo mexicano: Desde la Reforma hasta la Revolución (una interpretación)," *Historia Mexicana* 26, no. 1 (1985): 59–91.

2. Paul Gootenberg pithily sums up that view, citing, in particular, the work of E. Bradford Burns: "Urban elites—a tiny, defensive, dependent group—hegemonically [*sic*] foisted their estranged European conceptions of liberal order and property upon . . . [the] 'American' folk, rustic patriarchs and chaos-loving caudillos" ("Order and Progress in Developmental Discourse: The Case of Nineteenth-Century Peru," in *In Search of a New Order: Essays on the Politics and Society of Nineteenth-Century Latin America*, ed. Eduardo Posada-Carbó [London: ILAS, 1998], 61). I question "hegemonically" since, if it is argued that liberal elites had to *impose* their "liberal" policies on recalcitrant "subaltern" groups by force, then, by definition, those elites had *failed* to achieve Gramscian hegemony. Regarding Mexico in particular, see the historiographical examples cited in José Antonio Aguilar Rivera, "Tres momentos liberales en México (1820–90)," in *Liberalismo y poder: Latinoamérica en el siglo XIX*, ed. Iván Jaksic and Eduardo Posada-Carbó (Santiago: FCE, 2011), 119.

3. "Thus," observes Terry Rugeley, "began the quest for folk liberalism" (*Of Wonders and Wise Men: Religion and Popular Cultures in Southeast Mexico, 1800–1876* [Austin: University of Texas Press, 2001], 289). Regarding Mexico, notable contributions to the quest have been made by G. P. C. Thomson, "Bulwarks of Patriotic Liberalism: The National Guard, Philharmonic Corps and Patriotic Juntas in Mexico, 1847–88," *Journal of Latin American Studies* 22, no. 1 (1990): 31–68; G. P. C. Thomson and David G. LaFrance, *Patriotic Politics and Popular Liberalism in Nineteenth-Century Mexico* (Wilmington

DE: SR Books, 1995); and Florencia E. Mallon, *Peasant and Nation: The Making of Postcolonial Mexico and Peru* (Berkeley: University of California Press, 1995). As I mention later, recent studies have also identified and fleshed out forms of popular, including peasant and Indian, liberalism elsewhere in nineteenth-century Latin America: Cecilia Méndez, *The Plebeian Republic: The Huanta Rebellion and the Making of the Peruvian State, 1820–1850* (Durham NC: Duke University Press, 2005); and E. Gabrielle Kuenzli, *Acting Inca: National Belonging in Early Twentieth-Century Bolivia* (Pittsburgh: University of Pittsburgh Press, 2013).

4. Guillermo Palacios, ed., *Ensayos sobre la nueva historia política de México* (Mexico City: El Colegio de México, 2007) offers a useful *tour d'horizon*.

5. Sandra Kuntz Ficker, ed., *Historia económica de México: De la Colonia a nuestros días* (Mexico City: El Colegio de Mexico, 2010) is a good example of sensible revisionist synthesis; some ultrarevisionism, in contrast, goes way too far in its positive reevaluation of the Porfirian project and, I suspect, responds to presentist preferences and prejudices. In doing so, it often overlooks two obvious facts: first, as I later discuss, Porfirian *desarrollo hacia afuera* was driven forward by an authoritarian and highly illiberal state, and second, of course, it ended in sociopolitical disaster.

6. If only to avoid endless confusion and disagreement concerning the "explanandum" (liberalism) or, better, "explananda" (varieties of liberalism). In this context, a salutary lesson is provided by Ileana Rodríguez, *Liberalism at Its Limits: Crime and Terror in the Latin American Cultural Text* (Pittsburgh: University of Pittsburgh Press, 2009), which roams aimlessly through the—allegedly—"liberal" landscape of Latin America, at no point clarifying exactly what is being looked for; the only clear conclusion to emerge from this circumbendibus excursion is that, as Sellar and Yeatman would put it, liberalism was and is a thoroughly "Bad Thing."

7. Isaac Kramnick, *Republicanism and Bourgeois Radicalism: Political Ideology in Late Eighteenth-Century England and America* (Ithaca NY: Cornell University Press, 1990), 2, offers a fair summation of the scholarly consensus regarding (political) liberalism as "a political theory of individual rights, consent and a limited state." See also Joyce Appleby, *Liberalism and Republicanism in the Historical Imagination* (Cambridge MA: Harvard University Press, 1992), 1, on the "core affirmations" of liberalism as traditionally understood in the United States. I have also found the following historical-philosophical studies useful: D. J. Manning, *Modern Liberalism* (London: Dent, 1976); C. B. MacPherson, *The Life and Times of Liberal Democracy* (Oxford: Oxford

University Press, 1977); Alan Ryan, *The Making of Modern Liberalism* (Princeton NJ: Princeton University Press, 2012); and, in particular, Stuart Hall, "Varieties of Liberalism," in *Politics and Ideology*, ed. James Donald and Stuart Hall (Milton Keynes: Open University, 1986), 34–69.

8. Manning, *Liberalism*, 57–58. Raúl Coronado, *A World Not to Come: A History of Latino Writing and Print Culture* (Cambridge MA: Harvard University Press, 2013), 7–15, seems to think that "Hispanic liberalism," by virtue of its invocation of older notions of law and representation, "some originating as far back as the medieval period," stands apart from "the dominant account of the Enlightenment, revolution and modernity" characteristic of "Anglo America and Protestant northwestern Europe." Not only is Coronado asserting nothing very new (about "Hispanic liberalism"); he also seems entirely unaware that "Anglo-American" liberalism also has much older, also medieval roots: Magna Carta, habeas corpus, common law, and parliamentary representation for starters.

9. James C. Scott, *Domination and the Arts of Resistance: Hidden Transcripts* (New Haven CT: Yale University Press, 1989), 2. This is a key point that is often stressed in the Latin American context. It is one reason for being skeptical about intellectual history approaches, already mentioned, that focus narrowly on the great *pensadores* and their ideational commerce: political reality was often far removed from—or, we might say, "relatively autonomous" of—such intellectual lucubrations. The gap between theory and practice also means that, as I later mention, we encounter plenty of self-styled liberals (including Liberals with a capital *L*) whose practice is hardly liberal and may, indeed, be strikingly illiberal. There are also (not least in Latin America) plenty of Conservatives who adopt liberal stances. And there are liberals who never call themselves Liberals (the United States, after all, has never had a Liberal Party). Thus, while such self-styled—"emic"—labels matter, it is much more interesting and consequential to note what people (be they "Liberals" or "Conservatives" or something else) actually *did* than what they called themselves.

10. Much the same can be said of the relationship between liberalism and republicanism (which in turn links to the "Continental/British" distinction mentioned above in n. 8). If, greatly simplifying matters, we take "republicanism" at face value (thus, to denote support for a republic over a monarchy), then, clearly, republicanism may or may not be liberal (it could also be conservative, clerical, oligarchical, authoritarian, etc.), and liberalism may or may not be republican (since constitutional monarchies can be unquestionably

liberal; indeed, the most solidly liberal states in modern Europe—Denmark, Norway, Sweden, the Netherlands—also happen to be monarchies). Given that the Brazilian Empire was more durably liberal than many contemporary Latin American republics, the point is relevant to our discussion. There is, I am aware, a more specific notion of "republicanism" and "republican liberty" that derives from Machiavelli; I am not persuaded that this notion— questionable even in the European context—is at all helpful when it comes to Latin America. See Ellen Meiksins Wood, *Liberty and Property: A Social History of Western Political Thought from Renaissance to Enlightenment* (London: Verso, 2012), 18, 50–55, 228–29; and Roberto Gargarella, *Latin American Constitutionalism, 1810–2010* (Oxford: Oxford University Press, 2013), 7–11, to which I return in n. 20 below.

11. Frank Safford, "Politics, Ideology and Society in Post-independence Spanish America," in *The Cambridge History of Latin America*, vol. 3, *From Independence to c. 1870*, ed. Leslie Bethell (Cambridge: Cambridge University Press), 347–422, which remains one of the best syntheses of Latin American politics and ideology in the earlier nineteenth century, also proposes three stages: early liberalism, conservative reaction, and revived liberalism (see 353). I follow a similar chronology, but focusing on liberalism, I don't count the conservative reaction (though, of course, I take it into account as a causal factor). My third stage thus differs from—and falls outside of—Safford's typology/chronology, which necessarily ends ca. 1870. Also, my stages are approximate generations. Aguilar Rivera, "Tres momentos liberales," focusing on Mexico, also deals in generations, though he chooses to call them "moments" (in tacit homage to his fellow intellectual historian Pocock, perhaps?); however, his "moments," in terms of both chronology and content, are quite similar to mine, even if his nomenclature differs: (1) "liberal consensus," 1820–40; (2) "extemporaneous dissent," 1840–76; and (3) "metamorphosis and death of liberalism," 1876–1900. A roughly similar chronology also underlies Timo H. Schaefer, *Liberalism as Utopia: The Rise and Fall of Legal Rule in Post-colonial Mexico, 1820–1900* (Cambridge: Cambridge University Press, 2017).

12. Charles Hale, *Mexican Liberalism in the Age of Mora, 1821–1853* (New Haven CT: Yale University Press, 1968), 79.

13. Safford, "Politics, Ideology and Society," 353, 361; David Bushnell, *The Making of Modern Colombia: A Nation in Spite of Itself* (Berkeley: University of California Press, 1993), 84; Ralph Lee Woodward, "The Liberal-Conservative Debate in the Central American Federation, 1823–1840," in *Liberals, Politics and Power: State Formation in Nineteenth-Century Latin America*, ed. Vincent C. Peloso

and Barbara Tenenbaum (Athens: University of Georgia Press, 1996), 62, 67; Carmen McEvoy, "De la República jacobina a la República práctica: Los dilemas del liberalismo en el Perú, 1822–1872," in Jaksic and Posada-Carbó, *Liberalismo y poder*, 211. Eduardo Posada-Carbó, "La tradición liberal colombiana del siglo XIX de Francisco de Paula Santander a Carlos A. Torres," in the same volume, discerns "three great moments" in the trajectory of Colombian liberalism: "from initial moderation in the early decades of independence, when the aim was to build the state (*el orden estatal*); to radicalization at mid-century, based on a fundamental belief in the supreme value of liberty; to, at the end of the century, renewed moderation, valuing above all security and the law . . . while accepting a greater economic role for government" (174).

14. Rule that could hardly be called "liberal," even if the Bourbon Reforms embodied a modest dose of economic liberalism. Nils Jacobsen, *Mirages of Transition: The Peruvian Altiplano, 1780–1930* (Berkeley: University of California Press, 1993), 137, captures the scale of political change in the southern Andes, which went beyond constitutional design: as a local Indian *kuraka* (chief) observed, "In the five years since independence it has been notable that . . . servile submission is beginning to disappear. . . . [T]hose accustomed to see the Indians tremble find that the world is lost and there is no respect and subordination anymore."

15. Klaus Gallo, Nancy Calvo, and Roberto de Stefano, *Los curas de la revolución* (Buenos Aires: Emecel, 2002); McEvoy, "De la República jacobina," 213; Austen Ivereigh, "The Shape of the State: Liberals and Catholics in the Dispute over the Law 1420 of 1884 in Argentina," in *The Politics of Religion in an Age of Revival*, ed. Austen Ivereigh (London: ILAS, 2000), 169.

16. Aguilar Rivera, "Tres momentos liberales," 122, considers anticlericalism to be diagnostic of liberalism ("the liberal ideal type was simultaneously antimilitarist and anticlerical"), which seems to me questionable. After all, some Latin American liberals were devout Catholics who eschewed anticlericalism, as were some of their nineteenth-century French counterparts; while in Britain, that great paladin of nineteenth-century Liberalism, William Gladstone, was also a devout (some would say sanctimonious) High Church Anglican (incidentally, he was seen as a role model by the Anglophile Colombian president Rafael Núñez: Posada-Carbó, "La tradición liberal," 170–71).

17. Bushnell, *The Making of Modern Colombia*, 92. Despite its very different political trajectory, Brazil seems to follow a similar chronology: Roderick J. Barman, *Brazil: The Forging of a Nation, 1798–1852* (Stanford CA: Stanford University Press, 1988), 224.

18. Simon Collier, *Chile: The Making of a Republic, 1830–1865* (Cambridge: Cambridge University Press, 2003), 122–23, 132. This ideological bipartisanship, particularly pronounced in Chile, helped make possible the later Liberal/Conservative "Fusion" of the 1850s: see 211, 250. On Mexico, see Aguilar Rivera, "Tres momentos liberales," 125–26.

19. David Rock, *Argentina, 1516–1987* (Berkeley: University of California Press, 1987), 98–99, 101; Klaus Gallo, *Bernardino Rivadavia: El primer presidente argentino* (Buenos Aires: Edhasa, 2012).

20. Safford, "Politics, Ideology and Society," 365–66. Gargarella, *Latin American Constitutionalism*, 7–11, introduces, along with the conventional liberal/conservative dichotomy, a third political model, which he calls "republican or radical," characterized by "political majoritarianism," "moral populism," and a commitment to the Rousseauian "General Will." Harking back to the French Jacobins, this model was espoused, Gargarella argues, by the Chilean radical Francisco Bilbao. However, Bilbao was, Gargarella concedes, an "exceptional" (i.e., very unusual) figure, and the "republican or radical model" had scant success in "translating its main proposals into solid constitutional projects, supported by a significant sectors of society." Its chief role, it seems, was to provide a "phantom" against which rival projects/movements reacted. Some of Gargarella's "republican radicals" look to me like radical liberals who, following Jacobin precedent, favored the top-down imposition of their ideals, which they often espoused with a measure of moral certitude. In short, I am not convinced that this third category is sufficiently clear and significant to warrant its place in the nineteenth-century political pantheon (of Latin America).

21. Richard Graham, *Politics and Patronage in Nineteenth-Century Brazil* (Stanford CA: Stanford University Press, 1990), 51, offers a good example (Diogo Antonio Feijó); an earlier case might be Alexandre Pétion, the Haitian ally of Bolívar and champion of Spanish American independence who, after taking power in 1807, "crafted an increasingly autocratic regime," circumventing the democratic provisions of the 1816 Constitution: Laurent Dubois, *Haiti: The Aftershocks of History* (New York: Metropolitan Books, 2012), 60–61. Vincent C. Peloso concludes that in Peru during the guano era, "save for one heady interlude, liberal politicians abandoned principles in favor of power" ("Liberals, Electoral Reform and the Popular Vote in Mid-Nineteenth-Century Peru," in Peloso and Tenenbaum, *Liberals, Politics and Power*, 204). This "situational" logic was not confined to liberals. Bushnell, *The Making of Modern Colombia*, 91, notes "the particular appeal of federalism

for factions out of power" and, on 118–19, describes how Mariano Ospina Rodríguez (a Conservative of liberal inclination), "though he had embraced federalism, took a generous interpretation of the powers still vested in the central authorities" after he became president in 1857. Santa Anna is another very obvious example of opportunistic pragmatism, although charting his ideological gyrations, both in and out of office, would require a monster endnote: those gyrations are sympathetically recounted in Will Fowler, *Santa Anna of Mexico* (Lincoln: University of Nebraska Press, 2007).

22. Safford, "Politics, Ideology and Society," 359.

23. Fowler, *Santa Anna*, 161. Aguilar Rivera, "Tres momentos liberales," 130–31, stresses that the 1836 Constitution represented "centralist liberalism," which, in terms of its formal content, may well be true, but this reminds us that "conservatives" could also be liberals, at least in the minimal sense of favoring constitutional rule, division of powers, and (limited) political representation. Practice, of course, might be different, and in the mid-nineteenth century, liberal/conservative polarization increased, especially regarding the (separate) question of church/state relations.

24. Barbara Tenenbaum, *The Politics of Penury: Debts and Taxes in Mexico, 1821–1856* (Albuquerque: University of New Mexico Press), chaps. 1, 2.

25. Safford, "Politics, Ideology and Society," 353.

26. John Lynch, *Caudillos in Spanish America, 1800–1850* (Oxford: Clarendon Press, 1992), 59–60.

27. Collier, *Chile*, chap. 2 and, on the 1833 Constitution in particular, 123, 132, 134. On Rosas as "conservative dictator," see Lynch, *Caudillos*, chap. 6 (quotation from 250). Ivereigh, "The Shape of the State," 170, quotes the comment of the papal nuncio that, in the battle between *unitarios* and *federalistas* in 1830, "the pious stood with the Federation" (i.e., with Rosas).

28. Tulio Halperín Donghi, *The Contemporary History of Latin America* (Durham NC: Duke University Press, 1993), 106; Woodward, "The Liberal-Conservative Debate," 59.

29. Bushnell, *The Making of Modern Colombia*, 95; Enrique Ayala Mora, *Ecuador del siglo XIX: Estado nacional, ejército, iglesia y municipio* (Quito: Universidad Andina Simón Bolívar, 2011), 75.

30. Halperín, *The Contemporary History*, 101, notes how "European observers" saw Francia's regime as "an extreme case of reaction against liberalism," but it was a reaction against an external threat, not an internal reality.

31. On this phenomenon—the so-called *regresso*—see Graham, *Patronage and Politics*, 51–52, and Barman, *Brazil*, 196–201.

32. See the insightful analysis of Antonin Tibesan, "The Peruvian Church at the Time of Independence in the Light of Vatican II," *The Americas* 26, no. 4 (April 1970): 363, 367.

33. Bushnell, *The Making of Modern Colombia*, 97–99.

34. Woodward, "The Liberal-Conservative Debate," 66.

35. Peter V. N. Henderson, *Gabriel García Moreno and Conservative State Formation in Ecuador* (Austin: University of Texas Press, 2008), 63, 83.

36. Graham, *Politics and Patronage*, 171.

37. Safford, "Politics, Ideology and Society," 353–54; Guy Thomson, ed., *The European Revolutions of 1848 and the Americas* (London: ILAS, 2002). It is worth adding that "1848" should be seen as a bundle of ideas and inspirations (liberal, radical, nationalist). Also, in order to avoid the kind of crude diffusionism whereby Latin America is seen as a "reflex" society passively absorbing foreign (and, nowadays, "transnational") influences, we should stress that "1848" would not have had the impact it did had not Latin America, for its own domestic reasons, been ripe to react.

38. Aguilar Rivera, "Tres momentos liberales," 140, quotes Francisco Zarco on the "open war" that must be waged against "custom" if "physical, moral, intellectual, political, economic and social advance" was to be achieved.

39. Wilfrid H. Calcott, *Liberalism in Mexico, 1857–1929* (Hamden CT: Archon Books, 1965), chaps. 1–3, though old, provides a useful overview; Richard N. Sinkin, *The Mexican Reform, 1855–1876: A Study in Liberal Nation-Building* (Austin: ILAS, 1979) also remains a cogent analysis.

40. Collier, *Chile*, 80, 251, notes a "liberal renewal" beginning in the late 1840s and, by the 1860s, becoming an "irresistible tide"; Bushnell, *The Making of Modern Colombia*, 101, discerns a "mid-century conjuncture" characterized by a fresh "ascendancy of liberalism," specifically in Mexico, Colombia, and Argentina.

41. Collier, *Chile*, 84, 135–36; Bushnell, *The Making of Modern Colombia*, 111–12.

42. Safford, "Politics, Ideology and Society," 384. Chilean anticlericalism, signaled by the "affair of the sacristan" (1854), is discussed in Collier, *Chile*, 193, 199–202. On midcentury Peruvian liberalism, see Mark Thurner, *From Two Republics to One Divided: Contradictions of Postcolonial Nationmaking in Andean Peru* (Durham NC: Duke University Press, 1997), 44–46; Sarah C. Chambers, *From Subjects to Citizens: Honor, Gender, and Politics in Arequipa, Peru, 1780–1854* (University Park: Penn State University Press, 1999), 231–32; and Paul Gootenberg, *Between Silver and Guano: Commercial Policy and the State in Postindependence Peru* (Princeton NJ: Princeton University Press,

1989), 131, which sees the creation of a "genuinely liberal fiscal regime" ca. 1850. As Tibesan, "The Peruvian Church," 369, stresses, the church that the resurgent liberals confronted was now more conservative and ultramontane, which added to the potential polarization; Collier, *Chile*, 194, also discerns "an increasingly militant temper" within the Chilean church.

43. In the 1860s and 1870s, Argentine elections were held in the atria of parish churches so that "the citizens meet their electoral obligations under God's supreme protection" (Hilda Sabato, *The Many and the Few: Political Partici- pation in Republican Buenos Aires* [Stanford CA: Stanford University Press, 2001], 56–59). Ivereigh, "The Shape of the State," 172, 174, notes how church/ state relations were relatively uncontentious in Argentina between 1852 and 1880; potential differences between liberals and (political) Catholics were "masked by the need for consensus." Minor squabbles did occur, but in the interior provinces, where they did not compromise national political stability. The contrast between Argentina (where, in Negretto's words, "synthesis and compromise" characterized the mid-nineteenth-century liberal revival) and Colombia (where polarization resulted) is underscored by Posada-Carbó, "La tradición liberal," 174.

44. Thus, the radical Colombian liberal José María Samper not only harbored "a vehement hostility" toward organized religion, a hatred of Bolívar, and a "disdain for everything Spanish" but also displayed "that Jacobin spirit that defended the necessity of revolution"; thus, as he put it in 1861, the goal of revolution was "to destroy everything and create everything anew" (Posada- Carbó, "La tradición liberal," 166–67). As Alan Ryan observes, "One can irreparably damage liberal values by trying to implement them by force" (Ryan, *The Making of Modern Liberalism*, 122).

45. For example, in Ecuador the civil war of 1859–60 marked the defeat of the liberals (led by the *guayaquileño* president Francisco Robles) and the rise to power of García Moreno (recently returned from European exile) and his clerical/conservative (highland) supporters: Henderson, *Gabriel García Moreno*, 38–61. In Peru, too, the "triumphant export liberalism" of the guano age (roughly the 1850s and 1860s), associated with the figure of Ramón Castilla (president 1845–51 and 1854–62), did not last; the liberal Constitution of 1856 proved "short-lived," being modified by amendments that central- ized power and limited the franchise. Meanwhile, the guano boom—and with it government finances—went bust, and a disastrous foreign war was compounded by domestic rebellions. The outcome by the 1880s was "the era of the Second 'Militarism,'" characterized by "repression and exclusion"

and "an official discourse that 'othered' the subaltern classes" (Chambers, *From Subjects to Citizens*, 231); see also Peter Flinders Klaren, *Peru: Society and Nationhood in the Andes* (New York: Oxford University Press, 2000), 167–68, 169, 175, 194.

46. Compare, in Argentina, Julio Roca's slogan: "peace and administration" (Rock, *Argentina*, 155). To avoid possible misunderstanding, I should stress that my "developmental" (*desarrollista*) liberalism, a label for a sort of national project, has nothing to do with—and, indeed, tends to be antithetical to—MacPherson's "developmental" democracy (which I encountered only recently), an ideology that relates to individual fulfillment and is, in fact, much closer to my "social liberalism": see MacPherson, *The Life and Times of Liberal Democracy*, chap. 3. The classic study of Porfirian "developmental liberalism" is Charles A. Hale, *The Transformation of Liberalism in Late Nineteenth-Century Mexico* (Princeton NJ: Princeton University Press, 1989). A useful recent addition to the literature is Leonardo Lomelí Vanegas, *Liberalismo oligárquico y política económica: Positivismo y economía política del Porfiriato* (Mexico City: FCE, 2018), which, as the title makes clear, prefers the generic label "oligarchic" to describe the Porfirian brand of "liberalism."

47. Bushnell, *The Making of Modern Colombia*, 102–3, 131–33; Rock, *Argentina*, 123, 125–26; Brooke Larson, *Trials of Nation-Making: Liberalism, Race, and Ethnicity in the Andes, 1810–1910* (New York: Cambridge University Press, 2004), 45–46. Peru's somewhat precocious liberal project was also made possible by an export boom and rapid integration into global markets (thanks to guano): Klaren, *Peru*, 158–72.

48. So far, I have used "liberal" (lowercase *l*) to denote parties, leaders, policies, and movements that seem to fit the generic model of "liberalism" as defined and described by, for example, Manning, *Modern Liberalism*, and Ryan, *The Making of Modern Liberalism*, but with the caveat that these are both somewhat Platonic/philosophical studies that only tangentially engage with the real world of history. For example, Ryan has no index entries for Gladstone, Lloyd George, Mazzini, Woodrow Wilson, or—perhaps no surprise—Juárez. My approach is therefore closer to Hall, "Variants of Liberalism," 44–45, when he tries to address the "historical conditions of existence" of liberalism in particular contexts. As already mentioned (n. 9 above), in the "real world" not all liberals called themselves "Liberal," nor did they belong to "Liberal" parties (a distinction noted by Collier, *Chile*, 251). By the late nineteenth century, Latin America had acquired several Liberal (uppercase *L*) parties. But again, the appearance of "Liberal" in the

name is not cast-iron evidence of the liberal credentials of an individual, party, or regime: consider, for example, the "harsh dictatorship" of "Liberal" president Estrada Cabrera in Guatemala: Ciro F. Cardoso, "The Liberal Era, c. 1870–1930," in *Central America Since Independence*, ed. Leslie Bethell (Cambridge: Cambridge University Press, 1991), 60–61. Compare, by way of analogy, the many examples of so-called democratic, socialist, and people's parties in history, parties that have been neither democratic, nor socialist, nor particularly popular, the Democratic (*sic*) Party in the postbellum southern United States being yet another glaring misnomer.

49. Bushnell, *The Making of Modern Colombia*, 140–43; Posada-Carbó, "La tradición liberal," 168–69; Schaefer, *Liberalism as Utopia*, 8; and Gargarella, *Latin American Constitutionalism*, chap. 2, on "fusion Constitutionalism," alias "the Liberal-Conservative compact." Prior to 1880, Frédéric Martínez observes, Colombian liberals enunciated a "civilizing discourse" that stressed democracy, civil rights, and anticlericalism; after 1880 that discourse was "inverted," and emphasis was placed on "solid public order . . . political centralization, restriction of the suffrage and of civil liberties, and the re-Catholicization of the country by a reinforced Church" ("Las desilusiones del orden público: Los comienzos de la Policía Nacional en Colombia, 1891–98," in *In Search of a New Order: Essays on the Politics and Society of Nineteenth-Century Latin America*, ed. Eduardo Posada-Carbó [London: ILAS, 1998], 153). The "Fusion" of liberals and conservatives in Chile in the 1860s may be comparable (see Collier, *Chile*, 250–51), while in Brazil, for all its political idiosyncrasy, liberals and conservatives also converged after midcentury (see Graham, *Politics and Patronage*, 169, 171).

50. Ciro F. S. Cardoso's *Cambridge History* chapter covering Central America from 1870 to 1930 is titled "The Liberal Era" (n. 51 above); Peloso and Tenenbaum, introduction to Peloso and Tenenbaum, *Liberals, Politics and Power*, 19, call the "latter half" of the nineteenth century the "era of liberal domination"; while Jeremy Baskes concludes his study of transatlantic commerce by noting the onset of "the Liberal age" in the latter half of the nineteenth century: *Staying Afloat: Risk and Uncertainty in Spanish Atlantic World Trade, 1760–1820* (Stanford CA: Stanford University Press, 2013), 280.

51. "Progress" and occasionally "civilization" were the preferred terms at the time, but historians who should know better are very fond of introducing the cuckoo concept of "modernity" into the nest, where it brashly shoves these originals aside. Sometimes these same historians even put this demonstrably anachronistic and culturally loaded concept in the mouths of historical

actors who, to change the metaphor, are thus converted into ventriloquist's dummies. Oddly, these historians also make much of actors' "agency" and "voice," characteristics not usually associated with dummies.

52. Collier, *Chile*, 251; Aguilar Rivera, "Tres momentos liberales," 144, citing Justo Sierra on the "slow and painful" advance of liberal principles. See also Hale, *The Transformation of Liberalism*, 93, 96, on the advocacy of an "honorable tyranny" by Mexican liberals (so-called). It is worth noting that the "developmental" liberal project was not confined to Latin America. Italy, in this and other respects, displayed similar characteristics: in the late nineteenth century a "decidedly statist" Piedmontese liberalism enacted an authoritarian and centralizing "reform from above," happy "to sacrifice freedom and the rule of law to the claims of order and authority." In particular, "more obviously than in any other of the major European nations, the new relations of production had to be artificially imposed by an increasingly intrusive state" (Richard Bellamy, *Liberalism and Modern Society* [University Park: Penn State University Press, 1992], 105–9).

53. Gootenberg, "Order and Progress," 66.

54. Jacobsen, *Mirages of Transition*, 146, where the author refers appositely to these as "pseudo-liberal practices" whose "pseudo" character was detected and denounced by "those few individuals in the altiplano who at midcentury continued to fight for the emancipation of the Indians."

55. Jacobsen, *Mirages of Transition*, 305, citing a *cuzqueño* landowner.

56. Cecilia Méndez, "Incas Sí, Indios No: Notes on Peruvian Creole Nationalism and Its Contemporary Crisis," *Journal of Latin American Studies* 28, no. 1 (February 1996): 197–225 (quote from 218).

57. Larson, *Trials of Nation-Making*, 117, 213–18.

58. Though that icon of Victorian liberalism John Stuart Mill, "in his best East India Office manner," also conceded that, since "uncivilized races" disliked and avoided "continuous labour of an unexciting kind," it followed that "a civilized government, to be really advantageous to them, will require to be to a considerable degree despotic" (Bellamy, *Liberalism and Modern Society*, 28). I assume Mill would consider shoveling bird shit or tapping rubber trees in the sweltering bug-ridden Amazon to be "unexciting."

59. These are all late nineteenth- and early twentieth-century examples, but again, the pioneer of such repressive export commodity booms was Peruvian guano, which first displayed the distinctive combination of "liberalism" and labor coercion: Gootenberg, "Order and Progress," 66. I would add that the extreme examples also tend to correlate with the extractive exploitation of

finite resources: guano, nitrates, lumber, and rubber. As nonrenewables, these encouraged a predatory, get-rich-quick approach; their exploitation often took place in remote and/or harsh environments; and exploitation involved arduous, unhealthy work—all factors that militated in favor of coercive rather than voluntaristic labor recruitment. I discuss this phenomenon in Alan Knight, "Mexican Peonage: What Was It and Why Was It?" *Journal of Latin American Studies* 18 (May 1986): 41–74.

60. The boom in exports, coupled with the influx of foreign investment, bolstered state finances, thus making states more capable of repression, but booms also expanded the opportunities for private profiteering and peculation. The classic case was that of Julio César Arana's Peruvian Amazon Company, which created a powerful and oppressive politico-economic fief dedicated to the exploitation of rubber along the Putumayo River; we might note that the company "flagship" ("of evil fame" in local reports) was the launch *Liberal*: Angus Mitchell, ed., *The Amazon Journal of Roger Casement* (Dublin: Lilliput Press, 1997), 83.

61. Roberto Gargarella, *The Legal Foundations of Inequality: Constitutions in the Americas, 1776–1860* (Cambridge: Cambridge University Press, 2010), chap. 1; Alan Knight, *The Mexican Revolution*, 2 vols. (Cambridge: Cambridge University Press, 1986), 1:65–68, 68–69.

62. Sabato, *The Many and the Few*, 18.

63. Peloso and Tenenbaum, introduction, 26.

64. Thus, the Marxist theorist Plekhanov considered Herbert Spencer—something of a liberal icon in Latin America—to be "a conservative anarchist" (Juan Soriano, *Anarquistas: Cultura y política libertaria en Buenos Aires, 1890–1910* [Bueno Aires: Manantial, 2001], 69n18). On Spencer's appeal, see Posada-Carbó, "La tradición liberal," 171–72; and Hale, *The Transformation of Liberalism*, 184–85, 204–19.

65. Gargarella, *The Legal Foundations of Inequality*, 47–48, argues that Latin American constitutions of loosely liberal (but "radical" or "populist" liberal) character, such as Uruguay's (1813) and Mexico's (Apatzingán, 1814), were designed to "establish . . . alter, modify or totally abolish" the government in the interests of the people and their "happiness." Possibly this formulation sounds rather more anarchistic than is warranted: "totally abolish the government" perhaps means simply "get rid of the current administration" (a Lockean rather than a Bakuninist stance). Nevertheless, the kinship between liberalism and anarchism is evident.

66. C. A. M. Hennessy, *The Federal Republic in Spain* (Oxford: Clarendon Press, 1962), 28–31, 252, 253–54. Guy Thomson's study of Andalusian radical movements also suggests some kinship and elision between radical liberalism and anarchism: *The Birth of Modern Politics in Spain: Democracy, Association and Revolution, 1854–75* (Basingstoke: Palgrave Macmillan, 2010).

67. Soriano, *Anarquistas*, 38. Anarchist and radical liberal nomenclature also displayed some kinship: thus, clubs and newspapers carried names like *Luz* (Light), *Progreso* (Progress), *Sol* (Sun), *Aurora* (Dawn), *Evolución* (Evolution), and *Nueva Era* (New era): Soriano, *Anarquistas*, 43. It seems plausible that this semantic kinship was also connected to Freemasonry, although I have no hard evidence of this link. Carlos A. Forment, *Democracy in Latin America, 1760–1900*, vol. 1, *Civic Selfhood and Public Life in Mexico and Peru* (Chicago: University of Chicago Press, 2003) contains a wealth of information and ideas about Mexican and Peruvian associational life, but the political dimension is rather buried in the mass of data.

68. Knight, *Mexican Revolution*, 1:44–47. The PLM leaders, exiled to the United States, where they rubbed shoulders with the radicals of the IWW, arguably tacked toward anarchosyndicalism, an evolved species of anarchism that moved beyond libertarian individualism to espouse collectivist organization and insurrectionary action, including the transformational general strike.

69. Lowell Blaisdell suggests that "the innocuous-sounding name of the party" served to mislead potential American donors and supporters: quoted in Claudio Lomnitz, *The Return of Comrade Ricardo Flores Magón* (New York: Zone Books, 2014), 31.

70. Suriano, *Anarquistas*, 48, mentions several radicals who migrated to anarchism in the 1900s, including Arturo Montesano, Félix Basterra, and Alberto Ghiraldo. Posada-Carbó, "La tradición liberal," 163, notes the appeal of Proudhon in Colombia, an appeal partly explained by the radical liberal and anarchist attachment to extreme federalism. On Sandino, see Volker Wünderich, "El nacionalismo y el espiritualismo de Augusto C. Sandino en su tiempo," in *Encuentros con la historia*, ed. Margarita Vannini (Managua: Instituto de Historia de Nicaragua, 1995), 293. I return to Sandino as liberal nationalist later.

71. Alan Knight, "Salinas and Social Liberalism in Historical Context," in *Dismantling the Mexican State?*, ed. Rob Aitken, Nikki Craske, Gareth A. Jones, and David E. Stansfield (Basingstoke: Macmillan, 1996), 1–23.

72. Jesús Reyes Heroles, *El liberalismo mexicano*, 3 vols. (Mexico City: FCE, 1974), vol. 3, chaps. 7, 8.

73. Gargarella, *The Legal Foundations of Inequality.*

74. James O. Morris, *Elites, Intellectuals and Consensus: A Study of the Social Question and the Industrial Relations System in Chile* (Ithaca NY: Cornell University Press, 1966); Eduardo A. Zimmermann, *Los liberales reformistas: La cuestión social en la Argentina, 1890–196* (Buenos Aires: Sudamericana / Universidad de San Andrés, 1995); Paulo Drinot, *The Allure of Labor: Workers, Race and the Making of the Peruvian State* (Durham NC: Duke University Press, 2011), 19–20. In Britain, too, socieconomic changes in the late nineteenth century placed a "severe strain" on classic (mid-Victorian, laissez-faire) liberalism, engendering a "new liberalism" typified by Hobhouse, Hobson, and Marshall: see Bellamy, *Liberalism and Modern Society*, 15, 47–57; Hall, "Variants of Liberalism," 62–63; and MacPherson, *The Life and Times of Liberal Democracy*, 69–76. It may be worth clarifying that while in Europe industrialization stood at the heart of the "social question," in Latin America, where industrialization was more sketchy, it was the growth of cities, of urban squalor, and of a supposedly degenerate and dangerous lumpenproletariat that provoked particular concern.

75. Again, there are clear European parallels: Hall, "Variants of Liberalism," 62–66, and Bellamy, *Liberalism and Modern Society*, 34, which reminds us that Mill, typically combining paternalism and liberalism, advocated Irish land reform. Greg Grandin, "The Liberal Tradition in the Americas: Rights, Sovereignty and the Origins of Liberal Multilateralism," *American Historical Review* 117, no. 1 (February 2012): 68–91, in an interesting but somewhat confusing article, posits a fundamental divergence between Latin American social democracy (i.e., a progressive form of what I am calling social liberalism) and the United States' adherence to a doctrine of individual rights (much closer to classic laissez-faire liberalism). Latin America thus managed to "socialize hemispheric liberalism," asserting the "active role of the state" and producing a distinctive "sovereignty–social rights complex." (One reason why the article is confusing, to my mind, is its arbitrary yoking together of sovereignty and individual/social rights, two enormous questions whose relationship, both philosophical and historical, is highly debatable. They do not necessarily benefit from being crunched together, especially in a short essay.) My concern is with the "social rights" bit of the "complex," which, Grandin asserts, stands as Latin America's "contribution to global social democracy" (a bold claim!). Yet in reality Latin America is one of the least "social democratic" parts of the world: states have historically spent relatively little on social welfare, and what they have spent has often been

regressive, redounding to the benefit of the middle class (compare northern and western Europe or Asian countries such as Japan, Taiwan, and South Korea). Grandin's trump card is the Mexican Constitution of 1917, which can reasonably be seen as an example of the "social rights complex" (his phrase) or of "social liberalism" (mine). But the trump card is in fact something of a joker, since that constitution was—like many—honored in the breach, and it certainly did *not* usher in a social-democratic society. Indeed, Mexico after 1940 witnessed regressive policies, modest state spending, and growing inequality; neither women nor Indians benefited much from their alleged "social rights"; and when state intervention did dramatically increase during the 1970s, it was associated with corruption, clientelism, and economic failure. "Social rights" were more rhetorical flannel than political reality. In fact, it would make more sense to conclude that for most of the twentieth century, the Americas as a whole (including the United States and Latin America but not Canada) lagged way behind Europe when it came to "social rights," which is another way of saying that European "social liberalism" was more powerful and efficacious, especially after 1945, than anything seen in the Americas south of the forty-ninth parallel (with the possible honorable but minor exceptions of Costa Rica and Uruguay).

76. Of course, the Catholic Church also recognized the "social question" and proposed its own solutions, which, following Rerum Novarum (1891), included electoral engagement and the advocacy of social reform that was neither liberal nor socialist: Drinot, *The Allure of Labor*, 22–23; and Stephen J. C. Andes, *The Vatican and Catholic Social Activism in Mexico and Chile* (Oxford: Oxford University Press, 2014). As I discuss in chapter 3, the rival claims of church and state, now advanced in the context of an increasingly "massified" political society, provoked a fresh bout of anticlericalism, especially in revolutionary Mexico after 1913.

77. Rodney D. Anderson, *Outcasts in Their Own Land: Mexican Industrial Workers, 1906–1911* (DeKalb: Northern Illinois University Press, 1976), chap. 3; Charles Bergquist, *Labor in Latin America: Comparative Essays on Chile, Argentina, Venezuela and Colombia* (Stanford CA: Stanford University Press, 1986), 48–59, 132; Rock, *Argentina*, 187, 202; Suriano, *Anarquistas*, 52–56; Drinot, *Allure of Labor*, 17, 21–22; John W. F. Dulles, *Anarchism and Communism in Brazil* (Austin: University of Texas Press, 1973), 17–39.

78. Knight, *Mexican Revolution*, 1:432–35. Compare President Pardo's reformist response to the Peruvian general strike of 1919: David Parker, "Peruvian

Politics and the Eight-Hour Day: Rethinking the 1919 General Strike," *Canadian Journal of History / Annales Canadiennes d'Histoire* 30, no. 3 (1995): 417–38.

79. Manning, *Liberalism*, 101–3; Bellamy, *Liberalism and Modern Society*, 35–57.

80. Lars Peterson, "From Anarchists to 'Anarcho-Batllistas': Populism and Labor Legislation in Uruguay," in *In Defiance of Boundaries: Anarchism in Latin American History*, ed. Geoffroy de Laforcade and Kirwin Shaffer (Gainesville: University Press of Florida, 2015), chap. 5.

81. The phrase derives from the concept of "really existing socialism" as applied to the Soviet Union and other socialist states of the twentieth century. Another way of describing this broad approach would be in terms of Stuart Hall's inquiry into "liberalism's historical conditions of existence," that is, liberalism as it "applied to specific societies" in terms of time, place, and class relations: Hall, "Variants of Liberalism," 44. For a similar argument cogently deployed by way of criticizing the so-called Cambridge school of political thought for its concentration on "'discourses,' utterances or 'language situations,'" "the social conditions" of the day being "deliberately excluded," see Wood, *Liberty and Property*, 28.

82. I make no apology for citing Hall, "Variants of Liberalism," 44–45, 67, again. While it is certainly crude and reductionist to attribute "really existing liberalism" (my phrase) to one unified class (the bourgeoisie) or one monolithic movement (such as the "bourgeois revolution"), nevertheless, as Hall emphasizes, "the theoretical ideas first formulated in the materialist theory are absolutely essential" to our understanding of historical phenomena; those foundational ideas include the derivation of ideology from "actual social relations," above all, class relations (since "social being determines consciousness not—as we imagine—vice versa"). It's a point that some scholars of Latin America, stumbling about in a fog of "idealist" or "ideational" assumptions, seem to have lost sight of.

83. In what follows, I mostly deal in countries—for example, contrasting Argentina with Mexico—but, of course, most Latin American countries were composed of diverse regions; hence, national generalizations are necessarily aggregative and therefore broad-brush. More precise comparisons could be pitched at a regional level: for example, the Mexican Bajío resembled, say, the Central Valley of Chile more than the Guatemalan highlands, which closely resembled neighboring southern Mexico. I am taking what I see as the dominant politico-economic sector to stand for the country as a whole: so in the case of Argentina, it is the pampas and the littoral, not the

northwest; for Chile, it is the Central Valley; for Mexico, the central/south heartland (from Jalisco to Oaxaca, with Mexico City sitting in the middle).

84. On the long hiatus, see Halperín Donghi, *The Contemporary History*, 74.

85. Thus, in the 1860s, the regime of Maximilian in Mexico respected the status quo regarding property rights, and the liberal *desamortización* was not rolled back. If some clerical ultras regretted this outcome, most well-to-do conservatives were content. When property rights clashed with religiosity, the former won: see Robert H. Duncan, "Maximilian and the Construction of the Liberal State, 1863–1866," in *The Divine Charter: Constitutionalism and Liberalism in Nineteenth-Century Mexico*, ed. Jaime E. Rodríguez O. (Lanham MD: Rowman and Littlefield, 2005), 152–53.

86. Robert H. Holden, *Mexico and the Survey of Public Lands* (DeKalb: Northern Illinois University Press, 1994); Rock, *Argentina*, 107–8, 139–40. Erick D. Langer, *Economic Change and Rural Resistance in Southern Bolivia, 1880–1930* (Stanford CA: Stanford University Press, 1989), 21–22, 133–35, describes a similar sell-off of public lands in the Bolivian lowlands (the work, as it happens, of Conservatives).

87. Jacobsen, *Mirages of Transition*, 126, 198, 201, describes an "avalanche of hacienda expansion" in the southern Peruvian highlands in the late nineteenth century, while Larson, *Trials of Nation-Making*, 222, refers to a "massive alienation of indigenous land" throughout Bolivia between 1880 and 1930; for particular examples, see Langer, *Economic Change*, 20–21, 63, 65–66.

88. Karl Marx, *Capital*, 2 vols. (London: Dent, 1957), 2:793. The process that Marx discerned in Europe (especially England) was faster and more complete than that which affected Latin America: the English peasantry was eliminated; that of Latin America was squeezed and reduced. By way of putting a little flesh on the dry bones of "primary accumulation," we could quote the Indians of San Pablo Tecuantepec, in the municipality of Jilotepec, Estado de México, Mexico, who in 1858 complained that their community had been "extinguished" (by liberal legislation) and, "lacking resources for our very necessary subsistence, we went to augment the number of vagrants and beggars in the cities" (Carmen Salinas Sandoval and Diana Birrichaga Gardida, "Conflicto y aceptación ante el liberalismo: Los pueblos del Estado de México, 1856–1876," in *Los pueblos indios en los tiempos de Benito Juárez [1847–1872]*, ed. Antonio Escobar Ohmstede [Mexico City: UABJO/UAM, 2007], 247).

89. Jacobsen, *Mirages of Transition*, 195–96, gives good examples of the "weapons of the weak"—"ruses, tricks and plain common sense" that Peruvian livestock herders deployed in order to fool their superiors; on which, see also Juan

Martínez Alier, *Haciendas, Plantations and Collective Farms: Agrarian Class Societies—Cuba and Peru* (London: Frank Cass, 1977), 45, 86, which quotes one hacienda manager (1945) on how "the Indian, as a good Indian, is like a piece of granite when he is not willing to understand."

90. This classic dilemma faced President Francisco Madero when he had to deal with the Zapatista insurgency in 1911–13: as a good liberal, he deplored repression and attempted negotiation, but in the end he gave the green light to a brutal counterinsurgency campaign. See Knight, *Mexican Revolution*, 1:261–63, 316–17.

91. Jim Handy, *Gift of the Devil* (Boston: South End Press, 1984), 72; Jacobsen, *Mirages of Transition*, 304, citing the early twentieth-century opinions of local landlords, officials, and bosses (*gamonales*). Tristan Platt, "Liberalism and Ethnocide in the Southern Andes," *History Workshop Journal* 17 (1984): 7, 15, stressing "liberalism's . . . connotations of ethnocide and cultural imperialism" in the southern Andes, cites the grim prognosis of a creole mine owner in 1860s Bolivia: "The Indians will continue [in brutal subjection] for many more centuries if we do not wrench them finally from that shadowy path." Note also Chambers, *From Subjects to Citizens*, 251; and chapter 5 of this book, where I give further examples.

92. John Womack Jr., *Zapata and the Mexican Revolution* (New York: Knopf, 1969); Evelyn Hu-Dehart, *Yaqui Resistance and Survival: The Struggle for Land and Autonomy* (Madison: University of Wisconsin Press, 1984); Roberto Condarco Morales, *Zárate, el temible "Willka" historia de la rebelión indígena de 1899* (La Paz: Imprenta Renovación, 1983); Kuenzli, *Acting Inca*, chap. 1; Langer, *Economic Change*, chap. 4; Jacobsen, *Mirages of Transformation*, 209, 339–41; Klaren, *Peru*, 248.

93. Alfred Crosbie, *Ecological Imperialism: The Biological Expansion of Europe, 900–1900* (Cambridge: Cambridge University Press, 2004), xv.

94. Tulio Halperín Donghi, "Argentina: Liberalism in a Country Born Liberal," in *Guiding the Invisible Hand: Economic Liberalism and the State in Latin America*, ed. Joseph L. Love and Nils Jacobsen (New York: Praeger, 1988), 99–116. A somewhat similar notion has been floated in respect to Venezuela: from the early nineteenth century, argues Reuben Zahler, "a government led by civilians and guided by liberalism came to dominate the Venezuelan state" (*Ambitious Rebels: Remaking Honor, Law and Liberalism in Venezuela, 1780–1850* [Tucson: University of Arizona Press, 2013], 60). Indeed, if we took a global bird's-eye view, we could conclude, along with Frank Safford, that a "dominant liberal ideology" prevailed in Latin America—or, indeed, the

Americas—following the wars of independence: Safford, "Politics, Ideology and Society," 350. Thus, for all the failures and backsliding of the liberal project in Latin America, it compares favorably to the experience of Asia, Africa, and even much of Europe.

95. Natalio Botana, *El orden conservador: La política argentina entre 1880 y 1916* (Buenos Aires: Editorial Sudamericana, 1977); Paula Alonso, *Jardines secretos, legitimizaciones públicas: El Partido Autonomista Nacional y la política argentina de fines del siglo XIX* (Buenos Aires: Edhasa, 2010).

96. Roy Hora, *Landowners of the Argentine Pampas: A Social and Political History, 1860–1945* (Oxford: Oxford University Press, 2001), 142–47.

97. Fernando López-Alves, "The Authoritarian Roots of Liberalism: Uruguay, 1810–1886," in Peloso and Tenenbaum, *Liberals, Politics and Power*, 111–33. In the same volume, David Bushnell, "Assessing the Legacy of Liberalism," 284, concludes that Uruguay's two historic parties, the Blancos and Colorados, both came to subscribe to broadly liberal beliefs and practices (liberalism, therefore, was not a monopoly of the Colorados); their differences had more to do with "cultural style and external alliances than programmatic substance." In other words, we see another example of late nineteenth-century party-political convergence, though one that, given the socioeconomic context, was distinctly favorable to democratization.

98. In these cases—as in Brazil—the state played a role in encouraging and even subsidizing European immigration (so, again, this was no doctrinaire laissez-faire, night-watchman state), but this kind of state intervention in the labor market was very different from that undertaken by repressive regimes in Indo-America. And as Barrington Moore rightly reminded us some years ago, the means by which landlords recruit workers and organize production in agrarian societies have profound consequences for those societies and their political regimes: Barrington Moore Jr., *The Social Origins of Dictatorship and Democracy: Lord and Peasant in the Making of the Modern World* (Boston: Beacon Press, 1966). For an interesting application of Moore's thesis to Latin America, see Evelyne Huber and Frank Safford, eds., *Agrarian Structure and Political Power: Landlord and Peasant in the Making of Latin America* (Pittsburgh: University of Pittsburgh Press, 1995).

99. Sabato, *The Many and the Few*, 32–33, 43–46. This was also the urban/public space that enabled anarchism to flourish in Argentina: see Suriano, *Anarquismo*, 39–40. However, as Carlos Forment has argued, a vigorous, if more apolitical, associational life could also flourish under illiberal regimes, such as Mexico's Porfiriato: *Democracy in Latin America*, chap. 11. In fact, the

bulk of Forment's Mexican examples cluster in the 1870s, and he correctly observes that after 1880 there was a "resurgence of authoritarian politics" that "weakened democratic life." Nevertheless, he concludes (or hypothesizes?) that "citizens continue[d] imagining and practicing sovereignty of the people under adverse conditions." The "imagining" is plausible (but largely hypothetical); the "practicing" seems to me questionable.

100. Which I use in part to avoid the overworked and very general term "oligarchic" or the ill-advised "neofeudal." Rock, *Argentina*, 152, refers to the Tucumán landed elite of the late nineteenth century as "neo-seigneurial," which also comes close (and reminds us, again, that these forms do not denote whole countries but rather regions and sectors within what are often highly diverse countries). "Patrimonialism" at least has a respectable (Weberian) conceptual ancestry. See Max Weber, *The Theory of Social and Economic Organizaton* (New York: Free Press, 1964), 347–48, and for a useful résumé, Julien Freund, *The Sociology of Max Weber* (Harmondsorth: Penguin, 1972), 238–42. I add the "neo-" prefix to flag that this is no ancient, "traditional," prescriptive authority.

101. Arnold Bauer, *Chilean Rural Society from the Conquest to 1930* (Cambridge: Cambridge University Press, 1975) is the classic study; on Brazil, I found Billy Jaynes Chandler, *The Feitosas and the Sertão dos Inhamuns: The History of a Family and a Community in Northeastern Brazil, 1700–1930* (Gainesville: University Press of Florida, 1972) particularly illuminating. Colombia may also offer parallels: it witnessed factional conflict between elites who operated a system of "entrenched sociopolitical clientelism" (Bushnell, "Assessing the Legacy of Liberalism," 116); however, the strength of the historic parties meant that conflict—both electoral and violent—occurred within a structured national political system in which ideological differences mattered.

102. Brian Loveman, *Struggle in the Countryside: Politics and Rural Labor in Chile, 1919–1973* (Bloomington: Indiana University Press, 1976).

103. Thus, to young Liberals from the provinces (such as Atacama), Chile's "hacienda-dominated Central Valley" seemed like a bastion of stodgy tradition, "at least a century behind" the more progressive North: Collier, *Chile: The Making of a Republic*, 197–98.

104. Loveman, *Struggle in the Countryside*, chaps. 7–10; Shepard Forman, *The Brazilian Peasantry* (New York: Columbia University Press, 1975), 181–202.

105. Woodward, "The Liberal-Conservative Debate," 64–65; Ivereigh, "The Shape of the State," 169; Chambers, *From Subjects to Citizens*, 238; Gallo, Calvo, and De Stefano, *Los curas*.

106. John Lynch, "The Catholic Church in Latin America, 1830–1930," in *The Cambridge History of Latin America*, vol. 4, *c. 1870 to 1920*, ed. Leslie Bethell (Cambridge: Cambridge University Press, 1986), 529–30, 539–40, 541–42; Tibesan, "The Peruvian Church."

107. Bushnell, *The Making of Modern Colombia*, 117.

108. Ivereigh, "The Shape of the State," 177–80.

109. David Rock, *Politics in Argentina, 1890–1930: The Rise and Fall of Radicalism* (Cambridge: Cambridge University Press, 1975), 74, 76–77.

110. Forman, *The Brazilian Peasantry*, chap. 6.

111. Eric Van Young, "The Raw and the Cooked: Popular and Elite Ideology in Mexico, 1800–21," in *The Middle Period in Latin American History*, ed. Mark Szuchman (Boulder CO: Lynne Rienner, 1989), 75–102.

112. Robert Redfield, *Peasant Society and Culture* (Chicago: University of Chicago Press, 1956), 70–71.

113. See n. 3 above.

114. On the "class belongingness" of liberalism, see Hall, "Variants of Liberalism," 47, 55, 63. An ideology such as liberalism may also show a distinct spatial distribution (as I shall mention shortly). However, it is a moot point whether "regional" differences (e.g., in terms of liberal versus conservative allegiances) are really class, social, or sectoral differences that happen to be mapped geographically. Thus, if—for example—Colombian coffee producers tended to be liberal, then regions of coffee production will show up as liberal on the political map: the socioeconomic attachment reveals itself spatially. On the other hand, there may be regional differences that are, as it were, "relatively autonomous" of prior socioeconomic determinants. For example, as I later mention, outlying states or provinces, whether in Mexico or Colombia, have tended toward federalism (and liberalism) in opposition to the conservative "center," an antagonism that cannot be reduced to prior socioeconomic factors (save perhaps taxation).

115. Claudio Veliz, *The Centralist Tradition in Latin America* (Princeton NJ: Princeton University Press, 1980), 151–53, 170, where the author extends the argument concerning liberalism's alien and imported character to Spain. See also n. 2 above. Gabriel L. Negretto and José Antonio Aguilar Rivera, "Rethinking the Legacy of the Liberal State in Latin America: The Cases of Argentina (1853–1916) and Mexico (1857–1910)," *Journal of Latin American Studies* 32, no. 2 (2000): 362–65; Safford, "Politics, Ideology and Society," 355. In a sense, the provenance of liberalism—or any other "ism"—is not the crucial question; diffusionist debates about provenance can become sterile and inconclusive,

since it is often difficult, if not impossible, to determine which "isms" or which bit of which "isms" are imported as opposed to domestically fashioned. Christianity, after all, came out of the Middle East before it "conquered" Europe and, much later, the Americas. And when it got to the Americas it incorporated indigenous elements, as it had done previously in Europe. Ideas and "isms" are not like basic commodities (sugar and tobacco, coffee and potatoes), for which the balance sheet of the "Columbian exchange" can be confidently compiled. The important thing is how and why successive "isms" catch on and the impact they then have on politics and society. That said, it is, of course, true that events and trends in Europe and the United States had a direct impact in Latin America, for example, the revolutions of 1848: Thomson, *The European Revolutions*.

116. An alternative political-science model that avoids cooking metaphors could be derived from Pierre Ostiguy's interesting mapping of modern Argentine politics, in which conventional East/West distinctions (related to conventional questions of economic distribution) are combined with a North/South axis involving, at the top, more cosmopolitan and cerebral articulations and, at the bottom, those that are more nationalistic, nativist, and emotive: Pierre Ostiguy, "Argentina's Double Political Spectrum: Party System, Political Identities and Strategies, 1944–2007," Kellogg Institute, Notre Dame, working paper no. 361 (2009). Thus, both the Argentine Left and Right embody these contrasting—politico-cultural?—tendencies, creating a fourfold schema. A similar model could be applied to the nineteenth century, perhaps contrasting liberalism (high and low) and conservatism (ditto); indeed, though his focus is the later twentieth century, Ostiguy sees this outcome as rooted in nineteenth-century precedents.

117. Bushnell, *The Making of Modern Colombia*, 110–11. Of course, these same Catholic Conservative critics espoused a "European" religion, deferred to an Italian pope, and were keen to import European Jesuits to spread the faith.

118. Knight, *Mexican Revolution*, 1:160.

119. David Sowell, "Artisans and Tariff Reform: The Sociopolitical Consequences of Liberalism in Early Republican Spanish America," in Peloso and Tenenbaum, *Liberals, Politics and Powers*, 166–85. On the role of liberal artisans in Arequipa, Peru, see Chambers, *From Subjects to Citizens*, 229–30, 234, 248, 250.

120. Anderson, *Outcasts in Their Own Land*, chap. 6.

121. Chambers, *From Subjects to Citizens*, 229–30, 234, 248, 250; Bushnell, *The Making of Modern Colombia*, 112.

122. Womack, *Zapata*, 7–8, 393, 399–400; Peter F. Guardino, *Peasants, Politics, and the Formation of Mexico's National State: Guerrero, 1800–1857* (Stanford CA: Stanford University Press, 1996), chap. 6; Fernando Díaz Díaz, *Caudillos y caciques: Antonio López de Santa Anna y Juan Alvarez* (Mexico City: El Colegio de México, 1972); Sinkin, *The Mexican Reform*, 33–35.

123. Bushnell, *The Making of Modern Colombia*, 107; Frank Safford, "Reflections on Internal Wars in Nineteenth-Century Latin America," in *Rumours of Wars: Civil Conflict in Nineteenth-Century Latin America*, ed. Rebecca Earle (London: ILAS, 2000), 17.

124. Peter F. Guardino, *The Time of Liberty: Popular Political Culture in Oaxaca, 1750–1850* (Durham NC: Duke University Press, 2005), chap. 5. About a century later, in Michoacán, we encounter a somewhat similar terminology: the "partido de la hilacha" (ragamuffin party) represented agrarista radicals in opposition to the well-to-do "partido de la seda" (silk party): Guillermo Ramos Arizpe and Salvador Rueda Smithers, *Una visión subalterna del pasado a través de la histroria oral: Jiquilpán, 1895–1920* (Jiquilpán: Centro de Estudios de la Revolución Mexicana "Lázaro Cárdenas," 1984), 328.

125. Woodward, "The Liberal-Conservative Debate," 64. By way of translation I have opted for "lackeys" instead of Woodward's *serviles*. Again, a century later, we find Sandino referring to Nicaraguan Conservatives as *cachurecos* (twisted or deformed): Gregorio Smelser, *Sandino: The Testimony of a Nicaraguan Patriot* (Princeton NJ: Princeton University Press, 1990), 71.

126. Chambers, *Subjects to Citizens*, 228.

127. By "clan" I mean regionally defined politico-social networks that are typically based on extended kinship, such as Brazil's *parentelas*: see Linda Lewin, *Politics and Parentela in Paraíba: A Case Study of Family-Based Oligarchy in Brazil* (Princeton NJ: Princeton University Press, 1987); and Chandler, *The Feitosas*; note also Womack, *Zapata*, 7, 108.

128. Luis González, *Pueblo en vilo: Microhistoria de San José de Gracia* (Mexico City: El Colegio de México, 1972), 44, 73, 126, 152, 176.

129. Bushnell, *The Making of Modern Colombia*, 111–12; Thomson, "Bulwarks of Patriotic Liberalism."

130. Rick Shenkman, *Just How Stupid Are We? Facing the Truth about the American Voter* (New York: Basic Books, 2008) admittedly deals—in accessible style—with contemporary American public opinion, but then America is the cultural homeland of rational choice theory.

131. Alan Knight, "The Mentality and Modus Operandi of Revolutionary Anti-clericalism," in *Faith and Impiety in Revolutionary Mexico*, ed. Matthew Butler (New York: Palgrave Macmillan, 2007), 21–56.

132. Jean-Pierre Bastian, *Disidentes: Sociedades protestantes y revolución en México, 1872–1911* (Mexico City: FCE, 1989).

133. On Sandino's mystical, including spiritualist, bent, see Smelser, *Sandino*, 25–26, 41.

134. Chambers, *From Subjects to Citizens*, 238–39; Knight, "The Mentality," 34.

135. The Liberal governor of the province of Vélez, in eastern Colombia, promoted a female suffrage law as early as 1853 (he was, we are told, "of radical doctrinaire leanings, [and] also appears to have had a politically forceful wife"), but the measure was annulled by the national Supreme Court before it could be implemented: Bushnell, *The Making of Modern Colombia*, 108–9. Effective female suffrage did not become the norm in Latin America for another hundred years.

136. Chambers, *From Subjects to Citizens*, 246–47.

137. Thus, in 1920s Mexico, anticlericalism tended to be a male preoccupation foisted upon women (and children): Patience Schell, *Church and State Education in Revolutionary Mexico City* (Tucson: University of Arizona Press, 2003), 181. Suriano, *Anarquistas*, 38, quotes a 1906 anarchist newspaper to the effect that while the men in the family typically "have portraits of their favorite sociologists hung over the head of the bed," the mother and daughter "have statues of the Virgin and other saints and read nothing except a stupid prayer-book." I return to this gendered pattern of church/state politics in chapter 3.

138. Thus, an 1870 report from Estado de México describes how, in the Zumpango district, corporate land had been widely distributed, to the "great good" of the people, while municipal revenue and land values had increased: Salinas Sandoval and Birrichaga Gardida, "Conflicto y aceptación," 231. See also Antonio Escobar Ohmstede and Ana María Gutiérrez Rivas, "El liberalismo y los pueblos indígenas en las Huastecas, 1856–85," in *Los pueblos indios en los tiempos de Benito Juárez (1847–1872)*, ed. Antonio Escobar Ohmstede (Mexico City: UABJO/UAM, 2007), 253–98; and Charles Berry, *The Reform in Oaxaca* (Lincoln: University of Nebraska Press, 1981).

139. Womack, *Zapata*, chap. 2.

140. Knight, *Mexican Revolution*, 1:416–23.

141. Hall, "Variants of Liberalism," 41.

142. I offer this by way of proof that I am not a 100 percent materialist. More like 95 percent.

143. Though there had been earlier efforts: Jean Meyer, "La Ley Lerdo y la des-amortización de las comunidades en Jalisco," in *La sociedad indígena en el Centro y el Occidente de México*, ed. Pedro Carrasco (Zamora: El Colegio de Michoacán, 1986); Escobar Ohmstede and Gutiérrez Rivas, "El liberalismo," 259–60.

144. Salinas Sandoval and Birrichaga Gardida, "Conflicto y aceptación," 228, 230–31; Escobar Ohmstede and Gutiérrez Rivas, "El liberalismo," 269, 274–75, 287–88.

145. Escobar Ohmstede and Gutiérrez Rivas, "El liberalismo," 269–71; Robert H. Holden, *Mexico and the Survey of Public Lands* (DeKalb: Northern Illinois University Press, 1994); Schafer, *Liberalism as Utopia*, chap. 5.

146. Womack, *Zapata*, 16–17, 37–42.

147. Escobar Ohmstede and Gutiérrez Rivas, "El liberalismo," 276–77, 278–79.

148. Similarly, Peru's "heroic modernizer," President Manuel Pardo (1872–76), drew inspiration from "the democratic smallholder economy and frontier expansion of North America"; however, his dream of "Huancayo as a kind of mestizo Cincinnati" was never realized: Gootenberg, "Order and Progress," 69, 71.

149. The Zapatistas and other Mexican agrarian rebels are often glibly termed "communalists" on the assumption that they favored collective corporate or communal property over individual private freehold. This seems mistaken, or at least much exaggerated. Oddly, the assumption tends to be made by radical historians who, in emphasizing Zapatista "communalism," tend to echo the scare stories of Porfirian conservatives (who denounced Zapatista "Communism" and "Bolshevism"). "Communal" is confusing, since it can refer to (1) how the land is worked and (2) how it is owned. Regarding the latter, Mexican villages—not least those of Morelos—were thoroughly familiar with freehold property, and villagers were not averse to buying, selling, and renting land. Of course, some genuinely "communal" lands (e.g., woods and pastures) were better left as commons. But arable farmland could take many forms. We should distinguish more carefully between an attachment to communal/corporate landholding as the *summum bonum*—an end in itself, reflecting ancient communal tradition—and the defense of peasant access to land in whatever form it might come (sometimes communal/corporate, sometimes not). In other words, peasants were often pragmatic, as they had to be.

150. The American "social liberal" (as I would call him) Herbert Croly summed it up neatly: he sought "Jeffersonian goals" (a free, smallholding democracy)

by "Hamiltonian means" (i.e., by exercising the reformist power of the state): Ryan, *The Making of Modern Liberalism*, 477. For a good recent study of the ejido and Mexico's pioneer land reform, see Helga Baitenmann, *Matters of Justice: Pueblos, the Judiciary and Agrarian Reform in Revolutionary Mexico* (Lincoln: University of Nebraska Press, 2020).

151. We can usefully compare agrarian trends and peasant protest throughout Latin America, but only Mexico experienced a major popular revolution leading to a sweeping land reform during the "liberal" period under consideration (roughly 1870–1930). Agrarian reform did not become a staple feature of the Latin American political economy until the 1950s and 1960s, when, of course, the Alliance for Progress also sought to incorporate it within a broader liberal/capitalist framework. But that is another story.

152. Méndez, "Incas, Sí, Indios, No."

153. Kuenzli, *Acting Inca*, 62–63.

154. Sinkin, *The Mexican Reform*, 37.

155. Bushnell, *The Making of Modern Colombia*, 93, 115. Ecuador displays a similar political geography (conservative highland Quito versus liberal lowland Guayaquil): Ayala Mora, *Ecuador del siglo XIX*, 53–54.

156. Collier, *Chile*, 197–98; Chambers, *From Subjects to Citizens*, 250.

157. Woodward, "The Liberal-Conservative Debate," 62–63, 70–72.

158. Woodward, "The Liberal-Conservative Debate," 64.

159. Knight, *Mexican Revolution*, 1:115–27.

160. What Eric Van Young, *The Other Rebellion: Popular Violence, Ideology, and the Mexican Struggle for Independence, 1810–1821* (Stanford CA: Stanford University Press, 2001), 483, calls *campanilismo*: "The tendency of villagers to see the social and political horizon as extending metaphorically only as far as the view from their church bell tower."

161. Safford, "Reflections on Internal Wars," 21–22.

162. Lynch, *Caudillos*, 230–31, 233–34.

163. Bushnell, *The Making of Modern Colombia*, 91, 98, 111–12; Lynch, *Caudillos*, 236–37; James E. Sanders, "Subaltern Strategies of Citizenship and Soldiering in Colombia's Civil Wars," in *Military Struggle and Identity Formation in Latin America*, ed. Nicola Foote and René D. Harder Horst (Gainesville: University Press of Florida, 2010), 28.

164. Méndez, *The Plebeian Republic*; Chambers, *From Subjects to Citizens*; Kuenzli, *Acting Inca*. Chambers, *From Subjects to Citizens*, 225, describing the 1834 loosely liberal-federalist revolt against Gamarra, quotes a somewhat bemused journalist observing events in Arequipa: "The barracks became crowded and,

by some kind of magic spell, the people that have viewed military enlistment with horror were transformed into a town of soldiers." "Manpower," to which some might object, seems appropriate in this context, the soldiers being, it seems very likely, all men.

165. In two senses: they followed the liberal program of Madero—or the more radical Partido Liberal Mexicano—and they also harked back to the liberal tradition of Juárez and the Reforma.

166. Wünderich, "El nacionalismo," 293. A recent study that expertly explores Sandino's eclectic philosophy is Alejandro Bendaña, *Sandino: Patria y libertad* (Managua: Anamá, 2016).

167. Foote and Horst, *Military Struggle*, contains several good case studies.

168. Thus, Latin America, a region of nation-states, however imperfect, was more like western Europe rather than eastern Europe, the Middle East, or most of Africa and Asia, where empires prevailed. I realize, of course, that Britain, France, and Spain were imperial powers, but domestically they operated as nation-states—albeit, as I mention in chapter 5, nation-states that arguably embodied forms of internal colonialism, most obviously in Ireland.

169. Manning, *Liberalism*, 92–93.

170. I don't want to get into the thorny debates about the origins and character of Spanish American independence, about which we have heard a lot in recent years. However, I am inclined to think that (1) liberal and patriotic opposition to colonial rule has been overly downplayed in favor of explanations that stress external contingency (e.g., the Napoleonic invasion of Spain) and (2) the viability of the Spanish Empire (absent that invasion) has been exaggerated. The key question is whether, had no invasion occurred, Spain would have conceded political and economic rights in its American colonies (or "kingdoms," if you prefer) and whether such concessions would have satisfied liberal and patriotic (and other) malcontents, thus ensuring the robust survival of a reformed Spanish Empire, perhaps even "commonwealth." As I suggest in the introduction, I have my doubts.

171. Even after independence, Latin American liberals often entertained a healthy dislike of Spain and things Spanish; thus, the Colombian José María Samper, writing in 1878, defined the radical liberalism of his youth in terms of anticlericalism, anti-Bolivarianism, and "an open disdain for everything of Spanish provenance" (Posada-Carbó, "La tradición liberal," 166–67).

172. Van Young, *The Other Rebellion*, 315–20 (though the author might question whether *national* legitimation was an issue); Henderson, *Gabriel García Moreno*, 30, 63, 69, 82, 107; Roderick Barman, *Citizen Emperor: Pedro II*

and the Making of Brazil, 1825–91 (Stanford CA: Stanford University Press, 1999), 9–11. Catholic nationalism, of course, faced the tricky problem of Rome, which, under Pius IX, was making ambitious claims to ultramontane authority. Conservatives might scorn the liberals' affection for, say, the United States, but liberals could point to the conservatives' deference to Rome, the pope, and the Jesuits.

173. Chalmers Johnson, *Peasant Nationalism and Communist Power: The Emergence of Revolutionary China* (Stanford CA: Stanford University Press, 1962).

174. By the time it took power, the PAN had become a liberal party (in the ideological sense), and while it remained rather ambivalent about Juárez, it could embrace Madero, the "apostle of Mexican democracy," not least because several members of the Madero family were prominent in its ranks. It could also appeal to Catholic *guadalupanista* nationalism.

175. Woodward, "The Liberal-Conservative Debate," 60, where the author notes: "In Nicaragua the Walker episode had so discredited the liberals that they would not regain political control until 1893."

176. By the later nineteenth century, Manning, *Liberalism*, 97, notes, the association of liberalism and nationalism had faded (in Europe), and nationalism was increasingly seen to lie on the right of the political spectrum. There is a very simple—which is not to say complete—explanation for this. By then, the battle for the nation-state in Europe was being won, and the old multiethnic empires were in headlong retreat: Italy and Germany were united, Greece and most of the Balkans had thrown off Ottoman rule, and with the First World War, the ancient Habsburg Empire would fragment into a series of fragile nation-states. Nationalism and liberal self-government now went their separate ways. Meanwhile, the acquisition of empires elsewhere made Europeans leery of "Third World" nationalism.

177. Again, the use of "manpower" is not careless: voters were almost always men, as were the vast majority of soldiers. That is not to say that women did not play other roles in liberal movements, of course.

3. RELIGION AND CONFLICT

1. Those exceptions include Celedonio Jarauta, a Spanish priest and ex-Carlist based in Veracruz who mounted a fierce guerrilla resistance against the American invaders of Mexico in the 1840s: Daniel Molina Alvarez, *La pasión del Padre Jarauta* (Mexico City: Gobierno de la Ciudad de México, 1999). Eighty years later, Father José Reyes Vega—nicknamed "Pancho Villa in a cassock"—was a ruthless commander of the Catholic "Cristero" rebels

combating the revolutionary state: Jean A. Meyer, *The Cristero Rebellion* (Cambridge: Cambridge University Press, 1976), 55, 57, 74–75. During the War of the Triple Alliance (1864–70) the notorious Paraguayan priest Fidel Maíz commanded a battalion at the battle of Itá-Ybaté, allegedly annihilating a sizeable Brazilian force: Harrison Gaylord Warren, *Paraguay and the Triple Alliance: The Postwar Decade, 1869–1878* (Austin: University of Texas Press, 1978), 172. In Guatemala, Francisco González Lobos, the "guerrilla priest," played an important and very violent role in the country's turbulent nineteenth-century politics: Douglass Sullivan-González, *Piety, Power and Politics: Religion and Nation Formation in Guatemala 1821–1871* (Pittsburgh: University of Pittsburgh Press, 1998), 92–98.

2. As E. P. Thompson's classic analysis of Methodism illustrated, the sociopolitical role of religion can be highly ambivalent, at the same time inculcating hard work, abstinence, and deference while also promoting working-class organization and solidarity: *The Making of the English Working Class* (London: Penguin, 1963), chap. 11.

3. Sullivan-González, *Piety, Power and Politics*, 56, 60–61, 100–101, gives examples of clerical peace-making in Guatemala. John Lynch, *New Worlds: A Religious History of Latin America* (New Haven CT: Yale University Press, 2012), 131, quotes a Chilean political official who in 1854, when "faced by turbulence in the mining zone" of Atacama, declared that "religion and the law, the Church and the prison, are powerful means to stem the torrent of corruption which threatens us." Lynch notes a similar rationale at work in the Peruvian highlands (146). By way of contrast, see n. 69 below.

4. Haiti, being arguably "Latin," deserves inclusion, though I cannot give it the attention it merits. Regarding Spanish America, Mexico bulks large, since, as I have mentioned, it is the country I know best and, more importantly, it witnessed the most serious church/state conflict.

5. The year 1900 is a meaningless date, and 1914 carries less significance for Latin America than for Europe. The year 1930, the onset of the Great Depression, is a conventional watershed. While it lacks any clear-cut "religious" significance, it has the advantage of ensuring the inclusion of Mexico's Cristero War (1926–29), the biggest religious war in Latin American history.

6. Miguel Angel Centeno, *Blood and Debt: War and the Nation-State in Latin America* (University Park: Penn State University Press, 2002).

7. Father Jarauta has been mentioned (n. 1). U.S. commanders sought to restrain anti-Catholic actions on the part of their ill-disciplined troops, but they often

failed. One consequence of American anti-Catholicism (e.g., the looting of churches) was the defection of Irish American soldiers who went over to the enemy, forming the famous St. Patrick's Battalion: Peter Guardino, *The Dead March: A History of the Mexican-American War* (Cambridge MA: Harvard University Press, 2017), 117–20, 250–63.

8. See the excellent study by Ada Ferrer, *Insurgent Cuba: Race, Nation and Revolution, 1868–1898* (Chapel Hill: University of North Carolina Press, 1999). In the 1890s, Cuban Protestants—few in number—appear to have favored the patriot cause and occasionally suffered popular reprisals: Louis A. Pérez, *On Becoming Cuban* (New York: HarperCollins, 2001), 55–60.

9. William F. Sater, *Chile and the War of the Pacific* (Lincoln: University of Nebraska Press, 1986), 47.

10. Here, I follow a typology of violence previously sketched in Alan Knight, "War, Violence and Homicide in Modern Mexico," in *Murder and Violence in Modern Latin America*, ed. Eric A. Johnson, Ricardo D. Salvatore, and Pieter Spierenburg (Chichester: John Wiley, 2013), 12–48.

11. Paul Collier and Anke Hoeffler, "Greed vs Grievance in Civil War," *Oxford Economic Papers* 56 (2004).

12. E. J. Hobsbawm, *Primitive Rebels: Studies in Archaic Forms of Social Movement in the 19th and 20th Centuries* (Manchester: Manchester University Press, 1974), chap. 2. I discuss "social banditry" further in chapter 1. Of course, when bandits such as Pancho Villa were sucked into social revolutions their role dramatically changed; mercenary motives were then swamped by social demands and commitments.

13. As I note in chapter 1, bandits were rarely anticlerical and often respected priests (perhaps because local *curas* were not worth robbing anyway). A good example of today's narco saints is Mexico's San Jesús Malverde (Culiacán, Sinaloa): see James H. Creechan and Jorge de la Herrán García, "Without God or Law: Narcoculture and Belief in Jesús Malverde," *Religious Studies and Theology* 24, no. 2 (2005): 5–57. Colombia also has several such cults.

14. "Instrumental" versus "affective" raises several problems that cannot be addressed here. But I will suggest that, in many historical instances, the two happily coexist: wars are fought to advance instrumental policies cold-bloodedly, even casually, formulated by elites, but on the ground, the common foot soldiers may fight "hot-bloodedly," their aggression stoked by drink, drugs, berserker rage, or ideological "fanaticism" (whether religious, nationalist, ethnic, or political).

15. For a good study of "honor" and its association with crime and interpersonal violence, see Pablo Piccato, *The Tyranny of Opinion: Honor in the Construction of the Mexican Public Sphere* (Durham NC: Duke University Press, 2010).

16. On this pervasive syndrome, see, for example, Edward Wright-Ríos, *Revolutions in Mexican Catholicism: Reform and Revelation in Oaxaca, 1887–1934* (Durham NC: Duke University Press, 2009), 33–35; Sol Serrano, *Qué hacer con Dios en la República?* (Santiago: FCE, 2008), 39. The infant William Hudson, visiting Buenos Aires for the first time in the 1840s, was much impressed by a ritzy religious fiesta involving a "great attendance of fashionable people": at the church door the women, "beautifully dressed," filed in, while the men, numbering some "four or five hundred," milled about in the street, "conversing in an animated way" until the church bells signaled the end of the service and the women reemerged to join their male companions: W. H. Hudson, *Far Way and Long Ago* (London: J. M. Dent, 1951), 82.

17. Wright-Ríos, *Revolutions in Mexican Catholicism*, 27–28. The opposite of this view posits that humans are programmed (e.g., by a so-called God gene or god center in our brains) to be innately religious. This is also erroneous. I have no serious expertise in this field (and the issue is peripheral to the historical analysis presented here), but I found Daniel Dennett, *Breaking the Spell: Religion as a Natural Phenomenon* (London: Penguin, 2007) both interesting and convincing: see 82–83, 138–40.

18. The colonial church "did a great deal of political work," both institutionally and ideologically: for a good analysis, see Matthew D. O'Hara, *A Flock Divided: Race, Religion, and Politics in Mexico, 1749–1857* (Durham NC: Duke University Press, 2010), quote from 162.

19. D. A. Brading, *The First America* (Cambridge: Cambridge University Press, 1991), chap. 11, recounts a classic case of conflict between church and state: the quarrel between Bishop Palafox of Puebla and the viceroy of New Spain, the count of Salvatierra, in the 1640s. The bone of contention was the Jesuit Order, which, threatened by Palafox, allied with the viceroy. In other words, what was at issue was not the basic alliance of throne and altar (or the religious monopoly of the Catholic Church) but rather how the parties to that alliance—and the beneficiaries of that monopoly—would distribute the resulting power and privileges.

20. D. A. Brading, *Miners and Merchants in Bourbon Mexico* (Cambridge: Cambridge University Press, 1971), 27.

21. Lynch, *New Worlds*, 109.

22. Brading, *The First America*, chap. 20.

23. In Brazil clerical celibacy was something of a myth: Clarence H. Haring, "Church-State Conflict in Nineteenth-Century Brazil," in *The Conflict between Church and State in Latin America*, ed. Frederick B. Pike (New York: Knopf, 1964), 155. For Peru, see Jeffrey Klaiber, SJ, *The Catholic Church in Peru, 1821–1985* (Washington DC: Catholic University of America Press, 1992), 185–90.

24. As William Taylor observes, colonial Catholicism had a schizoid character (my term, not his): churches were often the focal point of community life, while religious rites and fiestas forged social solidarity. But clerical authority, in its immediate, quotidian, and local form, was frequently resented: "The parish priest might be hated and ridiculed by villagers, but the church and its grounds were sacred places, connecting the past to the present and future" (*Drinking, Homicide, and Rebellion in Colonial Mexican Villages* [Stanford CA: Stanford University Press, 1979], 118). For examples of popular protest against priests often spurred by excessive clerical fees, see Taylor, *Drinking, Homicide, and Rebellion*, 134, 137; and Terry Rugeley, *Of Wonders and Wise Men: Religion and Popular Cultures in Southeast Mexico, 1800–1876* (Austin: University of Texas Press, 2001), 43–44, 47, 50, 58.

25. One of many Mexican anticlerical protests occurred at Pozontepec, Oaxaca, in 1758: the *cura* raised his fees, his parishioners complained, there were "insults and shoves" leading to a "general tumult." "That night . . . the priest's house was set on fire and the priest himself narrowly escaped the flames in his underwear" (Taylor, *Drinking, Homicide, and Rebellion*, 134). In central Mexico, riotous protests of this kind were common, but there were very few fatalities (i.e., they followed a fairly moderate script, being rowdy and violent but rarely lethal). More radical rebellions involving a wholesale repudiation of the institutional church and even priest killings were confined to the outer extremities of New Spain: New Mexico, Chiapas, and Yucatán.

26. Protestants remained a small minority, usually of urban middle-class makeup, well into the twentieth century. A cosmopolitan port like Valparaíso might, in the 1850s, boast a couple of Protestant churches (a quarter of the town's total) catering to the foreign community, but elsewhere, an American resident commented, Chile remained resolutely Catholic: "No progress is made in the conversion of the natives to Protestantism and I do not see how there is to be a change in this respect" (Mrs. George Merwin, *Three Years in Chile* [Carbondale: Southern Illinois University Press, 1966], 27, 31, 76). Only in recent decades has Protestantism, chiefly evangelical Protestantism, made major advances in Latin America, especially in Brazil and Central America;

now, however, the converts are found among the poorer sections of the population: see David Stoll, *Is Latin America Turning Protestant? The Politics of Evangelical Growth* (Berkeley: University of California Press, 1990).

27. Of course, it is difficult to assess the depth of freethinking under a regime that systematically imposed religious orthodoxy and repressed religious deviance. Perhaps freethinking was, sub rosa, more widespread than it appears: compare Tim Whitmarsh, *Battling the Gods: Atheism in the Ancient World* (London: Faber & Faber, 2016). However, the regimes of classical antiquity were more tolerant of religious dissent than those of post-Tridentine Iberian America. During the nineteenth century, of course, toleration gradually spread, and freethinking acquired institutional vehicles such as political clubs and parties, Masonic lodges, and literary/cultural associations. But the scale of freethinking remains something of a mystery.

28. David Nicholls, *From Dessalines to Duvalier* (Cambridge: Cambridge University Press, 1979), 31.

29. João José Reis, *Slave Rebellion in Brazil* (Baltimore MD: Johns Hopkins University Press, 1993) is a fine study.

30. Robert L. Paquette, *Sugar Is Made with Blood: The Conspiracy of La Escalera and the Conflict between Empires over Slavery in Cuba* (Middletown CT: Wesleyan University Press, 1990) graphically describes the 1843 uprising, noting the part played by African religious influences such as festivals, "kings," drums, amulets, "magic," and "witchcraft" (109, 181, 234, 237, 242–43, 256). During the Cuban Wars of Independence in the later nineteenth century, some vestigial elements of these phenomena remained, but they were marginal, at best "facilitating" factors in a struggle that, though metaphorically called a "holy war," hinged on race, class, and nationalism (not religion): Ferrer, *Insurgent Cuba*, 35, 37, 86, 107.

31. For the sake of simplicity I am—anachronistically—using modern national designations of regions that, before independence, carried different colonial labels.

32. There is a huge literature on this process of "syncretism": a perceptive study focused on southeastern Mexico is Rugeley, *Of Wonders and Wise Men*.

33. D. A. Brading, *Mexican Phoenix: Our Lady of Guadalupe; Image and Tradition across Five Centuries* (Cambridge: Cambridge University Press, 2001), 43, 55–58, 214–15.

34. William Taylor, *Magistrates of the Sacred: Priests and Parishioners in Eighteenth-Century Mexico* (Stanford CA: Stanford University Press, 1996)

is an authoritative study of Catholic conversion and organization in late colonial Mexico.

35. Taylor, *Magistrates of the Sacred*, chap. 3.

36. Michael T. Taussig, *The Devil and Commodity Fetishism in South America* (Chapel Hill: University of North Carolina Press, 1980), 148, 218, where the Pachamama is contrasted with "El Tío" (literally, "the Uncle"), a diabolical figure, complete with horns and phallus, whose cult flourished among Bolivia's miners.

37. Alberto Flores Galindo, "In Search of an Inca," and Tristan Platt, "The Andean Experience of Bolivian Liberalism," both in *Resistance, Rebellion and Consciousness in the Andean Peasant World*, ed. Steve J. Stern (Madison: University of Wisconsin Press, 1987), chaps. 7, 10.

38. F. Calderón de la Barca, *Life in Mexico* (London: Dent, n.d. [1842]), 147–48. One reason why the clergy, especially the lower clergy, opposed Spanish rule was the Bourbons' recent record of anticlericalism and fiscal avarice; furthermore, after 1808, Spain had fallen under the partial control of the godless French. On the divisions among the late colonial clergy in Mexico, see Nancy M. Farriss, *Crown and Clergy in Colonial Mexico, 1758–1821: The Crisis of Ecclesiastical Privilege* (London: Athlone Press, 1968). Brian Connaughton further suggests that the middle and lower clergy (not the high-flying bishops) generally served in their regions of origin; hence, their views regarding church and state, royalism and independence, and postindependence politics tended to reflect local sentiment: "La larga cuesta del conservadurismo mexican, del disgusto resentido a la propuesta partidaria, 1789–1854," in *El conservadurismo mexicano en el siglo XIX (1810–1910)*, ed. Humberto Morales and William Fowler (Puebla: BUAP, 1999), 173, 177.

39. Nancy Calvo, Roberto de Stefano, and Klaus Gallo, *Los curas de la revolución* (Buenos Aires: Emece, 2002).

40. Emilia Viotti da Costa, *The Brazilian Empire* (Chapel Hill: University of North Carolina Press, 2000), 8–9.

41. Lynch, *New Worlds*, 126; on Mexico, see Michael P. Costeloe, *Church and State in Independent Mexico* (London: Royal Historical Society, 1978), 75.

42. Serrano, *Qué hacer con Dios*, 64–65; Klaiber, *The Catholic Church*, 45; Lynch, *New Worlds*, 127.

43. This supposed connection is often summed up in the glib aphorism that "there are no atheists in a foxhole" (or "in the trenches"). I have no idea if this is a statistically proven—or even provable—generalization. On the reassertion of peasant autonomy made possible by a weakened state and

landlord class, see John Tutino, *From Insurrection to Revolution in Mexico: The Social Bases of Agrarian Violence, 1750–1940* (Princeton NJ: Princeton University Press, 1986), chap. 6.

44. Assessing the impact of freethinking in the nineteenth century is difficult. Ideological repression sharply diminished after independence (though it did not disappear), so we might assume that (covert) freethinking was more common than the patchy evidence suggests. On the other hand, I suspect that some of that evidence may derive from horrified Catholics who denounced mild religious dissent as red-blooded atheism. Interestingly, some of the most outspoken critics of Catholicism were products of the seminary: for example, Lorenzo de Zavala and Andrés Quintana Roo had both studied at the Mérida seminary (Yucatán, Mexico), where they were taught by Pablo Moreno, said to be the doyen of Yucateco "Jacobinism" and, according to Catholic sources, a "mocker of the Bible . . . suspected of crude atheism" (Costeloe, *Church and State*, 10).

45. Pamela Voekel, *Alone before God: The Religious Origins of Modernity in Mexico* (Durham NC: Duke University Press, 2001). See also Connaughton, "La larga cuesta," 175, 177, which notes that, in contrast to their counterparts in Puebla, the clergy of Jalisco and Zacatecas, in the liberal/federalist fringe, applauded patriotism and progress, stressing that "progress" was "eminently Christian and providential." See also Klaiber, *The Catholic Church*, 60–63; and Serrano, *Qué hacer con Dios*, 84–85, on the appeal of Lamennais and Montalembert in Chile.

46. Lynch, *New Worlds*, 147–49.

47. John Lynch, "The Catholic Church in Latin America, 1830–1930," in *The Cambridge History of Latin America*, vol. 4, *c. 1870 to 1930*, ed. Leslie Bethell (Cambridge: Cambridge University Press, 1986), 530–31.

48. Erika Pani, coord., *Conservadurismo y derechas en la historia de México*, 2 vols. (Mexico City: FCE, 2010) offers some fresh perspectives on Mexican conservatism, which, we might say, has recently been rescued from "the enormous condescension of posterity."

49. David Brading, "Ultramontane Intransigence and the Mexican Reform," in *The Politics of Religion in an Age of Revival*, ed. Austen Ivereigh (London: ILAS, 2000), 141.

50. Richard N. Sinkin, *The Mexican Reform, 1855–76* (Austin: University of Texas Press, 1979) provides a good overview.

51. Helen Delpar, *Red Against Blue: The Liberal Party in Colombian Politics, 1863–1899* (Tuscaloosa: University of Alabama Press, 1981).

52. David Bushnell, *Colombia: A Nation in Spite of Itself* (Berkeley: University of California Press, 1993), 94–95.

53. Bushnell, *Colombia*, 91–92, 129–30, 148–49; Delpar, *Red Against Blue*, 118–19.

54. Rosas, a "conventional Catholic," took a tough line toward the church, which he "protected . . . [but] also dominated and manipulated." He spurned papal authority and, having invited the Jesuits back to Argentina, expelled them again when they refused to collaborate: John Lynch, *Argentine Caudillo: Juan Manuel de Rosas* (Lanham MD: SR Books, 2001), 84–85. Similarly, in Paraguay, the church was "reduced to impotence" by the Francia dictatorship (1814–40), perhaps the most extreme example of Gallican statism in Latin America. The eclipse of the church persisted under the authoritarian regimes of Carlos Antonio López (1840–62) and Francisco Solano López (1862–70): the latter, indeed, had a bishop shot by firing squad and required priests—under duress, if necessary—to divulge the secrets of the confessional: Harrison Gaylord Warren, *Paraguay and the Triple Alliance: The Postwar Decade, 1869–1878* (Austin: University of Texas Press, 1978), 150, 169–72.

55. Roderick J. Barman, *Citizen Emperor: Pedro II and the Making of Brazil, 1825–91* (Stanford CA: Stanford University Press, 1999), 253–58.

56. In Mexico and Colombia, too, the Conservative clerical highlands confronted the Liberal coastal lowlands. Although economic factors (protectionism versus free trade) counted, the relative strength of the institutional church was crucial. On the weakness of the church and the state in coastal Colombia, see Eduardo Posada-Carbó, *The Colombian Caribbean: A Regional History, 1870–1950* (Oxford: Clarendon Press, 1996), 30.

57. Peter V. N. Henderson, *Gabriel García Moreno and State Formation in the Andes* (Austin: University of Texas Press, 2008).

58. Ralph Lee Woodward, *Rafael Carrera and the Emergence of the Republic of Guatemala* (Athens: University of Georgia Press, 1993).

59. Brian Hamnett, *Juárez* (London: Longman, 1993) provides a good overview.

60. On the mutation of liberalism under Díaz (a topic touched on in chapter 2), see Charles A. Hale, *The Transformation of Liberalism in Late Nineteenth-Century Mexico* (Princeton NJ: Princeton University Press, 1989).

61. Karl M. Schmidt, "The Díaz Conciliation on State and Local Levels, 1876–1911," *Hispanic American Historical Review* 40, no. 4 (November 1960): 511–32.

62. Lynch, *New Worlds*, 242–44; Manuel Ceballos Ramírez, *El catolicismo social: Un tercero en discordia, Rerum Novarum, la "cuestión social" y la movilización de los católicos mexicanos (1891–1911)* (Mexico City: El Colegio de México, 1991). For a good analysis of the dynamic impact of papal ultramontane activism

combined with Catholic resurgence in opposition to the anticlericalism of presidents Juárez and Lerdo, see Brian Stauffer, "The Routes of Intransigence: Mexico's 'Spiritual Pilgrimage' of 1874; The Globalization of Ultramontane Catholicism," *The Americas* 75, no. 2 (April 2018): 291–324, which reaches the convincing conclusion that the espousal of ultramontanism in Mexico, especially west-central Mexico, was in good measure local, popular, and autonomous: it was "neither a slavish imitation of Europe, nor a simple Roman imposition" (322).

63. Luis González y González, *Pueblo en vilo: Microhistoria de San José de Gracia* (Mexico City: El Colegio de México, 1995), 95–98. Born in Sahuayo, close by, Padre Othón was educated at the seminary at Zamora, where he acquired a visceral hostility to the Liberal regime and project of the 1850s and after. It is worth noting that San José was not an ancient community; it was a nineteenth-century creation recently carved out of the internal frontier by mestizo settlers—which, it seems likely, made it more receptive and malleable to Padre Othón's social engineering project.

64. On Núñez's middle-of-the-road policy toward the church (which gave the church a privileged position, not least regarding education, while maintaining freedom of religion), see Delpar, *Red Against Blue*, 135. As Delpar notes, Núñez "always considered himself a Liberal" but favored order and (economic) progress, to which end he stressed the "general usefulness of religion when it served a social function" (75–77). It may also be relevant that his second wife, Soledad Román, whom he married in 1877, was an "extremely devout" Conservative (128).

65. Klaiber, *The Catholic Church*, 99–101; quote from Lynch, *New Worlds*, 204.

66. Lynch, *New Worlds*, 205, where the author also notes—correctly, I think— that the honeymoon between the church and Leguía (whose authoritarian rule was ended by a coup in 1930) signaled the risks for the church in such relationships. When Leguía fell, the archbishop of Lima "quietly left Peru to spend the rest of his life in Spain," leaving behind "a Church which had sought influence and lost credibility, a model of Church-state relations not uncommon in the Church's history." One suspects that Lynch may be thinking in particular of Catholic connivance with the "bureaucratic-authoritarian" regimes that afflicted the Southern Cone of Latin America in the 1960s through the 1980s (which lies beyond the scope of this discussion).

67. O'Hara, *A Flock Divided*, 163, 166.

68. O'Hara, *A Flock Divided*, 171–73, recounts the case of San Bartolomé Naucalpán, near Mexico City, where, in the 1770s, the church authorities imposed

a Spanish official on the grounds that the "tradition of Indian control over local devotions and cofradías . . . needed to be changed." The local people petitioned and protested (whether successfully or not remains unclear).

69. Taylor, *Drinking, Homicide, and Rebellion*, 119–20. Priests occasionally played the peace-maker, persuading the insurgents to lay down their weapons—mostly sticks, stones, and farm implements—and to seek a negotiated settlement with the authorities. But such outcomes were greatly outnumbered by those in which the priest was a target and victim. In general, Taylor argues, "the voices of spiritual reason and moral authority counted for little in subduing these village outbursts."

70. Slatta, *Gauchos*, 41. W. H. Hudson, *Far Way and Long Ago*, 142, illustrates the inaccessibility of priests on the pampas.

71. Francis Baylies to Secretary of State, July 24, 1832, in *Diplomatic Correspondence of the U.S.: Inter-American Affairs, 1831–60*, vol. 1, *Argentina*, ed. William R. Manning (Washington DC: Carnegie Endowment for International Peace, 1932), 131.

72. Jews and Protestants were sometimes conflated. William Hudson, growing up in mid-nineteenth-century rural Argentina, recalls that his mother, a devout New England Protestant, was popular with the local people, but "it was a grief to some who were much attached to her that she was not of their faith. She was a Protestant, and what that exactly meant they didn't know, but they supposed it was something very bad. Protestants, some of them held, had been concerned in the crucifixion of the Saviour" (Hudson, *Far Way and Long Ago*, 276).

73. Peter Guardino, *Peasants, Politics, and the Formation of Mexico's National State: Guerrero, 1800–1857* (Stanford CA: Stanford University Press, 2002), 63. This bizarre brand of popular anti-Semitism appears to have had quite deep roots in colonial Mexico: when the Tzeltal, Tzotzil, and Chol Maya rebelled against Spanish rule in Chiapas in 1712 they explicitly rejected the Catholic Church but retained Christian rituals and beliefs; "they called the Spaniards Jews, demons and devils." See Kevin Gosner, *Soldiers of the Virgin: The Moral Economy of a Colonial Maya Rebellion* (Tucson: University of Arizona Press, 1992), 143. Popular anti-Semitism was no doubt sustained, in part, by convivial fiestas that involved Judas-burning and depictions of villainous Jews (and Romans): Rodney Gallop, *Mexican Mosaic* (London: Quiller Press, 1990), 114–15, 141, gives examples based on his observations in the 1930s.

74. Paul Gootenberg, *Between Silver and Guano: Commercial Policy and the State in Postindependence Peru* (Princeton NJ: Princeton University Press, 1989), chap. 3. I touch on this theme in chapter 5.

75. Desmond Gregory, *Brute New World: The Rediscovery of Latin America in the Early Nineteenth Century* (London: British Academic Press, 1992), 35, 76, 105–6, 130, 142–43, 152.

76. Merwin, *Three Years in Chile*, 77, comments that in Valparaiso, public processions of the Host had provoked "constant difficulties between the natives and the heretic foreigners" until the authorities, concerned for public order and the preservation of the port's vital commerce, banned such processions. Nevertheless, as of the 1850s, they continued unabated in Santiago and other towns where "intolerance and superstition . . . are unchecked." Isaac Holton, an American Protestant who traveled widely in Colombia in the 1850s, regularly followed the prudent advice of his (Catholic) interlocutors, who advised him to take off his hat when in church or when a religious procession passed by, since "a Protestant who remained covered is liable to have things thrown at him." And if his "conscience did not permit [him] to kneel in mass," he should at least "stand where [his] nonconformity could not be seen" (Isaac F. Holton, *New Granada: Twenty Months in the Andes* [Carbondale: Southern Illinois University Press, 1967], 12, 40, 58, 126, 145, 183).

77. Hudson, *Far Away and Long Ago*, 130, note also 142.

78. Klaus Gallo, *The Struggle for an Enlightened Republic: Buenos Aires and Rivadavia* (London: ILAS, 2006); Baylies to Secretary of State, July 24, 1832, in Manning, *Diplomatic Correspondence*, 131, reported—rather simplistically—that as part of his ambitious "schemes of improvement," Rivadavia sought "the overthrow of the Priesthood" but that in doing so he incurred the enmity of "sacerdotal power," a "united and powerful body whose influence with the people he found he had greatly underrated."

79. Ariel de la Fuente, *Children of Facundo: Caudillo and Gaucho Insurgency during the Argentine State Formation Process (La Rioja, 1853–1870)* (Durham NC: Duke University Press, 2000), 54–55.

80. John Lynch, *Massacre in the Pampas, 1872* (Norman: University of Oklahoma Press, 1998), 3. See also Richard W. Slatta, *Gauchos and the Vanishing Frontier* (Lincoln: University of Nebraska Press, 1992), 169–74.

81. Lynch, *Massacre*, 75–82.

82. Lynch, *Massacre*, 4, 34, which notes that fifty-six Britons were killed in incidents of this kind in just five years (1865–70). Slatta, *Gauchos*, 168–69, mentions earlier xenophobic attacks; furthermore, although the perpetrators were

typically gauchos (occasionally military deserters), quintessential members of the landed elite, like Rosas's cousin Tomás Anchorena, also "hated foreigners, whom he considered liberal, heretical thieves." There is some evidence that, irrespective of religion and culture, such xenophobic sentiments derived partly from the classic clash between pastoral and arable communities, between big stock raisers (and their cowboys), on the one hand, and settler farmers, who often happened to be immigrants, on the other.

83. Eric R. Wolf and Edward C. Hansen, "Caudillo Politics: A Structural Analysis," *Comparative Studies in Society and History* 9 (1967): 168–79, remains a suggestive overview of the transition from personalist caudillo rule to "order and progress" regimes, a theme that I touch on in chapter 5.

84. The Maya insurgency had lasted over fifty years, dating back to the bloody "Caste War" of the 1840s. The rebels were sustained by the cult of the Speaking Cross, which, after decades of reciprocal brutality, was finally crushed by the Mexican army in 1901. See Nelson A. Reed, "Juan de la Cruz, Venancio Puc and the Speaking Cross," *The Americas* 53, no. 4 (1997): 497–523, which argues that the cult was, strictly speaking, neither messianic nor millenarian but an example of insurrectionary ethnic resistance inspired by a syncretic folk religion.

85. Paul Vanderwood, *The Power of God Against the Guns of Government* (Stanford CA: Stanford University Press, 1998). In this, as in other cases, the balance of secular (political, economic) factors versus religious (whether "folk Catholic" or millenarian) is open to debate: I take the view that Vanderwood overdoes the religious at the expense of the secular: Alan Knight, "Rethinking the Tomóchic Rebellion," *Mexican Studies / Estudios Mexicanos* 15, no. 2 (Summer 1999): 373–93.

86. Robert Levine, *Vale of Tears: Revisiting the Canudos Massacre in Northeast Brazil, 1893–1897* (Berkeley: University of California Press, 1995); Todd A. Diacon, *Millenarian Vision, Capitalist Reality: Brazil's Contestado Rebellion, 1912–1916* (Durham NC: Duke University Press, 1991).

87. Ralph della Cava, *Miracle at Joaseiro: A Political and Economic History of a Popular Religious Movement in Brazil, 1889–1934* (New York: Columbia University Press, 1968).

88. María Isaura Pereira de Queiroz, "Messiahs in Brazil," *Past and Present* 31 (July 1965): 62–86.

89. Any such casualty figures are highly speculative, given not only the unreliable data but also the slippery categories. For example, does wartime mortality include those caused by increased disease and hunger, often among civilians,

or solely battlefield deaths? Jean A. Meyer, *The Cristero Rebellion* (Cambridge: Cambridge University Press, 1976), 178, gives a "tentative" figure of one hundred thousand "combatants killed during three years of war," which presumably means battlefield deaths, broadly defined. This would represent about 1 in every 140 Mexicans; by way of comparison, the armed revolution of the preceding decade (which went on for ten years) may have caused the death in battle of 1 in 35. However, the Cristiada was highly concentrated in the center-west of the country; relative to the total population of the six states chiefly involved (Jalisco, Michoacán, Zacatecas, Aguascalientes, Guanajuato, and Colima = 3.5 million), the death toll was about the same (one in thirty-five). A final caveat: the one hundred thousand include losses suffered by the federal army and its agrarista allies. If we take only Cristero deaths (forty thousand, according to Meyer), the regional toll would have been about one in ninety. However, I find it slightly surprising that by this count the Cristeros suffered lighter casualties than the federals.

90. Meyer, *The Cristero Rebellion*, which is an abridged English translation of *La Cristiada*, 3 vols. (Mexico City: Siglo XXI, 1973).

91. Jennie Purnell, *Popular Movements and State Formation in Revolutionary Mexico: The Agraristas and Cristeros of Michoacán* (Durham NC: Duke University Press, 1999). In Mexico and elsewhere, outside authorities often provoked violent resistance when they interfered with local cults: Porfirio Díaz's brother was castrated and killed by local people after he razed the town of Juchitán and "defiled and mutilated the town's patron saint, San Vicente Ferrer" (Francie R. Chassen-López, *From Liberal to Revolutionary Oaxaca: The View from the South, Mexico 1867–1911* [University Park: Penn State University Press, 2004], 327–28). The significance of the Cristero War is that the outside authorities—the new revolutionary state—were much more radical, systematic, and determined.

92. Alan Knight, "The Mentality and Modus Operandi of Revolutionary Anticlericalism," in *Faith and Impiety in Revolutionary Mexico*, ed. Matthew Butler (New York: Macmillan, 2007), chap. 1. Among the more eloquently outspoken anticlericals of the revolution was Francisco J. Múgica, who, like some of his anticlerical predecessors (see n. 33 above), had been educated at a Catholic seminary, in his case, in the clerical (*mocho*) city of Zamora: Anna Ribera Carbó, *Francisco J. Múgica: El presidente que no tuvimos* (Mexico City: FCE, 2019). The anticlerical notion that women were particularly susceptible to clerical wiles was, no doubt, based partly on patriarchal prejudice; however, it seems clear that in the twentieth century, as in the nineteenth, women

tended to be more loyal churchgoers than men, and female organizations played a key role in the associational life of the church.

93. Meyer, *Cristero Rebellion*, 75, records 90 priests "executed" during the three years of the Cristero War. By contrast, 6,788 Spanish priests, monks, and nuns were reported killed during the three years of the Spanish Civil War, the great majority in the late summer of 1936: Stanley G. Payne, *The Spanish Civil War* (Cambridge: Cambridge University Press, 2012), 113. Even allowing for the fact that Mexico's population in 1926 was about two-thirds that of Spain in 1936, the contrast remains.

4. THE LITTLE DIVERGENCE

1. Sometimes overmuch. That is, a good deal of recent historiography, perhaps particularly that associated with the *nouvelle vague* of cultural history, prefers to address small, often idiosyncratic, case studies, drawing on a narrow range of sources and spurning efforts at considered comparisons, broad general-izations, or structural explanations. The latter, implicitly or explicitly, have been interred in the great graveyard of defunct "grand theory" and discarded "metanarratives." I should clarify that throwaway references to colonialism, transnationalism, patriarchy, and the rest in no way constitute considered comparisons or structural explanations; very often they are just formulaic genuflections, not considered analytical commitments.

2. Florencia E. Mallon, *Peasant and Nation: The Making of Postcolonial Mexico and Peru* (Berkeley: University of California Press, 1995).

3. Jeffrey Klaiber, SJ, *The Catholic Church in Peru, 1821–1985* (Washington DC: Catholic University of America Press, 1992), 99–101.

4. In a recent volume exploring the Mexico-Peru comparison, David Nugent seems to think that his Chachapoyas (Peru) case study provides a refutation of Max Weber's theory of the state, which it doesn't (and, indeed, couldn't), but then Nugent does not seem to have grasped that theory very well. See "Notes on the 'Afterlife': Forced Labor, Modernization and Political Paranoia in Twentieth-Century Peru," in *State Formation in the Liberal Era: Capitalisms and Claims of Citizenship in Mexico and Peru*, ed. Ben Fallaw and David Nugent (Tucson: University of Arizona Press, 2020), 221.

5. Thus producing an ordered "hierarchy of causes" and their reciprocal rela-tionships, not simply a "random jumble" or undifferentiated shopping list: E. H Carr, *What Is History?* (Harmondsworth: Penguin, 1964), 89.

6. By "nods of mutual recognition" I mean passing comparisons (or contrasts), which, in this case, link Peru and Mexico without exploring or clarifying

the link. For example, Mark Thurner, *From Two Republics to One Divided: Contradictions of Postcolonial Nationmaking in Andean Peru* (Durham NC: Duke University Press, 1997), 101, when he refers to the meeting between the Indian leader Pedro Atusparia and the criollo General Andrés Cáceres in Lima in 1886, regrets—in knowing but elliptical terms—that "Atusparia was no Emiliano Zapata, and Cáceres no Pancho Villa (nor, indeed, even a Venustiano Carranza)." Explicit Peru-Mexico comparisons that have proved useful in trying to develop the analysis presented here include Mallon, *Peasant and Nation*; D. A. Brading, *The First America: The Spanish Monarchy, Creole Patriots and the Liberal State, 1492–1866* (Cambridge: Cambridge University Press, 1992); Peter Guardino and Charles Walker, "The State, Society and Politics in Peru and Mexico in the Late Colonial and Early Republican Periods," *Latin American Perspectives* 19, no. 2 (Spring 1992): 10–43; and Nils Jacobsen and Hans-Jürgen Puhle, *The Economies of Mexico and Peru during the Late Colonial Period, 1760–1810* (Berlin: Colloquium-Verlag, 1986).

7. The literature is extensive (if a little dated): Clark Kerr et al., eds., *Industrialism and Industrial Man* (Cambridge MA: Harvard University Press, 1960) is a foundational text; a recent and useful survey is provided by Brigitte Unger and Frans van Waarden, "Introduction: An Interdisciplinary Approach to Convergence," in *Convergence or Diversity? Internationalization and Economic Policy Response*, ed. Unger and Waarden (Aldershot: Avebury, 1995), 1–35.

8. Kenneth Pomerantz, *The Great Divergence: China, Europe and the Making of the Modern World Economy* (Princeton NJ: Princeton University Press, 2000).

9. Stephen Haber, ed., *Why Latin America Fell Behind: Essays on the Economic History of Brazil and Mexico, 1800–1914* (Stanford CA: Stanford University Press, 1997).

10. A good example of sophisticated economic analysis concerning "Atlantic economy convergence" between ca. 1830 and 1940 is provided by Kevin H. O'Rourke and Jeffrey G. Williamson, *Globalization and History: The Evolution of a Nineteenth-Century Atlantic Economy* (Cambridge MA: MIT Press, 1999), quote from 3.

11. These categories are not, of course, watertight, but they offer a conventional—and useful—"trichotomous" way of organizing a mass of historical data: the political, which deals with state power, broadly defined; the economic, which relates to Polanyi's "material-means provisioning process"; and the cultural (or "sociocultural"), which has to do with the broad realm of ideas, beliefs, and symbolic practices. I return to this triad in chapter 5.

12. By "accidental" I don't mean entirely "undetermined" or "uncaused" events (like the movement of Schrödinger's subatomic particles, which are entirely irrelevant to historical explanation); I mean simply those events that could easily have turned out differently, regarding which counterfactuals are entirely plausible and valid. Thus, it is plausible to consider a Mexico in which Villa beats Obregón at the Battle of Celaya in 1915; it is not plausible to posit a Mexico in which railways are never built (though, following Robert Fogel's example, we may conduct a useful thought experiment concerning a hypothetical railwayless Mexico in order to calibrate the impact that railways actually had).

13. Enrique Krauze, *Plutarco E. Calles: Reformar desde el origen* (Mexico City: FCE, 1988).

14. Perhaps the coincidence was not entirely random: dense pre-Conquest populations tended to congregate in the temperate highlands rather than the hot coastal lowlands, and it was in the highlands that accessible mineral deposits could be found precisely because of geological uplift at the boundaries of tectonic plates. Which is why the same regions are also prone to earthquakes.

15. James Lockhart and Stuart B. Schwartz make the point for Spanish South America, where they see the independence movement "rigorously retracing in reverse the path of the sixteenth-century conquest" (*Early Latin America: A History of Colonial Spanish America and Brazil* [Cambridge: Cambridge University Press, 1983], 419–20). Mexico also broadly fits the bill, since, like Peru, its independence lagged behind that of Argentina, Venezuela, and Colombia.

16. "Futile" in that such a far-fetched comparison will yield neither meaningful broad generalizations nor specific insights regarding the individual cases. The Mexico-Peru comparison is more promising in both respects, but especially the second.

17. James Mahoney, *Colonialism and Postcolonial Development: Spanish America in Comparative Perspective* (New York: Cambridge University Press, 2010); Hillel David Soifer, *State Building in Latin America* (New York: Cambridge University Press, 2015).

18. I originally wrote, "Peru suffered from weaker integration," but it would be rashly normative to assume that "integration"—whether political or economic—was a good thing or lack of integration a bad thing. Since we are dealing with authoritarian colonial states ruling highly unequal stratified societies, it is arguable that "integration" implied greater social control,

military coercion, and fiscal extraction (which, after all, were the principal goals of the Bourbon reformers). In short, it was not necessarily better to be a more "integrated" Mexican than a less "integrated" Peruvian.

19. Soifer, *State Building*, 40, sees nineteenth-century Lima (including the port of Callao) as a primate city, eclipsing Mexico City in terms of its urban "primacy" (even more surprisingly, it scores more highly than Santiago [de Chile]). However, as Soifer acknowledges, the conclusion is skewed by the availability and dating of census material, and perhaps more important, statistical measurements of primacy based purely on population ratios do not necessarily capture the preeminence of a city in terms of its political, economic, and/or cultural influence.

20. Alberto Flores Galindo, *Buscando un Inca: Identidad y utopía en los Andes* (Mexico City: Grijalbo, 1993), 274, which also quotes an American traveler to Peru in the 1860s, E. G. Squier, who observed that "for every native of the capital (Lima) who has visited Cuzco, there are a hundred who have visited Paris" (275). Even if the observation is statistically questionable, it helps explain, as Flores Galindo observes, why "a national consensus was impossible" in nineteenth-century Peru.

21. Nils Jacobsen and Hans-Jürgen Pühle, introduction to Jacobsen and Pühle, *The Economies*, 1–25.

22. Jacobsen and Pühle, introduction, 9.

23. Mexico raised 11.6 pesos per capita of revenue in the 1790s, compared to 6.3 pesos in Bolivia (Upper Peru) and 3.5 pesos in Peru: Alejandra Irigoin, "Representation Without Taxation, Taxation Without Consent: The Legacy of Spanish Colonialism in America," *Revista de Historia Económica / Journal of Iberian and Latin American Economic History* 34, no. 2 (September 2016): 169–208, table 2.

24. Ilona Katzew, *Casta Images of Race in Eighteenth-Century Mexico* (New Haven CT: Yale University Press, 2004).

25. Any such estimate must necessarily be tentative and approximate, given both the paucity of reliable sources and the fluidity of ethnic categories. The Peruvian figure (60 percent of the population being Indian in the 1790s) seems to be broadly accepted: see Paul Gootenberg, "Population and Ethnicity in Early Republican Peru: Some Revisions," *Latin American Research Review* 26, no. 5 (1991): 111; Shane J. Hunt, "Growth and Guano in Nineteenth-Century Peru," Discussion Paper no. 34 (1973), 11, Woodrow Wilson School, Princeton University; and Peter F. Klarén, *Peru: Society and Nationhood in the Andes* (New York: Oxford University Press, 2000), 146.

Mahoney, *Colonialism and Postcolonial Development*, 154–55, suggests a roughly similar figure for Mexico, as does Gonzalo Aguirre Beltrán, whose estimate seems to be accepted by the doyen of Mexican demographic studies, Robert McCaa: see his succinct résumé, "The Peopling of Mexico from Origins to Revolution," in *The Population History of North America*, ed. Michael R. Haines and Richard Steckel (New York: Cambridge University Press, 2000), 264–65. Alexander von Humboldt reckoned on a lower figure: see Alejandro de Humboldt, *Ensayo político sobre el reino de la Nueva España* (1822; Mexico City: Porrúa, 1991), 51, which states that Indians constituted 40 percent of the "kingdom of Mexico."

26. As Charles F. Walker observes, "In Peru, the lines dividing Indians and non-Indians were more sharply drawn than in the other center of colonial Spanish America, Mexico, and intermediate groups, although important, were comparatively less significant" (*Smouldering Ashes: Cuzco and the Creation of Republican Peru, 1780–1840* [Durham NC: Duke University Press, 1999], 11).

27. Guardino and Walker, "State, Society and Politics," 11–12; Carlos Forment, *Democracy in Latin America, 1760–1900*, vol. 1, *Civic Selfhood and Public Life in Mexico and Peru* (Chicago: University of Chicago Press, 2003), 54. Thus, when the Indian leader Pedro Atusparia met with the criollo Andrés Cáceres in 1886, they conversed in Quechua (see n. 6 above). It would be hard to envisage a Mexican counterpart of this cross-class, transethnic linguistic encounter outside of specific ethnocultural regions (such as Yucatán, where Maya was widely spoken, and not just by Indians).

28. Mallon, *The Defence of Community*, 73; Nils Jacobsen, *Mirages of Transition: The Peruvian Altiplano, 1780–1930* (Berkeley: University of California Press, 1993), 129, 275. I later mention the continuation—or revival—of coercive labor recruitment during both the nineteenth century (*enganche* and debt peonage) and the twentieth (the *conscripción vial* [compulsory road-building] of the 1920s and 1930s).

29. D. A. Brading and Harry E. Cross, "Colonial Silver Mining: Mexico and Peru," *Hispanic American Historical Review* 52, no. 4 (1972): 545–79.

30. John Tutino, *From Insurrection to Revolution in Mexico: Social Bases of Agrarian Violence, 1750–1940* (Princeton NJ: Princeton University Press, 1988), 59, 71.

31. See McCaa, "The Peopling of Mexico," citing Aguirre Beltrán, 264–65, and Gootenberg, "Population and Ethnicity," 111, giving Peruvian estimates for the 1790s. The figures are plausible—even if the respective proportion of Indians in the two countries was similar—because Peru harbored a much bigger

Black (slave) and *pardo* (free Black and mulatto) population. It should be stressed that the categories of mestizo—and, indeed, indio/indígena—were and for generations would remain highly fluid and subjective: Alan Knight, "Racism, Revolution and Indigenismo: Mexico, 1910–40," in *The Idea of Race in Latin America, 1870–1940*, ed. Richard Graham (Austin: University of Texas Press, 1990), chap. 3; François Bourricaud, *Cambios en Puno* (Mexico City: INI, 1967), 6–11.

32. Richard J. Salvucci, *Textiles and Capitalism in Mexico: A History of the Obrajes, 1539–1840* (Princeton NJ: Princeton University Press, 1987), 18.

33. The lyrical view of the "spiritual conquest" was expressed by Robert Ricard, *The Spiritual Conquest of Mexico* (1933; Los Angeles: University of California Press, 1974). For an appropriately magisterial survey of the mature Mexican colonial church, see William B. Taylor, *Magistrates of the Sacred: Priests and Parishioners in Eighteenth-Century Mexico* (Stanford CA: Stanford University Press, 1999), which stresses the success of conversion and, we could say, of Catholic religious hegemony. Simple statistical analysis does not help much by way of explaining these phenomena: the ratio of priests to population in Peru and Mexico does not seem to have been radically different. Taylor, *Magistrates of the Sacred*, 78, gives a figure of 6,827 "male diocesan and regular priests" in Mexico in 1810, which, for a population of perhaps 5.25 million, suggests 1 priest to 769 inhabitants (I am using Robert McCaa's plausible deflation of Humboldt's figure of over 6 million). For Peru, Klaiber, *The Catholic Church*, 38, suggests a population-to-priest ratio of 667 on the eve of independence. Antonine Tibesar's more detailed breakdown by dioceses suggests 851, though with noticeable regional variations, as one would expect. See his "The Peruvian Church at the Time of Independence in the Light of Vatican II," *The Americas* 26, no. 4 (1970): 349–50.

34. Taylor, *Magistrates of the Sacred*, 288–91, 295–96, which notes the connection between Guadalupanismo and "proto-patriotism," the most obvious and well-known example of which was the discursive and iconographic invocation of the Virgin by patriot forces in the War of Independence; see also Hugh M. Hamill Jr., *The Hidalgo Revolt: Prelude to Mexican Independence* (Gainesville: University Press of Florida, 1966), 133–34, and D. A. Brading, *Mexican Phoenix: Our Lady of Guadalupe; Image and Tradition across Five Centuries* (Cambridge: Cambridge University Press, 2001), 228–30. On the broader question of Mexican protopatriotism, the classic text is Brading, *The First America*, chaps. 14, 20; note also D. A. Brading, *The Origins of Mexican Nationalism* (Cambridge: Cambridge University Press, 1985).

35. Klaiber, *The Catholic Church*, 13 and (for the nineteenth century) 49. Tibesar's figures confirm that priests were thinner on the ground in the highlands: in 1820 the ratio of population to priests in the diocese of Cuzco stood at 1,800, compared to a Peruvian average of 851 or, by way of contrast, 359 in the diocese of Arequipa. Kenneth Mills notes the "obsession with the place of idolatry in [Peruvian] Indian society" in the seventeenth and eighteenth centuries, when harshly repressive campaigns of extirpation were carried out, proof that the Indian population's "deepening relationship with Catholicism" lagged some way behind the process of conversion in Mexico: Kenneth Mills, "The Limits of Religious Coercion in Mid-colonial Peru," *Past and Present* 145 (November 1994): 88, 120.

36. Taylor, *Magistrates of the Sacred*, 66–67.

37. William Taylor, *Drinking, Homicide, and Rebellion in Colonial Mexican Villages* (Stanford CA: Stanford University Press, 1979), chap. 4. The contrast between local, limited Mexican protest and more general, radical Andean uprising is well drawn by Sergio Serulnikov, *Conflictos sociales e insurrección en el mundo colonial andino* (Mexico City: FCE, 2006), 10–14.

38. On local protests, see Eric Van Young, *The Other Rebellion: Popular Violence, Ideology, and the Mexican Struggle for Independence, 1810–1821* (Stanford CA: Stanford University Press, 2001). Two books by Peter F. Guardino are particularly good at capturing the political and discursive break signaled by independence as it affected two major regions of Mexico: *Peasants, Politics, and the Formation of Mexico's National State: Guerrero, 1800–1857* (Stanford CA: Stanford University Press, 1996), and *The Time of Liberty: Popular Political Culture in Oaxaca, 1750–1850* (Durham NC: Duke University Press, 2005).

39. There are legitimate objections to these terms, but I use them, faute de mieux, to describe dissidence that goes beyond backward-looking, prescriptive (whether "naive monarchist" or even "neo-Incaic") protest and, instead, justifies rebellion in terms of broader and newer notions of citizenship, republicanism, and protopatriotism, notions that, of course, transcend narrowly local loyalties (even if local grievances still provide crucial fuel for the protest). On the reactive/proactive distinction, see Charles Tilly, "Major Forms of Collective Action in Western Europe, 1500–1975," *Theory and Society* 3, no. 3 (1976): 365–75. Forment, *Democracy in Latin America*, 94, comparing the wars of independence in Mexico and Peru, presents a similar contrast (albeit in different and idiosyncratic terms): "In contrast to the Mexicans, the majority of Peruvians were not yet convinced that they had achieved adulthood and become rational, disciplined persons" (i.e., citizens).

40. Hamill, *The Hidalgo Revolt*; Taylor, *Magistrates of the Sacred*, 295.

41. See Gary Gosner, *Soldiers of the Virgin: The Moral Economy of a Colonial Maya Rebellion* (Tucson: University of Arizona Press, 1992); and Andrew L. Knaut, *The Pueblo Revolt of 1680: Conquest and Resistance in Seventeenth-Century New Mexico* (Norman: University of Oklahoma Press, 1995).

42. Brian R. Hamnett, *The End of Iberian Rule on the American Continent, 1770–1830* (Cambridge: Cambridge University Press, 2017) provides a good analysis of the Cuzco revolt of 1814–15, noting that when the rebel leaders—successfully—appealed for mass support from the Indian population of the southern highlands, they thereby "transformed an originally creole-led movement into a popular insurrection comparable to Hidalgo's in 1810–11" (170). On the Great Andean Revolt of the 1780s—and, indeed, previous midcentury rebellions—and their enduring legacy, see Mallon, *Defence of Community*, 48–49; Kenneth J. Andrien, *Andean Worlds: Indigenous History, Culture and Consciousness under Spanish Rule, 1532–1825* (Albuquerque: University of New Mexico Press, 2001), 211–28; and Thurner, *From Two Republics*, 134–35, 138, which notes that the 1780s revolt cast a long shadow, stretching right across the nineteenth century. On the Peruvian War of Independence, including the role of Cuzco, see John Fisher, "Royalism, Regionalism, and Rebellion in Colonial Peru, 1808–1815," *Hispanic American Historical Review* 59, no. 2 (1979): 232–57. Forment, *Democracy within Latin America*, 67, 83, makes a particularly sharp distinction between Mexico, where the people responded to Spain's crisis "by proclaiming their independence," and Peru, where, "in contrast, [they] responded by proclaiming their loyalty to the Spanish monarchy," albeit on new "adult" terms. While Forment arguably overdoes the contrast, he is right, I think, to discern a clear distinction—or divergence—and to stress, by way of explanation, the importance of "local dynamics in each colony," thus dissenting from those many historians who emphasize "socio-political dynamics within Spain" as the key determinants of Latin American outcomes.

43. My own view of the Mexican independence struggle is that it was fueled by popular grievances (triggered but not fundamentally caused by external events, such as Napoleon's invasion of Spain) and that the colonial regime therefore faced serious—perhaps insuperable—problems when it came to restoring royalist order and legitimacy: Alan Knight, *Mexico: The Colonial Era* (Cambridge: Cambridge University Press, 2002), 304–30. This view departs from what seems to be the new orthodoxy regarding both Mexico and Spanish America more broadly, which stresses external etiology (so

the Napoleonic invasion is not just a trigger but a fundamental cause) and plays down the internal tensions of the late colonial empire.

44. These cases could be seen as representing the three basic categories of Spanish colonial political economy: mining-and-agricultural economies based on a large exploited Indian population (concentrated in the highlands), tropical lowland plantation economies worked by black slaves, and relatively underpopulated temperate lowland pastoral economies.

45. I am, therefore, following those historians who see the first half of the nineteenth century as part of a so-called middle period (ca. 1750–1850), which, in socioeconomic if not political terms, displays continuities with the late colonial past and differs from the later nineteenth-century phase of export-led growth and related state-building. Some historians push the "middle period" into the twentieth century (so it runs from ca. 1750 to ca. 1930), but this seems to me a step way too far.

46. Flores Galindo, *Buscando un inca*, 275–76, notes a marked decline in the three principal sources of (traditional) authority as the colony gave way to the independent republic: state officials (with *corregidores* and *intendentes* being replaced by [weaker] prefects), parish priests (evidence of a debilitated church), and traditional Indian leaders (*curacas*). This collective eclipse favored the rise of *gamonales* (local bosses: in Mexico they would be *caciques*), who combined landed resources and unofficial powers based on coercion and clientelism.

47. Julio Cotler, *Clases, estado y nación en el Perú* (Lima: Instituto de Estudios Peruanos, 1978), 69, 71. On the phenomenon of *gamonalismo* (see n. 46 above), note Flores Galindo, *Buscando un inca*, 294–95; and Manuel Burga and Alberto Flores Galindo, *Apogeo y crisis de la república aristocrática* (Lima: Ediciones "Rikchay Perú," 1979), 104–13. *Caudillismo*, a variety of patron-client relationship, typically involving a good measure of violence, could be limited to a locality or could stretch across an entire region or state/department; either way, it represented a powerful centrifugal force. *Caudillismo* and *caciquismo* are close conceptual cousins, in some cases interchangeable, according to authorial taste. The main difference, in my view, is that *caciques* tended to denote smaller local bosses for whom violence was one of several mechanisms of control and co-optation, while caudillos were typically grander figures, some of regional or even national stature, who, given their capacity for extensive violence, might be considered "warlords." I should add that the Argentines have a perverse linguistic habit of calling their caciques (local bosses) caudillos.

48. However, the head tax (*contribución*), an updated version of the old Indian tribute, was much more significant in Peru than in Mexico, where yields had drastically declined toward the end of the colony: Barbara Tenenbaum, *The Politics of Penury: Debts and Taxes in Mexico, 1821–56* (Albuquerque: University of New Mexico Press, 1986), 5, 13. Cash-strapped Conservative governments later sought to revive the tax, provoking protest in southern/Indian zones such as Guerrero and Oaxaca in the 1840s: Guardino, *Peasants, Politics*, 147–77; and Benjamin T. Smith, *The Roots of Conservatism in Mexico: Catholicism, Society and Politics in the Mixteca Baja, 1750–1962* (Albuquerque: University of New Mexico Press, 2012), 111. In Peru, the head tax was much more important, yielding some 40 percent of government revenue, and during the nineteenth century, it was recurrently abolished (1812, 1824, 1854) and then reimposed (1813, 1826, 1866), according to the exigencies of state finances: see Walker, *Smoldering Ashes*, 188–89; and Thomas M. Davies, *Indian Integration in Peru: A Half Century of Experience, 1900–1948* (Lincoln: University of Nebraska Press, 1974), 19–20, 29–30. However, because of the chronic weakness of the Peruvian state, especially in the highlands, the head tax never yielded the revenue that it should have, given demographic realities: see Jacobsen, *Mirages of Transition*, 130–32; and Thurner, *From Two Republics*, 36–37, 41, 83.

49. Paul Gootenberg, *Between Silver and Guano: Commercial Policy and the State in Postindependence Peru* (Princeton NJ: Princeton University Press, 1989), 8. I touch on these topics again in chapter 5.

50. Mallon, *Defence of Community*, 54; Jacobsen, *Mirages of Transition*, 133–34, which notes that after independence the "fledgling central state" could not bolster provincial elites, as the Bourbon state had done; as a result, Indian communities enjoyed an "increased breathing space," the product of "their own assertiveness . . . and the continued weakness of provincial elites."

51. The classic version of the argument is made—convincingly, I think—by Tristan Platt in respect to Bolivia (Upper Peru): *Estado boliviano y ayllu andino: Tierra y tributo en el Norte de Potosí* (Lima: Instituto de Estudios Peruanos, 1982). For Peru, the significance of the "colonial pact" is rather harder to disentangle: see Thurner, *From Two Republics*, 47, 97; and Carmen McEvoy, *Forjando la nación: Ensayos de historia republicana* (Lima: PUCP, 1999), 102–3. In Spanish American as in other European colonies, the *capitación*, apart from yielding income, also served to propel "native" taxpayers into the money economy (and the labor market) by obliging them to raise cash. Thus, in Peru, the abolition of the tax in 1854, by relaxing this obligation,

tended to weaken the ties linking Indian communities to broader markets while reinforcing subsistence production. In Mexico, as already mentioned, the head tax never assumed the same fiscal and political importance and, indeed, by the time of independence was a minor and fast-declining tax.

52. In postindependence Peru, too, the common people appear to have had greater access to weaponry, for example, in Arequipa: Sarah C. Chambers, *From Subjects to Citizens: Honor, Gender, and Politics in Arequipa, 1780–1854* (University Park: Penn State University Press, 1999), 145.

53. Guardino, *Peasants, Politics*, 137–39. Although I think that this phenomenon—popular political mobilization under a liberal republican banner—was probably more pronounced in Mexico, Peru also experienced, in the same period, similar processes of protest and mobilization that, whether or not they were associated with a formally liberal or republican ideology, indicated a new more egalitarian ("plebeian") political activism: see Chambers, *From Subjects to Citizens*; and Cecilia Méndez, *The Plebeian Republic: The Huanta Rebellion and the Making of the Peruvian State, 1820–1850* (Durham NC: Duke University Press, 2005).

54. John Tutino, *From Insurrection to Revolution in Mexico: Social Bases of Agrarian Violence, 1750–1940* (Princeton NJ: Princeton University Press, 1988), 237–38, 255–56. In the Peruvian highlands, too, Mallon notes, peasants "revert[ed] to subsistence" after independence, thus reversing "the advances made by commercial capital" in the late colonial period: *The Defence of Community*, 54.

55. Tutino, *From Insurrection to Revolution*, chap. 6 and 356. See also Brooke Larson, *Trials of Nation-Making: Liberalism, Race and Ethnicity in the Andes, 1810–1910* (Cambridge: Cambridge University Press, 2004), 147, where the useful "compression/decompression" model is attributed to Tulio Halperín Donghi.

56. Adrian J. Pearce, "Re-indigenization and Native Languages in Peru's Long Nineteenth Century (1795–1940)," in *History and Language in the Andes*, ed. Paul Heggarty and Adrian J. Pearce (New York: Palgrave Macmillan, 2011), 135–63.

57. Gootenberg, *Between Silver and Guano*, 161–62, which shows that guano exports rose from zero in 1840 to over half a million tons in 1854, by which time it constituted 74 percent of Peru's total exports.

58. At its peak, the guano boom supplied 80 percent of government revenue; meanwhile, thanks to guano, total government revenue grew fivefold, and government spending, further buoyed by foreign loans, grew eightfold. See Heraclio Bonilla, "Peru and Bolivia from Independence to the War of the

Pacific," in *The Cambridge History of Latin America*, vol. 3, *From Independence to c. 1870*, ed. Leslie Bethell (Cambridge: Cambridge University Press, 1985), 551–52.

59. Gootenberg, *Between Silver and Guano*, 82. Over half of the guano revenue went to the government payroll: 29 percent to the bureaucracy and 25 percent to the military: Bonilla, "Peru and Bolivia," 552. On the Lima/provincial power balance, see Chambers, *From Subjects to Citizens*, 42–43. Alfonso W. Quiroz, *Domestic and Foreign Finance in Modern Peru, 1850–1950: Financing Visions of Development* (Basingstoke: Macmillan, 1993), 24–28, analyzes state/foreign business relations. Peru's guano boom was therefore unusual in that it made possible extensive foreign borrowing, even in the absence of a stable political regime that could offer credible across-the-board guarantees to foreign investors: see Catalina Vizcarra, "Guano, Credible Commitments and Sovereign Debt Repayments in Nineteenth-Century Peru," *Journal of Economic History* 69, no. 2 (2009): 358–87.

60. The labor demands of the guano industry were very small: perhaps a thousand shit shovelers were at work, these being convicts or Chinese coolies; hence, the wage bill was a negligible 4 percent of total production costs. See Bonilla, "Peru and Bolivia," 551. Dragooning or luring Indians from the highlands therefore made no sense (until later in the century, when the growing production of cash crops such as sugar and cotton generated a much greater demand for labor on the coast). The guano boom did, however, make possible the abolition of the head tax (see n. 51 above); however, in doing so, it may have further disarticulated the coastal market economy and that of the peasant highlands. At the time of abolition, there were still over twenty-five thousand slaves in Peru; their owners were compensated to the tune of 7.6 million pesos. The slaves, of course, got nothing. See Bonilla, "Peru and Bolivia," 552.

61. Peter F. Klarén, *Modernization, Dislocation, and Aprismo: Origins of the Peruvian Aprista Party, 1870–1932* (Austin: University of Texas Press, 1973), 4–5. Mallon, *Defence of Community*, 59, also notes an economic upturn in the (agricultural) economy of the interior after 1870 but attributes this to local and regional demand rather than links to the coastal economy.

62. Thurner, *From Two Republics*, 45–46; Gootenberg, *Imagining Development*, 207, who observes that the guano boom produced "a consolidating state remarkably 'autonomous' of civil and regional society." Thus, in the 1860s, as the guano boom petered out, the state's writ still ran haltingly, if at all, in the interior: "The law of the Republic was a dead letter in the southern Andean provinces" (McEvoy, *Forjando la nación*, 112).

63. The question of guano "linkages," being complicated and debatable, cannot be further discussed here. Some historians place greater weight on, for example, the impact of railway-building, financed by guano revenue: Larson, *Trials of Nation-Making*, 151. However, the consensus remains, I think, that such linkages were very tenuous. That does not necessarily mean that the guano industry was an isolated "enclave": Shane J. Hunt, "Growth and Guano in Nineteenth-Century Peru," in *The Latin American Economies: Growth and the Export Sector 1880–1930*, ed. Roberto Cortés Conde and Shane J. Hunt (New York: Holmes and Meier, 1985), 287–89, has persuasively argued that a better description would be a "rentier economy" characterized by abundant foreign exchange, an overvalued exchange rate, the atrophy of import-substitution industries, and—"perhaps the most pernicious effect"—a "rentier psychology" involving "wastefulness . . . extravagance . . . [and] conspicuous consumption." A plausible parallel would be the Amazon rubber boom of the early twentieth century, which affected Brazil (and, to a lesser degree, Peru), again in boom-and-bust fashion, without developing durable and positive linkages to national economies. However, the rubber boom represented a much smaller share of both national exports and GDP.

64. Robert McCaa, "The Peopling of Nineteenth-Century Mexico: Critical Scrutiny of a Censured Century," *Statistical Abstract of Latin America* 30 (1993): 603–33, estimates that the demographic losses (i.e., primarily but not solely deaths) generated by political upheaval and foreign invasion between 1810 and 1870 at 2.5 million. This enormous figure includes both the bloody War of Independence (1810–21) and the loss of two hundred thousand (living) Mexicans who found themselves under U.S. sovereignty after 1848. Even discounting that loss, the toll taken by war and rebellion after independence is very significant (substantially greater, I would suggest, than equivalent Peruvian losses).

65. That is not to discount President Polk's nakedly aggressive ambitions; however, by refusing to cut a deal over Texas and pursuing the vain hope of a Mexican reconquest, Santa Anna—and others—played into Polk's hands: Will Fowler, *Santa Anna of Mexico* (Lincoln: University of Nebraska Press, 2007), 226–27, 249; and Peter F. Guardino, *The Dead March: A History of the Mexican-American War* (Cambridge MA: Harvard University Press, 2017), 20–30.

66. The economic story of ca. 1840–70 has not been that deeply researched; such consensus as there is suggests, at best, very sluggish growth. See Enrique Cárdenas Sánchez, *Cuando se originó el atraso económico de México: La economía*

mexicana en el largo siglo XIX, 1780–1920 (Madrid: Editorial Biblioteca Nueva, 2003), 103 ff.

67. Manuel González, a compliant crony, was a fairly inept presidential stand-in for Díaz for the period 1880–84, after which Díaz returned and amended the constitution to allow successive reelections down to 1910. More importantly, the first half of the Porfiriato (1876–ca. 1890) was a period of political stabilization, infrastructural investment, and economic growth (probably associated with stable real wages), while from the 1890s we see, in contrast, processes of political ossification, sociopolitical repression, and falling living standards.

68. Sandra Kuntz Ficker and Paolo Riguzzi, eds., *Ferrocarriles y vida económica en México, 1850–1950* (Zinacantepec: El Colegio Mexiquense, 1996).

69. Thomas P. Passananti, "'Nada de papeluchos!': Managing Globalization in Early Porfirian Mexico," *Latin American Research Review* 42, no. 1 (2007): 101–28. Cárdenas, *Cuando se originó*, chap. 5, which gives aggregate figures showing annual growth (1877–1910) of 4.1 percent (GDP) and 7.5 percent (for exports), or, in per capita terms, 2.8 percent and 4.7 percent, respectively (189).

70. On the regressive politics of the Porfiriato, see Alan Knight, "The Mexican State, Porfirian and Revolutionary, 1876–1930," in *State and Nation Making in Latin America and Spain*, ed. Miguel A. Centeno and Agustín E. Ferrero (Cambridge: Cambridge University Press, 2013), 116–38. Paul H. Garner, *Porfirio Díaz* (London: Routledge, 2001) is rather more charitable.

71. William F. Sater, *Andean Tragedy: Fighting the War of the Pacific, 1879–1884* (Lincoln: University of Nebraska Press, 2007) offers a fine account of the war. Though Chile was a less formidable opponent than the United States, Peru was also a less formidable antagonist than Mexico. And there are some significant parallels (although they do not apply to the very different French Intervention in Mexico): Chile, like the United States, carried out a smash-and-grab raid on a weaker neighbor, making off with valuable territorial gains without seeking "regime change"; Chile, like the United States, was helped by superior weaponry and supplies, command of the sea (eventually), and the debilitating divisions suffered by its adversary.

72. By the 1870s guano exports and revenues were falling fast, and although nitrate exploitation partially plugged the gap, Peru's political economy entered into a prolonged crisis, which global depression and the outbreak of the War of the Pacific (1879) exacerbated: see Gootenberg, *Between Silver and Guano*, 135–36.

73. The transition from Juárez to Díaz is contentious: while Juárez's defeat of Maximilian and "restoration of the republic" obviously made possible the subsequent Porfiriato, orthodox ("liberal") historiography tended to distance the two, stressing the discontinuity between the liberal-democratic Juárez and the authoritarian Díaz. But some historians see greater continuity: Laurens Ballard Perry, *Juárez and Díaz: Machine Politics in Mexico* (DeKalb: Northern Illinois University Press, 1978); note also Timo H. Schaefer, *Liberalism as Utopia: The Rise and Fall of Legal Rule in Post-colonial Mexico, 1820–1900* (New York: Cambridge University Press, 2017), 161, 164.

74. Mallon, *Peasant and Nation.*

75. For contrasting views about popular (Peruvian) involvement in the War of the Pacific, see Heraclio Bonilla, "The Indian Peasantry and 'Peru' during the War with Chile," and Florencia E. Mallon, "Nationalist and Antistate Coalitions in the War of the Pacific: Junín and Cajamarca, 1879–1902," both in *Resistance, Rebellion and Consciousness in the Andean Peasant World, 18th to 20th Centuries*, ed. Steve J. Stern (Madison: University of Wisconsin Press, 1987), 219–79.

76. Justo Sierra—arguably the "organic intellectual" of the Porfiriato—maintained that victory in 1867 had "earned [Mexico] the incontestable right to call itself a nation" and that, as Díaz took power in 1876, "the country's real desire, manifested everywhere, was peace" (*The Political Evolution of the Mexican People* [Austin: University of Texas Press, 1969], 343, 359).

77. Peru suffered a severe export slump—arguably the worst in Latin American history—when the guano boom ended. Estimates of Peruvian output and growth therefore depend crucially on the chosen starting point, as table 1 suggests.

TABLE 1. Peru and Mexico: Exports/GDP per capita in U.S. dollars

	1870	1890	1910
Peru	10/160	3/44	9/75
Mexico	4/27	5/43	9/58

Note: I have rounded figures to the nearest whole number. The Peruvian figures are in current U.S. dollars; the Mexican figures are in U.S. dollars of 1900. For that reason, Mexico's figures for 1870 and 1890 should be slightly decreased, those of 1910 increased. But I do not think the adjustment greatly alters the big picture. Thus, over the forty-year period 1870–1910 Mexico's per capita GDP roughly doubled, while Peru's more than halved (in other words, the Mexican annual growth was +1.9 percent and the Peruvian –1.9

percent). But for the twenty years 1890–1910 (when, following the guano bust and the War of the Pacific, Peru played rapid catch-up) the respective rates of growth were +1.5 percent and +2.7 percent.

   Source: Created by the author from Victor Bulmer-Thomas, *The Economic History of Latin America Since Independence* (New York: Cambridge University Press, 2014), 74, 485–86, 489.

78. William Summerhill has convincingly argued that in Mexico railways produced a substantial fall in transport costs, to the benefit of the economy (more than they did in Brazil): "Transport Improvements and Economic Growth in Brazil and Mexico," in Haber, *How Latin America Fell Behind*, 93–117. I know of no comparable Mexico-Peru comparison. However, there is good evidence that Peruvian railways were commercially less successful: see Hunt, "Growth and Guano," 286–87.

79. Garner, *Porfirio Díaz*, 11.

80. Lewis Taylor, "Society and Politics in Late Nineteenth-Century Peru: Contumazá, 1876–1900," Working Paper no. 11 (1990), University of Liverpool ILAS, convincingly questions the traditional notion of the late nineteenth-century Peruvian Sierra as an isolated and archaic "feudal" redoubt but stresses "the chronic weakness of the Peruvian state which lacked legitimacy, authority and a monopoly of coercive power" (17).

81. See the summation of Civilista ideology as represented by the party's founding father, Manuel Pardo ("organic intellectual of the nascent ruling class"), in Gootenberg, *Imagining Development*, 72–74: *desarrollo hacia afuera* (outward-looking development), premised on exports and railways. But as the author observes, Pardo was "a deeply flawed architect of bourgeois Peru" who exemplified "a superficial, and thus doomed, neo-colonial mentality."

82. This argument is based on the notion that the revolution—even more clearly than the struggle for independence—involved genuine popular grievances and mobilization and was not foisted on a gullible or inherently violent people by either devious agitators or meddlesome foreigners. Such "explanations" were the staple of conservative critics of the revolution, and they still surface, suitably diluted, in some recent "revisionist" studies.

83. Klarén, *Peru*, 209; Jacobsen, *Mirages of Transition*, 339–43.

84. On Peruvian banditry, see the excellent study by Lewis Taylor, *Bandits and Politics in Peru: Landlords and Peasants in Hualgayoc, 1900–30* (Cambridge: Cambridge University Press, 1986). We can contrast this chronic disorder with Mexico's Pax Porfiriana, built upon tough rural policing and the suppression of endemic banditry: Paul T. Vanderwood, *Disorder and Progress:*

Bandits, Police and Mexican Development (Lincoln: University of Nebraska Press, 1981).

85. Klarén, *Modernization, Dislocation, and Aprismo*, 19–20, 32, 38, 41–42, 104, on the sugar strikes of 1917 and 1921 and their repression, on which see also Michael J. Gonzales, *Plantation Agriculture and Social Control in Northern Peru, 1875–1933* (Austin: University of Texas Press, 1985), chap. 8.

86. Indeed, even in Mexico, where industrialization was more advanced than in Peru, the urban working class was too small and weak to achieve substantial gains by itself; rather, it took advantage of a massive popular—above all, peasant—uprising to press its case and, after 1915, to forge a useful alliance with the infant revolutionary state. Ernest Gruening, a perceptive observer, exaggerated only somewhat when he declared that the feisty Mexican labor movement of the 1920s was more the creation ("the palpable product") than the creator of the revolution: *Mexico and Its Heritage* (London: Stanley Paul, 1928), 335.

87. Friedrich Katz, ed., *Riot, Rebellion and Revolution: Rural Social Conflict in Mexico* (Princeton NJ: Princeton University Press, 1988), especially chaps. 2 and 17 by John Coatsworth ("Patterns of Rural Revolt in Latin America: Mexico in Comparative Perspective") and Katz ("Rural Rebellions after 1810"), convincingly demonstrates the breadth and impact of Mexican popular protest through the nineteenth century and after. John Womack Jr., *Zapata and the Mexican Revolution* (New York: Knopf, 1969), chap. 2, offers a graphic case study of ruling-class arrogance provoking popular agrarian protest.

88. On Porfirian peonage, notably in southeastern Mexico, see Allen Wells and Gilbert M. Joseph, *Summer of Discontent, Seasons of Upheaval: Elite Politics and Rural Insurgency in Yucatán, 1876–1915* (Stanford CA: Stanford University Press, 1996), chap. 6; and Sarah Washbrook, *Producing Modernity in Mexico: Labour, Race and the State in Chiapas, 1876–1914* (Oxford: Oxford University Press, 2012). Moramay López-Alonso, *Estar a la altura: Una historia de los niveles de vida en México, 1850–1950* (Mexico City: FCE, 2015) offers original and convincing anthropometric evidence of declining height during the later Porfiriato: see 154–55.

89. Rodney Anderson, *Outcasts in Their Own Land: Mexican Industrial Workers, 1906–11* (DeKalb: Northern Illinois University Press, 1976) remains the best study.

90. Friedrich Katz, *The Secret War in Mexico: Europe, the United States and the Mexican Revolution* (Chicago: University of Chicago Press, 1981), 3.

91. On Peruvian peasant revolts in the 1880s, provoked by both landlord abuses and state exactions (taxation and military recruitment), see Larson, *Trials of Nation-Making*, 157–58; and Thurner, *From Two Republics*, 45–46, 81–82, 118. My strong impression is, first, that state fiscal demands were the biggest grievance and, second, that landlords provoked protest by virtue of their aggressive quest for *labor* rather than *land*—the classic syndrome evident in agrarian societies where land was relatively abundant and peasants, retaining access to land, had to be coerced or cajoled into working for landed estates. In the earlier nineteenth-century this syndrome was evident in Mexico (hence, rural revolts were often related to fiscal demands). But by the time of the Porfiriato, when the state could secure ample funding from foreign trade, land had become the key issue, especially in central and parts of northern Mexico.

92. Juan Martínez Alier, *Haciendas, Plantations and Collective Farms: Agrarian Class Societies—Cuba and Peru* (London: Frank Cass, 1977), chap. 3, though focusing on a slightly later period in Peruvian agrarian history, persuasively emphasizes the highland peasantry's dogged resistance to (pastoral) landlords, which often foiled the latter's efforts at expansion and innovation.

93. Alan Knight, *The Mexican Revolution* (Cambridge: Cambridge University Press, 1986), 1:78–115.

94. Both Peru and, to a lesser extent, Mexico also resorted to the importation of Chinese coolies—foreign peons, we could say, recruited by means of an international *enganche* system. But the primary source of labor, particularly in Mexico, remained national.

95. Burga and Flores Galindo, *La república aristocrática*, 62–63; Mallon, *Defence of Community*, 62, 73; Thurner, *From Two Republics*, 46; and, for a useful overview, Eduardo Bedoya Garland, "Bonded Labor, Coercion and Capitalist Development in Peru," https://core.ac.uk/download/pdf/39087445.pdf.

96. Martínez Alier, *Haciendas, Plantations and Collective Farms*, 68–70, provides good examples of such resistance in a context of vague property boundaries, old land disputes, and weak state control: hacienda employees who sought to assert the landlord's rights were "cursed, clubbed and hit with rocks"; as one ruefully commented, "It is not very comforting to face and argue with 50 to 300 half-drunken members" of an irate Indian community. It may be that community resistance of this kind was more effective in extensive pastoral landscapes than in areas of intense arable farming, which could be more feasibly fenced and policed.

97. Michael J. Gonzales, "Neo-colonialism and Indian Unrest in Southern Peru, 1867–1898," *Bulletin of Latin American Research* 6, no. 1 (1987): 7 (quote), 18, 21–22.

98. Jeffrey Bortz, *Revolution within the Revolution: Cotton Textile Workers and the Mexican Labor Regime, 1910–1923* (Stanford CA: Stanford University Press, 2008); Aurora Gómez-Galvarriato, *Industry and Revolution: Social and Economic Change in the Orizaba Valley, Mexico* (Cambridge MA: Harvard University Press, 2013), which contains valuable statistical data showing that there were real improvements in the pay and conditions of workers following—and thanks to—the armed revolution. Both of these studies concern the textile workers—the biggest group of manufacturing workers in Mexico—but other *organized* labor groups (railwaymen, miners, electricians, petroleum workers) also benefited: see the eyewitness account in Gruening, *Mexico and Its Heritage*, 336–90.

99. Given both his intransigent temper and his solid political base, Calles was more radical in his treatment of the church than Obregón. Matthew Butler, *Faith and Impiety in Revolutionary Mexico* (Basingstoke: Palgrave Macmillan, 2007) provides a good sample of recent research. I discuss this "Jacobin" syndrome further in chapter 7 of this book.

100. Knight, "Racism, Revolution and Indigenismo." For a good example of Indian upward mobility following the revolution, even in the relatively "nonrevolutionary" state of Yucatán, see Robert Redfield, *The Folk Culture of Yucatán* (Chicago: University of Chicago Press, 1941), 150, which describes how, in Dzitas, the revolution, by "putting town government largely in the hands of the Indians," created "a serious discrepancy between the present institutions and the patterns of subordination and superordination" characteristic of the "old culture."

101. We now have numerous good regional studies of "la revolución hecha gobierno" in different Mexican states and regions: see, for example, Carlos Martínez Assad, ed., *Balance y perspectivas de los estudios regionales en México* (Mexico City: UNAM, 1990); Thomas Benjamin and Mark Wasserman, eds., *Provinces of the Revolution: Essays on Mexican Regional History, 1910–1929* (Albuquerque: University of New Mexico Press, 1990).

102. Thus, an Indian rebellion in Puno in 1866–67 aroused lively fears in the local elite, fears that, one of its members declared, harked back to the "terrifying events of 1780 and 1814" (McEvoy, *Forjando la nación*, 91). In this respect, we might draw a parallel with Yucatán, where the memory of the Maya Caste

War was still alive, ethnic divisions were deeply etched, and, after 1910, elites were distinctly leery of popular mobilization; hence, when revolutionary transformation finally came to Yucatán in 1915, it came "from without" in the form of northern proconsuls and their invading forces: Gilbert M. Joseph, *Revolution from Without: Yucatán, Mexico and the United States, 1880–1924* (Durham NC: Duke University Press, 1997). Soon after, however, Yucatán produced its own social-reformist movements and state administrations, which were genuinely "indigenous" (in both senses of the word).

103. As my references show, this brief discussion of Leguía and the *oncenio* owes a good deal to Paulo Drinot, ed., *La Patria Nueva: Economía, sociedad y cultura en el Perú, 1919–1930* (Raleigh NC: Editorial a Contracorriente, 2018).

104. On the use of conscripted labor for road-building (the *conscripción vial*), see Steve Stein, *Populism in Peru: The Emergence of the Masses and the Politics of Social Control* (Madison: University of Wisconsin Press, 1980), 60–62; and Mario Miguel Mena Bazán, "Caminos, campesinos y modernización vial," in *Trabajos de historia: Religión, cultura y política en el Perú, siglos XVII–XX*, ed. Dino León Fernández (Lima: UNMSM, 2011), 301–34. On commitment to strong government, see Pablo Luna, "El Estado de la 'Patria Nueva' o la victoria de las estructuras," in Drinot, *La Patria Nueva*, 35–82. And on indigenismo, see Fiona Wilson, "Leguía y la política indigenista: Movilizaciones alrededor de la ciudadanía indígena, décadas de 1910–30," in Drinot, *La Patria Nueva*, 139–68.

105. Regarding land reform, Calles distributed about four million hectares during his presidency (after which he lapsed into a more conservative posture); his efforts were supported by powerful grassroots organizations and *agraristas políticos*, themselves products of the armed revolution. In Morelos, for example, Zapatista veterans held power during the 1920s. Regarding labor, Leguía was more proactive; his discourse—and, more important, his policies regarding health, housing, and social security—have been seen as constituting a "Labour State": Paulo Drinot, *The Allure of Labor: Workers, Race and the Making of the Peruvian State* (Durham NC: Duke University Press, 2011). However, Leguía was quite prepared harshly to repress strikes, and there was, to my knowledge, no counterparts of Luis Morones and the CROM operating at the higher echelons of government (to the disgust of capitalists, both foreign and Mexican).

106. "Instrumental" is Paulo Drinot's description: see "Introducción: La Patria Nueva de Leguía a través del siglo XX," in Drinot, *La Patria Nueva*, 5. Similar evaluations are given by Davies, *Indian Integration*, 93; and Klarén,

Modernization, Dislocation, and Aprismo, 62–63, who notes the disillusionment, "large-scale defection," and subsequent repression by the regime of young *indigenista* radicals. Wilson, "Leguía y la política indigenista," 141, argues that Leguía's discursive innovations with regard to *indigenismo* (he was the first president to "turn the Indian into an integral part of the State's political discourse") did not translate into effective practice, not least due to the stubborn resistance of landlords and *gamonales*.

107. On Leguía's deference toward the United States, see Drinot, "Introducción," 16–17; Cotler, *Clases, estado y nación*, chap. 4; and Stein, *Populism in Peru*, 53–54. Both Calles and Leguía were keen on public health projects, but when Peru faced a serious yellow fever outbreak in 1919, Leguía's response was to invite Henry Hanson, an American representative of the Rockefeller Foundation, who, even though he "barely spoke Spanish [and] despised what he perceived as the ignorance and resistance of the population," was given "power over the entire incipient health system" for over two years: Marcos Cueto and Steven Palmer, *Medicine and Public Health in Latin America: A History* (New York: Cambridge University Press, 2013). The foundation also played a major role in Mexican public health campaigns, starting in the 1920s, and by the 1940s it was also pioneering the green revolution. While again displaying a good deal of intrusive paternalism, the foundation's engagement with the Mexican state was, in my inexpert judgment, rather more nuanced and negotiated; it involved, for example, extensive training of Mexican experts: Anne-Emanuelle Birn, "Public Health or Public Menace? The Rockefeller Foundation and Public Health in Mexico, 1920–1950," *Voluntas: International Journal of Voluntary and Non-profit Organizations* 7, no. 1 (1996): 35–56.

108. On Callista education policy and cultural nationalism—which was not just an elite intellectual sport but an important feature of public art, the labor movement, and public schooling—see Mary Kay Vaughan, *State, Education and Social Class in Mexico, 1880–1928* (DeKalb: Northern Illinois University Press, 1982), esp. chap. 8; and John Lear, *Picturing the Proletariat: Artists and Labor in Revolutionary Mexico, 1908–1940* (Austin: University of Texas Press, 2017).

109. British diplomats, chastened by the Mexican expropriation of the Anglo-American oil companies in 1938, pointed to the reassuring gulf that separated Cardenista Mexico from the Peru of President Benavides. Here, reported the British minister in Lima, "[the] present government disapproves very strongly of [the] Mexican government," and indeed, given supposed Mexican collusion with Aprista subversives, the Peruvians were "much relieved that

there is no longer a Mexican Ambassador in Lima." President Benavides, in a public speech, had even given "a strong hint that Peru, while under his government, has no intention of following Mexico away from the Church and towards socialism" (Forbes to Foreign Office, March 29, 1938; and Marlowe, Annual Report, February 23, 1938, FO 371/21488/A2445 and A1382, UK National Archives, Kew, London).

110. William Shakespeare, *Julius Caesar*, act 3, scene 2, line 80.

111. I would make a sharp distinction between, on the one hand, normative evaluations (value judgments about who or what is *morally* good or bad) and technical judgments (about who or what is good or bad in terms of *objective outcomes*). So St. Francis was a good man (value judgment), but Lionel Messi is a good footballer (objective fact). Similarly, irrespective of any moral considerations, Calles achieved more—was more successfully radical—than Leguía. Neither, of course, would win an ethical beauty contest.

112. Leguía, it should be recalled, had been a member of the Civilista Party prior to the 1919 coup. The historians I have in mind are Nelson Manrique and Carmen McEvoy: see Drinot, "Introducción," 22. True, some commentators have also seen continuities linking Leguía and APRA (which I find less plausible): Drinot, "Introducción," 9.

113. I have explored such counterfactuals more fully in Alan Knight, "The Mexican Revolution: Five Counterfactuals," in *El siglo de la Revolución Mexicana*, ed. Jaime Bailón Corres, 2 vols. (Mexico City: INEHRM, 2000), 1:35–64.

114. Michael Snodgrass, *Deference and Defiance in Monterrey Workers, Paternalism and Revolution in Mexico, 1890–1950* (New York: Cambridge University Press, 2003), 25–29.

115. Barrington Moore Jr., *Social Origins of Dictatorship and Democracy: Lord and Peasant in the Making of the Modern World* (Harmondsworth: Penguin, 1967), chap. 8, which includes one passing reference to Latin America (438).

116. Clearly, events post-1950 are beyond my brief. But we could note, simply as illustrative straws in the wind, the unusual—nationalist and reformist—role played by the Peruvian regular army after 1968 or the extreme violence and antistate radicalism of Peru's Sendero Luminoso, which contrast with the ideology and practice of Mexico's EZLN, whose very name derives, of course, from a patriotic revolutionary hero.

5. EMPIRE AND COLONIALISM

1. Chalmers Johnson, *Blowback: The Costs and Consequences of American Empire* (New York: Henry Holt, 2000); Niall Ferguson, *Empire: The Rise and Decline*

of the British World Order and the Lessons for Global Power (New York: Basic Books, 2001); Niall Ferguson, *Colossus: The Rise and Fall of the American Empire* (London: Penguin Books, 2012); Deepak Lal, *In Praise of Empires: Globalization and Order* (New York: Palgrave Macmillan, 2004); Max Boot, *The Savage Wars of Peace: Small Wars and the Rise of American Power* (New York: Basic Books, 2002); John Darwin, *After Tamerlane: The Rise and Fall of Global Empires, 1400–2000* (London: Penguin Books, 2008); Charles S. Maier, *Among Empires: American Ascendancy and Its Predecessors* (Cambridge MA: Harvard University Press, 2009). For good overviews of recent boosters and critics of U.S. imperialism, see Lloyd C. Gardner and Marilyn B. Young, eds., *The New American Empire* (New York: W. W. Norton, 2005); and Michael Mann, *Incoherent Empire* (London: Verso, 2005), 1–14, 252–67. Symptomatic of the times though they may be, I omit from serious consideration such examples of simplistic Anglo-Saxon boosterism as Walter Russell Mead, *God and Gold: Britain, America and the Modern World* (New York: Knopf, 2007); and Andrew Roberts, *A History of the English-Speaking People Since 1900* (New York: HarperCollins, 2007).

2. Sir John Wheeler-Bennet, *A Wreath to Clio: Studies in British, American and German Affairs* (London: Macmillan, 1967), 19. Some thirty years on, Deepak Lal echoes Wheeler-Bennett, lamenting that "empires have unfairly got a bad name, not least in US domestic politics"—which is unfortunate, he says, since "the world needs an American pax to provide both global peace and prosperity" ("In Defense of Empire," in *The Imperial Tense: Prospects and Problems of American Empire*, ed. Andrew J. Bacevich [Chicago: Ivan R. Dee, 2003], 45). I am not sure if it is significant that in 2003 Lal was content to "defend" empire, while a year later he had moved up a gear and was "praising" it (compare n. 1).

3. On the notion of international hegemony, see Robert O. Keohane, *After Hegemony: Cooperation and Discord in the World Political Economy* (Princeton NJ: Princeton University Press, 1984). For what it's worth, the great British public appears to agree with the boosters of empire: according to a recent Yougov poll, 33 percent of respondents believe that Britain's dependencies were "better off" for being colonized, as against 17 percent who thought they were "worse off" (39 percent were neutral, and 12 percent "don't know"). Similarly, 32 percent were "proud" of the empire, while only 19 percent were "ashamed." Within Europe, only the Dutch are prouder of their imperial past. See Robert Booth, "Alarming Survey Shows UK Leading the World in Yearning for an Empire," *The Guardian*, March 11, 2020, 23. (Incidentally, the survey information does not justify the hyperbolic headline.)

4. Bernard Porter, "We Don't Do Empire," *History Today* 55, no. 3 (March 2005).

5. W. C. Sellar and R. J. Yeatman, *1066 and All That* (London: Methuen, 1930): a brilliant spoof of traditional history, including, as its subtitle proclaims, "103 Good Things, 5 Bad Kings and 2 Genuine Dates."

6. Maier, *Among Empires*, 7. Regarding definitions of "informal empire," see the recent—and sensible—résumé by Manuel Llorca-Jaña, *The British Textile Trade in South America in the Nineteenth Century* (New York: Cambridge University Press, 2012), 285–90. Debating definitions can seem sterile, but the importance of using the correct concepts correctly becomes sharply apparent when, for example, one reads that the French invasion of Mexico in the 1860s (which involved a French army of some forty thousand, plus Belgian, Austrian, and Mexican allies, sustaining a European "emperor" in the face of widespread resistance) was a species of "informal [*sic*] empire." How many boots on the ground do we need before "formality"—in the sense of direct coercive control—is conceded? Was the German occupation of France in 1940 an "informal" occupation? See Edward Shawcross, *France, Mexico and Informal Empire in Latin America, 1820–1867* (Basingstoke: Palgrave Macmillan, 2018). The author also asks why the French intervention in Mexico "was a failure, while other French imperial projects, most notably in Algeria and Indochina, proved to be much more enduring" (5). Note that "failure" is oddly contrasted with "enduring." Perhaps the author recoiled from denoting the bloody and finally disastrous history of French imperialism in Algeria and Indochina as a "success."

7. Maier, *Among Empires*, 90–91. Margery Perham, *Colonial Sequence, 1930–1949* (London: Methuen, 1967), 92, while noting the specificity of British "indirect rule," pioneered by Lugard in northern Nigeria and then deployed elsewhere in British colonial Africa, observes that as a "general principle in the government of subject peoples . . . we can find examples [of indirect rule] all through the [British] Empire and all through history."

8. The point is hardly new or original: as I later mention, the Roca-Runciman Treaty of 1933 allegedly made Argentina an "honorary member" of the British Empire (at least as regards trade and tariffs), and economic historians have productively explored the Argentina/Australia comparison: see John Fogarty, Ezequiel Gallo, and Héctor Diéguez, eds., *Argentina y Australia* (Buenos Aires: Instituto Torcuato di Tella, 1979); and for the Canadian comparison, Carl E. Solberg, *The Prairies and the Pampas: Agrarian Policy in Canada and Argentina, 1880–1930* (Stanford CA: Stanford University Press, 1987). Donald Denoon, *Settler Capitalism: The Dynamics of Dependent Development in the*

Southern Hemisphere (Oxford: Clarendon Press, 1983), a particularly ambitious and original study, pairs three British dominions (Australia, New Zealand, and South Africa) with three Latin American republics (Argentina, Uruguay, and Chile); unfortunately, his stimulating work went almost unnoticed in Latin American circles. Indeed, transcontinental comparison of this kind remains—increasingly, perhaps—a marginal interest, and the great majority of historians of Latin America—including Argentina—have little interest in or knowledge of the history of the dominions, just as historians of the latter are usually indifferent to Latin America. James Belich, *Replenishing the Earth: The Settler Revolution and the Rise of the Anglo-World, 1783–1939* (Oxford: Oxford University Press, 2011) is a welcome—partial—exception.

9. Johnson, *Blowback*, 35–36. Such a pattern is, arguably, an ancient imperialist—or "colonialist"—stratagem, evident, for example, in the "loosely linked maritime empire of the Republic of Genoa in the Mediterranean," the Portuguese thalassocracy of the sixteenth century, or even the British Empire prior to its massive nineteenth-century territorial expansion: Jürgen Osterhammel, *Colonialism: A Theoretical Overview* (Princeton NJ: Markus Wiener, 1997), 9–10.

10. Like "control," "legitimacy" should also be seen as occupying some sort of continuum: it varies over time and, like beauty, is often in the eye of the beholder. (The same, incidentally, is true of "nation"-states and their respective regimes.) Puerto Rico, acquired by war in 1898, occupied—and still occupies—an anomalous position within the American body politic. It displays clear-cut "colonial" characteristics: the Foraker Act of 1900 instituted "a new colonial structure" and reduced the island's population to "colonial subjects": César J. Ayala and Rafael Bernabe, *Puerto Rico in the American Century: A History Since 1898* (Chapel Hill: University of North Carolina Press, 2007), 52. However, American sovereignty over the island is also broadly accepted (ergo, is seen as "legitimate") both within the United States and around the world; Puerto Rican opinion, even if it is critical of the anomalies of "commonwealth" status, overwhelmingly prefers statehood to independence.

11. Thus, in the circum-Caribbean in the 1910s through the 1930s, "the US Marines took over many of the functions of the state—least so in Nicaragua . . . more so in Haiti . . . and completely in the Dominican Republic" (Alan McPherson, *The Invaded: How Latin Americans and Their Allies Fought and Ended U.S. Occupation* [Oxford: Oxford University Press, 2014], 1).

12. P. J. Cain and A. G. Hopkins, *British Imperialism: Innovation and Expansion, 1688–1914* (London: Longman, 1993), 285; Darwin, *After Tamerlane*, 313.

13. Celia Wu, *Generals and Diplomats: Britain and Peru, 1820–1840* (Cambridge: CLAS, 1991), 5. Hypotheticals aside, in the 1860s the French did attempt to set up a European-style monarchy in Mexico—"luckless Mexico," as Peruvian president Ramón Castilla lamented at the time: Carmen McEvoy, *Forjando la nación: Ensayos de historia republicana* (Lima: PUCP, 1999), 80–81. Castilla was well aware of the risk of European aggression, since Peru, allied with Chile, was then involved in a naval conflict with Spain. And in 1859, the Ecuadorian president, Gabriel García Moreno, flirted with the idea of a French protectorate: Ronn Pineo, *Ecuador and the United States: Useful Strangers* (Athens: University of Georgia Press, 2007), 42–43. These—like American filibustering in Central America—were serious matters, but there were also crackpot adventurers, like the Frenchman Orélie-Antoine de Tounens, who in the 1850s attempted to make himself ruler of the "Kingdom of Araucania and Patagonia" in southern Chile. Arrested and deported, he made three further abortive attempts to realize his deranged monarchical dream. See Simon Collier and William F. Sater, *A History of Chile, 1808–1994* (Cambridge: Cambridge University Press, 1996), 96.

14. Ronald Robinson, "The Excentric Idea of Imperialism, with or without Empire," in *Imperialism and After: Continuities and Discontinuities*, ed. Wolfgang J. Mommsen and Jürgen Osterhammel (London: Allen and Unwin, 1986), 267–90. Assessing "metropolitan" versus "peripheral" causality is central to debates about British imperialism; in the U.S. case, where "formal" imperialism has been much rarer, the issue is less often raised, which tends to result in a bias toward "metropolitan" explanations (the United States calls the tune to which its [informal] dependencies dance). This seems to me mistaken: there are—changing the metaphor—plenty of examples of the (dependent) tail wagging the (metropolitan) dog. I therefore agree with Michael Hunt when he argues that analysis of American expansion too often "omits the world in which Americans achieved their ascendancy," thus ignoring the "powerful pressures and trends . . . that sometimes smoothed their way and at other times made it rocky, even impassable" (*The American Ascendancy: How the United States Gained and Wielded Global Dominance* [Chapel Hill: University of North Carolina Press, 2007], 3). Paul K. MacDonald, "Those Who Forget Historiography Are Doomed to Republish It: Empire, Imperialism and Contemporary Debates about American Power," *Review of International Studies* 35, no. 1 (2009): 66, similarly calls for greater scholarly attention to be paid to the local "microfoundations of American imperial influence," which may explain how "the local political environment . . . allows

the US to translate its material and ideational capabilities into control in certain countries, but not others."

15. The classic chronicle of conquistador Bernal Díaz is peppered with references to gold (and silver): *The Conquest of New Spain* (Harmondsworth: Penguin, 1983), 17, 19, 26, 27, 33, 34, 35, 36, 37, 39, 40, 42, 43 (and so on). Thirty years earlier Columbus had displayed a similar bullionist mentality: Pierre Vilar, *A History of Gold and Money* (London: Verso, 1984), 63–66.

16. Perhaps this is an equation too far: clearly, "security" and "prestige" are not synonymous, even though there are clear connections, for example, in the way that "security"—possessing powerful armed forces—may be seen to enhance "prestige," while "prestige" may in turn bolster security. However, to avoid the multiplication of categories, I am choosing to lump these two attributes together, the chief justification being that they relate to the power, influence, and role of the state, as opposed to economic and cultural actors (such as businessmen and missionaries).

17. This trio of motives—roughly, (geo)political power, cultural proselytization, and economic advantage—crops up frequently (albeit in different semantic guises): for example, Darwin, *After Tamerlane*, 269 (commerce, culture, and coercion) and 311–12 (Dr. Livingstone's "Christianity, commerce and civilization"); C. A. Bayly, *The Birth of the Modern World, 1780–1914* (Oxford: Blackwell, 2004), 7 ("economic changes, ideological constructions and mechanisms of the state"); or Philip S. Golub, *Power, Profit and Prestige: A History of American Imperial Expansion* (London: Pluto Press, 2010). Mann, *Incoherent Empire*, 11, 13, proposes a fourfold typology of power: "military, political, economic and ideological" (the triple formulation collapses "military" and "political" into a single category on the grounds that both involve state action). The same trio is evident across a broad range of historical and social-scientific inquiry, beyond imperialism or great power policy: thus, David Priestland, *Merchant, Soldier, Sage: A New History of Power* (London: Penguin, 2012) identifies three dominant and recurrent "castes" who are the carriers, respectively, of economic, politico-military, and cultural-religious power. This trio, in turn, harks back to the ancient medieval society of estates: peasants who work, soldiers who fight, and priests who pray. For a more theoretical version of this familiar threesome, see W. G. Runciman, *The Social Animal* (London: HarperCollins, 1998), 67–69.

18. H. S. Ferns, *Britain and Argentina in the Nineteenth Century* (Oxford: Clarendon Press, 1960), chap. 3; Klaus Gallo, *Las invasiones inglesas* (Buenos Aires: Eudeba, 2004).

19. John Mayo, "Consuls and Silver Contraband on the West Coast of Mexico in the Era of Santa Anna," *Journal of Latin American Studies* 19, no. 2 (1987): 389–411.

20. As Macaulay famously put it, writing of Frederick the Great: "In order that he might rob a neighbour whom he had promised to defend, black men fought on the coast of Coromandel and red men scalped each other by the great lakes of North America" (Thomas Babington Macaulay, *On Frederick the Great* [New York: Useful Knowledge, 1882], 32).

21. Llorca-Jaña, *The British Textile Trade*, questions some received opinions and convincingly stresses the importance of British exports—chiefly textiles—to Latin America in the first half of the nineteenth century; thus, between 1820 and 1849 Latin America took an average of 21 percent of British exports, while the United States took only 16 percent (35). A couple of qualifications are important: the increase in *volume* of (textile) exports exceeded the increase in *value* (basically, textiles got much cheaper), and the impact in Latin America was appreciably greater in the Southern Cone (Llorca-Jaña's focus: Chile and Argentina) than, for example, in Mexico, Central America, or Andean America. I return to this question of import consumption later.

22. Given Roosevelt's dismemberment of a sovereign state (Colombia) in the pursuit of American hemispheric power, I find it hard to swallow Anders Stephanson's observation that Woodrow Wilson "intervened in Latin America, Mexico above all, far more than the imperial Roosevelt" (*Manifest Destiny: American Expansion and the Empire of Right* [New York: Hill & Wang, 1995], 114). Wilson's two interventions in Mexico (the 1914 occupation of Veracruz and the 1916–17 Punitive Expedition) were both limited and ineffectual. The first was gratuitous and ill-advised, the second, arguably, unavoidable in the circumstances, and neither had a decisive impact on the course of the Mexican Revolution. The story in Central America and the Caribbean was very different: there, American intervention was more violent, intrusive, and prolonged.

23. On the global strategic imperatives that prompted British expansion in Africa, see the classic study of Ronald Robinson, John Gallagher, and Alice Denny, *Africa and the Victorians: The Official Mind of Imperialism* (London: Macmillan, 1961).

24. Britain, of course, did not become a full-scale democracy (for men, at least) until 1918. During the nineteenth century, Bernard Porter writes, British diplomats remained "an exclusive bunch," self-contained and self-regarding; unlike other British politico-administrative elites, they avoided "institutional

takeover" by the rising middle class; and, it is worth adding, they were not appointed according to an American-style spoils system. In short, they could function relatively free from "extraneous considerations" (such as public opinion), and "the conduct of British diplomacy was uniquely concentrated and aloof" ("British Foreign Policy in the Nineteenth Century," *Historical Journal* 23, no. 1 [1980]: 193–201, 194). Occasionally, it is true, public opinion intruded upon elite foreign policymaking (e.g., the "Bulgarian atrocities" and Gladstone's Midlothian campaign of 1879–80), but there was no Latin American equivalent of that emotive issue.

25. The famous quotation (which comes in several versions) seems to derive originally from James Creelman, *On the Great Highway: The Wanderings and Adventures of a Special Correspondent* (Boston: Lothrop Publishing Co., 1901), 177–78. Some have questioned its veracity. The important point is that U.S. interventions in Latin America (such as Cuba in 1898 or, indeed, Cuba in 1961–62) excited lively domestic interest and controversy: as the French ambassador in Washington observed in 1898 regarding Spain and Cuba, "a sort of bellicose fury has seized the American nation" (Lewis L. Gould, *The Spanish-American War and President McKinley* [Lawrence: University Press of Kansas, 1982], 37). Again, no British intervention in Latin America aroused comparable public interest.

26. Nineteenth-century American policy-makers saw the world through "an ideological lens that presupposed rivalry between republics and monarchies" and proclaimed "ideological solidarity with the new states of Spanish America" (although, increasingly, "solidarity" proved quite compatible with aggression and expansion): Jay Sexton, *The Monroe Doctrine: Empire and Nation in Nineteenth-Century America* (New York: Hill & Wang, 2011), 11, 75. On the corporate ethic, see Thomas F. O'Brien, *The Revolutionary Mission: American Enterprise in Latin America, 1900–1945* (Cambridge: Cambridge University Press, 1996), 1–6.

27. However much the domestic British economy may have been premised on a kind of "gentlemanly capitalism" controlled by interlocking elites who gave priority to the City and finance (see Cain and Hopkins, *British Imperialism*), it did not follow that they sought to *export* this distinctive brand of "gentlemanly capitalism"—for example, to Latin America. As I later suggest, the British wanted the Latin American elites with whom they dealt to abide by certain basic rules (keeping order, honoring contracts, paying debts, respecting property rights); thereby, "capitalism" could thrive to mutual advantage. But there was nothing particularly "gentlemanly" about this arrangement. In fact,

the British often preferred congenial thuggish caudillos to ineffectual high-minded "gentlemen." Lord Palmerston may have viewed the brutal Argentine dictator Rosas "with horror," but "he considered that such tyrants were at least in control of their countries and were governments that could be referred to and dealt with" (Andrew Graham-Yooll, *Imperial Skirmishes: War and Gunboat Diplomacy in Latin America* [Oxford: Signal Books, 2002], 76). Seventy years later, the same logic was at work when the British government recognized—and, up to a point, supported—the Mexican counterrevolutionary dictator Victoriano Huerta.

28. The United States emerged from the Second World War globally dominant, but it still had to reckon with the victorious Soviet Union; forty years later, following the collapse of the Soviet Union, the United States possessed—in the words of neocon advocate Charles Krauthammer—"the strength and the will to lead a unipolar world, unashamedly laying down the rules of world order" (see Lloyd Gardner, "Present at the Culmination," in Gardner and Young, *The New American Empire*, 17; see also Mann, *Incoherent Empire*, 10). It didn't last: Russian imperialism reasserted itself (in different guise), the Middle East proved a morass, and China emerged as a formidable political and economic rival.

29. Desmond Gregory, *Brute New World: The Rediscovery of Latin America in the Early Nineteenth Century* (London: British Academic Press, 1992), 35, quoting Maria Graham; Francis Bond Head, *Journeys across the Pampas and among the Andes* (Carbondale: Southern Illinois University Press, 1967), 16; Wu, *Generals and Diplomats*, 37, citing W. B. Stevenson. A generation later, an American traveler visiting Valparaiso commented on the "magnificent stores" full of European imports; hence, "an old resident who removed to New York a few months since sent back to Valparaiso to buy dresses for his daughter" (Mrs. George B. Merwin, *Three Years in Chile* [Carbondale: Southern Illinois University Press, 1966], 28).

30. Rory Muir, *Wellington: The Path to Victory, 1769–1814* (New Haven CT: Yale University Press, 2013), 185–86.

31. Rory Miller, *Britain and Latin America in the Nineteenth and Twentieth Centuries* (London: Longman, 1993), chap. 4. Llorca-Jaña, *The British Textile Trade*, takes a more positive view of the British trade performance (see n. 21 above). For a shrewd eyewitness account of how and why early British mining ventures failed, see Head, *Journeys across the Pampas*, chap. 15.

32. Between 1905 and 1914 Latin America as a whole took 23 percent of British overseas investment, compared to just 6 percent for the "dependent colonies"

of the empire (i.e., excluding India and the "white dominions"): Gary B. Magee and Andrew S. Thompson, *Empire and Globalisation* (Cambridge: Cambridge University Press, 2010), 174.

33. D. C. M. Platt, "The Imperialism of Free Trade: Some Reservations," *Economic History Review* 21, no. 2 (1968): 296–306 (quote from 305).

34. On the East India Company as a protagonist of "primitive mercantilism," see Eric Stokes, "The First Century of British Colonial Rule in India: Social Revolution or Social Stagnation?" *Past and Present* 58 (1973): 143–44. Hence, British radicals regarded the company as a "despotic encumbrance" (Darwin, *After Tamerlane*, 262).

35. Llorca-Jaña, *The British Textile Trade*, 275–76, rightly reminds us of the importance of such mundane but neglected matters as improvements in packaging. Thus, the use of tarpaulin, coupled with the switch from wooden- to iron-hulled ships, ensured that British textiles arrived in good condition and did not have to be sold at a discount; insurance premiums were also cut as a result. Similarly, the unspectacular growth of transatlantic networks of credit and the use of bills of exchange laid the foundation for enhanced trade: Miller, *Britain and Latin America*, 94–95.

36. Patrick K. O'Brien, "The Costs and Benefits of British Imperialism, 1846–1914," *Past and Present* 120, no. 1 (1988): 186–94, shows that, compared to European powers, to the "white dominions," and to the United States, Britain was heavily—and no doubt regressively—taxed in order to maintain the empire and its global commercial interests, with the Royal Navy absorbing "an increasingly large part" of these heavy outlays (190).

37. Stephen D. Krasner, "State Power and the Structure of International Trade," *World Politics* 28 (1976): 317–47, broadly confirms—with some time lags—the hypothesis that "(global trade) openness is more likely to occur during periods when a key state is in its ascendency" (323). It should be added that foreign trade was never as crucial to the American economy as it was to the British, who, between 1855 and 1910, derived 50–60 percent of GNP from foreign trade; the American figure between 1900 and 1980 was 6–18 percent. Hence, in the past as in the present, the Americans were more disposed to play fast and loose with free trade (consider Smoot-Hawley, Nixon, Trump . . .). Data from Barbara Stallings, *Banker to the Third World: U.S. Portfolio Investment in Latin America* (Berkeley: University of California Press, 1987), 44–45.

38. C. R. Fay, *Imperial Economy and Its Place in the Formation of Economic Doctrine 1600–1932* (Oxford: Clarendon Press, 1934), chap. 6.

39. Peter Alhadeff, "Dependency, Historiography and Objections to the Roca Pact," in *Latin America: Economic Imperialism and the State*, ed. Christopher Abel and Colin Lewis (London: ILAS, 1985), 367–78; Alan D. Dye, "Cuba and the Origins of the US Sugar Quota," *Revista de Indias* 65 (2005): 193–218.

40. Thomas C. Mills, "Anglo-American Relations in South America during the Second World War and Postwar Economic Planning" (PhD diss., Brunel University, 2009), 22–26.

41. David Rock, *The British in Argentina: Commerce, Settlers and Power, 1800–2000* (Basingstoke: Palgrave Macmillan, 2018), 265, 273. Nearly a century later, with Britain greatly diminished as an economic power, the UK establishment still retains an unshakable faith in the commercial value of visits by the Prince of Wales to Latin America (e.g., Prince Charles schmoozing in Colombia and Mexico in 2014). There is not a sliver of evidence to support this faith, the questioning of which (as I know from personal experience) is not well received by the British diplomatic establishment.

42. This decisive trend affected Latin American countries differently: Brazil had historically cultivated good relations with the United States, a policy that was adroitly pursued by Getulio Vargas during the Second World War. Furthermore, the American and Brazilian economies were complementary, in part because of the American thirst for coffee, a product that had to be imported (thus, in 1913 the United States took 32 percent of Brazil's exports, compared to just 5 percent of Argentina's). Argentina, historically tied to Britain, had a history of uneasy relations with the United States, which, during the Second World War, were exacerbated by exaggerated American fears of Argentine sympathy for the Axis. Furthermore, while the Argentine economy neatly complemented the British, its chief exports competed with those of the United States; hence, as Argentine imports from the United States increased (from 15 percent of total imports in 1913 to 23 percent in 1929) and exports to the United States lagged (8 percent of total exports in 1929), so the bilateral trade deficit burgeoned. On the U.S.-Argentine political relationship during the Second World War, see C. A. MacDonald, "The Politics of Intervention: The United States and Argentina, 1941–1946," *Journal of Latin American Studies* 12, no. 2 (1980): 365–96. The trade data are from Victor Bulmer-Thomas, *The Economic History of Latin America Since Independence* (Cambridge: Cambridge University Press, 1994), 74, 159.

43. These were, in the words of Sir John Fisher (1904), "the five keys that lock up the world" (Barry Gough, *Pax Britannica* [New York: Palgrave Macmillan, 2014], 36).

44. It is a poignant historical coincidence that the pocket battleship *Von Spee* was named after Admiral Maxilian Von Spee, the German naval commander at the Battle of the Falkland Islands, in which he and his two sons were killed.

45. The Venezuelan border dispute, notable for the belligerent language and the "flagrant inaccuracies" of Secretary of State Richard Olney's declaration of American policy, is a classic example of a minor power (Venezuela) seeking to advance its local interests by inveigling a great power (the United States) into a dispute with a rival great power (Britain) but then finding that it lacked any control over the ensuing process: R. A. Humphreys, "Anglo-American Rivalries and the Venezuelan Crisis of 1895," *Transactions of the Royal Historical Society* 17 (1967): 131–64 (quote from 151). On British deference, see also Walter LaFeber, *The Panama Canal: The Crisis in Historical Perspective* (New York: Oxford University Press, 1989), 14–15; and P. A. R. Calvert, *The Mexican Revolution: The Diplomacy of Anglo-American Conflict, 1910–1914* (Cambridge: Cambridge University Press, 1968).

46. Luce's 1941 article can be read in Michael J. Hogan, ed., *The Ambiguous Legacy: U.S. Foreign Relations in the "American Century"* (Cambridge: Cambridge University Press, 1999), 11–29.

47. A few illustrative statistics: the share of Latin American exports (eight major countries) that went to the United States rose from 19 percent in 1913 to 30 percent in 1930 and 43 percent in 1954: Krasnick, "State Power," 331. U.S. investment in Latin America rose from $1.6 billion (in current dollars) to $5.4 billion in 1929 (during which period the ratio of portfolio to direct investment shifted from 22:78 to 32:68): Bulmer-Thomas, *The Economic History*, 161. British investment in Latin America stood at around $4 billion in 1913 (between two and three times the U.S. total); fifteen years later, the figure remained about $4 billion (£800 million), now only 75 percent of the U.S. total: Miller, *Britain and Latin America*, 121; Arthur Salter, "Foreign Investment," Essays in International Finance, Princeton University, no. 12 (1951): 18, which gives a figure of £800 million of British investment in Latin America in 1930.

48. Dexter Perkins, *A History of the Monroe Doctrine* (London: Longman, 1960), 72–74, 115–38. Perkins rightly points out that in the latter case, the U.S. government made clear its opposition to Napoleon III's avowedly anti-American project and, once the Civil War was over, exerted pressure to bring it to an end. That said, Perkins adds, "It is possible that without American diplomatic action the Mexican adventure would have ended exactly as it did" (137), that is, in French defeat and withdrawal. Rather than "it is possible," I would say "it is pretty certain."

49. The most obvious extension of "Monrovian" claims came with the (Theodore) Roosevelt Corollary of 1904, which declared that in order to maintain the exclusion of extra-American powers from the Continent, the United States had the right and duty to enforce law, order, and the protection of property throughout the Americas, thus exercising an "international police power": see Sexton, *The Monroe Doctrine*, 233–34; Perkins, *A History*, 240–43.

50. Nancy Mitchell, *The Danger of Dreams: German and American Imperialism in Latin America* (Chapel Hill: University of North Carolina Press, 1999) cogently argues that subjective factors—German "bombast" and American "paranoia" (223–24)—fanned the flames of a conflict out of all proportion to the objective interests and, indeed, the specific policies that were in play.

51. The historiography of this episode is extensive and often contentious: a useful overview is provided by Thomas G. Paterson, "United States Intervention in Cuba, 1898: Interpretations of the Spanish-American-Cuban-Filipino War," *History Teacher* 29, no. 3 (1998): 341–46.

52. Dana G. Munro, *The United States and the Caribbean Republics, 1921–1933* (Princeton NJ: Princeton University Press, 1974) provides a detailed "official" view; McPherson, *The Invaded*, offers an alternative (peripheral/bottom-up) perspective.

53. Mitchell, *The Danger of Dreams*, shows how domestic U.S. interests—the press, the navy, and ambitious politicians—grossly inflated the threat of German aggression in Latin America, especially the Caribbean. Theodore Roosevelt is a classic example: "Roosevelt beat the drum of the German threat—until he became vice-president. Then he precipitately dropped his dire predictions and professed his desire to cooperate with Berlin" (218). Woodrow Wilson also abruptly changed tack in 1915 "when the idea of a German threat was useful" (222). Unfortunately, once they were built up, such bogeymen could not so easily be banished (223).

54. Jules R. Benjamin, *The United States and Cuba: Hegemony and Dependent Development, 1880–1934* (Pittsburgh: University of Pittsburgh Press, 1977), 138–70, offers a good account of Welles's proconsular role, which involved direct political intervention, in clear contradiction of FDR's incipient Good Neighbor Policy. Following in Theodore Roosevelt's footsteps, Welles justified this by means of a sophistic argument that Benjamin aptly calls the "Welles Corollary" (145).

55. The toppling of the Arbenz government in Guatemala is particularly interesting, since it involved the application—much closer to home—of the tactics that the United States had successfully deployed the previous year

in Iran: Stephen G. Rabe, *Eisenhower and Latin America* (Chapel Hill: University of North Carolina Press, 1988), chap. 3; and Piero Gleijeses, *Shattered Hope: The Guatemalan Revolution and the United States, 1944–1954* (Princeton NJ: Princeton University Press, 1992), which makes clear that national geopolitical motives rather than the specific economic interests of the United Fruit Company were the key determinants of U.S. policy.

56. Kenneth D. Lehman, *Bolivia and the United States: A Limited Partnership* (Athens: University of Georgia Press, 1999), chap. 4.

57. On U.S. destabilization of the Goulart government and support for the military coup of 1964 in Brazil, see the résumé by Anthony W. Pereira, "The US Role in the 1964 Coup in Brazil: A Reassessment," *Bulletin of Latin American Research* 37, no. 1 (2018): 5–17.

58. "British policy followed the principle of extending control informally if possible, and formally if necessary" (John Gallagher and Ronald Robinson, "The Imperialism of Free Trade," *Economic History Review* 6, no. 1 [1953]: 13).

59. Robert E. Quirke, *An Affair of Honor: Woodrow Wilson and the Occupation of Veracruz* (New York: W. W. Norton, 1967), 68, 77, 115. The recurrent delusion of "liberating" invasions, from Bonaparte to Bush, is noted by Marilyn B. Young, "Imperial Language," in Gardner and Young, *The New American Empire*, 32–33. Indeed, the delusion is even older: for early modern examples, see Anthony Pagden, *Peoples and Empires* (London: Phoenix Press, 2002), 95.

60. Indeed, Aberdeen engaged in a rare moment of (British) critical introspection: "After shedding much blood, (we have given) him (General Rosas) just grounds for complaint against us" (Ferns, *Britain and Argentina*, 250). See also Miller, *Britain and Latin America*, 35, 52.

61. Bryce Wood, *The Making of the Good Neighbor Policy* (New York: Columbia University Press, 1961).

62. Lars Schoultz, *Beneath the United States: A History of U.S. Policy Toward Latin America* (Cambridge MA: Harvard University Press, 1998), 253. See also Bruce J. Calder, *The Impact of Intervention: The Dominican Republic during the U.S. Occupation of 1916–1924* (Austin: University of Texas Press, 1984), 239; James Dunkerley, *Power in the Isthmus: A Political History of Central America* (London: Verso, 1990), chap. 3. Even if the broad trend is clear, each national story had its quirks. The U.S. representative in the Dominican Republic did not welcome Trujillo's initial coup, but in seizing power, Trujillo relied on the (U.S.-trained) National Guard, and soon enough, he secured U.S. endorsement. As I mentioned in the introduction, FDR's (alleged) statement—regarding either Somoza or Trujillo—that

"he may be a sonofabitch, but [at least] he's our sonofabitch" is very likely apocryphal, but it captures a basic truth: that when it came to U.S. policy in the circum-Caribbean, supposed realpolitik trumped democratic niceties.

63. Geir Lundestad, "'Empire by Invitation' in the American Century," *Diplomatic History* 23, no. 2 (April 1999): 189–217.

64. Victor Kiernan, *Imperialism and Its Discontents* (New York: Routledge, 1995), 98–99, also observes that prior to imperial intervention and conquest, "a surprisingly high proportion of Africa and Asia, including both India and China, [was] under alien or half-alien rule"; by way of example, he cites "Matabele dominance over the Mashonas" in southern Africa. While the same argument is certainly relevant to the sixteenth-century Spanish conquest of Mexico and Peru, it does not hold (or, rather, it holds negatively) for postindependence Latin America, where, notwithstanding its undoubted socioethnic cleavages, the original conquest was three centuries old, and the resulting colonies/countries thus enjoyed a measure of historical longevity and (with qualifications, e.g., in Central America) a shared common national identity.

65. Jorge I. Domínguez, *Cuba: Order and Revolution* (Cambridge MA: Belknap Press, 1978), chaps. 2 and 3, sees the U.S.-Cuban relationship passing through successive phases: first, a phase of "empire" (i.e., a formal protectorate, 1902–33), then—partly in response to nationalist protest, evident in the 1933 Revolution—"hegemony" (informal control and influence, 1933–58). The triumph of the Castro revolution in 1959, of course, ushered in a third phase, one of mutual hostility. Central America charts a rather different trajectory: compared to Cuba (and most of the countries covered in this essay), the governments of Central America, apart from presiding over small, weak countries within the United States' self-designated sphere of influence, were also particularly "improvisational" (i.e., weak, fragmented, and illegitimate). They were, therefore, unusually vulnerable to U.S. intervention and control; indeed, their leaders also actively sought that intervention. Thus, in 1911 the president of Nicaragua, Adolfo Díaz, offered the United States a protectorate; nine years later, Manuel Estrada Cabrera, president of Guatemala, similarly told the U.S. representative—so the latter reported—that he "placed . . . the fate of the country in our hands and would agree to abide by any decision which we made" (Robert H. Holden, *Armies Without Nations: Public Violence and State Formation in Central America, 1821–1960* [Oxford: Oxford University Press, 2004], 25–28, 27).

66. On Smith's insistence on the key role of the state and of the "social and institutional framework of society" in the development of market society,

see David McNally, *Political Economy and the Rise of Capitalism: A Reinterpretation* (Berkeley: University of California Press, 1988), 250–56 (quote from 251). For a somewhat "Smithian" discussion of the sociopolitical conditions necessary (but at the time sadly lacking) if British trade, investment, and immigration were to succeed in newly independent Latin America, see Head, *Journeys across the Pampas*, chap. 15.

67. John Harriss, Janet Hunter, and Colin Lewis, eds., *The New Institutional Economics and Third World Development* (London: Routledge, 1997). Some versions of this thesis—versions that Smith would not have endorsed—are crudely macho (as well as being wrong): "The hidden hand of the market will never work without a hidden fist. McDonald's cannot flourish without McDonnell Douglas" (Thomas Friedman, quoted in Young, "Imperial Language," 41).

68. Karl Polanyi, *The Great Transformation* (1944; Boston: Beacon Press, 1957) is the locus classicus; see also Rodney Hilton, ed., *The Transition from Feudalism to Capitalism* (London: NLB, 1976).

69. Alan McFarlane, *The Origins of English Individualism: The Family, Property and Social Transition* (Oxford: Blackwell, 1978).

70. Stephen R. Platt, *Imperial Twilight: The Opium War and the End of China's Last Golden Age* (London: Atlantic Books, 2018), 43.

71. Arnold J. Bauer, *Goods, Power, History: Latin America's Material Culture* (Cambridge: Cambridge University Press, 2001), chap. 5. As I later note, however, consumer desire did not guarantee consumer purchases, and the caveat "urban" excludes the majority of Latin American inhabitants.

72. Regina Akel, *Benjamin Disraeli and John Murray: The Politician, the Publisher and the Representative* (Liverpool: Liverpool University Press, 2016), 12–13, 79–80.

73. Carlos Marichal, *A Century of Debt Crises in Latin America: From Independence to the Great Depression, 1820–1930* (Princeton NJ: Princeton University Press, 1989), chap. 2.

74. Bauer, *Goods, Power, History*, 130; D. C. M. Platt, *Latin America and British Trade, 1806–1914* (London: Adam & Charles Back, 1972), 67; Charles Darwin, *The Voyage of the Beagle* (London: Marshal Cavendish, 1987), 116. Bauer notes that it was cheaper for Costa Rican coffee exporters to send their Europe-bound produce eight thousand miles by sea around Cape Horn rather than three hundred miles over the mountains to Limón, on the Atlantic coast (132). See also Miguel Jaramillo Baanante, "El impacto de la apertura al comercio internacional sobre la economía regional del

extremo norte peruano, 1780–1877," in *Estado y mercado en la historia del Perú*, ed. Carlos Contreras and Manuel Gave (Lima: PUCP, 2002), 233–34; and Kim A. Clark, *The Redemptive Work: Railway and Nation in Ecuador, 1895–1930* (Wilmington DE: SR Books, 1998), 18–21. For a fuller discussion of land transport costs, note Llorca-Jaña, *The British Textile Trade*, 346–50.

75. Isaac Holton, *New Granada: Twenty Months in the Andes* (Carbondale: Southern Illinois University Press, 1967), 65, 66, 121, 140, 182, 197, where the author also points out that, given the scant consumption of imported goods, import taxes were of little use to the cash-strapped national treasury. Two caveats are in order: first, Colombia was probably an extreme case (its communications were unusually difficult, its capital stood far inland, and it lacked dynamic exports); second, the material poverty that struck foreign travelers should not be taken to indicate basic human deprivation—on the contrary, food seems to have been fairly cheap and abundant.

76. Richard Alan White, *Paraguay's Autonomous Revolution, 1810–1840* (Albu-querque: University of New Mexico Press, 1978) contrives to present Francia's Paraguay as a bold and successful example of quasi–state socialism, which saved the republic from the chronic dependency suffered by other newly independent Latin American countries. A more realistic analysis that stresses economic regression is provided by Mario Pastore, "Trade Contraction and Economic Decline: The Paraguayan Economy under Francia, 1810–1840," *Journal of Latin American Studies* 26, no. 3 (1994): 539–95. Francia was unusual in exerting authoritarian power for decades; in Peru, comparable xenophobic and protectionist lobbies (which sought, foreigners feared, a "Chinese path" for their country) were strident and often effective, but they were offset by the counterweight of urban, coastal cosmopolitanism, which finally prevailed in the late 1840s. See the excellent analysis in Paul Gootenberg, *Between Silver and Guano: Commercial Policy and the State in Postindependence Peru* (Princeton NJ: Princeton University Press, 1989), 70–80 (quote 76).

77. Tulio Halperín Donghi, *Politics, Economics and Society in Argentina in the Revolutionary Period* (Cambridge: Cambridge University Press, 1975), chap. 2, shows how the economy of the Río de la Plata, though it benefited by escaping Spanish mercantilist controls and gaining access to British commerce, suffered from chronic violence, arbitrary taxation, the flight of Spanish capital, and the breakup of the trade network that had linked the littoral to the silver economy of Upper Peru (soon to be Bolivia). Similar, if less severe, dislocations were evident throughout Spanish America.

78. Barbara A. Tenenbaum, *The Politics of Penury: Debt and Taxes in Mexico, 1821–1856* (Albuquerque: University of New Mexico Press, 1986).

79. John Lynch, *New Worlds: A Religious History of Latin America* (New Haven CT: Yale University Press, 2012), 185–86.

80. Gregory, *Brute New World*, 37, 76, 105–6, 130, 142–43, 152. I touch on this topic in chapter 3 of this book.

81. Miller, *Britain and Latin America*, chap. 4.

82. Graham-Yooll, *Imperial Skirmishes*, chap. 6; David McLean, *War, Diplomacy and Informal Empire: Britain and the Republics of La Plata, 1836–1853* (London: British Academic Press, 1995).

83. Gootenberg, *Between Silver and Guano*, 18–19, is unequivocal: "Overseas political interests did indeed intervene massively in Peruvian affairs in a push for free trade, far more, in fact, than historians ever imagined"; to that extent, the "imperialist" charge is fully justified. However, Gootenberg also shows, those interests were conspicuously unsuccessful, at least until post-1850. See also Mario Rodríguez, *A Palmerstonian Diplomat in Central America: Frederick Chatfield, Esq.* (Tucson: University of Arizona Press, 1964). Britain used its naval power to end the slave trade to Brazil (a case, perhaps, of "moral imperialism"): see Leslie Bethell, *The Abolition of the Brazilian Slave Trade* (Cambridge: Cambridge University Press, 1970). But in general, British and other foreign merchants in imperial Brazil relied on collaborative relations with a sympathetic regime and (slave-owning) elite: Eugene Ridings, *Business Interest Groups in Nineteenth-Century Brazil* (Cambridge: Cambridge University Press, 1994), 330, 334–36.

84. For contrasting policies and opinions at the time of the Tripartite Intervention in Mexico, see Jean Meyer, ed., *Memorias del simposio internacional 5 de mayo* (Puebla: El Colegio de Puebla, 2013).

85. On the "aggressive and interventionist mood" that affected the Foreign Office in the 1840s, see Miller, *Britain and Latin America*, 51 ff.

86. Bayly, *Birth of the Modern World*, 139–40. The same author's *Imperial Meridian: The British Empire and the World, 1780–1830* (London: Longman, 1989) is similarly persuasive: "The dominant ideological character of [the] Second British Empire was aristocratic, autocratic and agrarianist. By contrast, free trade and early 'liberal' ideas were much more characteristic of what might be called the 'Third' empire, which emerged in the 1830s and after" (137).

87. Gallagher and Robinson, "Imperialism of Free Trade," 2–3, produce an impressive list of territory "occupied or annexed" by Britain between 1840 and 1870, that is, during the supposed flood tide of free trade.

88. Miller, *Britain and Latin America*, 51. Here, Palmerston explicitly brackets Latin America with China and Portugal.

89. Gootenberg, *Between Silver and Guano*, 4, refers to "the usual behind-the-scenes arm-twisting by U.S. and British diplomats" who sought a reduction in Peru's protective tariffs in the 1830s; the British also "chose to throw political support" behind those who might favor free trade, such as General Santa Cruz and his short-lived Peru-Bolivia Confederation (19). The Americans, though keen rivals of the British, also actively espoused the free-trade cause: U.S. consuls "enthusiastically jumped into the messy ring of local political struggles" and mounted "a relentless series of political interventions" (20). Neither the British nor the Americans were successful in these efforts. Nor was Peru peculiar. In Mexico at the same time, the British also actively favored Santa Anna, believing him to be more sympathetic to free trade and British interests: Will Fowler, *Santa Anna of Mexico* (Lincoln: University of Nebraska Press, 2007), 205. But like many who dealt with Santa Anna, they found that he flattered to deceive.

90. Gallagher and Robinson, "The Imperialism of Free Trade"; Platt, "The Imperialism of Free Trade."

91. Bauer, *Goods, Power and History*, chap. 5; Gootenberg, *Between Silver and Guano*, 48, 62–63, which notes the paucity of European imports in upcountry Peru during the 1820s and 1830s, as well as the corresponding vigor of the "backwoods artisans" who, in alliance with "provincial merchants . . . rustic caudillos and municipal authorities," campaigned against the entry of foreign merchants and their goods, sometimes resorting to violence. Thus, prior to 1840, foreigners were chiefly confined to the coast. Clothes were a partial exception to this de facto protectionism, since, despite steep land transport costs, imported British textiles could undercut artisan products, even when the latter were manufactured far from the coast—for example, in the *obrajes* of the Ecuadorian highlands. See Manuel Chiriboga, *Jornaleros, grandes propetarios y exportación cacaotera, 1790–1925* (Quito: UASB, 2013), 106.

92. Stephen C. Topik and Allen Wells, *The Second Conquest of Latin America: Coffee, Henequen and Oil during the Export Boom, 1850–1930* (Austin: University of Texas Press, 1998). There is some scope for confusion here: the first conquest, clearly, was that of Cortés and Pizarro in the sixteenth century; John Lynch sees the Bourbon Reforms of the later eighteenth century as a "second conquest": see *The Spanish American Revolutions, 1808–1826* (London: Weidenfeld & Nicholson, 1973), 7, 16. If that usage is accepted, then the tighter integration of Latin America into the expanding global economy

of the later nineteenth century (along with its political and technological concomitants) would, strictly speaking, be a *third* conquest. Whatever the preferred enumeration, the significance of that integrative process is clear; I would also suggest that it was more consequential than the Bourbon Reforms.

93. Ronald Robinson, "Non-European Foundations of European Imperialism: Sketch for a Theory of Collaboration," in *Theories of Imperialism*, ed. Roger Owen and Bob Sutcliffe (London: Longman, 1972), 120–30.

94. The trajectory is well summarized in H. S. Ferns, "Argentina: Part of an Informal Empire?" in *The Land That England Lost: Argentina and Britain, a Special Relationship*, ed. Alistair Hennessy and John King (London: British Academic Press, 1992), chap. 2.

95. As Pellegrini proclaimed, "Rather than suspend service on the debt, I would renounce the presidency" (Miller, *Britain and Latin America*, 54–55).

96. Lance Davis reasonably suggests that "an empire without coercion is hardly an empire at all; and it is certainly not an exploitative empire" ("The Late Nineteenth-Century British Imperialist: Specification, Qualification and Controlled Conjectures," in *Gentlemanly Capitalism and British Imperialism: The New Debate on Empire*, ed. Raymond E. Dumett [London: Routledge, 2014], 83). Davis here seems to me to conflate two dimensions of "empire": the presence (or absence) of coercion, which I go on to discuss, and the role of "exploitation" (a rather more vague, which is not to say irrelevant, concept). It is not clear to me—or, I would guess, to many—that "exploitation" requires explicit coercion; in other words, we can easily envisage "exploitative" relationships that do not involve force (e.g., in families, companies, churches, and even universities). Is there any good reason to believe that international relationships are entirely different?

97. Ferns, *Britain and Argentina*, chap. 14; H. S. Ferns, "The Baring Crisis Revisited," *Journal of Latin American Studies* 24, no. 2 (1992): 241–73.

98. Rory Miller, "The Grace Contract, the Peruvian Corporation and Peruvian History," *Ibero-Amerikanische Archiv* 9 (1983): 319–43.

99. See the interesting comparison between Latin America (including Peru and Mexico) and Egypt, Morocco, Tunisia, and other "Old World" examples presented in Juan Flores Zendejas, "Sovereign Debt and European Interventions in Latin America," Working Paper of the Paul Bairoch Institute of Economic History, Geneva (2020). One small query: the author cites the French Intervention in Mexico (1861–66) as evidence of "the possibility of debt default leading to foreign intervention" (and, of course, such a "possibility" existed)

(11). But the French Intervention was not primarily a debt-collecting exercise: after all, the British debt was much greater, but the British did not boldly and foolishly march up-country (nor, indeed, did the Spaniards). Geopolitical considerations, including Napoleonic delusions, were key to French policy.

100. Teresa A. Meade, *"Civilizing" Rio: Reform and Resistance in a Brazilian City, 1889–1930* (University Park: Penn State University Press, 1997), 6–7.

101. "A major theme in the history of Anglo-Argentine relations is the replacement of power by law as a modus operandi," Ferns observes (of the nineteenth century), but, he adds, "the possibility of a reversal of this theme was always in the minds of Argentine political leaders" ("Argentina," 56). Miller, *Britain and Latin America*, 59, also suggests that the occasional naval coercion could cast a long shadow.

102. Miriam Hood, *Gunboat Diplomacy: Great Power Pressure in Venezuela, 1895–1905* (London: Allen and Unwin, 1983).

103. Ferns, *Britain and Argentina*, 152, 235, 239; Wilkins B. Winn, "Reports of British Diplomats Concerning the Status of Protestantism in Latin America in 1851," *Journal of Church and State* 10, no. 3 (1968): 137–44. Francis Bond Head describes how, in the Argentine interior, the locally influential but politically disaffected priests of San Juan took the governor prisoner and required the city jailer to publicly burn the recent decree that, "to encourage the settlement of the English in this province, had lately granted to strangers [*sic*] religious toleration" (*Journeys across the Pampas*, 18). "Strangers" is, presumably, a translation of *extranjeros* (foreigners).

104. Peru is a good and somewhat precocious example: by ca. 1850, thanks to the guano boom, the influx of revenue, and the triumph of new political elites, wedded to a project of *desarrollo hacia afuera* (export-led development), foreign interests now enjoyed a much more congenial environment. But the most basic prerequisite was sound sociopolitical order: as Gootenberg, *Between Silver and Guano*, 79, observes, "An institutionalized relationship among foreign diplomacy, free-trade finance and liberal state-building . . . first required the consolidation of political stability in Peru." And that could only be brought about by Peruvians; it could not be imposed from without by meddlesome imperialists. This phenomenon—the displacement of force from external "imperialist" actors to domestic elites and governments—has already been mentioned in respect to U.S. policy in the circum-Caribbean in the early twentieth century. Putting it simply, armed intervention could be scaled back because reliable "local" coercive mechanisms were now in place, typically controlled by "collaborating elites."

105. "Internal colonialism" is, like many useful big concepts, somewhat loose and shapeshifting. It has been deployed, I think correctly and creatively, to describe enduring features of Latin American societies such as Mexico (the case I happen to know best): see Pablo González Casanova, "Internal Colonialism and National Development," *Comparative International Development* 1, no. 4 (1965): 27–37. However, "internal colonialism" has also been discerned in sub-Saharan Africa, Russia, the Balkans, the United States, and the United Kingdom (where the so-called Celtic fringe figures—not altogether convincingly—as a kind of "colonial" periphery within Britain). Apart from raising specific empirical queries, this very broad usage—which includes ancient collective inequalities, often of ethnic/cultural character, within well-established nation-states—risks including too much. My own usage is more focused, specific, and—to use an ugly term—"processual." I argue that, roughly between 1860 and 1930, much of Latin America underwent socioeconomic changes that were also apparent in the contemporary colonial empires, changes that involved state-building, social control, technological innovation, coercive labor recruitment, and ruthless economic transformation. This was not an obstinately enduring state of affairs but a dynamic process that was actively pushed forward by (noncolonial) states and their national elites. In Britain, that process—which Marx described as one of "primary accumulation"—had already happened centuries earlier, but in the colonies it was recent and ongoing: see Karl Marx, *Capital* (London: J. M. Dent, 1957), vol. 2, chaps. 24, 25.

106. Bulmer-Thomas, *The Economic History*, 114–15.

107. Emily Rosenberg, "Foundations of United States International Financial Power: Gold Standard Diplomacy, 1900–1905," *Business History Review* 59, no. 2 (1985): 169–202.

108. Thomas P. Passananti, "The Politics of Silver and Gold in an Age of Globalization: The Origins of Mexico's Monetary Reform of 1905," *América Latina en la Historia Económica* 30 (2008): 67–95.

109. William Schell Jr., "Money as Commodity: Mexico's Conversion to the Gold Standard," *Mexican Studies / Estudios Mexicanos* 12, no. 1 (1996): 67–89; Luis Cerda, "Causas económicas de la Revolución mexicana," *Revista Mexicana de Sociología* 53 (1991): 307–47.

110. The 1880s witnessed a "veritable flood of foreign finance"; however, this followed hefty state investment on the part of so-called liberal regimes: see Colin M. Lewis, "The Financing of Railway Development in Latin America, 1850–1914," *Ibero-Amerikanisches Archiv* 9 (1983): 255–78 (quote

on 266). Two additional points are of interest: first, Cuba—the last major formal colony in Latin America—was a pioneer of railway building, but the railways were all private and nearly all foreign-owned; second, by the 1900s, Latin American states were beginning to claw back control of their mature railway systems by means of greater regulation or even direct ownership, the establishment of Mexico's National Railways in 1906 being a key example: see Arturo Grunstein, *Consolidados: José Yves Limantour y la formación de los Ferrocarriles Nacionales de México* (Mexico City: Conaculta, 2013).

111. Argentina and Uruguay were linked by cable in 1867, and direct transatlantic communication reached South America in the 1870s. Apart from accelerating commercial news and decisions, the telegraph gave metropolitan governments faster and closer control over their diplomatic representatives in Latin America, thus curbing their previous proconsular autonomy. However, it also fostered more intense and sometimes sensationalist reportage ("media hype," in today's jargon), as famously occurred in respect to Cuba in 1898. See the interesting analysis of John A. Britton, *Cables, Crises and the Press: The Geopolitics of the New International Information System in the Americas, 1866–1903* (Albuquerque: University of New Mexico Press, 2013).

112. Daniel R. Headrick, *The Tools of Empire: Technology and European Imperialism in the Nineteenth Century* (Oxford: Oxford University Press, 1981), 182–83; Lewis, "The Financing of Railway Development," 262, notes the parallels between Latin America and India.

113. Breech-loading rifles, usually German Mausers, became standard issue in Argentina, Brazil, and Chile in the 1890s: Peter M. Beattie, *The Tribute of Blood: Army, Honor, Race, and Nation in Brazil, 1864–1945* (Durham NC: Duke University Press, 2001), 79, 213, 309. When the Mexican Revolution began in 1910, the pioneer rebels—equipped, at best, with Winchester repeating rifles—were outgunned by the Federal army and their more formidable Mausers: Santiago Portillo, *Una sociedad en armas: Insurrección antirreleccionista en México, 1910–1911* (Mexico City: Colegio de México, 1995), 356. The eventual success of the revolution indicated not the military weakness of the old regime but the fact that the rebels, in order to defeat first Díaz (1910–11) and then Huerta (1913–14), had to raise, supply, and deploy large conventional armies capable of confronting the Federals in open battle. For colonial comparisons in respect to weaponry, see Kiernan, *Imperialism and Its Discontents*, 123–28; and Headrick, *Tools of Empire*, pt. 2.

114. Alistair Hennessy, *The Frontier in Latin American History* (London: Edward Arnold, 1978), 83–85, 147; Nelson A. Reed, *The Caste War of Yucatán* (Stanford

CA: Stanford University Press, 2001); Evelyn Hu-Dehart, *Yaqui Resistance and Survival: The Struggle for Land and Autonomy, 1821–1910* (Madison: University of Wisconsin Press, 2016), chaps. 5, 6; Collier and Sater, *A History of Chile*, 95–97; and for a detailed "bottom-up" perspective, Florencia E. Mallon, *Courage Tastes of Blood: The Mapuche Community of Nicolás Ailío and the Chilean State, 1906–2001* (Durham NC: Duke University Press, 2005), chap. 2; Carlos Martínez Sarasola, "The Conquest of the Desert and the Free Indigenous Communities of the Argentine Plains," in *Military Struggle and Identity Formation in Latin America*, ed. Nicola Foote and René D. Harder Horst (Gainesville: University Press of Florida, 2010), chap. 9.

115. Paul J. Vanderwood, *The Power of God Against the Guns of Government: Religious Upheaval in Mexico at the Turn of the Nineteenth Century* (Stanford CA: Stanford University Press, 1998); Robert M. Levine, *Vale of Tears: Revisiting the Canudos Massacre in Northeastern Brazil, 1893–1897* (Berkeley: University of California Press, 1995); Todd A. Diacon, *Millenarian Vision, Capitalist Reality: Brazil's Contestado Rebellion, 1912–1916* (Durham NC: Duke University Press, 1991), 122; Erick D. Langer, "Andean Rituals of Revolt: The Chayanta Rebellion of 1927," *Ethnohistory* 3 (1990), which observes how the swift defeat of the rebellion "showed the repressive power of the state when it mobilized police forces and soldiers armed with machine guns and cannons, arms which the Indians"—who wielded "clubs and sticks"—"could never hope to match" (237).

116. Reed, *The Caste War*, 95, 299, 371.

117. Frederick M. Nunn, *Yesterday's Soldiers: European Military Professionalism in South America, 1890–1940* (Lincoln: University of Nebraska Press, 1983). Roughly, German military (army) influence prevailed in Argentina and Chile, French influence in Brazil and Peru. Chile, given its incipient reputation as the "Prussia of South America," then supplied military expertise elsewhere in Latin America, notably Ecuador, Colombia, and El Salvador.

118. Alan Rouquié, *The Military and the State in Latin America* (Berkeley: University of California Press, 1989), 77, notes that Chilean military cadets still wore the pickelhaube in the 1980s. A rare statistical analysis of military recruitment and ethnicity is given by Richard N. Adams, "Race and Ethnicity in the Guatemalan Army, 1914," in Foote and Horst, *Military Struggle*, chap. 5. Based on 259 recruits from the Department of San Marcos, the data show that the ratio of Indians to Ladinos (3:1) roughly reflected the balance in both the departmental and the national populations as a whole (4:1): see 114. So Indians were only slightly more liable to recruitment than Ladinos.

However, while six of seven corporals were Indians, the officers all appear to have been Ladinos (125); indeed, the National Military Academy was, from its inception in the 1870, a preserve of the "better families," and "the possibility of Indian participation did not arise" (108).

119. Nunn, *Yesterday's Soldiers*, 25, 66. Some argue that this early French influence may have contributed to the unusually nationalist, populist, and developmentalist bent of the Peruvian army, which became politically decisive after 1968: Rouquié, *The Military and the State*, 78–79.

120. Todd A. Diacon, *Stringing Together a Nation: Cândido Mariano da Silva Rondon and the Construction of a Modern Brazil, 1906–1930* (Durham NC: Duke University Press, 2004); Raymond B. Craib, *Cartographic Mexico: A History of State Fixations and Fugitive Landscapes* (Durham NC: Duke University Press, 2004). Of course, the two processes often went together. As Craib narrates, in 1887 President Díaz despatched a surveying team to map and "divide the communal lands of the Yaqui and Mayo Indians in Sonora," in northwestern Mexico. He instructed the team leader to "direct [the Indians] in their labors such that they might enjoy the benefits of progress and bring them to civilization," and—"seeing like a state," we might say—he even stipulated the "rigorously rational" way that the land should be divided up and thus made suitable for settlement, production, and taxation (164–68, quotes on 165, 167; cf. James C. Scott, *Seeing Like a State* [New Haven CT: Yale University Press, 1998]). The Yaquis did not agree; as the project faltered, a big American "colonization company" was brought in to carry it through, and the simmering Yaqui rebellion gathered strength, eventually merging into the Mexican Revolution of 1910 (see Hu-Dehart, *Yaqui Resistance*).

121. Diacon, *Millenarian Vision*, 149–50. Central America followed the trend, as dispersed caudillo-led forces cohered into recognizable national armies from the 1870s, bringing about a "significant enlargement in the isthmian states' capacities for violence." However, since—with the exception of Costa Rica—these were "improvisational" states (see n. 64), the result was continued political violence and praetorianism: see Holden, *Armies Without Nations*, 37–41.

122. Not that the Mexican *rurales* were as ruthless and efficient as the old Porfirian myth depicted: Paul J. Vanderwood, *Disorder and Progress: Bandits, Police and Mexican Development* (Lincoln: University of Nebraska Press, 1981), chaps. 5–11. On Colombia, where national policing came relatively late, see Frédéric Martínez, "Las desilusiones del orden público: Los comienzos de la

Policía Nacional en Colombia, 1891–98," in *In Search of a New Order: Essays on the Politics and Society of Nineteenth-Century Latin America*, ed. Eduardo Posada-Carbó (London: ILAS, 1998).

123. Richard W. Slatta, *Gauchos and the Vanishing Frontier* (Lincoln: University of Nebraska Press, 1992), chap. 7.

124. Bulmer-Thomas, *Economic History*, 93–94. Daniela Marino, "La desamortización de las tierras de los pueblos (centro de México, siglo XIX): Balance historiográfico y fuentes para su estudio," *América Latina en la Historia Económica* 16 (2001): 33–43, offers a useful survey of what is a large and growing literature on Mexico, much of it regional or local in focus. On the Andean region (Peru, Bolivia, Ecuador, Colombia), which, along with Mexico, was the most seriously affected by this process, see Brooke Larson, *Trials of Nation-Making: Liberalism, Race and Ethnicity in the Andes, 1810–1910* (Cambridge: Cambridge University Press, 2004), 48–49, 86–93, 97–102, 142–44, 163 (the "yeomanry" quote), 213–28. Three features of this long and complicated process need to be clarified: first, though legal and constitutional measures may have mandated *desamortización*, it required economic incentives and suitable political circumstances to bring it about; second, some peasant societies doggedly resisted the process (or, in a few cases, took advantage of it to bolster a freehold peasantry); and third, in those extensive lowland regions (Cuba, Brazil, coastal Peru) where slave plantations had existed for centuries, serving commercial markets, this decisive transformation of landholding was unnecessary—labor regimes might change (as slavery was abolished), but the plantation was already a firm fixture and faced no recalcitrant challenge on the part of a traditional peasantry.

125. Hennessy, *The Frontier*, 83–85, 147; Collier and Sater, *A History of Chile*, 95–97; Mallon, *Courage Tastes of Blood*, chap. 2.

126. Bulmer-Thomas, *The Economic History*, 57–78; Topik and Wells, *The Second Conquest*; Gilbert M. Joseph, *Revolution from Without: Yucatán, Mexico and the United States, 1880–1924* (Cambridge: Cambridge University Press, 1982), chaps. 1, 2; David Rock, *Argentina, 1516–1987* (Berkeley: University of California Press, 1987), 131–52; Steven Topik and Mario Samper, "The Latin American Coffee Commodity Chain: Brazil and Costa Rica," in *From Silver to Cocaine: Latin American Commodity Chains and the Building of the World Economy, 1500–2000*, ed. Steven Topik, Carlos Marichal, and Zephyr Frank (Durham NC: Duke University Press, 2006), 118–46; Rosemary Thorp and Geoffrey Bertram, *Peru 1890–1977: Growth and Policy in an Open Economy* (London: Macmillan, 1978), chap. 4; Nils Jacobsen, *Mirages*

of Transition: The Peruvian Altiplano, 1780–1930 (Berkeley: University of California Press, 1993).

127. Richard Gott, "Latin America as a White Settler Society," *Bulletin of Latin American Research* 26, no. 2 (2007): 269–89. While I applaud Gott's effort to integrate Latin American history into a broader global context, I don't think the "white settler" thesis fits very well: white settlement in (formal) colonies such as New Zealand and British East Africa involved the direct displacement by recent "white" newcomers of dense existing populations, often of "peasants," who strenuously resisted the process (hence the Maori Wars and the Mau-Mau Rebellion). While the Spanish Conquest of the sixteenth century triggered such processes—and laid down an enduring ethnic/racial inequality—the nineteenth century was a different story: the tidal wave of genuine "white settlers"—mostly Spaniards and Italians—flooded into Argentina, Uruguay, and southern Brazil, none of which was an Indian/"brown"/peasant society (later, in the twentieth century, a secondary wavelet of white settlement similarly affected Cuba and Venezuela). Where dense Indian/"brown"/peasant societies persisted in Mexico, Central America, and the Andean region, European immigration was scant, since labor was abundant, and so wages were low; of course, in these regions racism was centuries old.

128. Fogarty, Gallo, and Diéguez, *Argentina y Australia*; Solberg, *The Prairies and the Pampas*, in which the contrast between Canadian and Argentine land tenure is neatly summarized: in Canada, the federal government's "massive land-distribution program" created a mosaic of "small, individually owned farms," while in Argentina, a policy of laissez-faire—indeed, "no national land policy existed in Argentina"—allowed "a small group of wealthy and powerful owners" to dominate the pampas, while direct cultivation devolved to a mass of relatively poor, highly mobile tenant farmers. Aside from demography and economics, the Canadian system encouraged "well-organized rural communities, strong cooperative institutions and powerful agrarian political movements"—all of which were (relatively) lacking in Argentina (52).

129. E. P. Thompson, "Time, Work-Discipline and Industrial Capitalism," *Past and Present* 38 (1967): 56–97.

130. Arnold T. Bauer, "Rural Workers in Spanish America: Problems of Peonage and Oppression," *Hispanic American Historical Review* 59, no. 1 (1979): 58–59.

131. Friedrich Hassaurek, *Four Years among the Ecuadorians* (Carbondale: Southern Illinois University Press, 1967), 72, III, notes how, in wartime, dragooned Indians also had to act as military porters; Clark, *Redemptive Work*, 79–80,

85, 91–92; Mario Miguel Mena Bazán, "Caminos, campesinos y modernización vial," in *Trabajos de historia: Religión, cultura y política en el Perú,
siglos XVII–XX*, ed. Dino León Fernández (Lima: UNMSM, 2011), 301–
34; Eduardo Bedoya Garland, "Bonded Labour, Coercion, and Capitalist
Development in Peru," *Quaderns de l'Institut Catalana d'Antopologia* 10
(1997): 9–38; Chiriboga, *Jornaleros*, 193–201; Clark, *Redemptive Work*, 75–76,
81–83; David McCreery, "'An Odious Feudalism': Mandamiento Labor and
Commercial Agriculture in Guatemala," *Latin America Perspectives* 13, no.
1 (1986): 99–117. In Guatemala, it seems, proletarianizing the Indians, apart
from being risky, was (as economists like to say) suboptimal: since coffee
was a highly seasonal crop, it made sense to draft seasonal labor from the
highlands when demand was high, thus avoiding the cost of supporting a
large superfluous labor force through the low season.
132. Joseph, *Revolution from Without*, 76. Contemporary references to Latin America's lazy natives are legion, for example: Hassaurek, *Four Years*, 41, 70, 90;
Holton, *New Granada*, 42, 44, 118–19, 220; Head, *Journeys across the Pampas*,
8–9, 14–15, 160. There was, of course, a nugget of reality lurking inside this
glob of racism: foreigners who were used to an established capitalist economy
in which proletarians, lacking their own means of production, were obliged
to work at the going—often very low—rate were taken aback when they
discovered that Latin American peasants and hunter-gatherers who had
not yet been proletarianized were unresponsive to cash incentives unless the
latter were both substantial and attractive (i.e., they enabled workers to buy
goods that they needed or wanted). And even if workers could be secured,
they came and went according to those needs/wants, sleeping off San Lunes,
seeking "target wages," and effectively working "part-time," whether on a
weekly or an annual basis. Thus, Hassaurek, *Four Years*, 113, complains that
"mechanics will work for three or four days and then suddenly stay away,
especially when they have succeeded in getting some money in advance."
See also Clark, *Redemptive Work*, 86. Developmental economists refer to
this phenomenon as the "S-shape labor supply curve."
133. Barbara Weinstein, *The Amazon Rubber Boom, 1850–1920* (Stanford CA:
Stanford University Press, 1983); Michael Edward Stanfield, *Red Rubber,
Bleeding Trees: Violence, Slavery and Empire in Northwest Amazonia, 1850–1933*
(Albuquerque: University of New Mexico Press, 1998), chap. 3. For reasons
I cannot explain, Ecuadorian rubber production—in contrast to Brazilian
and Peruvian—was the work of "smaller producers" who recruited Indian
labor on the basis of "negotiation" involving "patron-client relations." Not

that Ecuador was a stranger to repression and violence: when highland Indians rebelled against forced labor demands in 1871 they were "brutally repressed"; the local (Conservative) landlords called for exemplary executions, while their coastal (Liberal) rivals "thought that it would be much more instructive if the defeated rebels were sent to work on coastal plantations" (Clark, *Redemptive Work*, 29, 79).

134. Sarah Washbrook, *Producing Modernity in Mexico: Labour, Race and the State in Chiapas, 1876–1914* (Oxford: Oxford University Press, 2012), chaps. 7, 8; the phrase comes from Stanfield, *Red Rubber*, 41.

135. I discuss this mutation further in chapter 2. On the global appeal of positivism, see Johannes Feichtinger, Franz L. Fillafer, and Jan Surman, eds., *The Worlds of Positivism: A Global Intellectual History, 1770–1930* (Basingstoke: Palgrave Macmillan, 2017), especially part 1, which deals—in rather "intellectual" terms, as the title suggests—with Brazil, the Ottoman Empire, and British India.

136. Stanfield, *Red Rubber*, 41, notes how a Brazilian governor defended the use of coercion "by arguing that Indians forced to paddle canoes would become better citizens, as they learned 'love of work, love of family and of order.'" The so-called liberal revolutions/regimes evident in Central America from the 1870s were particularly illiberal, given that they were accompanied by enhanced centralized coercion and social control: Holden, *Armies Without Nations*, 37–38. There were, it should be said, some more enlightened aspects of positivistic politics: for example, the deployment of applied science in the interest of sanitation and public health. Thus, it has been suggested, late nineteenth-century Latin America saw the rise of "sanitarian states," which promoted—sometimes in heavy-handed fashion—vaccination programs, urban sanitation measures, and campaigns against major killers such as cholera and yellow fever: see Marcos Cueto and Steven Palmer, *Medicine and Public Health in Latin America: A History* (New York: Cambridge University Press, 2015), chap. 2. Needless to say, there are again clear "colonial" parallels.

137. In what follows I focus on Sarmiento, whose global vision is particularly striking. Justo Sierra took a narrower (Mexico-focused) view. However, his positivistic diagnosis of what Mexico needed and what President Díaz offered is broadly similar: given a wayward people steeped in "alcohol and ignorance," governed by backward warlords ("primitive satraps"), and afflicted by "savage hordes" of guerrillas, Mexico suffered from "an acute disease which required a drastic cure" at the hands of a strong leader commanding a powerful army; European immigrants were also essential, "for only European blood can keep the level of our civilization . . . from sinking" (Justo Sierra, *The*

Political Evolution of the Mexican People [Austin: University of Texas Press, 1969], 342–68). Jürgen Osterhammel, *The Transformation of the World: A Global History of the Nineteenth Century* (Princeton NJ: Princeton University Press, 2014), chap. 17, offers an interesting and genuinely "global"/"transnational" analysis of how the dichotomy of "civilization and exclusion" played out across the world (Sarmiento gets a mention [828]). Much of the analysis, however, focuses on the twin phenomena of slavery (and its aftermath) and anti-Semitism, the second of which is marginal to Latin America. Scant attention is paid to Latin American coercive labor systems (apart from Brazilian chattel slavery), and the portrait of the "Latin American hacienda" (683–84) is both cursory and questionable.

138. Domingo F. Sarmiento, *Facundo: Or, Civilization and Barbarism* (New York: Penguin, 1998), 44, 87, 20. See also 59 (more Cossacks) and 15, where the Argentine pampas "bring to mind the wilds of Asia," while the "lonely line of wagons" that crosses the wilderness resembles "the caravan of camels" that traverses the plains of Mesopotamia. Sarmiento was not the first Argentine to invoke Arab and Asiatic tropes: back in the 1820s, a colleague of the liberal/progressive President Bernardino Rivadavia invited him to take a walk beyond the familiar city center ("truly European in its habits, customs, and appearance") and, just a few blocks away, to contemplate a different world, the world of the slums (*arrabales*), that was "Arab, Abyssinian, Tartar and semi-savage" (Klaus Gallo, *Bernardino Rivadavia: El primer presidente argentino* [Buenos Aires: Edhasa, 2012], 105). Foreign travelers to Argentina regularly echoed such tropes as well: Slatta, *Gauchos*, 7, 21, 43.

139. Sarmiento, *Facundo*, 60, 95. Nicolas Shumway, *The Invention of Argentina* (Berkeley: University of California Press, 1991), 134, notes that Sarmiento, when in full Byronic flight, might seem to be "drawn to the titanic personality of the caudillo," but in terms of practical policy, "he consistently sought to eradicate gaucho and Indian life (by extermination if necessary), exclude dissenters, and force survivors into his vision of civilization: a modern, Europeanized Argentina."

140. Sarmiento, *Facundo*, 16, 20, 50, 59.

141. Sarmiento, *Facundo*, 126–27.

142. Darwin's account was based on the eyewitness account of a "very intelligent man," part of a company of 200 "banditti-like soldiers" who had recently pursued an Indian band of 110, "men, women and children," who were "nearly all taken or killed, for the soldiers sabre every man." The children were spared "to be sold or given away as servants or rather as slaves," but "all the women who appear above twenty years old are massacred in cold blood."

"When I exclaimed that this seemed rather inhuman," Darwin reports, his interlocutor answered, "Why, what can be done? They breed so" (Darwin, *Voyage of the Beagle*, 95–96). See also 113, 121, where Darwin observes that the "favourite occupation" of Estanislao López, governor of Santa Fé, was "hunting Indians: a short time since he slaughtered forty-eight, and sold the children at the rate of three or four pounds apiece."

143. Diana Sorensen Goodrich, *Facundo and the Construction of Argentine Culture* (Austin: University of Texas Press, 1996), 109–17.

144. Goodrich, *Facundo*, 115–17. Of course, Sarmiento's views were not shared by all his compatriots: Lucio V. Mansilla, twenty years his junior, who knew a great deal more about the Indians of the pampas, took a much more sympathetic and nuanced view: see *A Visit to the Ranquel Indians* (Lincoln: University of Nebraska Press, 1997). However, Argentine policy—including the "Conquest of the Desert"—carried the hallmark of Sarmiento's thinking. Contemporary critics of Sarmiento such as Alberdi and Echeverría nevertheless agreed with him on many of the ingredients of his prescription: "railroads, better river transportation, new sea-ports, private ownership of land and foreign invest-ment" (Shumway, *The Invention of Argentina*, 135; see also Slatta, *Gauchos*, 164–65). Furthermore, it has been argued that members of the "generation of '80," dominant between 1880 and 1916, typified by President Roca, and charac-terized by a progressive, positivistic, cosmopolitan, and elitist philosophy, were the intellectual children of Sarmiento: "In reality, the generation of '80 simply carried to their final outcome the principles of the civilizing policy whose brilliant champion had been Sarmiento" (José Luis Romero, *El desarrollo de las ideas en la sociedad argentina del siglo XX* [Mexico City: FCE, 1965], 16).

145. Georges Clemenceau, *South America Today* (London: T. Fisher Unwin, 1911), 81–82, 136, 138.

146. On the Anglophilia of the likes of Rui Barbosa, André Rebouças, Joaquim Nabuco, Viscount Mauá, and others, see Richard Graham, *Britain and the Onset of Modernization in Brazil, 1850–1914* (Cambridge: Cambridge University Press, 1968), 58, 61, 102, 210–13, 256, 268. Goodrich, *Facundo*, 94–95, 117, notes Sarmiento's admiration of the United States (notwithstanding the Civil War).

147. Sierra, *Political Evolution*, 361.

6. HOVERING DWARF

1. Since revolutions are processes whose start and stop dates are often hard to fix, I use the familiar dates, even if they are not conceptually consistent: the

Mexican and Bolivian revolutions started—in terms of successful violent rebellion—in 1910 and 1952, respectively, but the Cuban Revolution started before 1959, the latter being the date of the revolution's assumption of power. I omit putative Central American revolutions—notably the Sandinista in Nicaragua—for want of space and expertise. Contemporary commentators clearly saw these as the big three "social" revolutions of Latin America, worthy of comparison and contrast: Bolivia was "unique in South America in having passed through a profound social revolution" (Holliday to Foreign Office, November 3, 1960, FO 371/148758, AX 1015/22); furthermore, "Bolivia has had a social revolution more on the Mexican rather than the Cuban pattern" (Canadian ambassador, Lima, "Political, Social and Economic Conditions in Bolivia," December 15, 1961, in FO 371/162722, AX 1015/16). FO denotes British Foreign Office records housed in the UK National Archives, Kew, London.

2. This raises an interesting question: Why did these three revolutions—four if we were to include Nicaragua—fall within the American sphere of diplomatic and economic interest (as compared to Britain's Southern Cone sphere, namely, Argentina and Uruguay)? First, prior to 1952, the United States' commercial and diplomatic interest in Bolivia was quite small; only after the revolution did this poor, remote, landlocked country begin to figure prominently in the United States' rapidly burgeoning Cold War agenda. The story is well told in Kenneth D. Lehman, *Bolivia and the United States: A Limited Partnership* (Athens: University of Georgia Press, 1999). In contrast, Mexico and Cuba—and, we could add, Nicaragua—had fallen squarely within the American orbit since ca. 1900, if not before. A facile conclusion might be that American penetration provoked nationalist reactions and eventually revolution, but in fact the Mexican and Cuban revolutions, though certainly nationalistic, were less anti-American than often supposed. In both cases, however, the impact of American trade and investment profoundly affected the political economy of the two countries, leading to popular agrarian rebellion (especially in Mexico) and capricious ups and downs in export volumes and values (in Cuba and Bolivia, where sugar and tin were, respectively, the dominant exports). The Southern Cone, where British capital dominated, lacked a mass peasantry (so popular agrarian rebellion was largely off the agenda), and its integration into world—especially British—markets tended to be less destabilizing, since the demand for beef and grain was less elastic than that for sugar or industrial minerals such as tin.

3. Compare the useful comparative study by Cole Blasier, *Hovering Giant: U.S. Responses to Revolutionary Change in Latin America* (Pittsburgh: University of Pittsburgh Press, 1985).

4. Edward W. Said, *Orientalism* (New York: Vintage Books, 1979). Given the eager acceptance of Said's perspective, not least by those who may know little or nothing about the Arab/Islamic world, it is worth noting the telling critique of Robert Irwin, *For Lust of Knowing: Orientalists and Their Enemies* (London: Penguin, 2007). When it comes to these grand geocultural groupings and the "clash of civilisations" to which (some commentators glibly assert) they give rise, Latin America is distinctly anomalous: Is it part of "the West," perhaps "l'extrême occident," as Alain Rouquié called it? Or does it belong to some variegated "Third World," to be lumped in with Africa and Asia (but Asia minus Japan)? The first view, it seems to me, has some limited merit, but in general, I find these broadbrush geocultural categories to be more trouble than they're worth, so I don't feel any obligation to use them, still less to strive to clarify a confusion of their own making.

5. A somewhat scholastic but useful distinction that derives from Thomas Hobbes, *Leviathan*, chap. 15.

6. Lars Schoultz, *Beneath the United States* (Cambridge MA: Harvard University Press, 1998), xvi–xvii, prefers "mind-set" and on 1–13 gives some good early nineteenth-century examples.

7. Alan Knight, "U.S. Anti-imperialism and the Mexican Revolution," in *Empire's Twin: U.S. Anti-imperialism from the Founding Era to the Age of Terrorism*, ed. Ian Tyrrell and Jay Sexton (Ithaca NY: Cornell University Press, 2015), chap. 5.

8. Blasier, *Hovering Giant*; Stephen G. Rabe, *Eisenhower and Latin America: The Foreign Policy of Anticommunism* (Chapel Hill: University of North Carolina Press, 1988), 77–83, 117–33. British observers noted the contrast: Holliday, La Paz to Foreign Office, November 21, 1960, FO 371/148758, AX 1015/27.

9. The term was coined, in the context of British imperialism, by Ronald Robinson and John Gallagher with Alice Denny, *Africa and the Victorians: The Official Mind of Imperialism* (London: Macmillan, 1961). It may be disputed whether an American "official mind" existed, at least prior to 1945 (I recall hearing Ernest May query its existence in a discussion at the time of the centenary of 1898), but I note that some expert scholars are happy to use it: for example, Jay Sexton, "The U.S. in the First Age of Decolonization," paper presented at the workshop "The Geopolitics of Independence in the Caribbean 1800–70," Nuffield College, Oxford, May 10, 2012. Of course, times change, and right now (2020), in the era of President Trump, the very notion of an "official mind" sounds slightly oxymoronic.

10. Thus, President Eisenhower had the good sense—or good luck—to rely heavily on the perceptive Bolivian advice of his younger brother, Milton, whose "rich and varied career" included trips to Latin America, while in contrast, his policy toward Guatemala was influenced by the knuckle-headed views of Robert Patterson (U.S. ambassador to Guatemala, 1948–51), inventor of the famous "duck test" (if it looks, swims, and quacks like a duck, it's a duck, i.e., a Communist). See Rabe, *Eisenhower and Latin America*, 28–29, 66–68, 80, 82, 135–36, 141–42; and Richard H. Immerman, *The CIA in Guatemala* (Austin: University of Texas Press, 1982), 102.

11. Ronald Robinson, "Non-European Foundations of European Imperialism: Sketch for a Theory of Collaboration," in *Studies in the Theory of Imperialism*, ed. Roger Owen and Bob Sutcliffe (London: Longman, 1972), 120–23. I discuss this question further in chapter 5 of this book. I realize that "geopolitics" implies a kind of "mindset," a way of viewing the world, and that geopolitical decisions and policies do not arise "neutrally" from "objective" situations. But I would argue that facts on the ground relating to considerations of geography, military capability, economic assets, and "excentric" or "peripheral" politics, all of which are autonomous of metropolitan perceptions, are crucial and often determining.

12. Not least because, as I suggest in chapter 5, the British operated with a career diplomatic service and, especially in respect to Latin America, could largely insulate policy-making from an intrusive legislature and public opinion; in the United States, things were different. The British admiral commanding in Mexican waters in 1914 commented on the remarkable latitude enjoyed by his American counterpart, Admiral Fletcher, which he attributed in part to the fact that "in America, unlike England, they had no trained diplomatists" (Cradock to Admiralty, February 19, 1914, FO 371/2026, 91/11154).

13. F. W. Maitland, *Selected Historical Essays* (Cambridge: Cambridge University Press, 1957), 91.

14. British investment in Mexico on the eve of the revolution stood at approximately $700–800 million, compared to perhaps $1 billion of U.S. investment; however, British trade was substantially less than American and declining: P. A. R. Calvert, *The Mexican Revolution: The Diplomacy of Anglo-American Conflict, 1910–1914* (Cambridge: Cambridge University Press, 1968), 19–20; Paolo Riguzzi, *Reciprocidad imposible? La política del comercio entre México y Estados Unidos, 1857–1938* (Mexico City: El Colegio Mexiquense, 2003), 170, 173–74.

15. Cowdray's own words in the memo of a conversation with U.S. ambassador Walter Hines Page, London, January 9, 1914, Cowdray Papers, box A4, Science Museum, London. For a detailed and sympathetic portrayal of Cowdray, see Paul Garner, *Leones británicos y águilas mexicanos: Negocios, política e imperio en la carrera de Weetman Pearson en México, 1889–1919* (Mexico City: FCE, 2013).

16. Riguzzi, *Reciprocidad imposible?*, 173.

17. Thus, as part of this balancing act, President Salinas (1988–94), as he embarked on his neoliberal project of economic opening, sought European (and Japanese) investment as a counterweight to the United States. But when he found that Europe—Germany in particular—was immersed in its own post-1989 integration process, he opted for NAFTA, abandoning balance for a regulated but dependent relationship with the United States. The Davos meeting of February 1990 appears to have been a turning point: Carlos Salinas de Gortari, *México: Un paso difícil a la modernidad* (Barcelona: Plaza & Janes, 2000), chap. 2, esp. 49–52.

18. There is a large, diverse, and sometimes polemical literature: Calvert, *The Mexican Revolution*, chap. 2, offers a balanced resume of 1910–11; see also Jonathan C. Brown, *Oil and Revolution in Mexico* (Berkeley: University of California Press, 1993), 173–75, for the probably marginal role of the oil companies.

19. The major American interests in Mexico may not have been unanimous, but there was clear support for the Porfirian old regime and suspicion of Madero: William Schell Jr., *Integral Outsiders: The American Colony in Mexico City, 1876–1911* (Wilmington DE: SR Books, 2001), 184. John Mason Hart, *Empire and Revolution: The Americans in Mexico Since the Civil War* (Berkeley: University of California Press, 2002) offers abundant examples of American interests benefiting from their close liaison with the Porfirian regime.

20. Calvert, *The Mexican Revolution*, 110–11; Friedrich Katz, *The Secret War in Mexico: Europe, the United States and the Mexican Revolution* (Chicago: University of Chicago Press, 1981), 46–49.

21. "It was essential to give the new [Huerta] government immediate support," urged the British minister, since it "affords good prospects of stability" (Stronge to Foreign Office, February 21, March 3, 1913, FO 371/6269/8498, 10599).

22. Contrary to some assertions, President Wilson was not myopically focused on democracy ("teach[ing] South America to elect good men"); he also believed that the Mexican Revolution embodied social aspirations—not

least land reform—that demanded political attention: Spring-Rice, Washington, to Foreign Office, February 7, 1914, FO 371/2025, 91/7144. Two Foreign Office comments on Wilson's opinion stated: "impossible to understand" and "very disappointing reading." The Germans, in particular, inclined to this second view (though some British observers concurred); however, the British ambassador in Washington believed that to see Wilsonian policy as a "skilfully conducted campaign with a view to making a military intervention a necessity and even a popular necessity" was to "interpret American politics in terms of the German General Staff" (but then the ambassador in question, Cecil Spring-Rice, was a very high-minded fellow who was responsible for converting Holst's "Jupiter the Bringer of Jollity" into the maudlin hymn "I Vow to Thee My Country"): Spring-Rice to Foreign Office, January 23, 1914, FO 371/2025, 91/5205.

23. Hohler's comment on the pamphlet *The Mexican Situation from a Mexican Point of View*, published by the Confidential Agency of the Constitutional Government of Mexico, Washington DC, December 1, 1913, in Spring-Rice to Foreign Office, February 14, 1914, FO 371/2025, 91/8667.

24. F. Goodchild (Mazatlán banker) to W. Hearn, December 18, 1913, FO 371/2025, 91/4058; report of Consul Holms, Guadalajara, February 11, 1914, enclosed in Carden to Foreign Office, February 18, 1914, FO 371/2025, 91/10096; and Holms, again, September 1, 1914, FO 371/2031, 91/52831, when, following the victory of the revolutionaries, Holms continued to regard them as "villainous people in every sense of the word. Their appearances, manners, gestures and conversation were those of brigands."

25. Admiral Cradock, Veracruz, to Admiralty, February 19, 1914, in FO 371/2025, 91/11154.

26. Comment of Percy Furber in Foreign Office meeting also attended by Lord Cowdray, June 23, 1914, FO 371/2029, 91/29368.

27. Calvert, *The Mexican Revolution*.

28. Calvert, *The Mexican Revolution*, 233–34. The nefarious role of the Japanese was also blamed—and, again, greatly exaggerated: Hohler to Grey, March 11, 1914, FO 371/2025, 91/10934,

29. A Canadian diplomat noted how some "conservative upper-class Bolivians" maintained that "the United States had really instigated the agrarian reform movement in Bolivia," a "thesis" that the experienced rural sociologist Richard Patch "dismissed as quite absurd," since—he countered—"the violent agrarian reform which took place in 1952–53 was a grassroots or spontaneous movement which forced the hand of the government" (report

by the Canadian ambassador to Peru, December 15, 1961, in FO 371/162722, AX 1015/16).

30. Thus, while the Veracruz invasion was clearly designed to weaken and topple Huerta, some historians seem determined to construe it—against all the evidence—as an attempt by the United States to arrest the course of the revolution, a remarkable example of dogma trumping data. See, for example, William Appleman Williams, *America Confronts a Revolutionary World: 1776–1976* (New York: William and Morrow, 1976), 21, 140, which stresses Wilson's "counterrevolutionary" policy in Mexico.

31. Williams, *American Confronts*, 27, which notes that by ca. 1900 that commitment was "highly qualified" (137). In the case of Mexico, however, Woodrow Wilson, in conversation with Hohler, was explicit: "He knew of no instance in history in which political advance had been made by benefits from above: they all had to be gained by the efforts and the blood of the elements from below, of those who were struggling to be free" (Hohler memo, February 11, 1914, in Spring-Rice to Grey, February 14, 1914, FO 371/2025, 91/8667). One might be tempted to dismiss this comment as mere flannel; however, it was an opinion guaranteed to dismay Wilson's interlocutor, and more important, it informed Wilson's policy toward Mexico in 1913–14.

32. William Roger Louis, *Imperialism at Bay: The United States and the Decolonization of the British Empire, 1941–1945* (Oxford: Oxford University Press, 1977), chap. 6; Williams, *America Confronts*, 143–44; on Mexico's economic-nationalist challenge to U.S. business interests, see Robert Freeman Smith, *The United States and Revolutionary Nationalism in Mexico, 1916–1932* (Chicago: University of Chicago Press, 1972).

33. W. Langley, minute on Spring-Rice to Foreign Office, February 8, 1914, FO 371/2025, 91/5906, which questions the view that U.S. intervention in Mexico should be avoided at all costs; in fact, Langley argues, "it would be desirable if thereby an end could be put to the present situation" of chaos and civil war.

34. The British foreign secretary, the Liberal Sir Edward Grey, told the U.S. ambassador that President Wilson's "altruism" might be suitable in the case of a "great civilized country" like Britain or the United States (or, he might have said, Italy, since his Liberal forerunners had supported national self-determination at the time of the Risorgimento), "but Mexico was really an Indian state"; hence, "altruism" was a waste of time (Grey to Barclay [Washington DC], July 2, 1914, FO 371/2029, 91/30568).

35. Hohler compared Mexico's Indians—over 75 percent of the population, he alleged—to Egypt's fellaheen: "People such as those needed a firm but benevolent hand: firmness to control them within the bounds of order and benevolence to educate them and elevate their moral standards" (memo of February 11, 1914, FO 371/2025, 91/8667). As I argue in chapter 5, colonial attitudes of this kind were common among European observers of Latin America, but they were also shared by a good many elite Latin Americans.

36. Quotations from F. Goodchild (Mazatlán banker) to W. Hearn, December 18, 1913, FO 371/2025, 91/4058, and Hohler, memo of February 11, 1914, FO 371/2025, 91/8667.

37. Emily S. Rosenberg and Norman L. Rosenberg, "From Colonialism to Professionalism: The Public-Private Dynamic in United States Foreign Financial Advising, 1898–1929," *Journal of American History* 74 (June 1987): 59–82. Further examples are given in chapter 5.

38. However, a parliamentary question—asking whether "the whole territory of the Mexican Republic, or only its northern provinces, were within the sphere of influence of the US," as southern Persia was in a designated British "sphere"—prompted a clear-cut negative from the Foreign Office: there was no such analogy. British deference to the United States was informal and pragmatic but no less compelling for that. See FO 371/2025, 91/9998.

39. Sounded out by General Leonard Wood, who dissented from President Wilson's policy toward Mexico and suggested a multilateral Great Power intervention, British ambassador Spring-Rice told the general that he was "quite sure the British Government would never even entertain such an idea; that they would never send a man to Mexico" (Spring-Rice memo, February 12, 1914, FO 371/2025, 91/8667). See also W. Langley to Directors of the Sonora (Mexico) Land and Timber Co., March 3, 1914, FO 371/2025, 91/8940.

40. Thurstan to Foreign Office, March 20, 1917, FO 371/2966, 91/88967.

41. Holms to King, August 4, 1924, FO 723/57. Holms goes on to compare the killing of Rosalie Evans to the execution by the Germans of Nurse Edith Cavell, "who also died in defence of what she deemed to be the right."

42. For this reason, Lorenzo Meyer, *Su Majestad Británica contra la Revolución Mexicana, 1900–1950* (Mexico City: El Colegio de México, 1991), though lively and informative, greatly exaggerates the significance of the conflict, certainly for Britain, perhaps also for Mexico.

43. A depiction in which U.S. ambassador Josephus Daniels happily colluded.

44. Dutton-Pegram to Rees, January 4, 1939, FO 723/256.

45. George Philip, *Oil and Politics in Latin America* (Cambridge: Cambridge University Press, 1982), 206–7. The boss in question, Henri Deterding, "was incapable of conceiving of Mexico as anything but a Colonial Government to which you simply dictated orders" (Assheton's words).

46. Rosa King, *Tempest over Mexico* (London: Methuen, 1936), 63, 122, 276, 293–94, 295.

47. Rosa King report in Hohler to Foreign Office, November 30, 1914, FO 371/2031, 91/76893.

48. One recalls Kipling's "new-caught, sullen peoples, half-devil and half-child" (*The White Man's Burden*, 1899). See Hohler to Foreign Office, November 30, 1914, FO 371/2031, 91/76893 and FO (EWJL) minutes.

49. King to Foreign Office, May 3, 1924, FO 204/582, comments on soon-to-be-president Calles paying homage at Zapata's tomb and recalls Zapata, "whose deeds of cruelty when he laid waste the state of Morelos . . . earned him the name of the Attila of Mexico." Of course, Federal generals Victoriano Huerta, Juvencio Robles, and Pablo González were the chief culprits when it came to "laying waste" to Morelos.

50. Graham Greene, *The Lawless Roads* (London: Longman, 1939). In Marie-Françoise Allain, *The Other Man: Conversations with Graham Greene* (Harmondsworth: Penguin Books, 1984), Greene concedes that "I made my journey through Mexico in 1938 with the aim of denouncing the religious persecution" (118). The dyspeptic quality of *The Lawless Roads* may have something to do with the fact that while he was in Mexico, Greene suffered both dysentery and what he called "ticks on my backside" (Allain, *The Other Man*, 17, 53). On the other hand, Greene claimed that "if a country interests me I like to study it in depth" (56), from which one might conclude that Greene not only did not like Mexico but also wasn't much interested in it.

51. The revolutionaries being "bandits" and "criminals," who had given Mexico "twenty-five years of graft, bloodshed and bankruptcy" (Evelyn Waugh, *Mexico: An Object Lesson* [Boston: Little, Brown, 1939], 67–68, 84).

52. John Carey, *The Intellectuals and the Masses* (London: Faber, 1992). A distaste for consumerism and materialism often consorted with anti-Americanism, which Greene, for one, admitted to be one of his few consistent traits: Allain, *The Other Man*, 93–94. Similar anti-American sentiments, of course, fueled British elite philo-Communism, as in the cases of the "Cambridge spies"—Burgess, MacLean, Philby, and Blunt.

53. Allain, *The Other Man*, 49. This admission—made in the 1980s—is all the more striking since Greene had regularly visited Panama, Nicaragua, and

Cuba (the latter, six times between 1957 and 1966), and he recounts long conversations with both Torrijos and Castro, among others.

54. By way of illustration, British investment in Mexico (1913) was about $800 million (current U.S. dollars), compared to $220 million in Cuba and only $2 million in Bolivia: J. Fred Rippy, "British Investments in Latin America, End of 1913," *Journal of Modern History* 19, no. 3 (1947): 226–34. Forty years later, at the time of the Bolivian and Cuban Revolutions, British investment stood at $30 million in Cuba and—though I have not been able to get reliable data—even less in Bolivia.

55. Tin, which represented the bulk (approximately 70 percent) of Bolivia's exports, was subject to severe vicissitudes due to both fluctuating wartime demand (e.g., 1939–45 and 1950–52) and the dogmatic efforts of the postwar Truman administration to combat economic nationalism in Latin America, efforts that, counterproductively, helped precipitate the nationalist revolution of 1952: Glenn J. Dorn, "Pushing Tin: U.S.-Bolivian Relations and the Coming of the National Revolution," *Diplomatic History* 35, no. 2 (2011): 203–28. Meanwhile, tin was also a bone of contention in the old story of Anglo-American economic competition in Latin America: Olivia Saunders, "Preserving the Status Quo: Britain, the United States, and Bolivian Tin, 1946–56," *International History Review* 38 (2016): 551–72.

56. Daniel Rubiera Zim, "Straining the Special Relationship: British and U.S. Policies toward the Cuban Revolution, 1959–1961," *Cuban Studies* 33 (2002): 73, 84–85. I have been unable to come up with data for Bolivia ca. 1952, though British investment there would have been substantially less.

57. The American economic stake in Cuba dwarfed the United Kingdom's stake. Total U.S./Cuba trade averaged some $860 million a year during the 1950s, nearly twelve times greater than UK trade ($75 million), while U.S. investment in the island was thirty-two times greater than British investment ($960 million as against $30 million): data compiled from Leland L. Johnson, "U.S. Business Interests in Cuba and the Rise of Castro," Rand Corporation Paper (June 1964), 4; and Servando Valdés Sánchez, "Anglo-Cuban Diplomacy: The Economic and Political Links with Britain, 1945–60," *International Journal of Cuban Studies* 8, no. 1 (2016): 56–73. Of course, the sociopolitical impact of American economic predominance is another matter. Louis Pérez, pointing out that, "following World War II, Cubans were integrated into North American economic structures more fully than ever before," goes on to argue that this "close linkage," coupled with "economic stagnation in the 1950s," "all but guaranteed to raise Cuban frustration,"

which contributed to the revolution: Louis A. Pérez Jr., *Cuba and the United States: Ties of Singular Intimacy* (Athens: University of Georgia Press, 1990), 226, 228–29. However, the years preceding the Cuban Revolution (1952–57) did not see economic stagnation; U.S. investment rose substantially; and, if British reports can be trusted, Cuban political grievances had more to do with Batista's authoritarianism and corruption than with American "domination" and consequent "frustration." See also Morris H. Morley, "The U.S. Imperial State in Cuba, 1952–1958: Policymaking and Capitalist Interests," *Journal of Latin American Studies* 14, no. 1 (1982): 144, 148–51.

58. U.S. food aid to Bolivia significantly increased following the 1952 Revolution, but economic aid and credit soared after 1960, growing sixfold in four years, when, in the wake of the Cuban Revolution, Bolivia became "something of a showcase for the Alliance for Progress" (Lehman, *Bolivia*, 118–19, 136). The British ambassador to Bolivia concurred: "In foreign affairs the United States Government [was] . . . the dominating partner," a "domination" that the Alliance for Progress only reinforced: Holliday, La Paz, to Foreign Office, January 1, 1962, FO 371/162721, AX 1011/1.

59. Lehman, *Bolivia*, 135–36. Again, British sources shed light on American policy-making, showing, for example, that Cuba's turn to the USSR after 1959 was not an unfortunate and unforeseen consequence of the American economic boycott but rather the deliberate objective of U.S. policy, which, Washington wrongly believed, would discredit Castro both within and beyond Cuba and thus contribute to his speedy downfall: Zim, "Straining the Special Relationship," 80.

60. On the United States and Britain against Germany, see Katz, *The Secret War*; Nancy Mitchell, *The Danger of Dreams: German and American Imperialism in Latin America* (Chapel Hill: University of North Carolina Press, 1999); Friedrich E. Schuler, *Mexico between Hitler and Roosevelt: Mexican Foreign Relations in the Age of Lázaro Cárdenas, 1934–1940* (Albuquerque: University of New Mexico Press, 1998).

61. Walter LaFeber, *The New Empire: An Interpretation of American Expansion, 1860–1898* (Ithaca NY: Cornell University Press, 1963), 218–29, 281–82.

62. Regarding policy-making "lenses" (a.k.a. stereotypes, "core beliefs," or "cognitive maps"), see Lars Schoultz, *National Security and United States Policy toward Latin America* (Princeton NJ: Princeton University Press, 1987), 12, 14, 30.

63. Fordham, Havana, to Foreign Office, January 16, 1957, FO 371/126467, AK 1015/3. President Eisenhower's brother, Milton, noted the propensity of Latin

American *políticos* to play the Communist card as a "way to get action out of the United States" (Schoultz, *National Security*, 15).

64. "Political, social and economic considerations in Bolivia," report by the Canadian ambassador to Peru, December 15, 1961, in FO 371/162722, AX 1015/16. In this context, it is also worth noting that neighboring states contributed to these perceptions, no doubt with a view to their own interests: "Peruvians like to represent Bolivia as a simmering kettle of Communism," reported the British representative in La Paz (J. Thynne Henderson to Foreign Office, February 22, 1960, FO 371/148756, AX 1011/1).

65. Fordham, Havana, to Foreign Office, August 30, 1957, FO 371/26470, AK 1052/2.

66. As Ambassador J. Garnett Lomax (La Paz) put it, rather stating the obvious, "HMG's aversion to Communism in any form was open and unconcealed" (to Foreign Office, January 26, 1950, FO 371/81859, AX 1015/4).

67. Immerman, *The CIA in Guatemala*, 102.

68. Holliday, La Paz, to Foreign Office, November 3, 1960, FO 371/148758, AX 1015/22 (and note the telltale "indoctrination"). Ten years earlier, we read of Soviet agents, "liberally supported with funds from Moscow," who sought to create "a state of complete disorder in the Republic, by progressive steps: revolution, civil war, with the final eclipse of all authority to be contrived by an Indian uprising" (J. Garnett Lomax, La Paz, to Foreign Office, May 5, 1950, FO 371/81858, AX 1013/1).

69. Fordham, Havana, to Foreign Office, July 8, 1957, FO 371/126467, AK 1015/28.

70. J. Garnett-Lomax, La Paz, to Foreign Office, April 12, 1950, FO 371/81859, AX 1015/11. At the same time, a secondary domino theory also did the rounds, imputing external subversion not to the Communists but to Argentina's Peronist government, an imputation that the British, perhaps, were particularly disposed to credit and that may even have had some tenuous basis in fact. See J. Garnett-Lomax, La Paz, to Foreign Office, January 26, 1950, FO 371/81859, AX 1015/4. Of course, this fear rapidly petered out in the 1950s.

71. Holliday, La Paz, to Foreign Office, January 1, 1962, FO 371/162721, AX 1011/1. A year earlier, Holliday had reported that while there was considerable sympathy for the Cuban Revolution in Bolivia, the Bolivian Revolution of 1952 had been "on quite different lines" from the Cuban, and it was therefore "dangerous to equate any future revolution in Latin America with the Cuban Revolution" (November 21, 1960, FO 371/148758, AX 1015/27).

72. Bullock to Foreign Office, August 19, 1964, FO 371/174429, AX 1015/53.

73. Mary Kay Vaughan, *The State: Education and Social Class in Mexico, 1880–1928* (DeKalb: Northern Illinois University Press, 1982), 39; Herbert S. Klein, "Social Change in Bolivia Since 1952," in *Proclaiming Revolution*, ed. Merilee S. Grindle and Pilar Domingo (Cambridge MA: Harvard University Press, 2003), 236; Pérez, *Cuba and the United States*, 227.

74. Victor Bulmer-Thomas, *The Economic History of Latin America* (Cambridge: Cambridge University Press, 1994), 223, 444.

75. In 1910 Mexico had 280 telephones per 100,000 population, Bolivia (1952) 367, and Cuba (1959) 3,183: B. R. Mitchell, *International Historical Statistics: The Americas and Australasia* (Detroit: Gale Research, 1983), 747, 751. In the Mexican case, it is clear that having a telephone did not necessarily mean having a functioning telephone. I don't know whether the Cuban and Bolivian telephone systems were any better.

76. Catholic political mobilization took off with the initial Madero revolution of 1910; later, even after the original Partido Católico Nacional was eliminated and the armed rebels of the Cristiada were, more or less, defeated, new—supposedly apolitical—Catholic mass organizations sprang up and flourished under the banner of Acción Católica, beginning in the early 1930s, a decade that also witnessed the rapid rise of the militant Unión Nacional Sinarquista and the—discreetly Catholic—Partido Acción Nacional. In Bolivia, the Falange Socialista Boliviano played a somewhat similar role, acquiring a "strongish following among students," in the army, and even, allegedly, among Bolivia's miners: Holliday to Foreign Office, March 27, 1962, FO 371/162722, AX 1015/12. Interestingly, Cuba harbored no comparable Catholic/clerical/right-wing party or movement.

77. The squatters and subsistence farmers of the Sierra Maestra assumed an important role in Cuba's "peasant war" after 1956, but in previous years the *colonos*—"la clase más cubana"—had successfully pressed their nationalist and socioeconomic claims in the political arena. In the case of Bolivia, veterans' organizations, products of the Chaco War, also played a part in prerevolutionary mass politics.

78. Which, though not officially recognized, "adopted such threatening resolutions that the warders petitioned the authorities to disband it. In the investigation which followed the Union succeeded in getting the prison governor and his assistant placed on trial on a variety of major charges" ("Report on Labour Affairs Bolivia, April and May 1956," in J. Garnett-Lomax to Foreign Office, July 13, 1956, FO 371/120480, AX 2181/5).

79. Holliday, La Paz, to Foreign Office, October 17, 1960, FO 371/148748, AX 1015/22.

80. Again, the figures are suggestive: in 1921 Mexico had 69 university students per 100,000 population (and many of those students were in fact quite conservative and antirevolutionary); Bolivia in 1950 had 153, and Cuba in 1959 had 300: Mitchell, *International Historical Statistics*, 877, 878, 881. The growth in numbers was driven by the expansion in particular of public higher education, which tended to produce a more radical student body—hence the marked shift in Mexican student politics between the revolutionary period (ca. 1910–40) and the generation of the 1950 and 1960s and beyond. The latter generation is well covered, for Mexico City, by Jaime Pensado, *Rebel Mexico: Student Unrest and Authoritarian Political Culture during the Long Sixties* (Stanford CA: Stanford University Press, 2013).

81. Fordham, Havana, to Foreign Office, March 14, 1957, FO 371/126467, AK 1015/12. J. B. Vincent, minute on Fordham, Havana, to Foreign Office, March 14, 1957, FO 371/126467, AK 1015/12, concludes that student activism is "endemic in Cuba" and explains the demonstrable bravery of students who confronted Batista's ruthless repression in terms of a bizarre cod-psychology: "The excitement of organizing a coup of this nature would drug the fears of death of the organizers."

82. The Organización Regional Interamericana de Trabajadores was established in Mexico City in 1951 under the aegis of the American Federation of Labor. Replacing the Confederación Interamericana de Trabajadores (1948), it was designed to combat Communist and leftist trade unionism in the Americas: Moisés Poblete Troncoso and Ben G. Burnett, *The Rise of the Latin American Labor Movement* (New Haven CT: College and University Press, 1960), 140–46. ORIT bulletins can be found enclosed with reports from La Paz: for example, J. Garnett-Lomax to Foreign Office, May 15, 1956, FO 371/120480, AX 2181/4.

83. UN technical assistance in Bolivia was "wholly ineffective," since "the defects which [the mission] was sent to remedy, it seems to have adopted, in its zeal to be self-effacing and anonymous" ("Report on Labour Affairs Bolivia," August–September 1956, FO 371/120480, AX 2181/7).

84. "Peripheral" states also played the "soft-power" game. Mexico was a Latin American pioneer, as the new revolutionary regime of the 1920s deployed cultural resources—the country's pre-Hispanic heritage and the didactic murals of Rivera and others—to influence American opinion both official and public: Alan Knight, "History, Heritage, and Revolution: Mexico,

c.1910–c.1940," *Past and Present* 226, supp. 10 (2015): 299–325. Cuba had few such "soft" assets (unless we include sun, beaches, and mojitos), while Bolivia, lying off the tourist beaten track, was slow to capitalize on its pre-Hispanic past. Even when it did, the results—at least in jaded British eyes—were unimpressive: the British ambassador sniffily reported that when Bolivia's director of archaeology, Carlos Ponce Sanjinés, took His Royal Highness the Duke of Edinburgh on a personal tour of the ruins of Tiwanaku, "neither HRH nor I were much impressed by the ruins or by Sr Ponce" (Holliday, La Paz, to Foreign Office, September 16, 1963, FO 371/168565, AX 1015/24).

85. Or, indeed, the Bolivian military. Their relations with the United States are beyond the scope of this chapter, but the British were well aware that U.S. aid to Bolivia had a military dimension. At the parade celebrating the tenth anniversary of the revolution in April 1962, the army deployed a "large amount of new motorized and mechanized equipment of US origin"; indeed, so new was the hardware and so perfunctory its preparation that "the US 'friendship' labels were still visible" on the equipment. In contrast, the peasant militia still carried "the rifles handed out to them in 1952" (Holliday, La Paz, to Foreign Office, April 10, 1962, FO 371/162722, AX 1015/14).

86. Hohler, Mexico City, to Foreign Office, October 20, 1914, FO 371/2031/68897.

87. Compare Ruth Berins Collier and David Collier, *Shaping the Political Arena* (Princeton NJ: Princeton University Press, 1991).

88. Holliday, La Paz, November 3, 1960, FO 371/148758, AX 1015/22. Had Holliday been fortifying himself with a little coca on the way?

89. Katz, *The Secret War*, 350–78.

90. As Paolo Riguzzi rightly points out, the notion that the Allied war effort depended crucially on Mexican oil supplies is greatly exaggerated: see Paolo Riguzzi and Patrica de los Ríos, *Las relaciones México–Estados Unidos, 1756–2020*, vol. 2, *Destino no manifiesto? 1867–2010* (Mexico City: UNAM, 2012), 175–77. On the Anglo-American dimension of the Zimmermann Telegram, see the cogent study of Thomas Boghardt, *The Zimmermann Telegram: Intelligence, Diplomacy and America's Entry into World War I* (Annapolis MD: Naval Institute Press, 2012).

91. In order to gauge Mexican public opinion during the war and in the absence of relevant polling data, the British dispatched diplomats to Mexico City cinemas to watch the newsreels and report on public reactions to salient events in the war, such as the fall of France and the Battle of the River Plate.

92. J. Thynne Henderson, La Paz, to Foreign Office, February 22, 1960, FO 371/148756, AX 1011/1.

93. Holliday, La Paz, to Foreign Office, October 17, 1960, FO 371/148758, AX 1015/22.

94. Holliday, La Paz, to Foreign Office, October 17, 1960.

95. J. Garnett-Lomax, La Paz, January 26, 1950, FO 371/81859, AX 1015/4.

96. Though Holman noted the "fickle nature and temperament of the ordinary Cuban" and dismissed the assault on the Moncada barracks on July 23, 1953, as "just another hair-brained [*sic*] or suicide escapade" undertaken by "hotheads" (Havana, January 13, 1953, and July 29, 1953, FO 371/103376, AK 1015/1, AK 1015/15).

97. J. Garnett-Lomax, La Paz, May 5, 1950, FO 371/81858, AX 1013/1.

98. Thus, under Batista, government censorship severely limited the spread of news, and "one is obliged to rely largely for one's information on oral reports and rumours of which there is no lack" (Fordham, Havana, January 22, 1957, FO 371/126467, AK 1015/8).

99. Stuart Sutherland, *Irrationality* (Harmondsworth: Penguin, 1992), 9–10.

100. Carden to Foreign Office, January 25, 1914, FO 371/2025, 91/3575, which adds that his French and German colleagues agreed with his diagnosis.

101. Carden to Foreign Office, February 6, 1914, FO 371/2025, 91/5540.

102. Carden to Foreign Office, February 7, 1914, FO 371/2025, 91/5736. President Wilson was "badly informed," Carden later added, "if he thinks there is any reasonable prospect of Constitutionalist forces being strong enough to take the capital" (which, of course, they did six months later): Carden to Foreign Office, February 13, 1914, FO 371/2025, 91/6705.

103. Bullock to Foreign Office, August 19, 1964, FO 371/174429, AX 1015/53.

104. Fordham to Foreign Office, January 30, 1957, FO 371/126465, AK 1011/1. One wonders what corroborative evidence enabled the Foreign Office to credit Fordham's report.

105. Fordham to Foreign Office, October 23, 1957, FO 371/126467, AK 1015/45.

106. This is particularly true of Mexico and Cuba, where the capital remained in the hands of the government until rebels from the "provinces" seized power in 1914 and 1959, respectively. Bolivia, where the revolution involved a major urban insurrection in La Paz, was a different case.

107. By "sociocultural" I refer to the education and recruitment of entrants to the Foreign Service, which, for want of expertise, I have not attempted to evaluate. Of course, this specific factor cannot be isolated from broader trends, such as decolonization abroad and, perhaps, Britain's own changing class relations (e.g., the electoral victory of the Labour Party in 1945, the advent

of the welfare state, and the political salience of British trade unions in the 1950s and 1960s).

7. WORKERS AND PEASANTS

1. Since discussions about revolutions—their character and consequences—often hinge upon chronological distinctions (which phase of a putative revolution are we discussing?), I should clarify that I follow a fairly conventional approach: the Mexican Revolution began in 1910; it involved a decade of destructive civil war, followed by two further decades (1920–40) when the infant revolutionary state consolidated its authority and undertook a program of radical social reform. After ca. 1940 a new generation entered power, pursuing policies that can no longer be considered "revolutionary"; thereafter, the revolution lived on chiefly as memory and myth.

2. David Hackett Fischer, *Historical Fallacies: Towards a Logic of Historical Thought* (New York: HarperCollins, 1970), 166–67.

3. I am here rehearsing ideas previously advanced (probably for the benefit of Latin Americanist readers) elsewhere: Alan Knight, "The Mexican Revolution: Bourgeois, Nationalist or Just a 'Great Rebellion'?" *Bulletin of Latin American Research* 4, no. 2 (1985): 1–37; and Knight, "Revolución social: Una perspectiva latinoamericana," in *Revoluciones y revolucionarios en el mundo hispano*, ed. Manuel Chust (Castelló: Universitat Jaume I, 2002), 191–228.

4. The "lumping" versus "splitting" dichotomy was, it seems, coined by Charles Darwin; for historians, however, the locus classicus is J. H. Hexter's critique of Christopher Hill, "The Burden of Proof," *Times Literary Supplement*, October 24, 1975.

5. The King: "Is it a revolt?" The Duke: "No, Sire, it is a revolution." Simon Schama considers it "entirely possible that this exchange took place" (*Citizens: A Chronicle of the French Revolution* [New York: Knopf, 1989], 420). Whatever the truth of the anecdote, the distinction revolt/revolution has passed into mainstream analysis: Samuel P. Huntington, *Political Order in Changing Societies* (New Haven CT: Yale University Press, 1968), 75; Jack A. Goldstone, *Revolutions: A Very Short Introduction* (Oxford: Oxford University Press, 2014), 8.

6. Clearly, success/failure is a continuum, with clear-cut cases at each extreme and debatable cases clustered in the middle. When discussing outcomes in this way—which I think is an entirely legitimate and even necessary task for historians—it is helpful to clarify whether the criteria of success or failure should, on the one hand, be derived from the revolutionary actors themselves

358 NOTES TO PAGES 193–194

(did they achieve what they set out to do?) or, on the other hand, be introduced ex post facto by the historian (who might, for example, ask: Did the revolution enhance democracy, welfare, GDP growth, or social mobility?). I discuss this, apropos of Mexico, in "Fué un éxito la Revolución mexicana?" in *La Revolución cósmica: Utopías, regiones y resultados, México, 1910–1940* (Mexico City: FCE, 2015), 165–96. The second (ex post) analytical approach is important, given that revolutions—like wars—typically have unintended consequences that may prove more important than the planned outcomes of participants: a ubiquitous phenomenon stressed by, among others, Christopher Hill. See the discussion and criticism of so-called consequentialism by Neil Davidson, *How Revolutionary Were the Bourgeois Revolutions?* (Chicago: Haymarket Books, 2012), 466–67 and chap. 19. Given even a modicum of "consequentialism," it follows that some would-be "revolutions" underperform and turn out to be mere "revolts," while in a few cases, a series of revolts (not necessarily endowed with purposive and transformational "revolutionary" goals) can snowball and produce a radical "revolution." The Mexican independence movement of 1810 was such a snowballing phenomenon; so, in many respects, was the 1910 Revolution.

7. Coups, barracks revolts, and (literally) "pronouncements," the latter being a species of revolt, often local and limited in character, accompanied by a statement of political intent (hence, the "pronouncement"). They could be seen, at a pinch, as a kind of elite "bargaining by rebellion" analogous to the famous "bargaining by riot" analyzed by Eric Hobsbawm—or, in the Mexican colonial context, by William Taylor: see Will Fowler, ed., *Forceful Negotiations: The Origins of the Pronunciamiento in Nineteenth-Century Mexico* (Lincoln: University of Nebraska Press, 2010); Eric J. Hobsbawm, *Laboring Men: Studies in the History of Labor* (Garden City NY: Doubleday, 1967), 7–26; William Taylor, *Drinking, Homicide, and Rebellion in Colonial Mexican Villages* (Stanford CA: Stanford University Press, 1979), chap. 4. Terms such as *pronunciamiento* are, of course, "emic" in the sense that they are concepts used by the historical actors themselves; as historians, we should take such terms seriously while recognizing that "etic" (roughly, ex-post, "social-scientific") concepts such as "bargaining by riot" and "internal war" and "collective action" may also be crucial for understanding what went on.

8. Piero Gleijeses, *Shattered Hope: The Guatemalan Revolution and the United States, 1944–1954* (Princeton NJ: Princeton University Press, 1991). Fidel Castro's first attempt at armed insurrection—the attack on the Moncada barracks in 1953—was a costly failure; six years later the outcome was different. As

I note elsewhere in this volume, Eric Hobsbawm, following Orlando Fals Borda, considered the Colombian Violencia (1948–58) to be a "frustrated social revolution" (*Viva la Revolución: Hobsbawm on Latin America* [London: Little, Brown, 2016], 82–83).

9. Mike Rapport, *1848: Year of Revolution* (London: Little, Brown, 2009), 264; Jack Grey, *Rebellions and Revolutions: China from the 1800s to the 1980s* (Oxford: Oxford University Press, 1990), 76. Despite its failure, Taiping had important, if unforeseen, consequences by way of weakening the landed elite and the imperial state.

10. Huntington, *Political Order*, 264; Theda Skocpol, *States and Social Revolutions* (Cambridge: Cambridge University Press, 1979), xi, 3–5.

11. I am, rather riskily, summing up a very big and complicated debate. Of course, a weaker hypothesis—that the French Revolution *contributed* to a long-term feudal-to-capitalist transition—is more plausible, but it raises two questions: How big a push did the revolution deliver to the transition? Was that push essential in order to achieve it?

12. Though the American War of Independence is often seen as the pioneer anticolonial revolution, the Revolt of the Netherlands (1566) is a plausible earlier candidate; it, too, combined "anticolonial" and patriotic (nationalist?) sentiments with broader political and sociocultural aspirations: Geoffrey Parker, *The Dutch Revolt* (London: Pelican, 1985), 33 (patriotism), 46 (anticolonialism).

13. The Chinese Revolution was characterized by a "class-inflected anti-imperialist nationalism" (rather than, we could infer, a "nationalist-inflected class conflict"): S. A. Smith, *Revolution and the People in Russia and China: A Comparative History* (Cambridge: Cambridge University Press, 2008), 7.

14. Huntington, *Political Order*, 265–66. For a brief critique of "modernity" as an organizing concept, see Alan Knight, "When Was Latin America Modern? A Historian's Response," in *When Was Latin America Modern?*, ed. Nicola Miller and Stephen Hart (New York: Palgrave Macmillan, 2007), chap. 4.

15. Leon Trotsky, *The History of the Russian Revolution*, 3 vols. (London: Sphere Books, 1965), 1:15. Hobsbawm, too, seems to propose law-like generalizations: Danton, he tells us, "embodied the amoral, Falstaffian, free loving and free spending which *always* emerges initially in social revolutions until overpowered by the hard puritanism that *invariably* comes to dominate them" (*The Age of Revolution, 1789–1848* [New York: New American Library, 1962], 95, emphasis added). Albert Soboul, reviewing French revolutionary historiography, is rather more cautious: "The history of the Revolution,

like any historical subject, is structured and thus thinkable, scientifically knowable. . . . The goal of the historian is to achieve, if not certitudes, at least probabilities or networks of probabilities, or even better, as Georges Lefebvre said, tendential laws" (*Understanding the French Revolution* [London: International Publishers, 1988], 271). On revolutionary stages, see Crane Brinton, *The Anatomy of Revolution* (New York: Prentice Hall, 1965); see also George S. Pettee, *The Process of Revolution* (New York: Harper & Brothers, 1938). Brinton focused on stages within the (ongoing) revolutionary process; an alternative "stage" theory addresses revolutionary etiology, arguing that revolutions are—often? typically? invariably?—preceded by a common pattern sometimes known as the "J-curve" (a phase of improvement followed by a sharp downturn): see James C. Davies, "Toward a Theory of Revolution," *American Sociological Review* 27, no. 1 (1962): 5–19. While such a pattern may sometimes occur (and ingenious devotees of the theory can easily squeeze the facts to fit), plenty of revolutions display no such "prodromic" pattern.

16. Brinton, to be fair, included England and the United States among his four cases (along with France and Russia); however, many subsequent studies tend to regard 1789 as the big bang of the revolutionary universe, sometimes arguing that revolution is an essentially "modern" phenomenon, "modern" being defined as post-1789 (e.g., Huntington, *Political Order*, 264–65). In similar fashion, François-Xavier Guerra, *Le Méxique: De l'ancien régime à la Révolution*, 2 vols. (Paris: L'Harmattan, 1985) devotes a great deal of effort and erudition to shoe-horning revolutionary Mexico into an unsuitable francocentric theoretical model. The perceptive reader will note that in the course of this chapter, I deploy an arguably "francocentric" concept (Jacobinism) in order to make sense of the Mexican Revolution (and others); I leave it to that reader to decide if I am being waywardly inconsistent or judiciously open-minded.

17. The first needs no introduction; W. W. Rostow, *The Stages of Growth: A Non-Communist Manifesto* (Cambridge: Cambridge University Press, 1960), like the Marxists whom he criticizes, suffers from vaulting ambition (both historical and theoretical); in contrast, Alexander Gerschenkron, *Economic Backwardness in Historical Perspective* (Cambridge MA: Belknap Press, 1962) and Albert O. Hirschman, "The Political Economy of Import-Substituting Industrialization in Latin America," *Quarterly Journal of Economics* 82, no. 1 (February 1968): 1–32, offer staged models of development that are more historically and geographically circumscribed, hence rather more convincing and useful.

18. The most significant trend in recent (roughly post-1970) Mexican revolutionary historiography has been the focus on regional and local experiences (and divergences); in which respect, Mexican historiography has emulated—among others—English and French trends. The result for Mexico and other countries has been a necessary fragmentation of what had previously been seen as nationally monolithic movements. However, a key question remains: whether, when viewed from the right angle, some sort of mosaic pattern is discernible or whether it really is just "one damn thing after [or next to] another." In other words, we are back to "lumping" versus "splitting."

19. Huntington, *Political Order*, 272 (on Russia); Colin Jones, *The Great Nation: France from Louis XV to Napoleon* (London: Penguin, 2003), 544; Friedrich Katz, *The Secret War in Mexico: Europe, the United States and the Mexican Revolution* (Chicago: University of Chicago Press, 1981), 3. Not that the fallibility of political predictions is confined to revolutions, of course. It is par for the course—any course.

20. It is probably useful, even necessary, to distinguish between (1) fiscal and other pressures generated by quotidian international rivalry (including perceived foreign threats), which were important in the gestation of the French Revolution; (2) the domestic impact of actual international war (conscription, inflation, defeat), evident in Russia in 1917 and Germany in 1918–19; and (3) foreign intervention—alien "boots on the ground"—that impinges on a revolution in progress, such as France in 1792, Russia in 1918, or China in 1937.

21. As Atatürk himself observed regarding the Allied intervention, "If the enemy had not stupidly come here, the whole country might have slept on heedlessly" (Anthony Mango, *Atatürk* [London: Overlook Press, 2004], 217). For a good recent study of Russo-Ottoman warfare and its consequences, see Michael A. Reynolds, *Shattering Empires: The Clash and Collapse of the Ottoman and Russian Empires, 1908–1918* (Cambridge: Cambridge University Press, 2011).

22. Chalmers Johnson, *Peasant Nationalism and Communist Power: The Emergence of Revolutionary China* (Stanford CA: Stanford University Press, 1963); Smith, *Revolution and the People*, 34–35. A less well-known example would be the Makhnovschina—the anarchist rebellion led by Nestor Makhno in southern Ukraine—which also flourished as a result of its dogged resistance to the invading armies of the Central Powers: Michael Malet, *Nestor Makhno in the Russian Civil War* (London: LSE, 1982), 13–20.

23. In other words, absent these American interventions, the outcome of the revolution would have been much the same. Alan Knight, *U.S.-Mexican*

Relations, 1910–1940: An Interpretation (La Jolla CA: CUSMS, 1987) summarizes this somewhat heretical view; for a counterargument stressing the depth of Mexican anti-Americanism and the decisive character of U.S. intervention, see John Mason Hart, *Empire and Revolution: The Americans in Mexico Since the Civil War* (Berkeley: University of California Press, 2002).

24. The revolution was "autonomous" of the United States in two senses: American policy did not determine its outcome (as, arguably, it had at the time of the 1933 Revolution), and the 1956–59 revolution was not driven by overriding anti-American sentiments. See Jorge I. Domínguez, *Cuba: Order and Revolution* (Cambridge MA: Belknap Press, 1978), 141–42; again, this is not necessarily the orthodox view. Interestingly, while the United States actively sought to overthrow the Cuban revolutionary regime (and, in doing so, bolstered it), American policy toward a roughly contemporaneous Latin American revolution—that of Bolivia in 1952—involved cajolery rather than coercion and, being more subtle, proved more successful: see Kenneth D. Lehman, *Bolivia and the United States: A Limited Partnership* (Athens: University of Georgia Press, 1999).

25. Alan Knight, "La Revolución cósmica," in Knight, *La Revolución cósmica*, 138–39. More specifically, I totted up 384 notional permutations: a meaningless exercise, except inasmuch as it shows the enormous variation of potential combinations. My "local/regional" attachment corresponds to what Smith, *Revolution and the People*, 37, calls "native-place identity."

26. John Womack Jr., *Zapata and the Mexican Revolution* (New York: Knopf, 1969) remains the classic study. *Agrarista* refers to an activist (or program) seeking land reform; I retain the original because the standard English translation, "agrarian," gives rise to confusion, given that the "agrarians" of, say, the Po Valley in Italy were, in fact, big landowners who actively supported fascism in opposition to rural workers. The initial ambivalence of this sentence (constellation, syndrome, persuasion, coalition) derives from genuine authorial doubt as to which term serves best.

27. In the Mexican context (and, of course, some others), there may also be an ethnic or racial component. Comparative students of revolution often offer some sort of typology on these lines (i.e., combining social class and other—e.g., cultural—attributes): Huntington, for example, identifies four collective actors: middle-class intelligentsia, peasantry, proletariat, and urban lumpenproletariat: *Political Order*, 278, 291. My discussion of statist socialism is brief not because it is unimportant but because my analytical point of departure is Mexico, in which this outcome did not materialize: in other

words, the Mexican Revolution, though arguably a "great" "social" revolution, did not create a socialist (Marxist-Leninist) state, as happened in Russia, China, and Cuba, hence my preferred comparisons with, for example, France and Turkey.

28. "Republican/authoritarian" states can acquire "dynastic" qualities (the Somoza family of Nicaragua being a classic case), but such dynasties tend to be short-lived, not least because they lack the prescriptive and sacred legitimacy that underpinned monarchical and imperial dynasties. It did not help, of course, that—as I mention in chapter 5—Somoza (senior) was a "son-of-a-bitch" (as FDR possibly said).

29. "Perhaps the most important and obvious but also most neglected fact about successful great revolutions is that they do not occur in democratic political systems" (Huntington, *Political Order*, 275). Clearly, Huntington does not consider the Nazi overthrow of Weimar as a "great" revolution, in which respect I think he is probably right. Pinochet's destruction of Chilean (social) democracy provides a more recent comparable example. However, Huntington adds a rider that events have clearly called into question: "The absence of successful revolutions against communist dictatorship suggests that the crucial distinction between them and more traditional autocracies may be precisely this capacity to absorb new social groups."

30. Erik J. Zürcher, *The Young Turk Legacy and Nation Building: From the Ottoman Empire to Atatürk's Turkey* (London: I. B. Tauris, 2010), 76–83, 102–4. As I mention in the introduction, I appreciate Professor Zürcher's advice regarding Turkish history; similarly, Dr. Ayçse Yarar gave me some useful bibliographical guidance. Needless to say, any errors are my fault.

31. "We must save Russia," Kornilov declared, ". . . even if we have to set fire to half the country and shed the blood of three-fourths of all the Russians" (Arno J. Mayer, *The Furies: Violence and Terror in the French and Russian Revolutions* [Princeton NJ: Princeton University Press, 2000], 254).

32. Thus, François-Xavier Guerra's equation of the Mexican with the French Revolution (see n. 17) is conceptually flawed, since it treats the republican and positivistic Porfiriato as if it were a monarchical ancien régime. (Interestingly, Guerra's later work focused on the Latin American independence period, for which this kind of perspective is much more suitable.) Regarding the Huerta regime, Michael C. Meyer, *Huerta: A Political Portrait* (Lincoln: University of Nebraska Press, 1972) is a brave effort at revisionist reinterpretation; Alan Knight, *The Mexican Revolution*, 2 vols. (Lincoln: University of Nebraska Press, 1990), vol. 2, chap. 1, esp. 94–103, expresses skepticism.

33. Radetksy and Windischgrätz, though "men on horseback," were loyal servants of the Austrian emperor (whose legitimacy was far from spent), and they harbored no presidential/republican—or "neodynastic"—ambitions; thus, they enabled the Habsburg Empire to survive 1848 intact: Rapport, *1848*, 265–66. On the Guatemalan counterrevolution, see Gleijeses, *Shattered Hope*.

34. The "peasants" in question were chiefly inhabitants of "free" (i.e., independent) villages, many of them of ancient lineage; rancheros were, roughly, yeoman farmers, ranging from dirt poor to well-to-do (a rural petty bourgeoisie, perhaps). Both should be distinguished from hacienda (large estate) employees, many of them resident peons (laborers). "Folk liberalism" denotes the strong popular and patriotic movement—and its associated myths—that arose in mid-nineteenth-century Mexico under the leadership of Benito Juárez in opposition to the Conservatives, the Catholic Church, and French invaders who propped up the empire of Maximilian. As mentioned in chapter 2 of this book, I floated this notion many years ago: Alan Knight, "El liberalismo mexicano: Desde la Reforma hasta la Revolución (una interpretación)," *Historia Mexicana* 26, no. 1 (1985): 59–91; it has been more deeply and expertly analyzed by, among others, Guy P. C. Thomson and David G. LaFrance, *Patriotism, Politics, and Popular Liberalism in Nineteenth-Century Mexico* (Wilmington DE: SR Books, 1999); and Florencia E. Mallon, *Peasant and Nation: The Making of Postcolonial Mexico and Peru* (Berkeley: University of California Press, 1995).

35. Knight, *Mexican Revolution*, 1:55–71, 388–448.

36. "Democratic" in the sense of representative electoral democracy buttressed by basic freedoms of expression and organization in a manner described by Robert Dahl, *On Democracy* (New Haven CT: Yale University Press, 1998), esp. chap. 8.

37. The Society of Ottoman Liberals, led by Prince Sabahettin, represented the liberal, constitutionalist, decentralizing wing of the nascent Ottoman Committee for Union and Progress (CUP), out of which sprang the Young Turk movement; however, it was rapidly marginalized by the centralizing, nationalist, and (I argue) "Jacobin" military wing, typified by Atatürk: Zürcher, *Young Turk Legacy*, 98–99, 117. On Liang Ch'i-ch'ao and the Chinese Constitutionalists, see P'eng-yüan Chang, "The Constitutionalists," in *China in Revolution: The First Phase, 1900–1913*, ed. Mary Clabaugh Wright (New Haven CT: Yale University Press, 1978), chap. 3. Negrín, prime minister of Spain during the Civil War, pursued "domestic policies designed

to consolidate a liberal market-based economy and a parliamentary polity" (Helen Graham, *The Spanish Republic at War, 1936–1939* [Cambridge: Cambridge University Press, 2002], 338), while a British observer, lamenting Cuba's lurch to the left in 1961, exaggerated only somewhat when he concluded that "this is all a far cry from the liberal, democratic Cuba that 90% of Fidel Castro's supporters had in mind when they rallied to his banner in the first days of 1959" (Marchant to Foreign Office, "Annual Report for 1961," January 1962, FO 371/162308).

38. Francisco J. Romero Salvadó, *The Spanish Civil War: Origins, Course and Outcomes* (Basingstoke: Palgrave Macmillan, 2005), 29–30; compare Knight, *Mexican Revolution*, 1:443–45. Potentially, the emphasis on education could lead to clashes with organized religion, especially in Catholic countries such as Spain and Mexico. Jacobinism (discussed below) thus represented, in part, a radical, statist, and coercive adaptation of (moderate, laissez-faire) liberalism. Moderate liberals such as Madero, however, avoided the taint of anticlericalism and welcomed Catholic democratic mobilization. As Mexico's Constitutional Congress of 1916–17 made clear, the liberal/Jacobin split continued long after Madero's fall and assassination in 1913.

39. F. Gilbert Chan, "Sun Yat-sen and the Origins of Kuomingtang Reorganization," in *China in the 1920s*, ed. F. Gilbert Chan and Thomas H. Etzold (New York: New Viewpoints, 1976), 17–19. Like China, Ottoman Turkey was a "semicolony" subject to both formal foreign controls (the capitulations) and informal foreign meddling in domestic politics: Feroz Ahmad, *The Young Turks: The Committee of Union and Progress in Turkish Politics, 1908–14* (New York: Columbia University Press, 2010), 56–57.

40. Given the notional starting point (constitutional liberalism [CL]) and three potential outcomes (military counterrevolution [MCR], socialist revolution [SR], and Jacobin revolution [JR]), it would be possible to devise schematic time lines: thus, Mexico would be CL → MCR → JR, China would CL → MCR → SR, and so on. Of course, such a scheme involves heroic (or irresponsible) "lumping": it would need to be qualified in terms of regional variations, as already mentioned; it might benefit from additional categories (such as fascist counterrevolution [FCR], which I mention in conclusion); and it would need to recognize arguably hybrid forms. Thus, Bonapartism and Kemalism blended MCR and JR, although the blend—the balance of the two components—was different, Kemalism being, in my (inexpert) view, rather less "counterrevolutionary" than Bonapartism. Note that "counterrevolutionary" status depends not just on the content of the "counterrevolutionary"

regime or "ism" but also on the character of the previous regime (or "ism") that it overthrows.

41. A. J. P. Taylor, evaluating the role of Cavour in the Italian Risorgimento, is even more dismissive: Cavour's policy was "more Utopian than that of any radical," since "he imagined that Italy could be brought into being solely by the moderate liberals—the most useless of all classes in a revolution" (*Englishmen and Others* [London: Hamish Hamilton, 1956], 33). A counterexample might be India, where an incipient representative democracy incubated for decades under the later Raj. The conclusion that democracy may need time to bed down is not necessarily a concession to culturalist or prescriptive thinking (à la Edmund Burke); it may also derive from rational-actor and game-theory models, which posit reiterative "games" involving a "tit-for-tat" strategy such that, on the basis of cumulative experience, losers accept results and winners do not seek to eliminate losers from the game entirely. So the game goes on, and democracy gradually beds down. See Adam Przeworksi, *Democracy and the Market* (Cambridge: Cambridge University Press, 1991), 24–25.

42. Alan Knight, "The Working Class and the Mexican Revolution, c. 1900–1920," *Journal of Latin American Studies* 16 (1984): 51–79. A good illustration of class/cultural "synergies" is dress: the Parisian workers were sans-culottes, "recognizable by their dress," whom Robespierre contrasted with the "golden breeches" of the well-to-do: see Albert Soboul, *The Sans-Culottes: The Popular Movement and Revolutionary Government 1793–1794* (New York: Doubleday, 1972), 2. In Mexico, too, class tensions were defined in terms of "sandal versus shoe" and "rags (*hilacha*) against silk." In 1940s Argentina, of course, Perón's working-class followers were famously known as the *descamisados* (shirtless).

43. On the repression of organized labor in late Porfirian Mexico, see Rodney D. Anderson, *Outcasts in Their Own Land: Mexican Industrial Workers, 1906–1911* (DeKalb: Northern Illinois University Press, 1976).

44. Huntington, *Political Order*, 271–72; Ernesto Guevara, *Reminiscences of the Cuban Revolutionary War* (Harmondsworth: Penguin, 1969), 63. "Los del llano" (the people of the plain), whom Guevara contrasted with "los de la sierra" (the mountain people), the former being the urban resistance, which Guevara tended to disdain, the latter the rural guerrillas, whom he led and whose role he inflated (and unwisely generalized beyond Cuba, hence his own defeat and death in Bolivia in 1967).

45. As Soboul puts it in highly schematic form: in revolutionary Paris "concentration of capital had not yet, by gathering [journeymen] in . . . factories,

given rise to that concentration of men so favourable to awakening class solidarity and operating the mass conversion which guarantees its surge forward" (*The Sans-Culottes*, 257–58). See also Soboul, *Understanding the French Revolution*, 89; and Patrice Higonnet, *Goodness Beyond Virtue: Jacobins during the French Revolution* (Cambridge MA: Harvard University Press, 1998), 117, which quotes the Girondin Lanthenas: "The artisan is the true defender, the sincere friend of the Revolution."

46. Important though the war was, it did not create a militant proletariat ex nihilo: the major strikes and repression of 1905–6 and 1912–14 showed that a working class existed—in Marx's terms—both *an sich* (as a matter of empirical fact) and *für sich* (endowed with grievances and solidarity): Smith, *Revolution and the People*, 32.

47. St. Petersburg in 1917 had a population of 2.4 million, five times bigger than Mexico City, which at 476,000 was by far the largest city in Mexico. The northeastern city of Monterrey ("Mexico's Chicago"), which, proportionately, was a more industrial city than the capital, had a population of fewer than 90,000.

48. Smith, *Revolution and the People*, 196, 201.

49. John Lear, *Workers, Neighbors, and Citizens: The Revolution in Mexico City* (Lincoln: University of Nebraska Press, 2001), 50–60, 74–75.

50. Joel Beinin, *Workers and Peasants in the Modern Middle East* (Cambridge: Cambridge University Press, 2001), 86.

51. Huntington, *Political Order*, 265.

52. J. H. Hexter, "Storm over the Gentry," in *Reappraisals in History* (London: Longman, 1961), 117–52. Hexter, it should be added, disagrees with this interpretation of the origins of the English Civil War.

53. What is more, there is no good evidence to suggest that the industrial proletariat was fast overtaking the artisan population; in fact, the trend in the late Porfiriato seems to have been the reverse, as factory production (e.g., of leather goods and cigarettes) achieved productivity gains on the basis of a small labor force, while a mass artisan population—some in dire straits because of factory competition—languished in declining cities such as Guanajuato. At the same time, economic and technological change generated new forms of "artisan"—small workshop—production involving, for example, printers, electricians, car mechanics, and photographers. A more nuanced analysis would therefore demand a typology of different— perhaps "old" and "new"—artisan populations: Knight, *Mexican Revolution*, 1:131–32.

54. On Mexico City's literacy rate, see Lear, *Workers, Neighbours, and Citizens*, 53. Of course, Mexico City's higher literacy rate was also linked to its large middle class and service sector; however, I doubt that these factors alone accounted for the striking differential between the capital and the rest of the country, and "impressionistic" evidence (e.g., the capital's vigorous "penny press") confirms the existence of a large working-class reading public.

55. Mary Lynn McDougall, "Popular Culture, Political Culture: The Case of Lyon, 1830–1850," *Historical Reflections / Réflexions Historiques* 8, no. 2 (1981): 27–41; E. J. Hobsbawm, *Primitive Rebels* (Manchester: Manchester University Press, 1971), chap. 8; E. P. Thompson, *The Making of the English Working Class* (Harmondsworth: Penguin, 1968), 436–40. Regarding Spain and the role of literate artisans, especially in the South, see Guy P. C. Thomson, *The Birth of Modern Politics in Spain: Democratic Association and Revolution, 1854–75* (Basingstoke: Palgrave Macmillan, 2009); and Jerome R. Mintz, *The Anarchists of Casas Viejas* (Chicago: University of Chicago Press, 1984). It is worth noting that in those regions of northern Spain (Asturias and the Basque Country) where heavy industry—mining, steel, and shipbuilding—predominated, the mobilized working class inclined more to socialism than to anarchism.

56. Smith, *Revolution and the People*, 76.

57. Knight, *Mexican Revolution*, 1:63.

58. Andrew Grant Wood, *Revolution in the Street: Women, Workers, and Urban Protest in Veracruz, 1870–1927* (Wilmington DE: SR Books, 2001).

59. On the "House of the World Worker," see Ana Ribera Carbó, *La Casa del Obrero Mundial: Anarcosindicalismo y revolución en México* (Mexico City: INAH, 2010). Lear, *Workers, Neighbors, and Citizens*, 171–76, notes the pioneering role of printers and stonemasons while listing other occupational components of the early Casa: "teachers, carpenters, shoemakers . . . bricklayers, boilermakers, painters, textile workers, [and] streetcar workers." This initial nucleus then "attempted to bring women and less skilled workers into its ranks" (e.g., seamstresses, telephonists, and cigarette factory workers).

60. Lear, *Workers, Neighbors, and Citizens*, 168, 170, 174–75.

61. Lear, *Workers, Neighbors, and Citizens*, 58. *Gachupín*—of disputed derivation—was an old popular derogatory term for "Spaniard" dating back to colonial times.

62. China was probably the extreme case, followed by the Ottoman Empire / Turkey, with Mexico some way behind: Smith, *Revolution and the People*, 33, and Beinin, *Workers and Peasants*, 78–79. It is worth noting that, contrary to

some traditional accounts, the foreign bosses whom Mexican workers resented were more often *gachupines* (Spaniards) than *gringos* (North Americans), the explanation for which would have to take into account both cultural/historic and—perhaps more important—social/structural factors (e.g., the role of Spaniards as estate foremen, factory managers, and corner-shop retailers).

63. Apart from the case of Veracruz, already mentioned, stevedores played a prominent role in labor mobilization in the ports of Tampico, Mazatlán, and Acapulco. The railways—mostly foreign-owned—were also notable (and unusual) because of tensions between Mexican and foreign—chiefly American—skilled workers.

64. Lear, *Workers, Neighbors, and Citizens*, 274–88.

65. Some Casa activists, such as Antonio Díaz Soto y Gama, actually joined the Zapatistas; however, their ambivalent reception suggests that the urban radicals' disdain for ignorant peasants was sometimes matched by peasant suspicion of city slickers: see Samuel Brunk, "Zapata and the City Boys: In Search of a Piece of the Revolution," *Hispanic American Historical Review* 73, no. 1 (1993): 33–65.

66. Charles Tilly, *The Vendée* (New York: Wiley and Sons, 1967), 336–39; P. M. Jones, *The Peasantry in the French Revolution* (Cambridge: Cambridge University Press, 1988), 227–28.

67. The story is well told in Barry Carr, *El movimiento obrero y la política en México, 1910–29* (Mexico City: Ediciones Era, 1981).

68. Charles S. Maier, *Leviathan 2.0: Inventing Modern Statehood* (Cambridge MA: Harvard University Press, 2014).

69. Knight, *Mexican Revolution*, 1:160–61. A related distinction, which for want of space I will not pursue, concerns "competitive," "reactive," and "proactive" forms of popular—including peasant—protest: see Charles Tilly, *From Mobilization to Revolution* (New York: Random House, 1978), 50–51.

70. Knight, *Mexican Revolution*, 1:115–27. I should clarify: though most *serrano* groups hailed from highland zones in, for example, Chihuahua, Durango, Oaxaca, and (northern) Puebla, some (e.g., in the Yucatán interior) were lowland people who occupied remote, similarly recalcitrant frontier regions. The *serrano* category roughly corresponds to Eric Wolf's "peasantry located in . . . a peripheral area beyond the normal control of the central power," a collective actor that Wolf correctly identifies in several major revolutions: Eric R. Wolf, *Peasant Wars of the Twentieth Century* (London: Faber, 1973), 293.

71. The distinction is explored by Ronald Waterbury, "Non-revolutionary Peasants: Oaxaca Compared to Morelos in the Mexican Revolution," *Comparative*

Studies in Society and History 17 (October 1975): 410–42 (although the "non-revolutionary" label demands qualification).

72. It would take too long to discuss all these diverse affiliations. One in particular, millenarianism, deserves mention, if only to suggest some skeptical deflation. Eric Hobsbawm's seminal *Primitive Rebels* started a whole field of hares, some of which—such as banditry—were well worth pursuing. But Hobsbawm's stress on millenarianism has arguably contributed to an exaggeration of such religious, revivalist, and, perhaps, "irrational" ideologies/programs, whether in Spain (see the convincing caveats in Mintz, *The Anarchists of Casas Viejas*, xi, 5–6, 275) or in Mexico, where I have queried the imputed messianic or millenarian quality of popular protest during both the independence movement of the early nineteenth century and the late nineteenth-century Porfiriato: Alan Knight, "Crítica: Eric Van Young, *The Other Rebellion* y la historiografía mexicana," *Historia Mexicana* 54, no. 1 (2004): 445–515; and Knight, "Rethinking the Tomóchic Rebellion," *Mexican Studies / Estudios Mexicanos* 15, no. 2 (1999): 373–93. To put it bluntly, most peasant movements, including those in Mexico, were a lot more materialist than they were millenarian, and to the extent that their motivations were "ideational," the "ideas" involved were, again, more mainstream and secular than millenarian (or messianic). Even the devoutly religious Cristero rebels of the 1920s were orthodox Catholics respectful of clerical authority. Of course, genuinely millenarian/messianic movements have flourished (e.g., in Brazil), but in that context they more often eschewed revolution and represented instead a desperate quest for social order in a violent and anomic society: María Isaura Pereira de Queiroz, "Messiahs in Brazil," *Past and Present* 31 (1965): 62–86.

73. James C. Scott, *The Moral Economy of the Peasant: Rebellion and Subsistence in Southeast Asia* (New Haven CT: Yale University Press, 1976), vii, 2–34, 157–91.

74. Wolf, *Peasant Wars*. Wolf's argument is structural: long-term shifts in markets and production squeezed the "traditional" (independent, household-based, often subsistence-oriented) peasantry. Apart from being structural, these shifts were fairly recent results of late nineteenth-century globalization. At the same time, peasants and others were vulnerable to short-term crises associated with either harvest failure (an ancient story) or fluctuations in the business cycle (a relatively new phenomenon). On the eve of the revolution (1907–10), Mexico suffered both forms of conjunctural crisis.

75. Annie Moulin, *Peasantry and Society in France Since 1789* (Cambridge: Cambridge University Press, 1992), 88; Johnson, *Peasant Nationalism*.

76. Malet, *Nestor Makhno*. Perhaps it is not the final defeat of Spanish anarchism in 1939 that is notable so much as the movement's survival as a powerful popular movement as late as that date, a time when anarchist movements elsewhere in Europe—or Latin America—were spent forces. Clearly, Spain displayed particular characteristics favorable to anarchism: corrupt authoritarian governments; a powerful, socially repressive Catholic Church; a large impoverished peasantry (alongside a fairly small industrial proletariat); and strong regional and localist sentiments, hostile to Madrid. See the perceptive essay by Edward Malefakis, "La Revolución social," in *La guerra civil Española*, ed. Edward Malefakis (Madrid: Taurus, 2006), chap. 15.

77. Maier, *Leviathan 2.0*, 161.

78. The Romanov repression of Stenka Razin and Pugachev—or the Manchu dynasty's defeat of Taiping—would be examples of the first; in the 1920s and 1930s Mussolini and Franco made a priority of crushing leftist peasant movements. In El Salvador in 1932 and Guatemala after 1954, the task fell to the regular army, acting on the orders of authoritarian and fiercely anti-Communist "oligarchs."

79. The "communal" identity and practices of peasants are often stressed, which might make collectivization seem a logical and even welcome outcome. But as far as I know, collectivization has more often been imposed from above than willed from below. This may reflect the countercurrent of peasant "individualism" (a standard historical, sociological, and literary trope well captured in the novels of Balzac). The circle can be somewhat squared by arguing that collectivization was resisted—and so had to be forcibly imposed—because it was usually an alien project foisted on reluctant communities by city-based political elites and that forms of voluntarist peasant collectivism—for example, Spanish anarchism and, with qualifications, the Mexican land reform—appealed precisely because they were both homegrown and consistent with a large measure of individualism, at least at the level of the peasant household.

80. Schama, *Citizens*, 787. Higonnet, *Goodness Beyond Virtue*, 144, is even more emphatic: "The Jacobins were enamored of private property." See also 102, 124, 141.

81. Thus, Albert Soboul writes of "the fundamental opposition of two revolutionary temperaments facing the [with regard to?] problem of the state and the dictatorship . . . 'sans-culottism' and Jacobinism" (*Understanding the French Revolution*, 65).

82. Thus, the aggressive itinerant *déchristianeur* Claude Javogues lumped together "those rhinoceroses known as the rich and the priests" (Michel Vovelle, *1793: La révolution contre l'église: De la raison à l'être suprême* [Brussels: Complexe, 1988], 199).

83. Thompson, *Making of the English Working Class*, chap. 5. Bernardino Rivadavia, the progressive, cosmopolitan, and anticlerical (first) president of Argentina, was excoriated by Catholic critics for being a Jacobin: Klaus Gallo, *Bernardino Rivadavia: Primer presidente argentino* (Buenos Aires: Edhasa, 2012), 109, 117. Mexico's self-styled Jacobins are discussed in what follows. I am referring in the first instance to "emic" Jacobinism—the Jacobinism that dared speak its name (or that was invoked by contemporary critics). But the argument that follows also deals, more importantly, with "etic" Jacobinism—that is, a form of Jacobinism espoused by groups (such as the Young Turks) who, though they might not have used the term, followed in Jacobin footsteps.

84. Certainly the Bolsheviks liked to invoke the French Jacobins, endorsing, if not their particular policies, then at least their revolutionary intransigence: Trotsky, *History of the Russian Revolution*, 1:31, 86, 2:13–14, 115. Note also Maier, *Leviathan 2.0*, 245.

85. Moulin, *Peasantry and Society*, 38–39.

86. Eugen Weber, *Peasants into Frenchmen* (Stanford CA: Stanford University Press, 1976), chaps. 18, 19, 20. On Mexican schooling and related church/state confllct, see Mary Kay Vaughan, *Cultural Politics in Revolution: Teachers, Peasants and Schools in Mexico, 1930–1940* (Tucson: University of Arizona Press, 1997).

87. Alan Knight, "The Mentality and Modus Operandi of Revolutionary Anticlericalism," in *Faith and Impiety in Revolutionary Mexico*, ed. Matthew Butler (New York: Palgrave Macmillan, 2007), 21–56. The more educated revolutionaries—those who tended to dominate the grand formal debates, for example, during the Constituent Congress of 1916–17—regularly invoked the Jacobin label, often in proud and positive terms; thus, of the 738 pages of volume 1 of the transcript of those debates, 47 contained one or more "Jacobin" references (*El diario de los debates del Congreso Constituyente, 1916–1917*, 2 vols. [Mexico City: INEHRM, 2017]). These references tended to cluster in the debates concerning the church and education.

88. Regarding the politico-ideological kinship of the French Third Republic and the Mexican revolutionary regime, an Italian journalist, observing Mexico in the late 1920s, described the country as "a fief of the Masonic Second International" and President Calles as "a Herriot in Mexican military

riding boots," Edouard Herriot being the political personification of the Third Republic, from the 1920s through the 1950s, and, as it happens, an accomplished and sympathetic historian of Jacobinism: Jean Meyer, *La Cristiada*, vol. 2, *El conflicto entre la Iglesia y el Estado* (Mexico City: Siglo XXI, 2005), 16; Francis de Tarr, *The French Radical Party: From Herriot to Mendès-France* (Westport CT: Greenwood Press, 1980), chap. 3. Tarr's portrait of the French Radicals—the "spiritual heirs of the Jacobins" who harked back to "the immortal principles of 1789"—depicts a party that, in terms of its republicanism, nationalism, hostility to both Marxism and Catholicism, and rhetorical attachment to "Reason and Progress," bears close comparison with Mexico's "revolutionary" party.

89. Jürgen Buchenau, *Plutarco Elías Calles and the Mexican Revolution* (Lanham MD: SR Books, 2007) is a solid recent biography.

90. The "big boss" role meant that Calles controlled the political system—including the infant PNR (Partido Nacional Revolucionario)—without actually serving as president (though he did intermittently hold ministerial posts); under his tutelage, three presidents served (1928–34), until President Lázaro Cárdenas (1934–40) sloughed off Callista control and reasserted the preeminence of the presidency in 1935–36.

91. The validity of these charges could be disputed ad infinitum. On the specific question of Catholic/clerical hostility to the revolution, there is solid evidence of Catholic support for the counterrevolutionary coup and regime of Victoriano Huerta in 1913–14; however, as (some) revolutionary leaders cranked up their anticlerical measures, often citing this support by way of justification, so Catholic hostility to the revolution grew, and both sides found themselves in a cycle of mutual recrimination and confrontation that culminated in the bloody Cristero War of 1926–29.

92. It is worth mentioning that the church, while depicted as backward and obscurantist, proved quite capable of using these new methods and technologies to its own ends; thus, in the 1920s and 1930s, Mexico witnessed a battle for hearts and minds conducted by somewhat similar means on both sides. In terms of "soft power," we might say, they cancelled each other out, but the state retained the ultima ratio of coercive power and, especially when Calles was in control, was not afraid to use it. Cárdenas, in contrast, was more conciliatory.

93. On Garrido Canabal, the radical anticlerical boss of the state of Tabasco, see Carlos Martínez Assad, *El laboratorio de la Revolución: El Tabasco garridista* (Mexico City: Siglo XXI, 1979). Like their French Jacobin counterparts,

some Mexican anticlericals performed quasi-proconsular roles, bringing their radical measures to what they saw as benighted provinces in need of redemption from outside. The classic case was Salvador Alvarado in Yucatán: Gilbert M. Joseph, *Revolution from Without: Yucatán, Mexico and the United States, 1880–1924* (Chapel Hill: University of North Carolina Press, 1998).

94. The Cristeros took their name from their war cry, "Viva Cristo Rey" (Long live Christ the king). The classic study is Meyer, *La cristiada*. The parallel with France has echoes down to today: Pope John Paul II, at a stroke, beatified ninety-nine martyrs of the French "reign of terror," as well as twenty-five Cristeros slain by the Mexican state in the 1920s: "Pope Beatifies 99 Martyrs of Reign of Terror," *New York Times*, February 20, 1984, 2; Felipe Cobián, "25 mártires cristeros serán beatificados," *Proceso* (Mexico City), June 13, 1992.

95. "The Revolution could not destroy traditional religion in the soul of the people" (Soboul, *Understanding the French Revolution*, 133). Paul Froese argues—somewhat polemically—that the Bolshevik "plot to kill God" failed, but it should be noted they did manage to sideline him for several decades: Paul Froese, *The Plot to Kill God: Findings from the Soviet Experiment in Secularization* (Berkeley: University of California Press, 2008).

96. Alan Knight, "Popular Culture and the Revolutionary State in Mexico, 1910–1940," *Hispanic American Historical Review* 74, no. 3 (1994): 393–444.

97. Alan Knight, "Superstition in Mexico: From Colonial Church to Secular State," *Past and Present* 199 (2008): 229–70.

98. The material incentives provided by American evangelical churches also helped.

99. Jean Meyer, a revisionist historian of—but not an uncritical apologist for—Catholic resistance to the Mexican Revolution reckons that ninety priests were executed during the three years of the Cristero insurrection (1926–29): *The Cristero Rebellion* (Cambridge: Cambridge University Press, 1976), 75. By way of comparison, it has been estimated that 6,832 priests, monks, and nuns were killed during a similar period in the Spanish Civil War: Stanley Payne, *Spanish Catholicism: An Historical Overview* (Madison: University of Wisconsin Press, 1984), 168. Adjusting for the difference in total population—Spain's being 60 percent greater than Mexico's—does not negate the contrast.

100. Froese, *The Plot to Kill God*. While containing some useful data, Froese's analysis strikes me as tendentious (and scarcely helped by his apparent inability to read Russian).

101. Smith, *Revolution and the People*, 78–79. See also p. 80 for a Chinese parallel.

102. The Church of England, with its censorious morality and intimate ties to the ruling elite, was a pale imitation of the Catholic Church; hence, English Jacobinism—also, we might say, a pale imitation of its French counterpart—expressed anticlerical and rationalist views: Thompson, *Making of the English Working Class*, 182, 201, 493, 512–13, 771.

103. Margaret E. Crahan, "Catholicism in Cuba," *Cuban Studies* 19 (1989): 3–24.

104. Maier, *Leviathan 2.0*, 223–24, ventures a passing comparison between Mexico and Turkey. Trotsky, too, noted some parallels—not, it should be said, very convincingly. He brackets Mustafa Kemal (a nationalist Jacobin) with Porfirio Díaz (an authoritarian oligarch) and Stalin (a Communist autocrat and creator of a command economy): Davidson, *How Revolutionary?*, 434. Davidson seeks to justify this bizarre juxtaposition by speculating—in the conjectural form of a rhetorical question—that perhaps "the Stalinist regime was in effect a 'bureaucratic substitute for the bourgeoisie'" (435). Make of that what you will. On the Ottoman story, see Stanford E. Shaw and Ezel Kural Shaw, *History of the Ottoman Empire and Modern Turkey*, vol. 2, *Reform, Revolution and Republic: The Rise of Modern Turkey, 1808–1975* (Cambridge: Cambridge University Press, 1977), chaps. 2, 3; M. Sukru Hanioglu, *A Brief History of the Late Ottoman Empire* (Princeton NJ: Princeton University Press, 2008), chaps. 4, 5. Hanioglu points out that the Hamidian regime was not a "simple reversion to the patrimonial, pre-Tanzimat style of government"; rather, it followed "an ambitious agenda of bureaucratic modernization" involving banking and currency reform, railway-building, and a strong dose of francophile positivism—all diagnostic features of Mexico's Porfiriato (123, 128–29, 135–41). In short, this was a kind of "revolution from above." See Barrington Moore Jr., *The Social Origins of Dictatorship and Democracy* (London: Penguin, 1967), 438, who omits the Ottoman Empire / Turkey from his analysis but briefly mentions Latin America in passing.

105. Dudley Ankerson, *Agrarian Warlord: Saturnino Cedillo and the Mexican Revolution in San Luis Potosí* (DeKalb: Northern Illinois University Press, 1984), 141.

106. Atatürk was born in 1880 or 1881—see M. Sukru Hanioglu, *Atatürk: An Intellectual Biography* (Princeton NJ: Princeton University Press, 2011), 17—which made him slightly younger than many of his fellow Young Turk leaders, who had been born in the 1870s: Zürcher, *Young Turk Legacy*, 100. They were therefore very close contemporaries of the Mexican revolutionary generation: Madero, b. 1873, Calles, b. 1877, Villa, b. 1878, Zapata, b. 1879, Obregón, b. 1880. On Young Turk statism, see Zürcher, *Young Turk Legacy*, 117. Mexican

revolutionary concerns about national weakness and vulnerability to foreign threats (hence, the need to *forjar patria* [forge the fatherland]) are exemplified by Manuel Gamio, *Forjar patria* (Mexico City: Porrúa, 1916) and Salvador Alvarado, *La reconstrucción de México*, 2 vols. (Mexico City: J. Ballesca, 1919), both of whom could well have written these words of Atatürk: "We shall follow the road to civilization and get there. Those who halt on the road . . . will be drowned by the roaring flood of civilization" (David Hotham, *The Turks* [London: John Murray, 1972], 23).

107. The phrase is taken from Lynn Hunt, *Politics, Culture and Class in the French Revolution* (Berkeley: University of California Press, 1984), 205. Young Turk intellectual influences are traced by Hanioglu, *Atatürk*, 181; and Zürcher, *Young Turk Legacy*, 114.

108. Hanioglu, *Atatürk*, 192.

109. Hanioglu, *Atatürk*, 192.

110. Hanioglu, *Atatürk*, 194, and on the specific reforms, 209, 214; the author goes on (223) to contrast this grand scheme with the "mainly cosmetic" program implemented by Reza Shah in Iran. On education, see Zürcher, *Young Turk Legacy*, 112–14.

111. Hanioglu, *Atatürk*, 12.

112. Hanioglu, *Atatürk*, 6, 194, where Atatürk is descibed as "an omnivorous autodidact unsystematically synthesizing ideas from a range of sources"— much like Calles, who in his somewhat nomadic prerevolutionary career had briefly worked as a schoolteacher. The breadth of Calles's political and economic interests is apparent in his voluminous correspondence, housed in the archives of the Fidecomiso Archivos Plutarco Elías Calles y Fernando Torreblanca in Mexico City.

113. Zürcher, *Young Turk Legacy*, 119–21; Hanioglu, *Atatürk*, 205; Knight, *Mexican Revolution*, 2:240–50.

114. Hanioglu, *Atatürk*, 195–96; Alan Knight, "History, Heritage and Revolution," *Past and Present* 226 (2015): 299–325. The French Jacobins also dabbled in traditional symbols, such as "the monarchic Hercules and the ludovician sun" (Higonnet, *Goodness Beyond Virtue*, 70).

115. *Fronterizos* being people from the Mexican (northern) borderlands, including the state of Sonora. See Knight, *Mexican Revolution*, 2:236. Calles, combining both northern and patriarchal superiority, called the center-west state of Jalisco "the henhouse of the Republic" because it was full of clucking Catholic women: Meyer, *La Cristiada*, 1:9. Garibaldi, the patriotic paladin of the Italian Risorgimento, born in (French) Nice, a native speaker of

the Ligurian dialect, never wholly comfortable in Italian, displayed a keen "frontier-consciousness and exaggerated nationalism" (Denis Mack Smith, *Garibaldi* [London: Hutchinson, 1957], 11). Stalin, too, "could not escape his ethnic origins. His heavily accented Russian betrayed him as a man of the borderlands" (Alfred J. Rieber, "Stalin, Man of the Borderlands," *American Historical Review* 106, no. 5 [December 2001]: 1652). Rieber extends his borderlands thesis—perhaps excessively—to include other radical polit-ical outsiders: Hitler, Pilsudski, Gyula Gömbös, and Corneliu Codreanu. Cromwell and (pace Rieber) Mao do not fit the pattern; a (weak) case might be made for Fidel Castro (a native of Cuba's Oriente province, far to the east of Havana), a strong one for Che Guevara, who, when he sought to revolutionize Cuba (successfully) and Bolivia (unsuccessfully), was a foreign interloper.

116. Hunt, *Politics, Culture and Class*, 184, 186; see also Vovelle, *1793*, 200–201. In contrast, Higonnet, *Goodness Beyond Virtue*, 104, stresses the strong local roots of the Jacobin *clubbistes*.

117. By and large, Mexican Indians (perhaps 15 percent of the population) partic-ipated in the armed revolution as campesinos (peasants) or as members of particular communities or factions; there was little by way of self-consciously "tribal," still less "pan-Indian," mobilization. Such mobilization had to await the late twentieth century. Clearly, the ethnic minorities of the late Ottoman Empire were larger, more vocal, and more militant; in some cases (e.g., the Greeks) they could look to powerful foreign backers—which Mexican Indians lacked.

118. This would seem to be true of both Mexico and Turkey, where, in recent decades, administrations have abandoned traditional anticlerical policies (and, in Mexico at least, traditional nationalism). The election of a leftist populist (Andrés Manuel López Obrador) to the Mexican presidency in 2018 has produced a rhetorical shift back to (economic and cultural) nationalism, but the new president, despite hailing from the old anticlerical bastion of Tabasco, shows no signs of reviving anticlericalism and, like Turkey's pres-ident Erdoğan, rather likes to parade his religiosity.

Selected Bibliography

This is a selected bibliography that includes the great majority but not all of the sources cited in the text and endnotes. A small number of "one-off" references that are marginal to the main themes are not listed below.

Abel, Christopher, and Colin Lewis, eds. *Latin America: Economic Imperialism and the State*. London: ILAS, 1985.

Ahmad, Feroz. *The Young Turks: The Committee of Union and Progress in Turkish Politics, 1908–14*. New York: Columbia University Press, 2010.

Allain, Marie-Françoise. *The Other Man: Conversations with Graham Greene*. Harmondsworth: Penguin, 1984.

Alonso, Paula. *Jardines secretos, legitimizaciones públicas: El Partido Autonomista Nacional y la política argentina de fines del siglo XIX*. Buenos Aires: Edhasa, 2010.

Anderson, Rodney D. *Outcasts in Their Own Land: Mexican Industrial Workers, 1906–1911*. DeKalb: Northern Illinois University Press, 1976.

Andes, Stephen J. C. *The Vatican and Catholic Social Activism in Mexico and Chile*. Oxford: Oxford University Press, 2014.

Andrien, Kenneth J. *Andean Worlds: Indigenous History, Culture and Consciousness under Spanish Rule, 1532–1825*. Albuquerque: University of New Mexico Press, 2001.

Ankerson, Dudley. *Agrarian Warlord: Saturnino Cedillo and the Mexican Revolution in San Luis Potosí*. DeKalb: Northern Illinois University Press, 1984.

Ayala, César J., and Rafael Bernabe. *Puerto Rico in the American Century: A History Since 1898*. Chapel Hill: University of North Carolina Press, 2007.

Ayala Mora, Enrique. *Ecuador del siglo XIX: Estado nacional, ejército, iglesia y municipio*. Quito: Universidad Andina Simón Bolívar, 2011.

Bacevich, Andrew J., ed. *The Imperial Tense: Prospects and Problems of American Empire*. Chicago: Ivan R. Dee, 2003.

Baitenmann, Helga. *Matters of Justice: Pueblos, the Judiciary and Agrarian Reform in Revolutionary Mexico*. Lincoln: University of Nebraska Press, 2020.

Barman, Roderick J. *Brazil: The Forging of a Nation, 1798–1852*. Stanford CA: Stanford University Press, 1988.

———. *Citizen Emperor: Pedro II and the Making of Brazil, 1825–91*. Stanford CA: Stanford University Press, 1999.

Bastian, Jean-Pierre. *Disidentes: sociedades protestantes y revolución en México, 1872–1911*. Mexico City: FCE, 1989.

Bauer, Arnold J. *Chilean Rural Society from the Conquest to 1930*. Cambridge: Cambridge University Press, 1975.

———. *Goods, Power, History: Latin America's Material Culture*. Cambridge: Cambridge University Press, 2001.

Bauer, Arnold T. "Rural Workers in Spanish America: Problems of Peonage and Oppression." *Hispanic American Historical Review* 59, no. 1 (1979): 34–63.

Bayly, C. J. *The Birth of the Modern World, 1780–1914*. Oxford: Blackwell, 2004.

———. *Imperial Meridian: The British Empire and the World, 1780–1830*. London: Longman, 1989.

Beattie, Peter M. *The Tribute of Blood: Army, Honor, Race, and Nation in Brazil, 1864–1945*. Durham NC: Duke University Press, 2001.

Belich, James. *Replenishing the Earth: The Settler Revolution and the Rise of the Anglo World, 1783–1939*. Oxford: Oxford University Press, 2011.

Bellamy, Richard. *Liberalism and Modern Society*. University Park: Pennsylvania State University Press, 1992.

Bendaña, Alejandro. *Sandino: Patria y libertad*. Managua: Anamá, 2016.

Benin, Joel. *Workers and Peasants in the Modern Middle East*. Cambridge: Cambridge University Press, 2001.

Benjamin, Jules R. *The United States and Cuba: Hegemony and Dependent Development, 1880–1934*. Pittsburgh: University of Pittsburgh Press, 1977.

Benjamin, Thomas, and Mark Wasserman, eds. *Provinces of the Revolution: Essays on Mexican Regional History, 1910–1929*. Albuquerque: University of New Mexico Press, 1990.

Bergquist, Charles. *Labor in Latin America: Comparative Essays on Chile, Argentina, Venezuela and Colombia*. Stanford CA: Stanford University Press, 1986.

Berry, Charles. *The Reform in Oaxaca*. Lincoln: University of Nebraska Press, 1981.

Bethell, Leslie. *The Abolition of the Brazilian Slave Trade*. Cambridge: Cambridge University Press, 1970.

Blasier, Cole. *Hovering Giant: U.S. Responses to Revolutionary Change in Latin America*. Pittsburgh: University of Pittsburgh Press, 1985.

Blok, Anton. "The Peasant and the Brigand: Social Banditry Reconsidered." *Comparative Studies in Society and History* 14 (1972): 495–504.

Boghardt, Thomas. *The Zimmermann Telegram: Intelligence, Diplomacy and America's Entry into World War I*. Annapolis MD: Naval Institute Press, 2012.

Bonilla, Heraclio. "Peru and Bolivia from Independence to the War of the Pacific." In *The Cambridge History of Latin America*, vol. 3, *From Independence to c. 1870*, edited by Leslie Bethell, 539–82. Cambridge: Cambridge University Press, 1985.

Boot, Max. *The Savage Wars of Peace: Small Wars and the Rise of American Power*. New York: Basic Books, 2002.

Bortz, Jeffrey. *Revolution within the Revolution: Cotton Textile Workers and the Mexican Labor Regime, 1910–1923*. Stanford CA: Stanford University Press, 2008.

Botana, Natalio. *El orden conservador: La política argentina entre 1880 y 1916*. Buenos Aires: Editorial Sudamericana, 1977.

Bourricaud, François. *Cambios en Puno*. Mexico City: INI, 1967.

Brading, D. A., ed. *Caudillo and Peasant in the Mexican Revolution*. Cambridge: Cambridge University Press, 1980.

———. *The First America: The Spanish Monarchy, Creole Patriots and the Liberal State, 1492–1866*. Cambridge: Cambridge University Press, 1992.

———. *Mexican Phoenix: Our Lady of Guadalupe; Image and Tradition across Five Centuries*. Cambridge: Cambridge University Press, 2001.

———. *The Origins of Mexican Nationalism*. Cambridge: Cambridge University Press, 1985.

Brading, D. A., and Harry E. Cross. "Colonial Silver Mining: Mexico and Peru." *Hispanic American Historical Review* 52, no. 4 (1972): 545–79.

Brinton, Crane. *The Anatomy of Revolution*. New York: Prentice Hall, 1965.

Britton, John A. *Cables, Crises and the Press: The Geopolitics of the New International Information System in the Americas, 1866–1903*. Albuquerque: University of New Mexico Press, 2013.

Brown, Jonathan C. *Oil and Revolution in Mexico*. Berkeley: University of California Press, 1993.

Brunk, Samuel. "Zapata and the City Boys: In Search of a Piece of the Revolution." *Hispanic American Historical Review* 73, no. 1 (1993): 33–65.

Buchenau, Jürgen. *Plutarco Elías Calles and the Mexican Revolution*. Lanham MD: SR Books, 2007.

Bulmer-Thomas, Victor. *The Economic History of Latin America Since Independence*. New York: Cambridge University Press, 2014.

Burga, Manuel, and Alberto Flores Galindo. *Apogeo y crisis de la república aristocrática*. Lima: Ediciones "Rikchay Perú," 1979.

Bushnell, David. *The Making of Modern Colombia: A Nation in Spite of Itself*. Berkeley: University of California Press, 1993.

Butler, Matthew, ed. *Faith and Impiety in Revolutionary Mexico*. New York: Palgrave Macmillan, 2007.

Cain, P. J., and A. G Hopkins. *British Imperialism: Innovation and Expansion, 1688–1914*. London: Longman, 1993.

Calcott, Wilfrid H. *Liberalism in Mexico, 1857–1929*. Hamden CT: Archon Books, 1965.

Calder, Bruce J. *The Impact of Intervention: The Dominican Republic during the U.S. Occupation of 1916–1924*. Austin: University of Texas Press, 1984.

Calvert, P. A. R. *The Mexican Revolution: The Diplomacy of Anglo-American Conflict, 1910–1914*. Cambridge: Cambridge University Press, 1968.

Carbó, Ana Ribera. *La Casa del Obrero Mundial: Anarcosindicalismo y revolución en México*. Mexico City: INAH, 2010.

Cárdenas Sánchez, Enrique. *Cuando se originó el atraso económico de México: La economía mexicana en el largo siglo XIX, 1780–1920*. Madrid: Editorial Biblioteca Nueva, 2003.

Cardoso, Ciro F. "The Liberal Era, c.1870–1930." In *Central America Since Independence*, edited by Leslie Bethell, 31–68. Cambridge: Cambridge University Press, 1991.

Carr, E. H. *What Is History?* Harmondsworth: Pelican, 1964.

Carrasco, Pedro, ed. *La sociedad indígena en el Centro y el Occidente de México*. Zamora: El Colegio de Michoacán, 1986.

Centeno, Miguel A. *Blood and Debt: War and the Nation-State in Latin America*. University Park: Pennsylvania State University Press, 2002.

Centeno, Miguel A., and Agustín E. Ferrero, eds. *State and Nation Making in Latin America and Spain*. Cambridge: Cambridge University Press, 2013.

Cerda, Luis. "Causas económicas de la Revolución mexicana." *Revista Mexicana de Sociología* 53 (1991): 307–47.

Chambers, Sarah C. *From Subjects to Citizens: Honor, Gender, and Politics in Arequipa, Peru, 1780–1854*. University Park: Pennsylvania State University Press, 1999.

Chan, F. Gilbert, and Thomas H. Etzold, eds. *China in the 1920s*. New York: New Viewpoints, 1976.

Chandler, Billy Jaynes. *The Bandit King: Lampião of Brazil*. College Station: Texas A&M University Press, 1978.

———. *The Feitosas and the Sertão dos Inhamuns: The History of a Family and a Community in Northeastern Brazil, 1700–1930*. Gainesville: University Press of Florida, 1972.

Chiriboga, Manuel. *Jornaleros, grandes propetarios y exportación cacaotera, 1790–1925*. Quito: UASB, 2013.

Clark, Kim A. *The Redemptive Work: Railway and Nation in Ecuador, 1895–1930*. Wilmington DE: SR Books, 1998.

Clemenceau, Georges. *South America Today*. London: T. Fisher Unwin, 1911.

Collier, Simon. *Chile: The Making of a Republic, 1830–1865*. Cambridge: Cambridge University Press, 2003.

Collier, Simon, and William F. Sater. *A History of Chile, 1808–1994*. Cambridge: Cambridge University Press, 1996.

Condarco Morales, Roberto. *Zárate, el temible "Willka" historia de la rebelión indígena de 1899*. La Paz: Imprenta Renovación, 1983.

Cortés Conde, Roberto, and Shane J. Hunt, eds. *The Latin American Economies: Growth and the Export Sector 1880–1930*. New York: Holmes and Meier, 1985.

Cotler, Julio. *Clases, estado y nación en el Perú*. Lima: Instituto de Estudios Peruanos, 1978.

Crahan, Margaret E. "Catholicism in Cuba." *Cuban Studies* 19 (1989): 3–24.

Craib, Raymond B. *Cartographic Mexico: A History of State Fixations and Fugitive Landscapes*. Durham NC: Duke University Press, 2004.

Crawley, Andrew. *Somoza and Roosevelt: Good Neighbour Diplomacy in Nicaragua, 1933–1945*. Oxford: Oxford University Press, 2007.

Crosbie, Alfred. *Ecological Imperialism: The Biological Expansion of Europe, 900–1900*. Cambridge: Cambridge University Press, 2004.

Cueto, Marcos, and Steven Palmer. *Medicine and Public Health in Latin America: A History*. New York: Cambridge University Press, 2013.

da Cunha, Euclides. *Rebellion in the Backlands*. Chicago: Phoenix Books, 1964.

Darwin, Charles. *The Voyage of the Beagle*. London: Marshal Cavendish, 1987.

Darwin, John. *After Tamerlane: The Rise and Fall of Global Empires, 1400–2000*. London: Penguin, 2008.

Davidson, Neil. *How Revolutionary Were the Bourgeois Revolutions?* Chicago: Haymarket Books, 2012.

Davies, Thomas M. *Indian Integration in Peru: A Half Century of Experience, 1900–1948.* Lincoln: University of Nebraska Press, 1974.

de Humboldt, Alejandro. *Ensayo político sobre el reino de la Nueva España.* Mexico City: Porrúa, 1991.

de Laforcade, Geoffrey, and Kirwin Shaffer, eds. *In Defiance of Boundaries: Anarchism in Latin American History.* Gainesville: University Press of Florida, 2015.

Denoon, Donald. *Settler Capitalism: The Dynamics of Dependent Development in the Southern Hemisphere.* Oxford: Clarendon Press, 1983.

Diacon, Todd A. *Millenarian Vision, Capitalist Reality: Brazil's Contestado Rebellion, 1912–1916.* Durham NC: Duke University Press, 1991.

———. *Stringing Together a Nation: Cândido Mariano da Silva Rondon and the Construction of a Modern Brazil, 1906–1930.* Durham NC: Duke University Press, 2004.

Díaz, Bernal. *The Conquest of New Spain.* Harmondsworth: Penguin, 1983.

Díaz Díaz, Fernando. *Caudillos y caciques: Antonio López de Santa Anna y Juan Alvarez.* Mexico City: El Colegio de México, 1972.

Domínguez, Jorge I. *Cuba: Order and Revolution.* Cambridge MA: Belknap Press, 1978.

Donald, James, and Stuart Hall, eds. *Politics and Ideology.* Milton Keynes: Open University, 1986.

Drake, Paul W. *Between Tyranny and Anarchy: A History of Democracy in Latin America, 1800–2006.* Stanford CA: Stanford University Press, 2009.

Drinot, Paulo. *The Allure of Labor: Workers, Race and the Making of the Peruvian State.* Durham NC: Duke University Press, 2011.

———, ed. *La Patria Nueva: Economía, sociedad y cultura en el Perú, 1919–1930.* Raleigh NC: Editorial a Contracorriente, 2018.

Dubois, Laurent. *Haiti: The Aftershocks of History.* New York: Metropolitan Books, 2012.

Dulles, John W. F. *Anarchism and Communism in Brazil.* Austin: University of Texas Press, 1973.

Dumett, Raymond E., ed. *Gentlemanly Capitalism and British Imperialism: The New Debate on Empire.* London: Routledge, 2014.

Dunkerley, James. *Power in the Isthmus: A Political History of Central America.* London: Verso, 1990.

Earle, Rebecca, ed. *Rumours of Wars: Civil Conflict in Nineteenth-Century Latin America.* London: ILAS, 2000.

Escobar Ohmstede, Antonio, ed. *Los pueblos indios en los tiempos de Benito Juárez (1847–1872).* Mexico City: UABJO/UAM, 2007.

Fallaw, Ben, and David Nugent, eds. *State Formation in the Liberal Era: Capitalisms and Claims of Citizenship in Mexico and Peru.* Tucson: University of Arizona Press, 2020.

Fay, C. R. *Imperial Economy and Its Place in the Formation of Economic Doctrine 1600–1932.* Oxford: Clarendon Press, 1934.

Feichtinger, Johannes, Franz L. Fillafer, and Jan Surman, eds. *The Worlds of Positivism: A Global Intellectual History, 1770–1930.* Basingstoke: Palgrave Macmillan, 2017.

Ferguson, Niall. *Colossus: The Rise and Fall of the American Empire.* London: Penguin Books, 2012.

———. *Empire: The Rise and Decline of the British World Order and the Lessons for Global Power.* New York: Basic Books, 2001.

Ferns, H. S. "The Baring Crisis Revisited." *Journal of Latin American Studies* 24, no. 2 (1992): 241–73.

———. *Britain and Argentina in the Nineteenth Century.* Oxford: Clarendon Press, 1960.

Fischer, David Hackett. *Historical Fallacies: Towards a Logic of Historical Thought.* New York: HarperCollins, 1970.

Fisher, John. "Royalism, Regionalism, and Rebellion in Colonial Peru, 1808–1815." *Hispanic American Historical Review* 59, no. 2 (1979): 232–57.

Flores Galindo, Alberto. *Buscando un Inca: Identidad y utopía en los Andes.* Mexico City: Grijalbo, 1993.

Fogarty, John, Ezequiel Gallo, and Héctor Diéguez, eds. *Argentina y Australia.* Buenos Aires: Instituto Torcuato di Tella, 1979.

Foote, Nicola, and René D. Harder Horst, eds. *Military Struggle and Identity Formation in Latin America.* Gainesville: University Press of Florida, 2010.

Forman, Shepard. *The Brazilian Peasantry.* New York: Columbia University Press, 1975.

Forment, Carlos A. *Democracy in Latin America, 1760–1900,* vol. 1, *Civic Selfhood and Public Life in Mexico and Peru.* Chicago: University of Chicago Press, 2003.

Fowler, Will, ed. *Forceful Negotiations: The Origins of the Pronunciamiento in Nineteenth-Century Mexico.* Lincoln: University of Nebraska Press, 2010.

———. *Santa Anna of Mexico.* Lincoln: University of Nebraska Press, 2007.

Freund, Julien. *The Sociology of Max Weber.* Harmondsworth: Penguin, 1972.

Froese, Paul. *The Plot to Kill God: Findings from the Soviet Experiment in Secularization.* Berkeley: University of California Press, 2008.

Gallagher, John, and Ronald Robinson. "The Imperialism of Free Trade." *Economic History Review* 6, no. 1 (1953): 1–15.

Gallo, Ezequiel. *La pampa gringa*. Buenos Aires: Editorial Sudamericana, 1983.

Gallo, Klaus. *Bernardino Rivadavia: El primer presidente argentino*. Buenos Aires: Edhasa, 2012.

———. *Las invasiones inglesas*. Buenos Aires: Eudeba, 2004.

Gallo, Klaus, Nancy Calvo, and Roberto de Stefano. *Los curas de la revolución*. Buenos Aires: Emecel, 2002.

Gamio, Manuel. *Forjar patria*. Mexico City: Porrúa, 1916.

Gardner, Lloyd C., and Marilyn B. Young, eds. *The New American Empire*. New York: W. W. Norton, 2005.

Gargarella, Roberto. *Latin American Constitutionalism, 1810–2010*. Oxford: Oxford University Press, 2013.

———. *The Legal Foundations of Inequality: Constitutions in the Americas, 1776–1860*. Cambridge: Cambridge University Press, 2010.

Garner, Paul. *Leones británicos y águilas mexicanos: Negocios, política e imperio en la carrera de Weetman Pearson en México, 1889–1919*. Mexico City: FCE, 2013.

———. *Porfirio Díaz*. London: Routledge, 2001.

Gerschenkron, Alexander. *Economic Backwardness in Historical Perspective*. Cambridge MA: Belknap Press, 1962.

Gleijeses, Piero. *Shattered Hope: The Guatemalan Revolution and the United States, 1944–1954*. Princeton NJ: Princeton University Press, 1991.

Goldstone, Jack A. *Revolutions: A Very Short Introduction*. Oxford: Oxford University Press, 2014.

Gómez-Galvarriato, Aurora. *Industry and Revolution: Social and Economic Change in the Orizaba Valley, Mexico*. Cambridge MA: Harvard University Press, 2013.

Gonzales, Michael J. "Neo-colonialism and Indian Unrest in Southern Peru, 1867–1898." *Bulletin of Latin American Research* 6, no. 1 (1987): 1–26.

———. *Plantation Agriculture and Social Control in Northern Peru, 1875–1933*. Austin: University of Texas Press, 1985.

González Casanova, Pablo. "Internal Colonialism and National Development." *Comparative International Development* 1, no. 4 (1965): 27–37.

González y González, Luis. *La ronda de las generaciones*. Mexico City: Editorial Clio, 1997.

———. *Pueblo en vilo: Microhistoria de San José de Gracia*. Mexico City: El Colegio de México, 1972.

Gootenberg, Paul. *Between Silver and Guano: Commercial Policy and the State in Postindependence Peru*. Princeton NJ: Princeton University Press, 1989.

———. "Population and Ethnicity in Early Republican Peru: Some Revisions." *Latin American Research Review* 26, no. 5 (1991): 109–57.

Gosner, Gary. *Soldiers of the Virgin: The Moral Economy of a Colonial Maya Rebellion.* Tucson: University of Arizona Press, 1992.

Gott, Richard. "Latin America as a White Settler Society." *Bulletin of Latin American Research* 26, no. 2 (2007): 269–89.

Gould, Lewis L. *The Spanish-American War and President McKinley.* Lawrence: University Press of Kansas, 1982.

Graham, Helen. *The Spanish Republic at War, 1936–1939.* Cambridge: Cambridge University Press, 2002.

Graham, Richard. *Britain and the Onset of Modernization in Brazil, 1850–1914.* Cambridge: Cambridge University Press, 1968.

———, ed. *The Idea of Race in Latin America, 1870–1940.* Austin: University of Texas Press, 1990.

———. *Politics and Patronage in Nineteenth-Century Brazil.* Stanford CA: Stanford University Press, 1990.

Graham-Yooll, Andrew. *Imperial Skirmishes: War and Gunboat Diplomacy in Latin America.* Oxford: Signal Books, 2002.

Grandin, Greg. "The Liberal Traditions in the Americas: Rights, Sovereignty and the Origins of Liberal Multilateralism." *American Historical Review* 117, no. 1 (February 2012): 68–91.

Greene, Graham. *The Lawless Roads.* London: Longman, 1939.

Gregory, Desmond. *Brute New World: The Rediscovery of Latin America in the Early Nineteenth Century.* London: British Academic Press, 1992.

Grey, Jack. *Rebellions and Revolutions: China from the 1800s to the 1980s.* Oxford: Oxford University Press, 1990.

Grindle, Merilee S., and Pilar Domingo, eds. *Proclaiming Revolution: Bolivia in Comparative Perspective.* Cambridge MA: Harvard University Press, 2003.

Gruening, Ernest. *Mexico and Its Heritage.* London: Stanley Paul, 1928.

Grunstein, Arturo. *Consolidados: José Yves Limantour y la formación de los Ferrocarriles Nacionales de México.* Mexico City: Conaculta, 2013.

Guardino, Peter F. *The Dead March: A History of the Mexican-American War.* Cambridge MA: Harvard University Press, 2017.

———. *Peasants, Politics, and the Formation of Mexico's National State: Guerrero, 1800–1857.* Stanford CA: Stanford University Press, 1996.

———. *The Time of Liberty: Popular Political Culture in Oaxaca, 1750–1850.* Durham NC: Duke University Press, 2005.

Guerra, François-Xavier Guerra. *Le Méxique: De l'ancien régime à la Révolution.* 2 vols. Paris: L'Harmattan, 1985.

Guevara, Ernesto. *Reminiscences of the Cuban Revolutionary War*. Harmondsworth: Penguin, 1969.

Haber, Stephen, ed. *Why Latin America Fell Behind: Essays on the Economic History of Brazil and Mexico, 1800–1914*. Stanford CA: Stanford University Press, 1997.

Haines, Michael R., and Richard Steckel, eds. *The Population History of North America*. New York: Cambridge University Press, 2000.

Hale, Charles A. *Mexican Liberalism in the Age of Mora, 1821–1853*. New Haven CT: Yale University Press, 1968.

———. *The Transformation of Liberalism in Late Nineteenth-Century Mexico*. Princeton NJ: Princeton University Press, 1989.

Halperín Donghi, Tulio. *The Contemporary History of Latin America*. Durham NC: Duke University Press, 1993.

———. "'Dependency Theory' and Latin American Historiography." *Latin American Research Review* 17, no. 1 (1982): 115–30.

———. *Politics, Economics and Society in Argentina in the Revolutionary Period*. Cambridge: Cambridge University Press, 1975.

Hamill, Hugh M., Jr. *The Hidalgo Revolt: Prelude to Mexican Independence*. Gainesville: University Press of Florida, 1966.

Hamnett, Brian R. *The End of Iberian Rule on the American Continent, 1770–1830*. Cambridge: Cambridge University Press, 2017.

Handy, Jim. *Gift of the Devil: A History of Guatemala*. Boston: South End Press, 1984.

Hanioğlu, M. Şükrü. *A Brief History of the Late Ottoman Empire*. Princeton NJ: Princeton University Press, 2008.

Harriss, John, Janet Hunter, and Colin Lewis, eds. *The New Institutional Economics and Third World Development*. London: Routledge, 1997.

Hart, John Mason. *Empire and Revolution: The Americans in Mexico Since the Civil War*. Berkeley: University of California Press, 2002.

———. *Revolutionary Mexico: The Coming and Process of the Mexican Revolution*. Berkeley: University of California Press, 1987.

Hassaurek, Friedrich. *Four Years among the Ecuadorians*. Carbondale: Southern Illinois University Press, 1967.

Head, Francis Bond. *Journeys across the Pampas and among the Andes*. Carbondale: Southern Illinois University Press, 1967.

Headrick, Daniel R. *The Tools of Empire: Technology and European Imperialism in the Nineteenth Century*. Oxford: Oxford University Press, 1981.

Heggarty, Paul, and Adrian J. Pearce, eds. *History and Language in the Andes*. New York: Palgrave Macmillan, 2011.

Henderson, Peter V. N. *Gabriel García Moreno and Conservative State Formation in Ecuador*. Austin: University of Texas Press, 2008.

Hennessy, Alistair. *The Frontier in Latin American History*. London: Edward Arnold, 1978.

Hennessy, Alistair, and John King, eds. *The Land That England Lost: Argentina and Britain, a Special Relationship*. London: British Academic Press, 1992.

Hennessy, C. A. M. *The Federal Republic in Spain*. Oxford: Clarendon Press, 1962.

Hexter, J. H. *Reappraisals in History*. London: Longman, 1961.

Higonnet, Patrice. *Goodness Beyond Virtue: Jacobins during the French Revolution*. Cambridge MA: Harvard University Press, 1998.

Hilton, Rodney, ed. *The Transition from Feudalism to Capitalism*. London: NLB, 1976.

Hirschman, Albert O. "The Political Economy of Import-Substituting Industrialization in Latin America." *Quarterly Journal of Economics* 82, no. 1 (February 1968): 1–32.

Hobsbawm, E. J. *The Age of Revolution, 1789–1848*. New York: New American Library, 1962.

———. *Bandits*. Harmondsworth: Penguin, 1972.

———. *Interesting Times: A Twentieth-Century Life*. London: Abacus, 2003.

———. *Laboring Men: Studies in the History of Labor*. Garden City NY: Doubleday 1967.

———. *Primitive Rebels: Studies in Archaic Forms of Social Movement in the 19th and 20th Centuries*. Manchester: Manchester University Press, 1974.

———. *Viva la Revolución: Hobsbawm on Latin America*. London: Little, Brown, 2016.

Holden, Robert H. *Armies Without Nations: Public Violence and State Formation in Central America, 1821–1960*. Oxford: Oxford University Press, 2004.

———. *Mexico and the Survey of Public Lands*. DeKalb: Northern Illinois University Press, 1994.

Holton, Isaac. *New Granada: Twenty Months in the Andes*. Carbondale: Southern Illinois University Press, 1967.

Hood, Miriam. *Gunboat Diplomacy: Great Power Pressure in Venezuela, 1895–1905*. London: Allen and Unwin, 1983

Hora, Roy. *Landowners of the Argentine Pampas: A Social and Political History, 1860–1945*. Oxford: Oxford University Press, 2001.

Huber, Evelyne, and Frank Safford, eds. *Agrarian Structure and Political Power: Landlord and Peasant in the Making of Latin America*. Pittsburgh: University of Pittsburgh Press, 1995.

Hu-Dehart, Evelyn. *Yaqui Resistance and Survival: The Struggle for Land and Autonomy.* Madison: University of Wisconsin Press, 1984.

Hunt, Lynn. *Politics, Culture and Class in the French Revolution.* Berkeley: University of California Press, 1984.

Hunt, Michael. *The American Ascendancy: How the United States Gained and Wielded Global Dominance.* Chapel Hill: University of North Carolina Press, 2007.

Huntington, Samuel P. *Political Order in Changing Societies, Societies.* New Haven CT: Yale University Press, 1968.

Immerman, Richard H. *The CIA in Guatemala.* Austin: University of Texas Press, 1982.

Irigoin, Alejandra. "Representation Without Taxation, Taxation Without Consent: The Legacy of Spanish Colonialism in America." *Revista de Historia Económica / Journal of Iberian and Latin American Economic History* 34, no. 2 (September 2016): 169–208.

Ivereigh, Austen, ed. *The Politics of Religion in an Age of Revival.* London: ILAS, 2000.

Jacobsen, Nils. *Mirages of Transition: The Peruvian Altiplano, 1780–1930.* Berkeley: University of California Press, 1993.

Jacobsen, Nils, and Hans-Jürgen Puhle, eds. *The Economies of Mexico and Peru during the Late Colonial Period, 1760–1810.* Berlin: Colloquium-Verlag, 1986.

Jaksic, Iván, and Eduardo Posada-Carbó, eds. *Liberalismo y poder: Latinoamérica en el siglo XIX.* Santiago: FCE, 2011.

Johnson, Chalmers. *Blowback: The Costs and Consequences of American Empire.* New York: Henry Holt, 2000.

———. *Peasant Nationalism and Communist Power: The Emergence of Revolutionary China.* Stanford CA: Stanford University Press, 1962.

Jones, Colin. *The Great Nation: France from Louis XV to Napoleon.* London: Penguin, 2003.

Jones, P. M. *The Peasantry in the French Revolution.* Cambridge: Cambridge University Press, 1988.

Joseph, Gilbert M. "On the Trail of Latin American Bandits: A Re-examination of Peasant Resistance." *Latin American Research Review* 25, no. 3 (1990): 7–53.

———. *Revolution from Without: Yucatán, Mexico and the United States, 1880–1924.* Durham NC: Duke University Press, 1997.

Katz, Friedrich. *The Life and Times of Pancho Villa.* Stanford CA: Stanford University Press, 1996.

———, ed. *Riot, Rebellion and Revolution: Rural Social Conflict in Mexico.* Princeton NJ: Princeton University Press, 1988.

————. *The Secret War in Mexico: Europe, the United States and the Mexican Revolution.* Chicago: University of Chicago Press, 1981.

Keohane, Robert O. *After Hegemony: Cooperation and Discord in the World Political Economy.* Princeton NJ: Princeton University Press, 1984.

Kiernan, Victor. *Imperialism and Its Discontents.* New York: Routledge, 1995.

King, Rosa. *Tempest over Mexico.* London: Methuen, 1936.

Klaiber, Jeffrey, SJ. *The Catholic Church in Peru, 1821–1985.* Washington DC: Catholic University of America Press, 1992.

Klarén, Peter F. *Modernization, Dislocation, and Aprismo: Origins of the Peruvian Aprista Party, 1870–1932.* Austin: University of Texas Press, 1973.

————. *Peru: Society and Nationhood in the Andes.* New York: Oxford University Press, 2000.

Knaut, Andrew L. *The Pueblo Revolt of 1680: Conquest and Resistance in Seventeenth-Century New Mexico.* Norman: University of Oklahoma Press, 1995.

Knight, Alan. "Crítica: Eric Van Young, *The Other Rebellion* y la historiografía Mexicana." *Historia Mexicana* 54, no. 1 (2004): 445–515.

————. "El liberalismo mexicano: Desde la Reforma hasta la Revolución (una interpretación)." *Historia Mexicana* 26, no. 1 (1985): 59–91.

————. *La Revolución cósmica: Utopías, regiones y resultados, México, 1910–1940.* Mexico City: FCE, 2015.

————. "Mexican Peonage: What Was It and Why Was It?" *Journal of Latin American Studies* 18, no. 1 (May 1986): 41–74.

————. *The Mexican Revolution.* 2 vols. Lincoln: University of Nebraska Press, 1990.

————. "The Mexican Revolution: Bourgeois, Nationalist or Just a 'Great Rebellion'?" *Bulletin of Latin American Research* 4, no. 2 (1985): 1–37.

————. *Mexico: The Colonial Era.* Cambridge: Cambridge University Press, 2002.

————. "Popular Culture and the Revolutionary State in Mexico, 1910–1940." *Hispanic American Historical Review* 74, no. 3 (1994): 393–444.

————. "Rethinking the Tomóchic Rebellion." *Mexican Studies / Estudios Mexicanos* 15, no. 2 (1999): 373–93.

————. "Revolución social: Una perspectiva latinoamericana." In *Revoluciones y revolucionarios en el mundo hispano*, edited by Manuel Chust, 191–228. Castelló: Universitat Jaume I, 2002.

————. "Superstition in Mexico: From Colonial Church to Secular State." *Past and Present* 199 (2008): 229–70.

————. *U.S.-Mexican Relations, 1910–1940: An Interpretation.* La Jolla CA: CUSMS, 1987.

———. "When Was Latin America Modern? A Historian's Response." In *When Was Latin America Modern?*, edited by Nicola Miller and Stephen Hart, 91–120. New York: Palgrave Macmillan, 2007.

———. "The Working Class and the Mexican Revolution, c. 1900–1920." *Journal of Latin American Studies* 16, no. 1 (1984): 51–79.

Knight, Alan, and Paulo Drinot, eds. *The Great Depression in Latin America.* Durham NC: Duke University Press, 2014.

Knight, Alan, and Wil Pansters, eds. *Caciquismo in Twentieth-Century Mexico.* London: Institute for the Study of the Americas, 2005.

Krauze, Enrique. *Plutarco E. Calles: Reformar desde el origen.* Mexico City: FCE, 1988.

Kuenzli, E. Gabrielle. *Acting Inca: National Belonging in Early Twentieth-Century Bolivia.* Pittsburgh: University of Pittsburgh Press, 2013.

Kuntz Ficker, Sandra, ed. *Historia económica de México: De la Colonia a nuestros días.* Mexico City: El Colegio de México, 2010.

Kuntz Ficker, Sandra, and Paolo Riguzzi, eds. *Ferrocarriles y vida económica en México, 1850–1950.* Zinacantepec: El Colegio Mexiquense, 1996.

LaFeber, Walter. *Inevitable Revolutions: The United States in Central America.* New York: W. W. Norton, 1984.

———. *The New Empire: An Interpretation of American Expansion, 1860–1898.* Ithaca NY: Cornell University Press, 1963.

———. *The Panama Canal: The Crisis in Historical Perspective.* New York: Oxford University Press, 1989.

Lal, Deepak. *In Praise of Empires: Globalization and Order.* New York: Palgrave Macmillan, 2004.

Langer, Erick D. "Andean Rituals of Revolt: The Chayanta Rebellion of 1927." *Ethnohistory* 3 (1990): 227–53.

———. *Economic Change and Rural Resistance in Southern Bolivia, 1880–1930.* Stanford CA: Stanford University Press, 1989.

Larson, Brooke. *Trials of Nation-Making: Liberalism, Race, and Ethnicity in the Andes, 1810–1910.* New York: Cambridge University Press, 2004.

Lear, John. *Picturing the Proletariat: Artists and Labor in Revolutionary Mexico, 1908–1940.* Austin: University of Texas Press, 2017.

———. *Workers, Neighbors and Citizens: The Revolution in Mexico City.* Lincoln: University of Nebraska Press, 2001.

Lehman, Kenneth D. *Bolivia and the United States: A Limited Partnership.* Athens: University of Georgia Press, 1999.

León Fernández, Dino, ed. *Trabajos de historia: Religión, cultura y política en el Perú, siglos XVII–XX.* Lima: UNMSM, 2011.

Levine, Robert M. *Vale of Tears: Revisiting the Canudos Massacre in Northeastern Brazil, 1893–1897*. Berkeley: University of California Press, 1995.

Lewin, Linda. *Politics and Parentela in Paraíba: A Case Study of Family-Based Oligarchy in Brazil*. Princeton NJ: Princeton University Press, 1987.

Lewis, Colin M. "The Financing of Railway Development in Latin America, 1850–1914." *Ibero-Amerikanische Archiv* 9 (1983): 255–78.

Llorca-Jaña, Manuel. *The British Textile Trade in South America in the Nineteenth Century*. New York: Cambridge University Press, 2012.

Lockhart, James, and Stuart B. Schwartz. *Early Latin America: A History of Colonial Spanish America and Brazil*. Cambridge: Cambridge University Press, 1983.

Lomelí Vanegas, Leonardo. *Liberalismo oligárquico y política económica: Positivismo y economía política del Porfiriato*. Mexico City: FCE, 2018.

Lomnitz, Claudio. *The Return of Comrade Ricardo Flores Magón*. New York: Zone Books, 2014.

López-Alonso, Moramay. *Estar a la altura: Una historia de los niveles de vida en México, 1850–1950*. Mexico City: FCE, 2015.

Love, Joseph L., and Nils Jacobsen, eds. *Guiding the Invisible Hand: Economic Liberalism and the State in Latin America*. New York: Praeger, 1988.

Loveman, Brian. *Struggle in the Countryside: Politics and Rural Labor in Chile, 1919–1973*. Bloomington: Indiana University Press, 1976.

Lundestad, Geir. "'Empire by Invitation' in the American Century." *Diplomatic History* 23, no. 2 (April 1999): 189–217.

Lynch, John. "The Catholic Church in Latin America, 1830–1930." In *The Cambridge History of Latin America*, vol. 4, *c. 1870 to 1920*, edited by Leslie Bethell, 527–95. Cambridge: Cambridge University Press, 1986.

———. *Caudillos in Spanish America, 1800–1850*. Oxford: Clarendon Press, 1992.

———. *Massacre in the Pampas, 1872*. Norman: University of Oklahoma Press, 1998.

———. *New Worlds: A Religious History of Latin America*. New Haven CT: Yale University Press, 2012.

———. *The Spanish American Revolutions, 1808–1826*. London: Weidenfeld & Nicholson, 1973.

MacPherson, C. B. *The Life and Times of Liberal Democracy*. Oxford: Oxford University Press, 1977.

Mahoney, James. *Colonialism and Postcolonial Development: Spanish America in Comparative Perspective*. New York: Cambridge University Press, 2010.

Maier, Charles S. *Among Empires: American Ascendancy and Its Predecessors*. Cambridge MA: Harvard University Press, 2009.

———. *Leviathan 2.0: Inventing Modern Statehood*. Cambridge MA: Harvard University Press, 2014.

Malefakis, Edward, ed. *La Guerra Civil española*. Madrid: Taurus, 2006.

Malet, Michael. *Nestor Makhno in the Russian Civil War*. London: LSE, 1982.

Mallon, Florencia E. *Courage Tastes of Blood: The Mapuche Community of Nicolás Ailío and the Chilean State, 1906–2001*. Durham NC: Duke University Press, 2005.

———. *Peasant and Nation: The Making of Postcolonial Mexico and Peru*. Berkeley: University of California Press, 1995.

Mann, Michael. *Incoherent Empire*. London: Verso, 2005.

Manning, D. J. *Modern Liberalism*. London: Dent, 1976.

Mansilla, Lucio V. *A Visit to the Ranquel Indians*. Lincoln: University of Nebraska Press, 1997.

Marichal, Carlos. *A Century of Debt Crises in Latin America: From Independence to the Great Depression, 1820–1930*. Princeton NJ: Princeton University Press, 1989.

Martínez Alier, Juan. *Haciendas, Plantations and Collective Farms: Agrarian Class Societies—Cuba and Peru*. London: Frank Cass, 1977.

Martínez Assad, Carlos, ed. *Balance y perspectivas de los estudios regionales en México*. Mexico City: UNAM, 1990.

———. *El laboratorio de la Revolución: El Tabasco garridista*. Mexico City: Siglo XXI, 1979.

Marx, Karl, *Capital*. 2 vols. London: Dent, 1957.

Mayer, Arno J. *The Furies: Violence and Terror in the French and Russian Revolutions*. Princeton NJ: Princeton University Press, 2000.

Mayo, John. "Consuls and Silver Contraband on the West Coast of Mexico in the Era of Santa Anna." *Journal of Latin American Studies* 19, no. 2 (1987): 389–411.

McCreery, David. "'An Odious Feudalism': Mandamiento Labor and Commercial Agriculture in Guatemala." *Latin America Perspectives* 13, no. 1 (1986): 99–117.

McEvoy, Carmen. *Forjando la nación: Ensayos de historia republicana*. Lima: PUCP, 1999.

McFarlane, Alan. *The Origins of English Individualism: The Family, Property and Social Transition*. Oxford: Blackwell, 1978.

McLean, David. *War, Diplomacy and Informal Empire: Britain and the Republics of La Plata, 1836–1853*. London: British Academic Press, 1995.

McNally, David. *Political Economy and the Rise of Capitalism: A Reinterpretation*. Berkeley: University of California Press, 1988.

McPherson, Alan. *The Invaded: How Latin Americans and Their Allies Fought and Ended U.S. Occupation*. Oxford: Oxford University Press, 2014.

Meade, Teresa A. *"Civilizing" Rio: Reform and Resistance in a Brazilian City, 1889–1930*. University Park: Penn State University Press, 1997.

Méndez, Cecilia. "Incas Sí, Indios No: Notes on Peruvian Creole Nationalism and Its Contemporary Crisis." *Journal of Latin American Studies* 28, no. 1 (February 1996): 197–225.

———. *The Plebeian Republic: The Huanta Rebellion and the Making of the Peruvian State, 1820–1850*. Durham NC: Duke University Press, 2005.

Mendoza Soriano, Reidezel. *Bandoleros y rebeldes*. 2 vols. Mexico City: Ediciones del Azar, 2013.

Merwin, Mrs. George B. *Three Years in Chile*. Carbondale: Southern Illinois University Press, 1966.

Meyer, Jean. *La Cristiada*, vol. 2, *El conflicto entre la Iglesia y el Estado*. Mexico City: Siglo XXI, 2005.

———, ed. *Memorias del simposio internacional 5 de mayo*. Puebla: El Colegio de Puebla, 2013.

Meyer, Lorenzo. *Su Majestad Británica contra la Revolución Mexicana, 1900–1950*. Mexico City: El Colegio de México, 1991.

Meyer, Michael C. *Huerta: A Political Portrait*. Lincoln: University of Nebraska Press, 1972.

Miller, Rory. *Britain and Latin America in the Nineteenth and Twentieth Centuries*. London: Longman, 1993.

———. "The Grace Contract, the Peruvian Corporation and Peruvian History." *Ibero-Amerikanische Archiv* 9 (1983): 319–43.

Mills, Kenneth. "The Limits of Religious Coercion in Mid-colonial Peru." *Past and Present* 145 (November 1994): 84–121.

Mintz, Jerome R. *The Anarchists of Casas Viejas*. Chicago: University of Chicago Press, 1984.

Mitchell, Nancy. *The Danger of Dreams: German and American Imperialism in Latin America*. Chapel Hill: University of North Carolina Press, 1999.

Mommsen, Wolfgang J., and Jürgen Osterhammel, eds. *Imperialism and After: Continuities and Discontinuities*. London: Allen and Unwin, 1986.

Moore, Barrington, Jr. *Injustice: The Social Bases of Obedience and Revolt*. London: Macmillan, 1978.

———. *The Social Origins of Dictatorship and Democracy: Lord and Peasant in the Making of the Modern World*. Boston: Beacon Press, 1966.

Moulin, Annie. *Peasantry and Society in France Since 1789*. Cambridge: Cambridge University Press, 1992.

Munro, Dana G. *The United States and the Caribbean Republics, 1921–1933*. Princeton NJ: Princeton University Press, 1974.

Nunn, Frederick M. *Yesterday's Soldiers: European Military Professionalism in South America, 1890–1940*. Lincoln: University of Nebraska Press, 1983.

O'Brien, Patrick K. "The Costs and Benefits of British Imperialism, 1846–1914." *Past and Present* 120, no. 1 (1988): 163–200.

O'Brien, Thomas F. *The Revolutionary Mission: American Enterprise in Latin America, 1900–1945*. Cambridge: Cambridge University Press, 1996.

O'Rourke, Kevin H., and Jeffrey G. Williamson. *Globalization and History: The Evolution of a Nineteenth-Century Atlantic Economy*. Cambridge MA: MIT Press, 1999.

Ortiz, Fernando. *Cuban Counterpoint: Tobacco and Sugar*. Durham NC: Duke University Press, 1995.

Osterhammel, Jürgen. *Colonialism: A Theoretical Overview*. Princeton NJ: Markus Wiener, 1997.

———. *The Transformation of the World: A Global History of the Nineteenth Century*. Princeton NJ: Princeton University Press, 2014.

Owen, Roger, and Bob Sutcliffe, eds. *Theories of Imperialism*. London: Longman, 1972.

Pagden, Anthony. *Peoples and Empires*. London: Phoenix Press, 2002.

Pansters, Wil G., ed. *Violence, Coercion and State-Making in Twentieth-Century Mexico*. Stanford CA: Stanford University Press, 2012.

Parker, Geoffrey. *The Dutch Revolt*. London: Pelican, 1985.

Passananti, Thomas P. "The Politics of Silver and Gold in an Age of Globalization: The Origins of Mexico's Monetary Reform of 1905." *América Latina en la Historia Económica* 30 (2008): 67–95.

Pastore, Mario. "Trade Contraction and Economic Decline: The Paraguayan Economy under Francia, 1810–1840." *Journal of Latin American Studies* 26, no. 3 (1994): 539–95.

Payne, Stanley. *Spanish Catholicism: An Historical Overview*. Madison: University of Wisconsin Press, 1984.

Peloso, Vincent C., and Barbara Tenenbaum, eds. *Liberals, Politics and Power: State Formation in Nineteenth-Century Latin America*. Athens: University of Georgia Press, 1996.

Pensado, Jaime. *Rebel Mexico: Student Unrest and Authoritarian Political Culture during the Long Sixties*. Stanford CA: Stanford University Press, 2013.

Pereira de Queiroz, Maria Isaura. "Messiahs in Brazil." *Past and Present* 31 (1965): 62–85.

Perez, Louis A., Jr. *Lords of the Mountain: Social Banditry and Peasant Protest in Cuba, 1878–1918*. Pittsburgh: University of Pittsburgh Press, 1989.

Perham, Margery. *Colonial Sequence, 1930–1949*. London: Methuen, 1967.

Perkins, Dexter. *A History of the Monroe Doctrine*. London: Longman, 1960.

Philip, George. *Oil and Politics in Latin America*. Cambridge: Cambridge University Press, 1982.

Piccato, Pablo. *City of Suspects: Crime in Mexico City, 1900–1931*. Durham NC: Duke University Press, 2001.

Pineo, Ronn. *Ecuador and the United States: Useful Strangers*. Athens: University of Georgia Press, 2007.

Platt, D. C. M. "The Imperialism of Free Trade: Some Reservations." *Economic History Review* 21, no. 2 (1968): 296–306.

———. *Latin America and British Trade, 1806–1914*. London: Adam & Charles Back, 1972.

Platt, Tristan. *Estado boliviano y ayllu andino: Tierra y tributo en el Norte de Potosí*. Lima: Instituto de Estudios Peruanos, 1982.

———. "Liberalism and Ethnocide in the Southern Andes." *History Workshop Journal* 17 (1984): 3–18.

Polanyi, Karl. *The Great Transformation*. 1944; Boston: Beacon Press, 1957.

Pomerantz, Kenneth. *The Great Divergence: China, Europe and the Making of the Modern World Economy*. Princeton NJ: Princeton University Press, 2000.

Portilla, Santiago. *Una sociedad en armas: Insurrección antirreleccionista en México, 1910–1911*. Mexico City: El Colegio de México, 1995.

Posada-Carbó, Eduardo, ed. *In Search of a New Order: Essays on the Politics and Society of Nineteenth-Century Latin America*. London: ILAS, 1998.

Priestland, David. *Merchant, Soldier, Sage: A New History of Power*. London: Penguin, 2012.

Przeworksi, Adam. *Democracy and the Market*. Cambridge: Cambridge University Press, 1991.

Quirke, Robert E. *An Affair of Honor: Woodrow Wilson and the Occupation of Veracruz*. New York: W. W. Norton, 1967.

Quiroz, Alfonso W. *Domestic and Foreign Finance in Modern Peru, 1850–1950: Financing Visions of Development*. Basingstoke: Macmillan, 1993.

Rabe, Stephen G. *Eisenhower and Latin America: The Foreign Policy of Anticommunism*. Chapel Hill: University of North Carolina Press, 1988.

Rapport, Mike. *1848: Year of Revolution*. London: Little, Brown, 2009.

Redfield, Robert. *The Folk Culture of Yucatán*. Chicago: University of Chicago Press, 1941.

———. *Peasant Society and Culture*. Chicago: University of Chicago Press, 1956.

———. *Tepoztlán: A Mexican Village*. Chicago: University of Chicago Press, 1930.

Reed, John. *Insurgent Mexico*. New York: D. Appleton, 1914.

Reed, Nelson A. *The Caste War of Yucatán*. Stanford CA: Stanford University Press, 2001.

Reyes Heroles, Jesús. *El liberalismo mexicano*. 3 vols. Mexico City: FCE, 1974.

Reynolds, Michael A. *Shattering Empires: The Clash and Collapse of the Ottoman and Russian Empires, 1908–1918*. Cambridge: Cambridge University Press, 2011.

Ridings, Eugene. *Business Interest Groups in Nineteenth-Century Brazil*. Cambridge: Cambridge University Press, 1994.

Riguzzi, Paolo. *Reciprocidad imposible? La política del comercio entre México y Estados Unidos, 1857–1938*. Mexico City: El Colegio Mexiquense, 2003.

Riguzzi, Paolo, and Patrica de los Ríos. *Las relaciones México–Estados Unidos, 1756–2020*, vol. 2, *Destino no manifiesto? 1867–2010*. Mexico City: UNAM, 2012.

Robinson, Ronald. "Non-European Foundations of European Imperialism: Sketch for a Theory of Collaboration." In *Studies in the Theory of Imperialism*, edited by Roger Owen and Bob Sutcliffe, 120–30. London: Longman, 1972.

Robinson, Ronald, John Gallagher, and Alice Denny. *Africa and the Victorians: The Official Mind of Imperialism*. London: Macmillan, 1961.

Rock, David. *Argentina, 1516–1987*. Berkeley: University of California Press, 1987.

———. *The British in Argentina: Commerce, Settlers and Power, 1800–2000*. Basingstoke: Palgrave Macmillan, 2018.

———. *Politics in Argentina, 1890–1930: The Rise and Fall of Radicalism*. Cambridge: Cambridge University Press, 1975.

Rodríguez, Mario. *A Palmerstonian Diplomat in Central America: Frederick Chatfield, Esq*. Tucson: University of Arizona Press, 1964.

Rodríguez O., Jaime E., ed. *The Divine Charter: Constitutionalism and Liberalism in Nineteenth-Century Mexico*. Lanham MD: Rowman and Littlefield, 2005.

———. *The Independence of Spanish America*. Cambridge: Cambridge University Press, 2009.

Romero, José Luis. *El desarrollo de las ideas en la sociedad argentina del siglo XX*. Mexico City: FCE, 1965.

Romero Salvadó, Francisco J. *The Spanish Civil War: Origins, Course and Outcomes*. Basingstoke: Palgrave Macmillan, 2005.

Rosenberg, Emily. "Foundations of United States International Financial Power: Gold Standard Diplomacy, 1900–1905." *Business History Review* 59, no. 2 (1985): 169–202.

Rostow, W. W. *The Stages of Growth: A Non-Communist Manifesto*. Cambridge: Cambridge University Press, 1960.

Rouquié, Alain. *The Military and the State in Latin America*. Berkeley: University of California Press, 1989.

Rugeley, Terry. *Of Wonders and Wise Men: Religion and Popular Cultures in Southeast Mexico, 1800–1876*. Austin: University of Texas Press, 2001.

Runciman, W. G. *The Social Animal*. London: HarperCollins, 1998.

Ryan, Alan. *The Making of Modern Liberalism*. Princeton NJ: Princeton University Press, 2012.

Sabato, Hilda. *The Many and the Few: Political Participation in Republican Buenos Aires*. Stanford CA: Stanford University Press, 2001.

———. *Republics of the New World: The Revolutionary Political Experiment in Nineteenth-Century Latin America*. Princeton NJ: Princeton University Press, 2018.

Safford, Frank. "Politics, Ideology and Society in Post-independence Spanish America." In *The Cambridge History of Latin America*, vol. 3, *From Independence to c. 1870*, edited by Leslie Bethell, 347–422. Cambridge: Cambridge University Press, 1985.

Said, Edward W. *Orientalism*. New York: Vintage Books, 1979.

Salinas, Salvador. *Land, Liberty and Water: Morelos after Zapata, 1920–1940*. Tucson: University of Arizona Press, 2018.

Salvucci, Richard J. *Textiles and Capitalism in Mexico: A History of the Obrajes, 1539–1840*. Princeton NJ: Princeton University Press, 1987.

Sarmiento, Domingo F. *Facundo: Or, Civilization and Barbarism*. New York: Penguin, 1998.

Sater, William F. *Andean Tragedy: Fighting the War of the Pacific, 1879–1884*. Lincoln: University of Nebraska Press, 2007.

Schaefer, Timo H. *Liberalism as Utopia: The Rise and Fall of Legal Rule in Postcolonial Mexico, 1820–1900*. Cambridge: Cambridge University Press, 2017.

Schama, Simon. *Citizens: A Chronicle of the French Revolution*. New York: Knopf, 1989.

Schell, Patience. *Church and State Education in Revolutionary Mexico City*. Tucson: University of Arizona Press, 2003.

Schell, William, Jr. *Integral Outsiders: The American Colony in Mexico City, 1876–1911*. Wilmington DE: SR Books, 2001.

———. "Money as Commodity: Mexico's Conversion to the Gold Standard." *Mexican Studies / Estudios Mexicanos* 12, no. 1 (1996): 67–89.

Schoultz, Lars. *Beneath the United States: A History of U.S. Policy Toward Latin America*. Cambridge MA: Harvard University Press, 1998.

———. *National Security and United States Policy toward Latin America*. Princeton NJ: Princeton University Press, 1987.

Schuler, Friedrich E. *Mexico between Hitler and Roosevelt: Mexican Foreign Relations in the Age of Lázaro Cárdenas, 1934–1940*. Albuquerque: University of New Mexico Press, 1998.

Schwartz, Rosalie. *Lawless Liberators: Political Banditry and Cuban Independence*. Durham NC: Duke University Press, 1989.

Scott, James C. *Domination and the Arts of Resistance: Hidden Transcripts*. New Haven CT: Yale University Press, 1989.

———. *The Moral Economy of the Peasant: Rebellion and Subsistence in Southeast Asia*. New Haven CT: Yale University Press, 1976.

———. *Seeing Like a State*. New Haven CT: Yale University Press, 1998.

Serulnikov, Sergio. *Conflictos sociales e insurrección en el mundo colonial andino*. Mexico City: FCE, 2006.

Sexton, Jay. *The Monroe Doctrine: Empire and Nation in Nineteenth-Century America*. New York: Hill & Wang, 2011.

Shaw, Stanford E., and Ezel Kural Shaw. *History of the Ottoman Empire and Modern Turkey*, vol. 2, *Reform, Revolution and Republic: The Rise of Modern Turkey, 1808–1975*. Cambridge: Cambridge University Press, 1977.

Shumway, Nicholas. *The Invention of Argentina*. Berkeley: University of California Press, 1991.

Sierra, Justo. *The Political Evolution of the Mexican People*. Austin: University of Texas Press, 1969.

Sinkin, Richard N. *The Mexican Reform, 1855–1876: A Study in Liberal Nation-Building*. Austin: ILAS, 1979.

Skocpol, Theda. *States and Social Revolutions*. Cambridge: Cambridge University Press, 1979.

Slatta, Richard W. *Gauchos and the Vanishing Frontier*. Lincoln: University of Nebraska Press, 1992.

———. "Introduction to Banditry in Latin America." In *Bandidos: The Varieties of Latin American Banditry*, edited by Richard W. Slatta. Westport CT: Praeger, 1987.

Smelser, Gregorio. *Sandino: The Testimony of a Nicaraguan Patriot*. Princeton NJ: Princeton University Press, 1990.

Smith, Benjamin T. *The Roots of Conservatism in Mexico: Catholicism, Society and Politics in the Mixteca Baja, 1750–1962*. Albuquerque: University of New Mexico Press, 2012.

Smith, Robert Freeman. *The United States and Revolutionary Nationalism in Mexico, 1916–1932*. Chicago: University of Chicago Press, 1972.

Smith, S. A. *Revolution and the People in Russia and China: A Comparative History*. Cambridge: Cambridge University Press, 2008.

Snodgrass, Michael. *Deference and Defiance in Monterrey: Workers, Paternalism and Revolution in Mexico, 1890–1950*. New York: Cambridge University Press, 2003.

Soboul, Albert. *The Sans-Culottes: The Popular Movement and Revolutionary Government 1793–1794*. New York: Doubleday, 1972.

———. *Understanding the French Revolution*. London: International Publishers, 1988.

Soifer, Hillel David. *State Building in Latin America*. New York: Cambridge University Press, 2015.

Solberg, Carl E. *The Prairies and the Pampas: Agrarian Policy in Canada and Argentina, 1880–1930*. Stanford CA: Stanford University Press, 1987.

Sorensen Goodrich, Diana. *Facundo and the Construction of Argentine Culture*. Austin: University of Texas Press, 1996.

Soriano, Juan. *Anarquistas: Cultura y política libertaria en Buenos Aires, 1890–1910*. Bueno Aires: Manantial, 2001.

Stallings, Barbara. *Banker to the Third World: U.S. Portfolio Investment in Latin America*. Berkeley: University of California Press, 1987.

Stanfield, Michael Edward. *Red Rubber, Bleeding Trees: Violence, Slavery and Empire in Northwest Amazonia, 1850–1933*. Albuquerque: University of New Mexico Press, 1998.

Stein, Steve. *Populism in Peru: The Emergence of the Masses and the Politics of Social Control*. Madison: University of Wisconsin Press, 1980.

Stephanson, Anders. *Manifest Destiny: American Expansion and the Empire of Right*. New York: Hill & Wang, 1995.

Stern, Steve J., ed. *Resistance, Rebellion and Consciousness in the Andean Peasant World, 18th to 20th Centuries*. Madison: University of Wisconsin Press, 1987.

Szuchman, Mark, ed. *The Middle Period in Latin American History*. Boulder CO: Lynne Rienner, 1989.

Taylor, Lewis. *Bandits and Politics in Peru: Landlord and Peasant Violence in Hualgayoc, 1900–30*. Cambridge: Centre for Latin American Studies, 1986.

Taylor, William B. *Drinking, Homicide, and Rebellion in Colonial Mexican Villages.* Stanford CA: Stanford University Press, 1979.

———. *Magistrates of the Sacred: Priests and Parishioners in Eighteenth-Century Mexico.* Stanford CA: Stanford University Press, 1999.

Tenenbaum, Barbara. *The Politics of Penury: Debts and Taxes in Mexico, 1821–1856.* Albuquerque: University of New Mexico Press, 1986.

Thompson, E. P. *The Making of the English Working Class.* Harmondsworth: Penguin, 1968.

———. *The Poverty of Theory and Other Essays.* Manchester: Merlin Press, 1978.

———. "Time, Work-Discipline and Industrial Capitalism." *Past and Present* 38 (1967): 56–97.

Thomson, Guy. *The Birth of Modern Politics in Spain: Democracy, Association and Revolution, 1854–75.* Basingstoke: Palgrave Macmillan, 2010.

———, ed. *The European Revolutions of 1848 and the Americas.* London: ILAS, 2002.

Thomson, Guy P. C., and David G. LaFrance. *Patriotic Politics and Popular Liberalism in Nineteenth-Century Mexico.* Wilmington DE: SR Books, 1995.

Thorp, Rosemary, and Geoffrey Bertram. *Peru 1890–1977: Growth and Policy in an Open Economy.* London: Macmillan, 1978.

Thurner, Mark. *From Two Republics to One Divided: Contradictions of Postcolonial Nation-Making in Andean Peru.* Durham NC: Duke University Press, 1997.

Tibesar, Antonine. "The Peruvian Church at the Time of Independence in the Light of Vatican II." *The Americas* 26, no. 4 (April 1970): 68–91.

Tilly, Charles. *Coercion, Capital and European States, AD 990–1992.* Oxford: Blackwell, 1992.

———. *From Mobilization to Revolution.* New York: Random House, 1978.

———. *The Vendée.* New York: Wiley and Sons, 1967.

Topik, Steven, Carlos Marichal, and Zephyr Frank, eds. *From Silver to Cocaine: Latin American Commodity Chains and the Building of the World Economy, 1500–2000.* Durham NC: Duke University Press, 2006.

Topik, Steven C., and Allen Wells. *The Second Conquest of Latin America: Coffee, Henequen and Oil during the Export Boom, 1850–1930.* Austin: University of Texas Press, 1998.

Trotsky, Leon. *The History of the Russian Revolution.* 3 vols. London: Sphere Books, 1965.

Tutino, John. *From Insurrection to Revolution in Mexico: Social Bases of Agrarian Violence, 1750–1940.* Princeton NJ: Princeton University Press, 1988.

Tyrrell, Ian, and Jay Sexton, eds. *Empire's Twin: U.S. Anti-imperialism from the Founding Era to the Age of Terrorism.* Ithaca NY: Cornell University Press, 2015.

Unger, Brigitte, and Frans van Waarden, eds. *Convergence or Diversity? Internationalization and Economic Policy Response*. Aldershot: Avebury, 1995.

Vanderwood, Paul J. *Disorder and Progress: Bandits, Police and Mexican Development*. Lincoln: University of Nebraska Press, 1981.

———. *Juan Soldado: Rapist, Murderer, Martyr, Saint*. Durham NC: Duke University Press, 2004.

———. *The Power of God Against the Guns of Government: Religious Upheaval in Mexico at the Turn of the Nineteenth Century*. Stanford CA: Stanford University Press, 1998.

Van Young, Eric. *The Other Rebellion: Popular Violence, Ideology, and the Mexican Struggle for Independence, 1810–1821*. Stanford CA: Stanford University Press, 2001.

Vaughan, Mary Kay. *Cultural Politics in Revolution: Teachers, Peasants and Schools in Mexico, 1930–1940*. Tucson: University of Arizona Press, 1997.

———. *State, Education and Social Class in Mexico, 1880–1928*. DeKalb: Northern Illinois University Press, 1982.

Veliz, Claudio. *The Centralist Tradition in Latin America*. Princeton NJ: Princeton University Press, 1980.

———, ed. *Obstacles to Change in Latin America*. New York: Oxford University Press, 1965.

———, ed. *The Politics of Conformity in Latin America*. New York: Oxford University Press, 1967.

Vilar, Pierre. *A History of Gold and Money*. London: Verso, 1984.

Villanueva Martín, Orlando. *Guadalupe Salcedo y la insurrección llanera, 1949–1957*. Bogotá: Universidad Nacional de Colombia, 2012.

Vovelle, Michel. *1793: La révolution contre l'église: De la raison à l'être suprême*. Brussels: Complexe, 1988.

Wald, Elijah. *Narcocorrido*. New York: HarperCollins, 2001.

Walker, Charles F. *Smouldering Ashes: Cuzco and the Creation of Republican Peru, 1780–1840*. Durham NC: Duke University Press, 1999.

Washbrook, Sarah. *Producing Modernity in Mexico: Labour, Race and the State in Chiapas, 1876–1914*. Oxford: Oxford University Press, 2012.

Waterbury, Ronald. "Non-revolutionary Peasants: Oaxaca Compared to Morelos in the Mexican Revolution." *Comparative Studies in Society and History* 17 (October 1975): 410–42.

Weber, Eugen. *Peasants into Frenchmen*. Stanford CA: Stanford University Press, 1976.

Weber, Max. *The Theory of Social and Economic Organization*. New York: Free Press, 1964.

Weinstein, Barbara. *The Amazon Rubber Boom, 1850–1920*. Stanford CA: Stanford University Press, 1983.

Wells, Allen, and Gilbert M. Joseph. *Summer of Discontent, Seasons of Upheaval: Elite Politics and Rural Insurgency in Yucatán, 1876–1915*. Stanford CA: Stanford University Press, 1996.

White, Richard Alan. *Paraguay's Autonomous Revolution, 1810–1840*. Albuquerque: University of New Mexico Press, 1978.

Williams, William Appleman. *America Confronts a Revolutionary World: 1776–1976*. New York: William and Morrow, 1976.

Wolf, Eric R. *Europe and the People without History*. Berkeley: University of California Press, 1982.

———. *Peasant Wars of the Twentieth Century*. New York: Harper and Row, 1973.

Womack, John, Jr. *Zapata and the Mexican Revolution*. New York: Knopf, 1969.

Wood, Andrew Grant. *Revolution in the Street: Women, Workers, and Urban Protest in Veracruz, 1870–1927*. Wilmington DE: SR Books, 2001.

Wood, Bryce. *The Making of the Good Neighbor Policy*. New York: Columbia University Press, 1961.

Wood, Ellen Meiksins. *Liberty and Property: A Social History of Western Political Thought from Renaissance to Enlightenment*. London: Verso, 2012.

Wright, Mary Clabaugh, ed. *China in Revolution: The First Phase, 1900–1913*. New Haven CT: Yale University Press, 1978.

Wu, Celia. *Generals and Diplomats: Britain and Peru, 1820–1840*. Cambridge: CLAS, 1991.

Zahler, Reuben. *Ambitious Rebels: Remaking Honor, Law and Liberalism in Venezuela, 1780–1850*. Tucson: University of Arizona Press, 2013.

Zimmermann, Eduardo A. *Los liberales reformistas: La cuestión social en la Argentina, 1890–1916*. Buenos Aires: Sudamericana / Universidad de San Andrés, 1995.

Zürcher, Erik J. *The Young Turk Legacy and Nation Building: From the Ottoman Empire to Atatürk's Turkey*. London: I. B. Tauris, 2010.

Index

Abalá, 38

Aberdeen, Lord, 148, 325n60

Acheson, Dean, 173, 191

Africa, 143, 163, 164, 165–66, 187; and
  African religion, 93–94, 282n30;
  scramble for, 13, 138, 166, 168

agrarian reform, 77, 79, 129–30, 132, 200,
  208, 209, 220n4, 225n21, 275n151,
  310n105, 347n29, 363n26, 372n79

agraristas, 77, 79, 129–30, 132, 200, 208,
  209, 220n4, 225n21, 310n105, 347n29,
  363n26, 372n79

Aguilar Rivera, José Antonio, 52, 252n11,
  253n16, 255n23

Alamán, Lucas, 52, 229n38

Algeria, 195, 314n6

Alliance for Progress, 186, 275n151

Alvarado, Salvador, 211, 375n93, 377n106

Alvarez, Juan, 73, 81, 122

Amazon basin, 31, 59, 164, 260n59, 303n63

anarchism, 21, 61, 63, 64, 204, 205, 206,
  212, 261n65, 262nn66–68, 262n70,
  273n137, 362n22, 369n55, 372n76

Anchorena, Tomás, 289n82

Andalusia, 208, 262n66

Andean America, 6, 7, 59, 67, 95–96, 155,
  163, 337n124

Anderson, Rodney, 73

Anenecuilco, 78

Anglophilia, 342n146

animism, 91, 94

anticlericalism, 8, 18, 52, 56, 61, 70–71,
  75–76, 82, 93, 99, 110–12, 204, 209–10,
  248n109, 253n16, 257n44, 273n137,
  281nn24–25, 284n44, 290n92, 366n38,
  373n82, 375n95

anti-Semitism, 107, 108, 287n73

Antonio the Counsellor, 109

APRA (Alianza Popular Revolucionaria
  Americana), 21, 105, 133, 231n47

Arabs, 165–66, 341n138

Arana, Julio César, 261n60

Arbenz, Jacobo, 324n55

Arellano Félix brothers, 41

Arequipa, 73, 74, 81, 275n164

Argentina, 58, 63, 68, 97, 105, 120, 122,
  137, 143, 144, 156–57, 158, 163, 167,
  331n101, 338n128, 341n138, 353n70

armaments, 334n113, 335n115

army. *See* military

Arriaga, Ponciano, 62, 64

Artigas, José Gervasio, 247n106

artisans, 61, 74, 77, 81, 203–4, 367n45, 368n53

Assheton, J. A., 179

Atacama Desert, 59, 278n3

Ataturk, Mustafa Kemal, 197, 213–17, 362n21, 376n104, 376n106, 377n112

atheism. *See* freethinking

Atusparia, Pedro, 292n6, 295n27

Augustine, Saint, 33

Australia, 137, 163

Austria-Hungary, 198, 200, 365n33

Aymara, 79, 81, 187

Azana, Manuel, 201

Azángaro, 130

Aztecs, 96, 119, 151

Badiraguato, 40

Bahía, 9, 94, 347n100

Bajío, 31, 46, 47, 119, 265n83

Bakunin, Mikhail, 207

baldíos (public lands), 162, 266n86

Balzac, Honoré de, 372n79

banditry, 25–48, 89, 90, 127, 235n13, 239n43, 239n46, 242n55, 247n105, 347n24, 350n51

Barcelona, 211

Baring Crisis, 157

Batista, Fulgencio, 147, 149, 182–83, 352n57, 357n98

Batlle y Ordóñez, José, 21, 64

Bayly, C. J., 154, 329n86

Bejucal, 30

Benavides, Oscar, 132, 311n109

Bergquist, Charles W., 222n12

Bernal, Heraclio, 234n8, 248n115

Bilbao, Francisco, 254n20

bipolarity, international, 182, 184, 185

Blair, Tony, 172

Blok, Anton, 27

Bogotá, 8, 73, 80, 153, 184

Bolívar, Simón, 53, 120, 254, 257n44

Bolivia, 7, 10, 22, 57, 58, 59, 66, 67–68, 79, 81, 93, 94, 95, 96, 121, 123, 161, 267n91; relations of, with the United States, 147, 148, 343n2, 352n58, 356n85, 363n24; revolution in (1952), 111, 147, 148, 169–91, 201, 342n1, 343n2, 347n27, 353n64, 353n66, 353n68, 353n71, 357n106

Bolshevism. *See* Communism

Bonapartism, 207, 209, 366n40

Bourbon reforms, 82, 92, 97, 142, 229n41, 253n14, 293n18

bourgeoisie, 3, 139, 195, 200, 203, 221n10, 265n82

Brading, David, 92

Brazil, 2, 6, 8, 9, 19, 27, 29, 30–31, 32, 37, 38–39, 43, 46–47, 54, 55, 63, 69, 70, 71, 73, 83, 90, 92, 93, 94, 97, 98, 122, 141, 144, 148, 155, 158, 163, 164, 186, 221n8, 225n20, 225n22, 242n57, 253n17, 254n21, 268n98, 272n127, 281n23, 281n26, 303n63, 306n78, 322n42, 329n83, 338n127, 340n146, 371n72; monarchy in, 19, 31, 54, 101, 104, 122, 154, 220n4, 251n10, 259n49; northeastern, 69, 71, 72, 73, 98, 161, 238n34, 239n39, 241n50; Republic in, 31, 104–5, 109, 221n8, 229n38

Brexit, 179

Brinton, Crane, 196

Britain: armed interventions of, in Latin America, 139, 154–55, 228n35, 349n39; and Church of England,

376n102; exports of, to Latin
America, 107, 139, 142, 152, 154, 155,
228n35, 318n21, 321n35; Foreign
Office of, 318n24, 325n85, 354n12,
357n107; and imperial nostalgia,
313n3; investment of, in Latin
America, 139, 142, 154, 228n35,
320n32, 323n47, 351n54; Royal Navy
of, 139, 143, 321n36. *See also* imperialism; India; White Dominions
British Honduras, 146
Buenos Aires, 9, 56, 68, 72, 139, 142, 144,
148, 150, 153, 157, 161, 257n16, 280n16,
341n138
Bushnell, David, 52, 251n21, 268n97,
269n101

caboclos, 69
Cabrera, Luis, 97
Cáceres, Andrés, 292n6, 295n27
caciques, 185, 220n3, 299nn46–47
Calderón de la Barca, Fanny, 244n67,
248n109
Callao, 157, 161
Calles, Plutarco Elías, 75, 79, 110, 111,
114, 115, 130, 131–32, 150, 178, 206,
210–11, 214, 215, 216, 309n99, 310n105,
311n107, 312n111, 350n49, 373n88,
374n90, 377n112, 377n115
Calvert, Peter, 135
campanilismo, 275n160
Canada, 137, 143, 163, 264, 338n128
Cananea, 63, 128
Canudos, 29, 109, 161
capitación (head tax), 53, 121, 300n48,
300n51, 302n60
Carden, Lionel, 146, 174, 175, 177, 181, 182,
190, 357n102

Cárdenas, Lázaro, 132, 178, 182, 210, 214,
216, 374n90
Carr, E. H., 223n15
Carranza, Venustiano, 46, 150, 190,
292n6
Carrera, Rafael, 53, 102
Casa del Obrero Mundial, 64, 204, 206,
369n59
caste distinctions, 52, 118, 120
caste wars, 119, 289n84, 309n102
Castilla, Ramón, 257n45, 316n13
Castlereagh, Lord, 148
Castro, Cipriano, 158
Castro, Fidel, 150, 184, 191, 359n8,
366n37, 377n115
Catholicism. *See* Church, Catholic; folk
Catholicism; social Catholicism
Cauca, 81
caudillos, 38, 39, 42, 43, 47, 68, 73, 74,
81, 101, 121, 122, 125, 161, 166, 185,
210, 244n71, 249n2, 289n83, 299n47,
320n27, 330n91, 330n121
Cavour, Camillo, 367n41
Cedillo, Saturnino, 213
Central America, 10, 12, 21, 52, 54, 58, 66,
67, 72, 80, 83, 94, 121, 140, 149, 154, 155,
226n23, 231n44, 316n13, 326nn64–65,
336n121, 338n127, 340n136
centralism, 52, 53, 54, 56, 58, 79, 84, 98,
100, 102, 255n23
Cervantes, Miguel de, 139
CGT (Confederación General de
Trabajadores), 206
Chalco, 122
Chandler, Billy Jaynes, 27, 38, 236n17
Charles, Prince, 322n41
Chávez, Hugo, 150
Chávez García, José Inés, 44, 47, 247n99
Chayanta, 68, 161

Chiapas, 43, 59, 120, 121, 129, 131, 164–65, 287n73

Chihuahua, 37, 38, 44, 45, 46, 129, 370n70

Chile, 2, 8, 9, 52, 53, 54, 56, 58, 63, 71, 89, 90, 105, 113, 121, 122, 123, 125, 154, 161, 184, 187, 212, 230, 254n18, 257n42, 259n49, 278n3, 281n26, 304n71, 316n13, 322n41, 364n29; Central Valley of, 69, 72, 73, 80, 101, 265n83, 269n103

China, 43, 83, 115, 123, 142, 150, 152, 155, 194, 195, 197, 201, 205, 206, 207, 209, 224, 230, 326n64, 360n9, 360n13, 362n30, 369n62

Chinese immigrants, 164, 302n60, 308n94

Church, Catholic, 5, 61, 70–71, 85, 103, 116, 153, 158, 199, 204, 221n10, 259n49, 264n76, 278n3, 354n76, 374nn91–92; and church-state conflict, 5, 87–112, 209, 211, 257n43, 280n18; and women, 75–76, 91, 110, 111, 158, 211, 273n137, 280n16, 290n92, 377n115. *See also* anticlericalism; *curas* (parish priests); Rome; ultramontanism

Churchill, Winston, 223n15

Cícero, Padre, 109

Científicos, 58, 103, 125, 126, 160, 165, 220n4

Civilistas (Peru), 126, 131, 133, 306n81, 312n112

civilization and barbarism, 106, 165, 166, 259n51, 260n58, 336n120, 340n137, 341n138

clans, 31, 74, 272n127

Clavijero, Francisco, 92

Clemenceau, Georges, 162

clergy. See *curas* (parish priests)

Cochabamba, 187

Cockcroft, George, 1

coffee, 31, 54, 154, 162, 221n8, 224n20, 225n21, 270n114, 322n42, 327n74, 339n131

cofradías (sodalities), 95, 106, 286n68

Cold War, 22, 115, 147, 149, 182–86, 233n56, 343n2

collaborating elites, 13, 156, 158, 182, 332n104

Collier, Simon, 52, 256n40, 257n42

Colombia, 7, 8, 9, 12, 18, 53–54, 58, 71, 74, 94, 105, 140, 153, 164, 220, 225, 245n83, 248n114, 288n76, 318n22, 328n75, 335n117; civil wars in, 52, 89, 101, 227n26; political parties in, 21, 52, 56, 66, 70, 72, 73, 80, 100–101, 105, 245n83, 252n13, 254n21, 257n43, 259n49, 262n70, 269n101, 270n114, 271n117, 273n135, 276n171; Violencia in, 227n27, 246n114, 259n49, 285n56, 328n56, 360n8

colonialism, internal, xv, 12, 14, 19, 159, 168, 276n168, 333n105

colonial legacy, 7, 88, 99, 107, 116, 151–52

colonial pact, 16, 300n51

Colorado Party (Uruguay), 64, 268n97

Columbus NM, 46

commodity booms, 123, 124, 260

communalism, 79, 151, 274n149, 336n120, 372n79

Communism, 65, 83, 132, 147, 172, 177, 178, 182, 183, 184, 191, 202, 206, 208, 209, 212–13, 231n47, 274n149, 345n10, 350n52, 352n63, 353n64, 355n82, 364n29, 373n84, 375n95, 376n104

comparisons, historical, 22–23, 193

compression, socio-economic, 122, 127, 130, 301n55

Comte, Auguste, 103, 125, 165, 214

Congo, 164
Conquest, Spanish, 116, 139, 338n127
consequentialism, 359n6
conservatism, 3, 8, 15, 18, 19, 20, 52, 53, 54,
    55, 56, 57, 58, 66, 71, 72, 73, 74, 77, 79,
    81, 84, 85, 89, 98, 99–103, 104, 105, 108,
    124, 126, 132, 150, 185, 202, 208, 209,
    221n10, 229n38, 251n9, 252n11, 254n18,
    255n21, 257n42, 259n49, 266n85,
    270n114, 274n149, 275n155, 277n172,
    285n56, 286n64, 300n48, 340n133,
    347n29
constitutions, 18, 19, 51, 53, 56, 84, 87, 98,
    99, 200–202, 208, 251n10, 253n14,
    254n20, 259n49, 337n124, 365n37,
    366n40; Brazilian, 101; of Cádiz,
    50, 52; Chilean, 255n27; Colombian,
    58; Ecuadorian, 54; Haitian, 254n21;
    Mexican, 52, 55, 178, 255n23, 264n75,
    303n68, 366n38; Nicaraguan,
    81; Peruvian, 257n45, 261n65;
    Uruguayan, 261n65
Contestado, 109, 161
contingency, 3, 4, 5, 276n170
convergence, 114–15, 120, 126
Coronado, Raúl, 251n8
corridos, 38, 242n57, 249n91
Costa Rica, 6, 7, 11, 23, 67, 264n75,
    327n74, 336n121
cotton, 46, 54, 123, 139, 142, 162, 238n34,
    302n60
counterfactuals, 115–16, 133, 293n12
counterrevolutions, 194, 199, 200, 201,
    372n78
cowboys, 7–8, 106–8, 162, 165, 224n20
Cowdray, Lord, 173
Creel/Terrazas faction, 45
Cristero Rebellion, 5, 87, 89, 109–12, 211,
    223nn16–17, 277n1, 278n5, 290n89,

291n93, 371n72, 374n91, 375n94,
    375n99
Croly, Herbert, 274n150
CROM (Confederación Regional
    Obrera Mexicana), 132, 185, 206,
    310n105
Cromwell, Oliver, 126, 377n115
crop determinism, 224n20
Crosbie, Alfred, 68
CTM (Confederación de Trabajadores
    de México), 206
Cuba, 120, 122, 142, 239n39, 279n8,
    333n110, 338n127, 355n80; banditry
    in, 27, 28, 30–32, 37, 44–46, 241n50,
    243n58, 244n74; relations of, with the
    United States, 140, 141, 146–50, 160,
    181, 183, 186, 226n23, 319n25, 326n65,
    351n57, 352n59, 363n24; revolution
    in, xiv, 11, 22, 111, 148, 169–91, 194,
    196, 197, 199, 201, 202, 206, 213, 230,
    326n65, 342n1, 343n2, 351n57, 353n71,
    354n77, 367n64; slavery in, 8, 94, 163,
    164, 229n38, 282n30, 337n134, 343n1,
    366n37; Wars of Independence
    in, 10, 43, 44, 89, 102, 195, 227n26,
    244n74, 282n30
Cuernavaca, 179
Culiacán, 40, 279n13
cultural turn, 170
Cunard Cummins, H., 178
Cunha, Euclides da, 29, 237n26, 244n73
curas (parish priests), 93, 96, 106,
    282n38, 284n45, 291n93, 296n33,
    297n35, 332n103
currency, 151, 159–60, 220n4, 376n104
Cuzco, 120, 294n20, 297n35, 298n42

Danton, Georges, 360n15
Darwin, Charles, 166, 341n42, 358n4

Darwin, John, 135, 317n17, 321n34
"death by government," 11
Denoon, Donald, 314n8
dependency theory, 8, 12, 17, 57, 136, 157, 230n43, 328n76
desamortización (disentailment), 56, 76–79, 83, 99, 266n85, 266n88, 273n138, 337n124
Deterding, Henri, 350n45
developmentalism. *See* liberalism
de Vries, Jan, 232n53
Díaz, Adolfo, 326n65
Díaz, Porfirio, 2–3, 60, 67, 77, 78, 103, 109, 125–28, 133, 160, 173–74, 175, 176, 200, 245n78, 290n91, 304n67, 305n73, 305n76, 336n120, 340n137, 376n104. *See also* Porfiriato
Díaz Soto y Gama, Antonio, 370n65
Diéguez, Manuel, 211
diffusionism, 22, 256n37, 270n115
disease, 20, 289, 311n107, 340n136
Disraeli, Benjamin, 152
divergence, 114–15, 120, 122, 126, 132
Dominican Republic, 137, 140, 147, 148, 186, 231n48, 315n11, 325n62
domino theory, 184, 353n70
drug trafficking. *See* narco crime
Durango, 37, 41, 44, 46, 370n70
Dutton-Pegram, Stanley, 179, 187
dyadic rivalry, 41, 74, 246n91
Dzitas, 309n100

Ecuador, xv, 7, 54, 59, 66, 70, 83, 94, 95, 101–2, 153, 164, 184, 257n45, 275n155, 316n13, 330n91, 338n131, 339n133
education, 5, 6, 45, 55, 59, 63, 70, 92, 102, 104, 110, 112, 132, 185, 186, 201, 204, 209, 210, 211, 212, 214, 248n109,

286n64, 311n108, 355n80, 366n38, 373n87
Egypt, 158, 177, 187, 331n99, 349n35
Eisenhower, Milton, 47, 345n10, 352n63
ejidos, 78–79, 208, 225n21
El Salvador, 72, 80, 372n78
emic/etic distinction, 73–74, 359n7, 373n83
empire. *See* imperialism
encomienda, 116, 118, 152
enganche, 129, 164, 295n28, 308n94. *See also* peonage
Erdogan, Recep Tayyip, 378n118
Escala, Erasmo, 89
Escandón, Pablo, 78
Estrada Cabrera, Manuel, 67, 259n48, 326n65
Evans, Rosalie, 178, 349n41

Facundo, Juan, 166
Falange Socialista Boliviano, 354n76
Falkland Islands (Malvinas), 145, 146, 154, 323n44
fascism, 20, 79, 182, 207, 208, 214, 221, 244n67, 363n26, 366n40
federalism, 52, 80, 100, 254n21, 270n114
Ferguson, Niall, 135, 136, 143
Fernández, Nicolás, 243n67
Fernando VII, 16, 82
Feuillants, 201
fiestas, 75, 91, 93, 95, 106, 110, 211, 281n24, 287n73
filibusters, 140, 316n13
Flores Galindo, Alberto, 16, 117, 294n20, 299n46
fog of war, 173, 189
folk Catholicism, 72, 95–96, 106, 198, 289n84
Fordham, Stanley, 191, 357n98

Forment, Carlos, 262n67, 268n99, 297n39, 298n42

Foucault, Michel, 222n14

France, 78, 92, 98, 102, 125, 152, 154, 167, 199, 211; revolution in, 78, 107, 194, 195, 196, 200, 201, 202, 205, 207, 209, 211, 212, 215, 221, 361n16, 364n27, 367n45, 373n88, 375n94; Third Republic of, 9, 74, 167, 209, 210, 373n88

Francia, José Gaspar Rodríguez de, 17, 54, 153, 255n30, 285n54, 328n76

Franco, Francisco, 212, 372n78

Frederick the Great, 318n20

freemasons, 62, 98, 108, 262n67, 282n27, 373n88

freethinking, 93, 98, 282n27, 284n44

free trade, 8, 52, 54, 57, 66, 77, 82, 102, 108, 135, 143, 160, 176, 285n56, 329n83, 330n89, 332n104

Froese, Paul, 212–13, 375n44

frontiers, 32, 89, 95, 161, 162, 166, 167, 225n21, 238n34, 240n43, 274n148, 286n63, 370n70, 377n115

FSTMB (Federación Sindical de Trabajadores Mineros de Bolivia), 183

fueros (judicial privileges), 54, 55, 99

Fukuyama, Francis, 23, 233n56

Gallagher, J. A., xiv, xv, 13, 14, 17, 155, 156, 228n34, 325n58, 329n87, 344n9

Gallieni, Joseph, 162

Gamarra, Agustín, 74, 275n164

gamonales, 130, 267n91, 299nn46–47, 311n106

García, Manuel, 37–38

García Moreno, Gabriel, 54–55, 59, 102, 257n45, 316n13

Gargarella, Roberto, 62, 254n20, 259n49, 261n65

Garibaldi, Giuseppe, 215, 377n115

Garrido Canabál, Tomás, 211

gauchos. *See* cowboys

Gavira, Gabriel, 204

generations, 9, 16, 18, 19, 40, 50, 55, 56, 60, 66, 84, 99, 122, 179, 198, 228n37, 241n46, 252n11, 342n144, 355n80, 358n1, 376n106

Genoa, 315n9

gentlemanly capitalism, 156, 228n35, 319n27

Germany, 22, 144, 145, 146, 158, 161, 179, 181, 182, 188, 202, 203, 214, 221n10, 277n176, 323n44, 324n50, 324n53, 335n117, 346n17, 347n22, 349n41, 362n20

Gerschenkron, Alexander, 196, 361n17

Giuliano, Salvatore, 27, 236n15

Gladstone, William, 253n16, 319n24

globalization, 22, 30, 138, 371n74

gold, 139–40, 317n15

gold standard, 2, 159–60

González, Manuel, 304n67

González Lobos, Francisco, 278n1

González y González, Luis, 232n53

Good Neighbor Policy, 149, 150, 216, 324n54

Gootenberg, Paul, 249n2, 256n42, 274n148, 306n81, 329n83, 330n89, 330n91, 332n104

Gott, Richard, 163, 338n127

Grace Contract, 157

Grafton, Anthony, 24

Granada (Nicaragua), 80

Grandin, Greg, 263n75

Great Andean Revolt. *See* Tupac Amaru (revolt)

Green, T. H., 64

Greene, Graham, 180, 212, 350n50, 350nn52–53

Green Revolution, 311n107

Grenada, 148

Grey, Edward, 348n34

Grey Automobile Gang, 30

Gruening, Ernest, 307n86

Guadalajara, 80

Guanajuato, 79, 229n38, 290n89, 368n53

guano, 122–23, 124, 125, 157, 254n21, 257n45, 258n47, 260n59, 301nn57–58, 302nn59–60, 302n62, 303n63, 304n72, 305n77, 332n104

Guantánamo, 137

Guatemala, 7, 21, 53, 67, 72, 73, 80, 102, 129, 147, 149, 164, 171, 186, 194, 197, 200, 259n48, 265n83, 278n1, 324n55, 326n65, 335n118, 339n131, 345n10, 372n78

Guayaquil, 8, 9, 102, 153, 275n155

Guerra, François-Xavier, 361n16, 364n32

Guerrero, 79

Guevara, Ernesto "Che," 202, 226n22, 367n44, 377n115

Guzmán, Joaquín "Chapo," 41

haciendas/hacendados. See landowners

Haiti, 88, 94, 137, 140, 147, 219n3, 225n21, 229n38, 254n21, 315n11

Hale, Charles, 65, 258n46, 260n52

Hall, Stuart, 265nn81–82

Halperín Donghi, Tulio, 68, 301n55, 328n77

Hamidian Regime (Ottoman Empire), 213, 376n104

Havana, 30, 31, 37, 142, 197

Haya de la Torre, Víctor Raúl, 133, 231n47

Hay-Pauncefote Treaty, 177

head tax. See *capitación* (head tax)

Hearst, William R., 141

hegemony, international, 21–22, 135–36, 145, 326n65; politico-ideological, 40, 57, 69, 71, 75, 92, 249n2, 296n33

henequen, 162, 220n4, 242n55

heretics, 107, 108, 154

Herriot, Edouard, 373n88

Hidalgo, Miguel, 96, 119, 120, 298n42

Hilferding, Rudolf, 12

Hirschman, Albert, 196, 261n17

Hobhouse, Leonard, 64, 263n74

Hobsbawm, E. J., xiii, 25–35, 38, 48, 73, 227n27, 233n1, 234n6, 236n15, 239n43, 359n7, 360n15

Hohler, Thomas B., 175, 177, 179, 187, 348n31, 349n35

Holliday, Gilbert, 187

Holms, P. G., 178, 349n41

Hood, Robin, 27, 33, 40, 90, 236n17, 239n43, 241n49

Hoover, Herbert, 149

Huanta, 59, 81

Huasteca, 76

Hudson, William H., 280n16, 287n72

Huerta, Victoriano, 174, 175, 177, 190, 200, 223n15, 320n27, 334n113, 346n21, 348n30, 350n49, 374n91

Hunt, Lynn, 215

Huntington, S. P., 199, 361n16, 363n27, 364n29

idolatry, 119, 297n35

immigrants, 8, 21, 68–69, 93, 107–8, 163, 268n98, 282n82, 338n127, 340n137

imperialism, 10, 135, 157–59, 163, 166, 171–72, 228n34, 316n14, 326n64; Belgian, 164; British, 13, 135, 137,

139–40, 142–48, 152, 154–55, 156, 157, 159, 161, 175, 179, 187, 228n35, 319n27, 325n58; "excentric" explanations of, xv, 14, 138, 158–59, 171, 228n34, 316n14, 345n111; formal, 14, 136–38, 147–48; French, 146, 149, 162, 314n6; informal, 13, 15, 126, 132, 136–38, 142, 148, 149, 154, 161, 186, 216, 329n83, 332n104; Portuguese, 141, 150, 151; resistance to, 17, 83, 85, 130, 142–43, 150–54; Spanish, 116, 139–40, 141, 142, 143, 146, 151–52, 326n64; U.S., 12, 136–37, 140, 141, 144, 145–47, 149, 160, 186, 216

Incas, 95, 96, 119, 127, 151, 224n18, 297n39

independence, 8, 9, 11, 12, 15, 16–18, 19, 50, 53, 83, 94, 119, 120–22, 141, 152, 195, 229n38, 229n42, 276n170, 293n15, 297n39, 298nn42–43, 303n64, 326n64, 334n112, 359n6, 367n41, 371n72

India, 13, 137, 143, 144, 145, 159, 161, 177, 181, 187, 240n46, 367n41

Indian religion, 93–96, 106, 287n68, 297n35

Indians, 8, 12, 43, 56, 59, 66, 67, 95–96, 102, 106, 109, 117–21, 131, 151, 161, 162, 163, 164, 166, 176, 179, 189, 216, 253n14, 260n54, 266nn88–89, 294n25, 295nn26–27, 295n31, 298n42, 299n44, 300n48, 300n51, 302n60, 308n96, 309n100, 309n102, 335n115, 335n118, 336n120, 338n127, 338n131, 340n133, 340n136, 341n139, 341n142, 342n144, 349n38, 353n68, 378n117. *See also* "lazy natives"

indigenismo, 20, 130–32, 311n106

indirect rule, 137, 314n7

Indo-America, 19, 21, 65–67, 68, 94–96, 163, 165, 229n4, 338n127

Ingenieros, José, 166

inquilinos (Chile), 69

integration, political, 6, 116–18, 125, 209, 224n19, 293n18; global, 21, 22, 66, 143, 158, 159, 258n47, 330n92, 343n2

internal colonialism, xv, 12, 14, 19, 159, 168, 276n168, 333n105

Iquique, 63

Iran, 349n38, 377n110

Iraq, 148

Ireland, 78, 163, 276n168

Irigoyen, Hipólito, 21, 70

Islam, 91, 94, 98, 214, 216

Italy, 64, 68, 82, 92, 212, 214, 221, 226n24, 260n52, 277n176, 348n34, 363n26, 367n41

IWW (Industrial Workers of the World), 262n68

Jacobinism, 53, 56, 58–59, 75, 84, 130, 131, 199, 201, 208–17, 254n20, 257n44, 284n44, 361n16, 365n37, 372n80, 373n83, 373nn87–88, 374n93, 376n102, 377n114

Jacobsen, Nils, 253n14, 260n54, 266n87, 267n91

Jalisco, 76, 79, 284n45, 290n89, 377n115

Japan, 22, 146, 166, 197, 207, 224n19, 240n43, 264n75, 344n4, 347n28

Jarauta, Celedonio, 277n1

J-curve, 360n15

Jeffersonian ideal, 76, 78, 79, 274n150

Jenks, Jeremiah, 160

Jesuits, 18, 92, 99, 102, 271n117, 277n172, 285n54

Jews, 107, 108, 287n22

Joseph, Gilbert, 28, 29, 48

Juárez, Benito, 47, 55, 60, 70, 76, 77, 78, 83, 103, 125, 258n48, 276n165, 277n174, 286n62, 305n73, 365n34

Juazeiro, 109
Juchitán, 290n91

Kahlo, Frida, 226n22
Kerensky, Alexander, 199
Keynes, J. M., 223n17
Kiernan, Victor, 25, 233, 326n64
King, Rosa, 179
Kipling, Rudyard, 187, 350n48
Kirchner, Cristina Fernández de, 150
Kirchner, Néstor, 150
Kirkpatrick, Jeane, 231n48
Kornilov, Lavr, 199, 354n31

labor coercion, 59, 118, 164, 260n59,
    295n28, 302n60, 333n105, 338n131,
    340n136. See also peonage; slavery
labor reform, 20, 47, 64, 132, 178, 200,
    220n4
Lal, Deepak, 135, 143, 313n2
La Laguna, 46, 129, 179, 187
Lampião (Virgulino Ferreira da Silva),
    27, 34, 37, 41, 43, 236n7, 240n46,
    241n49, 243n59, 244n70, 247n100,
    248n109
landowners, 3, 4, 37, 44, 69, 71, 76, 77–78,
    110, 118, 121, 123, 128, 129, 130, 162–63,
    164, 199, 200, 204, 220n3, 241n49,
    266n87, 267n91, 268n98, 283n43,
    308n91, 311n106, 338n128, 340n133,
    341n137, 363n27
land reform. See agrarian reform
La Paz, 185, 189
La Rioja, 108
Latin America: definition of, 7, 88,
    344n4; diversity of, 7–8, 85, 88,
    223n18, 229n41; scramble for, 138, 144,
    167, 168; "Second Conquest" of, 155,
    330n92

"lazy natives," 11, 67, 164, 165, 176–77,
    339n132, 340n136, 349n35
Leguía, Augusto, 20–21, 105, 114, 131–33,
    286n66, 310nn105–6, 311n107
Lenin, Vladimir, 12
León (Nicaragua), 80
Leo XIII, 103
Levi-Strauss, Claude, 71
Lewin, Linda, 27, 236n18, 238n34
liberalism, 46–85, 156, 162–63, 250n6,
    256n40, 258n48, 270n114; Catholic,
    97, 98; constitutional, 200, 208;
    developmental, 57–60, 80, 164,
    167, 168, 246n9, 257n46, 260n52,
    260n54, 260n59, 267n91, 340n136;
    institutional, 18, 19, 55, 56, 60, 65, 70,
    76, 99; and "liberal" period in Latin
    America, 1–2, 18, 50, 58, 259n50,
    267n94; neo-, 222n13, 230n43;
    patriotic, 126, 277n176; philosophy
    of, 51, 250n7; popular, 3, 49, 71–72,
    73, 74, 75–80, 198, 200, 204, 275n164,
    301n53, 365n34; social, 62–63,
    263n75, 274n150; typology of, 51–52,
    64–65, 251n8, 252n11, 254n20, 261n65,
    263nn74–75, 265n81
Lima, 8, 95, 117, 119, 123, 142, 225n20,
    286n66, 292n6, 294n20, 302n59,
    311n109
Limantour, José Yves, 160, 220n4
Lind, John, 175, 182
linguistic turn, 4, 232n53
literacy, 6, 30, 72, 73, 74, 98, 184, 204, 213,
    369n54
localism, 36, 42, 43, 74, 80, 81, 96, 111,
    119, 131, 215, 249n91, 275n60, 281n24,
    283n38, 287n68, 290n91, 363n25,
    372n76, 378n116
logging, 165

López, Carlos Antonio, 285n54

López, Estanislao, 342n142

López Obrador, Andrés Manuel, 222n13, 378n118

Lozada, Manuel, 82

Luce, Henry, 145

"lumping and splitting," 193, 198, 358n4, 362n18, 366n40

Lundestad, Geir, 149

Luxemburg, Rosa, 12

Lyautey, Hubert, 162

Lynch, John, 108, 278n3

Lyon, 204

Macartney, George, 152

Macaulay, Thomas B., 140, 318n20

Machado, Gerardo, 147

Machiavelli, Nicoló, 252n10

Madero, Francisco, 60, 64, 67, 72, 76–77, 80, 130, 174, 176, 198, 200–201, 205, 267n90, 277n174, 346n19

Magonismo, 62. See also Partido Liberal Mexicano (PLM)

Mahoney, James, 116

Maier, Charles, 135, 206, 208

Maitland, F. W., 173

Maíz, Fidel, 278n1

Makhno, Nestor, 208, 362n22

Mallon, Florencio, 113, 126

Malverde, Jesús, 40, 279n13

Malvinas. See Falkland Islands (Malvinas)

Mansilla, Lucio V., 342n144

Maoism, 131

Mapuche, 161

Mariátegui, José Carlos, 21, 231n47

Martí, José, 150

Marx, Karl, 65, 66, 88, 196, 207, 266n88, 333n105, 368n46

Marxist interpretations, 2–3, 12–13, 110, 129, 136, 195, 203, 222n12, 223n16, 261n64, 265n82, 368n46

masons. See freemasons

Maximilian of Habsburg, 83, 124, 266n85, 305n73, 365n34

Maya, 95, 109, 118, 128, 161, 287n84, 289n84, 295n27, 309n102

Mayo, 336n120

Mazamitla, 74

Melgarejo, Manuel, 59

Méndez, Cecilia, 59, 79

Méndez, Othón, 104, 286n63

Mendicoa, Isaac, 30, 237n28

Mendoza, 153

Mendoza, Camerino Z., 204

mercantilism, 18, 107, 118, 121, 141, 142, 143, 144, 321n34, 328n77

messianism, 19, 29, 31, 71, 109, 289n84, 371n72

mestizaje, 117–18

metanarratives, 3, 4, 23, 222n13, 291n1

Methodism, 204, 278n2

Mexican Communist Party (PCM), 178

Mexican Revolution, xv, 2, 3, 5, 9, 11, 20–21, 25–26, 30, 37, 43, 44, 47–48, 67, 76, 79, 81, 104, 109–12, 114, 127, 129–33, 145, 146, 148, 160, 173–80, 188–91, 193–217, 222n15, 234n6, 241n50, 242n56, 290n89, 306n82, 318n22, 334n113, 336n120, 343n1, 346n22, 347n24, 358n1, 363n27, 366n38, 373nn87–88, 376n106, 378n117

Mexico, 5, 19, 51–52, 55, 70, 72, 83, 102–3, 113–33, 144, 146, 154, 264n75, 298n43, 345n14, 349n38

Mexico City, 39, 106, 117, 203, 204, 237n28, 294n19, 368n47, 369n54

Mexico State (Estado de México), 76

Meyer, Jean, 110, 111, 220n89

Michoacán, 74, 76, 79, 100, 104, 245n86, 272n124, 290n89

microhistory, 232n53

military, 54, 55, 56, 69, 79, 84, 97, 111, 123, 131, 137, 148, 150, 161, 183, 190, 199, 200, 201, 207, 213, 216, 222n15, 239n41, 257n45, 276n164, 302n59, 308n91, 317n17, 334n113, 335nn117–18, 336n121, 356n85, 366n40

Mill, John Stuart, 72, 74, 85, 260n58, 263n75

millenarianism, 109, 207, 289n84, 371n72

Minas Gerais, 221n8

miners, 183, 283n36, 309n98, 354n76

mining, 42, 59, 66, 116, 118, 139, 160, 221n7, 267n91, 293n14

"mission," American, 141, 319n26

missions, 139, 141, 154

mita, 118

MNR (Movimiento Nacionalista Revolucionario), 79, 182–83, 184, 190, 214

modernity, 6, 30, 58, 195, 251n8, 259n51

Moncada barracks attack, 83, 97, 190–91, 357n96, 359n8

Monroe Doctrine, 146, 171, 323n48, 324n49

Monterrey, 80, 198, 368n47

Montevideo, 9, 72, 139, 142, 148

Moore, Barrington, Jr., 133, 240n45, 268n98, 312n115

Mora, José María Luis, 52, 60, 65, 72

Morelos (Mexico), 2, 31, 76, 120, 129, 179, 198, 246n91, 249n119, 274n149, 310n105, 350n49

Morelos, José María, 96, 120

Morrow, Dwight, 178

Moscow, 202, 205, 353n68

Mosquera, Tomás Cipriano, 54

Múgica, Francisco J., 211, 290n92

myths, historical, 1, 3, 6, 9, 15, 16, 27, 28, 35, 40, 126, 217, 225n22, 235n13, 358n1, 365n34

Nahuatl, 118

Napoleon Bonaparte, 16, 53, 107, 126, 142, 154, 200, 215, 276n170, 298n43

Napoleon III, 7, 83, 103, 124, 125, 323n48

narco crime, 12, 30, 34, 36, 38, 39–41, 48, 90, 238n31, 239n46, 242n57, 243n61

nationalism, 20, 39, 46, 80–84, 92, 98, 130–32, 149–50, 151, 176, 178, 201, 205, 214, 277n176, 282n30, 311n108, 326n64, 343n2, 351n55, 360n13, 362n22, 374n88, 377n115; Catholic, 89, 92, 150, 277n172, 277n174, 296n34; liberal, 62, 82–84. See also protonationalism

Native Americans. See Indians

Negrín, Juan, 201, 365n37

neo-Europes, 65–66, 68

neopatrimonialism, 66, 69, 71, 73, 85

Netherlands, 252n10, 360n12

new institutional economics, 151, 327n67

New Mexico, 119–20

newspapers, 72, 98, 103, 262n67

New Zealand, 315n8, 338n127

Nicaragua, 62, 72, 80, 81, 83, 137, 146, 147, 149, 160, 186, 231n48, 277n175, 326n65

Nigeria, 137, 261n59, 314n7

nitrates, 59, 139, 154

Nuevo León, 133

Núñez, Rafael, 58, 105, 253n16, 286n64

Oaxaca, 73, 76, 79, 100, 119, 129, 266n83

Obando, José María, 73, 81

Obregón, Alvaro, 130, 205, 293n12, 309n99

occidentalism, 170, 180
"official mind," 35, 171, 172, 344n9
oil. *See* petroleum
old regimes, prerevolutionary, 199–200
oligarchy, 2–3, 68, 132, 133, 158, 220nn3–4, 258n46
Opium Wars, 155
organized labor, 20, 132, 185, 187, 202–6, 254n78, 307n86, 309n98, 355n82, 358n107, 370n63. *See also* strikes
Orientalism, 170
Oriente (Cuba), 31–32, 191, 377n115
ORIT (Organización Regional Interamericana de Trabajadores), 186, 355n82
Orozco, Luis, 41
Ospina Rodríguez, Mariano, 225n21
Ostiguy, Pierre, 271n116
Ottoman Empire, 150, 187, 199, 201, 203, 366n39, 376n104, 378n117. *See also* Turkey
Oxford University, xiv, xvi

Pachamama, 93, 283n36
Palmerston, Lord, 155, 156, 320n27, 330n88
pampas (Argentina), 7–8, 106, 107, 108, 109, 161, 162, 165, 166, 265n83, 287n70
Panama, 80, 140, 148, 186, 350n53
Panama Canal, 140, 145, 146
papacy. *See* Rome
Paraguay, 10, 16, 17, 54, 84, 148, 153, 184, 227n28, 278n1, 285n54, 328n76
Paraíba, 238n34
Pardo, Manuel, 264n78, 274n148, 306n81
Paris, 158, 189, 202, 203, 294n20
parish priests. See *curas* (parish priests)
Parral, 39, 41
Parsons, Talcott, 115

Partido Antirreleccionista, 72
Partido Autonomista Nacional (PAN), 68
Partido Católico Nacional (PCN), 354n76
Partido Liberal Mexicano (PLM), 61, 262n68. *See also* Magonismo
Partido Nacional Revolucionario (PNR), 133, 210, 374n90
Partido Revolucionario Institucional (PRI), 40, 184, 210, 216, 222n13
Partido Socialista Popular (PSP), 183
Pascal, Blaise, 6, 223n17
Passananti, Tom, 125
Pasto (Colombia), 81
pastoralism, 7–8, 162, 165, 221n8, 289n82, 299n44, 308n92, 308n96
Patagonia, 316n13
Patch, Richard, 347n29
patrimonialism, 269n100
patriotism. *See* nationalism
Patterson, Richard C., 183, 344n10
Paz Estenssoro, Víctor, 183
Pearce, Adrian, 122
Pearson, Weetman. *See* Cowdray, Lord
peasants, 66, 68, 73, 78, 81, 106, 121, 128–29, 225n21, 365n34, 372n79; protest by, 67, 121–22, 127, 130, 202, 206–8, 233n4, 274n149, 275n151, 307n87, 308nn91–92, 308n96, 309n102, 371n72, 371n74
Pedro II, 54, 101, 122
Pellegrini, Carlos, 157
Peñaloza, Angel, 108
peonage, 118, 129, 131, 132, 164, 220n3, 224n20, 260n59, 307n88, 308n94. *See also* labor coercion
Pérez, Louis, 28, 351n57
periodization, 15, 18, 299n45
Perón, Juan Domingo, 150, 214, 367n42

Peru, 6, 20, 25, 31, 37, 58–59, 63, 66, 67, 68, 72, 73, 79, 80, 81, 96, 105, 113–33, 142, 154, 157, 164, 225n20, 239n37, 239n41, 253n14, 294n20, 329n83, 330n89, 330n91, 332n103, 336n119
Peru-Bolivia Confederation, 123, 330n89
Peruvian Corporation, 157
Pétion, Alexandre, 254n21
Petrograd, 119, 202, 205, 368n47
petroleum, 22, 144, 173, 175, 176, 181, 210, 246n95, 309n38, 346n18; expropriation of, in Mexico, 178, 179, 311n109; and World War II, 356n90
Philip, Duke of Edinburgh, 356n84
Philippines, 160
Pinochet, Augusto, 364n29
Pius IX, 70, 99, 103, 277n172
Pi y Margall, Francisco, 61
Platt, D. C. M., 155
Platt, Tristan, 267n91, 300n51
Poland, 187
police, 11, 26, 36, 44, 47, 108, 161–62, 247n98, 335n115, 336n122
Polk, James, 303n65
Pomerantz, Kenneth, 115
Porfiriato, 57, 58, 60, 77, 124–25, 186, 220n4, 239n39, 250n5, 286n99, 304n67, 340n137, 364n32. See also Díaz, Porfirio
Portales, Diego, 53, 58, 101, 122
Portugal, 92, 141, 151, 330n88
Posada-Carbó, Eduardo, xvi, 253n13, 257n43, 262n70
positivism, 2, 15, 19, 20, 57, 58, 60, 103, 104–5, 108, 109, 126, 165, 167, 220n4, 340n135, 342n144, 364n32, 376n104
postcoloniality, 9, 51, 150, 165, 226n24
Pozontepec, 28n25

Prestes, Luis Carlos, 184
primacy, urban, 294n19
primary accumulation, 66, 67, 266n88, 333n105
proactive protest, 119, 297n39, 370n69
Proal, Herón, 204
Protestantism, 75, 91, 93, 107, 108, 150, 153–54, 211, 213, 279n8, 281n26, 287n72, 288n76, 332n103
protonationalism, 82, 92, 118–20, 296n34, 297n39
Proudhon, J.-J., 262n70
Puebla, 80, 119, 129, 205, 280n19, 284n45
Puerto Rico, 137, 140, 142, 160, 315n10
Punitive Expedition (1916–17), 46, 197, 318n22
Puno, 130, 309n102
Putumayo, 131, 164, 261n60

Quechua, 117–18, 122, 295n27
Quintana Roo, Andrés, 284n44
Quito, xv, 8, 9, 153, 275n155

racism, 3, 59, 125, 127, 165, 166, 170, 171, 180, 187, 189, 191, 338n127, 339n132
Radical Party (Argentina), 21, 70, 72
Radical Party (France), 70, 71, 374n88
railways, 57, 66, 77, 78, 103, 108, 121, 122, 125, 126, 139, 143, 153, 156, 157, 160–61, 164, 167, 174, 176, 181, 236n18, 293n12, 303n63, 306n78, 333n110, 370n63, 376n104
rancheros, 5, 76, 122, 200, 365n34
Ranke, Leopold von, 24
reactive protest, 119, 297n39, 370n69
Reciprocity Treaty (U.S.-Cuban, 1934), 144
Reconquista, 139
Red Battalions, 205

Redfield, Robert, 71, 246n91, 309n10
Reed, John, 44
Reforma (Mexican "Reform"), 73, 76, 79, 81, 89, 100, 102, 124, 213, 227n16, 276n165
regionalism, 121, 221n8, 265n83, 269n100, 270n114. *See also* localism
religion, 5, 7, 8, 69–70, 87–112, 120, 198, 211–13, 257n44, 278n2, 280n17. *See also* animism; Church, Catholic; Islam; Protestantism
Remington, Frederic, 141
republicanism, 68, 97, 141, 199, 200, 209, 250n7, 251n10, 254n20, 297n39, 301n53
Rerum Novarum (1891), 70, 103, 264n76
revolts, colonial, 16, 119–20, 281n25, 287n73, 297n37
revolutions, 9–10, 28, 30, 39, 42–45, 169–91, 342n1; definition of, 8, 17, 18, 194–96, 202, 227nn26–27, 229n42, 234n6, 342n1, 358n1, 364n29; of 1848, 55, 123, 194, 200, 256n37, 270n115, 365n33; theories of, 193–99, 221n10, 265n82, 358n6, 360n15, 361n16, 362n18, 364n32, 366n40, 376n104. *See also* Bolivia; China; Cuba; France; Mexican Revolution
Reyes, Bernardo, 133, 160, 222n15
Reyes Heroles, Jesús, 62
Reyes Vega, José, 277n1
Río Blanco, 63, 128
Rio de Janeiro, 157–58
Río de la Plata, 229n41, 328n77
riots, 89, 106, 119, 127, 157–58, 184, 281n25, 287n69, 377n115
Risorgimento, 82, 123, 195, 348n34, 367n41
Rivadavia, Bernardino, 52–53, 108, 288n78, 341n338, 373n83

roads, 131, 152–53
Robinson, Ronald, 13, 138, 155, 156, 228n34
Roca, Julio, 68, 105, 257n46, 342n34
Roca-Runciman Treaty (1933), 144, 314n8
Rochefoucauld-Liancourt, duc de La, 194
Rockefeller Foundation, 311n107
Rodríguez, Enrique ("El Tallarín"), 249n119
Roman Empire, 36, 137
Rome, 36, 54, 97, 98–99, 100, 110, 111, 137, 211, 212, 277n172
Rondônia, 7, 23
Roosevelt, Franklin D., 21, 149, 231n48, 324n54, 325n62, 364n28
Roosevelt, Theodore, 140, 141, 318n22, 324n49, 324n53
Rosas, Juan Manuel de, xvi, 9, 53, 56, 101, 108, 122, 154, 166, 255n27, 285n54, 289n82, 320n27, 325n60
Rostow, W. W., 196
Rouquié, Alain, 335n118, 336n119, 344n4
Royal Dutch Shell, 179
royalism, 96, 207, 283n38
rubber, 59, 131, 164, 261n60, 303n63, 339n33
Rugeley, Terry, 249n3
Rumelia, 215
Rumi Maqui (revolt), 68, 127
Rumsfeld, Donald, 32, 136
Russia, 141, 146, 166, 183, 194, 195, 197, 199, 201–7, 209, 211, 213, 230n42, 320n28, 333n105, 361n16, 362n20, 364n27, 364n31, 373n84, 377n115. *See also* Soviet Union
Ryan, Alan, 258n48

Sacred Heart of Jesus, 102, 105, 114, 132

Safford, Frank, 56, 252n11, 254n20, 267n94

Said, Edward, 170, 222n14, 344n4

Saint Petersburg. *See* Petrograd

saints, 47, 93, 95, 245n83, 273n137, 279n13, 290n91, 375n94

Salcedo, Guadalupe, 248n114

Salinas de Gortari, Carlos, 62, 346n17

Salisbury, Lord, 157

Salonika, 215, 216

Salta, 153

Samper, José María, 257n44

San Bartolomé Naucalpán, 286n68

Sandino, Augusto César, 21, 62, 75, 81, 83, 147, 150, 272n125

San Francisco, 154

San José de Gracia, 74, 104, 232n53, 286n63

San Juan, 332n103

San Luis Potosí, 79

San Lunes, 163, 164, 177, 339n132

San Martín, José de, 120

San Pablo Tecuantepec, 266n88

sans-culottes, 202, 203, 209, 367n42, 372n81

Santa Anna, Antonio López de, 115, 124, 255n21, 303n65, 330n89

Santa Catarina (Brazil), 109

Santa Cruz (Bolivia), 189

Santa Cruz, Andrés de, 330n89

Santa Muerte, cult of, 40

São Paulo, 31, 225n20

Sarmiento, Domingo Faustino, 56, 64, 72, 165–66, 340n137, 341nn138–39, 342n144

Schismatic Church, Mexican, 211

schoolteachers, 208, 209, 337n112

Schoultz, Lars, 149, 344n6, 352n62

Schwartz, Rosalie, 28, 30, 37, 44, 239n40, 243n58, 248n107

Scott, James C., 51, 207, 336n120

Sellar, W. C., 136, 250n6

Sendero Luminoso, 131, 312n116

serranos, 80, 206–7, 370n70

sertão (Brazil), 27, 31, 43, 69

Shanghai, 202

Sicily, 27, 236n15

Sierra, Justo, 165, 167–68, 305n76, 340n137

Sierra Maestra (Cuba), 191, 354n77

silver, 139, 151, 152, 154, 159, 160, 246n95, 317n15

Silvino, Antonio, 236n18

Sinaloa, 36, 40, 41, 243n61, 279n13

sindicatos. *See* organized labor

Slatta, Richard, 28

slavery, 8, 73, 94, 152, 163–64, 167, 224n20, 229n38, 295n31, 299n44; abolition of, 19, 31, 73, 81, 94, 118, 123, 163–64, 220n4, 302n60, 337n124; and slave revolts, 94, 98, 282n30; and slave trade, 91, 94, 154, 163–64, 329n83

Smith, Adam, 151, 326n66

Soboul, Albert, 360n15, 367n45, 368n46, 372n81, 375n95

social Catholicism, 20, 104, 265n76

"social question," 20, 21, 62, 69, 70, 104, 263n74, 264n76

Society of Ottoman Liberals, 201, 365n37

soft power, 186, 355n84, 374n92

Soifer, Hillel, 116, 294n19

Solané, Gerónimo de, 108

Solano López, Francisco, 285n54

Somoza dynasty (Nicaragua), 21, 149, 231n48, 364n28

Sonora, 3, 9, 215, 216, 221n7, 336n120

South Africa, 143, 315n8, 326n64

Soviet Union, 115, 147, 181, 182, 183, 184, 265n81, 320n28, 325n59, 353n68. *See also* Russia

Spain, 61, 64, 68, 112, 151, 201, 204, 208, 211, 291n93, 375n99

Spaniards, 45, 94–95, 106, 108, 140, 150, 151, 204, 287n73, 332n99, 338n127, 369nn61–62

Spencer, Herbert, 58, 72, 85, 261n64

spiritual conquest, 116, 118, 296n33

spiritualism, 75

Spring-Rice, Cecil, 346n22

Stalin, Joseph, 87, 215, 376n104, 377n115

state capacity, 20, 47, 90, 104, 108, 122, 126, 127, 130, 132, 155–56, 162, 239n39, 241n50, 300n48, 302n62, 306n80; and state coercion, 128, 161–62, 239n41, 257n45, 260n52, 261n60, 268n98, 293n18, 335n115, 336n121, 339n133, 341n142

stevedores, 204, 205, 370n63

stockraising. *See* pastoralism

strikes, 63, 127, 225, 262n68, 310n105, 368n46

students, 184, 185, 354n76, 355nn80–81

Suez Canal, 140, 145, 147, 188

suffrage, 21, 52, 54, 177, 259n49, 273n175, 373n135

sugar, 8, 21, 94, 122, 123, 127, 154, 162, 224n20, 302n60, 343n2

Sun Yat-Sen, 199

superstition, 95, 106, 108

Sutton, Willie, 32, 44, 240n44

syncretism, religious, 96, 289n84

Tabasco, 31, 378n118

Taft, William H., 174

Taiping Rebellion, 123, 194, 360n9, 372n78

Tandil, 108

Tanzimat Period/Reform (Ottoman Empire), 213, 376n104

Tapia, Rafael, 204

Tarascans, 119

tariffs, 2, 54, 121, 220n4

Tawney, R. H., 203

taxation, 53, 117, 118, 121, 226n25, 294n23, 300n48, 308n91, 328n75

Taylor, A. J. P., 367n41

Taylor, Lewis, 239n37, 306n80

Taylor, William, 106, 118, 281n24, 287n69, 296n33

telegraph, 66, 103, 108, 125, 156, 161, 162, 236n18, 334n111

telephones, 47, 184, 354n75

Tenenbaum, Barbara, 121, 259n50

Tenochtitlán, 117

Texas, 115, 303n65

textiles, 22, 139, 140, 143, 155, 203, 318n22, 321n35, 330n91

Thompson, E. P., 2–3, 163, 233n1

Tijuana, 41

Tilly, Charles, 246n93, 297n39

tin, 181, 351n55

Tlahualilo Company, 179

Tlaxcala, 119, 129

tobacco, 30, 59, 224n20, 238n30, 270n115

Tocqueville, Alexis de, 51

Tomóchic, 109, 161, 289n85, 371n72

Torreón, 190

trade, foreign, 57, 65, 104, 107, 117, 138, 139, 140, 142, 143, 147, 152, 156, 157, 158, 161, 176, 229n41, 308n91, 318n21, 320n31, 343n2, 345n14, 351n57

trade unions. *See* organized labor

transport, 152–53, 327n74, 342n144. *See also* railways; roads

Triangular Plan, 181

tributary pact, 121, 300n51
Trotsky, Leon, 196, 223n15, 325n62
Trotskyism, 183
Trujillo, Rafael, 149, 231n48, 325n62
Tucumán, 225n20
Tupac Amaru (revolt), 16, 96, 119, 131,
    298n42, 309n102
Turkey, 166, 187, 197, 199, 201, 203, 205,
    213–17, 365n37, 369n62, 376n104,
    378n117
Turpin, Dick, 29
Tutino, John, 122, 223n16

Ukraine, 208, 362n22
ultramontanism, 64, 102, 103, 257n42,
    277n172, 285n62
United States, 115, 167, 316n14, 320n28,
    321n37, 324n53; investment of, in
    Latin America, 144, 323n47, 351n57;
    policy of, toward Latin America,
    21–22, 145, 146, 147, 169, 181–84, 186,
    188, 190, 228n36, 318n22, 319n26,
    322n42, 323n45, 323n48, 324n55,
    326n65, 330n89, 343n2, 345n10,
    345n12, 348n30, 363n24
urbanization, 63, 65, 104, 184
Urbina, Tomás, 44
Uruguay, 10, 19, 57, 58, 64, 89, 143,
    247n106, 261n65, 264n75, 268n97,
    315n8, 334n111, 338n127, 343n2

Valparaíso, 8, 142, 152, 281n26, 288n76,
    320n29
Vanderwood, Paul, 27, 32, 44
Van Young, Eric, 71, 275n160, 371n72
Vargas, Aurelio, 37
Vargas, Getulio, 221n8, 322n42
Vatican. See Rome
Veliz, Claudio, 72, 270n115

Vendée, 205, 211, 213
Venezuela, 2, 8, 70, 94, 101, 146, 148,
    267n94; Anglo-German naval
    blockade of, 158, 228n36; and border
    dispute, 145, 323n45
Veracruz, 8, 31, 42, 79, 148, 152, 161, 175,
    197, 204, 205, 224n18, 277n1, 318n22,
    348n30
Vergara, José Francisco, 89
Versailles Conference, 176
Vietnam, 195
Villa, Pancho, 25–26, 29, 37, 38–39,
    41, 42, 43, 44–47, 175, 190, 226n22,
    241n49, 243n59, 244n67, 244n71,
    244n78, 245n79, 279n12, 293n12
violence, 9, 11–12, 15, 29, 39, 40, 41, 43, 47,
    87–91, 93, 98, 99, 100, 102, 105–12, 131,
    154, 159, 163, 166, 211, 212, 227n31, 246n95,
    299n47, 312n116, 336n121, 339n133
Violencia (Colombia), 227n27, 248n114,
    360n8
Virgin Mary, 95, 96, 273n137
Virgin of Guadalupe, 95, 96, 118, 296n34
Vivanco, Manuel Ignacio de, 74
von Spee, Maximilian, 323n44
voodoo, 94

Walker, William, 83, 277n175
wars, international: Chaco War, 84,
    354n77; of the French Intervention
    (in Mexico), 81, 83, 89, 100, 103, 113,
    314n6, 323n48, 331n99; of indepen-
    dence, 11, 15, 18, 53, 98, 226n25, 296n34,
    297n39, 298n42; Mexican-American
    War, 89, 99, 124, 125–26, 149, 277n1;
    of the Pacific, 10, 30, 84, 89, 113, 123,
    125, 150, 157, 304n71, 305n75; Spanish-
    American War, 140–41, 319n25; of the
    Spanish Succession, 16, 17; and total

war, 197; of the Triple Alliance, 10, 30, 43, 49, 84, 89, 150, 195, 278n1, 282n30
Waugh, Evelyn, 180
Weber, Max, 90, 291n4
Welles, Sumner, 324n54
Wellesley, Arthur, 142
Wellington, Duke of, 154
Wheeler-Bennett, John, 135
White Dominions, 137, 314n8
white settler societies, 163, 338n127
Williams, Harvey Co., 181
Wilson, Henry Lane, 174
Wilson, Woodrow, 46, 148, 174–75, 190, 318n22, 324n53, 346n22, 348n31
witchcraft (*brujería*), 282n30
Witte, Sergei, 202
Wolf, Eric, 207, 370n70, 371n74
Wood, Leonard, 349n39
Woodward, Ralph Lee, 207, 272n125

xenophobia, 11, 15, 89, 107–8, 130, 143, 150, 176, 288n82, 328n76, 332n103, 369n62

Yaquis, 2–3, 67, 109, 128, 129, 161, 221n7, 336n120
Yeatman, R. J., 136, 250n6
Young Turks, 214, 215, 365n37, 373n83
Yuan Shih-Kai, 199
Yucatán, 38, 129, 161, 164, 220n2, 242n55, 281n25, 284n44, 296n27, 309n100, 310n102, 370n70, 375n93
Yugoslavia, 83

Zacatecas, 79, 100, 190, 284n45
Zapata, Emiliano, 31, 39, 77–78, 179, 180, 198, 208, 216, 245n79, 247n105, 249n119, 350n49
Zapatismo, 4, 39, 67, 73, 75, 76, 78, 129, 179, 198, 205, 208, 238n36, 244n77, 267n90, 274n149, 310n105, 370n65
Zárate, Pablo, 67–68
Zarco, Francisco, 256n38
Závala, Lorenzo de, 284n44
Zimmerman Telegram, 188
Zürcher, Erik J., xv, 364n30